SUPPLEMENT

TO THE

OFFICIAL RECORDS

OF THE

UNION AND CONFEDERATE ARMIES.

EDITED BY
Janet B. Hewett

ASSISTANT EDITORS
Jocelyn Pinson, Julia H. Nichols and Katherine Hill

CONTRIBUTING EDITORS
Gary Gallagher, Robert Krick, Lee Wallace, Theodore Savas, Robert E. L. Krick, William Marvel, Michael Cavanaugh, Peter Carmichael, Prof. William L. Shea, Arthur W. Bergeron, Jr., Michael Banasik, Silas Felton

PART II - RECORD OF EVENTS

Volume 52

Serial No. 64

BROADFOOT PUBLISHING COMPANY
Wilmington, NC
1997

"Fine Books Since 1970."
BROADFOOT PUBLISHING COMPANY
1907 Buena Vista Circle
Wilmington, North Carolina 28405

THIS BOOK IS PRINTED ON ACID-FREE PAPER.

ISBN No. 1-56837-275-2 (Set)

Contents

Records of Events

Records of events material for this volume has been transcribed from National Archives microfilm group M594 (Union) "Compiled Records Showing Service of Military Units. . . ." Individual reel references are cited following each unit.

OHIO TROOPS

- UNION -

Record of Events for Twenty-eighth Ohio Infantry, July 1861-June 1865.

Field and Staff

Station not stated, June 13-August 31, 1861.

Stationed at Camp Dennison, Ohio, July 16, 1861.
July 16.— Muster-in roll of the field and staff in the Second German Regiment of Ohio Foot Volunteers, commanded by Colonel [Augustus] Moor, called into the service of the United States by the President from July 16, 1861 (date of this muster) for the term of three years, unless sooner discharged. . . .

[THOMAS WOODRUFF] WALKER,
First Lieutenant,
Third Infantry, Mustering Officer.

Stationed at Camp Dennison, Ohio, July 22, 1861.
July 22.— Muster-in roll of the band in the Second German Regiment of Ohio Foot Volunteers, commanded by Colonel Augustus Moor, called into the service of the United States by the President from July 22, 1861 (date of this muster) for the term of three years, unless sooner discharged. . . .

T. W. WALKER,
First Lieutenant,
Third Infantry, Mustering Officer.

Stationed at Camp Anderson, [West] Virginia, September-October 1861.

Stationed at Gauley Bridge, [West] Virginia, November 1861-April 1862.

Stationed at Flat Top Mountain, May-June 1862.

Stationed at Camp near Fort Buffalo, Virginia, July-August 1862.

Stationed at camp near Sutton, [West] Virginia, September-October 1862.

Station not stated, not dated.
October 23, 1862.— Muster-out roll of the band of the Twenty-eighth Regiment of Ohio Infantry, Colonel A. Moor, from August 31, 1862 when mustered out of service of the United States. . . .

GEORGE [ILLEGIBLE],
Captain,
Fourth Regiment Infantry, Mustering Officer.

Stationed near Brownstown, [West] Virginia, November-December 1862.

Stationed at Buckhannon, [West] Virginia, January-February 1863.

Stationed at Jane Lew, [West] Virginia, March-April 1863.
April 25.— The General commanding the brigade having been advised of the intention of the enemy to capture Buckhannon, [West] Virginia, with the Federal forces there, ordered one battalion of the Twenty-eighth Regiment, Ohio Volunteer Infantry, under Colonel A. Moor, to take and hold a position on the Beverly Road and the other battalion, under Major [Ernest] Schache, to hold and occupy a position on the French Creek Road, which was done.
April 27-29.— All the forces belonging to the Fourth Separate Brigade having safely arrived at Buckhannon, [West] Virginia. General [Benjamin Stone] Roberts ordered [us] to destroy all the government property that could not be carried away and commenced to retreat towards Weston, [West] Virginia about 3 o'clock p.m. The Twenty-eighth Regiment, Ohio Volunteer Infantry, with two pieces of artillery, served as rear guard. From Weston, [West] Virginia the retreat was continued by a forced march to Clarksburg, [West] Virginia, where the regiment arrived on April 29. On account of a forced march by day and night without sleep or rest, six men of the regiment are missing and supposed to have fallen into the hands of the enemy.

Stationed opposite New Creek, [West] Virginia, May-June 1863.
June 16.— At 4 o'clock a.m. the regiment received marching orders from Headquarters, Infantry Forces, Fourth Brigade, Middle Department and, accordingly, left Weston, [West] Virginia at

6 o'clock in the morning of the same day. Arrived at Clarksburg, [West] Virginia, a distance of twenty-three miles, in the evening at 5 o'clock and then proceeded to the railroad depot at said place, where it received orders to be ready to leave at a moment's notice with the cars.

June 17.— In the morning at 8 o'clock the regiment left Clarksburg on the cars and arrived at New Creek, [West] Virginia on June 18 at 2 o'clock a.m., where the camp was put up.

June 20.— In the morning the regiment received orders to proceed to a new camp opposite New Creek, [West] Virginia and accordingly left the old campground on the same day at 1 o'clock p.m. Crossed the Potomac and encamped on the Maryland side opposite New Creek, [West] Virginia and about half a mile from the old camping ground, where the regiment remained ever since.

Stationed at Beverly, West Virginia, July 1863-February 1864.

Stationed at Bunker Hill, West Virginia, March-April 1864.

April 25.— Pursuant to orders received from Headquarters, First Brigade, First Infantry Division, Department of West Virginia, the Twenty-eighth Regiment, Ohio Volunteer Infantry left Beverly en route to Martinsburg, West Virginia. Marched the same day eighteen miles and bivouacked near Belington for the night.

April 26.— Marched twelve miles and encamped near Philippi, West Virginia.

April 27-May 1.— Reached Webster after marching twelve miles. Late in the night the regiment was furnished with transportation on the cars to proceed to Martinsburg, where the regiment arrived at 2 o'clock a.m. of April 29. Remained there until everything was unloaded and each man provided with five days' rations and 100 cartridges, which in all took about two hours. About 12 o'clock m. it took up the line of march again by the Winchester Turnpike. Marched twelve miles and encamped at Bunker Hill, West Virginia, where it remained until May 1.

Station not stated, May-June 1864.

May 1.— The Twenty-eighth Regiment, Ohio Volunteer Infantry, received marching orders and after marching eleven miles arrived on the afternoon at Winchester, Virginia and encamped there.

May 8-10.— Received again marching orders and pursuant to orders started on the march on the morning of May 10. After marching eighteen miles it arrived at Cedar Creek, where it encamped.

May 12.— In the morning it marched to Woodstock, Virginia, a distance of twelve miles, where the regiment encamped.

May 15-16.— In the morning it received orders to act as train guard. It marched with such to Mount Jackson, a distance of fourteen miles and back again to Woodstock, where it arrived on the morning of May 16 at 10 o'clock a.m. The same day the regiment marched a distance of sixteen miles and arrived the same evening at Camp Cedar Creek.

May 26.— In the morning it marched to Woodstock, a distance of fourteen miles, where it arrived in the evening.

May 28.— Marched to Mount Jackson, where it arrived the same day.

June 2.— Left [Mount Jackson] with the rest of the Army and marched that day twenty miles and arrived at Harrisonburg the same day in the evening.

June 4-5.— The line of march was taken up again. Reached Port Republic in the afternoon, when the regiment was ordered to move near the ford of the Shenandoah to cover the artillery and train while crossing. Arrived in camp, two miles from Port Republic at midnight. Stayed until 6 o'clock the next morning, when we left camp and marched cautiously forward, the enemy being reported but little in advance of us. The regiment marched through the woods parallel with the road and 150 yards from it. Having proceeded about three miles our advance met the enemy. Charged and took thirty-five prisoners. Shortly afterwards we formed in line of battle. Attacked the enemy who was in force in our front. Whipped and routed him after charging twice on his fortifications and camped on the battlefield for the night. The Twenty-eighth Regiment lost twenty-eight killed and 100 wounded.

June 6.— We marched fifteen miles and arrived at Staunton. Encamped one mile from that place.

June 10.— The regiment was ordered in the rear in charge of the prisoners taken in late battle.

June 14-24.— The regiment reached Beverly, West Virginia, having crossed the Shenandoah, Alleghanies and Cheat Mountains. Rested one day and proceeded to Webster to get transportation by railroad to Camp Morton, where it arrived with the prisoners (940) on June 24 and stayed there since.

Stationed at Camp Dennison, Ohio, July 23, 1864.
July 23.— Muster-out roll of the field and staff in the Twenty-eighth Regiment of Ohio Infantry Volunteers, commanded by Colonel Augustus Moor, called into the service of the United States by the President at Cincinnati, Ohio (the place of general rendezvous) on May 3, 1861 to serve for the term of three years from the date of enrollment, unless sooner discharged, from April 30, 1864 (when last paid) to July 23, 1864 when mustered out. The field and staff was organized by Colonel A. Moor at Cincinnati, Ohio in the month of June 1861 and marched thence to Camp Dennison, where it arrived July 6, a distance of seventeen miles. . . .

[JACOB MIDDLECOFF] EYSTER,
Captain,
Eighteenth United States Infantry, Mustering Officer.

Regiment

Stationed at camp, Flat Top Tannery, June 1862.
June 11-13.— Companies A and C were ordered as a reconnoitering party to Princeton. The vanguard was attacked by enemy pickets; returned their fire and killed one Rebel. Three companies of mounted Rebels, who were stationed at Princeton, retreated upon their approach. They entered Princeton; obtained all the information they could get about the enemy and returned to camp on Flat Top Mountain, where they arrived on the morning of June 13, having made a march of forty-five miles in two days. None hurt on our side.
June 18-19.— Companies D and F were ordered as a reconnoitering party on the Princeton Road. They reached Princeton June 19 in the morning and returned the same day to camp of Flat Top Mountain. They did not meet any part of the enemy.

Stationed at Summerville, [West] Virginia, October 1862.

Stationed at Brownstown, [West] Virginia, November-December 1862.

Stationed at Buckhannon, [West] Virginia, January-March 1863.

Stationed at Clarksburg, [West] Virginia, April 1863.
April 21.— First Lieutenant [Albert] Liomin, then in command of Company D, Twenty-eighth Regiment, Ohio Volunteer Infantry, was ordered on a scout to intercept a body of Confederate recruits, having received information from report to be on their way to Dixie. He left Buckhannon, [West] Virginia with his company at 8 o'clock p.m. and marched to the cross-roads at Hager's Creek, where he arrived at 3 o'clock a.m. the next day and having heard nothing of such a party, he proceeded on over the mountain near Lost Creek, where he was ordered to arrest some disloyal citizens.
April 24.— He arrested some disloyal citizens. He started from there in four different squads and taking different roads, scouting through all the hills and valleys on his way, where he assisted some more disloyal citizens. The company met again at Harrison Hager's Creek.
April 25.— The company started back to camp, where they arrived at 3 o'clock p.m. the same day.
[For record of events, see Field and Staff.]

Stationed opposite New Creek, [West] Virginia, June 1863.
[For record of events, see Field and Staff.]

Stationed at Beverly, West Virginia, July 1863.
July 1-2.— The Twenty-eighth Regiment, Ohio Volunteer Infantry, received marching orders and accordingly left camp near New Creek, West Virginia from where it started at 3 o'clock p.m. of the same day, proceeding by railroad towards Webster, West Virginia, where it arrived early in the morning of the next day. In the afternoon orders were received to provide with ten days' rations and proceed to Philippi, West Virginia, a distance of twelve miles, and encamp there until further orders. Arrived at Philippi, West Virginia at 8 o'clock in the evening.
July 6-7.— The regiment received orders to proceed on to Beverly, West Virginia. Left Philippi, West Virginia on July 6 at 8 o'clock and arrived at Beverly, West Virginia, a distance of thirty miles, at 12 o'clock m. next day where the regiment is stationed ever since.

Stationed at Beverly, West Virginia, August-October 1863.

Stationed at Beverly, West Virginia, November 1863.
November 1.— In compliance with General Orders No. 2, from Headquarters, First Separate Brigade, dated October 28, 1863, the Twenty-eighth Regiment, Ohio Volunteer Infantry left Beverly, West Virginia in the direction of Huttonsville, West Virginia, eleven miles distant.
November 5.— We met with Colonel William Jackson's forces at Mile Point, West Virginia. After a short skirmish Jackson's forces retreated to Droop Mountain, a distance of five miles from there, and took position.
November 6.— In the morning we attacked them and by a flank movement drove them from their position and pursued them for six miles. They admit a loss of 800 men killed, wounded and missing. The Twenty-eighth Regiment lost three killed and twenty-five wounded, of which four died since.
November 7.— We marched to Lewisburg, West Virginia, where we arrived the same day in the evening.
November 8-12.— We started back towards Beverly, West Virginia with the prisoners' train and captured cattle and one cannon left by the enemy and after five days' hard marching we arrived at Beverly, West Virginia on November 12, having been absent twelve days.

Stationed at Beverly, West Virginia, December 1863-March 1864.

Stationed at Bunker Hill, West Virginia, April 1864.
April 25-30.— The Twenty-eighth Regiment, Ohio Volunteer Infantry, received orders to march and accordingly left Beverly, West Virginia the same day. Marched sixteen miles; arrived at Belington, where it encamped for the night. Broke camp early next morning. Marched twelve miles and arrived at Philippi in the evening, where the regiment stayed until the next morning, when it took up the line of march again and proceeded to Webster, a distance of twelve miles. Arrived there at 2 o'clock p.m. the same day. Stayed until midnight, when orders were received to proceed to Martinsburg, West Virginia by railroad and arrived

there next morning; started to Bunker Hill, West Virginia, a distance of twelve miles the same day, where it arrived in the evening, on which place it still remained on April 30.

Stationed at Cedar Creek, Virginia, May 1864.
May 1-9.— The regiment received orders to march and left camp accordingly. Proceeded twelve miles and encamped one mile beyond Winchester, where it remained until May 9.
May 10.— Broke camp again. Marched eighteen miles and arrived at Cedar Creek towards evening.
May 12.— Started to Woodstock, a distance of fourteen miles, where it arrived in the evening of May 12.
May 15-16.— The regiment was ordered to guard the rear of the Army of the Shenandoah and marched to Mount Jackson, a distance of fourteen miles, where the regiment was ordered to the front as support. The rest of the infantry, who were then already engaged with the enemy near New Market, arrived on the battlefield with five companies (three being left at Woodstock to turn over some prisoners, they having been detailed as provost guard at that place). Two companies were sent out in pursuit of bushwhackers, who attacked the train and one company was detailed as pioneers with the advance to build a bridge over the Shenandoah, just in time to aid in covering retreat of the Army, after which the regiment was ordered to fall back beyond the Shenandoah and from there proceeded on to Cedar Creek, where we arrived on the morning of May 16 after marching all night.
May 26.— The regiment again marched to Woodstock.
May 28-June 1.— The regiment received marching orders. Again proceeded as far as [illegible] Hill, a distance of seventeen miles, where it arrived the same evening and remained there until June 1.

Stationed at Camp Carrington near Indianapolis, June 1864.
June 2.— The regiment received marching orders and left camp accordingly with the rest of the Army. Marched twenty miles and arrived at Harrisonburg.
June 4-5.— The line of march was taken up again. Reached Port Republic the afternoon, when the regiment was ordered to move near the ford of the Shenandoah to cover the artillery and train while crossing. Arrived in camp two miles from Port Republic at

midnight. Stayed until 6 o'clock next morning, when we left camp and marched cautiously forward, the enemy being reported but little in advance of us. The Twenty-eighth Regiment marched through the woods parallel with the road and 150 yards from it. Having proceeded about three miles our advance met the enemy. Charged and took thirty-five prisoners. Shortly afterwards we formed in line of battle. Attacked the enemy who was in force in our front. Whipped and routed him after charging twice on his fortifications and encamped on the battlefield for the night. The regiment left twenty-eight killed and 100 wounded.
June 6-10.— We marched fifteen miles and arrived at Staunton and encamped one mile from that place. Remained until June 10, when the regiment was ordered to the rear in charge of the prisoners taken in the last battle.
June 14-21.— The regiment reached Beverly, West Virginia, having crossed the Shenandoah, Alleghanies and Cheat Mountains. Rested one day and proceeded to Webster to get transportation by railroad to Camp Morton, where it arrived with the prisoners on June 21 and stayed there since.

Stationed at Cumberland, Maryland, October 1864.

Company A

Stationed at camp, Bulltown, [West] Virginia, June 13-August 31, 1861.

Stationed at Camp Dennison, July 6, 1861.
July 6.— Muster-in roll of Captain Schache's Company A, in the Second German Regiment of Ohio Foot Volunteers, commanded by Colonel Augustus Moor, called into service of the United States by President from July 6, 1861 (date of this muster) for the term of three years, unless sooner discharged. . . .

T. W. WALKER,
First Lieutenant,
Third Infantry, Mustering Officer.

Stationed at Camp Anderson, [West] Virginia, September-October 1861.

Stationed at Gauley Bridge, [West] Virginia, November 1861-April 1862.

Stationed at camp, Flat Top Tannery, May-June 1862.
May 15.— While in camp at French's Mill, [West] Virginia I received orders to take all the men off duty of my company and those of Company A, Thirty-fourth Ohio Regiment Infantry and proceed on a reconnoitering expedition by a bridle path across the East River Mountain towards Wolf Creek. The small command started at 3 o'clock p.m. and reached Wolf Creek about 6 o'clock p.m. The path leading from camp to Wolf Creek across the East River Mountain was very rugged and precipitous. The distance from French's Mill by this path is about eight miles. On Wolf Creek we came suddenly on the camp of Captain Corcoran's Company of Cavalry of Jenkins' notorious regiment. We attacked them vigorously; killed six, wounded four and made seven prisoners. The rest ran to the bushes, leaving their arms, accoutrements, field equipage, ammunition, and one wagon with provisions, in our hands. We killed also three horses and captured nine. None of the command was killed or wounded. After burning all the arms, ammunition, saddles, and everything else that could not be carried along, we recrossed the mountains and got into camp at French's Mill next morning at 6 o'clock a.m. About 9 o'clock in the evening on the same day news reached camp that Princeton had been attacked that day by the enemy in superior numbers. Orders were given immediately for the brigade to get ready for march. At 11 o'clock all troops were on the road from French's Mill to Princeton. A few miles from Princeton my company was ordered ahead of the column as skirmishers. We drove the enemy picket out of Princeton without any loss on our side. In consideration of my company having had no sleep for two nights and having been on duty and on march nearly three days, the same did take no further part in action.
May 17-18.— Near Princeton, [West] Virginia a general retreat having been concluded upon and carried into effect during the night from May 17 to May 18, my company marched with the regiment as far as our present camp.

May 26.— I was ordered with my company on a reconnaissance to the Blue Stone River. We drove in some of the enemy pickets on Rich Creek and Blue Stone [River] and made a march of thirty-four miles, going and returning in one day.
June 11-13.— My company was again ordered on a reconnoitering expedition with Companies C of the Twenty-eighth Ohio Regiment Infantry and E of the Thirty-fourth Ohio Regiment Infantry and one detachment of the Second Virginia Cavalry, the whole commanded by myself. Near Princeton our vanguard was attacked by the enemy's picket. Their fire was returned and one Rebel was killed. None hurt on our side. Company A and part of Company C were then deployed as skirmishers and succeeded in driving them in. Three companies of mounted Rebels who were stationed at Princeton retreated upon our approach. We entered Princeton, obtained all the information about the enemy we could get and returned to camp on Flat Top Mountain, where we arrived on the morning of June 13, having made a march of forty-five miles in two days.

Stationed at Munson's Hill, Virginia, July-August 1862.
July 5-20.— Captain E. Schache, Acting Major, and First Lieutenant [Frederick] Wiesing, Acting Company Commander, Company A, together with Company H, on detached service guarding haymaking parties.
July 23-29.— Arrested three Rebels and sent them to Headquarters.
August 5-7.— Company A went on a scouting party on the Wyoming Road and returned to camp August 7, having made a march of fifty-two miles and arrested a woman, notorious for having harbored bushwhackers.
August 12.— Went on a scouting party together with three companies of the Twelfth Ohio Regiment Infantry under command of Colonel [Jonathan D.] Hines. Marched to cross-roads within three miles of the enemy and encamped.
August 13-14.— Returned to Rich Creek. Company D of the Twelfth Ohio Regiment and Company A of the Twenty-eight Ohio Regiment proceeded then under command of Captain Schache to the Blue Stone River. They routed a small band of bushwhackers on a farm of that neighborhood. On their march back to Rich Creek they were in turn attacked by a gang of bushwhackers from an ambush. Private Myer, Company A, was

wounded. Sergeant Hunk and Private Hielmeyer are missing. Their fire was returned but with what effect could not be ascertained. In obedience to orders marched the same day back to camp. Arrived there at 1 o'clock a.m. of August 14, having this day made a march of thirty-six miles. At 7 o'clock left with the regiment for Washington, District of Columbia.

Stationed at Sutton, [West] Virginia, September-October 1862.

Stationed at Brownstown, [West] Virginia, November-December 1862.

Stationed at Buckhannon, [West] Virginia, January-February 1863.

Stationed at Buckhannon, [West] Virginia, April 10, 1863.

Stationed at Clarksburg, [West] Virginia, March-April 1863.

Stationed at New Creek, May-June 1863.

Stationed at Beverly, West Virginia, July 1863-February 1864.

Stationed at Bunker Hill, West Virginia, March-April 1864.

Stationed at Camp Carrington, Indiana, May-June 1864.

Stationed at Camp Dennison, Ohio, July 23, 1864.
July 23.— Muster-out roll of Captain Charles Drach's, late Captain E. Schache's, Company A, in the Twenty-eighth Regiment of Infantry, Ohio Volunteers, commanded by Colonel Augustus Moor, called into the service of the United States by the President at Camp Dennison, Ohio (the place of general rendezvous) on May 3, 1861 to serve for the term of three years from the date of enrollment, unless sooner discharged, from December 31, 1863 (when last paid) to July 23, 1864 when mustered out. The company was organized by Captain Ernest Schache at Cincinnati, Ohio in the month of June 1861 and marched thence to Camp

Dennison, Ohio, where it arrived July 6, a distance of seventeen miles. . . .

J. M. EYSTER,
Captain,
Eighteenth United States Infantry, Mustering Officer.

Station not stated, September-October 1864.

Stationed at Parkersburg, West Virginia, November 1864-April 1865.

Stationed at Wheeling, West Virginia, May-June 1865.

Company B

Stationed at camp, Bulltown, [West] Virginia, June 13-August 31, 1861.

Stationed at Cincinnati, Ohio, July 6, 1861.
July 6.— Muster-in roll of Captain [Albert] Ritter's Company B, in the Second German Regiment of Ohio Foot Volunteers, commanded by Colonel Augustus Moor, called into service of the United States by the President from July 6, 1861 (date of this muster) for the term of three years, unless sooner discharged. . . .

T. W. WALKER,
First Lieutenant,
Third Infantry, Mustering Officer.

Stationed at Camp Anderson, [West] Virginia, September-October 1861.

Stationed at Gauley Bridge, [West] Virginia, November 1861-April 1862.

Stationed at Flat Top Tannery, [West] Virginia, May-June 1862.
May 2.— Marched from Gauley Bridge to Fayetteville, [West] Virginia, fifteen miles.
May 8.— Grand Review by Brigadier-General [Jacob Dolson] Cox.

May 10.— Marched to Raleigh, twenty-five miles.
May 12-13.— Marched from Raleigh to Blue Stone River, thirty-nine miles.
May 14.— Marched to Princeton and from Princeton to Frenchville, [West] Virginia, seventeen miles.
May 17.— On May 10 Sergeant Sauer, Corporal Krausen and eleven privates were left at Fayetteville to guard some commissary stores. They followed the company and arrived at Princeton on May 16, when Humphrey Marshall had made an attempt to take Princeton. They immediately reinforced a company of the Thirty-seventh Ohio Volunteer Regiment and had a hard skirmish with the Rebels, although overpowered by them. They had to retreat and joined the company on May 17. One of the privates was slightly wounded.

Stationed near Fort Buffalo, Virginia, July-August 1862.

Stationed at Sutton, [West] Virginia, September-October 1862.

Stationed at camp, Brownstown, [West] Virginia, November-December 1862.

Stationed at camp near Buckhannon, [West] Virginia, January-February 1863.

Stationed at camp near Clarksburg, [West] Virginia, March-April 1863.

Stationed at camp near New Creek, [West] Virginia, May-June 1863.

Stationed at Beverly, West Virginia, July 1863-February 1864.

Stationed at Martinsburg, West Virginia, March-April 1864.

Stationed at Camp Carrington, Indiana, May-June 1864.

Stationed at Camp Dennison, Ohio, July 23, 1864.
July 23.— Muster-out roll of First Lieutenant August Greiff's Company B, in the Twenty-eighth Regiment of Ohio Infantry Volunteers, commanded by Colonel Augustus Moor, called into

the service of the United States by the President at Cincinnati (the place of general rendezvous) on May 3, 1861 to serve for the term of three years from the date of enrollment, unless sooner discharged, from December 31, 1863 (when last paid) to July 23, 1864 when mustered out. The company was organized by Captain Albert Ritter at Cincinnati in the month of June 1861 and marched thence to Camp Dennison, where it arrived July 6, a distance of seventeen miles. . . .

JAMES THOMPSON,
Captain,
Second United States Artillery, Mustering Officer.

Stationed at Cumberland, Maryland, September-October 1864.

Stationed at Wheeling, West Virginia, November 1864-April 1865.

Company C

Stationed at Bulltown, June 13-August 31, 1861.

Stationed at Camp Dennison, July 6, 1861.
July 6.— Muster-in roll of Captain Mathias Reiching's Company C, in the Second German Regiment of Ohio Foot Volunteers, commanded by Colonel Augustus Moor, called into service of the United States by the President, thereof, from July 6, 1861 (date of this muster) for the term of three years, unless sooner discharged. . . .

T. W. WALKER,
First Lieutenant,
Third Infantry, Mustering Officer.

Stationed at Camp Anderson, [West] Virginia, September-October 1861.

Stationed at Camp Gauley, November-December 1861.

Stationed at Gauley Bridge, [West] Virginia, January-April 1862.

Stationed at Flat Top Tannery, May-June 1862.

Stationed at camp near Fort Buffalo, [Virginia], July-August 1862.

Stationed at Sutton, [West] Virginia, September-October 1862.

Stationed at Brownstown, [West] Virginia, November-December 1862.

Stationed at camp, Buckhannon, [West] Virginia, January-February 1863.

Stationed at camp, Buckhannon, Virginia, April 10, 1863.

Stationed at Clarksburg, [West] Virginia, March-April 1863.

Stationed at New Creek, [West] Virginia, May-June 1863.

Stationed at Beverly, West Virginia, July 1863-February 1864.

Stationed at Bunker Hill, March-April 1864.

Stationed at Camp Carrington, Indianapolis, Indiana, May-June 1864.

Stationed at Camp Dennison, Ohio, July 23, 1864.
July 23.— Muster-out roll of Captain Albert Traub's Company C, in the Twenty-eighth Regiment of Ohio Infantry Volunteers, commanded by Colonel Augustus Moor, called into the service of the United States by the President at Camp Dennison, Ohio (the place of general rendezvous) on May 3, 1861 to serve for the term of three years from the date of enrollment, unless sooner discharged, from January 1, 1864 (when last paid) to July 23, 1864 when mustered out. . . .

J. M. EYSTER,
Captain,
Eighteenth United Stationed Infantry, Mustering Officer.

Stationed at Cumberland, Maryland, September-October 1864.

Stationed at Wheeling, West Virginia, November 1864-June 1865.

Company D

Station not stated, June 13-August 31, 1861.

Stationed at Cincinnati, Ohio, July 6, 1861.
July 6.— Muster-in roll of Captain Louis Frey's Company D, in the Second German Regiment of Ohio Foot Volunteers, commanded by Colonel Augustus Moor, called into service of the United States by the President from July 6, 1861 (date of this muster) for the term of three years, unless sooner discharged. . . .

T. W. WALKER,
First Lieutenant,
Third Infantry, Mustering Officer.

Stationed at Camp Anderson, [West] Virginia, September-October 1861.

Stationed at Gauley Bridge, [West] Virginia, November 1861-April 1862.

Stationed at Flat Top Tannery, May-June 1862.

Stationed at camp near Fort Buffalo, July-August 1862.

Stationed at camp near Sutton, [West] Virginia, September-October 1862.

Stationed at camp, Brownstown, [West] Virginia, November-December 1862.

Stationed at Buckhannon, January-February 1863.

Stationed at Buckhannon, April 10, 1863.

Stationed at Clarksburg, March-April 1863.
[For record of events, see Regiment.]

Stationed at camp opposite New Creek, [West Virginia], May-June 1863.

Stationed at Beverly, West Virginia, July 1863-February 1864.

Stationed at Bunker Hill, West Virginia, March-April 1864.

Stationed at Camp Carrington near Indianapolis, May-June 1864.

Stationed at Camp Dennison, Ohio, July 23, 1864.
July 23.— Muster-out roll of Captain Louis Frey's Company D, in the Twenty-eighth Regiment of Ohio Infantry Volunteers, commanded by Colonel Augustus Moor, called into the service of the United States by the President at Camp Dennison, Ohio (the place of general rendezvous) on May 3, 1861 to serve for the term of three years from the date of enrollment, unless sooner discharged, from December 31, 1863 (when last paid) to July 23, 1864 when mustered out. . . .

J. M. EYSTER,
Captain,
Eighteenth United Stationed Infantry, Mustering Officer.

Company E

Stationed at Bulltown, [West] Virginia, June 13-August 31, 1861.

Stationed at Camp Dennison, July 15, 1861.
July 15.— Muster-in roll of Captain Arthur Forbriger's Company E, in the Second German Regiment of Ohio Foot Volunteers, commanded by Colonel Augustus Moor, called into service of the United States by the President from July 15, 1861 (date of this muster) for the term of three years, unless sooner discharged. . . .

T. W. WALKER,
First Lieutenant,
Third Infantry, Mustering Officer.

Stationed at Camp Anderson, [West] Virginia, September-October 1861.

Stationed at camp, Gauley Bridge, November 1861-April 1862.

Stationed at Flat Top Tannery, May-June 1862.

Stationed at camp near Fort Buffalo, Virginia, July-August 1862.

Stationed at camp at Sutton, [West] Virginia, September-October 1862.

Stationed at camp, Brownstown, November-December 1862.

Stationed at camp near Buckhannon, January-February 1863.

Stationed at camp near Buckhannon, [West] Virginia, April 1, 1863.

Stationed at Clarksburg, [West] Virginia, March-April 1863.

Stationed at camp opposite New Creek, [West] Virginia, May-June 1863.

Stationed at Beverly, West Virginia, July 1863-February 1864.

Station not stated, March-April 1864.

Stationed at Camp Carrington near Indianapolis, Indiana, May-June 1864.

Stationed at Camp Dennison, Ohio, July 23, 1864.
July 23.— Muster-out roll of Captain Edwin Frey's, late Arthur Forbriger's, Company E, in the Twenty-eighth Regiment of Ohio Infantry Volunteers, commanded by Colonel Augustus Moor, called into the service of the United States by the President at Cincinnati, Ohio (the place of general rendezvous) on June 13, 1861 to serve for the term of three years from the date of enrollment, unless sooner discharged, December 31, 1863 (when last paid) to July 23, 1864 when mustered out. . . .

J. M. EYSTER,
Captain,
Eighteenth United Stationed Infantry, Mustering Officer.

Company F

Stationed at camp near Bulltown, [West] Virginia, June 13-August 31, 1861.

Stationed at Cincinnati, Ohio, July 6, 1861.

July 6.— Muster-in roll of Captain Henry Sommer's Company F, in the Second German Regiment of Ohio Foot Volunteers, commanded by Colonel Augustus Moor, called into service of the United States by the President from July 6, 1861 (date of this muster) for the term of three years, unless sooner discharged. . . .

T. W. WALKER,
First Lieutenant,
Third Infantry, Mustering Officer.

Stationed at Camp Anderson, [West] Virginia, September-October 1861.

Stationed at Gauley Bridge, [West] Virginia, November 1861-April 1862.

Stationed at Flat Top Tannery, May-June 1862.

Stationed at camp near Fort Buffalo, July-August 1862.

Stationed at camp near Sutton, [West] Virginia, September-October 1862.

Stationed at camp, Brownstown, [West] Virginia, November-December 1862.

Stationed at camp near Buckhannon, [West] Virginia, January-February 1863.

Stationed at Buckhannon, [West] Virginia, April 10, 1863.

Stationed at Clarksburg, [West] Virginia, March-April 1863.

Stationed at camp near New Creek, [West] Virginia, May-June 1863.

Stationed at Beverly, West Virginia, July 1863-February 1864.

Stationed at Bunker Hill, West Virginia, March-April 1864.

Stationed at Camp Carrington, Indiana, May-June 1864.

Actions, marches, etc., in which the company was engaged during the month of June.

June 1.— Company F was encamped with the regiment at Bush Hill near New Market, Virginia.

June 2.— Broke up camp and marched to Harrisonburg, Virginia, a distance of twenty-one miles, arriving there at about 6 p.m.

June 3.— Remained in camp at Harrisonburg.

June 4.— Marched to Port Republic, Virginia, arriving there about 3 p.m., then ordered to cover the crossing of the artillery train of the Army, commanded by Major-General [David] Hunter. The company was on duty with the regiment until 9 p.m., then crossed the Shenandoah River on pontoon bridge and one fork on a log. Marched through Port Republic on the Staunton Road and arrived at camp at about 11 p.m., having marched a distance of nineteen miles.

June 5.— At 4 a.m. the company marched with the regiment and was engaged in the battle of Piedmont and in supporting the artillery on the center until the infantry of the First Brigade, Infantry Division, became engaged with the enemy skirmishers. The company was then ordered forward with the regiment and having been assigned in the center of the First Brigade, took part in two charges upon the enemy's fortifications, the second resulting in storming the works, capturing many prisoners and defeating the enemy completely. Casualties: killed, one; wounded fifteen.

June 6.— Marched to Staunton, arriving there about 3 p.m., eleven miles.

June 7.— Marched about five miles with the regiment on different roads, covering the Pioneers while tearing up the railroad track and burning the bridges of the Central Virginia Railroad, then returned to Staunton (marched ten miles).

June 8-10.— Remained in camp at Staunton.

June 11.— Marched with the regiment towards Beverly, West Virginia, twenty-one miles, escorting about 1,000 Rebel prisoners.

June 12.— To Monterey, twenty-four miles.

June 13.— To Lee's fortifications. Crossed the Allegheny Mountains, twenty-four miles.

June 14.— Crossed Cheat Mountain and arrived at Huttonsville, West Virginia, twenty-four miles.
June 15.— To Beverly, twelve miles.
June 16.— Encamped at Beverly, West Virginia.
June 17.— Marched to the foot of Laurel Hill, ten miles.
June 18.— To Philippi, West Virginia, twenty miles.
June 19.— To Webster, twelve miles.
June 20.— Left Webster on the Northwest Virginia Railroad to Bellaire.
June 21-23.— Crossed the Ohio River on a ferry boat and traveled per Central Ohio Railroad via Xenia and Dayton, Ohio and Richmond, Indiana to Indianapolis, Indiana, where the company arrived with the regiment on June 22 about 6 p.m., then escorted the prisoners to Camp Morton, Indiana. Turned them over and was detailed until 1 a.m. on June 23, then marched to Camp Carrington, Indiana, where the company is yet stationed with the regiment.

Stationed at Camp Dennison, Ohio, July 23, 1864.
July 23.— Muster-out roll of Captain Henry Sommer's Company F, in the Twenty-eighth Regiment of Ohio Infantry Volunteers, commanded by Colonel Augustus Moor, called into the service of the United States by the President at Camp Dennison, Ohio (the place of general rendezvous) on May 3, 1861 to serve for the term of three years from the date of enrollment, unless sooner discharged, July 6, 1863 (when mustered in) to July 23, 1864 when mustered out. . . .

JAMES THOMPSON,
Captain,
Second United States Artillery, Mustering Officer.

Company G

Station not stated, June 13-August 31, 1861.

Stationed at Cincinnati, Ohio, July 6, 1861.
July 6.— Muster-in roll of Captain Tobias Nagel's Company G, in the Second German Regiment of Ohio Foot Volunteers, commanded by Colonel Augustus Moor, called into service of the

United States by the President from July 6, 1861 (date of this muster) for the term of three years, unless sooner discharged. . . .

T. W. WALKER,
First Lieutenant,
Third Infantry, Mustering Officer.

Stationed at Camp Anderson, [West] Virginia, September-October 1861.

Stationed at camp, Gauley Bridge, [West] Virginia, November 1861-April 1862.

Stationed at camp, Flat Top Tannery, [West] Virginia, May-June 1862.

Stationed at camp near Fort Buffalo, July-August 1862.

Stationed at camp at Sutton, [West] Virginia, September-October 1862.

Stationed at camp at Brownstown, [West] Virginia, November-December 1862.

Stationed at Buckhannon, [West] Virginia, January-February 1863.

Stationed at Buckhannon, [West] Virginia, April 10, 1863.

Stationed at Clarksburg, [West] Virginia, March-April 1863.

Stationed at camp near New Creek, [West] Virginia, May-June 1863.

Stationed at Beverly, West Virginia, July 1863-February 1864.

Stationed at Bunker Hill, West Virginia, March-April 1864.

Stationed at Indianapolis, Indiana, May-June 1864.

Stationed at Camp Dennison, July 23, 1864.
July 23.— Muster-out roll of Lieutenant Albert Liomin's Company G, in the Twenty-eighth Regiment of Ohio Infantry Volunteers, commanded by Colonel Augustus Moor, called into the service of the United States by the President of the United States at Camp Dennison, Ohio (the place of general rendezvous) on May 3, 1861 to serve for the term of three years from the date of enrollment, unless sooner discharged, July 6, 1863 (when mustered in) to July 23, 1864 when mustered out. The company was organized by Captain Tobias Nagel at Cincinnati, Ohio in the month of June. . . .

JAMES THOMPSON,
Captain,
Second United States Artillery, Mustering Officer.

Company H

Stationed at camp, Bulltown, [West] Virginia, June 13-August 31, 1861.

Stationed at Cincinnati, Ohio, July 6, 1861.
July 6.— Muster-in roll of Captain Bernhardt Eith's Company H, in the Second German Regiment of Ohio Foot Volunteers, commanded by Colonel Augustus Moor, called into service of the United States by the President from July 6, 1861 (date of this muster) for the term of three years, unless sooner discharged. . . .

T. W. WALKER,
First Lieutenant,
Third Infantry, Mustering Officer.

Stationed at Camp Anderson, [West] Virginia, September-October 1861.

Stationed at camp, Gauley Bridge, November 1861-April 1862.

Stationed at Flat Top Tannery, [West] Virginia, May-June 1862.

Stationed near Fort Buffalo, July-August 1862.

Stationed at camp near Sutton, [West] Virginia, September-October 1862.

Stationed at camp, Brownstown, [West] Virginia, November-December 1862.

Stationed at camp near Buckhannon, [West] Virginia, January-February 1863.

Stationed at camp near Buckhannon, [West] Virginia, April 1, 1863.

Station not stated, March-April 1863.

Stationed at camp opposite New Creek, May-June 1863.

Stationed at Beverly, West Virginia, July 1863-February 1864.

Stationed at Bunker Hill, West Virginia, March-April 1864.

Stationed at Camp Carrington, Indiana, May-June 1864.

Stationed at Camp Dennison, Ohio, July 23, 1864.
July 23.— Muster-out roll of Captain Auguste Fix's Company H, in the Twenty-eighth Regiment of Ohio Infantry Volunteers, commanded by Colonel Augustus Moor, called into the service of the United States by the President of the United States at Cincinnati, Ohio (the place of general rendezvous) on June 13, 1861 to serve for the term of three years from the date of enrollment, unless sooner discharged, from December 31, 1863 (when last paid) to July 23, 1864 when mustered out. . . .

J. M. EYSTER,
Captain,
Eighteenth United Stationed Infantry, Mustering Officer.

Company I

Stationed at camp, Bulltown, June 13-August 31, 1861.

Stationed at Camp Anderson, [West] Virginia, September-October 1861.

Stationed at camp, Gauley Bridge, November 1861-April 1862.

Stationed at camp, Flat Top Tannery, [West] Virginia, May-June 1862.

Stationed at camp near Fort Buffalo, Virginia, July-August 1862.

Stationed at camp near Sutton, [West] Virginia, September-October 1862.

Stationed at Brownstown, [West] Virginia, November-December 1862.

Stationed at camp near Buckhannon, [West] Virginia, January-February 1863.

Stationed at camp near Clarksburg, [West] Virginia, March-April 1863.

Stationed at camp near New Creek, [West] Virginia, May-June 1863.

Stationed at Beverly, West Virginia, July 1863-February 1864.

Stationed at Bunker Hill, West Virginia, March-April 1864.

Stationed at Camp Carrington, Indiana, May-June 1864.

Stationed at Camp Dennison, Ohio, July 23, 1864.
July 23.— Muster-out roll of Lieutenant Frederick Wiesing's Company I, in the Twenty-eighth Regiment of Ohio Infantry Volunteers, commanded by Colonel Augustus Moor, called into the service of the United States by President's proclamation at Camp Dennison, Ohio (the place of general rendezvous) on May 3, 1861 to serve for the term of three years from the date of enrollment, unless sooner discharged, from July 6, 1863 (when mustered in)

to July 23, 1864 when mustered out. The company was organized by Captain Maurice Wesalowski at Cincinnati, Ohio in the month of June 1861. . . .

JAMES THOMPSON,
Captain,
Second United States Artillery, Mustering Officer.

Company K

Stationed at Bulltown, June 13-August 31, 1861.

Stationed at Camp Dennison, July 16, 1861.
July 16.— Muster-in roll of Captain George Sommer's Company K, in the Second German Regiment of Ohio Foot Volunteers, commanded by Colonel Augustus Moor, called into service of the United States by the President from July 16, 1861 (date of this muster) for the term of three years, unless sooner discharged. . . .

T. W. WALKER,
First Lieutenant,
Third Infantry, Mustering Officer.

Stationed at Camp Anderson, [West] Virginia, September-October 1861.

Stationed at camp, Gauley Bridge, November 1861-April 1862.

Stationed at Flat Top Tannery, May-June 1862.

Stationed at camp near Fort Buffalo, July-August 1862.

Stationed at Sutton, [West] Virginia, September-October 1862.

Stationed at Brownstown, [West] Virginia, November-December 1862.

Stationed at Buckhannon, [West] Virginia, January-February 1863.

Stationed at Buckhannon, [West] Virginia, April 10, 1863.

Stationed at Clarksburg, [West] Virginia, March-April 1863.

Stationed at New Creek, [West] Virginia, May-June 1863.

Stationed at Beverly, West Virginia, July 1863-February 1864.

Stationed at Bunker Hill, West Virginia, March-April 1864.

Stationed at Indianapolis, Indiana, May-June 1864.

Stationed at Camp Dennison, Ohio, July 23, 1864.
July 23.— Muster-out roll of Captain J. Arnold Heer's, late Captain [Malte] Lauterbach's, late G. Sommer's, Company K, in the Twenty-eighth Regiment of Ohio Infantry Volunteers, commanded by Colonel Augustus Moor, called into the service of the United States by the President at Camp Dennison, Ohio (the place of general rendezvous) on May 3, 1861 to serve for the term of three years from the date of enrollment, unless sooner discharged, from July 16, 1863 (when mustered in) to July 23, 1864 when mustered out. . . .

JAMES THOMPSON,
Captain,
Second United States Artillery, Mustering Officer.

[M594-Roll #148]

Record of Events for Twenty-ninth Ohio Infantry, August 1861-June 1865.

Field and Staff

Station not stated, not dated.
December 30, 1861.— Muster-in roll of the field and staff in the Twenty-ninth Regiment of Ohio Infantry Volunteers, commanded by Colonel Lewis P. Buckley, called into the service of the

United States by the President from December 30, 1861 (date of this muster) for the term of three years, unless sooner discharged. . . .

HENRY BELKNAP,
Captain,
Eighteenth Infantry, Mustering Officer.

ALBERT [BALDWIN] DOD,
Captain,
Fifteenth Infantry, United States Army, Mustering Officer.

C. T. CHAFFIE.

Stationed at Camp Chase, muster-in to December 31, 1861.

Stationed at Camp Tyler near Paw Paw, [West] Virginia, January-February 1862.

Stationed in the field near New Market, Virginia, March-April 1862.
March 23.— In action at Winchester.

Stationed near Alexandria, May-June 1862.

Stationed at Culpeper, Virginia, August 18, 1862.

Stationed at Frederick City, Maryland, July-August 1862.
August 9.— The regiment engaged in the battle of Cedar Mountain.

Station not stated, September-October 1862.

Stationed at Dumfries, Virginia, November 1862-February 1863.

Stationed in the field, March-April 1863.

Stationed at Dumfries, Virginia, April 10, 1863.

Stationed near Sandy Hook, Maryland, May-June 1863.

Stationed at Governor's Island, New York Harbor, July-August 1863.

Stationed at Wauhatchie, Lookout Valley, Tennessee, September-October 1863.

Stationed at Cleveland, Ohio, November-December 1863.

Stationed at Bridgeport, Alabama, January-April 1864.

Stationed in the field, Georgia, May-June 1864.

Stationed at Pace's Ferry, Georgia, July-August 1864.

Stationed at Atlanta, Georgia, September-October 1864.

Stationed at Savannah, Georgia, November-December 1864.

Stationed in the field, South Carolina, January-February 1865.

Stationed in the field, North Carolina, March-April 1865.

Stationed near Louisville, Kentucky, May-June 1865.

Regiment

Station not stated, December 1861.

Stationed at Camp Kelley near Cumberland, Maryland, January 1862.
December 30, 1861.— This regiment was mustered into the service of the United States at Columbus, Ohio.
January 17-19, 1862.— Remained in Camp Chase until January 17, when it started to join General [illegible] Division at Camp Kelley near Cumberland, Maryland. Arrived at Camp Kelley January 19.

Stationed at camp near Paw Paw Tunnel, [West] Virginia, February 1862.

There have been monthly returns for this month made before this and, as several of the companies have lost their company records, a correct list of the men absent on account of sickness cannot be furnished.

The colonel commanding and the adjutant of this regiment during the year 1862 are out of the military service of the United States.

Stationed at Camp Kimball near Strasburg, Virginia, March 1862.

There has never been a monthly return of this regiment made out for this regiment before this and as some of the companies have lost their company records, it is impossible to furnish a correct list of those absent from the regiment during this month.

Stationed near New Market, Virginia, April 1862.

Stationed on the march, May 1862.

Stationed at Camp Wade near Alexandria, Virginia, June 1862.

Stationed at camp near Little Washington, Virginia, July 1862.

Stationed in the field, August 1862.
July 27.— Joined General [John] Pope's Army at Little Washington, Virginia. Moved with that Army in its campaign on the Rappahannock.
August 9.— Was engaged in action at Cedar Mountain.

Stationed at Frederick, Maryland, September 1862.
September 9.— Detached from the brigade on the march and ordered to report to Monocacy Bridge to handle and guard commissary and quartermaster stores.
September 26.— Moved from Monocacy to Frederick City, Maryland by orders of General [George Brinton] McClellan. Reported to Colonel [Samuel] H. Allen, Military Governor, Frederick City.

Stationed at Frederick City, Maryland, October 1862.

The regiment is on duty at Frederick City, Maryland as hospital nurses and guards.

Stationed at Frederick City, Maryland, November 1862.

Stationed at Dumfries, Virginia, December 1862-March 1863.

Stationed near Aquia [Creek] Landing, April-May 1863.

Stationed at Littlestown, Pennsylvania, June 1863.

Stationed near Kelly's Ford, Virginia, July 1863.

Stationed at Governor's Island, New York Harbor, August 1863.

Stationed en route for the Army of the Cumberland (Tennessee), September 1863.

Stationed at Wauhatchie, Tennessee, October-November 1863.

Stationed at Bridgeport, Alabama, December 1863.

HEADQUARTERS, DEPARTMENT OF THE CUMBERLAND,
Chattanooga, Tennessee,
December 21, 1863.

SPECIAL FIELD ORDERS, }
NO. 342. }
Extract No. 17.

Three-fourths of the Twenty-ninth Regiment, Ohio Volunteers having reenlisted as veteran volunteers, it will proceed to Cleveland, Ohio under command of Colonel [William T.] Fitch, who upon his arrived at that place will report through the governor of Ohio to the superintendent of the recruiting service for that state for furlough of thirty days, [which was] granted veteran volunteers, and for the reorganization and recruiting of the regiment. All men of the regiment who are not eligible to reenlist as veteran volunteers on account of having more than one year to serve will be permitted to accompany the regiment upon giving a promise in writing that they will so reenlist when they become eligible. All other individuals who fail to reenlist as veterans will be permanently transferred to some other regiment under the superintendence of Major-General [Joseph] Hooker, commanding the Eleventh and Twelfth Corps, and will not be allowed to accompany them on furlough. Captains Wilber F. Stevens and Jonas Schoonover and First Lieutenant Andrew Wilson will not be permitted to accompany the regiment but will, during its absence, be assigned to duty with some other command of the Twelfth Corps, they having manifested no interest in reenlisting their companies. At the expiration of the furlough the regiment will depart in a body for duty with its brigade. The quartermaster's department will furnish transportation for the regiment going and coming. By command of Major-General [George Henry] Thomas.

WILLIAM McMICHAEL,
Major and Assistant Adjutant-General.

JAMES B. STORER,
Adjutant.

Stationed at Bridgeport, Alabama, January-April 1864.

Station not stated, May-July 1864.

Stationed near Pace's Ferry, Georgia, August 1864.

Stationed at Atlanta, Georgia, September-October 1864.

Station not stated, November 1864.

Stationed at Savannah, Georgia, December 1864.

Stationed in the field, Georgia, January 1865.

Stationed in the field, South Carolina, February 1865.

Stationed near Goldsborough, North Carolina, March 1865.

Stationed at Raleigh, North Carolina, April 1865.

Stationed near Bladensburg, Maryland, May 1865.

Stationed near Louisville, Kentucky, June 1865.

Company A

Stationed at Camp Chase, August 14-December 31, 1861.

Stationed at Jefferson, Ohio, September 7, 1861.
September 7.— Muster-in roll of Captain William T. Fitch's Company A, in the Twenty-ninth Regiment of Ohio Volunteers, commanded by Colonel L. P. Buckley, called into the service of the United States by the President from September 7, 1861 (date of this muster) for the term of three years, unless sooner discharged. The company was organized by Captain William T. Fitch at Jefferson in the month of August and marched thence to Camp Giddings, where it arrived August 14. . . .

HENRY BELKNAP,
Captain,
Eighteenth Infantry, Mustering Officer.

Stationed at Camp Tyler near Paw Paw, [West] Virginia, January-February 1862.

Stationed near New Market, Virginia, March-April 1862.

Stationed at camp near Alexandria, Virginia, June 30, 1862.

Stationed at Culpeper, Virginia, August 18, 1862.

Stationed at Frederick City, Maryland, July-October 1862.

Stationed at Dumfries, Virginia, November 1862-February 1863.

Stationed at Dumfries, Virginia, April 10, 1863.

Stationed at Aquia Creek, March-April 1863.

Stationed in the field, May-June 1863.

Stationed at Governor's Island, New York Harbor, July-August 1863.

Stationed at Lookout Valley, Tennessee, September-October 1863.

Stationed at Cleveland, Ohio, November-December 1863.

Stationed at Bridgeport, Alabama, January-April 1864.

Stationed near Atlanta, Georgia, May-October 1864.

Stationed at Savannah, Georgia, November-December 1864.

Stationed in the field, South Carolina, January-February 1865.

Stationed in the field, North Carolina, March-April 1865.

Stationed near Louisville, Kentucky, May-June 1865.

Company B

Stationed at Camp Chase, August 19-December 31, 1861.

Stationed at Jefferson, Ohio, September 7, 1861.
September 7.— Muster-in roll of Captain Wilbur F. Stevens' Company, in the Twenty-ninth Regiment of Ohio Volunteers, commanded by Colonel Lewis P. Buckley, called into the service of the United States by the President from September 7, 1861 (date of this muster) for the term of three years, unless sooner discharged. The company was organized by Captain Wilbur F. Stevens at Pierpont in the month of August and marched thence to Jefferson, where it arrived August 19, a distance of twelve miles. . . .

HENRY BELKNAP,
Captain,
Eighteenth Infantry, Mustering Officer.

Stationed at Camp Tyler near Paw Paw, [West] Virginia, January-February 1862.

Stationed near New Market, Virginia, March-April 1862.

Stationed near Alexandria, Virginia, May-June 1862.

Stationed at Culpeper Court-House, Virginia, August 18, 1862.

Stationed at Frederick City, Maryland, July-October 1862.

Stationed at Dumfries, Virginia, November 1862-February 1863.

Stationed at Dumfries, Virginia, April 10, 1863.

Stationed in the field, March-April 1863.

Stationed near Sandy Hook, Maryland, May-June 1863.

Stationed at Governor's Island, New York, July-August 1863.

Stationed at Lookout Valley, Tennessee, September-October 1863.

Station not stated, November-December 1863.

Stationed at Bridgeport, Alabama, January-April 1864.

Stationed near Atlanta, Georgia, May-June 1864.
June 15.— This regiment in action. Charged the enemy's works at Pine Hill, Georgia.

Stationed at Pace's Ferry, Georgia, July-August 1864.

Stationed at Atlanta, Georgia, September-October 1864.

Stationed at Savannah, Georgia, November-December 1864.

Stationed in the field, South Carolina, January-February 1865.

Stationed in the field, North Carolina, March-April 1865.

Stationed near Louisville, Kentucky, May-June 1865.

Company C

Stationed at Camp Chase, August 26-December 31, 1861.

Stationed at Jefferson, Ohio, not dated.
September 7, 1861.— Muster-in roll of Captain Edward Hayes' Company, in the Twenty-ninth Regiment of Ohio Volunteers, commanded by Colonel L. P. Buckley, called into the service of the United States by the President from September 7, 1861 (date of this muster) for the term of three years, unless sooner discharged. The company was organized by Captain Edward Hayes at West Andover in the month of August and marched thence to Jefferson, where it arrived August 27, a distance of fourteen miles. . . .

HENRY BELKNAP,
Captain,
Eighteenth Infantry, Mustering Officer.

Stationed at Camp Tyler near Paw Paw, [West] Virginia, January-February 1862.

Stationed at New Market, Virginia, March-April 1862.

Stationed at camp, Alexandria, Virginia, May-June 1862.

Stationed at Culpeper Court-House, Virginia, August 18, 1862.

Stationed at Frederick City, Maryland, July-October 1862.

Stationed at Dumfries, Virginia, November 1862-February 1863.

Stationed at Dumfries, Virginia, April 10, 1863.

Stationed in the field, March-June 1863.

Stationed at Governor's Island, New York, July-August 1863.

Stationed in the field near Chattanooga, Tennessee, September-October 1863.

Stationed at Cleveland, Ohio, November-December 1863.

Stationed at Bridgeport, Alabama, January-April 1864.

Stationed in the field, Georgia, May-August 1864.

Stationed at Atlanta, Georgia, September-October 1864.

Stationed at Savannah, Georgia, November-December 1864.

Stationed in the field, South Carolina, January-February 1865.

Stationed in the field, North Carolina, March-April 1865.

Stationed near Louisville, Kentucky, May-June 1865.

Company D

Stationed at Jefferson, Ohio, September 27, 1861.
September 27.— Muster-in roll of Captain Pulaski C. Hard's Company, in the Twenty-ninth Regiment of Ohio Volunteers, commanded by Colonel L. P. Buckley, called into the service of the United States by the President from September 27, 1861 (date of this muster) for the term of three years, unless sooner discharged. . . .

HENRY BELKNAP,
Captain,
Eighteenth Infantry, Mustering Officer.

Stationed at Camp Chase, December 31, 1861.

Stationed at Camp Tyler near Paw Paw, [West] Virginia, January-February 1862.

Stationed near New Market, Virginia, March-April 1862.

Stationed at camp near Alexandria, May-June 1862.

Stationed at Culpeper Court-House, August 18, 1862.

Stationed at Frederick City, Maryland, July-August 1862.

Stationed at camp near Frederick City, Maryland, September-October 1862.

Stationed at Dumfries, Virginia, November-December 1862.

Stationed at Dumfries Landing, Virginia, January-February 1863.

Stationed at Dumfries Landing, Virginia, April 10, 1863.

Stationed at camp in the field, Virginia, March-April 1863.

Stationed at camp near Sandy Hook, Maryland, May-June 1863.

Stationed at Governor's Island, New York, July-August 1863.

Stationed at Wauhatchie, Tennessee, September-October 1863.

Stationed at Cleveland, Ohio, November-December 1863.

Stationed at Bridgeport, Alabama, January-April 1864.

Stationed near Atlanta, Georgia, May-June 1864.

Stationed near Chattahoochee River, Georgia, July-August 1864.

Stationed at Atlanta, Georgia, September-October 1864.

Stationed at Savannah, Georgia, November-December 1864.

Stationed in the field, North Carolina, January-April 1865.

Stationed near Louisville, Kentucky, May-June 1865.

Company E

Stationed at Jefferson, Ohio, September 27, 1861.
September 27.— Muster-in roll of Captain Horatio Luce's Company, in the Twenty-ninth Regiment of Ohio Volunteers, commanded by Colonel Lewis P. Buckley, called into the service of the United States by the President from September 27, 1861 (date

of this muster) for the term of three years, unless sooner discharged. . . .

HENRY BELKNAP,
Captain,
Eighteenth Infantry, Mustering Officer.

Stationed at Camp Chase, enrollment to December 31, 1861.

Stationed at Camp Tyler near Paw Paw, [West] Virginia, January-February 1862.

Stationed at Mount Jackson, Virginia, March-April 1862.

Stationed near Alexandria, Virginia, May-June 1862.

Stationed at Frederick City, Maryland, July-October 1862.

Stationed at Dumfries, Virginia, November 1862-February 1863.

Stationed at Dumfries, Virginia, April 10, 1863.

Stationed in the field, March-April 1863.

Stationed at Littlestown, Pennsylvania, May-June 1863.

Stationed at Governor's Island, New York, July-August 1863.

Stationed in the field, Tennessee, September-October 1863.

Stationed at Cleveland, Ohio, January 7, 1864.

Stationed at Bridgeport, Alabama, January-April 1864.

Stationed in the field near Marietta, Georgia, May-June 1864.

Stationed at Pace's Ferry, Georgia, July-August 1864.

Stationed at Atlanta, Georgia, October 31, 1864.

Stationed at Savannah, Georgia, November-December 1864.

Stationed in the field, South Carolina, January-February 1865.

Stationed in the field, North Carolina, March-April 1865.

Stationed near Louisville, Kentucky, May-June 1865.

Company F

Station not stated, not dated.

Muster-in roll of Captain John F. Morse's Company, in the Twenty-ninth Regiment of Ohio Foot Volunteers, commanded by Colonel Lewis P. Buckley, called into the service of the United States by the President from the date set opposite their names respectively, 1861, for the term of three years, unless sooner discharged. . . .

JOHN F. MORSE.

Stationed at Camp Chase, muster-in to December 31, 1861.

Stationed at Camp Tyler near Paw Paw, [West] Virginia, January-February 1862.

Stationed near New Market, Virginia, March-April 1862.

Stationed at Alexandria, May-June 1862.

Stationed near Culpeper, Virginia, August 18, 1862.

Stationed at Frederick City, Maryland, July-October 1862.

Stationed at Dumfries Landing, Virginia, November-December 1862.

Station not stated, January-February 1863.

Stationed at Dumfries, Virginia, April 10, 1863.

Stationed in the field, March-April 1863.

Station not stated, May-June 1863.

Stationed at Governor's Island, New York, July-August 1863.

Stationed at Lookout Valley, Tennessee, September-October 1863.

Stationed at Cleveland, Ohio, November-December 1863.

Stationed at Bridgeport, Alabama, January-April 1864.

Stationed in the field near Atlanta, Georgia, May-June 1864.

Stationed near Chattahoochee River, Georgia, July-August 1864.

Stationed at Atlanta, September-October 1864.

Stationed at Savannah, Georgia, November-December 1864.

Stationed in the field, South Carolina, January-February 1865.

Stationed near Raleigh, North Carolina, March-April 1865.

Stationed near Louisville, Kentucky, May-June 1865.

Company G

Stationed at Jefferson, Ashtabula County, Ohio, September 30, 1861.
September 30.— Muster-in roll of Captain John S. Clemmer's Company, in the Twenty-ninth Regiment of Ohio Volunteers . . . called into the service of the United States by the President from September 30, 1861 (date of this muster) for the term of three years, unless sooner discharged. . . .

HENRY BELKNAP,
Captain,
Eighteenth Infantry, Mustering Officer.

Stationed at Camp Chase, enrollment to December 31, 1861.

Stationed at Camp Tyler near Paw Paw, [West] Virginia, January-February 1862.

Stationed at Mount Jackson, Virginia, March-April 1862.

Stationed near Alexandria, Virginia, May-June 1862.

Stationed at Culpeper Court-House, August 18, 1862.

Stationed at Frederick City, Maryland, July-October 1862.

Stationed near Dumfries, Virginia, November 1862-February 1863.

Stationed at Dumfries, Virginia, April 10, 1863.

Stationed in the field, Virginia, March-April 1863.

Stationed in the field, Pennsylvania, May-June 1863.

Stationed at Governor's Island, New York, July-August 1863.

Stationed at Lookout Valley, Tennessee, September-October 1863.

Stationed at Cleveland, Ohio, November-December 1863.

Stationed at Bridgeport, Alabama, January-April 1864.

Stationed near Atlanta, Georgia, May-June 1864.

Stationed near Chattahoochee River, Georgia, July-August 1864.

Stationed at Atlanta, Georgia, September-October 1864.

Stationed at Savannah, Georgia, November-December 1864.

Stationed in the field, South Carolina, January-February 1865.

Stationed in the field, North Carolina, March-April 1865.

Stationed near Louisville, Kentucky, May-June 1865.

Company H

Station not stated, not dated.

Muster-in roll of Captain Jonas Schoonover's Company H, in the Twenty-ninth Regiment of Ohio Volunteers, commanded by Colonel Lewis P. Buckley, called into the service of the United States by the President from the date set opposite their names, respectively, for the term of three years, unless sooner discharged. . . .

ALBERT B. DOD,
Mustering Officer.

[ALVIN] C. VORIS.

C. T. CHAFFIE.

Stationed at Camp Chase, muster-in to December 31, 1861.

Stationed at Camp Tyler near Paw Paw, [West] Virginia, January-February 1862.

Stationed at New Market, Virginia, March-April 1862.

Stationed near Alexandria, Virginia, May-June 1862.

Stationed at Culpeper Court-House, Virginia, August 18, 1862.

Stationed at Frederick City, Maryland, July-August 1862.

Station not stated, September-October 1862.

Stationed at Dumfries, Virginia, November 1862-February 1863.

Stationed at Dumfries, Virginia, April 10, 1863.

Stationed in the field, Virginia, March-April 1863.

Stationed in the field, Maryland, May-June 1863.

Stationed at Governor's Island, New York, July-August 1863.

Stationed at Lookout Valley, Tennessee, September-October 1863.

Stationed at Cleveland, Ohio, November-December 1863.

Stationed at Bridgeport, Alabama, January-April 1864.

Stationed in the field near Marietta, Georgia, May-June 1864.

Stationed at Pace's Ferry, Chattahoochee River, Georgia, July-August 1864.

Stationed at Atlanta, Georgia, September-October 1864.

Stationed at Savannah, Georgia, November-December 1864.

Stationed in the field, South Carolina, January-February 1865.

Stationed at Bladensburg, Maryland, March-April 1865.

Stationed near Louisville, Kentucky, May-June 1865.

Company I

Stationed at Camp Giddings, Jefferson, Ohio, December 14, 1861.
October 14.— Muster-in roll of Captain Russell B. Smith's Company, in the Twenty-ninth Regiment of Ohio Volunteer, commanded by Colonel Lewis P. Buckley, called into service of the United States by the President from October 14, 1861 (date of this muster) for the term of three years, unless sooner discharged. . . .

WILLIAM J. HALE,
Mustering Officer.

C. T. CHAFFIE.

[ANDREW] J. FULKERSON.

Stationed at Camp Chase, to December 31, 1861.

Stationed at Camp Tyler new Paw Paw, [West] Virginia, January-February 1862.

Stationed near New Market, Virginia, March-April 1862.

Station not stated, May-June 1862.

Stationed at Frederick City, Maryland, July-August 1862.
August 9.— Battle of Cedar Mountain.

Stationed at Frederick, Maryland, September-October 1862.

Stationed near Dumfries Landing, Virginia, November-December 1862.

Stationed at Dumfries, Virginia, January-February 1863.

Stationed at Dumfries Landing, Virginia, April 10, 1863.

Stationed in the field, March-April 1863.

Station not stated, May-June 1863.

Stationed at Governor's Island, New York, July-August 1863.

Stationed at Lookout Valley, Tennessee, September-October 1863.

Stationed at Cleveland, Ohio, November-December 1863.

Stationed at Bridgeport, Alabama, January-February 1864.

Station not stated, March-April 1864.

Stationed near Atlanta, Georgia, May-October 1864.

Stationed at Savannah, Georgia, November-December 1864.

Stationed in the field, South Carolina, January-February 1865.

Stationed in the field, North Carolina, March-April 1865.

Stationed near Louisville, Kentucky, May-June 1865.

Company K

Station not stated, not dated.

Muster-in roll of Captain Alden P. Steele's Company, in the Twenty-ninth Regiment of Ohio Infantry Volunteers, commanded by Colonel Lewis P. Buckley, called into service of the United States by the President, Abraham Lincoln . . . for the term of three years, unless sooner discharged. . . .

C. T. CHAFFEE,
Mustering Officer.

Stationed at Camp Chase, muster-in to December 31, 1861.

Stationed at Camp Tyler near Paw Paw, [West] Virginia, January-February 1862.

Stationed near New Market, Virginia, March-April 1862.

Stationed near Alexandria, Virginia, May-June 1862.

Stationed at Culpeper Court-House, August 18, 1862.

Stationed at Frederick, Maryland, July-August 1862.

Station not stated, September-October 1862.

Stationed at Dumfries, November 1862-February 1863.

Stationed at Dumfries, Virginia, April 10, 1863.

Stationed near Aquia Creek, Virginia, March-April 1863.

Stationed at camp in the field, Pennsylvania, May-June 1863.

Stationed on Governor's Island, New York, July-August 1863.

Stationed at Lookout Valley, Tennessee, September-October 1863.

Stationed at Cleveland, Ohio, November-December 1863.

Stationed at Bridgeport, Alabama, January-April 1864.

Stationed in the field near Marietta, May-June 1864.

Stationed at Pace's Ferry, Georgia, July-August 1864.

Stationed at Atlanta, Georgia, September-October 1864.

Stationed at Savannah, Georgia, November-December 1864.

Stationed in the field, South Carolina, January-February 1865.

Stationed in the field, North Carolina, March-April 1865.

Stationed near Louisville, Kentucky, May-June 1865.

[M594-Roll #148]

———

Record of Events for Thirtieth Ohio Infantry, August 1861-June 1865.

Field and Staff

Stationed at Camp Ewing, October 31, 1861.

Station not stated, January-February 1862.

Stationed at Raleigh Court-House, [West] Virginia, March-April 1862.
April 17.— The regiment left Fayetteville, Fayette County, [West] Virginia and marched to Raleigh Court-House, distance twenty-five miles. Time consumed in marching, two days.

Station not stated, May-June 1862.

Stationed at Centreville, Virginia, July-August 1862.
August 15-20.— Left Camp Jones, Flat Top Mountain, [West] Virginia at 3.45 a.m. Arrived at Camp Piatt on Kanawha River, [West] Virginia on August 19 at 11.20 a.m. At 2.30 p.m. of same day left Camp Piatt by boat. At 8 p.m. of August 20 arrived at Parkersburg, [West] Virginia.
August 21-24.— At 7 p.m. left Parkersburg, [West] Virginia by railroad. At 9.40 a.m. of August 23 arrived at Washington, District of Columbia and at 10.25 a.m. of August 24 arrived at Warrenton Junction, Virginia.
August 27-29.— At 3.40 p.m. left Warrenton Junction on foot. At 8.30 a.m. of August 29 arrived at Centreville, Virginia, a total distance of 750 miles.

Stationed at Sutton, [West] Virginia, September-October 1862.

Stationed at Brownstown, [West] Virginia, November-December 1862.

Stationed at Young's Point, Louisiana, January-April 1863.

Stationed at Walnut Hill, Mississippi, May-June 1863.

Stationed at Camp Sherman, Mississippi, July-August 1863.

Stationed at Chickasaw, Alabama, September-October 1863.

Stationed near Bellefonte, Alabama, November-December 1863.

Stationed at Cleveland, Tennessee, January-February 1864.

Stationed near Kenesaw Mountain, Georgia, [March]-June 1864.
Three-fourths of the regiment having reenlisted as veterans, the commanding officer was directed per Special Orders No. 85, March 31, Headquarters, Fifteenth Army Corps, to proceed with same to Columbus, Ohio, reporting through the governor to superintendent of recruiting service of the state for reorganization and furlough.
April 2-9.— Accordingly, the regiment left Larkinsville, Alabama. Arrived in Columbus, Ohio April 9.

May 9.— Was furloughed until May 9, at which time it reassembled at same place.
May 10-22.— Left Columbus and rejoined the Army in the field at Kingston, Georgia on May 22.

No muster could be made on April 30, the regiment being furloughed and scattered without organization of the state of Ohio.

Stationed in the field, July-August 1864.

Stationed in the field, September-October 1864.
October 4.— Moved from camp at East Point, Georgia, following [John Bell] Hood's Army to Little River, Alabama.

Stationed at Fort McAllister, Georgia, November-December 1864.

Stationed at Lynch's Creek, South Carolina, January-February 1865.
January 16.— The regiment left Savannah, Georgia with the division to which it belongs for Beaufort, South Carolina, where it disembarked.
January 27.— It marched from thence and has accompanied General [William Tecumseh] Sherman's forces thus far through Carolina. It was engaged in the taking of Columbia, South Carolina, crossing the Saluda River in pontoon boats under the enemy's fire, where it lost one officer severely wounded.

Stationed in the field, North Carolina, March-April 1865.

Stationed aboard steamer Starlight, May-June 1865.

Regiment

Stationed at Camp Sewell, except Companies D, F, G, and I at Camp Sutton, September 1861.

Stationed at Camp Ewing, [West] Virginia, except Companies D, F, G, and I at Camp Sutton, [West] Virginia, October 1861.

Stationed at Camp Union, [West] Virginia, except Companies D, F, G, and I at Camp Sutton, [West] Virginia; Company K at Camp Huddleston, [West] Virginia, November 1861.

Stationed at Camp Union, Fayette Court-House, [West] Virginia, except Companies A four miles, Company G ten miles and Company H two miles south of Fayette Court-House, [West] Virginia; Companies F and K at Raleigh Court-House, [West] Virginia, December 1861.
December 17-22.— Companies D, F, G, and I left Sutton, [West] Virginia, where they had been stationed since September 5, under command of Lieutenant-Colonel [Theodore] Jones. Arrived at Fayette Court-House, a distance of twenty-eight miles on December 22.
December 29.— Companies F and K were detached to Raleigh Court-House.

Company A was detached four miles south of Fayette Court-House December —.

Company B was detached ten miles south of Fayette Court-House December —.

Stationed at Camp Union, [West] Virginia, except Company A, Company B twelve miles and Company G two miles south of Fayette Court-House; Companies F, H and I at Raleigh Court-House, January 1862.

Stationed at Camp Union, [West] Virginia outpost, except Companies F, I and K at Camp Hayes, [West] Virginia outpost, February 1862.

Stationed at Camp Union, Fayette County, [West] Virginia, March 1862.

Stationed at Camp Hayes, Raleigh Court-House, [West] Virginia, April 1862.
April 15.— Captain [Charles] Townsend's Company C, accompanied by an escort of twelve men, distributed 200 copies of the Constitution of West Virginia throughout Fayette and the adjoining counties.

April 17.— The regiment left winter quarters and moved south to the junction of White Oak and Loup Creeks, ten miles.
April 18.— Marched to Raleigh Court-House, fifteen miles.
April 22.— Sent ten wagons under escort of Lieutenant [Jeremiah] Hall, Company A, and twenty men to the marshes of Cole, fifteen miles west, for forage.
April 24.— Sent scout of 100 men under Captain [Elijah] Warner, Company E, into Greenbrier County, head of Lick Creek, to attack a cavalry force of the enemy reported fifty strong and to ambush at the crossing of New River an expected force of 150.
April 30.— Reviewed, inspected and mustered the regiment.

Stationed at camp, Flat Top, [West] Virginia, May 1862.
May 4.— The regiment left Raleigh. Marched south to crossing of Glade Creek, sixteen miles.
May 5.— Marched to Wolf Creek at the foot of Flat Top Mountain, sixteen miles.
May 6.— Marched to Princeton, twelve miles.
May 10.— Marched east to the mouth of East River, twenty miles.
May 17.— Marched west to Princeton, twenty miles.
May 18.— Marched north to the mouth of Rich Creek, nine miles.
May 19.— Marched north to the top of Flat Top Mountain, seventeen miles.

Stationed at Camp Jones, [West] Virginia, June 1862.
June 14.— The regiment [marched] from Camp Flat Top to Camp Jones, Flat Top Mountain, distance two miles. Time consumed in marching one hour.

Stationed at Camp Jones, [West] Virginia, July 1862.

Stationed at camp at Centreville, Virginia, August 1862.
[For record of events, see Field and Staff.]

Stationed at mouth of Antietam [Creek], Maryland, September 1862.

Stationed at Camp Sutton, [West] Virginia, October 1862.

Stationed at Camp Ruth Udell, [West] Virginia, November 1862.

Stationed at Brownstown, [West] Virginia, December 1862.

Stationed opposite Vicksburg, Mississippi, January 1863.

Stationed at Young's Point, Louisiana, February-April 1863.

Stationed at Walnut Hill, Mississippi, May-June 1863.

Stationed at Camp Sherman, Mississippi, July-August 1863.

Stationed on board steamer Adams, Mississippi River, September 1863.

Stationed at Chickasaw, Alabama, October 1863.

Stationed at Graysville, Georgia, November 1863.

Stationed near Bellefonte, Alabama, December 1863.

Stationed at Larkinsville, Alabama, January 1864.

Stationed at Cleveland, Tennessee, February-March 1864.

Stationed on the battlefield near Dallas, Georgia, April-May 1864.

Stationed in the field, June-August 1864.

Stationed at East Point, Georgia, September 1864.

Stationed in the field, October-November 1864.

Stationed at Fort McAllister, Georgia, December 1864.

Stationed in the field, South Carolina, January 1865.

Stationed at Lynch's Creek, South Carolina, February 1865.

Stationed near Goldsborough, North Carolina, March 1865.

Stationed in the field, North Carolina, April 1865.

Stationed near Washington, District of Columbia, May 1865.

Stationed on board steamer Starlight, June 1865.

Company A

Stationed at Camp Chase near Columbus, Ohio, August 14, 1861.
August 14.— Muster-in roll of Captain William W. Reilly's Company A, in the Thirtieth Regiment of Ohio Volunteers, commanded by Colonel Hugh Ewing, called into the service of the United States by the President from August 14, 1861 (date of this muster) for the term of three years, unless discharged. The company was organized by Captain William W. Reilly at Portsmouth in the month of July and marched thence to Camp Chase, where it arrived August 2, a distance of ninety-four miles. . . .

HOWARD STANSBURY,
Captain,
Topographical Engineers, Mustering Officer.

Stationed at Camp Chase near Columbus, Ohio, August 14, 1861.
July 28.— This company went into quarters at Portsmouth, from which time their term of service is commenced.

Stationed at Camp Ewing, [West] Virginia, October 31, 1861.

Station not stated, December 31, 1861.

Stationed at Camp Fowler, [January]-February 1862.

Stationed at Camp Hayes, [West] Virginia, March-April 1862.

Stationed at Camp Jones, [West] Virginia, May-June 1862.

Stationed at Centreville, Virginia, July-August 1862.

Stationed at Sutton, [West] Virginia, September-October 1862.

Stationed on board steamer Leonora, December 31, 1862.

Stationed at camp at Young's Point, Louisiana, January-February 1863.

Stationed at Young's Point, Louisiana, April 10, 1863.

Stationed at Drumgould's Bluff, Mississippi, March-April 1863.

Stationed at Walnut Hill, Mississippi, May-June 1863.

Stationed at Camp Sherman, Mississippi, July-August 1863.

Stationed at Chickasaw, Alabama, September-October 1863.

Stationed at Bellefonte, Alabama, November-December 1863.

Stationed at Cleveland, Tennessee, January-February 1864.

Stationed before Kenesaw Mountain, Georgia, [March]-June 1864.
The veterans of the company were on furlough in Ohio from April 9 to May 9, in consequence of which no periodical muster was made for the months of March and April.

Stationed near Jonesborough, Georgia, July-August 1864.

Stationed at Cave Spring, Georgia, September-October 1864.

Stationed at White Hall, Georgia, November-December 1864.

Stationed in the field, January-April 1865.

Stationed aboard steamer Starlight, May-June 1865.

Company B

Stationed at Camp Chase near Columbus, Ohio, August 14, 1861.
August 14.— Muster-in roll of Captain David Cunningham's Company B, in the Thirtieth Regiment of Ohio Volunteers, commanded by Colonel Hugh Ewing, called into the service of the

United States by the President from August 14, 1861 for the term of three years, unless discharged. The company was organized by Captain Cunningham at Cadiz in the month of July and marched thence to Camp Chase, where it arrived July 30, a distance of 130 miles. . . .

HOWARD STANSBURY,
Captain,
Topographical Engineers, Mustering Officer.

Stationed at Camp Ewing, [West] Virginia, October 31, 1861.

Stationed at outpost at McCoy's near Fayette, [West] Virginia, February 28, 1862.

Stationed at Camp Hayes, Raleigh, [West] Virginia, March-April 1862.

Stationed at Camp Jones, [West] Virginia, May-June 1862.

Station not stated, July-August 1862.

Stationed at Sutton, [West] Virginia, September-October 1862.

Station not stated, November-December 1862.

Stationed at Young's Point, Louisiana, January-April 1863.

Stationed at Walnut Hill, Mississippi, May-June 1863.

Stationed at Camp Sherman, Mississippi, July-August 1863.

Station not stated, September-October 1863.

Stationed at Bellefonte, Alabama, November-December 1863.

Stationed at Cleveland, Tennessee, January-February 1864.

Stationed at Kenesaw Mountain, Georgia, May-June 1864.

The company reenlisted as veterans under provisions of General Orders No. 191, War Department, series 1863.

April 2-9.— Left Larkinsville, Alabama with the regiment with orders to report at Columbus, Ohio, where the men were furloughed for thirty days from April 9.
May 10.— The regiment reorganized at Columbus, Ohio and returned to the field. In consequence of the men being absent on furlough, there could be no muster April 30, the period for muster.

Stationed at East Point, Georgia, July-August 1864.

Station not stated, September-October 1864.

Stationed at White Hall, Georgia, November-December 1864.

Stationed at Lynch's Creek, South Carolina, January-February 1865.

Stationed near Raleigh, North Carolina, March-April 1865.

Stationed on board steamer Starlight, May-June 1865.

Company C

Stationed at Camp Chase near Columbus, Ohio, August 15, 1861.
August 15.— Muster-in roll of Captain Charles Townsend's Company C, in the Thirtieth Regiment of Ohio Volunteers, commanded by Colonel Hugh Ewing, called into the service of the United States by the President from August 15, 1861 (date of this muster) for the term of three years, unless sooner discharged. The company was organized by Captain Charles Townsend at Downington in the months of July and August and marched thence to Columbus, where it arrived August 6, a distance of 246 miles. . . .

HOWARD STANSBURY,
Captain,
Topographical Engineers, Mustering Officer.

Stationed at Camp Ewing, [West] Virginia, October 31, 1861.

This is to certify that my company was full August 4 and ordered to Camp Chase August 6, at which place it arrived at 3 o'clock a.m. August 6, and that the roll containing the men's names was presented to Adjutant-General [Catharinus Putnam] Buckingham, upon which he ordered an election, which resulted as shown by the original muster roll, and that my company was assigned to the regiment and lettered as it now stands. The company was not mustered in on account of a number deserting, they being dissatisfied with the election of our first lieutenant, and that the company remained wanting a few of being full until it was recruited by sending back to Downington. First Lieutenant [Jeremiah L.] Carpenter resigned on account of the above-named dissatisfaction.

C. TOWNSEND,
Captain.

Stationed at Camp Union, Fayetteville, [West] Virginia, February 28, 1862.

Stationed at Camp Hayes, Raleigh, [West] Virginia, March-April 1862.
[For record of events, see Field and Staff.]

Stationed at Camp Green Meadows, [West] Virginia, May-June 1862.
May 1-4.— The company left Raleigh Court-House on march as convoy of a train and reached Princeton, a distance of forty-two miles, May 4.
May 10.— The company left Princeton with the regiment and reached East River, a distance of twenty-two miles, in the afternoon of the same day.
May 17.— The company left East River with the regiment and reached Princeton, a distance of twenty-two miles, the same day.
May 18-19.— The company commenced a march to Flat Top Mountain, which it reached May 19, a distance of twenty-four miles.
June 1.— The company left camp on Flat Top Mountain as part of a detachment of the First Provisional Brigade and reached Camp Green Meadows, a distance of fifteen miles, on the evening of the same day, where it remains at this time.

Station not stated, July-August 1862.

Stationed at camp, Summerville, [West] Virginia, September-October 1862.

Stationed on board steamer Leonora, November-December 1862.

Stationed at Young's Point, Louisiana, January-April 1863.

Stationed at Walnut Hill, Mississippi, May-June 1863.

Stationed at Camp Sherman, Mississippi, July-August 1863.

Stationed at Chickasaw, Alabama, September-October 1863.

Stationed at Bellefonte, Alabama, November-December 1863.

Stationed at Cleveland, Tennessee, January-February 1864.

Stationed at Kenesaw Mountain, Georgia, [March]-June 1864.
[For record of events, see Company B.]

Stationed near Jonesborough, Georgia, July-August 1864.

Stationed at Cave Spring, Georgia, September-October 1864.

Stationed at Fort McAllister, Georgia, November-December 1864.

Stationed at Lynch's Creek, South Carolina, January-February 1865.

Stationed in the field, North Carolina, March-April 1865.

Stationed at Memphis, Tennessee, May-June 1865.

Company D

Stationed near Columbus, Ohio, August 29, 1861.
August 28.— Muster-in roll of Captain John W. Fowler's Company D, in the Thirtieth Regiment of Ohio Volunteers, commanded by Colonel Hugh Ewing, called into the service of the

United States by the President from August 28, 1861 (date of this muster) for the term of three years, unless sooner discharged. The company was organized by Captain John W. Fowler at New Lexington in the month of August and marched thence to Camp Chase, Columbus, where it arrived August 26, a distance of eighty-three miles. . . .

HOWARD STANSBURY,
Captain,
Topographical Engineers, Mustering Officer.

Station not stated, August 16-December 31, 1861.

Stationed at Camp Union, [West] Virginia, January-February 1862.

Stationed at Camp Hayes, Raleigh Court-House, [West] Virginia, March-April 1862.
[For record of events, see Field and Staff.]

Stationed at Camp Jones, Mercer County, [West] Virginia, May-June 1862.

Stationed at Centreville, Virginia, July-August 1862.
[For record of events, see Field and Staff.]

Stationed at Camp Sutton, [West] Virginia, September-October 1862.

Marched from Centreville, Virginia via Munson's Hill, Washington, District of Columbia to Frederick City, Maryland.
September 14.— Also to South Mountain, Maryland. In battle there September 14.
September 17.— Then to Antietam and in battle September 17. Marched to Hancock, Virginia via National Pike. Took cars to Clarksburg, [West Virginia].
October 30.— Arrived at Sutton.

Stationed on board steamer Leonora, November-December 1862.

Marched from Sutton, [West] Virginia to Camp Ruth Udell, [West] Virginia. Marched on a scout to Logan Court-House and returned to camp. Marched to Camp Piatt, in all a distance of about 300 miles.

Stationed at Young's Point, Louisiana, January-February 1863.
Traveled on transport from Point Pleasant, [West] Virginia to Young's Point, Louisiana.

Stationed at Young's Point, Louisiana, March-April 1863.

Stationed at Walnut Hill, Mississippi, May-June 1863.
Went in transport to Milliken's Bend. Marched thence to Mitchell's Plantation. Marched to Milliken's Bend, then on transport to Young's Point, Louisiana. Marched across the point to below Warrenton; thence on transport to Grand Gulf.
May 19, 22.— Then marched to Walnut Hill in the rear of Vicksburg. Was in the battles of May 19 and 22. Our marching was about the distance of 115 miles, eighty of which was performed in three days. Distance of transport about eighty miles. Total about 195 miles.

Stationed at Camp Sherman, Mississippi, July-August 1863.
July 5-17.— Marched toward Jackson, Mississippi. Arrived in front of Jackson on July 10. Occupied the town on July 17.
July 23.— Started toward Black River on July 23, where we arrived and went into camp. Whole distance marched about seventy-five miles. Was engaged with the enemy while in front of Jackson.

Stationed at camp at Chickasaw Landing, Alabama, September-October 1863.
Marched from Camp Sherman to Vicksburg; thence on boat to Memphis. Marched to Tuscumbia, Alabama; thence back to Cherokee; thence to the Tennessee River at Chickasaw. Whole distance about 600 miles.

Stationed at Bellefonte, Alabama, November-December 1863.
Marched from Chickasaw Landing, Alabama to Chattanooga, Tennessee.
November 24-25.— Was engaged in battle at Chattanooga, in which I lost one killed, two mortally and six severely wounded (all enlisted men). Marched to near Bellefonte, Alabama. Whole distance marched about 275 miles.

Stationed at Cleveland, Tennessee, January-February 1864.

Marched from Bellefonte, Alabama to Larkinsville, Alabama; built winter quarters. Marched thence across Tennessee River to gap on top of Sandy Mountain. Thence to Tennessee River; thence to Lebanon, Alabama; thence back to Larkinsville. Marched to Cleveland, Tennessee via Chattanooga. Whole distance marched about 125 miles.

Stationed near Big Shanty, Georgia, [March]-June 1864.
April 2.— Left Larkinsville, Alabama on veteran furlough.
May 9.— Left home for the front. Arrived at Kingston, Georgia May ——. Marched to Dallas, Georgia. Was engaged in battle there.
May 27-June 30.— Also skirmishing and fighting from May 27 until the present time. Whole distance traveled since February 29 about 1,600 miles. The regiment being disbanded April 30 and consequently was not mustered.

Stationed at Jonesborough, Georgia, July-August 1864.

Stationed at Cave Spring, Georgia, September-October 1864.

Stationed at Fort McAllister, Georgia, November-December 1864.

Stationed at Lynch's Creek, South Carolina, January-February 1865.

Stationed in the field, North Carolina, March-April 1865.

Stationed on board steamer Starlight, May-June 1865.

Stationed near Washington, District of Columbia, May 31, 1865.
May 31.— Muster-out roll of Captain [Benjamin] Fowler, late J. W. Fowler, a detachment of Company D, in the Thirtieth Regiment of Ohio Veteran Infantry Volunteers, commanded by Lieutenant-Colonel [Emerson] P. Brooks, late Jones, called into the service of the United States by the President at New Lexington, Ohio (the place of general rendezvous) on August 20, 1862 to

serve for the term of three years from the date of enrollment, unless sooner discharged, from August 31, 1864 (when last paid) to May 31, 1865 when mustered out. The company was organized by Captain J. W. Fowler at Camp Chase, Ohio in the month of August 1861. . . .

JOHN C. NELSON,
Captain,
Seventieth Ohio Veteran Volunteers, Infantry,
Assistant Commissary of Musters,
Second Division, Fifteenth Army Corps, Mustering Officer.

Company E

Stationed at Camp Chase near Columbus, Ohio, August 29, 1861.
August 19.— Muster-in roll of Captain Elijah Warner's Company E, in the Thirtieth Regiment of Ohio Volunteers, commanded by Colonel Hugh Ewing, called into the service of the United States by the President from August 19, 1861 (date of this muster) for the term of three years, unless sooner discharged. The company was organized by Captain Elijah Warner at Jerome, Union County in the month of August and marched thence to Camp Chase near Columbus, where it arrived August 19, a distance of twenty miles. . . .

HOWARD STANSBURY,
Captain,
Topographical Engineers, Mustering Officer.

Stationed at Camp Ewing, [West] Virginia, August 19-October 31, 1861.

Stationed at Camp Union, [West] Virginia, January-February 1862.

Stationed at Camp Hayes, [West] Virginia, March-April 1862.

Stationed at Camp Green Meadows, [West] Virginia, May-June 1862.

Stationed at Centreville, Virginia, July-August 1862.

Stationed at Sutton, [West] Virginia, September-October 1862.

Stationed at Brownstown, [West] Virginia, November-December 1862.

Stationed at Young's Point, Louisiana, January-April 1863.

Stationed at Walnut Hill, Mississippi, May-June 1863.

Stationed at Camp Sherman, Mississippi, July-August 1863.

Stationed at Chickasaw, September-October 1863.

Stationed at Bellefonte, Alabama, November-December 1863.

Stationed at Cleveland, Tennessee, January-February 1864.

Stationed at Kenesaw Mountain, [March]-June 1864.
The company was absent in Ohio on veteran furlough, consequently was not mustered at the proper time.
April 2.— Left Larkinsville, Alabama.
May 21.— Returned to the front. All veterans marked with red ink.

Stationed near Jonesborough, Georgia, July-August 1864.

Station not stated, September-October 1864.

Stationed at White Hall, Georgia, November-December 1864.

Stationed in the field, South Carolina, January-February 1865.

Stationed in the field, North Carolina, March-April 1865.

Stationed aboard the steamer Starlight, May-June 1865.

Company F

Stationed at Camp Chase near Columbus, Ohio, August 31, 1861.
August 30.— Muster-in roll of Captain Charles J. Gibeaut's Company, in the —— Regiment of Ohio Volunteers, commanded

by Colonel Hugh Ewing, called into the service of the United States by the President from August 30, 1861 (date of this muster) for the term of three years, unless sooner discharged. The company was organized by Captain Charles J. Gibeaut's at Washington in the month of August and marched thence to Camp Chase, where it arrived August 21, a distance of 114. . . .

HOWARD STANSBURY,
Captain,
Topographical Engineers, Mustering Officer.

Stationed at Camp Hayes, [West] Virginia, January-February 1862.

Stationed at Camp Hayes, [West] Virginia, March-April 1862.

Since last muster there have been two changes of stations.

March 9-10.— First the company left Camp Hayes, [West] Virginia and arrived at Camp Union, [West] Virginia on March 10, distance twenty-six miles.

April 17-18.— Second, the company left Camp Union, [West] Virginia. Arrived at Camp Hayes on April 18, distance twenty-six miles.

Stationed at Camp Jones, [West] Virginia, May-June 1862.

Station not stated, July-August 1862.

August 15.— The company left Flat Top, [West] Virginia on Friday, August 15, and marched to Raleigh, [West] Virginia, distant twenty miles.

August 16.— The company left Raleigh, [West] Virginia on Saturday, August 16, and marched to Fayetteville, distant twenty-five miles.

August 17.— The company left Fayetteville on Sunday, August 17, and marched to Cannelton, distant twenty-two miles.

August 18.— The company left Cannelton Monday, August 18, and marched opposite Camp Piatt, distant seventeen miles, where we arrived at 11 a.m.

August 20-24.— From thence on we took boat for Parkersburg, [West] Virginia, where we arrived Wednesday, August 20. Here we bivouacked until Thursday, August 21. Took cars at 6 p.m.

for Washington City, District of Columbia, where we arrived at 9.40 a.m. Saturday, August 23, and was forwarded to Warrenton Junction, Virginia, arriving there Sunday, August 24.
August 27-29.— Wednesday, August 27, we left about 3 o'clock, arriving at Bristoe Station, Virginia, where we bivouacked. Left Bristoe Station and marched to Centreville, Virginia, arriving there on Friday, August 29, at 12 m.
September 1.— After marching and countermarching we arrived at Centreville again on September 1.

Stationed at Sutton, [West] Virginia, September-October 1862.

The company was engaged in the battles of South Mountain, Maryland and Antietam, Maryland and marched from Centreville, Virginia to Sutton, [West] Virginia, a distance of 336 miles, making the following marches:
September 1.— From Centreville, Virginia to Fairfax Court-House, Virginia.
September 2.— From Fairfax Court-House, Virginia to Fort Ramsay, Virginia.
September 6.— From Fort Ramsay to Washington City.
September 7-8.— From Washington City to Goshen Mill, Maryland.
September 9.— From Goshen Mill to Damascus, Maryland.
September 11.— From Damascus to Ridgeville, Maryland.
September 12.— From Ridgeville to Frederick City, Maryland.
September 13.— Frederick City to Middletown, Maryland.
September 14.— From Middletown to South Mountain, Maryland.
September 15-17.— From South Mountain to Antietam, Maryland.
October 8.— From Antietam to Hagerstown, Maryland.
October 9.— From Hagerstown to Clear Spring, Maryland.
October 10.— From Clear Spring to Hancock, Virginia.
October 12-13.— From Hancock the First Brigade of which Company F formed a part, marched into Pennsylvania and returned to Hancock on October 13 and took cars for Clarksburg, [West] Virginia.
October 14-30.— Arrived at Cumberland, Maryland and Company F returned to Hancock and in company with the division

train proceeded to march to Clarksburg, where it arrived October 25. From thence to Sutton, where it arrived October 30.

Stationed on steamer Leonora, Kanawha River, [West] Virginia, November-December 1862.

Stationed at Young's Point, Louisiana, January-February 1863.

Stationed at Young's Point, Louisiana, April 10, 1863.

Stationed at Milliken's Landing, Louisiana, March-April 1863.

Stationed at Walnut Hill, Mississippi, May-June 1863.

Stationed at Camp Sherman, Mississippi, July-August 1863.

Stationed at Chickasaw, Alabama, September-October 1863.

Stationed at Bellefonte, Alabama, November-December 1863.

Stationed at Cleveland, Tennessee, January-February 1864.

Stationed near Big Shanty Station, Georgia, [March]-June 1864.
[For record of events, see Company B.]

Stationed at Jonesborough, Georgia, July-August 1864.

Stationed at Cave Spring, Georgia, September-October 1864.

Stationed at White Hall, Georgia, November-December 1864.

Stationed in the field, South Carolina, January-February 1865.

Stationed at Raleigh, North Carolina, March-April 1865.

Stationed in the field, May-June 1865.

Company G

Stationed at Camp Chase near Columbus, August 28, 1861.
August 28.— Muster-in roll of Captain William H. Harlan's Company G, in the Thirtieth Regiment of Ohio Volunteers, commanded by Colonel Hugh Ewing, called into the service of the United States by the President from August 28, 1861 (date of this muster) for the term of three years, unless sooner discharged. The company was organized by Captain William H. Harlan at Steubenville in the month of August and marched thence to Camp Chase near Columbus, where it arrived August 18, a distance of 152 miles. . . .

HOWARD STANSBURY,
Captain,
Topographical Engineers, Mustering Officer.

Stationed at Camp Union, [West] Virginia, January-February 1862.

Stationed at Camp Hayes, Raleigh Court-House, [West] Virginia, March-April 1862.

Stationed at Camp Jones, [West] Virginia, May-June 1862.

Station not stated, September-October 1862.

Station not stated, December 31, 1862.

Stationed at Young's Point, Louisiana, January-April 1863.

Stationed at Walnut Hill, Mississippi, May-June 1863.

Stationed at Camp Sherman, Mississippi, July-August 1863.

Stationed at Chickasaw, Alabama, September-October 1863.

Stationed at Bellefonte, Alabama, November-December 1863.

Stationed at Cleveland, Tennessee, January-February 1864.

Stationed near Big Shanty, Georgia, [March]-June 1864.
[For record of events, see Company B.]

Stationed near Atlanta, Georgia, July-August 1864.

Station not stated, September-October 1864.

Stationed at White Hall, Georgia, November-December 1864.

Stationed in the field, January-February 1865.

Stationed in the field, North Carolina, March-April 1865.

Stationed on board steamer Starlight, May-June 1865.

Company H

Stationed at Camp Chase near Columbus, August 29, 1861.
August 29.— Muster-in roll of Captain Jacob E. Taylor's Company H, in the Thirtieth Regiment of Ohio Volunteers, commanded by Colonel Hugh Ewing, called into the service of the United States by the President from August 29, 1861 (date of this muster) for the term of three years, unless sooner discharged. The company was organized by Captain Jacob E. Taylor at Circleville in the month of August and marched thence to Camp Chase, where it arrived August 21, a distance of thirty miles. . . .

HOWARD STANSBURY,
Captain,
Topographical Engineers, Mustering Officer.

Stationed at Camp Ewing, [West] Virginia, August 21-October 31, 1861.

Stationed at Fayetteville, [West] Virginia, November-December 1861.

Stationed at Fayette Court-House, [West] Virginia, January-February 1862.

Stationed at Camp Hayes, Raleigh Court-House, [West] Virginia, March-April 1862.

April 16.— Company H, Thirtieth Regiment, moved from Camp Union, Fayette Court-House, West Virginia to Camp Hayes, Raleigh Court-House, [West] Virginia, a distance of twenty-five miles.

Stationed at Camp Jones, Mercer County, [West] Virginia, May-June 1862.

Stationed at Centreville, Virginia, July-August 1862.

Stationed at Sutton, [West] Virginia, September-October 1862.

Stationed on board steamer Leonora, Kanawha River, [West] Virginia, November-December 1862.

Stationed at Young's Point, Louisiana, January-April 1863.

Stationed at Walnut Hill, Mississippi, May-June 1863.

Stationed at Camp Sherman, Mississippi, July-August 1863.

Stationed at Chickasaw Landing, Alabama, September-October 1863.

Stationed at Bellefonte, Alabama, November-December 1863.

Stationed at Cleveland, Tennessee, January-February 1864.

Stationed near Kenesaw Mountain, Georgia, [March]-June 1864.

Stationed near Jonesborough, Georgia, July-August 1864.

Stationed at Cave Spring, Georgia, September-October 1864.

Stationed at White Hall, Georgia, November-December 1864.

Stationed in the field, South Carolina, January-February 1865.

Stationed at Raleigh, North Carolina, March-April 1865.

Stationed aboard steamer Starlight, May-June 1865.

Company I

Stationed at Camp Chase near Columbus, August 31, 1861.
August 30.— Muster-in roll of Captain George H. Hildt's Company I, in the Thirtieth Regiment of —— Volunteers, commanded by Colonel Hugh Ewing, called into the service of the United States by the President from August 30, 1861 (date of this muster) for the term of three years, unless sooner discharged. The company was organized by Captain George H. Hildt at New Philadelphia in the month of August and marched thence to Camp Chase, Columbus, Ohio, where it arrived August 23, a distance of 113 miles. . . .

HOWARD STANSBURY,
Captain,
Topographical Engineers, Mustering Officer.

Stationed at Camp Union, enrollment to February 28, 1862.

Stationed at Camp Hayes, March-April 1862.
March 9-10.— Marched from Beckley, Raleigh County, [West] Virginia to Fayetteville, [West] Virginia.
April 17-18.— Marched from Fayetteville to Beckley, Raleigh County, [West] Virginia, a distance of twenty-five miles.

Stationed at Camp Jones, [West] Virginia, May-June 1862.

Stationed at Upton's Hill, Virginia, July-August 1862.

Stationed at Sutton, [West] Virginia, September-October 1862.

Stationed on board steamer Leonora, Kanawha River, November-December 1862.

Stationed at Young's Point, Louisiana, January-April 1863.

Stationed at Walnut Hill, Mississippi, May-June 1863.

Stationed at Camp Sherman, Mississippi, July-August 1863.

Stationed at Chickasaw, Alabama, September-October 1863.

Stationed at Bellefonte, Alabama, November-December 1863.

Stationed at Cleveland, Tennessee, January-February 1864.

Stationed at Big Shanty, Georgia, [March]-June 1864.

Stationed at Jonesborough, Georgia, July-August 1864.

Stationed at Cave Spring, Georgia, September-October 1864.

Stationed at White Hall, Georgia, November-December 1864.

Stationed in the field, South Carolina, January-February 1865.

Stationed near Raleigh, North Carolina, March-April 1865.

Stationed at Memphis, Tennessee, May-June 1865.

Company K

Stationed at Camp Chase near Columbus, August 26, 1861.
August 26.— Muster-in roll of Captain William H. Ijams' Company K, in the Thirtieth Regiment of Ohio Volunteers, commanded by Colonel Hugh Ewing, called into the service of the United States by the President from August 26, 1861 (date of this muster) for the term of three years, unless sooner discharged. The company was organized by Captain William H. Ijams at Caldwell, Noble County, Ohio in the month of August and marched thence to Camp Chase near Columbus, where it arrived August 23, a distance of 123 miles. . . .

HOWARD STANSBURY,
Captain,
Topographical Engineers, Mustering Officer.

Stationed at Camp Ewing, October 31, 1861.

Stationed at Camp Hayes, Raleigh Court-House, [West] Virginia, November 1861-April 1862.

Stationed at Camp Jones, [West] Virginia, May-June 1862.

Station not stated, July-August 1862.

Stationed at Camp Sutton, [West] Virginia, September-October 1862.

Stationed at Brownstown, West Virginia, November-December 1862.

Station not stated, January-February 1863.

Stationed at Young's Point, Louisiana, March-April 1863.

Stationed at Walnut Hill, Mississippi, May-June 1863.

Stationed at Camp Sherman, Mississippi, July-August 1863.

Stationed at Chickasaw, Alabama, September-October 1863.

Stationed at Bellefonte, Alabama, November-December 1863.

Stationed at Cleveland, Tennessee, January-February 1864.

Stationed near Kenesaw Mountain, Georgia, [March]-June 1864.
[For record of events, see Company B.]

Stationed at Jonesborough, Georgia, July-August 1864.

Stationed at Cave Spring, Georgia, September-October 1864.

Stationed at White Hall, Georgia, November-December 1864.

Stationed in the field, South Carolina, January-February 1865.

Stationed near Raleigh, North Carolina, March-April 1865.

Stationed at Memphis, Tennessee, May-June 1865.

[M594-Roll #148]

Record of Events for Thirty-first Ohio Infantry, August 1861-June 1865.

Field and Staff

Stationed at Camp Chase near Columbus, September 27, 1861.
September 25.— Muster-in roll of the field and staff in the Thirty-first Regiment of Ohio Volunteers, commanded by Colonel Moses B. Walker, called into service of the United States by the president from September 25, 1861 (date of this muster) for the term of three years, unless sooner discharged. . . .

JOHN [RUFUS] EDIE,
Major,
Fifteenth Infantry, United States Army, Mustering Officer.

Station not stated, October 31, 1861.

Stationed at Somerset, Kentucky, December 31, 1861.

Stationed at camp near Nashville, Tennessee, January-February 1862.

Stationed at camp near Corinth, Mississippi, March-April 1862.

Stationed at Tuscumbia, Alabama, May-June 1862.

Stationed at Nashville, Tennessee, September 7, 1862.
September 7.— Muster-out roll of the band in the Thirty-first Regiment of Ohio Infantry Volunteers, commanded by Lieutenant-Colonel [Frederick William] Lister (Colonel M. B. Walker), called into the service of the United States by orders of

the President at Camp Chase, Ohio (the place of general rendezvous) on September 25, 1861 to serve for the term of three years. . . .

JOHN [HORNE] YOUNG,
Captain,
Fifteenth United States Infantry, Mustering Officer.

Station not stated, [July] 1862-April 1863.

Stationed at Camp Thomas, Tennessee, [May]-June 1863.

HEADQUARTERS, FIRST BRIGADE, THIRD DIVISION,
Fourteenth Army Corps, Camp Thomas, Tennessee,
July 23, 1863.

On June 30, the day according to law that this field and staff should have been mustered, it was in the face of the enemy on the march with all transportations left behind. Since which time and until the present time it has been impracticable to muster it for want of muster rolls, books and papers belonging to the field and staff.

[THOMAS] R. THATCHER,
Lieutenant,
Seventeenth Regiment, Ohio Volunteers,
Acting Assistant Commissary Sergeant,
First Brigade, Third Division.

Station not stated, July-August 1863.

Stationed at Chattanooga, Tennessee, September-December 1863.

Stationed at Ringgold, Georgia, March-April 1864.

Stationed in front of Kenesaw Mountain, May-June 1864.

Stationed at Atlanta, Georgia, July-August 1864.

Stationed at Rome, Georgia, September-October 1864.

Stationed at Savannah, Georgia, November-December 1864.

Stationed at Rocky Mount, South Carolina, January-February 1865.

Stationed in the field, North Carolina, March-April 1865.

Stationed near Louisville, Kentucky, May-June 1865.

Regiment

Stationed at Camp Dick Robinson, Kentucky, October 1861.

Stationed at Camp Dick Robinson, except Company H at Kentucky River, seven miles from Camp Dick Robinson, guarding bridge, November 1861.

Stationed at Somerset, Kentucky, except Company E at Kentucky River, December 1861.

Station not stated, except Company E at Kentucky River between Camp Dick Robinson and Nicholasville, Kentucky, guarding bridge, January 1862.

Stationed at Nashville, Tennessee, February 1862.

Station not stated, March 1862.

Stationed at field of Shiloh, Tennessee, April 1862.

Station near Corinth, May 1862.

Stationed at Elk River, Alabama, August 1862.

Station not stated, September-October 1862.

Stationed on the Cumberland [River], November 1862.

Stationed at Murfreesborough, December 1862-February 1863.

Stationed near Triune, Tennessee, March-May 1863.

Station not stated, June 1863.

Stationed at Camp Thomas, Winchester, Tennessee, July 1863.

Stationed at Battle Creek, Tennessee, August 1863.

Station not stated, September-December 1863.

Station not stated, April-May 1864.

Station not stated, July-August 1864.

Station not stated, October-December 1864.

Stationed near Sister's Ferry, Georgia, January 1865.

Stationed near Washington, District of Columbia, May 1865.

Stationed near Louisville, Kentucky, June 1865.

Company A

Stationed at Somerset, Kentucky, December 31, 1861.

Stationed at Camp Thomas near Nashville, January-February 1862.

Stationed at camp near Monterey, March-April 1862.
March 1.— First Lieutenant Samuel Lyons was promoted captain of Company E January 28 but refused to accept the commission. Was then transferred to Company C, still first lieutenant.
Received pay up to include December 31, 1862.

Stationed at Danville, Kentucky, [May]-August 1862.

Station not stated, [September]-December 1862.

Stationed near Triune, Tennessee, January-February 1863.

Stationed camp near Triune, Tennessee, April 10, 1863.

Station not stated, March-April 1863.

Stationed at Camp Thomas, Tennessee, May-June 1863.

Stationed at Battle Creek, Tennessee, July-August 1863.

Stationed at Chattanooga, September-December 1863.

Stationed near Ringgold, Georgia, March-April 1864.

Stationed in front of Kenesaw Mountain, May-June 1864.

Stationed at Jonesborough, Georgia, July-August 1864.

Stationed at Rome, Georgia, September-October 1864.

Stationed near Savannah, Georgia, November-December 1864.

Stationed in the field, South Carolina, January-February 1865.

Stationed in the field, North Carolina, March-April 1865.

Stationed near Louisville, Kentucky, May-June 1865.

Company B

Stationed at Camp Chase near Columbus, Ohio, August 10, 1861.
August 8.— Muster-in roll of Captain William W. Bowen's Company, in the Thirty-first Regiment of Ohio Volunteers, commanded by Colonel Moses B. Walker, called into the service of the United States by the President from August 8, 1861 (date of this muster) for the term of three years, unless sooner discharged. The company was organized by Captain William W. Bowen at Logan, Ohio in the month of August and marched thence to Camp Chase via Columbus, where it arrived August 9, a distance of fifty-four miles. . . .

HOWARD STANSBURY,
Captain,
Topographical Engineers, Mustering Officer.

Stationed at Somerset, Kentucky, December 31, 1861.

Station not stated, January-February 1862.

Stationed at camp near Corinth, March-April 1862.

Stationed at Louisville, Kentucky, May-August 1862.

Stationed at Murfreesborough, Tennessee, August 31, 1862-February 28, 1863.

Stationed near Triune, Tennessee, March-April 1863.

Stationed at Camp Thomas, Tennessee, May-June 1863.

Stationed at Battle Creek, Tennessee, July-August 1863.

Stationed at Chattanooga, Tennessee, September-December 1863.

Stationed at camp near Ringgold, Georgia, March-April 1864.

Stationed in the field, Georgia, May-June 1864.

Stationed at Atlanta, Georgia, July-August 1864.

Stationed at Rome, Georgia, September-October 1864.

Stationed near Savannah, Georgia, November-December 1864.

Stationed in the field, South Carolina, January-February 1865.

Stationed in the field, North Carolina, March-April 1865.

Stationed at Louisville, Kentucky, May-June 1865.

Company C

Stationed at Camp Chase, September 3, 1861.
September 3.— Muster-in roll of Captain Samuel R. Mott's Company C, in the Thirty-first Regiment of Ohio Volunteers, commanded by Colonel M. B. Walker, called into the service of the United States by the President from September 3, 1861 (date of this muster) for the term of three years, unless sooner discharged.

The company was organized by Captain S. R. Mott at Saint Mary's in the month of August and marched thence to Camp Chase, where it arrived September 2, a distance of 115 miles. . . .

HOWARD STANSBURY,
Captain,
Topographical Engineers, Mustering Officer.

Stationed at Camp Dick Robinson, September 3-October 31, 1861.

I certify that this is a true copy of the original muster, June 18, 1863.

ABRAM V. BARBER,
Lieutenant,
Commanding Company.

Stationed near Nashville, January-February 1862.

Stationed near Corinth, Mississippi, March-April 1862.

Stationed at Tuscumbia, Alabama, May-June 1862.

Station not stated, July 1862-February 1863.

Stationed at Triune, Tennessee, March-April 1863.

Stationed at Camp Thomas, Tennessee, May-June 1863.
[For record of events, see Field and Staff.]

Stationed at Sweeden's Cove, Tennessee, July-August 1863.

Stationed at Chattanooga, Tennessee, September-December 1863.

Stationed at Ringgold, Georgia, March-April 1864.

Stationed in the field near Atlanta, May-June 1864.

Stationed at camp in the field, July-August 1864.

Stationed at Rome, Georgia, September-October 1864.

Stationed near Savannah, Georgia, November-December 1864.

Stationed near Wateree River, South Carolina, January-February 1865.

Stationed in the field, North Carolina, March-April 1865.

Stationed at Louisville, Kentucky, May-June 1865.

Company D

Stationed at Camp Chase near Columbus, Ohio, September 7, 1861.
September 7.— Muster-in roll of Captain William H. Free's Company D, in the Thirty-first Regiment of Ohio Volunteers, commanded by Colonel Moses B. Walker, called into the service of the United States by the President from September 7, 1861 for the term of three years, unless sooner discharged. The company was organized by Captain William H. Free at New Lexington, Perry County, in the month of August and marched thence to Camp Chase near Columbus, where it arrived September 6, a distance of eighty-eight miles. . . .

HOWARD STANSBURY,
Captain,
Topographical Engineers, Mustering Officer.

Stationed at Somerset, Kentucky, December 31, 1861.

Stationed at Camp Thomas near Nashville, Tennessee, January-February 1862.

Stationed at camp near Monterey, Tennessee, March-April 1862.

Station not stated, May 1, 1862-January 1, 1863.

Stationed at Triune, Tennessee, January-April 1863.

Stationed at Camp Thomas, May-June 1863.

Stationed at Winchester, Tennessee, July-August 1863.

Stationed at Chattanooga, Tennessee, September-December 1863.

Stationed at Ringgold, Georgia, March-April 1864.

Stationed in the field, Georgia, May-June 1864.

Stationed at Jonesborough, Georgia, July-August 1864.

Stationed at Rome, Georgia, September-October 1864.

Stationed near Savannah, Georgia, November-December 1864.

Stationed in the field, South Carolina, January-February 1865.

Stationed in the field, North Carolina, March-April 1865.

Stationed at Louisville, Kentucky, May-June 1865.

Company E

Stationed at Camp Chase, September 19, 1861.
September 19.— Muster-in roll of Captain David H. Miller's Company E, in the Thirty-first Regiment of Ohio Volunteers, commanded by Colonel Moses B. Walker, called into the service of the United States by the President from September 19, 1861 (date of this muster) for the term of three years, unless sooner discharged. The company was organized by Captain David H. Miller at Reesville, Ohio in the month of September and marched thence to Camp Chase, where it arrived September 6, a distance of 110 miles. . . .

JOHN R. EDIE,
Mustering Officer.

Stationed at Camp Dick Robinson, Kentucky, August 27-November 1, 1861.
September 27-October 3.— The company left Camp Chase with the regiment. Arrived at Camp Dick Robinson, Kentucky October 3.

Stationed at Kentucky River Bridge, Kentucky, November-December 1861.
December 5.— The company was detached to remain at Kentucky River Bridge, Kentucky under command of Lieutenant George W. Reed.

Stationed at Camp Thomas near Nashville, Tennessee, January-February 1862.
Company E at last muster was on detached service at Kentucky River Bridge, Kentucky by orders of Colonel Walker, dated December 5, 1861.
February 4.— Lieutenant [Milton B. W.] Harman assumed command of the company at the above-named place.
February 7-17.— The company started according to orders to join the regiment at Somerset, Kentucky but met the regiment on the march to Lebanon, Kentucky via Danville. Arrived at Lebanon February 17.
February 19-25.— Started to Bardstown. Arrived there February 21 and marched for Louisville February 24. Arrived there February 25 and went on board the steamer same night, having marched 164 miles.
February 26-March 3.— Left Louisville. Arrived at Nashville, Tennessee March 3.

Stationed at camp near Corinth, Mississippi, March-April 1862.
January 28.— First Lieutenant Samuel D. Lyons was promoted from first lieutenant of Company A to captain of Company E but refused the commission.
March 18-April 13.— Second Lieutenant George W. Reed resigned. Second Lieutenant M. B. W. Harman was transferred from Company A to Company E, which he assumed command of February 4. The company was last mustered for pay at Camp Thomas, Tennessee. It marched from there March 18 to Clifton, Tennessee, where it arrived April 13.
April 19.— The regiment was transported by steamboat from there to Pittsburg Landing, from which place we have advanced slowly on account of heavy rains to this camp, seven miles north of Corinth, Mississippi.

Stationed at Tuscumbia, Alabama, May-June 1862.

Stationed at Louisville, Kentucky, July-August 1862.

Stationed at Murfreesborough, Tennessee, [September] 1862-February 1863.

Stationed at camp near Triune, Tennessee, March-April 1863.

Stationed at Camp Thomas, Tennessee, May-June 1863.
June 23.— The company marched from Triune, Tennessee in the general movement against the Rebel Army.
June 26.— The company was in the action of Hoover's Gap, in which the Rebels were driven from every position with loss. Four men of the company were wounded. Smith Dyer was severely wounded with a minie ball through both hips. William Simpson was severely wounded with a ball in the left foot. Irvin Valentine was wounded slightly with a rifle ball over the left eye. David T. Feigley was knocked down by a minie ball hitting his shelter tent —— accoutrements —— severely hurt but the skin was not broken.
July 1.— From Hoover's Gap the company participated in the series of movements that culminated in the capture of Tullahoma July 1, after which it continued the pursuit of the Rebel Army to Elk River, suffering for want of proper subsistence, the roads being so bad from recent rains as to detain supply trains.
July 6.— Lewis Valentine was accidentally shot while foraging for supplies, the ball entering the right breast broke the spine and killed him instantly.

Stationed at camp on Battle Creek, July-August 1863.

Stationed at Chattanooga, Tennessee, September-December 1863.

Stationed at Ringgold, Georgia, March-April 1864.

Stationed near Kenesaw Mountain, Georgia, May-June 1864.

Stationed near Atlanta, Georgia, July-August 1864.

Stationed at Rome, Georgia, September-October 1864.

Stationed at Savannah, Georgia, November-December 1864.

Stationed in the field, South Carolina, January-February 1865.

Stationed in the field, North Carolina, March-April 1865.

Stationed near Louisville, Kentucky, May-June 1865.

Company F

Station not stated, August 22-October 31, 1861.

Stationed at Camp Chase, September 21, 1861.
September 21.— Muster-in roll of Captain Amos J. Sterling's Company F, in the Thirty-first Regiment of Ohio Volunteers, commanded by Colonel M. B. Walker, called into the service of the United States by the President from September 21, 1861 (date of this muster) for the term of three years, unless sooner discharged. The company was organized by Captain Amos J. Sterling at Byhalia, Union County, in the month of August and marched thence to Camp Chase, where it arrived August 23, a distance of ninety-nine miles. . . .

JOHN R. EDIE,
Major,
United States Army, Fifteenth Infantry, Mustering Officer.

Stationed at Somerset, Kentucky, December 31, 1861.

Station not stated, January-April 1862.

Stationed at Winchester, Tennessee, May-June 1862.

Station not stated, [July]-October 1862.

Stationed at Murfreesborough, Tennessee, November 1862-February 1863.

Stationed at Triune, Tennessee, March-April 1863.

Stationed at Camp Thomas, Tennessee, May-June 1863.

Company H

Stationed at Camp Chase, September 23, 1861.
September 23.— Muster-in roll of Captain John H. Putnam's Company G, in the Thirty-first Regiment of Ohio Volunteers, commanded by Colonel Moses B. Walker, called into the service of the United States by the President from September 23, 1861 (date of this muster) for the term of three years, unless sooner discharged. The company was organized by Captain John H. Putnam at Newark, Ohio in the month of September and marched thence to Camp Chase, where it arrived September 13, a distance of thirty-three miles. . . .

JOHN R. EDIE,
Major,
United States Army, Fifteenth Infantry, Mustering Officer.

Station not stated, September 14-October 31, 1861.

Stationed at Somerset, Kentucky, December 31, 1861.

Station not stated, January-February 1862.

Stationed at Camp Shiloh, Tennessee, March-April 1862.

Stationed at Louisville, Kentucky, [May]-August 1862.

Stationed near Murfreesborough, Tennessee, [September] 1862-February 1863.

Stationed near Triune, Tennessee, March-April 1863.

Stationed at Camp Winfred, Tennessee, May-June 1863.

Station not stated, July-August 1863.

Stationed at Chattanooga, September-December 1863.

Stationed at Ringgold, Georgia, March-April 1864.

Stationed near Atlanta, Georgia, May-June 1864.

Stationed near Jonesborough, Georgia, July-August 1864.

Stationed at Rome, Georgia, September-October 1864.

Stationed at Savannah, Georgia, November-December 1864.

Stationed at Wateree, South Carolina, January-February 1865.

Stationed in the field, North Carolina, March-April 1865.

Stationed at Louisville, Kentucky, May-June 1865.

Company I

Stationed at Camp Chase, Ohio, September 24, 1861.
September 24.— Muster-in roll of Captain David C. Rose's Company, in the Thirty-first Regiment of Ohio Volunteers, commanded by Colonel Moses Walker, called into the service of the United States by the President from September 24, 1861 (date of this muster) for the term of three years, unless sooner discharged. The company was organized by Captain David C. Rose at Cardington in the month of August and marched thence to Camp Chase, where it arrived August 28, a distance of forty-two miles. . . .

JOHN R. EDIE,
Major,
United States Army, Fifteenth Infantry, Mustering Officer.

Stationed at Somerset, Kentucky, December 31, 1861.

Station not stated, January-April 1862.

Stationed at Louisville, Kentucky, May 1-September 1, 1862.

Stationed near Murfreesborough, Tennessee, September-December 1862.

Station not stated, January-February 1863.

Stationed near Triune, Tennessee, March-April 1863.

Stationed at Camp Thomas, Tennessee, May-June 1863.

Stationed at Battle Creek, Tennessee, July-August 1863.

Stationed at Chattanooga, Tennessee, [September]-December 1863.

Stationed at Ringgold, Georgia, January-April 1864.

Stationed in the front of Kenesaw [Mountain], Georgia, May-June 1864.

Stationed at [Jonesborough], Georgia, July-August 1864.

Stationed at Rome, Georgia, September-October 1864.

Stationed at Savannah, Georgia, November-December 1864.

Stationed near Wateree River, South Carolina, January-February 1865.

Stationed at Asbury Station, North Carolina, March-April 1865.

Stationed near Louisville, Kentucky, May-June 1865.

Company K

Stationed at Somerset, Kentucky, December 31, 1861.

Station not stated, January-February 1862.

Stationed in the field, March-April 1862.

Station not stated, [May] 1862-February 1863.

Stationed in the field, Tennessee, April 10, 1863.

Stationed in the field, March-April 1863.

Stationed at Camp Thomas, Tennessee, [May]-June 1863.
[For record of events, see Field and Staff.]

Stationed at Chattanooga, Tennessee, July-December 1863.

Stationed at Ringgold, Georgia, March-April 1864.

Stationed in the field, May-June 1864.

Stationed near Atlanta, Georgia, July-August 1864.

Stationed at Rome, Georgia, September-October 1864.

Stationed near Savannah, Georgia, November-December 1864.

Stationed in the field, South Carolina, January-February 1865.

Stationed in the field, North Carolina, March-April 1865.

Stationed at Louisville, Kentucky, May-June 1865.

[M594-Roll #148]

Record of Events for Thirty-second Ohio Infantry, July 1861-June 1865.

Detachment

Station not stated, not dated.
Muster and descriptive rolls of a detachment of drafted men and substitutes placed on duty as permanent garrison at Tod Barracks, Ohio by instructions from the War Department, dated October 24, 1864. Assigned to the Thirty-second Ohio Volunteer Infantry to complete the record of detachment to enable it to be

mustered out of the service, in accordance with instructions from the War Department, dated April 30, 1865.

JOHN W. SKILES,
Major,
Eighty-eighty Ohio Volunteer Infantry, Commanding Draft Rendezvous.

Field and Staff

Stationed at Cheat Mountain Summit, July 26-October 31, 1861.

Stationed at Camp Dennison, Ohio, August 31, 1861.
August 31.— Muster-in roll of the field and staff officers in the Thirty-second Regiment of Ohio Volunteers, commanded by Colonel Thomas H. Ford, called into the service of the United States by the President from August 31, 1861 (date of this muster) for the term of three years, unless sooner discharged. . . .

JOHN [RUFUS] EDIE,
Major,
Fifteenth Infantry, United States Army, Mustering Officer.

Stationed at Beverly, [West] Virginia, [November]-December 1861.

Stationed at McDowell, Virginia, March-April 1862.

Stationed near Middletown, Virginia, May-June 1862.
April 5.— The Thirty-second Regiment left Cheat Mountain. Moved eastward, passing through the Rebel camps, Greenbrier and Allegheny, onto Monterey, McDowell and over the Shenandoah Mountain to within a short distance of Staunton, at which point it was attacked by the advance guard of the united forces of Generals [Thomas Jonathan] Jackson and [Edward] Johnson, causing it to fall back to McDowell.
May 8.— Eight companies were engaged in the bloody battle of McDowell, having four killed and fifty-three wounded. Of the other companies, one was supporting a battery on an eminence opposite the battlefield, the other was left to guard the post at Beverly. On the evening of May 8 was ordered to fall back to Franklin to form a junction with the force commanded by Major-

General [John Charles] Frémont. It remained in Franklin ten days and then accompanied General Frémont on arduous march in the Shenandoah Valley to Port Republic.
June 8.— It was engaged in the battle of Cross Keys.
June 24.— From Port Republic it was ordered back and arrived at its present position on June 24.

Stationed at Winchester, Virginia, July-August 1862.

Station not stated, September-December 1862.

Stationed at Lake Providence, Louisiana, January-February 1863.

Stationed at Berry's Landing, Louisiana, April 10, 1863.

Stationed at Hard Times Landing, Louisiana, March-April 1863.

Stationed near Vicksburg, Mississippi, May-June 1863.
May 1.— The regiment marched from Bruinsburg on the Mississippi River and engaged in the battle of Port Gibson, Mississippi.
May 12.— Engaged in the battle of Raymond, Mississippi.
May 14.— [Engaged] at Jackson, Mississippi.
May 16.— [Engaged] at Champion's Hill, Mississippi. At the latter place the regiment charged and captured the First Mississippi (Rebel) Battery of eight guns. Thirty-five horses were killed. Wounded and captured nearly every man of the battery.
May 22.— Marched from thence to the rear of Vicksburg, Mississippi and engaged in the assault upon the enemy's works on May 22 and have since been encamped on the front line of the Federal approaches to the enemy's works.

Stationed at Vicksburg, Mississippi, July-December 1863.

Stationed at Bogue Chitto Creek, Mississippi, January-February 1864.

Stationed at Clifton, Tennessee, March-April 1864.

Stationed at Big Shanty, Georgia, May-June 1864.

Stationed near Flint River, Georgia, July-August 1864.

Stationed near Raleigh, North Carolina, March-April 1865.

Stationed at Louisville, Kentucky, May-June 1865.

Regiment

Stationed at Cheat Mountain Summit, [West] Virginia, October 1861.

Stationed at Beverly, [West] Virginia, November 1861.

Stationed at Beverly, [West] Virginia, December 1861.

Company A
December 9-13.— Company A left Cheat Mountain Summit, [West] Virginia December 9. A detachment of twenty-six men, under command of Lieutenant [Abraham] Norris, was engaged in the attack at Allegheny Camp December 13.

Company B
Company B left Cheat Mountain Summit, under orders, for Beverly, [West] Virginia, distance twenty-four miles. Reached Beverly the same day. A detachment was engaged in the attack at Camp Allegheny, distance fifty miles.

Company E
December 13.— A detachment of the company was engaged in the attack at Camp Allegheny December 13.

Company I
December 11-13.— A detachment of the company, under command of Captain [William Douglas] Hamilton and Lieutenant [Ulysses] Westbrook (numbering nineteen privates and two officers), left Beverly December 11 to combine with the forces of General [Robert Huston] Milroy in the attack upon the enemy's camp at Allegheny Camp, which commenced the morning of December 13. Kept up a constant fire until the ammunition gave

out. Retired in good order, having lost one private killed and two wounded.

Company K

December 13.— A detachment of this company was engaged in the battle at Allegheny Camp December 13. Fought bravely during the entire conflict and retired from the field with one private, L. H. Hess, severely wounded.

Stationed at Beverly, [West] Virginia, January-February 1862.

Stationed at Cheat Mountain, [West] Virginia, March 1862.

Stationed at Camp Cleveland, Ohio, December 1862.

Stationed at Camp Todd, Memphis, Tennessee, January 1863.

Stationed at Lake Providence, Louisiana, February 1863.

Stationed at Berry's Landing, Louisiana, March 1863.

Stationed at Utica, Louisiana, April 1863.

Stationed in the rear of Vicksburg, May-August 1863.

Stationed at Vicksburg, Mississippi, September 1863.

Company F [has] eighty-eight privates absent as artillerists [per] Special Orders No. 147, Headquarters, Third Division, Seventeenth Army Corps, Major-General John [Alexander] Logan.

Stationed at Vicksburg, Mississippi, October-November 1863.

Five sergeants, eight corporals and seventy-five privates of Company F absent, detached as artillery since September 23 [per] Special Orders No. 147, Major-General J. A. Logan.

Stationed near Vicksburg, December 1863.

Company F detached as artillerists [per] Special Orders No. 147, Major-General Logan.

Stationed at Vicksburg, Mississippi, January 1864.

Stationed at Livingston, Mississippi, February 1864.

Stationed at Mansfield, Ohio, March 1864.

Reenlisted as veteran volunteers and on furlough in Ohio for thirty days, in accordance with Special Orders No. 60, Headquarters, Seventeenth Army Corps March 4.

Stationed at Clifton, Tennessee, April 1864.

Stationed at Warrenton, Alabama, May 1864.

Stationed at Big Shanty, Georgia, June 1864.

Stationed near Atlanta, Georgia, July 1864.

Stationed at Flint River, Georgia, August 1864.

Stationed at East Point, Georgia, September 1864.

Stationed at Cave Spring, Georgia, October 1864.

Stationed at Oliver Station, Georgia, November 1864.

Stationed near Savannah, Georgia, December 1864.

Station not stated, June 1865.

Company A

Stationed at Camp Bartley, Ohio, August 27, 1861.

August 27.— Muster-in roll of Captain Jackson Lucy's Company, in the Thirty-second Regiment of Ohio Volunteers, commanded by Colonel Thomas H. Ford, called into the service of the United States by the President from August 27, 1861 (date of this muster) for the term of three years, unless sooner discharged. The company was organized by Captain Jackson Lucy at

Carrollton, Ohio in the month of July 1861 and marched thence to Camp Bartley, where it arrived August 7, 1861, a distance of 100 miles. . . .

JOHN R. EDIE,
Major,
Fifteenth Infantry, United States Army, Mustering Officer.

Stationed at Cheat Mountain, [West] Virginia, October 31, 1861.

Stationed at Beverly, [West] Virginia, December 31, 1861.

Stationed at Beverly, [West] Virginia, January-February 1862.

Stationed at McDowell, Virginia, March-April 1862.

Stationed at camp near Middletown, Virginia, May-June 1862.
May 8.— The company engaged at Bull Pasture Mountain near McDowell, Virginia. Corporal Thomas J. Hendria was killed. Lieutenant Augustus G. Hostetter, Sergeant William A. McAllister, Corporal Levi Ball, and Privates James A. Morrow, Daniel Weymar, and Lowman A. Ball were wounded.
May 9-10.— Marched from McDowell to Franklin, [West] Virginia.
May 25.— Commenced marching from Franklin, [West] Virginia. Passed Petersburg and Moorefield.
June 1.— Reached Strasburg. Marched in pursuit of General Jackson and his forces through Woodstock, Mount Jackson, New Market, and Harrisonburg.
June 8.— In the engagement at Cross Keys. Private Samuel B. McClellan wounded in the right foot by the explosion of a shell.

Stationed at Camp Sigel near Winchester, Virginia, July-August 1862.

Stationed at Camp Douglas, Illinois, September-October 1862.

Stationed at Camp Cleveland, Ohio, November-December 1862.

Stationed at Lake Providence, Louisiana, January-February 1863.

Stationed at Berry's Landing, April 10, 1863.

Stationed at camp at Hard Times Landing, Louisiana, March-April 1863.

Stationed at camp in the rear of Vicksburg, Mississippi, May-June 1863.
[For record of events, see Field and Staff.]

Stationed at Vicksburg, Mississippi, July-December 1863.

Stationed at Bogue Chitto Creek, Mississippi, January-February 1864.

Enlisted thirty-two veterans up to January 5.

February 3.— The company and regiment started on a march under General [Ulysses Simpson] Sherman.

February 5.— Met a portion of the enemy near Baker's Creek, Mississippi. Casualties: Captain McAllister wounded severely in the thigh; Corporal Lathan D. Cowgill, veteran volunteer, killed, and two privates wounded. Marched from there to Meridian, Mississippi by way of Jackson and Brandon.

March 3.— Returned to Vicksburg by way of Canton, having marched near 400 miles.

Stationed at Clifton, Tennessee, March-April 1864.

Stationed near Kenesaw [Mountain], Georgia, May-June 1864.

May 5-11.— We started from Clifton, Tennessee. Marched from there by way of Pulaski to Athens, Alabama, arriving at Athens on the evening of May 11.

May 19-25.— Marched from thence to Huntsville, Alabama and remained there until May 25, during which time the Seventeenth Army Corps was reorganized and on May 25 started from Huntsville to join General Sherman's Army by way of Decatur, Alabama and Rome, Georgia.

June 8.— Arrived at Acworth in the evening, having marched a distance of near 300 miles. Since which time we have been in the front and have been engaged in the different movements necessary for the advance of an Army against an enemy strongly entrenched.

Stationed at Jonesborough, Georgia, July-August 1864.

Stationed near Raleigh, North Carolina, March-April 1865.

Stationed at Louisville, Kentucky, May-June 1865.

Company B

Stationed at Camp Chase near Columbus, Ohio, August 21, 1861.
August 20.— Muster-in roll of Captain William A. Palmer's Company B, in the Thirty-second Regiment of Ohio Volunteers, commanded by Colonel Thomas H. Ford, called into the service of the United States by the President from August 20, 1861 (date of this muster) for the term of three years, unless sooner discharged. The company was organized by Captain William A. Palmer at Mechanicsburg in the month of August and marched thence to Camp Chase, Columbus, where it arrived August 9, a distance of thirty-eight miles. . . .

HOWARD STANSBURY,
Captain,
Topographical Engineers, Mustering Officer.

Stationed at Cheat Mountain Summit, [West] Virginia, October 31, 1861.

Stationed at Beverly, [West] Virginia, December 31, 1861.

Stationed at Beverly, [West] Virginia, January-February 1862.

Stationed at McDowell, Virginia, March-April 1862.

Stationed at camp near Middletown, Virginia, May-June 1862.
May 5.— Left McDowell.
May 7.— [Illegible] Gap in Shenandoah Mountain to McDowell.
May 8.— Supported a section of [Aaron C.] Johnson's Ohio Battery at the battle of Bull Pasture Mountain.
May 9-10.— Fell back toward Franklin. Reached there May 10.
May 25.— Left Franklin. Went twenty miles and on the succeeding days [marched] by way of Petersburg, Moorefield, Wardensville, Strasburg, Woodstock, Mount Jackson, New Market, Mount Jackson, Harrisonburg, under Major-General Frémont.

June 8-9.— [Arrived at] Port Republic June 9 after fighting the battle of Cross Keys June 8.

Then fell back to Middletown, marching from Franklin 178 miles and from May 1 to June 24 a distance of 220 miles.

Stationed at Camp Sigel, July-August 1862.

Stationed at Camp Douglas, Illinois, September-October 1862.

Stationed at Camp Cleveland, Ohio, November-December 1862.

Stationed at Lake Providence, Louisiana, January-February 1863.

Stationed at Berry's Landing, Louisiana, April 10, 1863.

Stationed at Hard Times Landing, Louisiana, March-April 1863.

Stationed at Vicksburg, Mississippi, May-June 1863.
[For record of events, see Field and Staff.]

Stationed at Vicksburg, Mississippi, July-August 1863.

Stationed at Vicksburg, Mississippi, September-October 1863.
September 14-16, 1862.— In the engagements fought at Harper's Ferry September 14, 15 and 16 and was taken prisoner at the time of the surrender of the Federal forces under Colonel [Dixon Stansbury] Miles at that place. Was paroled and sent to Camp Douglas, Illinois; thence to Camp Cleveland, Ohio.
January 20, 1863.— Was exchanged and ordered to Memphis, Tennessee January 20.
May 1.— It has served honorably in the fight at Port Gibson.
May 12.— [Engaged] at Raymond.
May 16.— [Engaged at] at Champion's Hill.
May 19-July 4.— Also at the siege of Vicksburg, Mississippi.

Stationed at Vicksburg, Mississippi, November-December 1863.

Stationed at Bogue Chitto Creek, Mississippi, [January]-February 1864.

Stationed at Clifton, Tennessee, March-April 1864.

Stationed at Big Shanty, Georgia, May-June 1864.

Stationed near Jonesborough, Georgia, July-August 1864.

Stationed at Marietta, Georgia, September-October 1864.

Stationed at Savannah, Georgia, November-December 1864.

Stationed at Cheraw, South Carolina, January-February 1865.

Stationed near Raleigh, North Carolina, March-April 1865.

Stationed at Louisville, Kentucky, May-June 1865.

Company C

Stationed at Camp Chase near Columbus, Ohio, August 31, 1861.
August 31.— Muster-in roll of Captain James B. Banning's Company C, in the Thirty-second Regiment of Ohio Volunteers, commanded by Colonel Thomas H. Ford, called into the service of the United States by the President from August 31, 1861 (date of this muster) for the term of three years, unless sooner discharged. The company was organized by Captain James B. Banning at Mount Vernon in the month of July and marched thence to Camp Bartley, where it arrived August 8, a distance of thirty-six miles. . . .

HOWARD STANSBURY,
Captain,
Topographical Engineers, Mustering Officer.

Stationed at Cheat Mountain Summit, [West] Virginia, October 31, 1861.

Stationed at Beverly, [West] Virginia, December 31, 1861.

Stationed at Beverly, January-February 1862.

Stationed at McDowell, March-April 1862.

Stationed at camp near Middletown, Virginia, May-June 1862.
May 8.— The company was engaged in the battle of McDowell, Virginia, then marched to Franklin, [West] Virginia. From thence to Harrisonburg, Virginia and engaged in the battle of Cross Keys.

Stationed near Winchester, Virginia, July-August 1862.
Marched back to Winchester, Virginia, where they are engaged in building fortifications.

Stationed at Camp Douglas, Illinois, September-October 1862.
September 2-3.— Left Winchester, Virginia and marched to Harper's Ferry, [West] Virginia, a distance of thirty-three miles. Arrived September 3.
September 13.— In action on Maryland Heights.
September 14.— Also engaged at Harper's Ferry in the evening and on the following morning until the surrender. Marched from Harper's Ferry, [West] Virginia to Annapolis, Maryland via Frederick City. From thence to Baltimore, Maryland by steamer. From thence to Chicago, Illinois via Pittsburgh, Pennsylvania and Cleveland, Ohio.
September 28.— Arrived at Chicago in the morning.

Stationed at Camp Cleveland, Ohio, November-December 1862.
November 30-December 1.— The Thirty-second Regiment was ordered from Camp Douglas, Illinois, where last mustered, to this place (Camp Cleveland, Ohio). Left Camp Douglas November 30 and arrived at this place December 1.

Stationed at Lake Providence, Louisiana, January-February 1863.

Stationed at Berry's Landing, Louisiana, April 10, 1863.

Stationed at Hard Times Landing, Louisiana, March-April 1863.
Removed from Providence, Louisiana, where last mustered, per steamer to Milliken's Bend, Louisiana. Marched from that point to Hard Times Landing, Louisiana.

Stationed at the rear of Vicksburg, Mississippi, May-June 1863.
[For record of events, see Field and Staff.]

Stationed at Vicksburg, Mississippi, July-December 1863.

Stationed at Bogue Chitto [Creek], Mississippi, January-February 1864.
February 3.— The company reenlisted 330 volunteers prior to February 3, at which time the regiment left Vicksburg, Mississippi with other troops under General Sherman and commenced the march to Meridian, Mississippi via Jackson.
February 5.— Corporal Josiah Bushfield was severely wounded in action near Baker's Creek, Mississippi. After arriving at Meridian the regiment returned by way of Canton, marching in all about 350 miles.

Stationed at Clifton, Tennessee, March-April 1864.
March 4.— Three-fourths of the regiment having reenlisted as veteran volunteers, the veteran portion, so reenlisted, left Vicksburg per steamer on March 4 and proceeded to Cincinnati, Ohio; thence by rail to Columbus, Ohio, where they were furloughed to their respective homes for thirty days, at the expiration of which time they reassembled at Columbus, Ohio. Went by cars to Cincinnati, Ohio; thence by steamboat to Cairo, Illinois.
April 28-30.— The regiment left with other troops, all under command of Brigadier-General [John Basil Turchin], and proceeded by steamer up the Tennessee River to Clifton, Tennessee, arriving at that place on April 30.

Stationed at Big Shanty, Georgia, May-June 1864.
May 5.— Left Clifton, Tennessee and marched to Huntsville, Alabama.
May 25-June 8.— From thence crossed the Cumberland Mountains via Decatur, Alabama and Rome, Georgia, joining the main Army under General Sherman at Acworth June 8, from which place we advanced with the Army to Big Shanty, the place of present muster.

Stationed near Jonesborough, Georgia, July-August 1864.
July 2-21.— The company and regiment left their position near Kenesaw Mountain, Georgia and marched to Nickajack Creek; thence via Marietta across the Chattahoochee River to Decatur, passing through which the enemy was met and attacked on July 21.

July 22.— We participated in the battle before Atlanta.

During the two engagements the company lost two killed, two wounded and two captured. The company participated in all the movements of Sherman's Army during the remainder of the siege of Atlanta up to August 31, when we were before Jonesborough, twenty-five miles south of Atlanta.

Stationed at Cave Spring, Georgia, September-October 1864.
September 1.— The regiment was in the advance upon Jonesborough, Georgia and after the evacuation of Atlanta, Georgia by the enemy returned to East Point, Georgia and there encamped.
October 1-3.— The regiment marched to Fairburn, Georgia. Returned on October 3.
October 4.— The regiment and company marched northward in the pursuit of [John Bell] Hood, passing through Kingston and Resaca, Georgia to Gaylesville, Alabama, where, after remaining some days, marched to Cave Spring, Georgia, making within October a distance marched of 350 miles.

Stationed at Savannah, Georgia, November-December 1864.

The company marched from Cave Spring, Georgia to Marietta.
November 13.— Left [Marietta] with Sherman's Army and marched through the interior of Georgia to Savannah, where it is now encamped. Marched in all from Cave Spring to Savannah, a distance of 400 miles.

Stationed in the field, South Carolina, January-February 1865.

Stationed near Raleigh, North Carolina, March-April 1865.

Stationed at Louisville, Kentucky, May-June 1865.

Company D

Stationed at Camp Bartley, Ohio, August 27, 1861.
August 27.— Muster-in roll of Captain William B. Bowland's Company, in the Thirty-second Regiment of Ohio Volunteers, commanded by Colonel Thomas H. Ford, called into the service of the United States by the President from August 27, 1861 (date

of this muster) for the term of three years, unless sooner discharged. The company was organized by Captain William B. Bowland at Mansfield, Ohio in the month of July and marched thence to Camp Bartley, where it arrived August 19, a distance of two miles. . . .

HOWARD STANSBURY,
Captain,
Topographical Engineers, Mustering Officer.

Stationed at Beverly, [West] Virginia, December 31, 1861-February [28], 1862.

Stationed at McDowell, Virginia, March-April 1862.

Stationed at Middletown, Virginia, May-June 1862.
May 7-8.— We were encamped on the east side of the Shenandoah Mountains, Virginia, when we were attacked by Johnson's and Jackson's combined forces. Lost our camp equipage for want of transportation and were compelled to fall back to McDowell, Virginia and were in the engagement at that place on May 8. Had four men wounded. Fell back to Franklin and joined Frémont's command at that place. Made the march to Harrisonburg.
June 8.— Was at the battle of Cross Keys ([Robert Cumming] Schenck's Brigade). Marched thence to Port Republic and have since fallen back to this place (Middletown, Virginia).

Stationed at Camp Sigel, Winchester, Virginia, July-August 1862.

Stationed at Camp Douglas, Chicago, Illinois, September-October 1862.

Stationed at Camp Cleveland, November-December 1862.

Stationed at Lake Providence, Louisiana, January-February 1863.

Stationed at Berry's Landing, Louisiana, April 10, 1863.

Stationed at Hard Times Landing, Louisiana, March-April 1863.

Stationed before Vicksburg, Mississippi, May-June 1863.
[For record of events, see Field and Staff.]

Stationed at Vicksburg, Mississippi, July-December 1863.

Stationed at Bogue Chitto [Creek], January-February 1864.
Enlisted twenty veterans to January 5, 1864.
February 3.— Started on a expedition commanded by General Sherman.
February 5.— Met a portion of the enemy near Baker's Creek and drove him through Clinton, Mississippi. Marched thence to Meridian by way of Jackson and returned by way of Canton, having marched a distance of nearly 350 miles.

Stationed at Clifton, Tennessee, March-April 1864.

Stationed near Big Shanty, Georgia, May-June 1864.

Stationed near East Point, Georgia, July-August 1864.

Stationed near Raleigh, North Carolina, March-April 1865.

Stationed at Louisville, Kentucky, May-June 1865.

Company E

Stationed at Camp Bartley near Mansfield, Ohio, August 27, 1861.
August 27.— Muster-in roll of Captain Milton W. Worden's Company, in the Thirty-second Regiment of Ohio Volunteers, commanded by Colonel Thomas H. Ford, called into the service of the United States by the President of the United States from August 27, 1861 (date of this muster) for the term of three years, unless sooner discharged. The company was organized by Captain Milton W. Worden at Mansfield, Ohio in the month of July and marched thence to Camp Bartley, where it arrived August 19, a distance of two miles. . . .

HOWARD STANSBURY,
Captain,
Topographical Engineers, Mustering Officer.

Stationed at Cheat Mountain Summit, [West] Virginia, October 31, 1861.

Stationed at Beverly, [West] Virginia, December 31, 1861-February [28], 1862.

Stationed at McDowell, Virginia, March-April 1862.

Stationed at camp near Middletown, Virginia, May-June 1862.
May 8.— The company was engaged in the bloody fight near McDowell, Virginia and lost its first lieutenant while bravely leading the company onward.
June 8.— The company was also present at the Cross Keys engagement but sustained no loss. Also accompanied General Frémont's column on the entire march from Franklin, [West] Virginia through the Shenandoah Valley.

Stationed at Winchester, Virginia, July-August 1862.

Stationed at Camp Douglas, Illinois, September-October 1862.

Stationed at Camp Cleveland, Ohio, November-December 1862.

Stationed at Lake Providence, Louisiana, January-February 1863.

Stationed at Berry's Landing, Louisiana, April 10, 1863.

Stationed at Hard Times Landing, Louisiana, March-April 1863.

Stationed at the rear of Vicksburg, May-June 1863.
[For record of events, see Field and Staff.]

Stationed at Vicksburg, Mississippi, July-December 1863.

Stationed at Bogue Chitto Creek, January-February 1864.

Stationed at Clifton, Tennessee, March-April 1864.

Stationed near Kenesaw Mountain, Georgia, May-June 1864.

Stationed near Jonesborough, Georgia, July-August 1864.

Stationed at Cave Spring, Georgia, September-October 1864.

Stationed at Savannah, Georgia, November-December 1864.

Stationed at Lynch's Creek, South Carolina, January-February 1865.

Stationed at Neuse River, North Carolina, March-April 1865.

Stationed at Louisville, Kentucky, May-June 1865.

Company F

Stationed at Clifton, Tennessee, to April 30, 1864.

Stationed at Big Shanty, Georgia, May-June 1864.

Stationed near Jonesborough, Georgia, July-August 1864.

Stationed at Savannah, Georgia, November-December 1864.

Stationed at Neuse River, North Carolina, March-April 1864.

Stationed at Louisville, Kentucky, May-June 1865.

Company G

Stationed at Camp Bartley near Mansfield, Ohio, August 31, 1861.
August 31.— Muster-in roll of Captain William D. Hamilton's Company, in the Thirty-second Regiment of Ohio Volunteers, commanded by Colonel Thomas H. Ford, called into the service of the United States by the President from August 31, 1861 (date of this muster) for the term of three years, unless sooner discharged. The company was organized by Captain William D. Hamilton at Zanesville in the month of August and marched thence to Camp Bartley, where it arrived August 27, a distance of 100 miles. . . .

HOWARD STANSBURY,
Captain,
Topographical Engineers, Mustering Officer.

Stationed at Cheat Mountain Summit, [West] Virginia, October 31, 1861.

Stationed at Beverly, [West] Virginia, December 31, 1861-February [28], 1862.

Stationed at camp near Middletown, Virginia, February 28-July 1, 1862.
March 1.— Company G, Thirty-second Ohio Volunteer Infantry, was temporarily detached from the regiment about March 1 to guard the post of Beverly, [West] Virginia, where we remained.
May 8.— John Eoff, a member of the company, was on May 8 acting orderly for Colonel [Thomas H.] Ford and was on that day killed in the battle of McDowell while fighting in Company E (Captain Worden) of said regiment.
June 1-28.— We then removed by orders to New Creek, [West] Virginia in order to rejoin our regiment, when we were ordered to take charge of a battery of Ellsworth guns (twenty) with orders to convey them to General Frémont's Headquarters at Middletown, Virginia, where we arrived June 28 and from which we have not been relieved.

Stationed at Winchester, Virginia, July-August 1862.

Stationed at Camp Douglas, Illinois, September-October 1862.

Stationed at Camp Cleveland, Ohio, November-December 1862.

Stationed at Lake Providence, Louisiana, January-February 1863.

Stationed at Berry's Landing, Louisiana, April 10, 1863.

Stationed at Hard Times Landing, Louisiana, March-April 1863.

Stationed near Vicksburg, Mississippi, May-June 1863.
[For record of events, see Field and Staff.]

Stationed at Vicksburg, Mississippi, July 1863-February 1864.

Stationed at Clifton, Tennessee, March-April 1864.

Stationed at Big Shanty, Georgia, May-June 1864.

Stationed near Jonesborough, Georgia, July-August 1864.

Stationed at Cave Spring, Georgia, September-October 1864.

Stationed near Savannah, Georgia, November-December 1864.

Stationed near Raleigh, North Carolina, March-April 1865.

Stationed at Louisville, Kentucky, May-June 1865.

Company H

Stationed at Camp Dennison, Ohio, September 5, 1861.
September 5.— Muster-in roll of Captain George M. Baxter's Company, in the Thirty-second Regiment of Ohio Volunteers, commanded by Colonel Thomas H. Ford, called into the service of the United States by the President from September 5, —— (date of this muster) for the term of three years, unless sooner discharged. . . .

JOHN R. EDIE,
Major,
Fifteenth Infantry, United States Army, Mustering Officer.

Stationed at Cheat Mountain Summit, [West] Virginia, October 31, 1861.

Stationed at Beverly, [West] Virginia, December 31, 1861-February [28], 1862.

Stationed at McDowell, Virginia, March-April 1862.

Stationed at camp near Middletown, Virginia, May-June 1862.
May 5.— The company marched from McDowell, Virginia over Shenandoah Mountain. Surprised by the united forces of Generals Jackson and Johnson. Private John Miller, missing while on picket, who was as we have learned since, taken prisoner May 7.

Stationed at camp near Winchester, Virginia, [July]-August 1862.

Stationed at Camp Douglas, Illinois, September-October 1862.

Stationed at Camp Cleveland, November-December 1862.

Station not stated, January-February 1863.

Stationed at Camp Logan, Louisiana, April 10, 1863.

Stationed at Hard Times Landing, Louisiana, March-April 1863.

Stationed at Vicksburg, Mississippi, May-June 1863.
[For record of events, see Field and Staff.]

Loss of the company up to the present three privates killed and second lieutenant and four privates wounded.

Stationed at Vicksburg, Mississippi, July-December 1863.

Stationed at Bogue Chitto Creek, Mississippi, January-February 1864.

Station not stated, March-April 1864.

Stationed at Big Shanty, Georgia, May-June 1864.
May 5.— The regiment marched from Clifton, Tennessee.
May 20.— Arrived at Huntsville, Alabama, after marching a distance of 109 miles.
June 10.— Marched from thence to Big Shanty, Georgia, where it arrived June 10, after marching a distance of 250 miles.

Stationed near Jonesborough, Georgia, July-August 1864.

Stationed near Savannah, Georgia, November-December 1864.

Stationed near Raleigh, North Carolina, March-April 1865.

Stationed at Louisville, Kentucky, May-June 1865.

Company I

Stationed at Camp Dennison, Ohio, September 7, 1861.
September 6.— Muster-in roll of Captain Jay Dyer's Company, in the Thirty-second Regiment of Ohio Volunteers, commanded by Colonel Thomas H. Ford, called into the service of the United States by the President from September 6, 1861 (date of this muster) for the term of three years, unless sooner discharged. . . .

HOWARD STANSBURY,
Captain,
Topographical Engineers, Mustering Officer.

Stationed at Cheat Mountain Summit, [West] Virginia, October 31, 1861.

Stationed at Beverly, [West] Virginia, December 31, 1861-February [28], 1862.

Stationed at McDowell, Virginia, March-April 1862.

Stationed at Middletown, Virginia, May-June 1862.
May 7-8.— First Lieutenant [Elijah] B. Adams, while on picket with a part of the company, was cut off at the cross-roads near Jennings' Gap but all escaped through the mountains and reached camp at McDowell on May 8, just as the fight at Bull Pasture Mountain commenced, in which the remainder of the company was engaged. In the fight the company lost one killed and four seriously and five slightly wounded. Marched that night and the next day to Franklin.
May 25-June 8.— Started from Franklin and marched to Petersburg. From Petersburg to Moorefield, from Moorefield to Wardensville to Strasburg. From Strasburg to Mount Jackson, from Mount Jackson to Harrisonburg. From Harrisonburg to Cross Keys, where the battle was fought, which bears that name, on June 8. The company sustained no loss at the battle.
June 9-24.— Marched to Port Republic and on June 10 to Harrisonburg, from Harrisonburg to Mount Jackson, from Mount Jackson to Strasburg, from Strasburg to camp near Middletown June 24.

Stationed at Winchester, Virginia, July-August 1862.

Stationed at Camp Douglas, Chicago, Illinois, September-October 1862.

Stationed at Camp Cleveland, November-December 1862.

Stationed at Lake Providence, Louisiana, January-February 1863.

Stationed at Berry's Landing, Louisiana, April 10, 1863.

Stationed at Hard Times Landing, Louisiana, March-April 1863.

Stationed in the rear of Vicksburg, Mississippi, May-June 1863.
[For record of events, see Field and Staff.]

Stationed at Vicksburg, Mississippi, July-August 1863.

I certify that my clothing account with all enlisted men that had overdrawn was settled to March 31, 1863. Those underdrawn have never had a settlement.

JOSEPH GLADDEN,
Captain,
Commanding Company I, Thirty-second Ohio Volunteer Infantry.

Stationed at Vicksburg, Mississippi, September-December 1863.

Stationed at Bogue Chitto Creek, January-February 1864.

Recruited forty-three veteran volunteers for three years or during the war up to January 1, 1864.

February 3.— Started on Sherman's expedition from Vicksburg, Mississippi. Encountered the enemy near Clinton, Mississippi. Had five men wounded, two being left in Clinton, it being dangerous to remove them on account of their wounds.

JOSEPH GLADDEN,
Captain,
Commanding Company I, Thirty-second Ohio Volunteer Infantry.

Stationed at Clifton, Tennessee, March-April 1864.

Stationed at Big Shanty, Georgia, May-June 1864.

Stationed near Jonesborough, Georgia, July-August 1864.

Station not stated, September-October 1864.

Stationed at Savannah, Georgia, November-December 1864

Stationed at Neuse River, North Carolina, March-April 1865.

Stationed at Louisville, Kentucky, May-June 1865.

Company K

Stationed at Camp Bartley near Mansfield, Ohio, August 31, 1861.

August 31.— Muster-in roll of Captain Wilson M. Stanley's Company, in the Thirty-second Regiment of Ohio Volunteers, commanded by Colonel Thomas H. Ford, called into the service of the United States by the President from August 31, 1861 (date of this muster) for the term of three years, unless sooner discharged. The company was organized by Captain Wilson M. Stanley at Coshocton in the month of August and marched thence to Mansfield, where it arrived August 30, a distance of 110 miles. . . .

JOHN R. EDIE,
Major,
Fifteenth Infantry, United States Army, Mustering Officer.

Stationed at Cheat Mountain Summit, [West] Virginia, August 15-October 31, 1861.

Stationed at camp, Beverly, [West] Virginia, November-December 1861.

Stationed at Beverly, [West] Virginia, January-February 1862.

Stationed at McDowell, March-April 1862.

Stationed at camp near Middletown, Virginia, May-June 1862.
May 8.— The company was in action at Bull Pasture Mountain near McDowell, Virginia. Corporal William Cox was wounded and has since died from effects of wounds. Sergeant James H. Pigman, Privates Jesse V. Crago, Alexander C. Ellis, John W. McChristian, and John Tym were wounded.
May 9-10.— Marched from McDowell to Franklin, [West] Virginia, distance thirty-four miles.
May 25.— Commenced marching from Franklin via Petersburg, Moorefield, Strasburg, Woodstock, Mount Jackson, New Market, and Harrisonburg.
June 8.— In action at Cross Keys. No casualties.
June 9.— Marched to Port Republic. Distance marched since leaving Franklin about 196 miles. Marched from Port Republic via Harrisonburg, New Market, Mount Jackson, Woodstock, and Strasburg to camp near Middletown, Virginia, distance sixty-seven miles.

Stationed at Camp Sigel near Winchester, Virginia, July-August 1862.

Stationed at Camp Douglas, Chicago, Illinois, September-October 1862.

Stationed at Camp Cleveland, Ohio, November-December 1862.

Stationed at Lake Providence, Louisiana, January-February 1863.

Stationed at Berry's Landing, Louisiana, April 10, 1863.

Stationed at Hard Times Landing, Louisiana, March-April 1863.

Stationed near Vicksburg, Mississippi, May-June 1863.
[For record of events, see Field and Staff.]

Stationed at Vicksburg, Mississippi, July-December 1863.

Stationed at Bogue Chitto Creek, Mississippi, January-February 1864.

Stationed at Clifton, Tennessee, March-April 1864.

Stationed at Big Shanty, Georgia, May-June 1864.

Stationed near Jonesborough, Georgia, July-August 1864.

Station not stated, September-October 1864.

Stationed at Neuse River, North Carolina, March-April 1865.

Stationed at Louisville, Kentucky, May-June 1865.

[M594-Roll #148]

Record of Events for Thirty-third Ohio Infantry, July 1861-June 1865.

Field and Staff

Stationed at Hazle Green, Kentucky, July 29-October 31, 1861.

Stationed at Camp Morrow, August 27, 1861.
August 27.— Muster-in roll of the field and staff of the Thirty-third Regiment of Ohio (Foot) Volunteers, commanded by Colonel Joshua [Woodrow] Sill, called into the service of the United States by the President of the United States from August 27, 1861 (date of this muster) for the term of three years, unless sooner discharged. . . .

[ROBERT BOWNE] HULL,
First Lieutenant,
Eighteenth Regiment, United States Infantry, Mustering Officer.

Stationed at Bacon Creek, Kentucky, November-December 1861.

Stationed at Nashville, Tennessee, January-February 1862.

Stationed at Camp Taylor, Huntsville, Alabama, [March]-May 1862.

Stationed at Louisville, Kentucky, [June]-August 1862.

Stationed at Murfreesborough, Tennessee, [September] 1862-April 1863.

Station not stated, May-June 1863.

Stationed at camp near Anderson, Tennessee, July-August 1863.

Stationed at Chattanooga, Tennessee, September-December 1863.

Stationed at Graysville, Georgia, [January]-April 1864.

Stationed at Kenesaw Mountain, Georgia, May-June 1864.

Station not stated, July-August 1864.

Stationed at Rome, Georgia, September-October 1864.

Stationed near Savannah, Georgia, November-December 1864.

Stationed in the field, South Carolina, January-February 1865.

Stationed in the field, North Carolina, March-April 1865.

Stationed near Louisville, Kentucky, May-June 1865.

Regiment

Stationed at Camp Jefferson, Bacon Creek, Kentucky, December 1861-January 1862.

Stationed at Camp Andrew Jackson, Tennessee, February 1862.

Stationed at Camp Van Buren near Murfreesborough, Tennessee, March 1862.

Stationed at Camp Taylor near Huntsville, Alabama, April 1862.

Stationed at Battle Creek, Tennessee, July 1862.

Stationed at camp near Bowling Green, Kentucky, October 1862.

Stationed at camp at Edgefield Junction, Tennessee, November 1862.

Stationed at Murfreesborough, Tennessee, January-May 1863.

Stationed at camp near Manchester, Tennessee, June 1863.

Stationed at Camp Scribner near Cowan Station, Tennessee, July 1863.

Stationed at camp near Anderson, Tennessee, August 1863.

Stationed at camp near Chattanooga, Tennessee, September-December 1863.

Stationed at Graysville, Georgia, January-April 1864.

Stationed near Dallas, Georgia, May 1864.

Station not stated, June 1864.

Stationed near Atlanta, Georgia, July-September 1864.

Station not stated, October 1864.

Stationed in the field, Georgia, November 1864.

Stationed at Savannah, Georgia, December 1864.

Stationed at Sister's Ferry, Georgia, January 1865.

Stationed in the field, South Carolina, February 1865.

Stationed at Goldsborough, North Carolina, March 1865.

Stationed in the field, North Carolina, April 1865.

Stationed near Washington, District of Columbia, May 1865.

Stationed at camp near Louisville, Kentucky, June 1865.

Company A

Stationed at Camp Morrow near Portsmouth, Ohio, August 27, 1861.
August 27.— Muster-in roll of Captain Samuel A. Currie's Company, in the Thirty-third Regiment of Ohio Volunteers, commanded by Colonel Joshua W. Sill, called into the service of the United States by the President of the United States from August 27, 1861 (date of this muster) for the term of three years, unless sooner discharged. . . .

R. B. HULL,
First Lieutenant,
Eighteenth Regiment, United States Infantry, Mustering Officer.

Stationed at Camp Jenkins, Kentucky, August 27-October 31, 1861.

Stationed at Camp Jefferson, Kentucky, November-December 1861.

Stationed at Murfreesborough, Tennessee, January-February 1862.

Stationed at Huntsville, Alabama, [March]-May 1862.

Stationed at Louisville, Kentucky, [June]-August 1862.

Stationed at Murfreesborough, Tennessee, [September] 1862-April 1863.

Stationed at camp near Winchester, Tennessee, May-June 1863.

Stationed near Anderson Station, Tennessee, July-August 1863.

Stationed at Chattanooga, Tennessee, September-December 1863.

Stationed at Graysville, Georgia, [January]-April 1864.

Stationed at Kenesaw Mountain, Georgia, May-June 1864.

Stationed at Atlanta, Georgia, July-August 1864.

Stationed at Rome, Georgia, September-October 1864.

Stationed at Savannah, Georgia, November-December 1864.

Stationed in the field, January-February 1865.

Stationed near Washington, District of Columbia, March-April 1865.

Stationed near Louisville, Kentucky, May-June 1865.

Company B

Stationed at Hazle Green, Kentucky, August 18-October 31, 1861.

Stationed at Camp Jefferson, Kentucky, November-December 1861.

Stationed at Camp Van Buren, January-February 1862.

Stationed at Camp Taylor, Huntsville, Alabama, [March]-May 1862.

Stationed at Louisville, Kentucky, [June]-August 1862.

Stationed at Murfreesborough, Tennessee, [September] 1862-April 1863.

Stationed at Manchester, Tennessee, May-June 1863.

Stationed at Anderson, Tennessee, July-August 1863.

Stationed at Chattanooga, Tennessee, September-December 1863.

Stationed at Graysville, Georgia, March-April 1864.

Stationed at Kenesaw Mountain, May-June 1864.

Stationed at Atlanta, Georgia, July-August 1864.

Stationed at Rome, Georgia, September-October 1864.

Stationed at Savannah, Georgia, November-December 1864.

Stationed in the field, January-February 1865.

Stationed near Washington, District of Columbia, March-April 1865.

Stationed near Louisville, Kentucky, May-June 1865.

Company C

Stationed at Camp Morrow near Portsmouth, August 27, 1861.
August 27.— Muster-in roll of Captain William H. Douglas' Company, in the Thirty-third Regiment of Ohio Volunteers, commanded by Colonel Joshua W. Sill, called into the service of the United States by the President of the United States from August 27, 1861 (date of this muster) for the term of three years, unless sooner discharged. The company was organized by Captain William H. Douglas at Camp Chase, Ohio in the month of August and marched thence to Camp Morrow, where it arrived August 18, a distance of ninety miles. . . .

R. B. HULL,
First Lieutenant,
Eighteenth Regiment, United States Infantry, Mustering Officer.

Stationed at Hazle Green, Kentucky, August 18-October 31, 1861.

Stationed at Camp Jefferson, Bacon Creek, Kentucky, November-December 1861.

Stationed at Nashville, Tennessee, January-February 1862.

Stationed at Huntsville, Alabama, [March]-May 1862.

Stationed at Decherd, Tennessee, [June]-August 1862.

Stationed in front of Murfreesborough, Tennessee, [September] 1862-April 1863.

Stationed in the field, May-June 1863.

Stationed at Anderson, Tennessee, July-August 1863.

Stationed at Chattanooga, Tennessee, September-December 1863.

Stationed at Graysville, Georgia, [January]-April 1864.

Stationed in the field, May-June 1864.

Stationed near Atlanta, Georgia, July-August 1864.

Stationed at Rome, Georgia, September-October 1864.

Stationed at Savannah, Georgia, November-December 1864.

Stationed in the field, North Carolina, January-April 1865.

Stationed near Louisville, Kentucky, May-June 1865.

Company D

Stationed at Hazle Green, Kentucky, August 17-October 31, 1861.

Stationed at Camp Jefferson, November-December 1861.

Stationed at camp near Murfreesborough, Tennessee, January-February 1862.

Stationed at Battle Creek, Tennessee, [March]-May 1862.

Stationed at Louisville, Kentucky, [June]-August 1862.

Stationed at Murfreesborough, Tennessee, [September] 1862-April 1863.

Stationed at camp in the field, May-June 1863.
June 4.— Marched from Murfreesborough, Tennessee.
June 25.— Skirmished seven hours at Hoover's Gap with no loss.

Stationed near Anderson Station, Tennessee, July-August 1863.

Stationed at Chattanooga, Tennessee, September-December 1863.

Stationed near Ringgold, Georgia, [January]-April 1864.

Stationed near Kenesaw Mountain, Georgia, May-June 1864.

Stationed near Atlanta, Georgia, July-August 1864.

Stationed near Rome, Georgia, September-October 1864.

Stationed at Savannah, Georgia, November-December 1864.

Stationed in the field, South Carolina, January-February 1865.

Stationed in the field, North Carolina, March-April 1865.

Stationed near Louisville, Kentucky, May-June 1865.

Company E

Stationed at Hazle Green, Kentucky, September 3-October 31, 1861.

Stationed at Camp Jefferson, November-December 1861.

Stationed at Murfreesborough, Tennessee, January-February 1862.

Stationed at Camp Taylor, Huntsville, Alabama, [March]-May 1862.

Stationed at Louisville, Kentucky, [June]-August 1862.

Stationed at Murfreesborough, Tennessee, [September] 1862-April 1863.

Stationed at Camp King, Tennessee, May-June 1863.

Stationed at Anderson, Tennessee, July-August 1863.

Stationed at Chattanooga, Tennessee, September-December 1863.

Stationed in the field, Georgia, [January]-August 1864.

Stationed at Rome, Georgia, September-October 1864.

Stationed in the field, November 1864-February 1865.

Stationed in the field, North Carolina, March-April 1865.

Stationed near Louisville, Kentucky, May-June 1865.

Company F

Stationed at Hazle Green, Kentucky, August 25-October 31, 1861.

Stationed at Camp Jefferson, Kentucky, November-December 1861.

Stationed at Camp Andrew Jackson, January-February 1862.

Stationed at Battle Creek, Tennessee, [March]-May 1862.

Stationed at Louisville, Kentucky, [June]-August 1862.

Stationed at Murfreesborough, Tennessee, [September] 1862-April 1863.

Station not stated, May-June 1863.

Stationed near Anderson, Tennessee, July-August 1863.

Stationed at Chattanooga, Tennessee, September-December 1863.

Stationed at Parker's Gap, Georgia, [January]-April 1864.

Stationed in the field, Georgia, May-August 1864.

Stationed at Rome, Georgia, September-October 1864.

Stationed near Savannah, Georgia, November-December 1864.

Stationed in the field, January-April 1865.

Stationed near Louisville, Kentucky, May-June 1865.

Company G

Stationed at Hazle Green, Kentucky, August 26-October 31, 1861.

Stationed at Camp Jefferson, November-December 1861.

Stationed at Nashville, Tennessee, January-February 1862.

Stationed at Huntsville, Alabama, [March]-May 1862.

Stationed at Louisville, Kentucky, [June]-August 1862.

Stationed at Murfreesborough, Tennessee, [September] 1862-April 1863.

Stationed at Camp King, Tennessee, May-June 1863.

Stationed at Anderson Station, Tennessee, July-August 1863.

Stationed at Chattanooga, Tennessee, September-December 1863.

Stationed at Graysville, Georgia, [January]-April 1864.

Stationed at Kenesaw Mountain, Georgia, May-June 1864.

Stationed near Atlanta, Georgia, July-August 1864.

Stationed near Rome, Georgia, September-October 1864.

Stationed at Martha's Vineyard, North Carolina, November-December 1864.

Stationed in the field, [January]-February 1865.

Stationed in the field, North Carolina, March-April 1865.

Stationed at Louisville, Kentucky, May-June 1865.

Company H

Stationed at Hazle Green, Kentucky, September 18-October 31, 1861.

Stationed at Camp Jefferson, Kentucky, November-December 1861.

Stationed at Shelbyville, Tennessee, January-February 1862.

Station not stated, [March]-May 1862.

Stationed at New Market, Kentucky, [June]-August 1862.

Stationed at Murfreesborough, Tennessee, [September] 1862-April 1863.

Stationed in the field, Middle Tennessee, May-June 1863.

Station not stated, July-August 1863.

Stationed at Chattanooga, Tennessee, September-December 1863.

Stationed at Graysville, Georgia, January-April 1864.

Stationed at Kenesaw Mountain, Georgia, May-June 1864.

Stationed in the field, Georgia, July-August 1864.

Stationed at Rome, Georgia, September-October 1864.

Stationed at Savannah, Georgia, November-December 1864.

Stationed at Goldsborough, North Carolina, January-February 1865.

Stationed in the field, North Carolina, March-April 1865.

Stationed near Louisville, Kentucky, May-June 1865.

Company I

Stationed at Hazle Green, Kentucky, September 10-October 31, 1861.

Stationed at Camp Jefferson, Kentucky, November-December 1861.

Stationed at Camp Andrew Jackson, January-February 1862.

Stationed at Camp Taylor, Huntsville, Alabama, [March]-May 1862.

Stationed at Louisville, Kentucky, [June]-August 1862.

Stationed at Murfreesborough, Tennessee, [September] 1862-April 1863.

Station not stated, May-June 1863.

Stationed near Anderson, Tennessee, July-August 1863.

Stationed at Chattanooga, Tennessee, September-December 1863.

Stationed at Atlanta, Georgia, [January]-August 1864.

Stationed near Gaylesville, Alabama, September-October 1864.

Stationed in the field, November 1864-April 1865.

Stationed at Louisville, Kentucky, May-June 1865.

Company K

Stationed at Hazle Green, Kentucky, October 9-31, 1861.

Stationed at Camp Jefferson, Kentucky, November-December 1861.

Station not stated, January-February 1862.

Stationed at Camp Taylor, Huntsville, Alabama, [March]-May 1862.

Station not stated, August 31-December 31, 1862.

Stationed at Murfreesborough, Tennessee, January-April 1863.

Station not stated, May-June 1863.

Stationed near Anderson, Tennessee, July-August 1863.

Stationed at Chattanooga, Tennessee, September-December 1863.

Stationed at Ringgold, Georgia, [January]-April 1864.

Stationed in the field, Georgia, May-June 1864.

Stationed at Atlanta, Georgia, July-August 1864.

Stationed at Rome, Georgia, September-October 1864.

Stationed at Savannah, Georgia, November-December 1864.

Stationed at Goldsborough, North Carolina, January-February 1865.

Stationed near Alexandria, Virginia, March-April 1865.

Stationed near Louisville, Kentucky, May-June 1865.

[M594-Roll #148]

Record of Events for Thirty-fourth Ohio Infantry, July 1861-January 1865.

Field and Staff

Stationed at Camp Dennison, August 7, 1861.
August 7.— Muster-in roll of field and staff in the Thirty-fourth Regiment of Ohio Volunteers, commanded by Colonel [Abraham] Sanders Piatt, called into the service of the United States by President from August 7, 1861 (date of this muster) for the term of three years, unless sooner discharged. . . .

[THOMAS WOODRUFF] WALKER,
Captain,
Third Infantry, Mustering Officer.

Stationed at Camp Franklin, Virginia, October 31, 1861.

Stationed at Barboursville, Cabell Court-House, [West] Virginia, November-December 1861.

Stationed at Camp Toland, [West] Virginia, January-February 1862.

Stationed at Fayetteville, [West] Virginia, March-April 1862.
March 18.— The regiment left Barboursville, [West] Virginia and moved to Gauley Bridge, a distance of about 140 miles.
April 7.— The regiment left Gauley Bridge, [West] Virginia and marched to Fayetteville, [West] Virginia, distance thirteen miles.

Stationed at Flat Top Mountain, [West] Virginia, May-June 1862.

Stationed at Post Raleigh Court-House, [West] Virginia, July-August 1862.
August 15.— Marched from Flat Top Mountain, [West] Virginia to this post, distance twenty-two miles.

Stationed at Camp Piatt, September-October 1862.
September 10.— The regiment was in the battle of Fayette Court-House, [West] Virginia and suffered very severely. Marched from Fayette Court-House to Charleston, [West] Virginia.
September 13-18.— Was in the battle of Charleston. Continued on our march to Point Pleasant, [West] Virginia via Ravenswood, arriving at our destination on September 18, a distance of 156 miles.
October 19.— Started from Point Pleasant and marched to Camp Piatt, a distance of sixty-five miles.

Station not stated, November-December 1862.

Stationed at Fayetteville, [West] Virginia, January-April 1863.

Stationed at Camp Piatt, West Virginia, May-August 1863.

Stationed at Camp Toland, Charleston, West Virginia, September-October 1863.

Stationed at Charleston, West Virginia, November-December 1863.
November 3.— The regiment marched for Lewisburg, West Virginia (whole distance 216 miles) and returned.
November 7-13.— Arrived and drove the enemy from the town. Destroyed camp tents and company stores, etc. Arrived here November 13.
November 16-20.— The regiment marched for Barboursville (whole distance and retired, ninety miles). Arrived there November 20.
December 8.— The regiment marched for Lewisburg (distance and retired, 216 miles). Drove the enemy beyond Greenbrier River without loss on side.

Stationed at Charleston, West Virginia, January-April 1864.

Stationed at Charleston, West Virginia, May-June 1864.
This regiment has been half mounted and half dismounted.

The dismounted forces have been engaged as follows.
May 9.— Cloyd's Mountain.
May 11.— New River Bridge.
June 18.— Lynchburg.

The mounted forces have been engaged as follows.
May 10.— Mountain Cove Gap.
May 13.— Salt Pond Mountain.
May 17.— New London.
June 18.— Lynchburg.
June 21.— Salem.

Marched from Charleston, West Virginia to Lynchburg and back to Charleston via Fayette, Princeton, Dublin, Blacksburg, Union, Blue Sulphur [Springs], Lewisburg, White Sulphur [Springs], Warm Springs, Staunton, Lexington, Liberty, Buchanan to Salem, New Market, Sweet Springs, Union, Lewisburg, Gauley to Charleston.

Mounted forces via Logan Court-House, Wyoming, Jeffersonville to Mountain Cove, Mechanicsburg, Dublin Station, Christiansburg and from Union to Lewisburg and there in connection with the infantry 1,000 miles.

Stationed at Charlestown, West Virginia, July-August 1864.
July 9-16.— The regiment left Charleston, West Virginia for Martinsburg, West Virginia, where it arrived July 16.
July 17.— Sent to Cherry Run.
July 19.— Returned to Martinsburg, West Virginia. Marched to near Winchester, Virginia.
July 20.— Engaged in action.
July 21.— Marched into Winchester.
July 24.— Engaged in action at Martinsburg.
July 26.— Crossed Potomac.
July 27.— Arrived at Sandy Hook, Maryland.
July 30.— Marched from Sandy Hook, Maryland.
August 2.— To Wolfsville Gap.
August 3.— To Monocacy, five miles from Frederick, Maryland.

August 6.— Marched to Sandy Hook, Maryland.
August 8.— Marched to Key's Ford, Virginia.
August 10.— Marched to Berryville, Virginia.
August 11.— To Stony Point.
August 12.— To Middletown and Cedar Creek.
August 16.— Left Cedar Creek near Strasburg, Virginia.
August 22.— Marched to Halltown. Built fortifications.
August 24.— Engaged. Six enlisted men wounded.
August 27.— Marched to Charlestown, West Virginia.
August 31.— At Charlestown, West Virginia.

Stationed at Cedar Creek, Virginia, September-October 1864.
September 3.— Marched from Charlestown, West Virginia to Berryville, a distance of nine miles.
September 8.— Marched from Berryville to Summit Point, four miles.
September 19.— Marched to Winchester, nine miles. Engaged the enemy. Lost ten killed and nine wounded.
September 20.— Marched from Winchester to Cedar Creek, fifteen miles.
September 21.— Marched from Cedar Creek to Strasburg, two miles.
September 22.— Marched to Fisher's Hill, four miles. Engaged the enemy. Lost nine wounded and two missing.
September 23.— Marched to Woodstock, eight miles.
September 24.— Marched from Woodstock to New Market, twenty-one miles.
September 25.— Marched from New Market to Harrisonburg, seventeen miles.
October 6.— Marched from Harrisonburg to Mount Jackson, twenty-two miles.
October 7.— Marched from Mount Jackson to Woodstock, fifteen miles.
October 8.— Marched to Fisher's Hill, eight miles.
October 11.— Marched to Cedar Creek, four miles.
October 19-20.— Engaged the enemy. Was driven beyond Middletown. Reformed and charged the "Johnnies," where we remained to date of muster. In action lost three killed, twelve wounded, and eighteen missing, not including Lieutenant-Colonel [Luther] Furney, who was taken prisoner and escaped October 20. Whole distance marched was 142 miles.

Stationed at Beverly, West Virginia, November-December 1864.

Regiment

Stationed at Camp Toland, Barboursville, [West] Virginia, except Company A at Red House [Shoal], [West] Virginia; Company G at —— Bridge, Cabell County, [West] Virginia, January 1862.

Stationed at Flat Top Tannery, [West] Virginia, May 1862.
May 1.— Detachment of five companies (E, H, K, G, and B) left Fayetteville, [West] Virginia and marched to Raleigh, [West] Virginia, a distance of twenty-five miles. Major [Freeman] E. Franklin in command of detachment.
May 10.— The remaining five companies, under command of Lieutenant-Colonel [John T.] Toland, left Fayetteville in Second Provisional Brigade and marched to Frenchville, [West] Virginia, distance eighty-two miles.
May 11-12.— Major F. E. Franklin's detachment left Raleigh Court-House, [West] Virginia and marched to Princeton, a distance of forty-five miles, arriving there May 12.
May 15.— The five companies under the command of Lieutenant-Colonel Toland were at Raleigh one day, where they arrived. Company A under Lieutenant [Henry C.] Hatfield and Company A, of Twenty-eighth Detachment commanded by Captain [Ernest] Schache of Twenty-eighth Regiment marched a distance of twelve miles across East River Mountains and attacked a Rebel outpost taking six prisoners and some property.
May 16.— Company A arrived in camp at Frenchville at 10 a.m., having marched a distance of twelve miles from Wolf Creek. Three companies (B, D and I) under command of Major F. E. Franklin were engaged with enemy at Princeton in a fight of four hours' continuance at night. Five companies under Lieutenant-Colonel Toland left Frenchville and marched to relief of Major F. E. Franklin at Princeton.
May 17.— They arrived in morning. At sunrise Companies E and K were engaged under Major Franklin with enemy and Company F, under Lieutenant-Colonel [Louis] von Blessingh of Thirty-seventh Ohio Volunteer Infantry.
May 18-19.— The regiment left Princeton and marched to Flat Top Mountain, a distance of twenty-two miles. Arrived May 19.

Stationed at Flat Top Mountain, [West] Virginia, June 1862.

Stationed at Flat Top Mountain Tannery, [West] Virginia, July 1862.

Stationed at Post Raleigh Court-House, [West] Virginia, August 1862.
August 22.— The regiment marched from Camp Flat Top Tannery, [West] Virginia to Post Raleigh, [West] Virginia, distance twenty-two miles.

Stationed at Point Pleasant, [West] Virginia, September 1862.
September 3-4.— The regiment left Raleigh Court-House, [West] Virginia and arrived in Fayetteville, [West] Virginia September 4, distance twenty-two miles.
September 10.— The regiment was engaged with Secesh forces in Fayette Court-House, [West] Virginia. Lost in killed two commissioned officers, eighteen enlisted men; wounded five commissioned officers and seventy-five enlisted men; missing one commissioned officer and thirty enlisted men for total casualties of [131]. Names of the killed were commissioned officers Samuel McCutcheon, First Lieutenant, Company C; Henry Hatfield, Captain, Company A (died four days after the action). Wounded commissioned officers were First Lieutenant [Charles] W. Boyd, Company B; First Lieutenant [Frank] B. Helwig, Company E; First Lieutenant [Ethan] A. Brown, Company H; Second Lieutenant Benjamin [J.] Ricker, Company A; Second Lieutenant [Andrew] S. Frazer, Company F. Second Lieutenant [Robert] B. Underwood, Company I, missing. Enlisted men killed Company A, William A. Wyatt, Sergeant; Samuel T. Beard, M. Burdeal, W. Kingler and P. Simmons; Company B, Fred Lewing (died since action); Company C, Boyce Egan, Luther Bouns, P. Mard; Company D, Willard King, Jr., Tool C. Getson, R. H. Treedecy; Company E, Alanon Petezel (died since action); Company F, none; Company G, Sam Ashton; Company H, Tuk O'Reilly (corporal); Company K, Levi Brooche (died since action). Wounded enlisted men, Company A, Sergeant Temple J. H. Ulsey, W. J. Rolls, L. J. Day, William H. Day, J. Donham, J. Clark, E. Hawkins; Company B, Corporals G. L. Johnson and A. J. Davis, Privates Van Hunter, Rossman, Jones, Thomas, and

William Crawford, M. Cahill, P. Varley, H. Simpson; Company C, M. Lawler; Company D, E. Calver, Beacox, Gregory, Rushton; Company E, Corporal John Sherrock, Privates Austin, Cox, Charlton, Evans, and Hollensburgh; Company F, Puckham, Shirten, Robbins, Laurie; Company F, Sergeant Packard, Privates Arey, Kirk, Kramer, Lafferty, Wright; Company H, Barry, Divire, Durre, Cheeseman, Elder, Golden, McCarthy, Walker, and Young; Company I, Annisier, Davison, Garvey, Clark; Company K, Kriger, Larger (corporal), Shearer, Shepherd, and Sergeant Oliver.

September 13.— On retreat. Made Charleston, [West] Virginia. Held the enemy in check all day at this point. Three enlisted men wounded.

September 16.— Ravenswood, [West] Virginia. Crossed the Ohio River at this point. Marched to Racine.

September 17.— Went on board steamer *Mary Cook.* Arrived at Point Pleasant, [West] Virginia.

September 19.— The regiment crossed the Ohio River from Point Pleasant to Fair Haven, Ohio.

September 27.— The regiment recrossed the river from Fair Haven, Ohio to Point Pleasant, [West] Virginia. Camped on left bank of Crooked Creek.

Stationed at Camp Piatt, [West] Virginia, October 1862.

October 20.— The regiment marched with the division fifteen miles up the Kanawha [River].

October 21.— Marched nine miles to Buffalo.

October 22.— Marched from Buffalo to Red House [Shoal], ten miles.

October 24.— Marched to mouth of Pocotaligo and had a slight skirmish with enemy.

October 28.— Marched four miles to Bolings.

October 29.— Marched fourteen miles to Two-Mile Shoal near Charleston.

October 30.— Marched through Charleston and twelve miles to Camp Enyart.

October 31.— Marched nine miles to Widow Tompkins'.

November 1.— Marched thirteen miles to Camp Huddleston, slightly skirmishing with the rear of some Rebel cavalry.

November 3.— Marched to Gauley Bridge, seven miles, and encamped.

Stationed at camp near Loup Creek, [West] Virginia, November 1862.

Stationed at Fayetteville, [West] Virginia, December 1862-April 1863.

Stationed at Camp Butler, Cannelton, [West] Virginia, May 1863.

Stationed at Camp Piatt, [West] Virginia, June 1863.

Stationed at Camp Piatt, West Virginia, July 1863.
July 13-20.— The regiment marched from Camp Piatt, West Virginia to Wytheville, Virginia via Raleigh Court-House, Wyoming Court-House, and Tazewell Court-House and returned July 20. Engaged in skirmish at Spangler's Mills July 14. Participated in engagement at Wytheville July 18. Engaged in skirmish at Abb's Valley July 20. The total distance marched was 550 miles.

Stationed at Camp Piatt, West Virginia, August 1863.

Stationed at Camp Toland, West Virginia, September 1863.

Stationed at Camp Toland, Charleston, West Virginia, October 1863.

Stationed at Camp Toland, Charleston, West Virginia, November 1863.

From Charleston, West Virginia the regiment with the rest of the brigade (Third Cavalry, Third Division, Department of West Virginia) marched in concert with General [William Woods] Averell's command against the enemy at Lewisburg, West Virginia. We destroyed his camp equipage and captured part of rear guard. Distance marched was 220 miles. From Charleston the regiment marched to Barboursville and returned. Enemy reported in force. Distance marched was eighty miles.

Stationed at Camp Toland, Charleston, West Virginia, December 1863.

Stationed at Charleston, West Virginia, January 1864.

Stationed at Camp Toland, Charleston, West Virginia, February-March 1864.

Stationed at Bunger's Mills near Lewisburg, West Virginia, April-May 1864.

Stationed at Charleston, West Virginia, June 1864.

Marched from Bunger's Mills, West Virginia to Lynchburg, Virginia via Blue Sulphur [Springs], Lewisburg, White Sulphur [Springs], Warm Springs, Staunton, Lexington, Liberty, Buchanan to Lynchburg and returned via Liberty, Salem, New Market, Sweet Springs, Union, Lewisburg, Gauley to Charleston. Distance was 450 miles.

Stationed at Halltown, West Virginia, except Company B at Cumberland, Maryland, July 1864.

July 6-17.— The regiment left Charleston, West Virginia for Martinsburg, West Virginia and arrived there July 17.

July 18.— Seven companies sent to Cherry Run as guard to Baltimore and Ohio Railroad. Three companies at Martinsburg as provost guard.

July 19.— Seven companies returned to Martinsburg and marched to Winchester.

July 20.— In action at Winchester, Virginia. Privates William Blackburn, Frank Wise, Patrick McGovern, Company C, were killed at Winchester. William Cross of Company E; John M. Ford and William Hozier, Company F; Pierce Hassett and Uriah Purkises, Company H; S. F. Stahl (corporal), and James Shepherd, Company K, wounded.

July 24.— Retreated from Winchester, Virginia to Bolivar Heights, West Virginia via Williamsport and Shepherdstown. Lieutenant-Colonel [John] W. Shaw, mortally, and Captain George W. McKay, wounded in action at Winchester, Virginia. Corporal Charles Bobbitt, Lewis Bobbitt, First Sergeant J. Wesley Smith, Company D; Sergeant J. M. Tarboy, James Ball, William Meshwert, William Strohmier, Company F; George T. Smith, Ben Pelle, Company G; Patrick Barry, Hugh Connor, Joseph Cohn, Edward Hullinger, H. C. Levens, John Neal, John

Rockhill, Company H; James R. Wilkinson, F. M. Pingry, Company K, killed in action at Winchester, Virginia. Corporal A. Perry, Company D; John Bailey, Company E; H. Eichelberger, Company G, wounded. Isaac Corbly, Company A; Edward Gleeson (mortally) and Pat Lawler, Company C; George E. Sweetland, D. Carnban, William Schuyler, Company D; William H. Miller, Alex Cross, and S. Stephenson, Company E; Corporal Dudley Beal, Frank Blessing, J. Bouser, Company F; Conrad Reichel, Company G; J. M. Phillips, Joseph Eichelberger, J. N. Floyd, Company K, wounded.
July 25.— Killed at Martinsburg, West Virginia, Sergeant Horace Martin, Company E. Wounded were William A. Patterson, Company F, and D. M. Hartsell, Company K.

Stationed at Charlestown, West Virginia, August 1864.
August 5.— Company D, Corporal Alexander McDonald, wounded near Charlestown, West Virginia. Leonard Biacox, Private, wounded near Charlestown, West Virginia.
August 13.— Captain George W. McKay died in the United States Hospital, Sandy Hook, Maryland from the effects of an amputation due to a wound to his right leg in action at Winchester, Virginia July 24.
August 16.— Samuel W. Stevenson died at Frederick, Maryland of wounds received at Martinsburg, West Virginia July 25.
August 24.— Company A, Francis M. Windsor wounded in action near Bolivar Heights, West Virginia in left shoulder. Edward McGrew's right thumb off in action near Bolivar Heights, West Virginia. Alex Cossau died at Frederick City, Maryland from wounds received in action at Winchester, Virginia July 24.

Stationed at Harrisonburg, Virginia, September 1864.

Stationed at Cedar Creek, Virginia, October 1864.

Stationed at Camp Russell, Virginia, November 1864.

Stationed at Beverly, West Virginia, December 1864.

Stationed at Cumberland, Maryland, January 1865.

Company A

Stationed at Camp Lucas, Ohio, July 27, 1861.
July 27.— Muster-in roll of Captain Thomas W. Rathbone's Company, in the Thirty-fourth Regiment of Ohio Volunteers, commanded by Colonel A. Sanders Piatt, called into the service of the United States by the President from July 27, 1861 (date of this muster) for the term of three years, unless sooner discharged. The company was organized by Captain Thomas W. Rathbone at Amelia in the month of July and marched thence to Camp Lucas, where it arrived July 27, a distance of four miles. . . .

T. W. WALKER,
[Captain],
Third Infantry, Mustering Officer.

Stationed at Camp Red House [Shoal], October 31, 1861.

Stationed at Camp Red House [Shoal], [West] Virginia, December 31, 1861.

Stationed at Camp Franklin, [West] Virginia, January-February 1862.
February 3.— Marched from Camp Red House [Shoal], [West] Virginia to Camp Franklin, [West] Virginia, a distance of seventy-five miles.

Stationed at Camp Union, Fayetteville, [West] Virginia, March-April 1862.
March 17-20.— The company moved from Camp Franklin, [West] Virginia to Gauley Bridge via Guyandotte and Gallipolis. Distance marched nearly 160 miles.
April 7.— Also marched from Gauley Bridge, [West] Virginia to Camp Union, Fayetteville, [West] Virginia, a distance of fifteen miles.

Stationed at Camp Flat Top Tannery, [West] Virginia, May-June 1862.
May [5].— Marched from Fayette Court-House to Raleigh Court-House, [West] Virginia, twenty-five miles.

May 12-14.— Marched from Raleigh Court-House, [West] Virginia to French's Mill, [West] Virginia, distance fifty-five miles.
May 15.— The company went on reconnaissance seven miles beyond French's Mill. Had skirmish with [Albert Gallatin] Jenkins' Cavalry.
May 16-17.— Returned to camp. Total distance marched was fourteen miles. Marched to Princeton during the night of May 16 and 17, eleven miles.
May 18.— Marched from Princeton, [West] Virginia to Flat Top Tannery, [West] Virginia, distance twenty-three miles.

Total distance marched, since last muster, was 118 miles.

Stationed at Post Raleigh Court-House, [West] Virginia, July-August 1862.
August 4-7.— The company marched to Camp Creek, distant seven miles from Flat Top Tannery, [West] Virginia and returned August 7.
August 16.— The company marched from Flat Top, [West] Virginia to Raleigh Court-House, [West] Virginia, distance twenty-two miles.

Stationed at Camp Enyart, [West] Virginia, September-October 1862.
September 10-17.— Engaged in action at Fayetteville, at 3 a.m. Retreated to Gauley Bridge and from thence to Charleston, [West] Virginia, from thence to Ravenswood, [West] Virginia, arriving there September 17. In the evening marched to Racine, Ohio.
September 18.— From there took steamboat to Point Pleasant, [West] Virginia, in all a distance of 156 miles.
October 20.— Started from Point Pleasant, [West] Virginia up the Kanawha Valley and by short marches reached Camp Enyart, [West] Virginia, a distance of sixty-five miles.

Station not stated, November-December 1862.

Stationed at Fayetteville, [West] Virginia, January-April 1863.

Stationed at Camp Piatt, West Virginia, May-August 1863.

Stationed at Camp Toland, West Virginia, September-October 1863.

Stationed at Camp Toland, West Virginia, November-December 1863.
November 3.— The regiment marched for Lewisburg, West Virginia, whole distance 216 miles, and returned.
November 7-12.— Arrived and drove the enemy from the town, destroying camp tents, company stores, etc. and arrived here November 12.
November 16-20.— The regiment marched for Barboursville, whole distance seventy miles, and arrived here November 20.
December 8.— The regiment marched for Lewisburg 216 miles and returned. Drove the enemy from the towns and beyond Greenbrier River without loss on roll.

Stationed at Charleston, West Virginia, January-April 1864.

Stationed at Charleston, West Virginia, May-June 1864.
May 1.— The company left Charleston, West Virginia. The first day marched ten miles to Camp Piatt.
May 2.— The second day marched to Peytona, eighteen miles.
May 3.— Third day to Chapmanville, twenty-five miles.
May 4.— To Logan Court-House, sixteen miles.
May 5.— The fifth day to Wyoming Court-House, thirty-one miles.
May 6.— Sixth day marched thirty miles.
May 7.— Seventh day to Abb's Valley, twenty-four miles.
May 8.— Eighth day skirmishing with the enemy and drove them beyond Tazewell Court-House; distance marched twelve miles.
May 9.— Ninth day to Stony Gap, twenty-eight miles.
May 10.— Tenth day marched thirty-five miles. Met the enemy at Cove Mountain Gap and fought them for five hours, when we were forced to fall back. The company lost three killed and seven wounded.
May 11-18.— Marched to Dublin Depot, distance forty miles; thence by way of Christianburg to Salt Pond Mountain, where we met the enemy and engaged them, the company losing corporal wounded; thence by way of Union Court-House to Lewisburg, where we arrived May 18, having marched 127 miles.

June 3.— The company left Lewisburg, marched via White Sulphur, Hot and Warm Springs to Staunton, distance 100 miles.
June 11-17.— Moved out from Staunton on the Lexington Pike, from Lexington to Buchanan; thence across the Blue Ridge to Liberty; thence to New London. Met the enemy; had a skirmish and lost one corporal wounded. We marched to within three miles of Lynchburg June 17, where we met and engaged the enemy. The company lost one private wounded.
June 18.— General engagement with the enemy but fell back fifteen miles during the night.
June 19.— Continued our retreat through Liberty. Had a heavy skirmish with the enemy here.

Continued our retreat through New Salem and thence by way of New Castle, Warm Springs, White Sulphur and Lewisburg down to the Kanawha Valley; thence Charleston, West Virginia, a distance of sixty-five miles. Whole distance marched during the month of May and June was 652 miles.

Stationed at Charlestown, July-August 1864.

Stationed at Cedar Creek, Virginia, September-October 1864.

Stationed at Beverly, West Virginia, November-December 1864.

Company B

Stationed at Camp Dennison, Ohio, September 2, 1861.
September 2.— Muster-in roll of Captain [Oliver] P. Evans' Company, in the Thirty-fourth Regiment of Ohio Volunteers, commanded by Colonel A. Sanders Piatt, called into service of the United States by the President of the United States from September 2, 1861 (date of this muster) for the term of three years, unless sooner discharged. . . .

T. W. WALKER,
Captain,
Third Infantry, Mustering Officer.

Stationed at Camp Red House [Shoal], October 31, 1861.

Stationed at Camp Paxton, Guyandotte, [West] Virginia, December 31, 1861.

Stationed at Camp Toland, Barboursville, [West] Virginia, January-February 1862.

Station not stated, March-April 1862.
March 16-19.— Moved with regiment from Barboursville, [West] Virginia to Gauley Bridge, [West] Bridge, arriving there March 19.
April 7.— Moved with regiment from Gauley Bridge to Fayetteville, distance thirteen miles.
April 17.— Marched from Fayetteville to McCoy's Farm, distance ten miles.

Stationed at Camp Flat Top Tannery, May-June 1862.
May 3.— Moved with left wing of battalion from Camp McCoy to Raleigh, distance fifteen miles.
May 11.— Left Raleigh with left wing.
May 12.— Arrived at Princeton, [West] Virginia, distance forty-four miles.
May 16-17.— Fought the battle of Princeton, [West] Virginia.
May 18.— Retreated back to Camp Flat Top Tannery, [West] Virginia, distance twenty-two miles.

Stationed at Raleigh Court-House, [West] Virginia, July-August 1862.
August 11.— Went scouting with forty-eight men to Camp Creek from Camp Flat Top Tannery, [West] Virginia. Came back same day, distance sixteen miles.
August 15.— Left Flat Top Tannery, [West] Virginia with the regiment. Came to Raleigh Court-House, [West] Virginia the same day, distance twenty miles.

Station not stated, September-October 1862.
September 3.— Marched from Raleigh, [West] Virginia, distance twenty-five miles.
September 10.— Fought the battle of Fayetteville, [West] Virginia.

September 11-17.— Retreated from Fayetteville, [West] Virginia to Point Pleasant, [West] Virginia.
October 20.— Moved from Point Pleasant, [West] Virginia.
October 31.— Camped at Loup Creek.

Whole distance marched during the months of September and October was 384 miles.

Stationed at Fayetteville, [West] Virginia, November-December 1862.

Marched from Loup Creek, [West] Virginia with regiment to Gauley, [West] Virginia, distance seven miles.

Went on scout to Fayetteville, [West] Virginia. Return to Gauley. Distance, twenty-four miles.

Moved with regiment from Gauley, [West] Virginia to Loup Creek, [West] Virginia, distance seven miles.

Moved with regiment to Fayetteville, [West] Virginia, distance nineteen miles.

Stationed at Fayette Court-House, [West] Virginia, January-February 1863.
February 20.— The company marched fourteen miles on scout.

Stationed at Fayette Court-House, West Virginia, March-April 1863.

Stationed at Camp Piatt, [West] Virginia, May-June 1863.
May 3.— The company marched from Fayette Court-House, [West] Virginia to Camp Reynolds, [West] Virginia, distance thirteen miles.
May 13.— Marched from Camp Reynolds to Loup Creek, [West] Virginia, distance five miles.
May 21.— Marched from Loup Creek to Fayette Court-House, [West] Virginia, distance eighteen miles.
May 23.— From Fayette Court-House, [West] Virginia to Camp Reynolds, [West] Virginia, distance thirteen miles.
May 25.— From Camp Reynolds, [West] Virginia to Camp Butler, distance ten miles.
May 28.— The regiment was mounted.
June 5.— To Camp Brownstown, distance ten miles.
June 6.— From Camp Brownstown to Camp Piatt, [West] Virginia at night, distance two miles.

Stationed at Camp Piatt, West Virginia, July-August 1863.

Stationed at Camp Toland, West Virginia, September-October 1863.

Stationed at Camp Toland, West Virginia, November-December 1863.
November 3.— The regiment marched for Lewisburg, West Virginia (whole distance and returned, 216 miles).
November 7-13.— Arrived and drove the enemy from town. Destroyed camp, tents, company stores, etc., and arrived here November 13.
November 16.— The regiment marched to Barboursville and returned, distance ninety miles.
December 8.— The regiment marched to Lewisburg (distance and returned, 216 miles), drove the enemy beyond Greenbrier River without loss on our side.

Stationed at Camp Toland, West Virginia, January-June 1864.

Stationed near Charlestown, West Virginia, July-August 1864.

Stationed at Cedar Creek, Virginia, September-October 1864.

Stationed at Beverly, West Virginia, November-December 1864.

Company C

Stationed at Camp Dennison, Ohio, August 15, 1861.
August 15.— Muster-in roll of Captain Austin T. Miller's Company, in the Thirty-fourth Regiment of Ohio Volunteers, commanded by Colonel A. Sanders Piatt, called into the service of the United States by the President from August 15, 1861 (date of this muster) for the term of three years, unless sooner discharged. The company was organized by Captain Austin T. Miller at Cincinnati in the month of July and marched thence to Camp Lucas, where it arrived August 5, a distance of seventeen miles. . . .

T. W. WALKER,
Captain,
Third Infantry, Mustering Officer.

Stationed at Camp Franklin, October 31, 1861.

Stationed at Camp Toland, Cabell Court-House, [West] Virginia, December 31, 1861.

Stationed at Camp Toland, [West] Virginia, January-February 1862.

Stationed at Camp Union, Fayetteville, [West] Virginia, March-April 1862.

Stationed at Camp Flat Top Tannery, [West] Virginia, May-June 1862.

Stationed at Post Raleigh Court-House, [West] Virginia, July-August 1862.

Stationed at camp near Loup Creek, [West] Virginia, September-October 1862.

Stationed at Fayette Court-House, [West] Virginia, November-December 1862.

Stationed at Fayetteville, [West] Virginia, January-April 1863.

Stationed at Camp Piatt, West Virginia, May-August 1863.

Stationed at Camp Toland, West Virginia, September-October 1863.
November 3.— The regiment marched for Lewisburg, West Virginia.
November 7-13.— Arrived and drove the enemy from town. Destroyed camp and company stores, etc. and arrived here November 13. Distance traveled 216 miles.
November 16.— The regiment marched to Barboursville, West Virginia and returned. Distance traveled ninety miles.
December 8.— The regiment marched to Lewisburg, West Virginia. Drove the enemy across Greenbrier River. Returned without the loss of a man. Distance traveled was 216 miles.

Stationed at Charleston, West Virginia, January-February 1864.
February 1-8.— Went on scout through Logan and Boone Counties and returned February 8. Distance traveled was 150 miles.

Stationed at Camp Toland, West Virginia, March-June 1864.

Stationed at Charlestown, West Virginia, July-August 1864.

Stationed in West Virginia, September-October 1864.

Stationed at Beverly, West Virginia, November-December 1864.

Company D

Stationed at Camp Lucas, Ohio, July 30, 1861.
July 30.— Muster-in roll of Captain Luther Furney's Company (Infantry), in the Thirty-fourth Regiment of Ohio Volunteers, commanded by Colonel A. Sanders Piatt, called into the service of the United States from July 30, 1861 (date of this muster) for the term of three years, unless sooner discharged. The company was organized by Captain Luther Furney at Kenton and Bellevue in the month of July and marched thence to Camp Lucas where it arrived July 31. . . .

T. W. WALKER,
[Captain],
Third Infantry, Mustering Officer.

Stationed at Camp Franklin, October 31, 1861.

Stationed at Camp Toland, [West] Virginia, December 31, 1861-February 28, 1862.

Stationed at Camp Union, [West] Virginia, March-April 1862.

Stationed at Camp Flat Top Tannery, [West] Virginia, May-June 1862.
May 14-16.— I left Raleigh in command of Companies D and I at 2 o'clock and arrived at Princeton, a distance of forty-six miles, at 11 a.m. on May 16. Reported to Major F. E. Franklin of the

Thirty-fourth Regiment, Ohio Volunteer Infantry. At 2 p.m. there was an alarm at the picket. We were ordered into line to await further orders. At 4 o'clock we were ordered out to reinforce the picket, where we met a large force under Humphrey Marshall. After engaging them in skirmishing for nearly four hours, we were compelled to retire.

Stationed at Raleigh Court-House, [West] Virginia, July-August 1862.

Stationed at Camp Piatt, September-October 1862.
September 4.— Left Raleigh, [West] Virginia. Marched to Fayetteville, distance of twenty-six miles, the same day.
September 10.— Remained there until we were attacked by a large force of the enemy commanded by [William Wing] Loring and [John Stuart] Williams. They attacked at 12 o'clock. The fight continued until after dark. During the night we received orders to fall back to Gauley, [West] Virginia. Loss was one killed and nine wounded, two taken prisoner. We were forced to fall back to Charleston, distance of thirty-seven miles.
September 13.— We were again attacked in the morning at 10 a.m. The fight continued until dark. Two men slightly wounded during the fight. We then were forced to retreat across the country to Ravenswood, distance sixty miles.
September 15.— Arrived in the morning; crossed the Ohio River and marched to Racine, Ohio, distance of twelve miles.
September 17.— Took the boat and went to Point Pleasant, [West] Virginia, distance of thirty-six miles.
October 20.— Remained there until, being reinforced, we advanced up the Kanawha River to [illegible] Creek, distance thirty miles.
October 24-30.— Arrived there and saw a small detachment of the enemy. After firing a few rounds the enemy retreated. We then advanced and marched to Charleston, arriving October 30, distance thirty miles.

Stationed at Camp Union, Fayetteville, [West] Virginia, November-December 1862.

Stationed at Fayetteville, [West] Virginia, January-April 1863.

Stationed at Camp Piatt, West Virginia, May-August 1863.

Stationed at Camp Toland, West Virginia, September-October 1863.
September 2-6.— The company left Camp Piatt, West Virginia; marched to Clarksburg by way of Sutton, West Virginia. Arrived at Clarksburg September 6, distance 160 miles.
September 12.— Left Clarksburg at night.
September 13.— Pursued a band of guerrillas near Glenville, West Virginia. Returned to Weston in the evening.
September 14-18.— Left Weston for Camp Piatt, West Virginia via Spencer, West Virginia. Arrived at camp September 18.
September 20.— Received orders to move Camp —— to Camp Toland near Charleston, West Virginia, distance ten miles.
October 20.— Received orders to march. Left camp at 6 p.m. Arrived at Boone Court-House.
October 22.— Left and arrived at Camp Toland October 23.

Stationed at Charleston, West Virginia, November-December 1863.
November 3.— The regiment marched for Lewisburg, distance and return of 216 miles (eight miles beyond).
November 7-13.— Arrived and drove the enemy from town, destroyed camp tents and commissary stores, etc. and arrived here November 13.
November 16-20.— The regiment marched for Barboursville, distance and return of ninety miles. Arrived here November 20.
December 8-19.— The regiment marched for Lewisburg, West Virginia, distance and return 200 miles. Arrived here on December 19.

Stationed at Camp Toland, West Virginia, January-February 1864.

Stationed at Charleston, West Virginia, March-June 1864.

Stationed in the field, July-August 1864.

Stationed at Cedar Creek, Virginia, September-October 1864.

Stationed at Beverly, West Virginia, November-December 1864.

Company E

Stationed at Camp Lucas, Ohio, August 1, 1861.
August 1.— Muster-in roll of Captain John W. Shaw's Company, in the Thirty-fourth Regiment of Ohio Volunteers, commanded by Colonel A. Sanders Piatt, called into the service of the United States from August 1, 1861 (date of this muster) for the term of three years, unless sooner discharged. The company was organized by Captain John W. Shaw at Bucyrus, Ohio in the month of July and marched thence to Camp Lucas, where it arrived August 1, a distance of 175 miles. . . .

T. W. WALKER,
[Captain],
Third Infantry, Mustering Officer.

Stationed at Camp Franklin, October 31, 1861.

Stationed at Camp Toland, [West] Virginia, December 31, 1861-February 28, 1862.

Stationed at Fayette Court-House, [West] Virginia, March-April 1862.
April 21-29.— Second lieutenant, one sergeant, one corporal, and twenty privates started from Fayette Court-House, [West] Virginia by order of Lieutenant-Colonel John T. Toland. Scouted up New River to Richmond's Ferry, from thence to Raleigh, [West] Virginia. Was absent eight days; returned to Fayette Court-House April 29.

Stationed at Flat Top Mountain, Mercer County, [West] Virginia, May-June 1862.
June 11.— The company left Flat Top Mountain, Mercer County, [West] Virginia at 6 a.m., fifty-eight in number, with two companies of Twenty-eighth Ohio Volunteers. Marched the first day seventeen miles and camped at Blue Stone River. Second platoon of this company was left three miles in rear.

June 12-13.— In the morning at 4 a.m. marched to Princeton; arrived at 10 a.m.; returned same day and camped overnight nine miles this side of Princeton. Proceeded to Camp Flat Top Mountain at 3 a.m. and arrived all safe and sound, the reconnaissance being a success.

Stationed at Post Raleigh Court-House, [West] Virginia, July-August 1862.

Stationed at Camp Piatt, September-October 1862.

Stationed at Fayetteville, [West] Virginia, November 1862-April 1863.

Stationed at Camp Piatt, [West] Virginia, May-June 1863.
May 27.— Furnished with horses and made mounted infantry. Marched with regiment from Camp Butler, fourteen miles.

Stationed at Camp Piatt, West Virginia, July-August 1863.

Stationed at Camp Toland, September-October 1863.
September 24.— The company marched from Camp Piatt west to Camp Toland, West Virginia.
October 20-24.— From Camp Toland to Boone Court-House and returned October 24.

The company has been in no engagement during the past two months.

Stationed at Camp Toland, West Virginia, November-December 1863.
November 2-12.— The company marched with the regiment to Lewisburg, a distance of 100 miles, and returned to camp November 12. During the march the company was in no engagement.
November 17-22.— The company went to Barboursville, West Virginia on a scout and returned to camp on November 22 without meeting the enemy.
December 8.— The company again marched to Lewisburg, West Virginia.

December 12.— The company was engaged in a small skirmish with the enemy, who was driven from their position without loss of a man.
December 19.— The company returned to camp.
Total distance marched, since last muster, was 550 miles.

Stationed at Camp Toland, West Virginia, January-February 1864.
January 15.— The company marched to Wayne Court-House, West Virginia without meeting the enemy and returned January 19. Total distance marched 210 miles.

Stationed at Camp Toland, Charleston, West Virginia, March-April 1864.

Stationed at Camp Toland, West Virginia, May-June 1864.

Stationed at Charlestown, West Virginia, July-August 1864.

Station not stated, September-October 1864.

Stationed at Beverly, West Virginia, November-December 1864.

Company F

Stationed at Camp Dennison, Ohio, September 7, 1861.
September 7.— Muster-in roll of Captain Samuel R. S. West's Company, in the Thirty-fourth Regiment of Ohio Volunteers, commanded by Colonel A. Sanders Piatt, called into service of the United States by the President from September 7, 1861 (date of this muster) for the term of three years, unless sooner discharged. . . .

T. W. WALKER,
Captain,
Third Infantry, Mustering Officer.

Stationed at Camp Franklin, Cabell County, [West] Virginia, October 31, 1861.

Stationed at Camp Toland, [West] Virginia, November-December 1861.

Stationed at Camp Franklin, [West] Virginia, January-February 1862.

Stationed at Camp Union, Fayetteville, Fayette County, [West] Virginia, March-April 1862.
March 17.— Company F, with Company A, marched from Camp Franklin, Mud Bridge, [West] Virginia to Barboursville (Camp Toland) Cabell County, [West] Virginia, a distance of twelve miles.
March 18-23.— Company F, with the regiment, moved from Barboursville to Gauley Bridge, [West] Virginia, a distance of 140 miles, where it arrived March 23.
April 7.— Company F marched with the regiment from Gauley Bridge, [West] Virginia to Fayetteville, Fayette County, [West] Virginia, a distance of fifteen miles.

Stationed at Camp Flat Top Tannery, [West] Virginia, May-June 1862.
May 10.— Company F marched from Fayetteville to Raleigh Court-House, [West] Virginia, twenty-five miles.
May 12.— Company F marched from Raleigh to foot of Flat Top Mountain, twenty miles.
May 13.— Company F marched to Blue Stone River, twenty miles.
May 14.— Company F marched to Frenchville, Mercer County, [West] Virginia, sixteen miles.
May 17.— Company F took part in an engagement with the Rebels at Princeton, [West] Virginia and lost two privates "missing in action," supposed to be wounded and prisoners *viz.*: Frank M. Curl and Anthony Ebleheart, also two privates seriously wounded *viz.*: James B. Winter and Alex C. Kyle. The company also lost (by reason of company wagon being captured) all of the company books and accounts, knapsacks, clothing, and a few arms and equipments.
May 18.— Company F marched by a circuitous route of fifty miles to Blue Stone River.

May 19.— Company F marched to Great Flat Top Mountain, fifteen miles.

Stationed at Camp Raleigh Post, July-August 1862.
August 15.— Marched from Great Flat Top Mountain to Raleigh Court-House (Camp Raleigh Post), a distance of twenty-three miles.

Stationed at Camp Piatt, September-October 1862.

Stationed at Fayette Court-House, November-December 1862.

Stationed at Fayette Court-House, [West] Virginia, January-February 1863.
February 20.— The company on scout. Marched twenty-six miles.

Stationed at Fayette Court-House, [West] Virginia, March-April 1863.

Stationed at Camp Piatt, [West] Virginia, May-June 1863.

Stationed at Camp Piatt, West Virginia, July-August 1863.
July 13-23.— The company was raid to East Tennessee and Virginia Railroad with Third Brigade (mounted) under command of the late Colonel John T. Toland, leaving Camp Piatt and returning July 23. Was engaged in the fight at Wytheville, Virginia July 18 and the different skirmishes incident to the march.

Stationed at Camp Toland, West Virginia, September-October 1863.

Stationed at Camp Toland, West Virginia, November-December 1863.
November 3-13.— The company, with regiment, marched to Lewisburg, found Rebels had evacuated company. The company, with regiment, returned November 13.
November 14-15.— The company on scout after guerrillas. Marched sixty-five miles. Returned on the evening of November 15.

December 8-21.— The company marched, with regiment, to Lewisburg; engaged the enemy, routed them and returned December 21.

Stationed at Camp Toland, West Virginia, January-February 1864.

Stationed at Charleston, West Virginia, March-April 1864.

Stationed at Camp Toland, West Virginia, May-June 1864.

Station not stated, July-October 1864.

Stationed at Beverly, West Virginia, November-December 1864.

Company G

Stationed at Camp Lucas, Ohio, August 20, 1861.
August 20.— Muster-in roll of Captain Charles G. Broadwell's Company, in the Thirty-fourth Regiment of Ohio Foot Volunteers, commanded by Colonel A. Sanders Piatt, called into the service of the United States by the President from August 20, 1862 (date of this muster) for the term of three years, unless sooner discharged. The company was organized by Captain Charles G. Broadwell at Cincinnati in the month of July and marched thence to Camp Lucas, where it arrived July 22, a distance of eighteen miles. . . .

T. W. WALKER,
[Captain],
Third Infantry, Mustering Officer.

Stationed at Camp Franklin, [West] Virginia, October 31, 1861.
Not have received any notice of it being our duty to keep a record of the marches of the company until we received into roll, am unable now to give dates. The company has not been engaged in any battle or skirmish or any very long or important marches.
September 15-19.— We left Camp Dennison, Ohio and arrived at Camp Enyart, [West] Virginia September 19.
Have been with the regiment actively engaged since between that point and Mud Bridge.

Stationed at Camp Toland, [West] Virginia, December 31, 1861.

Stationed at Camp Toland, [West] Virginia, January-February 1862.
January 7-8.— The company marched from Camp Toland, [West] Virginia to Lykins Mill (Camp Broadwell) starting in the afternoon and arriving on the evening of January 8, a distance of twenty-eight miles.
January 31.— It remained until marched to Camp Franklin, eighteen miles.
February 7.— It remained until it returned to Camp Toland, [West] Virginia, ten miles.

Stationed at Camp Union, Fayetteville, [West] Virginia, March-April 1862.
March 17-April 7.— Left Barboursville, [West] Virginia and marched to Guyandotte, a distance of seven miles. Embarked on steamboat the same evening. Disembarked at Loup Creek. Marched thence to Camp Gauley, [West] Virginia. Left Camp Gauley, [West] Virginia April 7 for Fayetteville, [West] Virginia, a distance of twelve miles, and arrived there the same night.

Stationed at Camp Flat Top Tannery, May-June 1862.
May 2.— Left Fayetteville at 12.30 p.m. Marched ten miles.
May 3.— Marched sixteen miles, arriving at Raleigh, [West] Virginia.
May 11.— Left Raleigh at 5 a.m. Marched twenty-nine miles.
May 12.— Marched sixteen miles and arrived at Princeton.
May 14.— Marched from Princeton to Frenchville, eleven miles.
May 16-17.— Left Frenchville at 9 p.m. for Princeton and entered Princeton at 7 a.m. May 17 and was detailed with Company H, Thirty-fourth Regiment, to scout the Raleigh Road for five miles and arrived back at camp at 11 a.m.
May 18.— Left Princeton on the retreat. Halted at Wolf Creek, nine miles, at 3 p.m.
May 19.— Left at 6 a.m. and arrived on the same evening at Camp Flat Top Tannery, fourteen miles, and twenty-three [miles] from Princeton.

Stationed at Raleigh Court-House, July-August 1862.
August 15.— Marched from Camp Flat Top Tannery to Raleigh Court-House, [West] Virginia, distance twenty-two miles.
August 23-27.— Marched on a scout to Richmond's Ferry at New River, a distance of twenty miles, and returned to Raleigh Court-House August 27.

Stationed at Camp Enyart, [West] Virginia, September-October 1862.
September 10.— Engaged in action at Fayetteville, [West] Virginia.
September 11-17.— At 3 a.m. retreated to Gauley Bridge and from thence to Charleston, [West] Virginia, from thence to Ravenswood, [West] Virginia, arriving there September 17. In the evening marched to Racine, Ohio.
September 18.— Took steamboat to Point Pleasant, [West] Virginia, in all a distance of 156 miles.
October 19.— Started from Point pleasant up the Kanawha Valley and by short marches reached Camp Enyart, a distance of sixty-five miles.

Stationed at Fayetteville, [West] Virginia, November 1862-April 1863.

Stationed at Camp Piatt, [West] Virginia, May-August 1863.

Stationed at Camp Toland, West Virginia, September 1863-June 1864.

Stationed at Charlestown, West Virginia, July-August 1864.

Stationed at Cedar Creek, Virginia, September-October 1864.

Stationed at Beverly, West Virginia, November-December 1864.

Company H

Stationed at Camp Franklin, [West] Virginia, October 31, 1861.

Stationed at Camp Toland, December 31, 1861.

Stationed at Camp Toland, [West] Virginia, January-February 1862.
January 6-10.— Company H under command Captain [Herman] C. Evans marched to Beech Fork, Cabell County, [West] Virginia, distance from Toland twenty miles, and there encamped three days.
January 11-13.— The company returned to Camp Toland, having performed a march over almost impassable roads and in extremely bad weather from the effects of which one sergeant, Samuel Balser, died and much sickness resulted.

Stationed at Fayetteville, [West] Virginia, March-April 1862.
Joseph Rigney, principal musician, and Richard Marsh, hospital steward, dropped on last muster roll by mistake. Transferred on this one, last aggregate too small by two.
March 19-23.— The company moved from Barboursville, [West] Virginia and arrived at Gauley Bridge March 23.
April 7.— The company marched from Gauley Bridge at 7 a.m. and arrived at Fayetteville, [West] Virginia at 4.30 p.m.

Stationed at Flat Top Tannery, May-June 1862.
May 2-3.— The company marched from Fayetteville, [West] Virginia and arrived at Raleigh, [West] Virginia May 3.
May 11-12.— The company marched from Raleigh, [West] Virginia and arrived at Princeton, [West] Virginia May 12.
May 14.— Left Princeton, [West] Virginia and arrived at French's Mill the same day. Distance from Princeton was eleven miles.
May 16-17.— Started from French's Mill and arrived at Princeton May 17, the battle of Princeton but our company was not actively engaged.
May 18-19.— Left Princeton and arrived at Flat Top Tannery, our present encampment, May 19.

Stationed at Post Raleigh Court-House, [West] Virginia, July-August 1862.
August 14.— The company went out on a scout. Marched some twenty-six miles, returning to Camp Flat Top Tannery, [West] Virginia at night. Object of the scout was to find Colonel [Jonathan D.] Hines of the Twelfth Ohio Regiment of Infantry for whom we had sealed orders.
August 15.— Left Camp Flat Top Tannery, [West] Virginia at 7 a.m. Arrived at Raleigh, [West] Virginia, our present encampment at night about 8 p.m. Distance from Camp Flat Top Tannery, [West] Virginia was twenty-two miles.

Stationed at Camp Piatt, [West] Virginia, September-October 1862.
September 3-4.— The regiment left Raleigh, [West] Virginia and arrived at Fayetteville, [West] Virginia September 4.
September 7.— The company went on a scout.
September 10.— Had an engagement with the enemy.
September 11-13.— Commenced our retreat from Fayetteville in the morning. Repulsed the enemy at Cotton Hill. Continued our retreat arriving at Charleston, [West] Virginia September 13, and again engaged the enemy, resuming our march at night, retreating via Ripley, [West] Virginia to Ravenswood, [West] Virginia on the Ohio River.
September 16.— Arrived at Racine, Ohio at night.
September 17.— Embarked on steamboats and went down the river, arriving at Point Pleasant, [West] Virginia after a march of 107 miles.
October 20.— Remained in camp at Point Pleasant, [West] Virginia until we commenced our march up the valley and are at present in camp at Camp Piatt, [West] Virginia, distant from Point Pleasant, [West] Virginia, sixty-four miles.

Stationed at Fayetteville, [West] Virginia, November-December 1862.
December 4.— The company marched from Loup Creek, [West] Virginia and arrived at Fayetteville, [West] Virginia in the afternoon of the same day.

Stationed at Fayetteville, [West] Virginia, January-February 1863.

Stationed at Fayette Court-House, [West] Virginia, March-April 1863.

Stationed at Camp Piatt, [West] Virginia, May-June 1863.
May 24.— The company was mounted and marched from Kanawha Falls, [West] Virginia to Camp Butler, [West] Virginia on the same day.
June 5.— Left Camp Butler and arrived at Brownstown the same day.
June 6.— Crossed river to Camp Piatt, [West] Virginia.

Stationed at Camp Piatt, West Virginia, July-August 1863.
July 13.— The company left Camp Piatt, West Virginia on scout to Wytheville, West Virginia.
July 18.— Arrived at Wytheville and was in the action of that day. Six of our men were missing.
July 25.— Returned to Camp Piatt.

Stationed at Camp Toland, West Virginia, September-October 1863.
September 24.— The company marched from Camp Piatt to Camp Toland, Charleston, West Virginia, distance nine miles.
October 20.— The company marched from Camp Toland to Peytona.
October 21.— From Peytona to Boone Court-House.
October 22.— From Boone Court-House to Camp Piatt.
October 23.— From Camp Piatt to Camp Toland. Entire distance marched was seventy miles.

Stationed at Camp Toland, West Virginia, November-December 1863.
November 2-7.— The company went to Lewisburg and arrived there November 7.
November 13.— Returned to Camp Toland; distance marched was 200 miles.

November 16.— On scout to Barboursville.
December 8-12.— Left Camp Toland and arrived at Lewisburg December 12.
December 19.— Returned to Camp Toland, West Virginia. Distance marched was 200 miles.

Stationed at Camp Toland, West Virginia, January-June 1864.

Stationed at Charlestown, West Virginia, July-August 1864.

Company I

Stationed at Camp Dennison, Ohio, August 10, 1861.
August 10.— Muster-in roll of Captain James A. Anderson's Company, in the Thirty-fourth Regiment of Ohio Volunteers, commanded by Colonel A. Sanders Piatt, called into service of the United States by the President from August 10, 1861 (date of this muster) for the term of three years, unless sooner discharged. . . .

T. W. WALKER,
Captain,
Third Infantry, Mustering Officer.

Stationed at Camp Franklin, October 31, 1861.

Stationed at Camp Toland, Cabell Court-House, [West] Virginia, December 31, 1861.

Stationed at Camp Toland, [West] Virginia, January-February 1862.

Stationed at Fayetteville, [West] Virginia, March-April 1862.

Stationed at Flat Top Mountain, [West] Virginia, May-June 1862.
May 16.— The company was in the battle at Princeton, [West] Virginia.

Stationed at Post Raleigh Court-House, [West] Virginia, July-August 1862.

Stationed at Camp Enyart, [West] Virginia, September-October 1862.
September 10.— Engaged in action at Fayetteville, [West] Virginia.
September 11-17.— At 3 a.m. retreated to Gauley Bridge and from thence to Charleston, [West] Virginia and from thence to Ravenswood, [West] Virginia, arriving there September 17. In the evening marched to Racine, Ohio.
September 18.— Took steamboat for Point Pleasant, [West] Virginia. Traveled in all a distance of 156 miles.
October 20.— In a.m. started from Point Pleasant up the Kanawha Valley and by short marches reached Camp Enyart, a distance of sixty-five miles.

Station not stated, November-December 1862.
The aggregate of the last muster roll was incorrect, being three more than it should have been. Three men that were discharged men included in the aggregate.

Stationed at Fayetteville, [West] Virginia, January-April 1863.

Stationed at Camp Piatt, West Virginia, May-August 1863.

Stationed at Camp Toland, West Virginia, September-October 1863.

Stationed at Camp Toland, West Virginia, November-December 1863.
November 3-12.— The company started for Lewisburg, West Virginia, a distance of over 100 miles and returned November 12.
November 16-20.— Started to Barboursville, West Virginia and returned November 20.
December 8-19.— A squad of the company, a large proportion being home in Ohio on furlough, started for Lewisburg, West Virginia and returned December 19.

Stationed at Camp Toland, West Virginia, January-February 1864.
February 4-8.— One sergeant, two corporals and twenty privates started out on a scout and returned February 8.

February 18.— Captain Underwood rejoined company from absence in Ohio on recruiting service.
February 20-27.— Captain, two sergeants, four corporals, a bugler, and twenty-three privates started out on scout and returned February 27.

Stationed at Camp Toland, West Virginia, March-April 1864.
April 10-13.— The captain and fifty-one enlisted men left camp and proceeded to the falls of Guyandotte River, a distance of sixty-six miles, and returned on April 13. The total number of miles traveled was 132.

Stationed at Camp Toland, West Virginia, May-June 1864.
May 1-10.— The company, with the regiment, started on a march going to Logan Court-House, from thence to Tazewell Court-House, and from thence to Cove [Mountain] Gap, where it encountered the enemy, losing two men killed and two wounded May 10.

From thence went to Lewisburg, by way of Dublin Depot and Christiansburg. After remaining in camp at Bunger's Mill, near Lewisburg, a few days started to Staunton by way of White Sulphur Springs, going from Staunton to Lexington and from thence to the front of Lynchburg, where the enemy was again encountered in force.
June 18.— The company, in front of Lynchburg, had two men wounded and one missing.
June 19-29.— The command fell back, skirmished with the enemy along the road to Lewisburg and arrived in Charleston June 29.

Stationed at Charlestown, West Virginia, July-August 1864.

Company K

Stationed at Camp Dennison, Ohio, August 10, 1861.
August 10.— Muster-in roll of Captain Thomas R. Smiley's Company, in the Thirty-fourth Regiment of Ohio Foot Volunteers, commanded by Colonel A. Sanders Piatt, called into service

of the United States by President from August 10, 1861 (date of this muster) for the term of three years, unless sooner discharged. . . .

T. W. WALKER,
Captain,
Third Infantry, Mustering Officer.

Stationed at Camp Franklin, October 31, 1861.

Stationed at Camp Toland, Cabell Court-House, [West] Virginia, November-December 1861.

Stationed at Camp Toland, January-February 1862.

Stationed at Camp Union, March-April 1862.

Stationed at Camp Flat Top Tannery, May-June 1862.
May 17.— The company was in the battle of Princeton.

Stationed at Raleigh Court-House, [West] Virginia, July-August 1862.
August 15.— The company marched from Flat Top Tannery to Post Raleigh Court-House, a distance of twenty-two miles.

Stationed at Camp Piatt, September-October 1862.
September 10.— The company under command of Lieutenant Brown on scout from Fayetteville, [West] Virginia to Laurel Creek, [West] Virginia and returned same evening. Distance marched was thirteen miles.
September 11.— Skirmish in morning at Fayetteville, [West] Virginia. Lieutenant Brown and Private Levi Borcher mortally wounded.

Stationed at Camp Union, Fayette Court-House, [West] Virginia, November-December 1862.
November 3.— Arrived at Gauley Bridge marching from Camp Piatt.
November 5-6.— Left Gauley Bridge for Fayette Court-House, Virginia on a scout and returned to Gauley Bridge November 6.

November 10.— Left Gauley Bridge for mouth of Loup Creek, a distance of seven miles.
December 6.— Left camp near mouth of Loup Creek for Fayette Court-House, [West] Virginia, a distance of sixteen miles, where we arrived December 6 at 2 p.m.

Stationed at Camp Union, Fayette Court-House, [West] Virginia, January-February 1863.
January 3-5.— The company left on a scout east of Fayette Court-House, [West] Virginia to Lick Creek, a distance of thirty-five miles. Captured eight of the enemy and returned to camp at Fayette Court-House, [West] Virginia January 5 after a march of seventy miles.
February 16.— The company left on a scout at 6 a.m. Marched a distance of eighteen miles and returned to camp same day at 6 p.m.

Stationed at Camp Union, Fayette Court-House, [West] Virginia, April 10, 1863.

Stationed at Fayetteville, West Virginia, March-April 1863.

Stationed at Camp Piatt, [West] Virginia, May-June 1863.
May 3.— The company marched from Fayette Court-House to Kanawha Falls, distance twelve miles.
May 20.— The company marched from Kanawha Falls to Fayette Court-House.
May 23.— Returned to Kanawha Falls, distance twenty-four miles.
May 25.— The company marched from Kanawha Falls to Camp Butler, distance ten miles.
June 5.— The company marched from Camp Butler to Camp Piatt, distance eighteen miles.

Stationed at Camp Piatt, West Virginia, July-August 1863.
July 13.— The company left Camp Piatt, West Virginia with regiment on a scout.
July 14.— Engaged in a skirmish with the enemy.
July 15.— Arrived at Raleigh Court-House at 6 a.m. Left Raleigh Court-House for Wytheville, West Virginia.

July 18.— Engaged in a skirmish with the enemy at Wytheville, West Virginia.
July 25.— Arrived at Camp Piatt, West Virginia; distance marched was 365 miles.

Stationed at Camp Toland, West Virginia, September-October 1863.
September 2-17.— The company left Camp Piatt, West Virginia and proceeded to Clarksburg, West Virginia to procure horses and rejoined the regiment on September 17, having marched 320 miles.

The regiment moved to Camp Toland, a distance of twelve miles.
October 20-23.— The regiment started on an expedition in search of Colonel [Henry M.] Beckley's Rebel Regiment in the evening. Rebs skedaddled and we returned to camp October 23, having marched seventy-five miles to Boone Court-House, West Virginia.

Stationed at Camp Toland, West Virginia, November-December 1863.
November 3-13.— The company left camp on a scout. Marched to Lewisburg. Returned November 13; distance marched 200 miles.
November 16-20.— The company left camp at 2 p.m. Marched to Barboursville, West Virginia. Returned November 20. Distance marched was eighty miles.
December 8-19.— The company left camp and marched to Lewisburg. Returned to December 19, distance 200 miles.

Stationed at Camp Toland, West Virginia, January-February 1864.

Stationed at Charleston, West Virginia, March-August 1864.

[M594-Roll #149]

Record of Events for Thirty-fifth Ohio Infantry, July 1861-September 1864.

Field and Staff

Stationed at Hamilton, Ohio, Camp Hamilton, Ohio, September 24, 1861.

September 24.— Muster-in roll of field and staff and band in the Thirty-fifth Regiment of Ohio Volunteers, commanded by Colonel Ferdinand Van Derveer, called into the service of the United States by the President from September 24, 1861 (date of this muster) for the term of three years, unless sooner discharged. . . .

[PATRICK HENRY] BRESLIN,
Captain,
Eighteenth United States Infantry,
United States Army Mustering Officer.

Stationed at Somerset, Kentucky, July 26-December 31, 1861.

Station not stated, February 28-April [30], 1862.

Stationed at Pelham, Tennessee, April 30-August 31, 1862.

Stationed at Nashville, Tennessee, September 24, 1862.

September 24.— Muster-out roll of regimental band in the Thirty-fifth Regiment of Ohio Foot Volunteers, commanded by Colonel Ferdinand Van Derveer, called into the service of the United States by order of the President at Hamilton, Ohio (the place of general rendezvous) on September 24, 1862 to serve for the term of three years from the date of enrollment, unless sooner discharged, from August 31, 1862 (when last mustered). . . .

JOHN [HORNE] YOUNG,
Captain,
Fifteenth United States Infantry, Mustering Officer.

Stationed at Gallatin, Tennessee, August 31-December 31, 1862.

Stationed at Concord Church, Tennessee, [January 1]-February 28, 1863.

Stationed at Triune, Tennessee, April 10, 1863.

Stationed at Camp Winford, Tennessee, February 28-June 30, 1863.

Stationed at Battle Creek, Tennessee, July-August 1863.

Stationed at Chattanooga, Tennessee, September-December 1863.

Stationed at Ringgold, Georgia, January-February 1864.

Stationed at Chattanooga, Tennessee, September 27, 1864.
September 27.— Muster-out roll of field and staff of the Thirty-fifth Regiment of Ohio Infantry Volunteers, commanded by Colonel Ferdinand Van Derveer, called into the service of the United States by the President at Hamilton, Ohio (the place of general rendezvous). . . .

WILLIAM [GEORGE] WEDEMEYER,
First Lieutenant,
Sixteenth United States Infantry, Mustering Officer.

Regiment

Station not stated, December 1861-November 1862.

Stationed at Branham Mills, Tennessee, December 1862.

Station not stated, January 1863.

Stationed at Concord Church, Tennessee, February 1863.

Station not stated, March 1863.

Stationed at Triune, Tennessee, April-May 1863.

Station not stated, June 1863.

Stationed at Camp Thomas, Tennessee, July 1863.

Stationed at Battle Creek, Tennessee, August 1863.

Station not stated, September 1863.

Stationed at Chattanooga, Tennessee, October 1863.

Station not stated, November 1863.

Stationed at Chattanooga, Tennessee, December 1863-January 1864.

Station not stated, February-March 1864.

Stationed at Ringgold, Georgia, April 1864.

Stationed at Burnt Hickory, Georgia, May 1864.

Stationed near Kenesaw Peaks, Georgia, June 1864.

Stationed in front of Atlanta, Georgia, July 1864.

Company A

Stationed at Hamilton, Ohio, August 20, 1861.
August 20.— Muster-in roll of Captain Joseph L. Budd's Company, in the Thirty-fifth Regiment of Ohio Volunteers, commanded by Colonel Ferdinand Van Derveer, called into the service of the United States by the President from August 20, 1861 (date of this muster) for the term of three years, unless sooner discharged. . . .

[THOMAS JEFFERSON] CRAM,
Captain,
United States Army, Mustering Officer.

Stationed at Somerset, Kentucky, December 31, 1861.

Station not stated, February 29, 1862.

Stationed at camp near Pittsburg Landing, March-April 1862.

Stationed at Pelham, Tennessee, April 30-August 31, 1862.

Stationed at Gallatin, Tennessee, August 31-December 31, 1862.

Stationed at camp at Concord Church, Tennessee, February 28, 1863.

Stationed at camp near Triune, Tennessee, April 10, 1863.

Stationed at Concord, Tennessee, February 28-June 30, 1863.

Stationed at Battle Creek, Tennessee, August 31, 1863.

Stationed at Chattanooga, Tennessee, June 30-December 31, 1863.

Stationed at Ringgold, Georgia, January-February 1864.

Stationed at Chattanooga, Tennessee, August 26, 1864.
August 26.— Muster-out roll of Captain Lewis F. Daugherty's (late of Captain J. L. Budd's) Company (A), in the Thirty-fifth Regiment of Ohio Infantry Volunteers, commanded by Colonel Ferdinand Van Derveer, called into the service of the United States by the President under act of Congress approved at Hamilton, Ohio (the place of general rendezvous) on August 20, 1861 to serve for the term of three years from the date of enrollment, unless sooner discharged, from December 31, 1863 (when last paid) to August 26, 1864 when discharged. The company was organized by Captain Joseph L. Budd at Lebanon, Ohio in the month of August 1861 and marched thence to Hamilton, Ohio, where it arrived August 15, a distance of twenty miles.

GEORGE [KAISER] SANDERSON,
First Lieutenant,
Fifteenth United States Infantry, Mustering Officer,
Assistant Commissary of Musters,
Third Division, Fourteenth Army Corps.

Company B

Stationed at Hamilton, Ohio, August 20, 1861.
August 20.— Muster-in roll of Captain Thomas Stone's Company, in the Thirty-fifth Regiment of Ohio Volunteers, commanded

by Colonel Ferdinand Van Derveer, called into the service of the United States by the President from August 20, 1861 (date of this muster) for the term of three years, unless sooner discharged. . . .

T. J. CRAM,
Mustering Officer.

Stationed at Somerset, Kentucky, August 9-December 31, 1861.

Station not stated, January-February 1862.

Stationed at camp near Pittsburg Landing, Tennessee, March-April 1862.

Stationed at Manchester, Tennessee, April 30-August 31, 1862.

Stationed at Gallatin, Tennessee, August 31-December 31, 1862.

Stationed at Concord Church, Tennessee, October 31, 1861-February 28, 1863.

Stationed at Triune, Tennessee, April 10, 1863.

Stationed at Camp Winford, February 28-June 30, 1863.

Stationed at mouth of Battle Creek, Tennessee, July-August 1863.

Stationed at Chattanooga, Tennessee, September-December 1863.

Stationed at Ringgold, Georgia, January-February 1864.

Stationed at Chattanooga, Tennessee, August 26, 1864.
August 26.— Muster-out roll of Captain Jonathan Henninger's Company (B), in the Thirty-fifth Regiment of Ohio Infantry Volunteers, commanded by Colonel F. Van Derveer, called into the service of the United States by the President at Hamilton, Ohio (the place of general rendezvous) to serve for the term of three years from the date of enrollment, unless sooner discharged, from August 20, 1861 (when mustered in) to August 26, 1864 when

discharged. The company was organized by Captain Thomas Stone at Hamilton, Ohio in the month of August 1861. . . .

GEORGE SANDERSON,
First Lieutenant,
Fifteenth United States Infantry, Assistant Commissary of Muster,
Third Division, Army Corps, Mustering Officer.

Company C

Stationed at Hamilton, Ohio, August 20, 1861.
August 20.— Muster-in roll of Captain [John] S. Earhart's Company, in the Thirty-fifth Regiment of Ohio Volunteers, commanded by Colonel Ferdinand Van Derveer, called into the service of the United States by the President from August 20, 1861 (date of this muster) for the term of three years, unless sooner discharged. . . .

T. J. CRAM,
United States Army Mustering Officer.

P. H. BRESLIN,
Captain,
Eighteenth Infantry, United States Army Mustering Officer.

Station not stated, August 20, 1861-February 28, 1862.

Stationed at camp near Pittsburg Landing, Tennessee, March-April 1862.

Stationed at Tuscumbia, Alabama, May-June 1862.

Stationed at Manchester, Tennessee, July-August 1862.

Stationed at camp near Gallatin, Tennessee, August 31-December 31, 1861.

Stationed at Camp Concord Church, Tennessee, [January 1]-February 28, 1863.

Stationed at camp near Triune, Tennessee, April 10, 1863.

Stationed at Concord, Tennessee, February 28-June 30, 1863.

Stationed at Battle Creek, Tennessee, July-August 1863.

Stationed at Chattanooga, Tennessee, September-December 1863.

Stationed at Ringgold, Georgia, January-February 1864.

Stationed at Chattanooga, Tennessee, August 26, 1864.
August 26.— Muster-out roll of Captain John Van Derveer's, late John S. Earhart's, Company (C), in the Thirty-fifth Regiment of Ohio Infantry Volunteers, commanded by Colonel Ferdinand Van Derveer, called into the service of the United States by the President under act of Congress approved at Hamilton, Ohio (the place of general rendezvous) on August 12, 1861 to serve for the term of three years from the date of enrollment, unless sooner discharged, from August 20, 1861 (when mustered) to August 26, 1864. The company was organized by Captain John S. Earhart at Hamilton, Ohio in the month of August 1861. . . .

GEORGE SANDERSON,
First Lieutenant,
Fifteenth United States Infantry,
Assistant Commissary of Musters, Third Division,
Fourteenth Army Corps, Mustering Officer.

Company D

Stationed at Camp Hamilton, Hamilton, Ohio, September 9, 1861.
September 9.— Muster-in roll of Captain Nathaniel Reeder's Company, in the Thirty-fifth Regiment of Ohio Volunteers, commanded by Colonel Ferdinand Van Derveer, called into the service of the United States by the President from September 9, 1861 (date of this muster) for the term of three years, unless sooner discharged. . . .

P. H. BRESLIN,
Captain,
Eighteenth Regiment, United States Infantry,
Mustering Officer.

Station not stated, August 26, 1861-February 28, 1862.

Stationed at camp near Pittsburg Landing, Tennessee, March-April 1862.

Stationed at Pelham, Tennessee, April 30-August 31, 1862.

Stationed at Gallatin, Tennessee, August 31-December 31, 1862.

Stationed at camp at Concord Church, Tennessee, [January 1]-February 28, 1863.

Stationed at Triune, Tennessee, April 10, 1863.

Stationed at Concord, Tennessee, February 28-June 30, 1863.

Stationed at camp on Battle Creek, Tennessee, July-August 1863.

Stationed at Chattanooga, Tennessee, September-December 1863.

Stationed at Ringgold, Georgia, January-February 1864.

Stationed at Chattanooga, Tennessee, September 8, 1864.
September 8.— Muster-out roll of Captain James H. Bones', late Nathaniel Reeder's, Company (D), in the Thirty-fifth Regiment of Infantry Ohio Volunteers, commanded by Colonel Ferdinand Van Derveer, called into the service of the United States by the President at Hamilton, Ohio (the place of general rendezvous) on September 9, 1861 to serve for the term of three years from the date of enrollment unless sooner discharged, from April 30, 1864 (when last mustered) to September 8, 1864, when mustered out. The company was organized by Captain Nathaniel Reeder at Hamilton, Ohio in the month of September 1861. . . .

WILLIAM G. WEDEMEYER,
First Lieutenant,
Sixteenth Infantry, United States Army,
Assistant Commissary of Musters,
D. C., Mustering Officer.

Company E

Stationed at Camp Hamilton, Hamilton, Ohio, September 9, 1861.
September 9.— Muster-in roll of Captain David M. Gans' Company (I), in the Thirty-fifth Regiment of Ohio Volunteers, commanded by Colonel Ferdinand Van Derveer, called into the service of the United States by the President from September 9 (date of this muster). . . .

P. H. BRESLIN,
Captain,
Eighteenth Regiment, United States Infantry, Mustering Officer.

Stationed at Somerset, Kentucky, September 1-December 31, 1861.

Station not stated, January-February 1862.

Stationed at camp near Pittsburg Landing, Tennessee, March-April 1862.

Stationed near Pelham, Tennessee, April 30-August 31, 1862.

Stationed at Gallatin, Tennessee, August 31-December 31, 1862.

Stationed at Concord Church, Tennessee, October 31, 1862-February 28, 1863.

Stationed at Triune, Tennessee, April 10, 1863.

Stationed at Concord Church, Tennessee, February 28-June 30, 1863.

Stationed at Battle Creek, Tennessee, July-August 1863.

Stationed at Chattanooga, Tennessee, September-December 1863.

Stationed at Ringgold, Georgia, January-February 1864.

Stationed at Chattanooga, Tennessee, September 8, 1864.
September 8.— Muster-out roll of Captain William H. C. Steele's, late Captain David M. Gans', Company (E), in the Thirty-fifth Regiment of Ohio Infantry Volunteers, commanded by Colonel Ferdinand Van Derveer, called into the service of the United States by the President at Hamilton, Ohio (the place of general rendezvous) on September 1, 1861 to serve for the term of three years from the date of enrollment, unless sooner discharged, from June 30, 1864 (when last mustered) to September 8, 1864 when mustered out. The company was organized by Captain David M. Gans at Hamilton, Ohio in the month of September 1861 and marched thence to Hamilton, Ohio, where it arrived September 1. . . .

WILLIAM G. WEDEMEYER,
First Lieutenant,
Sixteenth United States Infantry,
Assistant Commissary of Musters, D. C.,
Mustering Officer.

Company F

Stationed at Camp Hamilton, Hamilton, Ohio, September 9, 1861.
September 9.— Muster-in roll of Captain Oliver H. Parshall's Company (F), in the Thirty-fifth Regiment of Ohio Volunteers, commanded by Colonel Ferdinand Van Derveer, called into the service of the United States by the President from September 9, 1861 (date of this muster) for the term of three years, unless sooner discharged. . . .

P. H. BRESLIN,
Captain,
Eighteenth Regiment, United States Infantry,
United States Army, Mustering Officer.

Stationed at Somerset, Kentucky, September 5-December 31, 1861.

Station not stated, January-February 1862.

Stationed at camp near Pittsburg Landing, Tennessee, March-April 1862.

Stationed at Cherokee, Alabama, May-June 1862.

Stationed at camp near Pelham, Tennessee, July-August 1862.

Stationed at Camp Gallatin, Tennessee, August 31-December 31, 1862.

Stationed at Camp Concord Church, [January 1]-February 28, 1863.

Stationed at Triune, Tennessee, March-April 1863.

Stationed at Concord Church near Tullahoma, Tennessee, May-June 1863.

Stationed at Battle Creek, July-August 1863.

Stationed at Chattanooga, Tennessee, September-December 1863.

Stationed at Ringgold, Georgia, January-February 1864.

Stationed at Chattanooga, Tennessee, September 8, 1864.
September 8.— Muster-out roll of late Captain Oliver H. Parshall's Company (F), in the Thirty-fifth Regiment of Ohio Foot Volunteers, commanded by Colonel Ferdinand Van Derveer, called into the service of the United States by the President of the United States at Hamilton, Butler County, Ohio (the place of general rendezvous) on September 5, 1861 to serve for the term of three years from the date of enrollment, unless sooner discharged, from June 30, 1864 (when last mustered) to September 8, 1864 when mustered for discharge. The company was organized by Captain Oliver H. Parshall at Lebanon, Ohio in the month of

September 1861 and marched thence to Hamilton, Ohio, where it arrived September 5, a distance of twenty miles. . . .

WILLIAM G. WEDEMEYER,
First Lieutenant,
Sixteenth Infantry,
United States Army, Assistant Commissary of Musters,
D. C., Mustering Officer.

Company G

Stationed at Camp Hamilton, Hamilton, Ohio, September 24, 1861.

September 24.— Muster-in roll of Captain Samuel L'Hommedieu's Company, in the Thirty-fifth Regiment of Ohio Infantry Volunteers, commanded by Colonel Ferdinand Van Derveer, called into the service of the United States by the President from September 24, 1861 (date of this muster) for the term of three years, unless sooner discharged. . . .

P. H. BRESLIN,
Captain,
Eighteenth United States Infantry, Mustering Officer.

Stationed at Somerset, Kentucky, September 7-December 31, 1861.

Station not stated, January-February 1862.

Stationed at camp near Pittsburg Landing, Tennessee, March-April 1862.

Stationed at Pelham, Tennessee, April 30-August 31, 1862.

Stationed at Gallatin, Tennessee, August 31-December 31, 1862.

Stationed at Concord Church, Tennessee, January-February 1863.

Stationed at Triune, April 10, 1863.

Station not stated, May-June 1863.
June 29.— Deployed as skirmishers before Tullahoma, Tennessee. Captain Samuel L'Hommedieu wounded.

Stationed at camp on Battle Creek, July-August 1863.

Stationed at Chattanooga, Tennessee, September-October 1863.

Station not stated, November-December 1863.

Stationed at Ringgold, Georgia, January-February 1864.

Stationed at Chattanooga, Tennessee, September 23, 1864.
September 23.— Muster-out roll of Captain Samuel L'Hommedieu's Company (G), in the Thirty-fifth Regiment of Ohio Infantry Volunteers, commanded by Colonel Ferdinand Van Derveer, called into the service of the United States by the President at Hamilton, Ohio (the place of general rendezvous) on September 7, 1861 to serve for the term of three years from the date of enrollment, unless sooner discharged, from September 24, 1861 (when mustered) to September 23, 1864 when discharged. . . .

WILLIAM G. WEDEMEYER,
First Lieutenant,
Sixteenth Infantry, United States Army,
Assistant Commissary of Musters,
D. C., Mustering Officer.

Company H

Stationed at Camp Hamilton, Hamilton, Ohio, September 9, 1861.
September 9.— Muster-in roll of Captain Michael S. Gunckel's Company (H), in the Thirty-fifth Regiment of Ohio Volunteers, commanded by Colonel Ferdinand Van Derveer, called into the service of the United States by the President from September 9, 1861 (date of this muster) for the term of three years, unless sooner discharged. . . .

P. H. BRESLIN,
Captain,
Eighteenth Regiment, United States Infantry,
United States Army, Mustering Officer.

Station not stated, August 26, 1861-February 28, 1862.

Stationed at camp near Pittsburg Landing, Tennessee, March-April 1862.

Stationed at Pelham, Tennessee, April 30-August 31, 1862.

Stationed at Gallatin, Tennessee, August 31-December 31, 1862.

Stationed at Triune, Tennessee, [January 1]-February 28, 1863.

Stationed at Triune, Tennessee, April 10, 1863.

Stationed at Camp Winford, Tennessee, February 28-June 30, 1863.

Stationed at Battle Creek, Tennessee, July-August 1863.

Stationed at Chattanooga, Tennessee, September-December 1863.

Stationed at Ringgold, Georgia, January-February 1864.

Stationed at Chattanooga, Tennessee, September 8, 1864.
September 8.— Muster-out roll of Captain [Theodore] D. Mather's Company (H), in the Thirty-fifth Regiment of Ohio Foot Volunteers, commanded by Colonel Ferdinand Van Derveer, called into the service of the United States by the President of the United States at Hamilton, Ohio (the place of general rendezvous) on August 26, 1861 to serve for the term of three years from the date of enrollment, unless sooner discharged, from June 30, 1864 (when last mustered) to September 8, 1864 when mustered out. The company was organized by Captain M. S. Gunckel at Hamilton, Ohio in the month of August 1861 and marched thence to Hamilton, Ohio, where it arrived August 26. . . .

WILLIAM G. WEDEMEYER,
First Lieutenant,
Sixteenth Infantry, United States Army Mustering Officer.

Company I

Stationed at Cincinnati, Ohio, September 24, 1861.
September 24.— Muster-in roll of Captain Henry Mallory's Company, in the Thirty-fifth Regiment of Ohio Volunteers commanded by Colonel Ferdinand Van Derveer, called into the service of the United States by the President from September 24, 1861 (date of this muster) for the term of three years, unless sooner discharged. . . .

P. H. BRESLIN,
Captain,
Eighteenth Infantry, United States Army, Mustering Officer.

Station not stated, December 31, 1861-February [28], 1862.

Stationed at camp near Pittsburg Landing, Tennessee, March-April 1862.

Stationed at Manchester, Tennessee, April 30-August 31, 1862.

Stationed at Gallatin, Tennessee, August 31-December 31, 1862.

Stationed at camp near Triune, Tennessee, [January 1]-February 28, 1863.

Stationed at camp near Triune, Tennessee, April 10, 1863.

Stationed at Concord, Tennessee, February 28-June 30, 1863.

Stationed at Battle Creek, Tennessee, July-August 1863.

Stationed at Chattanooga, Tennessee, September-December 1863.

Stationed at Ringgold, Georgia, January-February 1864.

Stationed at Chattanooga, Tennessee, September 23, 1864.
September 23.— Muster-out roll of [Philip] Rothenbush's Company (I), in the Thirty-fifth Regiment of Ohio Infantry Volunteers, commanded by Colonel F. Van Derveer, called into the

service of the United States from the date of enrollment, unless sooner discharged, from June 30, 1864 (when last mustered) to September 23, 1864 when discharged. . . .

WILLIAM G. WEDEMEYER,
First Lieutenant,
Sixteenth Infantry,
United States Army, Assistant Commissary of Musters,
D. C., Mustering Officer.

Company K

Stationed at Camp Bourbon near Paris, Kentucky, November 5, 1861.

November 5.— Muster-in roll of Captain Joel K. Deardorf's Company, in the Thirty-fifth Regiment of Ohio Foot Volunteers, commanded by Colonel Ferdinand Van Derveer, called into the service of the United States by the President from November 5, 1861 (date of this muster) for the term of three years, unless sooner discharged. . . .

FERDINAND VAN DERVEER,
Colonel,
Commanding Thirty-fifth Regiment, Ohio Volunteers,
Mustering Officer.

Stationed at Camp Bourbon near Paris, Kentucky, November 5, 1861.

November 5.— The Thirty-fifth Regiment of Ohio Volunteers was organized at Hamilton about the month of September 1861 but before the company was mustered the regiment was ordered into active service in Kentucky, where at Camp Bourbon near Paris it was mustered into the service. . . .

FERDINAND VAN DERVEER,
Colonel,
Thirty-fifth Ohio Volunteers, Mustering Officer.

Stationed at Somerset, Kentucky, September 12-December 31, 1861.

Stationed at camp near Pittsburg Landing, Tennessee, March-April 1862.

Stationed at Pelham, Tennessee, April 30-August 31, 1862.

Stationed at Gallatin, Tennessee, August 31-December 31, 1862.

Stationed at Camp Concord Church, [January 1]-February 28, 1863.

Stationed at camp near Triune, Tennessee, April 10, 1863.

Stationed at Concord, Tennessee, February 28-June 30, 1863.

Stationed at camp on Battle Creek, Tennessee, July-August 1863.

Stationed at Chattanooga, Tennessee, September-December 1863.

Stationed at Ringgold, Georgia, January-February 1864.

Stationed at Chattanooga, Tennessee, September 23, 1864.
September 23.— Muster-out roll of late Captain Joel K. Deardorf's Company (K), in the Thirty-fifth Regiment of Ohio Infantry Volunteers, commanded by Colonel Ferdinand Van Derveer, called into the service of the United States by the President at Hamilton, Ohio (the place of general rendezvous) on September 12, 1861 to serve for the term of three years from the date of enrollment, unless sooner discharged, from November 5, 1861 (when mustered) to September 23, 1864 when discharged. . . .

WILLIAM G. WEDEMEYER,
First Lieutenant,
Sixteenth Infantry, United States Army,
Assistant Commissary of Musters, D. C., Mustering Officer.

[M594-Roll #149]

—

Record of Events for Thirty-sixth Ohio Infantry, August 1861-June 1865.

Field and Staff

Stationed at Camp Putnam, Marietta, Ohio, August 27, 1861.
August 27.— Muster-in roll of field and staff in the Thirty-sixth Regiment. . . .

HENRY BELKNAP,
Captain,
Eighteenth Infantry, Mustering Officer.

Stationed at Summerville, [West] Virginia, August 27, 1861-February 28, 1862.

Stationed at Meadow Bluff, [West] Virginia, May-June 1862.
May 12-23.— The regiment left Summerville, [West] Virginia; marched thence to Frankfort; thence to Lewisburg; thence to Jackson's River Depot, returning thence to Lewisburg, where it was engaged in the action with General [Henry] Heth on May 23, losing five killed and forty-one wounded, and six missing.

Of the wounded, four have since died. The regiment has since made an expedition to Salt Sulphur Springs, marching some eighty miles. The whole distance marched, since leaving Summerville, is about 350 miles.

Stationed at Centreville, [West] Virginia, July-August 1862.

Stationed at Sutton, [West] Virginia, September-October 1862.

Stationed at Charleston, [West] Virginia, November-December 1862.

Stationed at camp near Carthage, Tennessee, January-February 1863.

Station not stated, March-August 1863.

Stationed at Chattanooga, Tennessee, September 1863-February 1864.

Stationed at Gauley Bridge, West Virginia, March-April 1864.

Stationed at Charleston, West Virginia, May-June 1864.

Stationed near Charlestown, West Virginia, July-August 1864.

Stationed at Cedar Creek, Virginia, September-October 1864.

Stationed at Martinsburg, West Virginia, November-December 1864.

Stationed at Cumberland, Maryland, January-February 1865.

Stationed at Winchester, Virginia, March-April 1865.

Stationed at Wheeling, West Virginia, May-June 1865.

Regiment

Stationed at Summerville, [West] Virginia, October 1861.

Company A
October 24.— The company had an engagement with the enemy near Proctor's Ford, killing eight and wounding six, but sustained no loss except one wounded, James Speers.

Company B
October 14-17.— The company left Summerville on a scout and returned October 17. Marched a distance of fifty miles. Crossed Gauley at Brock's Ferry, scouting on the opposite side of the river. Recrossed at Stroud's Ferry, returning by Cranberry Road.
October 24-27.— The company was on a scout in the vicinity of Powell Mountain; traveled a distance of forty miles.

Stationed at Summerville, [West] Virginia, November 1861.

Company B
November 14.— Second Lieutenant [Robert] B. Carter, Sergeants Groover, Adney, Jones, Corporals Eaton, Holcomb, Dent, Mather, and thirty-eight privates by order of Colonel George Crook, left the post for the vicinity of Powell Mountain, encamped on Muddleby.
November 15-17.— Scoured the hills in the direction of Bear Glade settlement until November 17, when the detachment returned to camp.

Company G
November 19-22.— The company on a scout in direction of Meadow Bluff. The distance traveled over about seventy-five miles.

Stationed at Summerville, [West] Virginia, except Company A at Cross-Lanes, [West] Virginia, December 1861.

Company A
December 4.— By order of Colonel Crook, agreeable to Special Orders No. 51, Department of West Virginia, marched to this post at Cross-Lanes, [West] Virginia.
December 24.— Ordered three privates with two guides to scout in Greenbrier County, a distance of eighteen miles.
December 29.— Returned with five horses.
December 30.— Left again.
December 31.— Brought in camp fifty sheep.

Company B
December 16-31.— The company went on an expedition to Meadow Bluff, Greenbrier County under command of Major [Ebenezer B.] Andrews, returned December 31, having marched about eighty miles.

Company G
December 14-16.— The company on a scout into east corner of Nicholas County. Killed one Rebel.
December 27-28.— The company was on a scout into Greenbrier County, effected nothing.

Company H
December 20.— Privates William Monroe and Alph W. Lynch wounded in action in the expedition to Meadow Bluff.

Stationed at Summerville, [West] Virginia, except Company A at Cross-Lanes, January 1862.

Company E
January 3.— Private Dallman wounded in skirmish at Gardner's Store.

Company F
January 3.— Private James M. Malcomb wounded in skirmish at Gardner's Store.

Company G
Private Horace Hearn wounded in skirmish at Gardner's Store, Webster County, [West] Virginia; distance marched fifty miles.

Stationed at Summerville, [West] Virginia, except Company A at Cross-Lanes, [West] Virginia, February-April 1862.

Stationed at Meadow Bluff, [West] Virginia, May 1862.
May 23.— All the companies of the regiment, except Company B, were in the engagement which took place at Lewisburg.

Stationed at Meadow Bluff, [West] Virginia, June 1862.

Stationed at Meadow Bluff, [West] Virginia, July 1862.
Noncommissioned staff, Wallace S. Stanley, sergeant major; Thomas M. Turner, quartermaster sergeant; Samuel H. Dustin, commissary sergeant; Ebenezar Cory, principal musician, and the hospital steward Charles Washeushnuns.

Stationed at Centreville, [West] Virginia, August 1862.

Stationed at camp near mouth of Antietam, Maryland, September 1862.

Stationed at Sutton, [West] Virginia, October 1862.

Stationed at Charleston, [West] Virginia, November-December 1862.

Stationed at Portland, Kentucky, January 1863.

Stationed at camp near Carthage, Tennessee, February 1863.

Stationed at Carthage, Tennessee, March-May 1863.

Stationed at Tullahoma, Tennessee, June 1863.

Stationed at University Depot, Tennessee, July 1863.

Stationed at Jasper, Tennessee, August 1863.

Station not stated, September 1863.

Stationed at Chattanooga, Tennessee, October 1863-February 1864.

Stationed at Meadow Bluff, West Virginia, April-May 1864.

Stationed at Charleston, West Virginia, June 1864.

Stationed at Middletown, Maryland, July 1864.

Stationed near Charlestown, West Virginia, August 1864.

Stationed at Harrisonburg, Virginia, September 1864.

Stationed at Cedar Creek, Virginia, October 1864.

Stationed at Camp Russell, Virginia, November 1864.

Stationed at Martinsburg, West Virginia, December 1864.

Stationed at Camp Hastings near Cumberland, Maryland, January-March 1865.

Stationed near Winchester, Virginia, April 1865.

Stationed at Staunton, Virginia, May 1865.

Stationed at Wheeling, West Virginia, June 1865.

Company A

Stationed at Camp Putnam, Marietta, August 24, 1861.
August 24.— Muster-in roll of Captain Hiram [Fosdick] Devol's Company (A), in the Thirty-sixth Regiment of Ohio Volunteers, commanded by Lieutenant-Colonel Melvin Clarke, called into the service of the United States by the President from August 24, 1861 (date of this muster) for the term of three years, unless sooner discharged. The company was organized by Captain H. F. Devol at Lowell, Ohio in the month of July 1861 and marched thence to Camp Putnam, a distance of ten miles. . . .

HENRY BELKNAP,
Captain,
Eighteenth Infantry, Mustering Officer.

Stationed at Summerville, [West] Virginia, August 24-October 31, 1861.

Stationed at Cross-Lanes, [West] Virginia, [November 1]-April 30, 1862.

Stationed at Meadow Bluff, May-June 1862.

Stationed at Parkersburg, [West] Virginia, August 21, 1862.

Stationed at Camp Centreville, [West] Virginia, July-August 1862.

Stationed at Sutton, Braxton County, [West] Virginia, September-October 1862.

Stationed at Charleston, [West] Virginia, November-December 1862.

Stationed at camp near Carthage, Tennessee, January-April 1863.

Stationed at Tullahoma, Tennessee, May-June 1863.

Stationed at camp near Jasper, Tennessee, July-August 1863.

Stationed at Chattanooga, Tennessee, September 1863-February 1864.

Stationed at Gauley Bridge, West Virginia, March-April 1864.

Stationed at Charleston, West Virginia, May-June 1864.

Stationed at Harper's Ferry, West Virginia, August 30, 1864.
August 30.— Muster-out roll of detachment of enlisted men of Captain James G. Barker's Company (A), in the Thirty-sixth Regiment of Ohio Infantry Volunteers, commanded by Colonel Hiram F. Devol, called into the service of the United States by the President at Marietta, Ohio (the place of general rendezvous) on August 24, 1861 to serve for the term of three years from the date of enrollment, unless sooner discharged, from August 24, 1861 (when mustered into service) to August 30, 1864 when mustered out by reason of expiration of term of service. . . .

CYRUS [SWAN] ROBERTS,
Lieutenant,
One Hundred Fiftieth New York,
Assistant Commissary of Musters, Army of West Virginia,
Mustering Officer.

Stationed at Charlestown, West Virginia, July-August 1864.

Stationed near Strasburg, Virginia, September-October 1864.

Stationed at Martinsburg, West Virginia, November-December 1864.

Stationed at Camp Hastings, Maryland, January-February 1865.

Stationed at Winchester, Virginia, March-April 1865.

Stationed at Wheeling, West Virginia, May-June 1865.

Company B

Stationed at Camp Putnam, Marietta, Ohio, August 26, 1861.
August 26.— Muster-in roll of Captain William H. G. Adney's Company (B), in the Thirty-sixth Regiment of Ohio Volunteers commanded by Lieutenant-Colonel Melvin Clarke, called into the service of the United States by the President from August 26, 1861 (date of this muster) for the term of three years, unless sooner discharged. The company was organized by Captain William H. G. Adney at Vinton, Gallia County, Ohio in the month of August and marched thence to Camp Putnam, where it arrived August 12, 1861, a distance of seventy-five miles. . . .

HENRY BELKNAP,
Captain,
Eighteenth Infantry, Mustering Officer.

Stationed at Summerville, [West] Virginia, September 1861-April 1862.

Stationed at Meadow Bluff, [West] Virginia, May-June 1862.
May 31-June 1.— The company changed station leaving Summerville, [West] Virginia and arrived at Meadow Bluff June 1, a distance of forty miles.
June 22-25.— Marched from Meadow Bluff with remainder of the Thirty-sixth Regiment and Forty-fourth and Forty-seventh Ohio Volunteer Infantry into Monroe County, [West] Virginia via Centreville, Salt Sulphur Springs, and Union, and returned to this camp June 25, a distance of eighty miles.

Stationed at Parkersburg, [West] Virginia, August 21, 1862.

Stationed at Centreville, [West] Virginia, July-August 1862.

Stationed at Sutton, [West] Virginia, September-October 1862.

Stationed at Charleston, [West] Virginia, November-December 1862.

Stationed at Carthage, Tennessee, January-April 1863.

Stationed at Tullahoma, Tennessee, May-June 1863.

Stationed at Jasper, Tennessee, July-August 1863.

Stationed at Chattanooga, Tennessee, September 1863-February 1864.

Stationed at Gauley Bridge, West Virginia, March-April 1864.

Stationed at Charleston, West Virginia, May-June 1864.

Stationed at Charlestown, West Virginia, July-August 1864.

Stationed Cedar Creek, Virginia, September-October 1864.

Stationed at Harper's Ferry, September 3, 1864.
September 3.— Muster-out roll of Captain Edward P. Henry's Company (B), in the Thirty-sixth Regiment of Ohio Infantry Volunteers, commanded by Colonel Hiram F. Devol, called into the service of the United States by the President at Marietta, Ohio (the place of general rendezvous) on August 12, 1861 to serve for the term of three years from the date of enrollment, unless sooner discharged, from August 26, 1861 (when mustered). The company was organized by Captain W. H. G. Adney at Vinton, Ohio in the month of August 1861 and marched thence to Marietta, Ohio, where it arrived August 12, 1861, a distance of seventy-five miles. . . .

CYRUS S. ROBERTS,
Lieutenant,
One Hundred [Fiftieth] New York Volunteers, Mustering Officer.

Stationed at Cumberland, Maryland, November-December 1864.

Stationed at Camp Hastings, Maryland, January-February 1865.

Stationed at Winchester, Virginia, March-April 1865.

Stationed at Wheeling, West Virginia, May-June 1865.

Company C

Stationed at Camp Putnam, Marietta, Ohio, August 27, 1861.
August 27.— Muster-in roll of Captain John Beckley's Company (C), in the Thirty-sixth Regiment of Ohio Volunteers, commanded by Lieutenant-Colonel Melvin Clarke, called into the service of the United States by the President from August 27, 1861 (date of this muster) for the term of three years, unless sooner discharged. The company was organized by Captain John Beckley at Albany in the month of July and marched thence to Marietta, where it arrived July 31, 1861, a distance of fifty-two miles. . . .

HENRY BELKNAP,
Captain,
Eighteenth Infantry, Mustering Officer.

Stationed at Summerville, [West] Virginia, August 27, 1861-April 30, 1862.

Stationed at Meadow Bluff, [West] Virginia, May-June 1862.

The company was on a scout five days during the first part of May on Gauley River, Webster County, [West] Virginia. Distance marched was 100 miles.
May 12.— Left the post of Summerville, [West] Virginia with the regiment. Marched to Lewisburg, [West] Virginia, a distance of sixty miles. Marched with expedition under Colonel George Crook up the Virginia Central Railroad to Jackson's River Depot; distance marched ninety miles.
May 23.— Was engaged in the action at Lewisburg, [West] Virginia.
May 29.— Marched with the regiment to Meadow Bluff, [West] Virginia, distance fifteen miles.
June 22.— Marched with the expedition under Colonel Crook to Salt Sulphur Springs, [West] Virginia and returned June 25; distance marched eighty miles.

Total distance marched in the two months was 345 miles.

Stationed at Camp Union, Parkersburg, [West] Virginia, August 21, 1862.

Stationed at Centreville, [West] Virginia, July-August 1862.

Stationed at Sutton, [West] Virginia, September-October 1862.

Stationed at Charleston, [West] Virginia, November-December 1862.

Stationed at Carthage, Tennessee, January-April 1863.

Stationed in the field near Tullahoma, Tennessee, May-June 1863.

Stationed at Jasper, Tennessee, July-August 1863.

Stationed at Chattanooga, Tennessee, September 1863-February 1864.

Stationed at Gauley Bridge, West Virginia, March-April 1864.

Stationed at Charleston, West Virginia, May-August 1864.

Stationed at Harper's Ferry, West Virginia, August 31, 1864.
August 31.— Muster-out roll of enlisted man of Captain Benjamin F. Stearn's Company (C), in the Thirty-sixth Regiment of Ohio Infantry Volunteers, commanded by Colonel H. F. Devol, called into the service of the United States by the President at Marietta, Ohio (the place of general rendezvous) on August 27, 1861 to serve for the term of three years from the date of enrollment, unless sooner discharged, from August 27, 1861 (when mustered into service) to August 31, 1864 when mustered out of service. . . .

CYRUS S. ROBERTS,
Lieutenant,
One Hundred [Fiftieth] New York Volunteers,
Assistant Commissary of Musters, Army of West Virginia,
Mustering Officer.

Stationed at Cedar Creek, Virginia, September-October 1864.

Stationed at Martinsburg, West Virginia, November-December 1864.

Stationed at Camp Hastings, Maryland, January-February 1865.

Stationed at Winchester, Virginia, March-April 1865.

Stationed at Wheeling, West Virginia, May-June 1865.

Company D

Stationed at Camp Putnam, Marietta, Ohio, August 27, 1861.
August 27.— Muster-in roll of Captain William Dunham's Company (D), in the Thirty-sixth Regiment of Ohio Volunteers, commanded by Lieutenant-Colonel Melvin Clarke, called into the service of the United States by the President from August 27, 1861 (date of this muster) for the term of three years, unless sooner discharged. The company was organized by Captain William H. Dunham at Oak Hill, Jackson County, Ohio in the month of August and marched thence to Camp Marietta, Ohio where it arrived August 7, 1861. . . .

HENRY BELKNAP,
Mustering Officer.

Stationed at Summerville, [West] Virginia, August 27, 1861-April 30, 1862.

Stationed at Meadow Bluff, [West] Virginia, May-June 1862.

Stationed at Parkersburg, [West] Virginia, August 21, 1862.

Stationed at Centreville, [West] Virginia, July-August 1862.

Stationed at Sutton, [West] Virginia, September-October 1862.

Stationed at Camp Crook near Charleston, [West] Virginia, November-December 1862.

Stationed at camp near Carthage, Tennessee, January-February 1863.

Stationed at Carthage, Tennessee, March-April 1863.

Stationed in the field, May-August 1863.

Stationed at Chattanooga, Tennessee, September 1863-February 1864.

Stationed at Charleston, West Virginia, March-April 1864.

Stationed Camp Piatt, West Virginia, May-June 1864.

Stationed near Charlestown, West Virginia, July-August 1864.

Stationed at Cedar Creek, Virginia, September-October 1864.

Station not stated, November-December 1864.

Stationed at Camp Hastings, Maryland, January-February 1865.

Stationed at camp near Winchester, Virginia, March-April 1865.

Stationed at Wheeling, West Virginia, May-June 1865.

Company E

Stationed at Camp Putnam, Marietta, Ohio, August 26, 1861.
August 26.— Muster-in roll of Captain Warren Hollister's Company (E), in the Thirty-sixth Regiment of Ohio Volunteers, commanded by Lieutenant-Colonel Melvin Clarke, called into the service of the United States by the President from August 26, 1861 (date of this muster) for the term of three years, unless sooner discharged. The company was organized by Captain Warren Hollister at Woodsfield, Ohio in the month of August and marched thence to Marietta, where it arrived August 15, a distance of forty miles. . . .

HENRY BELKNAP,
Captain,
Eighteenth Infantry, Mustering Officer.

Stationed at Summerville, [West] Virginia, August 26, 1861-April 30, 1862.

Stationed at Meadow Bluff, [West] Virginia, May-June 1862.
May 23.— The company was engaged in the battle of Lewisburg, [West] Virginia.

Stationed at Parkersburg, [West] Virginia, August 18, 1862.

Stationed at Centreville, [West] Virginia, July-August 1862.

Stationed at Sutton, [West] Virginia, September-October 1862.

Stationed at Charleston, [West] Virginia, November-December 1862.

Stationed near Carthage, Tennessee, January-February 1863.

Stationed at Carthage, Tennessee, March-April 1863.

Stationed at Tullahoma, Tennessee, May-June 1863.

Stationed at Jasper, Tennessee, July-August 1863.

Stationed at Chattanooga, Tennessee, September 1863-February 1864.

Stationed near Charleston, West Virginia, March-April 1864.

Stationed at Charleston, West Virginia, May-June 1864.

Stationed near Charlestown, West Virginia, July-August 1864.

Stationed at Cedar Creek, Virginia, September-October 1864.

Stationed at Stephenson's Depot, Virginia, November-December 1864.

Stationed at Cumberland, Maryland, January-February 1865.

Stationed at Winchester, Virginia, March-April 1865.

Stationed at Wheeling, West Virginia, May-June 1865.

Company F

Stationed at Camp Putnam, Marietta, Ohio, August 26, 1861.
August 26.— Muster-in roll of Captain Thomas W. Moore's Company (F), in the Thirty-sixth Regiment of Ohio Volunteers, commanded by Lieutenant-Colonel Melvin Clarke, called into the service of the United States by the President from August 26, 1861 (date of this muster) for the term of three years, unless sooner discharged. The company was organized by Captain Thomas W. Moore in the month of August and marched thence to Camp Putnam, Marietta, where it arrived August 1, a distance of twelve miles. . . .

HENRY BELKNAP,
Captain,
Eighteenth Infantry, Mustering Officer.

Stationed at Summerville, [West] Virginia, October 31, 1861-April 30, 1862.

Stationed at Meadow Bluff, [West] Virginia, May-June 1862.

Station not stated, June 30, 1862.

Stationed at Centreville, [West] Virginia, July-August 1862.

Stationed at Sutton, [West] Virginia, September-October 1862.

Stationed at Charleston, [West] Virginia, November-December 1862.

Stationed at Carthage, Tennessee, January-April 1863.

Stationed at Manchester, Tennessee, May-June 1863.

Stationed at Jasper, Tennessee, July-August 1863.

Stationed at Chattanooga, Tennessee, September 1863-February 1864.

Stationed at Gauley Bridge, West Virginia, March-April 1864.

Stationed at Charleston, West Virginia, May-June 1864.

Stationed near Charlestown, West Virginia, July-August 1864.

Stationed at Cedar Creek, Virginia, September-October 1864.

Stationed at Cumberland, Maryland, November 1864-February 1865.

Stationed at Winchester, Virginia, March-April 1865.

Stationed at Wheeling, West Virginia, May-June 1865.

Company G

Stationed at Camp Putnam, Marietta, Ohio, August 26, 1861.
August 26.— Muster-in roll of Captain Jewett Palmer's, Jr., Company (G), in the Thirty-sixth Regiment of Ohio Volunteers commanded by Lieutenant-Colonel Melvin Clarke, called into the service of the United States by the President from August 26, 1861 (date of this muster) for the term of three years, unless sooner discharged. The company was organized by Captain Jewett Palmer, Jr., at Salem in the month of August and marched thence to Marietta, where it arrived August 12, a distance of twelve miles. . . .

HENRY BELKNAP,
Captain,
Eighteenth Infantry, Mustering Officer.

Stationed at Summerville, [West] Virginia, September 1861-April 1862.

Stationed at Meadow Bluff, [West] Virginia, May-June 1862.

Stationed at Parkersburg, [West] Virginia, August 21, 1862.

Stationed at Centreville, [West] Virginia, July-August 1862.

Stationed at Sutton, [West] Virginia, September-October 1862.

Stationed at Charleston, [West] Virginia, November-December 1862.

Stationed near Carthage, Tennessee, January-February 1863.

Stationed at Carthage, Tennessee, March-April 1863.

Stationed at Tullahoma, Tennessee, May-June 1863.

Stationed near Jasper, Tennessee, July-August 1863.

Stationed at Chattanooga, Tennessee, September 1863-February 1864.

Stationed at Gauley Falls, West Virginia, March-April 1864.

Stationed at Charleston, West Virginia, May-August 1864.

Stationed at Harper's Ferry, West Virginia, August 30, 1864.
August 30.— Muster-out roll of a detachment of Captain Homer C. Cherrington's Company (G), in the Thirty-sixth Regiment of Ohio Infantry Volunteers, commanded by Colonel Hiram F. Devol, called into the service of the United States by the President at Marietta, Ohio (the place of general rendezvous) on August 26, 1861 to serve for the term of three years, from the date of enrollment, unless sooner discharged, from August 26, 1861 (when mustered into service) to August 30, 1864 when mustered out of services by reason of expiration of term of service. The company was organized by Captain Jewett Palmer, Jr. . . .

CYRUS S. ROBERTS,
Lieutenant,
One Hundred [Fiftieth] New York Volunteers,
Assistant Commissary Musters, Army of West Virginia,
Mustering Officer.

Stationed at Cedar Creek, Virginia, September-October 1864.

Stationed at Cumberland, Maryland, November 1864-February 1865.

Stationed at Winchester, West Virginia, March-April 1865.

Stationed at Wheeling, Virginia, June 30, 1865.

Company H

Stationed at Camp Putnam, Marietta, Ohio, August 26, 1861.
August 26.— Muster-in roll of Captain William S. Wilson's Company (H), in the Thirty-sixth Regiment of Ohio Volunteers, commanded by Lieutenant-Colonel Melvin Clarke, called into the service of the United States by the President from August 26, 1861 (date of this muster) for the term of three years, unless sooner discharged. The company was organized by Captain William S. Wilson at Harrisonville Heights, Ohio in the month of August and marched thence to Marietta, where it arrived August 13, 1861, a distance of sixty miles. . . .

HENRY BELKNAP,
Captain,
Eighteenth Infantry, United States Army, Mustering Officer.

Stationed at Summerville, [West] Virginia, August 26, 1861-April 30, 1862.

Stationed at Meadow Bluff, [West] Virginia, May-June 1862.

Stationed at Parkersburg, [West] Virginia, August 21, 1862.

Stationed at Centreville, [West] Virginia, July-August 1862.

Stationed at Sutton, [West] Virginia, September-October 1862.

Stationed at Charleston, [West] Virginia, November-December 1862.

Stationed near Carthage, Tennessee, January-February 1863.
January 20.— This company has been in service nearly nineteen months and never lost a man by desertion until they were within one day's journey of home and were on the way to Nashville. Most of the men that deserted had not been home since they

enlisted. Twenty-five of them left, five of which have returned and more are on their way.

Stationed at Carthage, Tennessee, March-April 1863.

Stationed twelve miles south of Tullahoma, Tennessee, May-June 1863.

Stationed at Jasper, Tennessee, July-August 1863.

Stationed at Chattanooga, Tennessee, September 1863-February 1864.

Stationed at Meadow Bluff, West Virginia, March-April 1864.

Stationed at Charleston, West Virginia, May-June 1864.

Stationed at Charlestown, West Virginia, July-August 1864.

Stationed at Cedar Creek, Virginia, September-October 1864.

Stationed at Stephenson's Depot, Virginia, November-December 1864.

Stationed at Cumberland, Maryland, January-February 1865.

Stationed at Winchester, Virginia, March-April 1865.

Stationed at Wheeling, West Virginia, May-June 1865.

Company I

Stationed at Camp Putnam, Marietta, Ohio, August 27, 1861.
August 27.— Muster-in roll of Captain William S. Taylor's Company (I), in the Thirty-sixth Regiment of Ohio Volunteers, commanded by Lieutenant-Colonel Melvin Clarke, called into the service of the United States by the President from August 27, 1861 (date of this muster) for the term of three years, unless sooner discharged. The company was organized by Captain William S. Taylor at Chambersburg in the month of July and marched thence

to Camp Putnam, Marietta, where it arrived August 14, a distance of eighty miles. . . .

HENRY BELKNAP,
Captain,
Eighteenth Infantry, Mustering Officer.

Stationed at Summerville, [West] Virginia, August 27, 1861-April 30, 1862.

Stationed at Meadow Bluff, [West] Virginia, May-June 1862.

The company was on a scout of five days during the first part of May on Birch Creek in Nicholas County, [West] Virginia. Distance marched was 100 miles.

May 12.— Left the post of Summerville with the regiment. Marched to Lewisburg, [West] Virginia, a distance of sixty miles. Marched with the expedition under Colonel George Crook up the Virginia Central Railroad to Jackson's River Depot; distance marched ninety miles.

May 23.— Was engaged in the action at Lewisburg, [West] Virginia.

May 29.— Marched with the regiment to Meadow Bluff, a distance of fifteen miles.

June 22-25.— Marched with the expedition under Colonel Crook to Salt Sulphur Springs, [West] Virginia and returned June 25. Distance marched was eighty miles.

Total number of miles marched during the two months was 345.

Stationed at Parkersburg, [West] Virginia, August 21, 1862.

Stationed at Centreville, [West] Virginia, July-August 1862.

Stationed in the field, September-October 1862.

Stationed at Charleston, [West] Virginia, November-December 1862.

Stationed at Carthage, Tennessee, February 28, 1863.

Stationed at camp near Carthage, Tennessee, March-April 1863.

Stationed at camp near Tullahoma, Tennessee, May-June 1863.

Stationed at Jasper, Tennessee, July-August 1863.

Stationed at Chattanooga, Tennessee, September-October 1863.

Stationed at Chattanooga, Tennessee, November-December 1863.
November 25.— The company was engaged in the action at Missionary Ridge.

Stationed at Chattanooga, Tennessee, January-February 1864.

Stationed at Gauley Bridge, West Virginia, March-April 1864.

Stationed at Charleston, West Virginia, May-June 1864.
The company has marched 750 miles during the last sixty days.
May 9.— Was engaged in the action at Cloyd's Mountain.
June 18.— Was engaged in the action at Lynchburg, Virginia.

Stationed at Charlestown, West Virginia, July-August 1864.

Stationed at Cedar Creek, Virginia, September-October 1864.
September 19.— The company was engaged in the battle of Opequon [Creek].
September 23.— The company was engaged in the battle of Fisher's Hill.
October 19.— The company was engaged in the battle of Cedar Creek.
The company is serving as General Crook's escort.

Stationed at Martinsburg, West Virginia, November-December 1864.

Stationed at Cumberland, Maryland, January-February 1865.

Stationed at Winchester, Virginia, March-April 1865.

Stationed at Wheeling, West Virginia, May-June 1865.

Company K

Stationed at Camp Putnam, Marietta, Ohio, August 31, 1861.
August 31.— Muster-in roll of Captain Levi M. Stephenson's Company (K), in the Thirty-sixth Regiment of Ohio Volunteers, commanded by Lieutenant-Colonel Melvin Clarke, called into the service of the United States by the President from August 31, 1861 (date of this muster) for the term of three years, unless sooner discharged. The company was organized by Captain Levi M. Stephenson at Jackson in the month of August and marched thence to Marietta, where it arrived August 19, a distance of eighty-eight miles. . . .

HENRY BELKNAP,
Captain,
Eighteenth Infantry, Mustering Officer.

Stationed at Summerville, [West] Virginia, September 1861-April 1862.

Stationed at Meadow Bluff, [West] Virginia, May-June 1862.

Stationed at Parkersburg, [West] Virginia, August 21, 1862.

Stationed at Centreville, [West] Virginia, July-August 1862.

Stationed at Sutton, [West] Virginia, September-October 1862.

Stationed at Camp Crook, Charleston, [West] Virginia, November-December 1862.

Stationed at camp near Carthage, Tennessee, January-February 1863.

Stationed at Carthage, Tennessee, March-April 1863.

Stationed at Tullahoma, Tennessee, May-June 1863.

Stationed at Jasper, Tennessee, July-August 1863.

Stationed at Chattanooga, Tennessee, September 1863-February 1864.

Stationed at Montgomery's Ferry, West Virginia, March-April 1864.

Stationed at Charleston, West Virginia, May-June 1864.

Stationed at camp near Charlestown, West Virginia, July-August 1864.

Stationed at camp near Cedar Creek, Virginia, September-October 1864.

Stationed at Stephenson's Depot, Virginia, November-December 1864.

Stationed at Cumberland, Maryland, January-February 1865.

Stationed at Winchester, Virginia, March-April 1865.

Stationed at Wheeling, West Virginia, May-June 1865.

[M594-Roll #149]

Record of Events for Thirty-seventh Ohio Infantry, August 1861-June 1865.

Field and Staff

Stationed at Camp Clifton, August 3, 1861.
August 3.— Muster-in roll of field and staff in the Thirty-seventh Regiment of Ohio Volunteers, commanded by Colonel Edward Siber, called into service of the United States by the President

from August 3, 1861 (date of this muster) for the term of three years, unless sooner discharged. . . .

GEORGE COOK,
Captain,
Fourth Infantry, United States Army Mustering Officer.

Stationed at Camp Montgomery, October 31, 1861.

Stationed at Camp Clifton, [West] Virginia, February 28, 1862.

Stationed at mouth of Loup [Creek], [West] Virginia, March-April 1862.

Stationed at Raleigh, [West] Virginia, May-August 1862.

Stationed at Brownstown, [West] Virginia, September-October 1862.

Station not stated, October 8, 1862.
October 8.— Muster-out roll of the band of the Thirty-seventh Regiment of Ohio Volunteer Infantry (Colonel Edward Siber) when mustered out this October 8, 1862. . . .

RICHARD [ROSS] CRAWFORD,
Second Lieutenant,
Seventh Infantry, United States Army,
Inspector and Mustering Officer.

Stationed at Camp Piatt, [West] Virginia, November-December 1862.

Stationed at Young's Point, Louisiana, January-February 1863.

Stationed at Young's Point, Louisiana, April 10, 1863.

Stationed at Milliken's Bend, Louisiana, March-April 1863.

Stationed at Walnut Hill, Mississippi, May-June 1863.

Stationed at Camp Sherman, Mississippi, July-August 1863.

Stationed at camp on Tennessee River, September-October 1863.

Stationed at Bellefonte Station, Alabama, November-December 1863.

Stationed at Cleveland, Tennessee, January-February 1864.

Stationed near Kenesaw Mountain, Georgia, May-June 1864.
May 10.— The regiment arrived at Sugar Creek Valley, Louisiana by the way of Nashville and Chattanooga, where it joined its division of the Fifteenth Army Corps.
May 13-15.— Took part in the battle at Resaca. Marched then over Kingston to Dallas.
May 28-29.— Was engaged there in the action.
June 1.— Marched to New Hope Church.
June 5-10.— Left that place and arrived June 10 by the way of Acworth near the Kenesaw Mountain, where the regiment is at the present time fronting the enemy.

Stationed near Jonesborough, Georgia, July-August 1864.
July 2-12.— The regiment operated with the Fifteenth Army Corps in its operations on the northern bank of the Chattahoochee River in Georgia until July 12, when it marched to the left of [the] Army.

Crossed the Chattahoochee River at Roswell factories; participated in the destruction of the Atlanta and Augusta Railroad; advanced on Atlanta.
July 22.— Participated in the battle near Atlanta.
July 27.— After having been placed with the Fifteenth Army Corps to the right of the Army, participated in the battle.
July 28-August 26.— It confronted the enemy in his fortified position near Atlanta, when it marched toward Jonesborough, Georgia.
August 31.— Participated in the battle in the vicinity of Jonesborough, which caused the fall of Atlanta.

Stationed at Cave Spring, Georgia, September-October 1864.

Stationed near Savannah, Georgia, November-December 1864.

Stationed at Lynch's Creek, South Carolina, January-February 1865.

Stationed at Rogers' Cross-Roads, North Carolina, March-April 1865.

Stationed on board steamer Argonaut, May-June 1865.

Regiment

Stationed at Clifton, [West] Virginia, except Company A at mouth of Paint Creek; Company B at mouth of Loup Creek; Company D at Cannelton Steamboat Landing; Company F at Montgomery; Company H at Paint Creek; Company I at Morris' Farm, December 1861.

Company A

Detailed at Cannelton, had during the whole month detailed to furnish fifty laborers for the purpose of removing government stores from Cannelton Landing, loading and unloading steamboats.

Company B

Company B occupied, upon the orders of General [Jacob Dolson] Cox, the mouth of Loup Creek, nine miles from Clifton in order to cover the landing place there to be established. The same company remained at Loup Creek during the whole month, scouting parties having reported one intended attack of the enemy through Cabin Creek.

December 13.— Lieutenant-Colonel [Louis] von Blessingh left Clifton with Company F. Joined Company H at oil factory and scouted on this and the following days with these two companies as far as Coal River Valley, not finding an enemy, he returned with both companies to Clifton.

Company C

Captain [Charles] Hipp undertook repeated scouting expeditions through the mountains at Cabin Creek.

Company E

Stationed opposite Cannelton at Montgomery Landing. Had to assist Company A in this labor (extra duty) and at the same time to occupy the Kanawha Valley from there to Armstrong's Creek by pickets.

The remainder of the companies were daily occupied with drillings. The detached companies were relieved at the end of the month by others.

Company H

December 11.— Company H under command of Captain [Charles] Messner had been detached to the oil factory six miles upward Paint Creek for the purpose of occupying the passes leading to Cabin Creek and to Coal River marshes and was occupied in scouting on these passes as far as about fourteen miles from Clifton.

Stationed at Clifton, except Company A at mouth of Paint Creek; Company D at Montgomery Landing; Company G at Loup Creek; Company H at Morris' Farm, January 1862.

January 7.— Companies A, B, C, H, and I under command of Colonel Siber and Major [Charles] Ankele started from the Kanawha at Clifton upon an order from Brigadier-General Cox for the purpose of clearing the mountainous country between this river and the Guyandotte from the Rebel and robber camps who infested it.

January 8.— Company F, accompanied by a train for thirty pack horses loaded with provisions, followed.

January 9.— These companies having scouted up Paint and Cabin Creeks and having crossed the high mountain ridge between these creeks and the Big Coal River, were reunited in the valley of the Big Coal opposite the mouth of Big Laurel Creek in the evening. The force of the whole detachment amounted to 340 men and forty horses.

January 10.— Big Coal was forded under great difficulties and Big Laurel ascended as far as the fork of the passes. The whole detachment formed one column.

January 11.— The Pond Fork of Little Coal was reached and followed as far as the junction of the forks. All the inhabitants of this country being greatly inimical to the cause of the Union had fled into the mountains and woods.
January 12.— Little Coal River and the Spruce Fork of Little Coal were forded at Boone [Court-House], town (burned at a former period). The detachment was again divided in order to embrace a greater space. Companies B, C, F, and I under Major Ankele marched up Spruce Fork and reached the same evening on the county road Chapmanville on the Guyandotte River. Company H scouted up the Turtle Creek and rejoined Company A and the staff and train the same evening at Ballards on Spruce Fork. All the male inhabitants of this country being almost exclusively bushwhackers had left their homes and had fled, armed with rifles, to the other bank of the Guyandotte which river had in the meanwhile become unfordable.
January 13.— Major Ankele was consequently received by an unexpected and well directed rifle fire from all the houses and mills from the opposite bank of the river, when on this morning, he ascended the valley of Guyandotte on the march to Logan. Captain [Henry] Goeke of Company B was mortally wounded by this fire and Major Ankele made halt at three miles from Logan, reported to be fortified and still occupied by the enemy. Men of all companies however crossed swimming the Guyandotte, drove the concealed assassins in the road and burned the houses from which they had been fired at. The staff and remaining companies of the detachment reached the same evening, Chapmanville.
January 14.— Continued, upon the receipt of this news, their march early in the morning. The whole detachment was reunited at 8 o'clock in the morning three miles from Logan and the march to this place continued on both banks of the Guyandotte. The place was found empty. All the male inhabitants had retreated, armed, to the surrounding mountains which completely commanded the town. A band of cavalry appeared which with loss, was driven back on the road to Big Laurel. The pickets of the regiment were however continually fired at from the mountains and Corporal Belim of Company C was killed at this occasion. By the heavy rain which poured down during the day and the following night, the Guyandotte rose so high that a further pursuit of the enemy became impossible.

January 15.— Logan Court-House, which since long time had served as a shelter and a barrack for the Rebel band as well as the jail, were consequently set fire to in the morning and here upon abandoned.
January 16.— The detachment retreated unmolested through Crooked Creek and Hewitt's [Creek] to Spruce Fork to the site of Boone town. Little Coal had become unfordable.
January 17.— The passage of the river was effected under great difficulties. Four companies reached the same evening, Peytona on Big Coal, two remained at Ballardsville.
January 18-20.— On Little Coal the detachment remained at Peytona, a passage of Big Coal being impossible on account of the high water.
January 21.— The Kanawha was reached by Jens Creek at Brownstown. Company I was stationed at the depot of Cannelton. Company G at the depot of Loup Creek. Companies F and K at Clifton. The regiment covered consequently a space of twelve miles along the Kanawha and scouted a distance of more than fifty miles to the west.

Stationed at Clifton, except Company I at Loup Creek; Company K at Montgomery Landing, February 1862.

Company I under command of Captain [William J. Ch.] Kraus, has been detached to Loup Creek Landing, ten miles from Clifton, to guard government stores and occasional reconnoitering party have been sent up Loup Creek. Company K under command of Lieutenant [Andreas] Huber detailed at Montgomery Landing during the whole month to guard the depot at Cannelton. The eight companies remaining in Clifton were daily occupied in the fore and afternoon with battalion and company drill and skirmishing.

Stationed at Clifton, except Company C at Loup Creek; Company K at Montgomery Landing, March 1862.

Company C under command of Captain Charles Hipp relieved Company I.
March 1.— Captain Kraus at Loup Creek Landing ten miles from Clifton, to guard government stores and reconnoitering parties have occasionally been sent up Loup Creek.

Company K under command of Captain F. [M.] Stumpf detailed at Montgomery Landing during the whole month to put a picket across the river to guard the telegraph office at Cannelton and to keep up communication between Clifton and Loup Creek Landing. The eight companies remaining at Clifton were occupied with battalion and company drill as well as skirmishing in the forenoon and afternoon.
March 5.— A platoon of Company D, under command of Lieutenant [William] Konig undertook a scouting party up Hughes Creek on the right bank of Kanawha to reconnoiter the road to Summerville and reported at their return the road was clear and totally passable for squads of infantry as well as cavalry if the creek did not rise too rapidly.

Stationed at mouth of Loup Creek, Kanawha Valley, [West] Virginia, April 1862.
April 19.— The regiment marched from Clifton to the mouth of Loup Creek, a distance of ten miles on the left bank of the Kanawha, except Company C remained at Clifton until the removal of the quartermaster and commissary stores. Company K left the station at Montgomery and marched with regiment to Loup Creek. Company C had been stationed there before.
April 25.— Company E joined the regiment. The regiment was occupied with battalion and regimental drill as well as skirmishing in the forenoon and afternoon.

Stationed at Great Flat Top Mountain Tannery, May 1862.
May 2-3.— The regiment left mouth of Loup Creek and marched over Cotton Hill to Fayetteville, where it arrived in the morning of May 3, distance twenty-two miles. It was added to the Second Provisional Brigade of General Cox's Division.
May 9.— The nine first companies of the regiment marched with the brigade to Raleigh, a distance of twenty-eight miles. Company K remained in Fayetteville.
May 11-14.— The regiment marched with the brigade to Frenchville on the East River, where it arrived on May 14, a distance of fifty-eight miles.
May 15.— Companies A, H, C, and F, under command of Lieutenant-Colonel von Blessingh, made in connection with companies

of other regiments, reconnaissance upward the East River to Cross-Roads, where they encountered the enemy in force without engaging him.

May 16-17.— In the night the other five companies retreated with the rest of the brigade from Frenchville to Princeton, where the enemy, in the afternoon of the same day, had surprised the Headquarters of the commanding general and after a serious fight, driven back Company K, of the same regiment, to which in the meantime had here arrived under the command of Major Ankele from Fayetteville. In this comeback Major Ankele had been wounded and Company K suffered a loss of three killed, six wounded, and three missing. On the morning of May 17 the five above-named companies arrived with the brigade and the commanding General in Princeton without engaging the enemy, had taken position in the surrounding heights. The detachment left under the lieutenant-colonel consisting of Companies A, H, C of the Thirty-seventh Regiment and other companies of which retreated from Cross-Roads to Princeton encountered the enemy in its position and was repulsed after a short, serious engagement in which the above named companies suffered a loss of ten killed, forty wounded, and ten missing. The detachment reached [illegible] withstanding this without further loss. The division retreated to Flat Top Mountain.

Stationed at Flat Top Mountain Tannery, June 1862.

June 6.— The regiment was in camp at Flat Top Tannery with the Second Provisional Brigade of General Cox's Division and received payment for the month of March and April by Major Reese.

June 18-20.— Company C, under command of Lieutenant von Kyssinger (sixty-eight noncommissioned officers and privates) marched with one company of the Twelfth and two companies of the Twenty-eighth Regiments on a scouting expedition to Princeton and returned on June 20.

Stationed at Flat Top Tannery, [West] Virginia, July 1862.

The regiment was in camp at Flat Top Tannery.

July 17.— Company I (partly) on a scouting expedition took one prisoner, who pretended to be a lieutenant of the southern Army.

July 21-22.— Company B was on a scouting expedition to Blue Stone River.
July 26.— Companies A, H, C, F, and I marched to Raleigh.
August 1.— The remaining companies went to Raleigh to increase the garrison in said place.

Stationed at Raleigh, [West] Virginia, except Companies A and B at Fayetteville Court-House; Companies F and I at McCoy's Mill, August 1862.
August 10.— (Oceana). We left with the whole force the court-house without having met the enemy but after having encouraged the Union Home Guard of the county and caused several citizens to take the oath of allegiance.
August 12.— The detachment arrived at Raleigh Court-House.
August 19.— Companies F and K under command of Captain Stumpf marched to McCoy's Mill to guard the place.
August 27.— Company K was relieved by Company I and marched to Fayetteville.

The other companies are camping at Raleigh. Companies C as guard by the combined artillery. Companies H, D, G, and E serving as guards and building fortifications and breastworks.

Company A
August 13.— Company A marched to Fayetteville, where it has since been occupied with scouting and guarding post and quarter-master stores.

Company B
August 2-4.— Company B was on a scouting expedition on New River and Richmond's Ferry.
August 13.— Company B marched to Fayetteville with Company A.

Company G
August 2.— Company G, Captain [Frederick] Shoening marched on a scouting expedition to Wyoming Court-House to reconnoiter the county.

Companies H and I

August 2.— Companies H and I under command of Captain Messner marched on a scouting expedition to Wyoming Court-House to reconnoiter the county.

Detachment

August 5.— A detachment of sixteen men under command of Lieutenant Gustav Wintzer being sent out about four miles from the court-house and was attacked by [William] Straton's and [Vincent A.] Witcher's Rebel Cavalry and Lieutenant Wintzer, with six men of Company I and one of Company H, taken prisoner. One private killed. On the same day, one private of Company I was killed at Wyoming by Rebel scouts.

August 6.— Colonel Siber, with Company D and E and a detachment of [James L.] Wallar's Cavalry, marched to Trump's Farm to assist the above-named companies.

August 7.— He arrived at Wyoming Court-House.

Stationed at Camp Fair Haven, Point Pleasant, [West] Virginia, September 1862.

September 3.— The Companies H, C, D, G, and E marched to McCoy's Mill.

September 4.— With Companies F and L to Fayetteville, where Companies A, B and K were serving as guard.

September 10-11.— Companies B and F were sent out on Princeton Road for scouting and one and one-half miles distant from the town encountered the enemy in strong force. The companies retreated followed by the enemy who soon was engaged by the whole regiment. The Thirty-fourth and the combined artillery under command of First Lieutenant [William] Weste in a severe fight. The Rebels under General [William Wing] Loring attacked our breastworks and our position with a five-times stronger force, but we kept our position until night, being in a most fatiguing engagement from 11.30 a.m. until dark. At 3 o'clock in the night we commenced the retreat on the Gauley River, taking position on Cotton Hill and engaging there the Rebels for about one hour. After marching until night we camped on our arms at Montgomery. All our company wagons are lost with the company

books, clothes of officers, and soldiers killed, etc. by one attack of dismounted Rebels, who flanked the train on his way near Fayetteville at about 2 a.m. on September 10 at Point Pleasant.
September 12.— Crossed the river in the afternoon at Brownstown.
September 13.— Arrived at Charleston at 9 a.m. Another battle took place. Our regiment being on the north side of the Elk River, the engagement ended with darkness.

Three days and night marching brought us on the Ohio River at Ravenswood.
September 15-19.— Passing through Ripley, where we camped at night. Crossed the river in the afternoon and both by marching and steamboating arrived at Point Pleasant September 19. Our loss in dead, wounded and missing is considerable, with two killed, five wounded and sixty-two missing.
September 20.— Went in camp opposite the town.
September 26-30.— Recrossed being since in camp here.

The regiment was in camp near Point Pleasant doing guard and picket service and received pay for four months until September 1.

Stationed at Camp Loup Creek, [West] Virginia, October 1862.
October 15.— The regiment marched with Second Brigade commanded by Colonel Edward Siber to Ten-Mile Creek.
October 19.— To Eighteen-Mile Creek.
October 21.— To Buffalo.
October 22.— The regiment advanced seven miles on the Kanawha River Road.
October 23.— To Red House [Shoal], two miles.
October 24.— To Pocotaligo River.
October 28.— The regiment camped until marched four miles and camped on foot of Tyler Mountain.
October 29.— Marched to mouth of Cove River and crossing the Kanawha.
October 30.— To Brownstown.
October 31.— The regiment left Brownstown and marched to Clifton, thirteen miles.

Stationed at Gauley Bridge, [West] Virginia, November 1862.
November 3.— The regiment, after a two-day and night bivouac at Montgomery Landing and a day's march, arrived at mouth of Loup. Encamped there and ordered to march to Charleston.
November 10-12.— It left mouth of Loup. Marched that day to Slaughter's Creek, a distance of nineteen miles, and reached after crossing the Kanawha River opposite Charleston on November 12, marching that day a distance of seventeen miles.
November 16.— After encampment at Charleston of four days, the regiment was ordered to proceed to Gauley Bridge and marched to Camp Enyart, twelve miles distant.
November 17.— Marched to a place one-half mile above Cannelton.
November 18-30.— Reached Gauley Bridge, where it has been encamped since performing the guard and fatigue duties required by the necessities of the post at Gauley Bridge and of the regiment.

Stationed at Gauley Bridge, [West] Virginia, December 1862.
The regiment was stationed the whole month at Gauley Bridge, [West] Virginia.

Stationed at camp opposite Vicksburg, January 1863.
January 1-3.— The regiment embarked with General Hugh [Boyle] Ewing's Brigade at Camp Piatt, [West] Virginia and was shipped to Louisville, Kentucky, where it disembarked January 3.
January 9-31.— Camped there until it reembarked and shipped to Napoleon, Arkansas, where it joined General [John Alexander] McClernand's Fleet. From there the regiment moved down the Mississippi River on steamboats about two miles and a half below Vicksburg, where it is stationed this day.

Stationed at camp near Vicksburg, Mississippi in Louisiana, February 1863.

Stationed at Young's Point, Louisiana, March 1863.
March 1-17.— The regiment was stationed at Young's Point, Louisiana until March 17, when it embarked on board steamer *Fanny Ogden* and moved up the Mississippi River.

March 18-21.— Disembarked at Gwin's Plantation on the left bank of the Mississippi, where it bivouacked until March 21.
March 22-23.— In the morning it marched to the confluence of Muddy Creek and Steele's Bayou at which point it was again embarked on board steamer *Silver Wave* on which it proceeded upwards said bayou as far as Deer Creek, where it was disembarked on the evening of March 23.
March 24.— Bivouacked there during the night being all this time occupied with fatigue and guard duty. In the morning six companies proceeded up Deer Creek to reconnoiter the force of the enemy, three companies being taken up by guard and picket duty in and around the camp and one company was sent to the right bank of Deer Creek to protect Forces Plantation. Company G had some skirmishing with mounted Rebels, who, however, soon withdrew and did not approach any more.
March 26.— In the morning the regiment was embarked again on board gunboat *Carondelet* and first mortar grape.
March 27-31.— Returned to its old camp at Young's Point, Louisiana at night, where it is still stationed. The regiment had no loss on this expedition.

Stationed at Yazoo River on board steamer Chancellor, April 1863.
April 29.— The regiment was stationed on Young's Point, Louisiana engaged in doing guard and fatigue duty until the regiment embarked on board the steamer *Chancellor* and was taken to near Haynes' Bluff, Mississippi on the Yazoo River the same afternoon.
April 30.— After having arrived at that point, the Thirty-seventh Regiment was sent on picket in the morning; reembarked on board of the same boat and remained there until the afternoon of the same day, when the regiment again disembarked with the brigade and made some movements against the enemy. After dark the regiment returned to the boat and remained there.

Stationed at Walnut Hill near Vicksburg, Mississippi, May 1863.
May 1.— At Yazoo River. The regiment remained on board steamer *Chancellor* until evening, when the whole fleet returned to Young's Point and the men were disembarked.

May 2.— Early in the morning the tents were struck and the regiment with transportation, baggage, etc., was put aboard of the steamer *Chancellor* and taken to Milliken's Bend, and there disembarked, where the camp was put up.
May 3.— This afternoon the regiment again struck tents and was conveyed in two trips on steamer *Diligence* to Duckport and there went into camp.
May 9.— Here the regiment was occupied with guard and fatigue duty and scouting until orders came for the removal of the regiment to Young's Point, which was effected the same day.
May 13.— The regiment was constantly and strongly engaged in doing guard and fatigue duty until, camp equipage and baggage having been stored at Convalescent Camp at Young's Point, the regiment marched to Bowers Landing and was the same day put aboard of steamer *Forest Queen* on which it was conveyed to Grand Gulf, and there disembarked.
May 15.— Left Grand Gulf with brigade.
May 18.— Marched until the front, two and one-half miles from Vicksburg, was reached.
May 19.— During the forenoon the regiment took its position on the extreme right of General [Francis Preston] Blair's Division joining the left wing of General [Frederick] Steele's Division opposite the enemy's breastworks. During the afternoon and until night the regiment was heavily engaged in action upon the enemy works, sustaining a loss of forty-four killed and wounded.
May 20.— About noon fire upon the enemy's fortifications was reopened and lasted until nightfall. The regiment lost six killed and wounded. Among them were two officers killed.
May 22.— An attack was made in column by the brigade upon the enemy's fortifications which resulted in a repulse at great loss. The fire upon the enemy was kept up from the position which the regiment had taken after the repulse until night. Loss of the regiment on this day was forty killed and wounded. Lieutenant-Colonel von Blessingh having been wounded in action, Major Charles Hipp assumed command of the regiment.
May 28-31.— The regiment occupied the same position it had taken on May 22, watching the enemy closely at a distance of 100 yards from their works, until the regiment withdrew to a ravine 150 yards in the rear of its former position, where they are stationed at this date.

Stationed at Walnut Hill near Vicksburg, Mississippi, June 1863.

The regiment was occupying during the whole month the same position it held at the end of last month, engaged constantly in doing picket and fatigue duty.

Stationed at Camp Sherman near Vicksburg, Mississippi, July 1863.

July 4.— The regiment had the same position as last month until the surrender of Vicksburg took place and we received marching orders.

July 5.— Left camp at 7 a.m. Took the Bridgeport Road; turned off the road leading to Messinger's Ford; reached Fox's Plantation at 7 p.m., a distance of fifteen miles.

July 6.— Camped until 4 p.m. The regiment thence crossed Big Black River.

July 7-9.— Camped near Jeff Davis Plantation until 6 a.m. We reached a place called Ten Springs at 5 p.m. We then took the Clinton Road, and reached near Clinton, where we camped until 9 p.m. July 9.

July 10.— At 6 a.m. we marched and reached the enemy's works at 10 a.m. The regiment took position on the left of the brigade, the right of the brigade resting on the left of [the] Thirteenth Army Corps.

July 17.— The regiment was laying before Jackson, Mississippi making entrenchments and doing picket duty until morning when the enemy evacuated Jackson. We then marched in town and took position near the State House.

July 23.— We camped doing provost guard duty, etc. until we received orders to march back and to camp near [Big] Black River. The regiment left Jackson in the morning at 5 a.m.

July 25-31.— Reached Fox's Plantation at 12 a.m., where we have been camping since. The casualties in the regiment were as follows, Private F. Buhe of Company C, wounded in the left arm and amputated; G Muenzing of Company A, wounded in right shoulder.

Stationed on board of steamer Nashville, Mississippi River, September 1863.

September 27.— The regiment was stationed at Camp Sherman drilling and doing guard and fatigue duty until marched to Vicks-

burg and there was embarked on board the steamer *Nashville*, serving as escort to the steamer *Edward Walsh*.
September 28-29.— Left Vicksburg for a point fifteen miles below Greenville, where the boat reached September 29.
September 30.— Were still stationed there.

Stationed at camp on Tennessee River, Alabama, October 1863.
October 1-3.— The regiment was still on board of steamer *Nashville* en route for Memphis, Tennessee, which place was reached October 3.
October 4.— In the morning it was disembarked.
October 6-7.— Bivouacked in a camp near Memphis until evening, when it marched to Germantown, where it arrived in the afternoon of October 7.
October 9-15.— In the morning it marched with the train of the Thirteenth Army Corps to Corinth, Mississippi touching the villages of Moscow, La Grange and Pocahontas, and arrived at Corinth, Mississippi in the afternoon of October 15. Left Corinth the same day and marched to Clear Creek.
October 17-20.— The regiment bivouacked until left Clear Creek in the morning and marched via Iuka, Mississippi to Cherokee Station, Alabama, where it arrived in the night of October 20.
October 26-28.— Bivouacked there until it marched with the division to Tuscumbia to reconnoiter the enemy and returned to Cherokee Station on the evening of October 28.
October 30-31.— Left Cherokee Station in the morning and marched to Chickasaw, Alabama on the Tennessee River, where it is in bivouac, stationed now.

Stationed at camp in the field near Cleveland, Tennessee, November 1863.
November 2.— The regiment left Chickasaw, Alabama in the morning; crossed with the brigade the Tennessee River on the steamer *Nashville* and marched to Waterloo, Alabama, where it went into bivouac.
November 3.— Left Waterloo and marched to Florence, Alabama, where it bivouacked.
November 5-17.— During the night, marched from here over Blue [Water] Creek, Anderson's Creek, fork of Elk River, Bradshaw Creek, Cane Creek, Fayetteville, Tennessee; Bren Creek,

New Market, Maysville, Woodville Station, Scottsville, Bellefonte, Stevenson, [to Bridgeport, Alabama, where it arrived November 17.

November 19-20.— Crossed the Tennessee River on pontoon bridges and went into bivouac near Missionary Ridge November 20.

November 23-24.— Crossed the Tennessee River on pontoon boats in the night and fortified themselves before daybreak, advanced to Missionary Ridge and held a hill in front of the enemy during the night to hold communication with the First Brigade.

November 25.— In the morning Companies E and F were ordered on picket and the remaining eight companies were ordered with the Thirtieth Regiment, Ohio Infantry in connection with a brigade of the Fourth Division to charge the enemy works which was done twice without success and in which the regiment sustained a loss of five killed and thirty-three wounded among which are five officers wounded. After the repulse the regiment occupied the breastworks which the enemy had built the night previous until it was relieved.

After having taken three days' rations the regiment marched in pursuit of the enemy over Chickamauga Station and Cleveland in the vicinity of which it is in bivouac now.

Stationed at Bellefonte Station, Alabama, December 1863.

December 1-3.— The regiment having received orders to march to Knoxville without provisions and having detailed one officer and number of men as foraging party left bivouac near Cleveland and marched with the brigade via Charleston and Athens, crossing the Hiwassee River to Sweetwater and near Philadelphia where we struck the road leading to Morganton and reached the Little Tennessee River in the afternoon of December 3. Crossed the river and then marched through Morganton to near Maryville.

December 5.— We bivouacked.

December 6-7.— Marched back to Morganton; recrossed the river and marched on the Madisonville Road until December 7.

December 8.— Went to Tellico Plains.

December 10.— The regiment marched with the brigade towards North Carolina across the Unaka Mountains up to Fry's Farm.

December 13-19.— Bivouacked here until the morning, when we went back via Charleston, Cleveland, and Chattanooga to Bridgeport, where we arrived December 19.
December 26-31.— Bivouacked here until the regiment marched, with the brigade, to Bellefonte Station, Alabama, where it remains now.

Stationed at Burk's Pocket, De Kalb County, Alabama, January 1864.
January 7.— The regiment marched from Bellefonte Station to Larkinsville, Alabama, where it went into camp.
January 26-28.— Remained here employed in picket and guard duty until it marched with the brigade via Larkin's Landing to the Tennessee River; crossed the same on pontoons during the night and marched in two columns towards Smith's Gap. Had here some skirmishing with the enemy's pickets and captured some of them. Returned to the bivouac at Larkin's Landing January 28.
January 30.— Remained here until it crossed the river again on a pontoon bridge that had been built and marched to Burk's Pocket, De Kalb County, Alabama, where it is in bivouac now.

Stationed at Cleveland, Tennessee, February 1864.
February 1-2.— The regiment left Burk's Pocket and marched to Lebanon, arriving in the afternoon of February 2.
February 3-6.— It remained with the brigade awaiting an attack from the enemy, who, however, did not venture to appear, until we left Lebanon and marched back via Burk's Pocket and Larkin's Landing, where it recrossed the Tennessee River to Larkinsville and arrived here February 6.
February 11.— Remained here until again marching orders were received and marched with the brigade via Bridgeport, Stevenson and Chattanooga to Cleveland, Tennessee.
February 17-29.— Here it arrived and went into camp employed in heavy picket duty and it is stationed here now.

In the meantime three-fourths of the eligible men present of the regiment have reenlisted as veteran volunteers awaiting muster-in.

Stationed near Kenesaw Mountain, Georgia, March 1864.
March 18.— The regiment was stationed at Larkinsville, Alabama until it proceeded to Ohio on veteran furlough, three-fourths of the [eligible] number having reenlisted as veterans.

The report of this month could not be forwarded. The regiment was on veteran furlough at the end of the month of March.

Stationed at Cincinnati, Ohio, April 1864.
April 26.— The regiment assembled at Camp Cleveland the day of expiration of its thirty days' furlough and went by railroad to Cincinnati on its way to join the Fifteenth Army Corps.
April 30.— Left Cincinnati.

Stationed in the field near Dallas, Georgia, May 1864.
May 1.— The regiment arrived at Louisville, Kentucky.
May 2.— Left the same.
May 6.— Reached Chattanooga.
May 7.— The regiments received new muskets.
May 8.— Left and marched in a southern direction towards the front of our lines, escorting the quartermaster train of the First Division of the Fifteenth Army Corps.
May 10.— Arrived at Sugar Valley, where it joined its division.
May 13-15.— The regiment took part in the battle near Resaca, Georgia.
May 16.— It marched to Kingston.
May 23.— It remained in camp there until it marched towards Dallas, Georgia. L. von Blessingh commanding the regiment, left the regiment on sick leave and Major Charles Hipp took command.
May 25.— It reached the vicinity of Dallas.
May 28-29.— Took part in the actions near said Dallas.

Stationed near Kenesaw Mountain, Georgia, June 1864.
June 1.— The regiment marched with the Army Corps to the line near New Hope Church, previously occupied by the Twentieth Army Corps and took position there.
June 5-6.— Remained there until the enemy evacuated his entrenchments, then the regiment marched to Acworth and arrived there on June 6.

June 10.— Bivouacked there until it marched in a southerly direction and arrived at Big Shanty on the same day.
June 14.— The regiment held with its division the right of the Army Corps until it advanced more southeast and near the position of the enemy on the Kenesaw Mountain.
June 16.— In the evening the regiment occupied a part of our advanced lines and sent out its skirmishers.
June 19.— Remained in this position until the enemy again abandoned his position.
June 26.— The regiment advanced more near the Kenesaw Mountain, where it took position, all the time engaged in sending out skirmishing parties and supporting those of other regiment of the division until the regiment was moved towards the right of our line.
June 27.— Took part in the general assault on the enemy's works.
June 28.— The regiment within our fortified lines bivouacked.
June 30.— The regiment was mustered in and inspected by Major Charles Hipp, commanding the regiment.

Stationed near Atlanta, Georgia, July 1864.
July 2.— The regiment marched with the division to the extreme right of the Army on the Sandtown Road, Georgia, arrived at its position at 10 p.m. and threw up entrenchments.
July 3.— It participated in driving the enemy towards the Chattanooga and Atlanta Railroad and the Chattahoochee River.
July 4-12.— Supported the Sixteenth Army Corps in its attacks on the ——. From July 5-12 ——.

In the morning —— the Chattahoochee River.

Marched with the division to the extreme left of the Army.

July 14-17.— Crossed the Chattahoochee River near Roswell factory, where it remained in an entrenched position until July 17, when it marched in a southeasterly direction towards the Atlanta and Augusta Railroad.
July 18.— The latter was reached near Gibraltar (Stony Mound) and participated in the destruction of said railroad in that vicinity.
July 19.— It reached Decatur after having being engaged on the same day in the destruction of another portion of said railroad.

July 20.— It advanced along the line of said railroad towards Atlanta in line of battle, the enemy appearing in front to a point about three miles from Atlanta, where it took position and threw up entrenchments.
July 22.— The enemy having left its position of the previous day, the regiment advanced one mile and took position in the enemy's works in the forenoon. About 3.30 p.m. the enemy attacked the regiment in this position and being successful on our left, came in our rear and flank and forced the regiment to fall back to the position occupied before advancing on this day. Here the regiment rallied, advanced, and in about one hour from the time it fell back, recaptured the entrenchments held in the forenoon.
July 27.— The regiment remained until it marched to the extreme right of the Army.
July 28.— Coming in position the regiment was attacked by the enemy, having been thrown out as skirmishers. A general battle ensued, the enemy trying to take our position, in which he was foiled during the remainder of the day and repulsed with great loss to him. In this action, Major Charles Hipp, commanding the regiment, was severely wounded and Captain Carl Moritz took command.
July 30.— The regiment advanced its line and threw up entrenchments.

Stationed at Jonesborough, Georgia, August 1864.
August 26.— The regiment confronted the enemy in his fortified position near Atlanta, Georgia until it marched towards Jonesborough, Georgia, a distance of about thirty miles.
August 31.— It participated in the battle in the vicinity which caused the fall of Atlanta.

Stationed at East Point, Georgia, September 1864.
September 1-2.— The position defended by the regiment near Jonesborough on August 31 was held, all the while engaged in heavy skirmishing and engaging the enemy when the latter retreated in the following night.
September 3.— Was pursued as far as Lovejoy's Station.
September 5-7.— The regiment bivouacked in this vicinity until the regiment, being part of the rear guard of the Fifteenth Army Corps, returned to East Point, Georgia.

September 8-30.— It arrived and went into camp in which it remained during the month, occupying its time by erecting breastworks, drilling, and doing picket duty.

Stationed at Cave Spring, Georgia, October 1864.
October 4.— The regiment remained in camp near East Point, Georgia until it marched with the brigade to Ruff's Station, a distance of fifteen miles, to participate in the movement of the Army against the enemy under General [John Bell] Hood, who endeavored to destroy our communication with the north.
October 5-25.— After marching over Marietta, Kingston, Resaca, through Snake Creek Gap, Ship's Gap, La Fayette, Summerville, Alpine, Gaylesville, and crossing the Little River, Alabama, the regiment came up with the enemy's cavalry about five miles from Gadsden, Alabama, which after the regiment advanced in line of battle with the brigade, retreated, and on October 25 the regiment marched back to Little River.
October 26.— It arrived at Little River.
October 29-31.— Bivouacked until it marched in the direction of Rome, Georgia, crossing the Chattooga River, passing through Cedar Bluff; thence crossing the Coosa River and bivouacked within two miles of Cave Spring on October 31. The regiment had marched a distance of 311 miles.

Stationed at Summerville, Georgia, November 1864.
November 3-5.— The regiment bivouacked on its return from the pursuit of the enemy under General Hood at Cave Spring, Georgia until it marched over Cedartown, Pumpkin Vine, Powder Springs, crossing the Sandtown Road, and passing Nickajack Creek, to the Western and Atlantic Railroad, where it arrived in bivouac at Camp Smyrna near Ruff's Station November 5.
November 11.— Lieutenant-Colonel von Blessingh took command of the regiment.
November 13-15.— The regiment marched to Atlanta, distance twelve miles, and there having been equipped, marched out of Atlanta on November 15 as a part of the Army which under the command of Major-General [William Tecumseh] Sherman undertook the great invasion of the state of Georgia from the northwestern part to the southeastern border of said state.

The line of march the regiment made was over McDonough, Indian Springs, near which place it crossed the Ocmulgee River over Hillsborough, and Clinton.

November 22.— At the latter place the regiment went on picket with the Fifteenth Michigan Volunteer Infantry under command of Lieutenant-Colonel L. von Blessingh on the road leading to Macon, from where the enemy's cavalry tried to enter Clinton and cut off the train of the division. The regiment went in line of battle and the enemy was forced to retreat by the advancing skirmish line.

November 23-26.— The regiment remained near Clinton covering the rear of the division and marched on the same day towards Griswoldville and joined the division near said place after having crossed the Georgia Central Railroad; thence marched over Irwinton to the Oconee River, which it crossed November 26, when it resumed its march through the swamps.

November 30.— It arrived at Summerville, Georgia, where it bivouacked overnight. Distance marched from Atlanta to Summertown was 197 miles.

Stationed near Savannah, Georgia, December 1864.

December 1-8.— The regiment, with the Army of Major-General W. T. Sherman in Georgia, continued its march from Summerville towards the seacoast through the low and swampy country of Georgia and having passed [illegible] and Bulloch Counties of said state on the right southwest side of the Ogeechee River until December 8 when it crossed the Cannouchee River.

December 9-10.— Marched to the Savannah, Albany and Gulf Railroad and destroyed the same in connection with the other regiments of the brigade for about five miles. Having returned the same day to the Cannouchee River, it crossed the same the next day and also the Ogeechee River, the latter near the Ogeechee Canal, then marched towards Savannah within nine miles of which the regiment bivouacked.

December 12.— The regiment returned with the division to the Ogeechee River.

December 13.— Crossed it at King's Bridge, and advanced to Fort McAllister, which was invested and carried by assault with its entire garrison and armament.

December 17-18.— The regiment then bivouacked near the fort until it marched with the brigade to McIntosh, thirty miles southwest of Savannah on the Savannah, Albany and Gulf Railroad, which was reached on December 18.
December 20.— The regiment being engaged in destroying the railroad completely so that nothing of the same way left but the twisted iron rails until night.
December 21.— The regiment returned to the Ogeechee River and received on said return, an order to report at Corps Headquarters to take part in the contemplated assault on Savannah. In the meantime, Savannah being evacuated by the enemy, the regiment went in bivouac eleven miles from Savannah.
December 29.— Marched to within four miles of Savannah, where it remained up to this date. Distance marched was about 175 miles.

Stationed near Pocotaligo, South Carolina, January 1865.
January 2.— The regiment remained in bivouac four miles from Savannah, Georgia until it marched with the brigade to the southwestern side of Savannah and went into camp. The regiment here being engaged in working on the fortification of Savannah.
January 14.— It marched to Fort Thunderbolt.
January 15.— Was embarked on the steamer *Crescent* for Beaufort, South Carolina in the evening.
January 16.— Arrived at noon and went in bivouac three miles from the latter place.
January 26.— The regiment was ordered to march to Beaufort, South Carolina for unloading the train of the division from the boats.
January 30-31.— This finished, the regiment marched with the train in a northwesterly direction to close up on the division and went into bivouac near Pocotaligo, South Carolina, where it remained on January 31.

Stationed at Lynch's Creek, South Carolina, February 1865.
February 1.— The regiment rejoined the brigade at McPhersonville, South Carolina and marched in a northwesterly direction.
February 4.— Bivouacked at Angley's Post-Office.
February 5.— Crossed the Big Salkehatchie.

February 6.— Waded the Little Salkehatchie.
February 7.— Struck the South Carolina Railroad at Bamberg, South Carolina. Bivouacked two miles from town.
February 8.— The regiment went with the brigade on a reconnaissance to the South Edisto River and returned to camp.
February 10.— Crossed the South Edisto River.
February 12.— The regiment with the brigade waded the swamps one and one-half miles in breadth near the North Edisto River and crossed the river and assaulted the Rebel rifle pits on the left bank of the river and drove them out of their works, thereby effecting a crossing for the Corps.
February 14.— Passed through Sandy Run.
February 15.— Crossed Congaree Creek; bivouacked five miles from Columbia, South Carolina near the Congaree River.
February 16.— Crossed Saluda River four miles above Columbia, South Carolina.
February 17.— Was detached to the train as guards. The Corps crossed Broad River.
February 18.— Rejoined the brigade and marched to Section No. 7 on the South Carolina Railroad and began destroying the same.
February 19.— Completed the destruction and returned to Columbia.
February 20.— Continued the march with the brigade in a northeasterly direction.
February 21.— Crossed Dutchman's Creek.
February 22.— Crossed the Wateree River.
February 23.— Passed through Liberty Hill.
February 26-28.— Waded Lynch's Creek; made a reconnaissance in company with the Fifty-fourth Ohio Veteran Volunteers Infantry and returned the same evening. Bivouacked and remained there until February 28.

Stationed near Goldsborough, North Carolina, March 1865.
March 1.— Took up the line of march again.
March 3.— Crossed Black Creek.
March 4.— Marched through Cheraw, South Carolina.
March 5.— Crossed the Pee Dee River.
March 7.— Reached Laurel Hill, North Carolina.

March 9.— Crossed Lumber River. The regiment was detached from the brigade by order of Major-General [Oliver Otis] Howard to guard the Headquarters train of the department and Army of the Tennessee.
March 11.— Crossed Big and Little Rockfish Creeks; bivouacked one mile from Fayetteville, North Carolina.
March 12.— Rejoined the brigade, escorted a forage train and returned in the evening.
March 14.— Crossed Cape Fear River.
March 16.— Crossed South River.
March 19.— Marched all day and at night turned back to reinforce the Twentieth Army Corps.
March 20.— At daylight arrived there.
March 21-22.— Started for the front, took up our position in the line of battle near Mill Creek under fire of the enemy. The regiment suffered a loss of one man killed and three wounded. At 4 a.m. discovered that the enemy had fled on March 22 and we pushed out our skirmishers in pursuit. They closed up on the enemy rear guard. We took up our line of march for Goldsborough.
March 24.— Crossed the Neuse River, and passed through Goldsborough, North Carolina and occupied a camping ground.
March 31.— Camped at Goldsborough, North Carolina.

Stationed at Rogers' Cross-Roads, North Carolina, April 1865.
April 10.— The regiment marched with the brigade across the Wilmington Weldon Railroad, passed through Pikeville, North Carolina.
April 11.— Crossed Little River.
April 14.— Crossed Neuse River; marched through Raleigh, North Carolina; bivouacked two miles from town.
April 29.— Marched with the brigade in a northerly direction from Raleigh, North Carolina.
April 30.— Bivouacked at Rogers' Cross-Roads, North Carolina.

Stationed near Washington, District of Columbia, May 1865.
May 1.— Took up the line of march with the brigade; bivouacked for the night at Louisburg, North Carolina.
May 2.— Crossed Tar River.
May 3.— Passed through Warrenton, North Carolina. Bivouacked at Robinson's Ferry at the Roanoke River.

May 4.— Crossed the river.
May 7.— Reached Petersburg, Virginia.
May 9.— Crossed the Appomattox River.
May 13.— Pass through Richmond, Virginia.
May 17.— Passed through Fredericksburg, Virginia ——.
May 31.— This regiment was encamped near Washington, District of Columbia.

Stationed on board steamer Argonaut, June 1865.
June 1.— Were embarked on the Baltimore and Ohio Railroad.
June 3.— Arrived at Parkersburg, West Virginia.
June 4.— Embarked on steamer.
June 6.— Arrived at Louisville, Kentucky and went into camp.
June 25.— Again embarked on steamer and went down the Ohio River.
June 30.— Still en route.

Company A

Stationed at Cleveland, Ohio, September 9, 1861.
September 9.— Muster-in roll of Captain Lewis Quedenfeld's Company, in the Thirty-seventh Regiment of Ohio Volunteers, commanded by Colonel Edward Siber, called into the service of the United States by the President from September 9, 1861 (date of this muster) for the term of three years, unless sooner discharge. The company was organized by Captain Lewis Quedenfeld at Cleveland, Ohio in the month of August and marched thence to Camp Brown. . . .

HENRY BELKNAP,
Captain,
Eighteenth Infantry, Mustering Officer.

Stationed at Camp Montgomery, [West] Virginia, October 31, 1861.

Stationed at Clifton, [West] Virginia, November-December 1861.

Stationed at Camp Clifton, [West] Virginia, January-February 1862.

Stationed at mouth of Loup Creek, March-April 1862.

Stationed at Flat Top Tannery, May-June 1862.

Stationed at Fayetteville, [West] Virginia, July-August 1862.

Stationed at Camp Brownstown, September-October 1862.

Stationed at Camp Piatt, [West] Virginia, November-December 1862.

Stationed at Young's Point, Louisiana, January-February 1863.

Stationed at Young's Point, Louisiana, April 10, 1863.

Stationed at Milliken's Bend, Louisiana, March-April 1863.

Stationed at Walnut Hill, Mississippi, May-June 1863.

Stationed at Camp Sherman, Mississippi, July-August 1863.

Stationed at camp on Tennessee River, September-October 1863.

Stationed at Bellefonte, Alabama, November-December 1863.

Stationed at Cleveland, Tennessee, January-February 1864.

Stationed near Kenesaw Mountain, Georgia, May-June 1864.

Stationed near East Point, Jonesborough, Georgia, July-August 1864.

Stationed at East Point, Georgia, September 12, 1864.
September 12.— Muster-out roll of Captain John Hamm's, late Captain L. Quedenfeld's, Company A, in the Thirty-seventh Regiment of Ohio Infantry Volunteers, commanded by Lieutenant-Colonel Louis von Blessingh, late Colonel Siber, called into the service of the United States by the President at Cleveland, Ohio (the place of general rendezvous) on August 3,

1861 to serve for the term of three years from the date of enrollment, unless sooner discharged, from December 31, 1861 (when last paid) to September 12, 1864 when mustered out. The company was organized by Captain Lewis Quedenfeld at Cleveland, Ohio in the month of August 1861 and marched thence to Camp Brown, where it arrived August 15, a distance of two miles. . . .

[CHARLES JOHN] DICKEY,
First Lieutenant,
Thirteenth Infantry, Assistant Commissary of Musters,
Second Division, Fifteenth Army Corps, Mustering Officer.

Stationed at Cave Spring, Georgia, September-October 1864.

Stationed near Savannah, Georgia, November-December 1864.

Stationed near Lynch's Creek, South Carolina, January-February 1865.

Stationed in the field, Rogers' Cross-Roads, North Carolina, March-April 1865.

Stationed on steamer Argonaut No. 2 near Memphis, Tennessee, May-June 1865.

Company B

Stationed at Cleveland, Ohio, September 9, 1861.
September 9.— Muster-in roll of Captain Louis von Blessingh's Company (B), in the Thirty-seventh Regiment of Ohio Volunteers, commanded by Colonel Edward Siber, called into the service of the United States by the President from September 9, 1861 (date of this muster) for the term of three years, unless sooner discharged. The company was organized by Captain Louis von Blessingh at Toledo in the month of August and marched thence to Camp Brown, Cleveland, where it arrived August 26, a distance of 113 miles. . . .

HENRY BELKNAP,
Captain,
Eighteenth Infantry, Mustering Officer.

Stationed at Camp Montgomery, [West] Virginia, October 31, 1861.

Stationed at Post Loup Creek Landing, November-December 1861.

Stationed at Camp Clifton, [West] Virginia, January-February 1862.

Stationed at mouth of Loup Creek, March-April 1862.

Stationed at Flat Top Tannery, May-June 1862.

Station not stated, July-August 1862.

Stationed at Brownstown, September-October 1862.

Stationed at Camp Piatt, [West] Virginia, November-December 1862.

Stationed at Young's Point, Louisiana, January-February 1863.

Stationed at Young's Point, Louisiana, April 10, 1863.

Stationed at Milliken's Bend, Louisiana, March-April 1863.

Stationed at Walnut Hill, Mississippi, May-June 1863.

Stationed at Camp Sherman, Mississippi, July-August 1863.

Stationed at camp on Tennessee River, September-October 1863.

Stationed at Bellefonte Station, Alabama, November-December 1863.

Stationed at Cleveland, Tennessee, January-February 1864.

Stationed at Cincinnati, Ohio, March-April 1864.

Stationed in the field, Kenesaw, Georgia, May-June 1864.

Stationed at Jonesborough, Georgia, July-August 1864.

Stationed at East Point, Georgia, September 12, 1864.
September 12.— Muster-out roll of a detachment of Captain Carl Moritz's, late Captain Henry Goeke's, Company (B), in the Thirty-seventh Regiment of Ohio Infantry Volunteers, commanded by Lieutenant-Colonel Louis von Blessingh, late Colonel E. Siber, called into the service of the United States by the President at Cleveland, Ohio (the place of general rendezvous) on August 3, 1861 to serve for the term of three years from the date of enrollment, unless sooner discharged, from December 31, 1863 (when last paid) to September 12, 1864 when mustered out. . . .

C. J. DICKEY,
First Lieutenant,
Thirteenth Infantry, Assistant Commissary of Musters,
Second Division, Fifteenth Army Corps, Mustering Officer.

Stationed at Cave Spring, Georgia, September-October 1864.

Stationed near Savannah, Georgia, November-December 1864.

Stationed near Lynch's Creek, South Carolina, January-February 1865.

Stationed at Rogers' Cross-Roads, North Carolina, March-April 1865.

Stationed on board of steamer Argonaut, May-June 1865.

Company C

Stationed at Cleveland, Ohio, September 14, 1861.
September 14.— Muster-in roll of Captain Charles Hipp's Company (C), in the Thirty-seventh Regiment of Ohio Volunteers, commanded by Colonel Edward Siber, called into the service of the United States by the President from September 14, 1861 (date of this muster) for the term of three years, unless sooner discharged. The company was organized by Captain Charles Hipp at

Saint Marys in the month of September and marched thence to Camp Brown, Cleveland, Ohio, where it arrived September 5, a distance of 205 miles. . . .

HENRY BELKNAP,
Captain,
Eighteenth Infantry, Mustering Officer.

Stationed at Camp Montgomery, [West] Virginia, October 31, 1861.

Stationed at Clifton, [West] Virginia, November-December 1861.

Stationed at Camp Clifton, January-February 1862.

Stationed at mouth of Loup Creek, March-April 1862.

Stationed at Flat Top Tannery, May-June 1862.

Stationed at Camp Raleigh, July-August 1862.

Stationed at Camp Brownstown, September-October 1862.

Stationed at Camp Piatt, November-December 1862.

Stationed at Young's Point, Louisiana, January-February 1863.

Stationed at Young's Point, Louisiana, April 10, 1863.

Stationed at Milliken's Bend, Louisiana, March-April 1863.

Stationed at Walnut Hill, Mississippi, May-June 1863.

Stationed at Camp Sherman, Mississippi, July-August 1863.

Stationed on Tennessee River, September-October 1863.

Stationed at Bellefonte Station, Alabama, November-December 1863.

Stationed at Cleveland, Ohio, January-February 1864.

Stationed at Cincinnati, Ohio, March-April 1864.

Stationed near Kenesaw Mountain, May-June 1864.

Stationed near Jonesborough, Georgia, July-August 1864.

Stationed at East Point, Georgia, September 15, 1864.
September 15.— Muster-out roll of a detachment of Captain Henry Schmidt's, late Charles Hipp's (captain), Company (C), in the Thirty-seventh Regiment of Ohio Infantry, Veteran Volunteers, commanded by Lieutenant-Colonel Louis von Blessingh, late Colonel E. Siber, called into the service of the United States by the President at Cleveland, Ohio (the place of general rendezvous) on August 3, 1861, to serve for the term of three years from the date of enrollment, unless sooner discharged, from December 31, 1863 (when last paid) to September 15, 1864 when mustered out. The company was organized by Captain Charles Hipp at Saint Marys, Ohio in the month of September 1861 and marched thence to Camp Brown, Cleveland, Ohio, where it arrived September 15, 1861, a distance of 205 miles. . . .

C. J. DICKEY,
First Lieutenant,
Thirteenth Infantry, Assistant Commissary of Musters,
Second Division, Fifteenth Army Corps, Mustering Officer.

Stationed at Cave Spring, Georgia, September-October 1864.

Stationed near Savannah, Georgia, November-December 1864.

Stationed at Lynch's Creek, South Carolina, January-February 1865.

Stationed at Rogers' Cross-Roads, March-April 1865.

Stationed on board steamer Argonaut No. 2 near Memphis, Tennessee, May-June 1865.

Company D

Stationed at Cleveland, Ohio, September 19, 1861.
September 19.— Muster-in roll of Captain Julius Gustavus Eberhard's Company (D), in the Thirty-seventh Regiment of Ohio Volunteers, commanded by Colonel Edward Siber, called into the service of the United States by the President from September 19, 1861 (date of this muster) for the term of three years, unless sooner discharged. The company was organized by Captain Julius Gustavus Eberhard at Columbus, Ohio in the month of August and marched thence to Camp Brown, where it arrived August 28, a distance of 130 miles.

HENRY BELKNAP,
Captain,
Eighteenth Infantry, Mustering Officer.

Stationed at Camp Montgomery, [West] Virginia, October 31, 1861.

Stationed at Cannelton, [West] Virginia, November-December 1861.

Stationed at Camp Clifton, [West] Virginia, January-February 1862.

Stationed at mouth of Loup, March-April 1862.

Stationed at Flat Top Tannery, [West] Virginia, May-June 1862.

Stationed at Raleigh Court-House, [West] Virginia, July-August 1862.

Stationed at Brownstown, Kanawha Valley, September-October 1862.

Stationed at Camp Piatt, [West] Virginia, November-December 1862.

Stationed at Young's Point, Louisiana, January-February 1863.

Stationed at Young's Point, Louisiana, April 10, 1863.

Stationed at Milliken's Bend, March-April 1863.

Stationed at Walnut Hill, Mississippi, May-June 1863.

Stationed at Camp Sherman, July-August 1863.

Stationed at camp near Tennessee River, September-October 1863.

Stationed at Bellefonte, Alabama, November-December 1863.

Stationed at Cleveland, Tennessee, January-February 1864.

Stationed at Cincinnati, Ohio, March-April 1864.

Stationed at Kenesaw Mountain, Georgia, May-June 1864.

Stationed in the field, Jonesborough, Georgia, July-August 1864.

Stationed at East Point, Georgia, September 19, 1864.
September 19.— Muster-out roll of First Lieutenant Florentin Finn's, late J. G. Eberhard's, Company (D), in the Thirty-seventh Regiment of Ohio Infantry Volunteers, commanded by Colonel Louis von Blessing, late Colonel E. Siber, called into the service of the United States by the President at Cleveland, Ohio (the place of general rendezvous) on August 3, 1861 to serve for the term of three years from the date of enrollment unless sooner discharged, to September 19, 1864 when mustered out. The company was organized by Captain Eberhard at Columbus, Ohio in the month of August 1861 and marched thence to Camp Brown, Cleveland, where it arrived August 28, a distance of 130 miles. . . .

C. J. DICKEY,
First Lieutenant,
Thirteenth Infantry, Assistant Commissary of Musters,
Second Division, Fifteenth Army Corps, Mustering Officer.

Stationed at Cave Spring, Georgia, September-October 1864.

Stationed at camp near Savannah, Georgia, November-December 1864.

Stationed at Lynch's Creek, South Carolina, January-February 1865.

Stationed at Rogers' Cross-Roads, North Carolina, March-April 1865.

Stationed on steamer Argonaut, Mississippi River, May-June 1865.

Company E

Stationed at Camp Montgomery, [West] Virginia, October 31, 1861.

Stationed at Clifton, [West] Virginia, November-December 1861.

Stationed at Camp Clifton, [West] Virginia, January-February 1862.

Stationed at mouth of Loup Creek, March-April 1862.

Stationed at Flat Top Tannery, May-June 1862.

Station not stated, July-August 1862.

Stationed at Brownstown, September-October 1862.

Stationed at Camp Piatt, [West] Virginia, [November 1]-December 31, 1862.

Stationed at Young's Point opposite Vicksburg, Mississippi, January-February 1863.

Stationed at Young's Point, Louisiana, opposite Vicksburg, April 10, 1863.

Stationed at Milliken's Bend, Louisiana, March-April 1863.

Stationed at Walnut Hill, Mississippi, May-June 1863.

Stationed at Camp Sherman, Mississippi, July-August 1863.

Stationed at camp on Tennessee River, September-October 1863.

Stationed at Bellefonte, Alabama, November-December 1863.

Stationed at Cleveland, Tennessee, January-February 1864.

Stationed at Cincinnati, Ohio, March-April 1864.

Stationed at Big Shanty, Georgia, May-June 1864.

Stationed at Jonesborough, Georgia, July-August 1864.

Stationed at Cave Springs, [Georgia], September-October 1864.

Stationed near Savannah, Georgia, November-December 1864.

Stationed at Lynch's Creek, South Carolina, January-February 1865.

Stationed at Rogers' Cross-Roads, North Carolina, March-April 1865.

Stationed on board of steamer Argonaut, May-June 1865.

Company F

Stationed at Cleveland, Ohio, September 23, 1861.
September 23.— Muster-in roll of Captain [Anton] Vallendar's Company (F), in the Thirty-seventh Regiment of Ohio Volunteers, commanded by Colonel E. Siber, called into the service of the United States by the President from September 23, 1861 for the term of three years, unless sooner discharged. The company was organized by Captain A. Vallendar at Sandusky in

the month of September and marched thence to Camp Brown near Cleveland, where it arrived September 2, a distance of sixty-two miles. . . .

HENRY BELKNAP,
Captain,
Eighteenth Infantry, Mustering Officer.

Stationed at Camp Montgomery, [West] Virginia, October 31, 1861.

Stationed at Montgomery's Landing, [West] Virginia, November-December 1861.

Stationed at Camp Clifton, [West] Virginia, January-February 1862.

Stationed at mouth of Loup Creek, [West] Virginia, March-April 1862.

Stationed at Camp Flat Top Mountain Tannery, May-June 1862.

Stationed at McCoy's Mill, Fayette County, [West] Virginia, July-August 1862.

Stationed at Brownstown, [West] Virginia, September-October 1862.

Stationed at Camp Piatt, Virginia, November-December 1862.

Stationed at Young's Point, Louisiana, January-February 1863.

Stationed at Young's Point, Louisiana, April 10, 1863.

Stationed at Milliken's Bend, Louisiana, March-April 1863.

Stationed at Walnut Hill, Mississippi, May-June 1863.

Stationed at Camp Sherman, Mississippi, July-August 1863.

Stationed at camp on Tennessee River, Alabama, September-October 1863.

Stationed at Bellefonte Station, Alabama, November-December 1863.

Stationed at Cleveland, Tennessee, January-February 1864.

Stationed at Cincinnati, Ohio, March-April 1864.

Stationed at Kenesaw Mountain, Georgia, May-June 1864.

Stationed at Jonesborough, Georgia, July-August 1864.

Stationed at Cave Spring, Georgia, September-October 1864.

Stationed near Savannah, Georgia, November-December 1864.

Stationed near Lynch's Creek, South Carolina, January-February 1865.

Stationed at Rogers' Cross-Roads, March-April 1865.

Stationed on steamer Argonaut near Memphis, May-June 1865.

Company G

Stationed at Cleveland, Ohio, September 19, 1861.
September 19.— Muster-in roll of Captain Frederick Schoening's Company (G), in the Thirty-seventh Regiment of Ohio Volunteers, commanded by Colonel E. Siber, called into the service of the United States by the President from September 19, 1861 (date of this muster) for the term of three years, unless sooner discharged. The company was organized by Captain Frederick Schoening at Toledo in the month of August and marched thence to camp Brown, Cleveland, where it arrived September 3, a distance of 112 miles. . . .

HENRY BELKNAP,
Captain,
Eighteenth Infantry, Mustering Officer.

Stationed at Camp Montgomery, [West] Virginia, October 31, 1861.

Stationed at Clifton, [West] Virginia, November-December 1861.

Stationed at Camp Clifton, [West] Virginia, January-February 1862.

Stationed at mouth of Loup Creek, March-April 1862.

Stationed at Flat Top Tannery, May-June 1862.

Stationed at Camp Raleigh, July-August 1862.

Stationed at Brownstown, [West] Virginia, September-October 1862.

Stationed at Camp Piatt, [West] Virginia, November-December 1862.

Stationed at Camp Young's Point, Louisiana, January-February 1863.

Stationed at Young's Point, Louisiana, April 10, 1863.

Stationed at Milliken's Bend, Louisiana, March-April 1863.

Stationed at Walnut Hill near Vicksburg, Mississippi, May-June 1863.

Stationed at Camp Sherman, Mississippi, July-August 1863.

Stationed at camp on Tennessee River, September-October 1863.

Stationed at Bellefonte Station, Alabama, November-December 1863.

Stationed at Camp Cleveland, Tennessee, January-February 1864.

Stationed at Cincinnati, Ohio, March-April 1864.

Stationed at Kenesaw Mountain, May-June 1864.

Stationed near Jonesborough, Georgia, July-August 1864.

Stationed at East Point, Georgia, September 19, 1864.
September 19.— Muster-out roll of a detachment of late Captain Frederick Schoening's Company (G), in the Thirty-seventh Regiment of Ohio Infantry Volunteers, commanded by late Colonel Siber, Lieutenant-Colonel L. von Blessingh, called into the service of the United States by the President at Camp Brown, Ohio (the place of general rendezvous) on August 3, 1861 to serve for the term of three years from the date of enrollment, unless sooner discharged, from December 31, 1863 (when last paid) to September 19, 1864 when mustered out. . . .

C. J. DICKEY,
First Lieutenant,
Thirteenth Infantry, Assistant Commissary of Musters,
Second Division, Fifteenth Army Corps, Mustering Officer.

Stationed at Cave Spring, Georgia, September-October 1864.

Stationed near Savannah, Georgia, November-December 1864.

Stationed at Lynch's Creek, South Carolina, January-February 1865.

Stationed at Rogers' Cross-Roads, North Carolina, March-April 1865.

Stationed on board steamer Argonaut, May-June 1865.

Company H

Stationed at camp near Cannelton, [West] Virginia, August 3, 1861.
August 3.— Muster-in roll of Captain Charles Messner's Company (H), in the Thirty-seventh Regiment of Ohio Volunteers,

commanded by Colonel Edward Siber, called into the service of the United States by the President from August 3, 1861 (date of this muster) for the term of three years, unless sooner discharged. . . .

CHARLES ANKELE,
Major,
Thirty-seventh Ohio Volunteers,
United States Army, Mustering Officer.

Stationed at Camp Montgomery, [West] Virginia, October 31, 1861.

Stationed at Clifton, [West] Virginia, November 1861-February 1862.

Stationed at mouth of Loup Creek, [West] Virginia, March-April 1862.

Stationed at Flat Top Tannery, [West] Virginia, May-June 1862.

Stationed at Fair Haven, July-August 1862.

Stationed at Brownstown, [West] Virginia, September-October 1862.

Stationed at Camp Piatt, [West] Virginia, November-December 1862.

Stationed at Young's Point, Louisiana, January-February 1863.

Stationed at Young's Point, Louisiana, April 10, 1863.

Stationed at Milliken's Bend, Louisiana, March-April 1863.

Stationed at Walnut Hill, Mississippi, May-June 1863.

Stationed at Camp Sherman, Mississippi, July-August 1863.

Stationed at camp near Tennessee River, September-October 1863.

Stationed at Bellefonte, Alabama, November-December 1863.

Stationed at Cleveland, East Tennessee, January-February 1864.

Stationed at Cincinnati, Ohio, March-April 1864.

Stationed at Kenesaw Mountain, Georgia, May-June 1864.

Stationed near Jonesborough, Georgia, July-August 1864.

Stationed at Cave Spring, Georgia, September-October 1864.

Stationed near Savannah, Georgia, November-December 1864.

Stationed at Lynch's Creek, South Carolina, January-February 1865.

Stationed on the field, North Carolina, March-April 1865.

Stationed on board steamer Argonaut near Memphis, Tennessee, May-June 1865.

Company I

Stationed at camp near Cannelton, [West] Virginia, August 3, 1861.

August 3.— Muster-in roll of Captain William J. C. Kraus' Company, in the Thirty-seventh Regiment of Ohio Volunteers, commanded by Colonel Edward Siber, called into the service of the United States by the President from August 3, 1861 (date of this muster) for the term of three years, unless sooner discharged. . . .

CHARLES ANKELE,
Thirty-seventh Regiment, Ohio Volunteers,
United States Army, Mustering Officer.

Stationed at Camp Montgomery, [West] Virginia, October 31, 1861.

Station not stated, November-December 1861.

Stationed at Clifton, [West] Virginia, January-February 1862.

Stationed at mouth of Loup, March-April 1862.

Stationed at Flat Top Mountain Tannery, May-June 1862.

Stationed at McCoy's Mill, Fayette County, [West] Virginia, July-August 1862.

Stationed at Brownstown, Kanawha, September-October 1862.

Stationed at Camp Piatt, [West] Virginia, November-December 1862.

Stationed at Young's Point, Louisiana, January-February 1863.

Stationed at Young's Point, Louisiana, April 10, 1863.

Stationed at Milliken's Bend, Louisiana, March-April 1863.

Stationed at Walnut Hill, rear of Vicksburg, Mississippi, May-June 1863.

Stationed at Camp Sherman, Mississippi, July-August 1863.

Stationed at camp on Tennessee River, September-October 1863.

Stationed in Alabama, November-December 1863.

Stationed at Cleveland, Tennessee, January-February 1864.

Stationed at Cincinnati, Ohio, March-April 1864.

Stationed near Kenesaw Mountain, Georgia, May-June 1864.

Stationed at Jonesborough, Georgia, July-August 1864.

Stationed at Cave Spring, Georgia, September-October 1864.

Stationed near Savannah, Georgia, November-December 1864.

Stationed in the field, South Carolina, January-February 1865.

Stationed at Rogers' Cross-Roads, North Carolina, March-April 1865.

Stationed on board the steamer Argonaut near Memphis, Tennessee, May-June 1865.

Company K

Stationed at Clifton, [West] Virginia, October 3-December 31, 1861.

Stationed at Camp Clifton, [West] Virginia, January-February 1862.

Stationed at mouth of Loup Creek, March-April 1862.

Stationed at Flat Top Mountain Tannery, May-June 1862.

Station not stated, July-August 1862.

Stationed at Brownstown, September-October 1862.

Stationed at Camp Piatt, [West] Virginia, November-December 1862.

Stationed at Young's Point, January-February 1863.

Stationed at Young's Point, April 10, 1863.

Stationed at Milliken's Bend, March-April 1863.

Stationed at Walnut Hill, May-June 1863.

Stationed at Camp Sherman, Mississippi, July-August 1863.

Stationed a camp near Tennessee River, September-October 1863.

Stationed at Bellefonte, Alabama, November-December 1863.

Stationed at Cleveland, Tennessee, January-February 1864.

Stationed at Cincinnati, Ohio, March-April 1864.

Stationed near Kenesaw Mountain, Georgia, May-June 1864.

Stationed at Jonesborough, Georgia, July-August 1864.

Stationed at Cave Spring, Georgia, September-October 1864.

Stationed near Savannah, Georgia, November-December 1864.

Stationed at Lynch's Creek, January-February 1865.

Stationed at Rogers' Cross-Roads, North Carolina, March-April 1865.

Stationed on board steamer Argonaut, May-June 1865.

[M594-Roll #149]

———

Record of Events for Thirty-eighth Ohio Infantry, August 1861-June 1865.

Field and Staff

Stationed at Nicholasville, Kentucky, September 10, 1861.
September 10.— Muster-in roll of field and staff officers in the Thirty-eighth Regiment of Ohio Infantry Volunteers, commanded by Colonel Edwin D. Bradley, called into service of the United States by the President from September 10, 1861 (date of this muster) for the term of three years, unless sooner discharged. . . .

[EPHRAIM] MORGAN WOOD,
Captain,
Fifteenth Infantry, United States Army, Mustering Officer.

Stationed at Nicholasville, Kentucky, September 10, 1861.
September 10.— Muster-in roll of band in the Thirty-eighth Regiment of Ohio Infantry Volunteers, commanded by Colonel E. D. Bradley, called into the service of the United States by the President from September 10, 1861 (date of this muster) for the term of three years, unless sooner discharged. . . .

E. MORGAN WOOD,
Captain,
Fifteenth Infantry, United States Army, Mustering Officer.

Stationed at Camp Wild Cat, Kentucky, August 10-October 31, 1861.

Stationed at Somerset, Kentucky, January 6, 1862.

Station not stated, January-February 1862.
The regiment has been constantly on duty.
January 26-February 1.— By the aid of rafts crossed the swollen waters of Fishing Creek; joined in the pursuit of the Rebel forces and entered the entrenchments of the enemy at Mill Springs with the gallant forces who fought at Logan's Cross-Roads the day previous. Returned to Somerset and from thence crossed the Cumberland River on February 1.
February 7-25.— Was recalled and marched from thence to Louisville, Kentucky, which city we reached on February 25. Left Louisville on boats that night.
March 4.— Arrived at Nashville, Tennessee and encamped four miles from the city. The regiment is in good condition, well disciplined, and well in every respect compared with any troops in the field.

Station not stated, March-April 1862.
The regiment has been constantly on duty, is in good condition, well disciplined, and well in every respect compared with any troops in the field.

Stationed at camp near Louisville, June 30-September 1, 1862.

Stationed at Nashville, Tennessee, September 9, 1862.
September 9.— Muster-out roll of regimental band in the Thirty-eighth Regiment of Ohio Infantry Volunteers, commanded by Colonel [Edward] H. Phelps, late Colonel E. D. Bradley, called into the service of the United States by the President at Camp Tremble, Ohio (the place of general rendezvous) on September 10, 1861 to serve for the term of three years from the date of enrollment, unless sooner discharged. The band was organized by Colonel E. D. Bradley at Defiance, Ohio in the month of September 1861 and marched then to Camp Tremble, where it arrived September 10, 1861, a distance of two miles. . . .

JOHN [HORNE] YOUNG,
Captain,
Fifteenth United States Infantry, Mustering Officer.

Stationed at Bowling Green, Kentucky, September-October 1862.

Stationed at Murfreesborough, Tennessee, November-December 1862.
November 1-December 30.— Commenced our march from Rolling Fork near Lebanon, Kentucky; proceeded to Bowling Green, Kentucky, from thence to Gallatin. While here our regiment was divided and did guard duty on the Louisville and Nashville Railroad from Gallatin, Tennessee to Saundersville, and three miles south. After laying in this condition from four to five weeks we were ordered to Nashville, encamped a few days near the town, when we marched out on the Franklin Pike some fifteen miles. We then proceeded to make our way across the country to the Murfreesborough Pike and on the night of December 30 camped on that pike three miles northeast of La Vergne.
December 31.— In the morning the memorable battle of Stone's River opened. This regiment marched out towards the scene of action and was much embarrassed by the returning soldiers, who were leaving the field in a demoralized condition. We soon took up a position in front supporting the Fourth Michigan Battery, which throughout the action did fearful execution. Our loss during the action was six wounded.

Since then we have been in our present camp.

Stationed near Murfreesborough, Tennessee, March 1, 1863.
January 1-March 1.— This regiment was in the lines of the First Brigade, First Division, Fourteenth Army Corps at the battle of Stone's River and until close of that battle kept their position. During this time we aided in supporting the artillery upon our left and our strength was frequently used as skirmishers and assaulting parties on our front. After the evacuation of Murfreesborough, in connection with the First Brigade, we advanced and went into camp beyond the city, where we have been lying during the months of January and February doing heavy picket duty in front and acting as escort to trains over to Nashville and on diverse other occasions besides numerous scouts, etc.

Stationed at camp near Triune, Tennessee, March-April 1863.
During the months of March and April this regiment moved from Murfreesborough, Tennessee to their present location, a distance of some fifteen miles. Since that time we have continued to perform heavy picket duty besides being busily engaged in constructing fortifications and earthworks which should properly command our position. We have been in numerous foraging expeditions within the enemy's lines and frequently skirmishes have taken place yet nothing like a general engagement. The health of the regiment is good.

Stationed at Camp Winford, Tennessee, May-June 1863.
June 30.— The day according to law that the field and staff of this regiment should have been mustered, the regiment was in the face of the enemy and on the march with all transportation left behind, hence could not be mustered until the present time. This muster roll shows the true state of the field and staff of the Thirty-eighth Regiment, Ohio Volunteer Infantry.

Stationed in the field, Tennessee, July-August 1863.
July 10.— Headquarters, First Brigade, Third Division, Fourteenth Army Corps, Department of Cumberland at camp in the field near Elk River, Tennessee.

Stationed at Chattanooga, Tennessee, September-October 1863.
September 1-20.— Crossed Tennessee River at mouth of Battle Creek and proceeded toward Chattanooga. When four miles from

Crawfish Springs were detailed as train guard. In compliance with orders, marched in charge of trains of Fourteenth and Twenty-first Army Corps to Chattanooga. Arrived on evening of September 20. Crossed the river and reported to post for duty. Were given charge of the disposition of trains, foraging for animals, etc. Picket detail of one lieutenant and fifteen men were engaged in battle of Chickamauga September 19 and 20.

September 23.— This regiment recrossed to Tennessee River; joined its brigade and has since been employed building fortifications, guarding supply trains to Stevenson and Bridgeport, and doing heavy picket duty.

Strength aggregate 675.

Station not stated, November-December 1863.

This regiment has been with the division during the months of November and December.

November 23.— With the division was ordered to the front.

November 25.— Until 12 m. maneuvered in the front of and on the enemy's center which was strongly posted on Missionary Ridge, two and one-half miles in front of Chattanooga. At 3 p.m. began to advance on the enemy's position. The division was ordered to storm the works on the ridge, the regiment formed the extreme left of the line, advancing under a heavy fire of artillery and musketry, drove the enemy from his chosen position with great loss. Our loss is two commissioned officers killed (Colonel E. H. Phelps and John Lewis, Second Lieutenant, Company A) and three wounded, Captain [Edgar M.] Denchar, Lieutenant [Abram W.] Burgoyne and Lieutenant Joseph Newman, Company H. The enlisted men killed were seven and thirty-five wounded.

November 26.— The regiment followed after the enemy early in the morning, driving him through Ringgold, Georgia.

November 29-December 31.— Returned to Chattanooga and have remained in camp up to December 31, when they started home on furlough by virtue of having reenlisted.

Station not stated, January-February 1864.

Marched to Bridgeport, Alabama, where it was furnished transportation by railroad to Nashville, Tennessee, proceeding thence to Cairo, Illinois by water. After three days' delay at Cairo, transportation was furnished by railroad and the regiment proceeded via Odin, Illinois; Cincinnati, Ohio to Toledo, Ohio,

where it disbanded and each company proceeded to its place of original organization. Much suffering and some sickness was occasioned by the intensity of the cold. One man, a member of Company F, died at Cairo, Illinois.
February 17-29.— The regiment concentrated at Toledo, Ohio; proceeded by railroad to Camp Cleveland, Ohio. After four days' delay, proceeded by railroad via Columbus and Cincinnati, Ohio; Louisville, Kentucky and Nashville, Tennessee to Chattanooga, where we arrived February 29.

Stationed at Ringgold, Georgia, March-April 1864.

Stationed in the field near Marietta, Georgia, May-June 1864.

Stationed in the field, Georgia, July-August 1864.

Station not stated, September-October 1864.

Stationed near Savannah, Georgia, November-December 1864.

Stationed at Goldsborough, North Carolina, January-February 1865.

Stationed at Page's Station, North Carolina, March-April 1865.

Stationed near Louisville, Kentucky, May-June 1865.

Regiment

Station not stated, October 1861.

Stationed at Danville, Kentucky, except Company A at Lebanon, Kentucky, November 1861.
November 13-15.— Marched from London to Crab Orchard and encamped.
November 20-21.— Marched to Danville and encamped.
November 27.— Marched towards Lebanon, twelve miles, and encamped.
November 29-30.— Marched towards Somerset and encamped three miles north of Stanford.

Stationed at Somerset, Kentucky, except Company A at Lebanon, Kentucky, December 1861-January 1862.

Station not stated, February 1862.

Stationed near Columbia, Tennessee, March 1862.

Stationed at Camp Shiloh, April 1862.

Stationed at camp south of Corinth, Mississippi, May 1862.

Stationed at Tuscumbia, Alabama, June 1862.

Stationed near Winchester, Tennessee, July 1862.

Station not stated, September-December 1862.

Stationed at camp near Murfreesborough, Tennessee, January 1863.
December 31, 1862.— In the morning the regiment lay with the remainder of the brigade at La Vergne, some six miles distant from our advance lines in front of Murfreesborough. We were ordered hastily forward at sunrise and reached the field just as the right wing had succeeded in rallying from the surprise and confusion into which they had been thrown that morning. Advancing to the front we were assigned position on the left of the right wing near the center of the lines we held this position during the continuation of the battle and though not immediately engaged as a body, still occupied a responsible and at times dangerous position.

Stationed at Murfreesborough, Tennessee, February 1863.

Stationed at camp near Triune, Tennessee, March 1863.

Stationed at camp near Triune, Tennessee, April-May 1863.

Stationed at Camp Winford, Tennessee, June 1863.

Station not stated, August 1863.

Stationed at Chattanooga, Tennessee, September-October 1863.

Stationed at Chattanooga, Tennessee, November 1863.

This regiment has been with the division to which it is attached during this month (November).

November 23-25.— With the division, was ordered out and until 12 m. of November 25, marched and countermarched in front of the enemy's line who were strongly posted on Missionary Ridge two and one-half miles in front of Chattanooga. At 3 p.m. began to advance upon their works. This regiment, with the brigade, stormed the enemy's position and drove them with severe loss from the ridge below. . . . Have marched during the engagement and rout of the enemy about sixty miles.

Stationed at Napoleon, Ohio, December 1863.

Station not stated, January-February 1864.

Stationed at Ringgold, Georgia, March 1864.

Station not stated, April 1864.

Stationed at Burnt Hickory, May 1864.

May 10.— The regiment left Ringgold, Georgia; marched ten miles and encamped on a hill fronting Buzzard Roost.

May 11.— Left the railroad and by a succession of marches through Snake Creek Gap, arrived in front of Resaca, Georgia.

May 13-15.— It participated in the fight near that place, losing one man, First Sergeant Leonard Sindle, killed, and Private Lyman Skeels and Corporal John Kane, wounded.

From Resaca the regiment moved along the line of the Chattanooga and Atlanta Railroad through Calhoun, Adairsville, and Kingston as train guard. From Kingston the regiment again diverged from the railroad, almost daily skirmishing with the rear guard of the enemy until we arrived at this place.

Stationed near Marietta, June 1864.

June 1.— The regiment moved from Burnt Hickory, Georgia, moving in the direction of Dallas, Georgia.

June 2-14.— Near this place it, together with the division to which it belonged, engaged the enemy, and after five days skirmishing he was compelled to evacuate his position. On June 4 Hiram Huyk, Private, killed; John B. Brace, Private, Company D, wounded; Daniel Stevens, Private, Company G, wounded; James King, Private, Company K, wounded; James W. Graham, Private, Company G, wounded; William A. Carnakun, First Sergeant, Company E, wounded. This regiment, with the division, pursuing in the direction of Acworth, Georgia, where the enemy was again engaged on June 14. By continued pressing he was again compelled to fall to the Kenesaw Mountain, taking a position on Kenesaw Point in front of which the regiment, with the brigade and division, took position.

June 16.— John Rogers, Private, Company F, was wounded.

June 18.— Orion Cameron, Private, Company D, was wounded.

June 21.— Thomas Lonegan, Private, Company G, was wounded.

June 22.— David Kimkly, Private, Company C, wounded; John S. Cameron, Lieutenant, Company D (appointed but not mustered), wounded; Edward Metz, Lieutenant, Company G, wounded; Charles Vannes, Private, Company I, wounded; Lewis Fashbaugh, Private, Company I, wounded; Joel Young, Private, Company I, wounded; Jeff Milke, Private, Company I, wounded; John Hall, Corporal, Company I, wounded.

June 23.— William Tinney, Corporal, Company C, wounded; Daniel Lewis, Corporal, Company E, wounded; Washington Miser, Corporal, Company A, wounded; Samuel Bosh, Private, Company C, wounded; John A. Ginton, Private, [illegible].

June 30.— We had gained a position to the right and well to the rear of this point until we moved together with the division, about one-half mile to the right and about two miles from Marietta.

Stationed near Atlanta, Georgia, July 1864.

July 2.— It engaged the enemy in his works by skirmishing until night, when he evacuated his position, moving towards the Chattahoochee River. Took part in the pursuit of the enemy and finally drove him across the river, where the regiment with the division crossed.

July 7.— Jacob A. John, Private, Company K, was wounded in head slightly, returned to duty. Henry Whitmer, Private, Company B, wounded in shoulder and is in general hospital.

July 9.— August Prince, Private, Company C, wounded in hip severely and is in general hospital. German, Private, Company I, wounded in side severely and in general hospital. Michael Bost, Private, Company B, wounded in thigh severely and in general hospital. Amos Sowers, Corporal, Company C, wounded [illegible] slightly and returned to duty.
July 17.— Being on the front line, it moved in conjunction with the whole Army, which after severe fighting on the left succeeded in driving the enemy from his position.
July 21.— Daniel Climer, Private, Company B, wounded in head slightly and in general hospital.
July 22.— Steadily advanced until the enemy offered resistance within one and a half miles of Atlanta, where it still remains. Daniel Calkins, Company C, wounded in back severely and in general hospital.
July 23.— Franklin Stoy, Company E, wounded in leg severely and in general hospital. John Gideon, Company A, wounded in leg severely and in general hospital. George W. Myers, Private, Company E, wounded in foot slightly and returned to duty. Franklin Green, Company E, wounded in arm severely and in general hospital.
July 28.— James McQuillen, Company I, wounded in thigh severely and is in general hospital.

Station not stated, August 1864.
August 1.— This regiment was in the trenches in front of Atlanta which place it had occupied since July 22.
August 3.— The regiment moved about five miles to the right.
August 27.— Took position where it remained, but in the meantime we engaged in several skirmishes and charges, etc., until the regiment moved by the right crossing the Atlanta and West Point Railroad, marching in same circle around Atlanta.
August 31.— Struck the Macon and Western Central Railroad about fourteen miles south of Atlanta.

Stationed near Atlanta, Georgia, September 1864.

Stationed near Rome, Georgia, October 1864.
October 3.— The Thirty-eighth Regiment, Ohio Veteran Volunteer Infantry in pursuance with orders from General [William Tecumseh] Sherman left Atlanta, Georgia and entered upon the

campaign against the Rebel General [John Bell] Hood, who was operating in our —— with the view of cutting our communications with Chattanooga. This day the regiment marched eight miles, going into camp about 11 p.m., a terrific rainstorm prevailing.

October 4.— Marched seven miles with nothing worthy of note transpiring.

October 5.— Marched twelve miles and went into camp at 10 p.m.

October 6.— Marched five miles and encamped at noon.

October 7.— Went on a reconnaissance to Lost Mountain. Could find no traces of the enemy but could hear heavy cannonading to our right. In the evening returned to camp, having marched about ten miles.

October 8.— Marched six miles and went in camp near Acworth, Georgia.

October 10.— We remained until evening, when we were again ordered out and marched fifteen miles, camping on the Etowah River, having marched all night.

October 11.— Marched eighteen miles and went into camp near Kingston, Georgia.

October 12.— Marched fifteen miles in the direction of Rome.

October 13.— Lay in camp until 8 p.m., then marched eight miles in the direction of Calhoun.

October 14.— Marched eighteen miles, passing through Calhoun and encamping near Resaca.

October 15.— Marched ten miles and encamped on Red Vine Mountain.

October 16.— Marched eight miles passing through a portion of Snake Creek Gap.

October 17.— Lay in camp.

October 18.— Marched fifteen miles, crossing Waldron's Ridge.

October 19.— Marched eight miles and went into camp near Summerville on the Alabama Road.

October 20.— Marched twenty miles and encamped near Gaylesville.

October 29.— We remained until we marched thirty-one miles in the direction of Rome.

October 30.— Went to Rome, a distance of seven miles.

Stationed near Louisville, Georgia, November 1864.
November 2.— We encamped at Rome until the Thirty-eighth Regiment, Ohio Veteran Volunteer Infantry marched to Kingston, Georgia.
November 12.— It was encamped until, in conformity with the general movement southward, it marched sixteen miles in the direction of Atlanta, passing through Calhoun.
November 13.— Marched nine miles, passing through Acworth and encamping near Big Shanty.
November 14.— Marched twenty-three miles, passing through Marietta and encamping on Chattahoochee River.
November 15.— Marched into Atlanta, distance eight miles.
November 16.— Left Atlanta; marched fourteen miles, passing through Decatur.
November 17.— Marched fifteen miles, passing though Lithonia and Conyers Station.
November 18.— Marched eight miles, crossing Yellow River and passing through Covington.
November 19.— Marched twelve miles, passing through Sandtown.
November 20.— Marched eighteen miles.
November 21.— Marched eight miles, no opposition.
November 22.— Marched ten miles.
November 23.— Marched ten miles and encamped near Milledgeville, Georgia.
November 24.— Moved into the city.
November 25.— The regiment did provost duty until morning when the movement south was recommenced. The regiment moved fifteen miles this day.
November 26.— Marched fifteen miles, passing through Sandersville.
November 27.— Marched twenty-five miles during the day. Crossed the Ogeechee River. The Thirty-eight Regiment during the day was detached from the command and sent about five miles to the left for the purpose of burning a bridge across the Rocky Comfort Creek. This was successfully accomplished in the evening.
November 28.— The regiment rejoined the command in the morning with slight skirmishing during the day.

November 29-30.— Marched ten miles; crossed the Rocky Comfort Creek and passed through Louisville, Georgia going into camp about two miles from the village, where we remained during November 30.

Station not stated, December 1864.

Stationed in the field, Georgia, January 1865.
January 1-20.— The regiment was stationed near Savannah, Georgia until January 20, when the camp was broken up and the regiment entered upon the South Carolina campaign. This day the troops marched seven miles, when on account of the impassable condition of the roads, the regiment encamped at Turkey Hill.
January 25.— It remained there until it marched ten miles.
January 26.— Marched ten miles and encamped at Springfield, Georgia.
January 27-February 5.— Marched ten miles and encamped near Sister's Ferry, Georgia, where the regiment remained until February 5.

Station not stated, February-May 1865.

Stationed at Louisville, Kentucky, June 1865.

Company A

Stationed at Defiance, Ohio, September 10, 1861.
September 10.— Muster-in roll of Captain Charles Greenwood's Company, in the Thirty-eighth Regiment of Ohio Infantry Volunteers, commanded by Colonel E. D. Bradley, called into the service of the United States by the President from September 10, 1861 (date of this muster) for the term of three years, unless sooner discharged. . . .

E. MORGAN WOOD,
Captain,
Fifteenth Infantry, United States Army, Mustering Officer.

Stationed at Camp Wild Cat, Kentucky, August 26-October 31, 1861.

Stationed at Lebanon, December 31, 1861.

Station not stated, January-February 1862.

Stationed at Corinth, Mississippi, March-April 1862.

Stationed near Tuscumbia, Alabama, May-June 1862.

Stationed at Louisville, Kentucky, July-August 1862.

Stationed at Murfreesborough, Tennessee, September-December 1862.

Stationed at Murfreesborough, Tennessee, January-February 1863.
January 2.— At night at battle of Stone's River the company was ordered to the front as skirmishers, attacked the enemy and in the engagement had four men severely wounded.

Stationed at Triune, Tennessee, March-April 1863.

Stationed at camp near Elk River, Tennessee, May-June 1863.

Stationed at Battle Creek, Tennessee, July-August 1863.

Stationed at Chattanooga, Tennessee, September-October 1863.

Stationed at Ringgold, Georgia, November-December 1863.
November 25.— The company, with the regiment, was engaged in the battle of Missionary Ridge. Loss in action were second lieutenant killed and four enlisted men wounded.
December 31.— Twenty-eight men of the company reenlisted as veteran volunteers and started from Chattanooga on furlough to Ohio.

Stationed at Ringgold, Georgia, January-April 1864.

Stationed near Marietta, Georgia, May-June 1864.

Stationed near Jonesborough, Georgia, July-August 1864.

Stationed at Rome, Georgia, September-October 1864.

Stationed near Savannah, Georgia, November-December 1864.

Stationed in the field in South Carolina, January-February 1865.

Stationed at Page's Station, North Carolina, March-April 1865.

Stationed near Louisville, Kentucky, May-June 1865.

Company B

Stationed at Nicholasville, Kentucky, September 10, 1861.
September 10.— Muster-in roll of Captain William A. Choate's Company, in the Thirty-eighth Regiment of Ohio Infantry Volunteers, commanded by Colonel E. D. Bradley, called into the service of the United States by the President from September 10, 1861 (date of this muster) for the term of three years, unless sooner discharged. The company was organized by Captain William A. Choate at Napoleon, Ohio in the month of August and marched thence to Camp Tremble, where it arrived August 22, a distance of fifteen miles. . . .

E. MORGAN WOOD,
Captain,
Fifteenth Infantry, United States Army, Mustering Officer.

Stationed at Ringgold, Georgia, August 19-October 31, 1861.

Stationed at Somerset, Kentucky, November-December 1861.

Stationed at Camp Thomas near Nashville, Tennessee, January-February 1862.
September 23-25, 1861.— Left Camp Tremble, Defiance, Ohio in the extreme northwestern portion of the state by rail and arrived at Camp Dennison near Cincinnati, Ohio September 25.
October 2.— Left Camp Dennison; crossed the Ohio River at Cincinnati and came by rail to Nicholasville, Kentucky, a distance of 145 miles.
October 3-18.— Reached there and left there for Camp Dick Robinson October 18.

October 21-23.— Left Camp Dick Robinson and made a forced march to Camp Wild Cat, where we arrived the day after the victory of General [Albin Francisco] Schoepf over [Felix Kirk] Zollicoffer, which battle was fought October 22.

October 27-28.— Left Camp Wild Cat for Camp Calvert, eight miles distant. Alarm at night, extras thrown forward with the regiment to London, three miles distant, where we commenced fortifying in the morning.

November 15.— Was there engaged in fortifying and reconnaissances toward Cumberland Gap until, with the other regiments, we made the "celebrated retreat" from London to Crab Orchard, thereby suffering much from exposure and fatigue, causing much sickness and some deaths.

November 20.— Left Crab Orchard for Lebanon. Stopped at Danville and was paid off.

November 27.— Left Danville for Lebanon. Was ordered back same night to Somerset, via Danville and Stanford, which place we reached after a forced march December 2. Halted a few minutes and then marched to the Cumberland River the same day. The last day we marched twenty-one miles in seven hours but the flagging spirits of the men were buoyed up by the booming cannon of Zollicoffer's forces who were cannonading Colonel Hoskins' Regiment across the river. The Thirty-eighth was the first regiment to relieve him.

The company was constantly on duty from that time to the battle of Mill Springs. Suffered much from cold and exposure, on picket duty and reconnaissances, having frequently had to wade Fishing Creek, whose swift waters reached often to the arms of the men.

January 19, 1862.— Did not participate in the battle but by the aid of ropes, crossed the swollen waters of the latter creek, joined the pursuit of the Rebel forces and entered the entrenchments of the enemy with the gallant forces who fought at the cross-roads. Returned to Somerset and from thence was ordered into Tennessee.

February 1.— Crossed the Cumberland River.

February 7-25.— Was recalled and marched from thence to Louisville, Kentucky by way of Crab Orchard, Stanford, Danville, Bardstown, which city we reached February 25. The march was a long one (over 150 miles) and the company suffered much from the cold rains and snow storms. Had to leave a number [of men] sick at Somerset and Lebanon so that when we left Louisville for Nashville on boats at night, had but sixty-four enlisted men for duty. The men were much reduced by hard service at Somerset.

Station not stated, March-April 1862.
March 4.— Reached Nashville and encamped four miles from the [illegible]. Came to this city by boats by the Ohio and Cumberland Rivers. The company, since in service, has ever been on active duty. Has traveled by rail over 400 miles, by water over 600 miles and marched by land on the aggregate nearly 600 miles. The company is now in good condition, the well men in the best of condition, the sick rapidly recovering their strength. The discipline of the company is good and their services are the best evidences of their efficiency. Though on active duty ever since their organization, are well drilled, and will in every respect compare favorably with any troops in the field.

Stationed at Ringgold, Georgia, May-August 1862.

Stationed near Murfreesborough, Tennessee, August 31-December 31, 1862.

Stationed at Murfreesborough, Tennessee, January-February 1863.

Stationed at Triune, Tennessee, April 10, 1863.

Station not stated, March-April 1863.

Stationed at Camp Winford, May-June 1863.

Station not stated, July-August 1863.

Stationed at Chattanooga, Tennessee, September-October 1863.

Station not stated, November 1863-February 1864.

Stationed at Ringgold, Georgia, March-April 1864.

Stationed in the field near Marietta, Georgia, May-June 1864.

Stationed at Jonesborough, July-August 1864.

Stationed near Savannah, Georgia, November-December 1864.

Stationed near Raleigh, North Carolina, March-April 1865.

Stationed near Louisville, Kentucky, May-June 1865.

Company C

Stationed at Nicholasville, Kentucky, September 10, 1861.
September 10.— Muster-in roll of Captain [David S.] Tallerday's Company, in the Thirty-eighth Regiment of Ohio Infantry Volunteers, commanded by Colonel Edwin D. Bradley, called into the service of the United States by the President from September 10, 1861 (date of this muster) for the term of three years, unless sooner discharged. . . .

E. MORGAN WOOD,
Captain,
Fifteenth Infantry, United States Army, Mustering Officer.

Station not stated, September 10-October 31, 1861.

Stationed at Somerset, Kentucky, November-December 1861.

Stationed at Camp Thomas near Nashville, Tennessee, January-February 1862.

Stationed at Camp Muddy Creek, Tennessee, March-April 1862.

Stationed at camp near Tuscumbia, Alabama, May-June 1862.

Stationed at Winchester, Tennessee, July-August 1862.

Station not stated, September-December 1862.

Stationed at Murfreesborough, Tennessee, January-February 1863.

Stationed at Triune, Tennessee, March-April 1863.

Stationed at camp in the field near Elk River, Tennessee, May-June 1863.

Stationed at Camp Hog Valley, July-August 1863.

Stationed at Chattanooga, Tennessee, September 1863-February 1864.

Stationed at Ringgold, Georgia, March-April 1864.

Stationed in the field near Marietta, Georgia, May-June 1864.

Stationed in the field near Jonesborough, Georgia, July-August 1864.

Stationed near Savannah, Georgia, November-December 1864.

Stationed in the field, South Carolina, January-February 1865.

Stationed at Raleigh, North Carolina, March-April 1865.

Stationed near Louisville, Kentucky, May-June 1865.

Company D

Stationed at Nicholasville, Kentucky, September 10, 1861.
September 10.— Muster-in roll of Captain Benjamin Miller's Company, in the Thirty-eighth Regiment of Ohio Volunteers, commanded by Colonel E. D. Bradley, called into the service of the United States by the President from September 10, 1861 (date of this muster) for the term of three years, unless sooner discharged. The company was organized by Captain Benjamin Miller at Evansport, Ohio in the months of August and September and marched thence to Camp Tremble, where it arrived September 2, a distance of fourteen miles. . . .

E. MORGAN WOOD,
Captain,
Fifteenth Infantry, United States Army, Mustering Officer.

Stationed at Louisville, Kentucky, September 10-October 31, 1861.

Stationed at Somerset, Kentucky, November-December 1861.

Station not stated, January-February 1862.
September 23-25, 1861.— Left Camp Tremble, Defiance, Ohio in the extreme northern part of the state by rail and arrived at Camp Dennison near Cincinnati, Ohio September 25.
October 3-4.— Left Camp Dennison and crossed the river to Covington, Kentucky. Came by rail to Nicholasville, Kentucky, a distance of 145 miles, and reached there October 4.
October 18.— Left there for Camp Dick Robinson.
October 21-23.— Left Camp Dick Robinson and made a forced march to Camp Wild Cat, where we arrived the day after the victory of General Schoepf over Zollicoffer which battle was fought on October 22.
October 27-28.— Left Camp Wild Cat for Camp Calvert, eight miles distant. Alarm at night, was thrown forward with the regiment to London, three miles distance, when we commenced fortifying in the morning.
November 15.— Was there engaged in fortifying and reconnoitering until, with other Ohio [troops] we marched and drew back to Crab Orchard, suffering much from exposure and fatigue causing much sickness and some deaths.
November 20.— Left Crab Orchard for Lebanon. Stopped at Danville and was paid off.
November 27-December 2.— Left for Lebanon and ordered back same night to Somerset via Danville and Stanford, which place we reached after a forced march December 2. Halted a few moments and thence marched to the Cumberland River, making a march of two miles, the last day twenty-one miles in seven hours but the flagging spirits of the men were buoyed up by the booming of cannon of Zollicoffer's forces who were cannonading Colonel Hoskins' Regiment across the river. The Thirty-eighth was the first regiment to relieve him.

The company was constantly on duty from that time to the battle of Mill Springs. Suffered much from cold and exposure on picket duty and reconnaissances having frequently to wade Fishing Creek, whose swift waters often reached to the arms of the men.

January 19, 1862.— Did not participate in the battle but by the aid of ropes, crossed the swollen water of Fishing Creeks. Joined in the pursuit of the Rebel forces and entered the entrenchments of the enemy with the gallant forces who fought at the cross-roads. Returned to Somerset and from thence was ordered into Tennessee.

February 1.— Crossed the Cumberland River.

February 7-25.— Was recalled and marched from thence to Louisville, Kentucky by way of Crab Orchard, Stanford, Danville, and Bardstown, which city was reached February 25. The march was a long one over 150 miles and the company suffered much from the hard pains and snow storms. Had to leave men at Somerset, Danville, and Lebanon so that when we left Louisville for Nashville on boats the night of February 25, had but thirty-nine enlisted men for duty. The men were much reduced by hard service at Somerset.

March 4.— Reached Nashville; encamped four miles from the city. Came to the city by boats by the Ohio and Cumberland Rivers.

The company, since in service, has ever been in actual duty. Has traveled by rail over 400 miles, by water over 600 miles and marched by land in the aggregate nearly 600 miles. The company is now in good condition, the men in the best of condition, the sick rapidly recovering their strength. The discipline of the company is good though in active duty ever since their organization are well drilled and will in every respect compare with any troops probably in the field.

Station not stated, March-April 1862.

Stationed near Louisville, Kentucky, July-August 1862.

Stationed at Bowling Green, Kentucky, September-October 1862.

Stationed at Murfreesborough, November 1862-February 1863.

Stationed at camp near Triune, Tennessee, March-April 1863.

Stationed in the field, Tennessee, May-June 1863.

Stationed at Battle Creek, Tennessee, July-August 1863.

Stationed at Chattanooga, Tennessee, September-October 1863.

Station not stated, November 1863-February 1864.

Stationed in the field near Atlanta, Georgia, June 30, 1864.

Stationed eighteen miles south of Atlanta, Georgia, July-August 1864.

Stationed at Ringgold, Georgia, March-April 1864.

Stationed near Savannah, Georgia, November-December 1864.

Stationed near Raleigh, North Carolina, March-April 1865.

Stationed near Louisville, Kentucky, May-June 1865.

Company E

Stationed at Nicholasville, Kentucky, September 10, 1861.
September 10.— Muster-in roll of Captain Robert McQuilkin's Company, in the Thirty-eighth Regiment of Ohio Infantry Volunteers, commanded by Colonel E. D. Bradley, called into the service of the United States by the President from September 10, 1861 (date of this muster) for the term of three years, unless sooner discharged. The company was organized by Captain R. McQuilkin at Bryan, Ohio in the month of September and marched thence to Camp Tremble, Ohio, where it arrived September 8, a distance of twenty miles. . . .

E. MORGAN WOOD,
Captain,
Fifteenth Infantry, United States Army, Mustering Officer.

Stationed at Camp Wild Cat, Kentucky, September 3-October 31, 1861.

Stationed at Somerset, Kentucky, November-December 1861.

Station not stated, January-April 1862.

Stationed at Tuscumbia, Alabama, May-June 1862.

Stationed at Louisville, Kentucky, [July] 1-August 31, 1862.

Stationed at Bowling Green, Kentucky, September-October 1862.

Stationed at Murfreesborough, Tennessee, November 1862-February 1863.

Stationed at Triune, Tennessee, March-April 1863.

Stationed at Camp Winford, Tennessee, May-June 1863.
June 30.— The day according to law that this company should have been mustered, it was in the face of the enemy and on the march with all transportation left behind, hence could not be mustered until the present time. This muster roll shows the state of the company.

[THOMAS] R. THATCHER,
Lieutenant,
Seventeenth Regiment, Ohio Volunteer Infantry,
Assistant Adjutant and Inspector-General,
First Brigade, Third Division.

Stationed at camp on Battle Creek, Tennessee, July-August 1863.
July 10.— Headquarters, First Brigade, Third Division Army Corps, Department of the Cumberland. Camp on Elk River, Tennessee.

Stationed at Chattanooga, Tennessee, September-October 1863.

Station not stated, November 1863-February 1864.

Stationed at Ringgold, Georgia, March-April 1864.

Stationed in the field, Georgia, near Marietta, May-June 1864.

Stationed in the field, July-August 1864.

Stationed near Rome, Georgia, September-October 1864.

Stationed near Savannah, Georgia, November-December 1864.

Stationed in the field, North Carolina, March-April 1865.

Stationed near Louisville, Kentucky, May-June 1865.

Company F

Stationed at Nicholasville, Kentucky, September 10, 1861.
September 10.— Muster-in roll of Captain John H. Adams' Company, in the Thirty-eighth Regiment of Ohio Infantry Volunteers, commanded by Colonel E. D. Bradley, called into the service of the United States by the President from September 10, 1861 (date of this muster) for the term of three years, unless sooner discharged. The company was organized by Captain John H. Adams at Royal Oak, Ohio in the month of August and marched thence to Defiance, where it arrived August 26, a distance of seventeen miles. . . .

E. MORGAN WOOD,
Captain,
Fifteenth Infantry, United States Army, Mustering Officer.

Stationed at Camp Wild Cat, Kentucky, August 19-October 31, 1861.

Stationed at Somerset, Kentucky, November-December 1861.

Stationed at Camp Thomas near Nashville, Tennessee, January-February 1862.
This company has been with the regiment from its first organization and did its duty in every respect, marching from seven to twenty-five miles per day.

Stationed at Camp Muddy Creek, Tennessee, March-April 1862.

Stationed at camp near Tuscumbia, Alabama, May-June 1862.

Stationed at Louisville, Kentucky, [June] 30-August 31, 1862.

Stationed at Bowling Green, Kentucky, September-October 1862.

Stationed at Murfreesborough, Tennessee, November 1862-February 1863.

Stationed at camp at Triune, Tennessee, April 13, 1863.

Stationed at camp near ——, March-April 1863.

Stationed at camp in the field near Elk River, Tennessee, May-June 1863.

Stationed at Camp Battle Creek, Tennessee, July-August 1863.

Stationed at camp near Chattanooga, September-October 1863.

Stationed at Chattanooga, Tennessee, November-December 1863.
November 25.— This company, in connection with the regiment, took action in the engagement with the enemy at Missionary Ridge near Chattanooga in which it sustained a loss of two killed and five wounded, two of which have since died of their wounds.

Stationed at Chattanooga, Tennessee, January-February 1864.

Stationed at Ringgold, Georgia, March-April 1864.

Stationed in the field, Georgia, May-August 1864.

Stationed near Rome, Georgia, September-October 1864.

Stationed near Savannah, Georgia, November-December 1864.

Stationed at Goldsborough, North Carolina, January-February 1865.

Stationed in the field in North Carolina, March-April 1865.

Stationed at Louisville, Kentucky, May-June 1865.

Company G

Stationed at Nicholasville, Kentucky, September 10, 1861.
September 10.— Muster-in roll of Captain [William] Irving's Company, in the Thirty-eighth Regiment of Ohio Infantry Volunteers, commanded by Colonel Edwin D. Bradley, called into the service of the United States by the President from September 10, 1861 (date of this muster) for the term of three years, unless sooner discharged. The company was organized by Henry C. Boutin at Defiance in the month of September and marched thence to Camp Tremble, where it arrived September 5, a distance of one mile. . . .

E. MORGAN WOOD,
Captain,
Fifteenth Infantry, United States Army, Mustering Officer.

Stationed at Nicholasville, Kentucky, September-October 1861.

Stationed at Somerset, Kentucky, November-December 1861.

Stationed at Camp Thomas near Nashville, Tennessee, January-February 1862.
September 23-25, 1861.— Left Camp Tremble, Defiance, Ohio by rail. Arrived at Camp Dennison.
October 2-3.— Left Camp Dennison. Crossed the Ohio River at Cincinnati. Came by rail to Nicholasville, Kentucky, distance 112 miles, reached October 3.
October 18.— Left for Camp Dick Robinson.
October 21-23.— Left Camp Dick Robinson; made a forced march to Camp Wild Cat, when we arrived the day after the victory of General Schoepf over Zollicoffer, which battle was fought on October 22.
October 27.— Left Camp Wild Cat for Camp Calvert, eight miles distance. At night an alarm was given and in the morning before day, we were thrown forward with the regiment to London, three miles distant, when we immediately commenced fortifying.
November 15.— Was then engaged in fortifying and reconnoitering with other regiments towards Cumberland Gap until, with other regiments, we made the celebrated retreat from London to

Crab Orchard, suffering much from exposure and fatigue, causing much sickness and some deaths.
November 20.— Left Crab Orchard for Lebanon. Stopped at Danville and was paid off.
November 27.— Left Danville for Lebanon. Was ordered back the same night to Somerset via Danville and Stanford, which place we reached by a forced march.
December 2.— Halted a few moments and then marched to the Cumberland River the same day. The last day we marched twenty-one miles in seven hours but the flagging spirit of the men were buoyed up by the booming cannon of Zollicoffer's forces who were cannonading Colonel Hoskins' Regiment (Twelfth Kentucky) across the river. The Thirty-eighth was the First Regiment to relieve him. The company was constantly on duty from that time to the battle of Mill Springs, suffered much from cold and exposure on picket duty and reconnaissances, having been made frequently to wade Fishing Creek, when swift water was often to the armpits of the men.
January 19, 1862.— Did not participate in the battle but by the aid of ropes, crossed the swollen water of the creek, joined in the pursuit of the Rebels and entered the entrenchments of the enemy, with the gallant forces who fought at the cross-roads. Returned to Somerset and from thence was ordered into Tennessee.
February 1.— Crossed the Cumberland River.
February 7-25.— Was recalled and marched from thence to Louisville, Kentucky via Crab Orchard, Stanford, Danville, Lebanon, and Bardstown, when we arrived February 25. The march was a long one (over 150 miles) and the company suffered much from the cold rains and snow storms. Had to leave numbers sick at Somerset and Lebanon and when we left Louisville on the boats for this place (Nashville, Tennessee) we reported sixty-one men for duty, which was the night of February 25.
March 4.— Came by the way of the Ohio and Cumberland Rivers to Nashville, where we arrived and encamped about four miles from the city.

The company, since it has been in the service has been constantly on active duty, has traveled by rail over 400 miles, by water over 600 miles and marched by land in the aggregate nearly 600 miles. The company at present is in good condition, the sick are recovering generally, three have returned since we arrived here. The discipline of the company is good and though on active duty ever since their organization, were well drilled and will compare favorably with any troops in the field.

Stationed at Camp Corinth, Mississippi, March-April 1862.

Stationed at Tuscumbia, May-June 1862.

Stationed at Louisville, Kentucky, July-August 1862.

Stationed at camp near Bowling Green, Kentucky, September-October 1862.

Stationed at camp near Murfreesborough, Tennessee, November 1862-February 1863.

Stationed at Triune, Tennessee, April 10, 1863.

Stationed at camp near Triune, Tennessee, March-April 1863.

Station not stated, May-June 1863.
[For record of events, see Company F.]

Station not stated, July-August 1863.

Stationed at Chattanooga, Tennessee, September-October 1863.

Stationed at Chattanooga, Tennessee, November-December 1863.
November 23.— The regiment to which my company belongs marched out of the works at Chattanooga, Tennessee to attack the enemy then in possession of Lookout Mountain and Missionary Ridge.
November 25.— My company was deployed as skirmishers and drove the enemy's pickets to their works on the ridge. In this skirmish we lost Sergeant Daniel Bishop, wounded, and Private Joseph W. Scott, wounded.
November 26.— We followed the retreating enemy to Ringgold, Georgia but did not arrive in time to participate in the battle.
November 29.— We remained at Ringgold and during our stay there we took a part in tearing up and destroying the railroad until we returned to Chattanooga.

December 4.— Private Joseph W. Scott died from the effects of his wound.
December 11.— The regiment reenlisted as retired volunteers.
December 31.— Started for Ohio, where the regiment is to have thirty days' furlough after arriving in the state.

Stationed at Chattanooga, Tennessee, January-February 1864.

Stationed at Ringgold, Georgia, March-April 1864.

Stationed near Atlanta, Georgia, May-June 1864.

Stationed in the field, Georgia, July-August 1864.

Stationed at Rome, Georgia, September-October 1864.

Stationed at Savannah, Georgia, November-December 1864.

Stationed in the field, South Carolina, January-February 1865.

Stationed near Raleigh, North Carolina, March-April 1865.

Stationed near Louisville, Kentucky, May-June 1865.

Company H

Stationed at Nicholasville, Kentucky, September 10, 1861.
September 10.— Muster-in roll of Captain William Stoug's Company, in the Thirty-eighth Regiment of Ohio Infantry Volunteers, commanded by Colonel Edward D. Bradley, called into the service of the United States by the President from September 10, 1861 (date of this muster) for the term of three years, unless sooner discharged. . . .

E. MORGAN WOOD,
Captain,
Fifteenth Infantry, United States Army, Mustering Officer.

Stationed at Camp Wild Cat, Kentucky, September 1-October 31, 1861.

Stationed at Somerset, Kentucky, November-December 1861.

Station not stated, January-February 1862.

Stationed in the field before Corinth, Mississippi, March-April 1862.

Stationed at camp near Tuscumbia, Alabama, May-June 1862.

Stationed at Louisville, Kentucky, [July] 1-August 31, 1862.

Stationed near Bowling Green, September-October 1862.

Stationed near Murfreesborough, Tennessee, [November] 1, 1862-February 28, 1863.

Stationed near Triune, Tennessee, March-April 1863.

Stationed at camp in the field near Elk River, Tennessee, May-June 1863.

Stationed at mouth of Battle Creek, Tennessee, July-August 1863.

Stationed at Chattanooga, Tennessee, September-October 1863.

Stationed at Chattanooga, Tennessee, November-December 1863.

During the months of November and December this company has been camped at Chattanooga, Tennessee.

November 22.— The men were engaged in the erection of Fort Phelps with an average of twenty men per day and doing picket duty at an average of seven men per day.

November 23-25.— Moved toward the enemy maneuvering with the troops until the afternoon of November 25, when the order was given to charge Missionary Ridge. In the assault Sergeant N. W. Market was killed; Second Lieutenant Joseph Newman, Private George W. Clark and Henry P. Dellinger were wounded.

November 26.— This company was ordered to scour the woods for stragglers of the enemy. By 1 p.m. was recalled, having brought in forty-eight deserters. At 2 p.m. was ordered forward

with troops. At evening, camped on Ringgold Road, eight miles from Missionary Ridge. Henry P. Dellinger died of wounds.
November 27.— Marched early. Reached Ringgold at midnight.
November 28.— Marched four miles on Dalton Road, assisting in the destruction of railroad track and bridges. Returned to camp at Ringgold.
November 29.— Returned to camp at Chattanooga, Tennessee. Reenlistment as veteran volunteers continued and regiment prepared for furlough (of wounds).
December 12.— Lieutenant J. Newman died instead of December 14 as officially announced by "surgeon" in charge of Critchfield House, Chattanooga, Tennessee.
December 31.— Started from Chattanooga, Tennessee for northwestern Ohio.

Stationed at Chattanooga, Tennessee, January-February 1864.

During the months of January and February this company was on furlough with the regiment by virtue of having reenlisted as veteran volunteers.
January 14.— Arrived at Toledo, Ohio via Nashville, Tennessee; Cairo, Illinois; Sandoval, Illinois; and Cincinnati, Ohio. The regiment dispersed. This company dispersed at Bryan, Ohio.
February 18-29.— The regiment assembled at Toledo, Ohio and started for Chattanooga, Tennessee via Cleveland, Ohio; Cincinnati, Ohio; Seymour, Iowa; Louisville, Kentucky; Nashville, arriving at Chattanooga, Tennessee on February 29.

Stationed at Ringgold, Georgia, March-April 1864.

Stationed in the field, Georgia, May-June 1864.

Stationed near Atlanta, Georgia, July-August 1864.

Stationed near Savannah, Georgia, November-December 1864.

Stationed in the field, North Carolina, March-April 1865.

Stationed near Louisville, Kentucky, May-June 1865.

Company I

Stationed at Nicholasville, Kentucky, September 10, 1861.
September 10.— Muster-in roll of Captain [Moses Randolph] Brailey's Company, in the Thirty-eighth Regiment of Ohio Infantry Volunteers, commanded by Colonel E. D. Bradley, called into the service of the United States by His Excellency, Abraham Lincoln, President from September 10, 1861 (date of this muster) for the term of three years, unless sooner discharged. . . .

E. MORGAN WOOD,
Captain,
Fifteenth Infantry, United States Army, Mustering Officer.

Stationed at Camp Wild Cat, Kentucky, October 31, 1861.

Stationed at Somerset, Kentucky, November-December 1861.

Stationed at Camp Thomas near Nashville, Tennessee, January-February 1862.

Station not stated, March-April 1862.

Stationed at Tuscumbia, Alabama, May-June 1862.

Stationed at Louisville, Kentucky, July-August 1862.

Stationed at Gallatin, Tennessee, September-October 1862.

Stationed at Murfreesborough, Tennessee, November 1862-February 1862.

Stationed at Triune, Tennessee, April 10, 1863.

Stationed at camp near Triune, Tennessee, March-April 1863.

Stationed at Camp Winford, Tennessee, May-June 1863.

Stationed at Battle Creek, Tennessee, July-August 1863.

Stationed at Chattanooga, Tennessee, September-October 1863.

Station not stated, November 1863-February 1864.

Stationed at Ringgold, Georgia, March-April 1864.

Stationed in the field, Georgia, May-October 1864.

Stationed near Savannah, Georgia, November-December 1864.

Stationed in the field, South Carolina, January-February 1865.

Stationed in the field, North Carolina, March-April 1865.

Stationed near Louisville, Kentucky, May-June 1865.

Company K

Stationed at Nicholasville, Kentucky, September 1, 1861.
September 1.— Muster-in roll of Captain Rezin A. Franks' Company, in the Thirty-eighth Regiment of Ohio Infantry Volunteers, commanded by Colonel E. D. Bradley, called into the service of the United States by the President from September 1, 1861 (date of this muster) for the term of three years, unless sooner discharged. . . .

E. MORGAN WOOD,
Captain,
Fifteenth Infantry, United States Army, Mustering Officer.

Stationed at Camp Wild Cat, Kentucky, September 1-October 31, 1861.

Stationed at Somerset, Kentucky, November-December 1861.

Stationed at Camp Thomas near Nashville, Tennessee, January-February 1862.

Stationed at camp near Corinth, Mississippi, March-April 1862.

Stationed at Tuscumbia, Alabama, May-June 1862.

Stationed at Louisville, Kentucky, [July] 1-August 31, 1862.

Stationed in the field, September-October 1862.

Stationed near Murfreesborough, Tennessee, [October] 31-December 31, 1862.

Stationed at Murfreesborough, Tennessee, January-February 1863.

Stationed at Triune, Tennessee, March-April 1863.

Stationed at camp in the field near Elk River, May-June 1863.
June 30.— The day according to law that this company should have been mustered, it was in the face of the enemy on the march with all transportation left behind, hence would not be mustered until the present time. This muster roll shows the true state of the company.

T. R. THATCHER,
Lieutenant,
Seventeenth Regimen, Ohio Volunteer Infantry,
Assistant Adjutant and Inspector-General,
First Brigade, Third Division.

Stationed in the field, Tennessee, June 30-August 30, 1863.

Stationed at Chattanooga, Tennessee, August 30-October 31, 1863.

Stationed at Chattanooga, Tennessee, November-December 1863.
November 23.— This company, with the regiment, moved out of the works around Chattanooga to attack the enemy.
November 25.— Formed part of the storming force that charged Missionary Ridge in which it left one private killed, two non-commissioned officers and three privates severely wounded.
November 26.— It, with the regiment, pursued the enemy to Ringgold, Georgia. Did not arrived in time to take any part in the engagement.
November 29.— Returned to Chattanooga, Tennessee.

December 11.— Thirty-eight of its members reenlisted as veteran volunteers in compliance with General Orders No. 191, series 1863, War Department.

Stationed at Chattanooga, Tennessee, January-February 1864.

Stationed at Ringgold, Georgia, March-April 1864.

Stationed in the field, Georgia, May-August 1864.

Stationed near Rome, Georgia, September-October 1864.

Stationed near Savannah, Georgia, November-December 1864.

Stationed at Goldsborough, North Carolina, January-February 1865.

Stationed in the field, North Carolina, March-April 1865.

Stationed near Louisville, Kentucky, May-June 1865.

[M594-Roll #149]

Record of Events for Thirty-ninth Ohio Infantry, July 1861-June 1865.

Field and Staff

Stationed at Camp Dennison, Ohio, August 16, 1861.
August 16.— Muster-in roll of field and staff in the Thirty-ninth Regiment (Brigade) of Ohio Foot Volunteers, commanded by Colonel John Groesbeck, called into the service of the United States by the President from August 16, 1861 for the term of three years, unless sooner discharged. The regiment was organized by Colonel John Groesbeck at Camp Dennison, Ohio in the month of August 1861. . . .

[THOMAS WOODRUFF] WALKER,
First Lieutenant,
Third Infantry, Mustering Officer.

Stationed at Hudson, Missouri, September-October 1861.

Stationed at Palmyra, Missouri, [October] 31-December 31, 1861.

Stationed near New Madrid in the field, January-February 1862.

Station not stated, March-April 1862.

Stationed at Camp Clear Creek, Mississippi, May-June 1862.

Stationed at camp near Corinth, July 22, 1862.
July 22.— Muster-in roll of the band of the Thirty-ninth Regiment of Ohio Volunteer Infantry (Colonel John Groesbeck) from the date set opposite their names for three years, unless sooner discharged. . . .

BYRON KIRBY,
Second Lieutenant,
Sixtieth Infantry, United States Army,
Inspector and Mustering Officer.

Stationed at Camp Clear Creek, Mississippi, August 18, 1862.
August 18.— Muster-out roll of the field, staff, and band. . . .

CHARLES W. DUNSTAN,
Captain,
Assistant Adjutant-General, Mustering Officer.

Stationed at camp at Iuka, July-August 1862.
July 1.— In camp at Clear Creek, four miles south of Corinth, Mississippi.
July 21.— Inspected by Brigadier-General Inspector-General, Army of the Mississippi.
July 25.— Received Whitney rifles with sword bayonets.
August 2.— Struck tents and took up the line of march.
August 10.— The regiment detailed as escort to the remains of Brigadier-General [Joseph Bennett] Plummer.
August 18.— The regiment mustered by Colonel [Alfred W.] Gilbert in accordance with Orders No. —— to ascertain absentees.
August 20.— Marched fifteen miles and bivouacked for the night.

August 21.— Arrived at Iuka about 10 a.m.; went into camp on edge of town.
August 28.— Still in camp.
August 31.— Mustered for pay by Lieutenant-Colonel [Edward Follansbee] Noyes of the Thirty-ninth Ohio Volunteers Infantry, United States Army.

Stationed at camp at Corinth, [August] 30-October 31, 1862.
September 11.— Remained at Iuka.
September 12.— Marched to Clear Creek, a distance of twenty-four miles, and bivouacked.
September 14-17.— On a reconnaissance in direction of Iuka.
September 18.— Rejoined the division at Jacinto.
September 19.— Marched with the division a distance of sixteen miles. Had an engagement with the enemy near Iuka.
September 20.— Entered Iuka. The enemy withdrew during the night. Followed the retreating enemy ten miles from Iuka and bivouacked.
September 21.— Marched towards Jacinto (twenty miles) and bivouacked.
September 22-28.— Went into camp one and one-half miles from Jacinto and remained in camp until September 28.
September 29.— Marched to and bivouacked at Rienzi, a distance of nine miles.
September 30.— In bivouac at Rienzi.
October 1.— Marched through Kossuth and bivouacked on the Tuscumbia River.
October 3.— Marched to Corinth and took position in line of battle on the west side of town in support of Battery Robinett, the enemy being in front.
October 4.— Participated in the battle of Corinth.
October 5-7.— Pursuing the retreating enemy, marching forty miles.
October 8.— The regiment ordered on a reconnaissance in direction of Ripley.
October 9.— In bivouac near Ripley.
October 10.— Marched in direction of Corinth (twenty miles).
October 11.— Passed through Kossuth; bivouacked near Tuscumbia River.
October 12.— Marched into Corinth; encamped east of town inside of outer breastworks.

October 13-31.— In camp at Corinth, when the regiment was mustered for pay.

Stationed at camp near Corinth, November-December 1862.
November 2-7.— The regiment marched from Corinth, the place of last muster, and arrived at Grand Junction, Tennessee on November 7.
November 17.— Remained in camp near Grand Junction until the camp was removed five miles south of Holly Springs.
November 30.— The regiment joined part of a reconnaissance in force in the direction of the Tallahatchie River.
December 10.— Remained in camp seven miles south of Holly Springs until took up line of march for Oxford, Mississippi.
December 11.— Marched through the town of Oxford, Mississippi and encamped two miles south of it.
December 18.— Remained encamped here until the regiment was ordered to prepare three days' rations and go by rail to Jackson. Leaving camp and garrison equipage behind, left Oxford at 12 p.m.
December 19.— Arrived in Jackson. Bivouacked on the north side of Jackson that night.
December 20.— Formed part of a force under General [Jeremiah Cutler] Sullivan and marched nineteen miles in the direction of Lexington, Tennessee.
December 21.— Remained in bivouac near Jackson until the regiment was moved to Trenton, Tennessee by rail.
December 28-29.— Formed part of a force under General Sullivan and marched in the direction of Huntingdon, Tennessee and arrived there December 29.
December 31.— Remained there until the regiment again resumed the march with the First Brigade under command of Colonel [John Wallace] Fuller toward the Tennessee River. Sixteen miles from Huntingdon came upon the enemy under command of General [Nathan Bedford] Forrest, who had been engaged with Colonel [Cyrus L.] Dunham's Union Brigade during the day. Assisted to put the enemy to rout, in recapturing prisoners, guns and train, and in capturing a portion of the enemy's artillery and forces.

Stationed at Corinth, Mississippi, January-February 1863.

January 1.— After having collected the dead and wounded of the engagement the day before, the regiment marched with the command of General Sullivan in the direction of Lexington, Tennessee. After marching thirteen miles, bivouacked one mile south of Lexington.

January 2.— Resumed march towards Tennessee River. Marched twenty miles and bivouacked in cornfield. Rained during the night.

January 3.— Marched to the river, ten miles over a broken and hilly country. Found the enemy on the opposite bank. Drew the fire of artillery but without any injury. After maneuvering for some time, started to return, having then accomplished the object of driving the enemy across the river. Marched about eight miles, bivouacked on a plantation, occupying the houses to shelter the men from the rain, as it had been raining all day.

January 4.— Remained bivouacked.

January 5-7.— Moved in direction of Bethel on Mobile and Ohio Railroad, forty-five miles, arriving there on January 7.

January 8-9.— Remained until the regiment was ordered to Corinth, twenty-eight miles distant, arriving there January 9 and going into camp one mile south of town.

January 13.— The camp and garrison equipage arrived from Oxford.

January 16.— The regiment marched as escort to forage train with four days' rations.

January 18.— The regiment returned at dusk from march as escort having marching some fifty miles out and back on Purdy and Crooked Creek Roads.

February 28.— Remained in camp until date of muster.

Stationed at Corinth, Mississippi, April 15, 1863.

Stationed at Bear Creek, Alabama, March-April 1863.

Stationed at Memphis, Tennessee, May-August 1863.

Stationed at Iuka, Mississippi, September-October 1863.

Stationed at Columbia, Tennessee, November-December 1863.

Stationed at Athens, Alabama, January-February 1864.

Stationed at Decatur, Alabama, March-April 1864.

Stationed at Kenesaw Mountain, Georgia, May-June 1864.

Stationed at Jonesborough, Georgia, July-August 1864.

Stationed at Cave Spring, Georgia, September-October 1864.

Stationed at Savannah, Georgia, November-December 1864.

Stationed at Cheraw, South Carolina, January-February 1865.

Stationed at Neuse River, North Carolina, March-April 1865.
Summery. This command during the past two months has been engaged in operations with the Army under Major-General [William Tecumseh] Sherman in the North and South Carolinas.
March 21.— Took part in the action at Bentonville, North Carolina with a loss of four killed and seventeen wounded.

Stationed at Louisville, Kentucky, May-June 1865.
May 1-9.— The regiment marched from near Raleigh, North Carolina, place of last muster, to Manchester, Virginia via Henderson, Dinwiddie Court-House, Petersburg, and arrived at Manchester May 9.
May 12-19.— Marched to Alexandria via Richmond, Hanover Court-House, Fredericksburg, and arrived at Alexandria May 19.
May 23.— Marched to Long Bridge.
May 24.— Crossed the Potomac River; marched through Washington in review before the President of the United States. Encamped on the Bladensburg Road, three miles from the city.
June 5.— Moved from camp near Washington to depot Baltimore and Ohio Railroad in Washington and embarked on cars.
June 7.— Arrived at Parkersburg, West Virginia at 10 p.m.
June 8-10.— Embarked on transports at Parkersburg and arrived at Louisville June 10 and encamped near the city.
June 30.— The regiment was mustered by Colonel Daniel Weber.

Regiment

Stationed at Palmyra, Missouri, December 1861.

Stationed at Palmyra, Missouri, except Companies F, G and H at Syracuse, Missouri, January 1862.

Stationed in the field, February 1862.

Stationed in the field near New Madrid, Missouri, March 1862.

Stationed at camp on Corinth Road, Tennessee, April 1862.

Stationed at camp near Booneville, Mississippi, May 1862.

Stationed at Camp Clear Creek, Mississippi, June 1862.

Stationed at Camp Clear Creek, Mississippi, July 1862.

During the month the regiment has been encamped at Camp Clear Creek about four miles south of Corinth, Mississippi.
July 7.— Colonel Groesbeck, having resigned, left for Ohio.
July 21.— The regiment was inspected by Brigadier-General Smith, Inspector-General of the Army of the Mississippi.
July 25.— Received the Whitney rifle with sword bayonet in place of the Greenwood rifled musket furnished at Camp Dennison.

The health of the regiment has in general been good. Schools of instruction for company officers have been held daily and constant drills for the men. Company drill in the morning, battalion drill in the afternoon each day.

Stationed at Camp Iuka, Mississippi, except Companies A and E at Eastport, [Mississippi], August 1862.
August 10.— The regiment detailed as escort to the remains of General Plummer.
August 18.— The regiment mustered by Colonel Gilbert in accordance with Orders No. —— to ascertain absentees.

August 20.— Struck tents and took up the line of march for Iuka in company with whole brigade under command of Colonel [John Wilson] Sprague. Marched about fifteen miles and bivouacked for the night.
August 21.— Arrived at Iuka about 10 a.m., went into camp on edge of town.
August 28.— Still in camp.
August 31.— Mustered for pay by Lieutenant-Colonel E. F. Noyes of the Thirty-ninth Ohio Volunteer Infantry.

Stationed at Corinth, Mississippi, September 1862.

Stationed at camp at Corinth, October 1862.
October 1.— Marched through Kossuth and bivouacked on the Tuscumbia River.
October 3.— Marched to Corinth and took a position in line of battle on the west side of town in support of Battery Robinett.
October 4.— Participated in the battle of Corinth.
October 5-7.— Pursuing the retreating enemy, marching about forty miles.
October 8.— The regiment ordered on a reconnaissance in the direction of Ripley.
October 9.— In bivouac near Ripley.
October 10.— Marched in direction of Corinth, twenty miles.
October 11.— Passed through Kossuth. Bivouacked near Tuscumbia River.
October 12.— Marched into Corinth. Encamped east of town inside of outer breastworks.
October 13-31.— In camp at Corinth when the regiment was mustered for pay. Number of contrabands employed in the regiment was seventeen.

Stationed at camp near Lumpkin's Mill, Mississippi, November 1862.

Stationed at Corinth, December 1862.
December 10-11.— The regiment remained in camp seven miles south of Holly Springs until it took up line of march for Oxford, Mississippi, arriving on December 11.
December 18.— Moved by rail to Jackson, Tennessee.

December 20.— Forming part of a force under command of General Sullivan, marched nineteen miles in direction of Lexington, Tennessee.
December 21.— Returned to Jackson.
December 27.— Remained in bivouac near Jackson until the regiment moved by rail to Trenton, Tennessee.
December 28-29.— Forming part of a force under General Sullivan marched in direction of Huntingdon, Tennessee, arriving there December 29.
December 31.— Remained there until the regiment again resumed the march with the First Brigade under the command of Colonel Fuller, commanding brigade towards the Tennessee River, sixteen miles from Huntingdon. Came upon the enemy under command of General Forrest, who had been engaged with Colonel Dunham's Union Brigade during the day. Assisted to put the enemy to rout in recapturing prisoners, guns and train, and in capturing a portion of the enemy's artillery and forces.

Stationed at Corinth, Mississippi, January-March 1863.

Stationed at Corinth, Mississippi, April 1863.
April 20.— Remained in camp until marched that day to Burnsville, twenty-one miles, a portion of the distance over a very bad road. The line of march was in a southeasterly direction.
April 21.— Marched by way of Iuka to Bear Creek, seventeen miles and there formed junction with the division of General [Grenville Mellen] Dodge. A portion of this day's march was over very bad and muddy road and was in an easterly direction. Rained during most of the afternoon and a part of the following night.
April 22.— Remained in bivouac near Bear Creek.
April 23.— Marched sixteen miles in direction of Tuscumbia. Passed through a fine section of country.
April 24.— Marched to Tuscumbia, Alabama, eight miles, and bivouacked on the west side of the town. The enemy, who had occupied the place having left there in the morning, making no resistance to our advance.
April 25-26.— Remained in bivouac near Tuscumbia, Alabama.

April 27.— Resumed march in an easterly direction. Marched twelve miles. The day was hot and sultry and roads were muddy and heavy, it having rained the night before. Received orders to be ready to move at 5 o'clock in the morning.
April 28.— Remained in bivouac until 11 o'clock. Moved five miles to the front and took position on west bank of Town Creek. The enemy having made his appearance on the opposite side during the day but, after some shelling and skirmishing, retired.
April 29.— Remained in line until 6 o'clock in the morning, when the regiment took up line of march in a westerly direction. Marched twenty miles and bivouacked five miles west of Tuscumbia.
April 30.— Marched to Bear Creek, seventeen miles.

Stationed at Memphis, Tennessee, except Companies E and H, "north," May 1863.
May 1.— The regiment continued the march towards Corinth, crossing Bear Creek and marching to Burnsville, sixteen miles.
May 2.— Marched to Corinth, eighteen miles, and went into the camp formerly occupied.
May 12.— Remained in camp until the regiment moved with camp and garrison equipage to Memphis by rail.
May 13-31.— Went in camp near Memphis, where the regiment has remained since except forty-seven men of Company G, who were detailed on May 22 to guard prisoners to the north and 112 men of Companies E and H, who were detailed on May 29 to guard prisoners to the north.

Stationed at Memphis, Tennessee, June-September 1863.

Stationed at Iuka, Mississippi, October 1863.
October 18.— The regiment remained in camp at Memphis until it took up line of march to Iuka, Mississippi by way of La Grange and Corinth.

Stationed at Prospect, Tennessee, November 1863.

Stationed at Columbia, Tennessee, December 1863.
The regiment has been in camp at Prospect, Tennessee since last report.

December 26.— Four hundred eighty-nine men of the regiment reenlisted for three years.
December 27.— Were mustered in by Lieutenant Hoffman, United States Army.
December 29.— The regiment left Prospect en route for Ohio to receive furlough for thirty days in the state of Ohio. Leaving Prospect were six officers and the men who had not reenlisted, all in command of Captain John V. Drake, Company H.

Stationed at Cincinnati, Ohio, January 1864.
January 1.— The regiment embarked on transport at Nashville, Tennessee en route for Ohio.
January 2-6.— Arrived at Cairo; took cars for Camp Dennison, Ohio and arrived there January 6.
January 9.— The regiment was paid by Major [Dudley Woodbridge] Rhodes.
January 11.— Furloughed for thirty days.

The regiment is now on furlough in Ohio in accordance with Special Orders No. 48, Left Wing of Sixteenth Army Corps of December 29, 1863, having reenlisted as veteran volunteers.

Stationed at Athens, Alabama, February-March 1864.

Stationed at Decatur, Alabama, April 1864.

Stationed at Dallas, Georgia, May 1864.

Stationed at Kenesaw Mountain, Georgia, June 1864.

Stationed before Atlanta, Georgia, except Company F at Chattahoochee River, July 1864.

Stationed near Jonesborough, Georgia, except Company F at Chattahoochee, Georgia, August 1864.

Stationed at Atlanta, Georgia, September 1864.

Stationed at Van's Valley, Georgia, October 1864.

Stationed at Herndon, Georgia, November 1864.

Station not stated, December 1864.

Stationed in the field, South Carolina, January 1865.

Stationed at Goldsborough, North Carolina, March 1865.
The regiment during the present month formed a portion of the Army under General Sherman in the campaign through the Carolinas.
March 21.— Took part in the engagement near Bentonville, North Carolina, losing four killed and seventeen wounded, after which the regiment marched to Goldsborough with the Corps (Seventeenth).
March 24-31.— Arrived there and remained the remainder of the month.

Stationed at Neuse River, North Carolina, April 1865.

Stationed at Washington, District of Columbia, May 1865.

Stationed at Louisville, Kentucky, June 1865.
June 5.— Moved from camp near Washington to depot of Baltimore and Ohio Railroad in Washington and embarked on cars.
June 7.— Arrived at Parkersburg, West Virginia at 7 p.m.
June 8.— Embarked on transports at Parkersburg. Arrived at Louisville June —— and encamped near the city.
June 30.— The regiment was mustered by Colonel Daniel Weber.

Company A

Stationed at Camp Dennison, Ohio, July 31, 1861.
July 31.— Muster-in roll of Captain Henry T. McDowell's Company (A), in the Thirty-ninth Regiment of Ohio Foot Volunteers, commanded by John Groesbeck, called into the service of the United States by the President from July 31, 1861 (date of this muster) for the term of three years, unless sooner discharged. The company was organized by Captain Henry T. McDowell at Portsmouth, Ohio in the month of July 1861 and marched thence

to Camp Dennison, where it arrived August 2, 1861, a distance of 140 miles. . . .

T. W. WALKER,
First Lieutenant,
Third Infantry, Mustering Officer.

Stationed at Camp Benton, July 31-August 31, 1861.

Stationed at Camp Prentiss, Chillicothe, Missouri, September-October 1861.

Station not stated, [October] 31-December 31, 1861.
December 3-4.— Left Macon City and arrived at Saint Joseph on December 4.
December 5.— Took the field under the command of Brigadier-General [Benjamin Mayberry] Prentiss, our force consisting of five companies of Thirty-ninth Ohio, five companies of Illinois Sixteenth, Colonel Kimball's [illegible] Regiment, Cavalry, and Infantry, and four pieces of artillery under Lieutenant Guard. The whole number, 1,500, marched twelve miles the first day and pitched tents on Platte River Bottom.
December 6.— Marched eighteen miles the second day. Weather was very stormy and roads bad. Camped at Ridgely.
December 7.— Marched six miles the third day, arriving at Smithville.
December 8.— In the morning started for Liberty some twenty miles distant. Entered the town about 3 p.m., our second visit to that place.
December 11.— Remained here until Wednesday, making sixteen miles to Albany that day. On the route destroyed the ferry boat on Missouri River at Missouri City.
December 12-14.— On Thursday went to Richmond via Lexington; distance marched was twenty-eight miles. At Lexington threw a few shells into some of the houses on the river bank, dispersing some small bands gathered there to dispute our crossing the river. Arrived at Richmond about sundown. Camped at that place two days.
December 15.— Started for Carrollton. Pitched tents that night near the Missouri River at Shanghai Ferry and destroyed the boat at that point.

December 16-18.— In the evening reached Carrollton and stayed overnight. Took the road for Utica, arriving the evening of December 18 and took the Hannibal and Saint Joseph Railroad for Palmyra. Health of the company good throughout.

Station not started, January-February 1862.
February 12-14.— Left Palmyra, Missouri and arrived at Saint Louis February 14.
February 22-24.— Left Benton Barracks and arrived Commerce, Missouri February 24.

Stationed near Hamburg, Tennessee, March-April 1862.
March 1.— Forming part of the First Brigade, First Division, Army of Mississippi under General [John] Pope, took up the line of march from Hunter's Farm for New Madrid, Missouri.
March 3.— Arriving there, made a demonstration before the town and was fired upon by Fort Thompson and gunboats. Retired at dusk and camped one and one-half miles from the town.
March 7.— Formed part of a reconnaissance in force and was fired upon again from the upper fort and gunboats at 3 a.m.
March 13-14.— Marched on the fort and town. Took supporting distance in rear of a battery of four siege guns. Remained all day amid a shower of shot and shell and all night in a terrible and drenching rain and was relieved at daylight.
April 7.— Remained in camp until ordered to the river. Crossed the Mississippi in order to get position in the rear of Island No. 10. Marched six miles and camped.
April 8.— Marched to Tiptonville, where 6,000 of the enemy had surrendered to the command of General [Eleazer Arthur] Paine. Marched to Island No. 10 and camped.
April 9.— Took passage on steamer *N. W. Graham* for New Madrid.
April 13.— Remained in camp at New Madrid until we embarked on steamer *Admiral* for Fort Pillow.
April 14.— Arrived above the fort.
April 19-23.— Ordered to Pittsburg Landing and arrived there on April 23.
April 27.— Went into camp at Hamburg. Moved camp five miles in advance.
April 29.— Formed part of a reconnaissance in force and drove in the pickets of the enemy. Captured a number of prisoners. Returned to camp.

Stationed at Camp Clear Creek, Mississippi, May-June 1862.
May 1.— Left our camp and marched about five miles on the road to Farmington and encamped.
May 2.— In camp. General [Daniel] Tyler assumed command of the First Brigade, Second Division of which the Thirty-ninth formed a part.
May 4.— Marched to a point within two miles of Farmington.
May 8.— Forming part of the division of General [David Sloan] Stanley, was ordered out on an armed reconnaissance toward Corinth and got to within one mile of the outworks, when we fired on Rebel cavalry. Immediately a battery opened on us with shot and shell. Returned to camp at night.
May 17.— Moved our camp to Farmington, where we were protected by entrenchments and batteries.
May 28.— Marched toward Corinth and took a position about two miles from Corinth and dug rifle pits, a portion of our forces skirmishing all day with the enemy. We had one man mortally wounded in the thigh by a shell.
May 29.— Lay in the trenches all day.
May 30.— Ordered early in the morning toward Corinth. Our company and Company B thrown out as skirmishers. Kept near the main road in advance of the regiment and after some skirmishing with cavalry, were the first troops to enter the deserted works. At 6.40 a.m. the flags of the Thirty-ninth Ohio and Forty-second Illinois were the first planted. At 5 p.m. the same day started in pursuit of the Rebels, marching on the Danville Road. Encamped six miles from Corinth.
June 1.— Marched toward Booneville, leaving camp at 7 a.m. Encamped two miles north of Booneville.
June 3.— Marched to Booneville and returned to camp in the evening.
June 7.— Changed camp about two miles to the right.
June 11.— Returned to our old camp within six miles of Corinth.
June 12.— Changed camp about three-fourths of a mile to the left.
June 15.— Received payment for the months of March and April.
June 23.— Had regimental inspection.

Stationed at Camp Clear Creek, Mississippi, August 18, 1862.

Stationed at Eastport, Mississippi, July-August 1862.
August 20.— Left Camp Clear Creek near Corinth, Mississippi; marched eighteen miles.
August 21-31.— Marched thirteen miles to Eastport, Mississippi, where we are at present encamped.

Stationed at Corinth, Mississippi, September-October 1862.
September 12.— Remained at Iuka until marched to Clear Creek, a distance of twenty-four miles, and bivouacked.
September 14-17.— On a reconnaissance in the direction of Iuka.
September 18.— Rejoined the division at Jacinto.
September 19.— Marched with the division a distance of sixteen miles. Had an engagement with the enemy.
September 20.— Entered Iuka. The enemy withdrew through the night. Followed the retreating enemy ten miles from Iuka and bivouacked.
September 21.— Marched toward Jacinto twenty miles and bivouacked.
September 22-28.— Went into camp one and one-half miles from Jacinto and remained in camp until September 28.
September 29.— Marched to and bivouacked at Rienzi, a distance of nine miles.
September 30.— In bivouac at Rienzi.
October 1.— Marched through Kossuth and bivouacked on the Tuscumbia River.
October 3.— Marched to Corinth and took position in line of battle on the west side of the town in support of Battery Robinett, the enemy being in front.
October 5-7.— Pursued the retreating enemy, marching forty miles.
October 8.— The regiment ordered on a reconnaissance in direction of Ripley.
October 9.— In bivouac near Ripley.
October 10.— Marched in direction of Corinth, twenty miles.
October 11.— Passed through Kossuth. Bivouacked near Tuscumbia River.
October 12.— Marched into Corinth. Encamped east of town inside of outer breastworks.
October 13-31.— In camp at Corinth. Mustered for pay.

Stationed at Corinth, Mississippi, November-December 1862.
November 2-7.— The regiment marched from Corinth, the place of last muster, arrived at Grand Junction on November 7.
November 19.— Remained in camp near Grand Junction until moved the camp five miles south.
November 28.— Remained in camp until the regiment moved seven miles south of Holly Springs.
November 30.— The regiment formed a part of a reconnaissance in force in the direction of the Tallahatchie River.
December 10.— Remained in camp seven miles south of Holly Springs until took up line on march in direction of Oxford, Mississippi.
December 11.— Marched through the town of Oxford and encamped two miles south of it.
December 18-19.— Remained encamped here until the regiment was ordered to prepare three days' rations and go by rail (leaving camp and garrison equipage behind) to Jackson. Left Oxford at 12 p.m. and arrived in Jackson the next day. Bivouacked on the north side of Jackson that night.
December 20.— Formed part of a force under command of General Sullivan and marched nineteen miles in the direction of Lexington, Tennessee.
December 21.— Returned to Jackson.
December 27.— Remained in bivouac near Jackson until the regiment moved to Trenton, Tennessee by rail.
December 28-29.— The regiment formed part of a force under General Sullivan; marched in direction of Huntingdon, Tennessee; arrived there December 29.
December 31.— Remained until the regiment again resumed the march with the First Brigade under command of Colonel Fuller towards the Tennessee River, sixteen miles from Huntingdon. Came upon the enemy under command of General Forrest, who had been engaged with Colonel Dunham's Union Brigade during the day. Assisted to put the enemy to rout and in recapturing prisoners, guns, and train, and in capturing a portion of the enemy's artillery and forces.

Stationed at Corinth, Mississippi, January-February 1863.
February 28.— Remained in camp at Corinth until the date of muster.

Stationed at Corinth, Mississippi, April 15, 1863.

Stationed at Bear Creek, Alabama, March-April 1863.
[For record of events, see Regiment.]

Stationed at Memphis, Tennessee, May-June 1863.
May 1.— The regiment continued the march towards Corinth, crossing Bear Creek, marching to Burnsville, sixteen miles.
May 2.— Marched to Corinth, eighteen miles, and went into the camp formerly occupied.
May 12-June 30.— Remained until the regiment moved by rail to Memphis and encamped one mile south of the city, where the regiment has since remained doing guard duty until it was mustered June 30 for pay by Colonel Edward F. Noyes, Thirty-ninth Regiment, Ohio Volunteer Infantry.

Stationed at Memphis, Tennessee, July-August 1863.

Stationed at Iuka, Mississippi, September-October 1864.
October 18.— Remained in Memphis doing guard duty until marched to Germantown. Bivouacked in an open field.
October 19.— Marched to La Fayette.
October 20.— Marched to Moscow.
October 21.— Marched to within one mile of Saulsbury.
October 22.— Marched to Pocahontas.
October 23.— Marched to within eight miles of Chewalla.
October 24.— Marched to Corinth.
October 25.— Remained until received pay for July and August.
October 26.— Came to Burnsville by rail.
October 29.— Remained until marched to Iuka.
October 31.— Remained until mustered for pay.

Stationed at Columbia, Tennessee, November-December 1863.
December 31.— Move from camp about 3 o'clock and marched to Smith Station nearly ten miles. Got regiment into cars and started for Nashville. Experienced very cold weather. Arrived at Nashville about 9 p.m. at the regiment quarters in City Barracks.

Stationed at Athens, Alabama, January-February 1864.
January 1.— Got transportation on board transports and started at 4 p.m. for Cairo, Illinois.
January 3.— Arrived there at noon, proceeded to Camp Dennison to be paid and furloughed.
January 10.— Paid.
January 11.— Furloughed for thirty days.
February 11.— The regiment reorganized. Had orders to take the field immediately.
February 12-18.— The regiment embarked on transports *Arizona* and *Reserve*. Proceeded to Nashville and arrived there February 18. Took quarters in city hospital.
February 20-21.— The regiment took cars for Pulaski, Tennessee and arrived there February 21. The regiment marched from there to Prospect, Tennessee, about fifteen miles and arrived there in the evening.
February 22-23.— Marched from camp at 8 o'clock; took up line of march for Athens, Alabama and arrived there at 4 p.m. February 23.
February 29.— Remained in camp until day of muster.

Stationed at Decatur, Alabama, March-April 1864.

Stationed at Camp near Kenesaw Mountain, Georgia, May-June 1864.
May 1-4.— The company, with the regiment, took up line march from Decatur, Alabama and after three days successive marching, reached Woods Station on the Memphis and Charleston Railroad, a distance of fifty miles from Decatur. Here it took the cars and reached Chattanooga, Tennessee on May 4, a distance of fifty miles.
May 5.— Took up line of march from Chattanooga and brought up at Resaca, Georgia via Snake Creek Gap, a distance of about forty-five miles, serving with the Army of the Tennessee under command of Major-General [James Birdseye] McPherson.
May 16.— Was engaged in active operations against the enemy at Resaca until he evacuated. Then proceeded to Lay's Ferry, Oostenaula River, Georgia, a distance of five miles.
May 19.— Reached Kingston, Georgia, a distance of fifty miles from Lay's Ferry.

May 23-26.— Left Kingston and reached Dallas, Georgia on May 26, a distance of fifty miles. Was engaged in the operations against the enemy at Dallas, serving with the First Brigade, Fourth Division, Sixteenth Army Corps, Army of the Tennessee.
June 1.— Marched to Pumpkin Vine Creek, a distance of five miles.
June 5-6.— Took up line of march and reached Acworth, Georgia on June 6, a distance of ten miles.
June 10.— Moved to Big Shanty Station, Georgia, a distance of five miles.
June 12-30.— Took position in front of the enemy posted on Kenesaw Mountain and since that time have been engaged in this investment.

Stationed near Jonesborough, Georgia, July-August 1864.
July 1-3.— The company, with the regiment, lay at the foot of Kenesaw Mountain, Georgia until July 3, when we marched about twelve miles.
July 4.— In the morning the regiment was ordered to advance. After a march of three miles we met the enemy and after a severe skirmish, drove him into his earthworks near Ruff's Mill, Georgia. At 6 p.m. charged and drove him from his works with a loss of one man killed and one wounded in the company.
July 5.— Marched eight miles.
July 9.— Marched to Marietta, Georgia, fifteen miles.
July 10.— Marched to Roswell, factory, twelve miles.
July 11.— Crossed Chattahoochee River.
July 17.— Marched ten miles.
July 18.— Eight miles.
July 19.— Marched to Decatur, Georgia, ten miles.
July 20.— Marched three miles.
July 21.— Marched in rear of Seventeenth Army Corps.
July 22.— At 1 p.m. the enemy made an attack on our left. We were ordered to move at a double-quick to the rear to protect our ammunition and supply trains. There met the enemy; fought him three hours, and repulsed him with a loss of two men killed and eight wounded in the company.
July 27-August 26.— Marched to the right of the Army, twelve miles, where we were engaged in the investment of Atlanta, Georgia until August 26, when we fell back.
August 27.— Marched fifteen miles.

August 28.— Marched twelve miles.
August 29.— Destroyed Atlanta and Montgomery Railroad.
August 30.— Marched twelve miles to Jonesborough, Georgia.
August 31.— In line of battle on the right flank expecting an attack, the center being heavily engaged with the enemy, he having made the attack but was repulsed with severe loss.

Stationed at Van's Valley, Georgia, October 31, 1864.

Stationed at Savannah, Georgia, November-December 1864.
November 1.— Marched from Van's Valley to Cedartown, ten miles.
November 2.— Marched nine miles.
November 3.— Marched to Dallas, nineteen miles.
November 4.— Marched to Lost Mountain, ten miles.
November 5.— Marched twelve miles.
November 6.— Twelve miles. In camp at dark. Destroyed railroad from Big Shanty to Marietta.
November 7.— Marched to Peach Tree Creek, fourteen miles.
November 8.— Marched to Atlanta, eight miles.
November 16.— Marched with division twenty miles.
November 17.— Marched to Jackson, Georgia.
November 18.— Marched to Ocmulgee River, ten miles.
November 19.— Marched to Monticello.
November 20-22.— Marched to Gordon Station.
November 24.— Marched to Oconee River.
November 27.— Marched ten miles.
November 28.— Marched fifteen miles.
November 29.— Marched to Williams' Swamp, twelve miles.
November 30.— Marched to Ogeechee River at Sebastopol, ten miles.
December 1.— Marched seven miles along railroad and destroyed.
December 2.— Marched to Millen, eleven miles.
December 3.— Marched to Station No. 7.
December 4.— Marched to Cameron Station, fifteen miles.
December 5.— Marched to Horton.
December 6.— Drove enemy out of works at Little Ogeechee River.
December 7.— Marched along railroad, thirteen miles.

December 8.— Marched to Station No. 2.
December 9.— Marched to Station No. 1, ten miles.
December 10.— Marched and drove enemy into man works four miles from Savannah. During night built line of works 800 yards from enemy's.
December 12.— Still in position. Relieved by Fourteenth Army Corps. Moved to the right nine miles.
December 14.— Marched on forage expedition to Midway Church, thirty miles, and returned.
December 16-17.— Marched with division to Altamaha River, fifty miles to destroy Savannah, Albany and Gulf Railroad.
December 21.— Returned.
December 22.— Marched to Savannah and camped near Wassaw Sound, three miles from city.
December 31.— Still in camp.

Stationed near Cheraw, South Carolina, January-February 1865.

Stationed at Neuse River, North Carolina, March-April 1865.
March 21.— The company was engaged at the battle of Bentonville.
March 22.— In the morning skirmished through town and crossed the bridge over Mill Creek while burning, under a sharp skirmish fire from the enemy's rear guard.

Stationed at Louisville, Kentucky, May-June 1865.
May 1-20.— The company moved camp near Raleigh, North Carolina. Marched to Petersburg, Virginia; thence from Petersburg to Richmond, Virginia, then to Washington, District of Columbia, where it arrived on May 20.
May 24.— Passed in review.
June 5-11.— Camped near Washington until we took the cars en route for Louisville, Kentucky, where we arrived June 11.
June 26.— The company was detailed as provost guards at Seventeenth Army Corps Headquarters.
June 30.— It remained there until it was mustered for pay.

Company B

Stationed at Camp Dennison, Ohio, July 31, 1861.
July 31.— Muster-in roll of Captain John C. Fell's Company (B), in the Thirty-ninth Regiment of Ohio Foot Volunteers, com-

manded by Colonel John Groesbeck, called into the service of the United States by the President from July 31, 1861 (date of this muster) for the term of three years, unless sooner discharged. The company was organized by Captain John C. Fell at Marietta in the month of July and marched thence to Camp Colerain; thence to Camp Dennison, where it arrived August 2, a distance of 226 miles.

T. W. WALKER,
First Lieutenant,
Third Infantry, Mustering Officer.

Stationed at Camp Benton, July 31-August 31, 1861.

Stationed at Camp Prentiss near Chillicothe, Missouri, September-October 1861.

Stationed at Palmyra, Missouri, [October] 31-December 31, 1861.
December 4-5.— Arrived at Saint Joseph after receiving orders at Macon City from Brigadier-General Prentiss to proceed the following day and join him for the purpose of taking the field. Took up our line of march.
December 8-10.— Arrived at Liberty and lay in camp for two days.
December 11.— Marched to Albany.
December 12.— To Richmond via Camden [Point] and Lexington. At the latter place, we found from 2,000 to 3,000 Rebels. We threw from twenty to thirty shells over them and retired, they going one way, we the other.
December 15.— Marched to Shanghai, where we had a skirmish, killing one man and destroyed ferry boats.
December 16-21.— Marched for Chillicothe via Carrollton. From Chillicothe we came via railroad to Palmyra, where we arrived December 21.

Stationed at camp in the field near Commerce, Missouri, January-February 1862.
February 12-13.— Left station at Palmyra, Missouri in the morning for Saint Louis via Hannibal and Saint Joseph and North Missouri Railroad and arrived on February 13.

February 22.— Received orders to move and embarked on board steamer *Gladiator* for the south.
February 24.— Reached Commerce; disembarked and marched out some two miles and encamped.
February 28.— Left Commerce, Missouri with the regiment.

Stationed at camp on Corinth Road, March-April 1862.
March 3.— Arrived before New Madrid and advanced on the enemy as skirmishers. Had one man killed and there retired and encamped two and one-half miles in the rear.
March 13.— We stayed there until we again advanced on the enemy's works and took up a position in the rear of a siege battery, where we lay all day and night.
March 14.— Were relieved and went back to our camp.
April 7-8.— Crossed the Mississippi River. Marched to Tiptonville, Tennessee, where we arrived on April 8, went on a scout to Island No. 10 and arrived at that place the same day at sunset.
April 9.— We embarked on steamboat and went to New Madrid.
April 12-13.— Marched to river and embarked on steamboat and proceeded down the river to Fort Pillow; arrived in front of that place on April 13.
April 17-22.— We lay on board the boat until again started up the river to Pittsburg Landing, where we arrived on April 22 and encamped two miles from the landing.
April 27-30.— Marched south on the Corinth Road three miles and encamped, where we now are.

Stationed at camp near Corinth, Mississippi, May-June 1862.
May 1.— Left our camp near Hamburg Landing, Tennessee. Marched five miles and encamped.
May 4.— Remained in camp until marched nine miles. Encamped two miles from Farmington, Mississippi.
May 8.— Remained in camp until, forming part of General Stanley's Division, ordered out our reconnaissance towards Corinth. Marched within one-half mile of the enemy's works, where deployed as skirmishers. Drove in the enemy's pickets and advanced within 600 yards of a battery, which opened on us with shot and shell without doing any injury. Skirmishing lasted until evening, when we then returned to camp.
May 17.— We there remained until we moved our camp to Farmington.

May 24.— We were one of the five companies from our regiment ordered out to support a battery driving in the enemy's pickets.
May 28.— Marched towards Corinth about two miles. Dug rifle pits, during which time we were shelled by a Rebel battery about one mile from us on our left.
May 29.— In our trenches.
May 30.— Marched on Corinth. Deployed as skirmishers and advanced on the enemy's works, which we entered with but little firing on either side. We were the first to enter the works and marched in pursuit of the enemy on the Danville Road. Encamped six miles from Farmington.
June 1.— Marched towards Booneville. Encamped two miles north of that place.
June 3.— Marched to Booneville and returned to camp.
June 7.— Moved camp two miles.
June 11.— Returned within six miles of Farmington.
June 12.— Moved three-quarters of a mile to our present camp.

Station not stated, August 18, 1862.

Stationed at Iuka, Mississippi, July-August 1862.
July 1.— In camp at Clear Creek, four miles south of Corinth, Mississippi. Remained in camp.
July 21.— Inspected by Brigadier-General Smith, Inspector-General, Army of the Mississippi.
July 24.— Still at Camp Clear Creek. Received Whitney rifles with sword bayonets.
August 10.— The regiment detailed as escort to the remains of Brigadier-General Plummer.
August 18.— The regiment mustered by Colonel Gilbert in accordance with Orders No. 71 to ascertain absentees.
August 20.— Struck tents and took the line of march from Iuka, Mississippi. The company, with the whole brigade under Colonel Sprague, marched about fifteen miles and bivouacked for night.
August 21.— Arrived at Iuka, Mississippi about 10 a.m. Camped just outside of town.
August 28.— Still in camp.

Stationed at Corinth, Mississippi, September-October 1862.
September 1.— In camp at Iuka, Mississippi.

September 2-12.— Received orders to march but remained in camp until September 12, when we left Iuka for Clear Creek. Bivouacked near the old ground.
September 14.— Left Clear Creek. Reached and ordered to hold a cross-roads near Jacinto, Mississippi.
September 18.— General Stanley arrived with [illegible] division and started for Iuka, Mississippi.
September 19.— Reached Iuka, found the place occupied by General [Sterling] Price and hosts; whipped them and occupied the battlefield at night.
September 20.— Found the enemy had been badly beaten and the place evacuated. Started in pursuit of the flying enemy. Marched eight miles and found him too far in advance to effect a capture. Returned and marched by way of Jacinto.
September 22.— Reached Jacinto. Here received thirteen new recruits.
September 29.— Left Jacinto and marched for Rienzi.
October 1.— Left Rienzi en route for Corinth by way of Kossuth.
October 3.— Reached Corinth and found the place besieged by superior numbers of the enemy.
October 4.— Engaged in battle with the enemy and whipped [him], causing him to retreat, leaving his dead and wounded behind.
October 5.— Started in hot pursuit of the flying enemy.
October 7.— Arrived at Ripley, Mississippi and found the place evacuated and the enemy still flying. A few days were spent in camp. Received orders to return.
October 12.— Reached Corinth and were reviewed by General [William Starke] Rosecrans and went into camp just at edge of town.
October 22.— Still in camp. The company was sent out as foragers.
October 28.— Still in camp.
October 29.— The company was detailed to work on entrenchments.

Stationed at camp near Corinth, Mississippi, November-December 1862.
November 2-7.— The regiment marched from Corinth, Mississippi, the place of last muster, and arrived at Grand Junction, Tennessee November 7 and encamped near Grand Junction.

November 17.— Remained until the camp was removed five miles south.
November 28.— It remained until the regiment moved and marched seven miles south of Holly Springs.
November 30.— The regiment took part in a reconnaissance in force in the direction of the Tallahatchie River.
December 10.— The regiment took up line of march and moved to Oxford, Mississippi and encamped two miles south of that place.
December 18.— The regiment moved by rail to Jackson, Tennessee, leaving camp and garrison equipage behind.
December 20.— Formed part of force under General Sullivan and marched nineteen miles towards Lexington, Tennessee.
December 21.— Returned to Jackson.
December 27.— Remained in bivouac near Jackson until the regiment moved to Trenton by rail.
December 28-29.— Formed part of a force and marched in the direction of Huntingdon, Tennessee and arrived there December 29.
December 31.— Remained until it again resumed the march with the First Brigade under command of Colonel Fuller, commanding brigade, toward the Tennessee River, sixteen miles from Huntingdon. Came upon the enemy under command of General Forrest, who had been engaged with Colonel Dunham's Union Brigade. During the day assisted in putting the enemy to rout and recapturing prisoners, guns and trains, and in capturing a portion of the enemy's artillery and forces.

Stationed at Corinth, Mississippi, January-February 1863.
January 1.— After having collected the dead and wounded of the engagement of the day before, the regiment marched with the command of General Sullivan in the direction of Lexington, Tennessee. After marching thirteen miles bivouacked one mile south of Lexington.
January 2.— Resumed march towards Tennessee River. Marched twenty miles and bivouacked in cornfield. Rained during the night.
January 3.— Marched to the river ten miles over a broken and hilly country. Found the enemy on the opposite bank. Drew their fire of artillery but without any injury. After maneuvering

for some time, started to return, having accomplished the object of driving the enemy across the river. Marched about eight miles back. Bivouacked on a plantation occupying a house to shelter the men from the rain. It had been raining all day.
January 4.— Remained in bivouac.
January 5-7.— Moved in the direction of Bethel on Mobile and Ohio Railroad, forty-five miles, arriving January 7.
January 8-9.— Remained until the regiment was ordered to Corinth, twenty-three miles, arriving January 9 and going into camp one mile south of town.
January 13.— The company and garrison equipage arrived from Oxford.
January 16.— The regiment marched as escort to forage train with four days' rations.
January 18.— The regiment returned at dark from march as escort, having marched some fifty miles out and back on Purdy and Crooked Creek Roads.
February 28.— Remained in camp at Corinth until the date of muster.

Stationed at Corinth, Mississippi, April 15, 1863.

Stationed at Bear Creek, Alabama, March-April 1863.
[For record of events, see Regiment.]

Stationed at Memphis, Tennessee, May-June 1863.
May 1.— The regiment continued the march towards Corinth, crossing Bear Creek and marching to Burnsville, sixteen miles.
May 7.— Marched to Corinth, eighteen miles, and went into camp formerly occupied.
May 12.— Remained until the regiment moved by rail to Memphis and encamped one mile south of Memphis, where the regiment has since remained doing guard duty.
June 30.— Mustered for pay by Colonel Edward F. Noyes, Thirty-ninth Ohio Regiment.

Stationed at Memphis, Tennessee, July-August 1863.
July 1.— The company was in camp on Hernando Road, with regiment, one mile south of Memphis. Engaged in doing picket duty.

August 8.— Companies B and G detailed for special service at Memphis and Charleston Depot and ordered to report to Brigadier-General [Joseph Dana] Webster by order of Major [William] H. Lathrop, commanding regiment. Moved and camped near depot and are now engaged in furnishing guard and patrol for depot and escort with daily train for Grand Junction.
August 31.— Mustered and inspected for pay.

Stationed at Iuka, Mississippi, September-October 1863.
September 12.— The company turned over their arms, Whitney Rifles, and received in their place the Springfield rifle musket.
October 11.— The company, with Company G, went as guard with extra train to carry reinforcements to General Sherman, then attacked at Collierville. Arrived after the enemy had retreated.
October 13.— The company held an election in accordance with the laws of Ohio casting sixty-six votes for [John] Brough and one for [Clement Laird] Vallandigham.
October 17.— Relieved from duty at Memphis and Charleston Depot by a company of convalescents from Fort Pickering.
October 18.— Rejoined regiment. Received pay for the months July and August and marched with the brigade commanded by Colonel Fuller to Germantown.
October 19.— Marched to La Fayette.
October 20.— Marched to Moscow. Rained all night.
October 21.— Marched to Saulsbury.
October 22.— Marched to Pocahontas. Rained all night.
October 23.— Marched ten miles; camped on Shelton's Branch.
October 24.— Left Shelton's Branch and arrived at Corinth at 10.30 a.m. after marching about thirty miles around to avoid swamps.
October 26.— Went by rail to Burnsville.
October 29.— Marched to Iuka.
October 31.— The company was still at Iuka. Inspected and mustered for pay.

Stationed at camp near Columbia, Tennessee, November-December 1863.
December 31.— Moved from camp about 7 a.m. and marched to Smith Station, some ten miles and got on cars and started for Nashville. Experienced very cold weather. Arrived at Nashville about 9 p.m. The regiment was quartered in the City Barracks.

Stationed at Athens, Alabama, January-February 1864.
January 1-3.— Got transport on board transport and started at 4 p.m. for Cairo, Illinois and arrived there at noon of January 3. Got transport on cars for Cincinnati.
January 6.— Arrived there in the morning. Proceeded to Camp Dennison to be paid and furloughed.
January 10.— Paid.
January 11.— Furloughed for thirty days.
February 11.— The regiment reorganized. Has orders to take the field immediately.
February 12-18.— The regiment embarked on board transports *Arizona* and *Reserve*, proceeded to Nashville and arrived there February 18. Took quarters in City Hospital.
February 20-21.— Took cars for Pulaski and arrived there February 21. Marched from there to Prospect, Tennessee about fifteen miles.
February 22-29.— Arrived there in the evening. Moved from camp about 8 a.m. Took up line of march for Athens, Alabama. Arrived at 4 p.m. Remained in camp until February 29, day of muster.

Stationed at Decatur, Alabama, March-April 1864.

Stationed in the field, foot of Kenesaw Mountain, May-June 1864.
May 1-4.— The company, with the regiment, took up line of march from Decatur, Alabama and after three days successive marching, reached Woods Station on the Memphis and Charleston Railroad, a distance of fifty miles from Decatur, Alabama. Here it took the cars and reached Chattanooga, Tennessee on May 4, a distance of fifty miles.
May 5.— Took up line of march from Chattanooga and brought up at Resaca, Georgia via Snake Creek Gap, a distance of about forty-five miles, with the Army of Tennessee under the command of Major-General McPherson.
May 16.— Was engaged in active operations against the enemy at Resaca until he evacuated. The company then proceeded to Lay's Ferry, Oostenaula Creek, Georgia, a distance of five miles.
May 19.— Reached Kingston, a distance of fifty miles from Lay's Ferry.

May 25.— Left Kingston and reached Dallas, Georgia, a distance of fifty miles.
May 26.— Was engaged in the operations against the enemy at Dallas, Georgia with the First Brigade, Fourth Division, Sixteenth Army Corps, Army of the Tennessee.
June 1.— Marched to Pumpkin Vine Creek, a distance of five miles.
June 5-6.— Took up line of march and reached Acworth, Georgia on June 6, a distance of ten miles.
June 10.— Moved to Big Shanty Station, Georgia, a distance of five miles.
June 12-30.— Took position in front of the enemy posted on Kenesaw Mountain and since that time have been engaged in his investment.

Stationed near Jonesborough, Georgia, July-August 1864.
[For record of events, see Company A.]
July 4.— A loss of four men wounded in the company.
July 22.— Repulsed him with a loss of six men wounded in company.

Stationed at Cave Spring, Georgia, September-October 1864.
September 1.— In front of Jonesborough, Georgia.
September 2.— The enemy evacuated the place during the night and retreated southward. Marched four miles in pursuit to vicinity of Lovejoy's Station.
September 5.— Moved back during the night to Jonesborough.
September 6.— Marched four miles in direction of East Point.
September 7.— Marched eight miles.
September 8.— Marched four miles and camped one mile south of East Point.
September 10.— Moved camp to East Point.
September 20.— The regiment lay until it was detailed to go to Atlanta to put up hospital tents for the Department of the Tennessee.
October 4-5.— Remained on duty at Atlanta until the regiment joined the brigade in its march northward. Marched all night and camped five miles north of the Chattahoochee River.
October 6.— Marched all night and camped three miles from Marietta, Georgia.

October 9.— Marched to Big Shanty, nine miles, and bivouacked.
October 10.— Marched at 10 p.m. to Acworth, Georgia, seven miles.
October 11.— Marched at daylight to Cartersville, fifteen miles.
October 12.— Marched at daylight passing through Kingston and marched eighteen miles to a point seven miles from Rome.
October 13.— Started at 5 p.m. and marched all night to Adairsville, sixteen miles.
October 14.— Took cars for Resaca and after arriving there, made a reconnaissance at 7 p.m. to Snake Creek Gap, five miles. Drove the enemy two miles and returned to Resaca at 5 p.m.
October 15.— Marched at 7 a.m. to Snake Creek Gap and drove the enemy through and camped eighteen miles from Resaca.
October 16.— Marched eight miles and camped near the Blue Mountains.
October 17.— Marched at dark, crossing the mountains through Ship's Gap, and camped, making four miles.
October 18.— The regiment ordered to remain in rear and guard cross-roads while the whole Army train passed.
October 19.— Marched at 1 a.m. passing through Summerville and Alpine.
October 20.— We joined the brigade in the morning and marched to Gaylesville, Alabama, forty-nine miles from Blue Mountains.
October 29.— Moved from Gaylesville at 7 a.m., crossing the Chattooga and Coosa Rivers, passing through Cedar Bluff. Marched twelve miles and camped.
October 30.— Marched eighteen miles to Cave Spring, Georgia and camped in Van's Valley.
October 31.— The regiment in camp at Cave Spring, where it was mustered for pay.

Stationed near Savannah, Georgia, November-December 1864.
November 1.— The company, with the regiment, marched from Van's Valley to Cedartown, ten miles.
November 2.— Marched nineteen miles.
November 3.— Marched to Dallas, nineteen miles.
November 4.— Marched to Lost Mountain, ten miles.
November 5.— Marched to Smyrna Campground, twelve miles.
November 6-12.— In camp, where the regiment was paid until November 12 when marched to Atlanta, eight miles.

November 15-16.— Marched with division train, twenty miles.
November 17.— Marched to Jackson, seventeen miles.
November 18.— Marched to Ocmulgee River, ten miles.
November 19.— Marched through Monticello and Hillsborough, thirteen miles.
November 20-22.— Marched southward to Gordon, thirty-three miles.
November 24.— Marched eastward ten miles.
November 25.— Marched to Sandersville, nine miles.
November 26.— Marched to Oconee River, nine miles.
November 27.— Marched ten miles.
November 28.— Marched fifteen miles.
November 29.— Marched to Williams' Swamp, thirteen miles.
November 30.— Marched to Ogeechee River at Sebastopol Station, ten miles.
December 1.— Marched seven miles along the railroad destroying it.
December 2.— Marched to Millen, eleven miles.
December 3.— Marched to Station No. 7, nine miles.
December 4.— Marched to Cameron, fifteen miles.
December 5.— Marched to Horton Station, driving the enemy out of his works at the Little Ogeechee River, sixteen miles.
December 7.— Marched along the railroad, thirteen miles.
December 8.— Marched to Station No. 2, four miles.
December 9.— Marched to Station No. 1, ten miles.
December 10.— Marched six miles, driving the enemy into his works four miles from Savannah. During the night built works within 800 yards of the enemy.
December 11.— Still in position. In the evening relieved by Fourteenth Army Corps and marched nine miles to the right.
December 14-16.— Started on foraging expedition to Midway Church, thirty miles, and returned on December 16.
December 17-21.— Marched with First Division, Seventeenth Army Corps to the Altamaha River, destroying the Savannah, Albany and Gulf Railroad, fifty miles and returned on December 21.
December 24.— Marched to Savannah and camped near Wassaw Sound, three miles east of city.
December 29.— The Seventeenth Army Corps was reviewed by Major-General Sherman.

December 31.— Still in camp, where we were mustered for pay.

Stationed near Lynch's Creek, South Carolina, January-February 1865.
January 3.— Moved from Savannah, Georgia to Beaufort, South Carolina on transports.
January 13.— Commenced campaign in South Carolina.
February 3.— Drove the enemy from River's Bridge on the Salkehatchie.
February 9.— Crossed the South Edisto.
February 12.— Crossed the North Edisto and occupied Orangeburg.
February 17.— Crossed the Saluda and Broad Rivers and occupied Columbia.
February 22.— Passed through Winnsborough.
February 23.— Crossed the Wateree River.
February 24.— Passed through Liberty Hill.
February 27.— Occupied Lynch's Creek.
February 28.— Mustered for pay.

Stationed near Neuse River, North Carolina, March-April 1865.

Stationed near Louisville, Kentucky, May-June 1865.

Company C

Stationed at Camp Dennison, Ohio, July 31, 1861.
July 31.— Muster-in roll of Captain George [Washington] Baker's Company (C), in the Thirty-ninth Regiment of Ohio Foot Volunteers, commanded by Colonel John Groesbeck, called into the service of the United States by the President from July 31, 1861 (date of this muster) for the term of three years, unless sooner discharged. The company was organized by Captain George W. Baker at Athens, Ohio in the month of July and marched thence to Camp Colerain; thence to Camp Dennison, where it arrived August 2, a distance of 210 miles. . . .

T. W. WALKER,
First Lieutenant,
Third Infantry, Mustering Officer.

Stationed from Sedalia, Missouri, October 31, 1861.
August 18-20.— The company left Camp Dennison, Ohio on Sunday for Camp Benton, Saint Louis, Missouri at which place we arrived August 20.
September 6-8.— We remained there until we were ordered to Mexico, Missouri, arriving there on September 8. Left Mexico under General [Samuel Davis] Sturgis for Lexington, Missouri via Hudson and Utica.
September 18.— Arrived in sight of Lexington; went to Kansas City via Camden, Richmond and Liberty.
September 20.— Arrived at Kansas City.
October 15.— Left Kansas City to take position on the extreme right of [John Charles] Frémont's Grand Army by way of Pleasant Hill, Osceola and Bolivar.
October 20.— Arrived at Greenfield.
October 31.— Were inspected and mustered for pay. The company left Greenfield, Missouri at 5 p.m., forming part of Brigadier-General Sturgis' Brigade, under orders to join the Army of the West at Springfield.

Stationed at Syracuse, Missouri, November-December 1861.
November 1.— Arrived at Springfield about 5 p.m., marching about thirty-three miles.
November 9.— Remained in camp at that place until it formed part of the brigade commanded by Acting Brigadier-General [Joseph Gilbert] Totten in the Fifth Division of the Army under Acting Major-General Sturgis and took up the line of march for Warsaw by way of Bolivar and Quincy.
November 15-16.— Arrived at Warsaw and thence marched to Sedalia, the terminus of the Pacific Railroad and arrived there November 16.
December 3.— At Sedalia received pay and clothing.
December 8.— Remained in camp near Georgetown, until we received orders from Brigadier-General Pope to march to Syracuse forming part of the detachment of the Thirty-ninth Regiment, Ohio Volunteers under command of Lieutenant-Colonel A. W. Gilbert.
December 9.— Arrived at Syracuse and went into camp.
December 31.— Was inspected and mustered for pay.

GEORGE W. BAKER,
Commanding Company.

Stationed at Hunter's Farm, Scott County, Missouri, February 28, 1862.

Stationed near camp near Hamburg, Tennessee, April 30, 1862.
March 1.— Forming part of the First Brigade, First Division, Army of the Mississippi under General Pope, took up the line of march at Hunter's Farm for New Madrid, Missouri.
March 3.— Arrived there and made a demonstration before the town and was fired upon by Fort Thompson and gunboats. Retired at dusk and camped one and one-half miles from the town.
March 7.— Formed part of a reconnaissance in force and was fired upon again from the upper fort and gunboats.
March 13-14.— At 3 a.m. marched on the forts and town. Took supporting distance in rear of a battery of four siege guns. Remained all day amid a shower of shot and shell and all night in a terrible and drenching rain. Was relieved at daylight.
April 7.— Remained in camp until ordered to the river. Crossed the Mississippi in order to get position in rear of Island No. 10. Marched six miles and camped.
April 8.— Marched to Tiptonville, where 6,000 of the enemy had surrendered to the command of General Paine. Marched to Island No. 10 and camped.
April 9.— Took passage on steamer *N. W. Graham* for New Madrid.
April 13.— Remained in camp at New Madrid until ordered to Fort Pillow.
April 14.— Arrived at the above fort.
April 17.— Ordered to Pittsburg Landing.
April 23.— Arrived there and went into camp at Hamburg.
April 27.— Moved camp five miles in advance. Formed part of a reconnaissance in force.
April 29.— Drove in the picket of the enemy, captured a number of prisoners, and returned to camp.

GEORGE W. BAKER,
Commanding Company.

Station not stated, May-June 1862.
May 1.— Left our camp and marched about five miles on the road to Farmington and encamped.
May 2.— In camp. General Tyler assumed command of the First Brigade, Second Division of which the Thirty-ninth formed a part.
May 4.— Marched to a point within two miles of Farmington.
May 8.— Formed part of the division with General Stanley. Were ordered out in an armed reconnaissance toward Corinth and got to within one mile of the outworks, when we were fired upon by Rebel cavalry. Immediately a battery opened on us with shot and shell, returned to camp at night.
May 17.— Moved our camp to Farmington, where we were protected by entrenchments and batteries.
May 24.— Five companies ordered out to support a battery driving in the Rebel pickets.
May 28.— Marched toward Corinth and dug rifle pits. A portion of our forces skirmishing all day with the enemy. Had four men wounded by shot and shell.
May 29.— Stayed in trenches and skirmished.
May 30.— Ordered early in morning towards Corinth. Marched on main road and after some skirmishing with pickets, entered the deserted works at 6.40 a.m. The flags of the Thirty-ninth Ohio and Forty-second Illinois being the first planted. At 5 p.m. the same day started in pursuit of the Rebels, marching on the Danville Road. Encamped six miles from Corinth.
June 1.— Marched towards Booneville, leaving camp at 7 a.m. Encamped two miles north of Booneville.
June 3.— Marched to Booneville. Returned to camp.
June 7.— Changed camp about two miles to the right.
June 11.— Returned to our camp within six miles of Corinth.
June 12.— Changed camp about three-fourths of a mile to the left.
June 15.— Received payment for the months of March and April.
June 23.— Had regiment inspection.

Stationed at Camp Clear Creek, Mississippi, August 18, 1862.

Stationed at Iuka, Mississippi, July-August 1862.
July 1.— In camp at Clear Creek, Mississippi, four miles south of Corinth.
July 21.— Remained in camp. Inspected by Brigadier-General Smith, Inspector-General, Army of the Mississippi.
July 25.— Still at Camp Clear Creek. Received Whitney rifles with sword bayonets.
August 10.— The regiment detailed as escort to the remains of Brigadier-General Plummer.
August 18.— The regiment mustered by Colonel Gilbert in accordance with General Orders No. 58 to ascertain absentees.
August 20.— Struck tents and took up the line of march for Iuka. In company, whole brigade under command of Colonel Sprague marched about fifteen miles and bivouacked for the night.
August 21.— Arrived at Iuka about 10 a.m. Went into camp on edge of town.
August 28.— Still in camp.

Stationed at Corinth, Mississippi, October 31, 1862.

Stationed at Corinth, Mississippi, November-December 1862.
[For record of events, see Company A.]
November 17.— Remained in camp near Grand Junction until the camp was removed five miles south.

Stationed at Corinth, Mississippi, January-February 1863.
January 1.— After having collected the dead and wounded of the engagement the day before, the regiment marched with the command of General Sullivan in the direction of Lexington, Tennessee. After marching thirteen miles bivouacked one mile south of Lexington.
January 2.— Resumed march towards Tennessee River. Marched twenty miles and bivouacked in cornfield. Rained during the night.
January 3.— Marched to the river, ten miles over broken and hilly country. Found the enemy on the opposite bank. Drew their fire of artillery but without any injury. After reconnoitering for some time, we started to return having accomplished the object of driving the enemy across the river. Marched about

eight miles back; bivouacked on a plantation occupying the houses to shelter the men from the rain. It had been raining all day.

January 4.— Remained bivouacked.

January 5-7.— Moved in direction of Bethel on Mobile and Ohio Railroad, forty-five miles, arriving there on January 7.

January 8-9.— Remained until the regiment was ordered to Corinth, twenty-three miles, arriving there January 9 and going into camp one mile south of the town.

January 13.— The camp and garrison equipage arrived from Oxford.

January 16.— The regiment marched as escort to forage train with four days' rations.

January 18.— The regiment returned at dusk from march as escort, having marched some fifty miles out and back on Purdy and Crooked Creek Road.

February 28.— Remained in camp at Corinth until date of muster.

Stationed at Corinth, Mississippi, April 15, 1863.

Remained in camp at Corinth since last muster.

Stationed at Bear Creek, Alabama, March-April 1863.

[For record of events, see Regiment.]

Stationed at Memphis, Tennessee, May-June 1863.

May 1.— The regiment continued the march towards Corinth, crossing Bear Creek, marching to Burnsville, sixteen miles.

May 2.— Marched to Corinth, eighteen miles and went into the camp formerly occupied.

May 12.— Remained until the regiment moved by rail to Memphis and encamped one mile south of Memphis.

June 30.— The regiment has since remained doing guard duty until mustered for pay by Colonel Edward F. Noyes, Thirty-ninth Ohio Regiment.

Stationed at Memphis, Tennessee, July-August 1863.

Stationed at Iuka, Mississippi, September-October 1863.

Stationed at Columbia, Tennessee, December 31, 1863.
December 31.— Moved from camp about 7 o'clock and marched to Smith Station, some ten miles. Got regiment on cars and started for Nashville. Experienced very cold weather. Arrived at Nashville about 9 p.m. The regiment quartered in the City Barracks.

Stationed at Athens, Alabama, January-February 1864.
[For record of events, see Company B.]

Stationed at Decatur, Alabama, March-April 1864.
March 22-24.— Remained in camp at Athens until marched to Decatur, Alabama during the night and returned to Athens, Alabama on March 24, in all having marched thirty miles.
April 15.— Marched to Decatur, Alabama with camp and garrison equipage, a distance of fifteen miles.

During the months of March and April, the company was marched in all, forty-five miles.

Stationed at Kenesaw Mountain, Georgia, May-June 1864.

Stationed near Jonesborough, Georgia, July-August 1864.
July 1-3.— The company, with the regiment, lay at the foot of Kenesaw Mountain, Georgia until July 3, when we marched twelve miles.
July 4.— Were ordered to advance. After a march of two miles met the enemy and after a severe skirmish, drove him into his earthworks near Ruff's Mill, Georgia. At 6 p.m. charged and drove him from his works with a loss of —— killed and one wounded in Company B.
July 5.— Marched eight miles.
July 9.— Marched to Marietta, Georgia, fifteen miles.
July 10.— Marched to Roswell Factory, twelve miles.
July 11.— Crossed Chattahoochee River.
July 17.— Marched ten miles.
July 18.— Marched eight miles.
July 19.— Marched to Decatur, Georgia, ten miles.
July 20.— Marched three miles.

July 21.— Took position in rear of Seventeenth Army Corps.
July 22.— At 10 a.m. the enemy made an attack on our left. We were ordered to the rear double-quick to protect our ammunition and supply train. After a fight of three hours, we repulsed him with a loss of men killed and wounded in company, eight.
July 27-August 26.— Marched to the right of the Army twelve miles, where we were engaged in the investment of Atlanta, Georgia until August 26, when we fell back.
August 27.— Marched fifteen miles.
August 28.— Marched twelve miles.
August 29.— Destroyed Atlanta and Montgomery Railroad.
August 30.— Marched twelve miles to Jonesborough, Georgia.
August 31.— In line of battle expecting an attack. The enemy had attacked our center but were repulsed with severe loss.

Stationed at Van's Valley, Georgia, September-October 1864.

In front of Jonesborough, the enemy evacuated the place during the night. Marched southward in pursuit in vicinity of Lovejoy's Station four miles. Moved back in the night to Jonesborough.
September 6.— Marched in direction of East Point.
September 7.— Marched three miles.
September 8.— Marched four miles. Camped one mile south of East Point.
September 10.— Moved to East Point, where they rested.
September 20.— Detailed to put up hospital tents for the Department of Tennessee. Rejoined the brigade.
October 4.— Marched all night and camped five miles north of Chattahoochee.
October 6.— Marched all night and camped three miles from Marietta.
October 8.— Marched to Big Shanty, nine miles.
October 10.— Marched to Acworth.
October 11.— Marched to Cartersville, fifteen miles.
October 12.— Marched through Kingston. Camped eighteen miles from Resaca and seven miles from Rome, Georgia.
October 13.— Marched all night at Adairsville.
October 14.— Took the cars for Resaca, then marched to Snake Creek Gap. Drove the enemy and returned to Resaca at 5 a.m.
October 15.— Marched to Snake Creek Gap, drove the enemy through and camped eighteen miles from Resaca.

October 16.— Marched nine miles from Blue Mountain.
October 17.— Marched through Ship's Gap, four miles.
October 18.— The regiment ordered to remain and guard cross-roads while Army passed. Marched at [illegible]; passed through Summerville and rejoined brigade.
October 20.— Marched to Gaylesville, Alabama, forty-nine miles.
October 26.— Crossed the Chattooga and Coosa Rivers, passing through Cedar Bluff. Marched twelve miles and camped.
October 30.— Marched nineteen miles and camp.
October 31.— Regular camp at Cave Spring, where we mustered for pay.

Stationed near Savannah, Georgia, December 31, 1864.
November 1.— Marched from Van's Valley to Cedartown, ten miles.
November 2.— Marched nine miles.
November 3.— Marched to Dallas; passed through Van Wert.
November 4.— Marched to Lost Mountain, ten miles.
November 5.— Marched twelve miles.
November 6.— In camp at dark. Destroyed railroad from Big Shanty to Marietta.
November 12.— Marched to Peach Tree Creek.
November 14.— Marched to Atlanta, nine miles.
November 15-16.— Marched twenty miles.
November 17.— Marched to Jackson.
November 18.— Marched to Ocmulgee, ten miles.
November 19.— Marched to Monticello.
November 20-22.— Marched southward to Gordon Station.
November 24.— Marched to Oconee River.
November 27.— Marched ten miles.
November 28.— Marched thirteen miles.
November 29.— Marched to Williams' Swamp, ten miles.
November 30.— Marched to Ogeechee River at Sebastopol, ten miles.
December 1.— Marched seven miles along railroad, destroying it.
December 2.— Marched to Millen Station, eleven miles.
December 3.— To Horton Station.
December 6.— Drove the enemy out of works at Little Ogeechee River.
December 7.— Marched along railroad thirteen miles.

December 8.— Marched to Station No. 2, eleven miles.
December 9.— Marched to Station No. 1, ten miles.
December 10.— Marched driving the enemy into his main works four miles from Savannah. During the night built a line of works within 800 yards of the enemy still in position. Relieved by Fourteenth Army Corps. Moved nine miles to the right.
December 14.— Marched on forage expedition to Midway Church, thirty miles.
December 17.— Marched with division from Savannah River to destroy [Savannah, Albany and] Gulf Railroad.
December 21-22.— Returned and marched to Savannah and camped near Wassaw Sound, three miles out of city.
December 31.— Still in camp.

Stationed near Cheraw, South Carolina, January-February 1865.
January 1.— At Savannah, Georgia.
January 3-4.— Took steamer for Beaufort, South Carolina and arrived January 4.
January 5.— Remained until marched seven miles.
January 14.— Marched ten miles.
January 15.— Marched to Pocotaligo. Enemy evacuating.
January 20.— Made a reconnaissance to Salkehatchie River and returned to camp, a distance of eight miles.
January 21.— Marched to —.
January 22.— Returned to Pocotaligo.
January 26.— Made a reconnaissance to Salkehatchie. Returned to camp.
January 30.— Marched in a northwesterly direction. Camped near Salkehatchie River.
January 31.— Remained in camp.
February 1.— Moved and heavy skirmishing. Marched westward thirteen miles.
February 2.— Heavy skirmishing. Marched eight miles.
February 3.— Crossed Whippy Swamp and Salkehatchie River by wading and drove the enemy from their works.
February 7.— Marched twelve miles; camped at the railroad at Midway. Moved camp one mile.
February 12.— Marched and crossed South Edisto River and camp north of Orangeburg.
February 13.— Destroyed railroad and marched fourteen miles.

February 14.— Moved in direction of Columbia. Marched twelve miles.
February 15.— Marched nine miles.
February 16.— Crossed Congaree River.
February 17.— Crossed Saluda River and crossed Broad River. Marched through Columbia.
February 18.— Destroyed railroad all day.
February 19.— Remained in camp.
February 20.— Destroyed railroad and marched twelve miles.
February 21.— Marched twelve miles.
February 22.— Marched through Winnsborough.
February 23.— Crossed the Wateree River, marched ten miles.
February 24.— Marched though Silver Hill; marched eight miles.
February 25.— Marched fifteen miles.
February 26.— Crossed Little Lynch's Creek and marched eight miles.
February 27.— Crossed Big Lynch's Creek and marched four miles.
February 28.— Marched ten miles and camped and mustered.

Stationed in the field, March-April 1865.
March 1.— Remained in camp.
March 2-24.— Marched to Cheraw; thence to Fayetteville, from thence to Goldsborough, North Carolina, where we arrived March 24 after fighting battle of Bentonville.
April 10-14.— Remained until we marched for Raleigh, North Carolina, where we arrived April 14.
April 29.— Remained at Raleigh until marched north fourteen miles.
April 30.— Remained until we were mustered for pay.

Stationed at Louisville, Kentucky, May-June 1865.
May 1-9.— Marched toward Richmond; arriving there May 9. Marched from there to Washington, District of Columbia.
Arrived at Washington.
May 24.— Participated in the review of the Army of the Tennessee.
June 5.— Left Washington by railroad for Louisville.
June 1-30.— Arrived and have remained in camp near Louisville since.

Company D

Stationed at Camp Dennison, Ohio, July 31, 1861.
July 31– Muster-in roll of Captain [Christopher] A. Morgan's Company (D), in the Thirty-ninth Regiment of Ohio Foot Volunteers, commanded by Colonel John Groesbeck, called into the service of the United States by the President from July 31, 1861 (date of this muster) for the term of three years, unless sooner discharged. The company was organized by Captain Morgan at Cincinnati in the month of August and marched thence to Camp Colerain and thence to Camp Dennison, where it arrived August 2, a distance of forty-two miles. . . .

T. W. WALKER,
First Lieutenant,
Third Infantry, Mustering Officer.

Stationed in the field, Missouri, October 31, 1861.
August 18.— The company left Camp Dennison, Ohio for Camp Benton, Saint Louis, Missouri.
September 6-8.— Remained at that place until we were ordered to Mexico, Missouri. Arrived there September 8.
September 13.— Remained there until we left under General Sturgis for Lexington, Missouri via Hudson, Utica.
September 18.— Arrived in sight of Lexington and went to Kansas City via Camden, Richmond and Liberty.
September 20.— Arrived at Kansas City.
October 15-30.— Left Kansas City to take position on the extreme right of the Army under General Frémont via Pleasant Hill, Osceola and Bolivar and arrived at Greenfield October 30.
October 31.— Were inspected and mustered for pay previous to which the whole of the forces, of which Company D were a portion, were reviewed by General Sturgis. The company left Greenfield, Missouri at 5 p.m. forming part of Brigadier-General Sturgis' Brigade under orders to join the Army of the West at Springfield.

Stationed at Syracuse, Missouri, November-December 1861.
[For record of events, see Company C.]
November 14.— Arrived at Warsaw.

Stationed at Hunter's Farm, January-February 1862.
February 2-3.— The company remained at Syracuse, Missouri, the place of last muster, until formed part of the detachment of the Thirty-ninth Ohio Regiment under Lieutenant-Colonel Gilbert. It took up the line of march for Saint Louis via Boonville, Columbia, Fulton, Danville, Warrenton, and Saint Charles. We arrived at Boonville on the afternoon of February 3.
February 7.— We remained until we crossed the Missouri River and camped near New Franklin; thence forming part of the column under command of Colonel [William H.] Worthington of the Fifth Iowa Volunteers.
February 10.— We passed through Columbia.
February 12.— Through Fulton.
February 13.— Danville.
February 14.— Warrenton.
February 17.— Arrived at Saint Charles.
February 18.— Crossed the Missouri River.
February 19.— Arrived at Saint Louis and took up quarters at Benton Barracks, where we joined the regiment under Colonel Groesbeck.
February 22-24.— Left Benton Barracks under Groesbeck for Commerce, Missouri, taking passage on the steamer *Gladiator*. Arrived at Commerce February 24.
February 28.— We remained in camp until we took up the line of march for New Madrid, forming part of the First Brigade of the First Division of the Army of the Mississippi under General Pope and were mustered for pay while encamped on Colonel Hunter's Farm.

Stationed in camp near Hamburg, Tennessee, March-April 1862.
[For record of events, see Company C.]
April 13.— Remained in camp at New Madrid until embarked on steamer *Admiral* for Fort Pillow.

Stationed at Camp Clear Creek, May-June 1862.
May 1.— Left our camp and marched about five miles on the road to Farmington and encamped.
May 2.— General Tyler was in command of the First Brigade, Second Division of which the Thirty-ninth formed a part.

May 4.— Marched to a point within two miles of Farmington, where we were protected by entrenchments and batteries, forming part of the division of General Stanley. Were ordered on an armed reconnaissance towards Corinth. Got to within one mile of the outworks when we fired upon Rebel cavalry. Immediately a battery opened upon us with shot and shell. Returned to camp at night.
May 17.— Moved our camp to Farmington.
May 24.— Five companies were ordered out to support a battery driving in the picket.
May 28.— Marched towards Corinth and took a position within two miles of Corinth and dug rifle pits, a portion of our forces skirmishing with the enemy all day.
May 29.— Stayed in trenches.
May 30.— Early in the morning were ordered out. Marched in the main road and after some skirmishing entered the deserted works at 6.40 a.m. The flags of the Thirty-ninth and Forty-second Illinois being the first planted. At 5 p.m. the same day, started in pursuit of Rebels marching on the Danville Road. Encamped six miles from Farmington.
June 1.— Marched towards Booneville. Encamped two miles north of Booneville.
June 3.— Marched to Booneville. Returned to camp.
June 7.— Changed camp two miles to the right.
June 11.— Returned to old camp near Corinth.
June 12.— Changed camp three-fourths to the left.
June 15.— Received payment for March and April.
June 23.— Had regimental inspection.

Stationed at Camp Clear Creek, Mississippi, August 18, 1862.

Stationed at Iuka, Mississippi, July-August 1862.
[For record of events, see Company C.]
August 31.— Mustered for July and August.

Stationed at camp at Corinth, Mississippi, September-October 1862.
[For record of events, see Company A.]
October 4.— Participated in the battle of Corinth.

Stationed at camp near Corinth, Mississippi, November-December 1862.
November 2-7.— The regiment marched from Corinth, Mississippi, the place of last muster, and arrived at Grand Junction, Tennessee on November 7.
November 17.— Encamped near Grand Junction and remained until the camp was removed five miles south.
November 28.— It remained until the regiment marched seven miles south of Holly Springs.
November 30.— The regiment formed part of a reconnaissance in force in the direction of the Tallahatchie River.
December 10.— The regiment took up line of march and moved to Oxford, Mississippi and encamped two miles south of Oxford.
December 18.— The regiment moved by rail to Jackson, Tennessee, leaving camp and garrison equipage behind.
December 20.— Formed part of force under command of General Sullivan and marched nineteen miles in Lexington, Tennessee.
December 21.— Returned to Jackson.
December 27.— Remained in bivouac near Jackson until the regiment moved to Trenton by rail.
December 28-29.— Formed part of a force marched in direction of Huntingdon, Tennessee and arrived there December 29.
December 31.— Remained until it again resumed the march with the First Brigade under command of Colonel Fuller commanding brigade towards the Tennessee River. Sixteen miles from Huntingdon came upon the enemy under command of General Forrest who had been engaged with Colonel Dunham's Union Brigade during the day. Assisted to put the enemy to rout in recapturing prisoners, guns, and train and in capturing a portion of the enemy's artillery and forces.

Stationed at camp near Corinth, Mississippi, January-February 1863.
February 28.— Remained in camp at Corinth until the day of muster.

Stationed at camp near Corinth, Mississippi, April 15, 1863.

Stationed at camp on Bear Creek, March-April 1863.
[For record of events, see Regiment.]

Stationed at Memphis, Tennessee, May 30-June 30, 1863.
May 1.— The regiment continued the march toward Corinth, crossing Bear Creek and marching to Booneville, fifteen miles.
May 2.— Marched to Corinth, eighteen miles, and went into camp formerly occupied.
May 12.— Remained until regiment moved to Memphis by rail and encamped one mile south of town.
June 30.— The regiment has since remained doing guard duty until mustered for pay by Colonel E. F. Noyes of the Thirty-ninth Ohio Volunteer Infantry.

Stationed at Memphis, Tennessee, July-August 1863.

Stationed at Iuka, Mississippi, September-October 1863.
October 18-29.— Left Memphis and marched to this place, Iuka, Mississippi and arrived here on October 29. Nothing worthy of note occurred on the march.

Stationed at Columbia, Tennessee, November-December 1863.
December 31.— Moved from camp about 7 o'clock and marched to Smith Station some ten miles. Got regiment on cars and started for Nashville. Experienced very cold weather. Arrived at Nashville about 9 p.m. The regiment quartered in the City Barracks.

Stationed at Athens, Alabama, January-February 1864.
January 1-3.— Got transportation on board transport and started for Cairo, Illinois and arrived there at noon of January 3. Got transportation on cars for Cincinnati.
January 6.— Arrived there in the morning and proceeded to Camp Dennison to be paid and furloughed.
January 10.— Were paid.
January 11.— Furloughed for thirty days.
February 11.— The regiment reorganized with orders to take the field immediately.
February 12-18.— The regiment embarked on transports *Arizona* and *Reserve* and proceeded to Nashville and arrived there February 18 to take quarters in city hospital.

February 20-21.— The regiment took cars for Pulaski, Tennessee and arrived there February 21. The regiment marched from there to Prospect, Tennessee, about thirteen miles, and arrived there in the evening.
February 22-23.— Marched from camp about 8 o'clock. Took up lines of march for Athens, Alabama and arrived there at 4 p.m. February 23.
February 29.— Remained in camp until day of muster.

Stationed at Decatur, Alabama, March-April 1864.

Stationed at Kenesaw Mountain, Georgia, May-June 1864.

Stationed at Jonesborough, Georgia, July-August 1864.

Stationed at Cave Spring, September-October 1864.
[For record of events, see Company B.]

Stationed at Savannah, Georgia, November-December 1864.
November 1.— Marched from Van's Valley to Cedartown, ten miles.
November 2.— Marched nine miles.
November 3.— Marched to Dallas, passing Van Wert, nineteen miles.
November 4.— Marched to Lost Mountain, ten miles.
November 5.— Marched to Smyrna Campground, twelve miles.
November 6-12.— In camp. Marched to tear up railroad from Big Shanty to Marietta.
November 13.— Marched to Peach Tree Creek.
November 14.— To Atlanta, eight miles.
November 15-16.— Marched with division train twenty miles.
November 17.— Marched to Jackson, seventeen miles.
November 18.— Marched to Ocmulgee River, ten miles.
November 19.— Marched through Monticello to Hillsborough, thirteen miles.
November 20-22.— Marched southward to Gordon, thirty-three miles.
November 24.— Marched eastward ten miles.
November 25.— Marched to Sandersville, nine miles.
November 26.— Marched to Oconee River, nine miles.
November 27.— Marched to northwest ten miles.

November 28.— Marched fifteen miles.
November 29.— Marched to Williams' Swamp, thirteen miles.
November 30.— Marched to Ogeechee River at Sebastopol Station, ten miles.
December 1.— Marched seven miles along the railroad, destroying it.
December 2.— Marched to Millen, eleven miles.
December 3.— Marched to Station No. 7, nine miles.
December 4.— Marched to Cameron, fifteen miles.
December 5.— Marched to Horton Station, driving the enemy out of his works at the Little Ogeechee River, ten miles.
December 7.— Marched along railroad thirteen miles.
December 8.— Marched to Station No. 2, eleven miles.
December 9.— Marched to Station No. 1, ten miles.
December 10.— Marched six miles driving the enemy into his works four miles from Savannah. During the night built works within 800 yards of the enemy.
December 11.— Still in position. Relieved by Fourteenth Army Corps. Marched to [illegible], nine miles.
December 14-16.— Went on foraging expedition to Midway Church, thirty miles. Returned December 16.
December 17-21.— Marched with division to Altamaha River, fifty miles, destroying [Savannah, Albany and] Gulf Railroad and returning December 21.
December 24.— Marched to Savannah. Camped near Wassaw Sound three miles east of city.
December 31.— Still in camp.

Stationed near Cheraw, South Carolina, January-February 1865.

Stationed at Raleigh, North Carolina, March-April 1865.

Stationed at Louisville, Kentucky, May-June 1865.

Company E

Stationed at Camp Dennison, Ohio, July 31, 1861.
July 31.— Muster-in roll of Captain John S. Jenkins' Company (E), in the Thirty-ninth Regiment of Ohio Foot Volunteers, commanded by Colonel John Groesbeck, called into the service of the

United States by the President from the July 31, 1861 (date of this muster) for the term of three years, unless sooner discharged. The company was organized by Captain Jenkins at Mount Carmel, Clermont County in the month of July 1861 and marched thence to Camp Colerain, Hamilton County, Ohio, where it arrived the July 13, 1861, a distance of thirty miles. . . .

T. W. WALKER,
First Lieutenant,
Third Infantry, Mustering Officer.

Stationed at Camp Benton, Saint Louis, Missouri, July 31-September 1, 1861.

The company was recruited and organized by Captain John S. Jenkins and Lieutenant John J. Hooker and John Davis.

July 13.— Went into Camp Colerain, Hamilton County, Ohio under Colonel John Groesbeck.

August 2.— From thence to Camp Dennison, Hamilton County, Ohio, a distance of thirty miles.

August 18-20.— From thence to Camp Benton, Saint Louis, where it arrived on August 20. The company was the first company in camp of the Thirty-ninth Regiment, Ohio Volunteers, United States Army.

Stationed at Camp Prentiss, Chillicothe, Missouri, September-October 1861.

Stationed at Palmyra, Missouri, [October] 31-December 31, 1861.

December 3.— Left Macon City, Missouri under command of Brigadier-General Prentiss.

December 4.— Arrived at Saint Joseph.

December 5.— Marched to Platte River and encamped.

December 6.— Marched to Ridgely, eighteen miles.

December 7.— On account of rain marched only six miles to Smithville.

December 8.— Marched from Smithville to Liberty, eighteen miles.

December 11.— Remained until marched from Liberty to Albany, sixteen miles.

December 12.— Marched from Albany to opposite Lexington. The command threw a few shot and shell into the town which was answered by musketry doing no damage. In the afternoon marched to Richmond making total distance for the day of twenty-six miles.
December 13-15.— Remained at Richmond until December 15, when marched to Shanghai on the Missouri River. Was fired upon by musketry from the opposite bank, which was returned by us, killing two of the enemy and sinking their ferry boat.
December 16.— Marched to Carrollton, sixteen miles.
December 17.— Marched to Coloma, sixteen miles.
December 18-21.— Marched to Grand River Bridge on the Hannibal and Saint Joseph Railroad for Palmyra, arriving on the morning of December 21.

Stationed at camp in the field at Hunter's Farm, Missouri, January-February 1862.
February 12-13.— Left barracks at Palmyra, Missouri and arrived at Benton Barracks via Hannibal and Saint Joseph Railroad and North Missouri Railroad on the afternoon of February 13.
February 22-24.— Left Benton Barracks at noon. Marched to landing at Saint Louis. Took the steamboat *Gladiator* for Commerce, Missouri at which point arrived February 24 a.m. and encamped one and one-half miles west of the town.
February 28-29.— In a.m. took up line of march for New Madrid, Missouri. Marched thirteen miles and bivouacked at Hunter's Farm. The wagon train, owing to the bad roads, not arriving until next morning.

Stationed at camp on the Corinth Road, Tennessee, March-April 1862.
March 3.— Marched to within sight of New Madrid, Missouri. Formed in line of battle and proceeded within range of the enemy's guns, which opened upon us a heavy fire of shot and shell. After remaining exposed to their fire for some time without receiving any damage, we retired to camp about two miles from the enemy's batteries. Made several reconnaissances of the enemy's works at different —— receiving no injury from their fire.

March 13.— In conjunction with the several regiments and batteries comprising General Stanley's Division, marched before daylight to attack the enemy's works. Soon a heavy cannonading was commenced on both sides, being kept up all day without much intermission. Our company received no damage although greatly exposed to the shot and shell. At night a heavy storm arose which afforded good facility for the evacuation of the place by the enemy, which was accomplished during the night.
April 9.— The company, with the regiment, took an active part in the capture of Island No. 10.
April 12.— Left New Madrid on steamer for down the Mississippi River. Reached within four miles of Fort Pillow.
April 17-23.— Remained until returned up the Mississippi and Tennessee Rivers arriving at Hamburg Landing April 23.
April 30.— At present encamped about twelve miles northeast of Corinth, Mississippi.

Stationed at Camp Clear Creek near Corinth, Mississippi, May-June 1862.
May 1.— Moved from Hamburg Landing to within eleven miles of Corinth, Mississippi.
May 3.— Moved from above camp to two miles north of Farmington.
May 8.— Reconnoitered in force with General Pope's Division toward Corinth.
May 19.— Removed camp to Farmington.
May 28-29.— Advanced with whole force toward Corinth. Were shelled by Rebel batteries. Threw up entrenchments within fire of the Rebel battery. Bivouacked on nights of May 28 and 29.
May 30.— At 6 a.m. Thirty-ninth Regiment ordered to ascertain whether or not Corinth had been evacuated in company with Forty-seventh Illinois Regiment. Marched into Corinth. At 5 p.m. left entrenchments in pursuit of enemy. Marched eight miles and bivouacked.
June 3.— Marched to Booneville. At night First Lieutenant John J. Hooker ordered under arrest by Brigadier-General Stanley for writing a communication published in the *Cincinnati Daily Times* of April 19, 1862 charging him (General Stanley) with cruel treatment of the men under his charge on the night of April 8, 1862 at Island No. 10 by causing them to remain exposed to a severe storm when shelter was within a reasonable distance.

June 11.— Remained near there (bivouacked) until returned to old camp near Clear Creek, six miles south of Corinth.
June 30.— At present encamped there.

Stationed at Camp Clear Creek, Mississippi, August 18, 1862.

Stationed at Eastport, Mississippi, July-August 1862.
August 20-22.— Left Camp Clear Creek, Mississippi and marched to Iuka with regiment from whence in conjunction of Company A, was sent as detachment to Eastport, Mississippi, at which place arrived on the afternoon of August 22.

Stationed at camp near Corinth, Mississippi, September-October 1862.
September 12.— Remained at Iuka until marched to Clear Creek, distance twenty-four miles, and bivouacked.
September 14-17.— On a reconnaissance in the direction of Iuka.
September 18.— Rejoined the division at Jacinto.
September 19.— Marched a distance of sixteen miles. Had an engagement with the enemy.
September 20.— Entered Iuka, the enemy having gone during the night. Followed the enemy ten miles from Iuka and bivouacked.
September 21.— Marched towards Jacinto, twenty miles, and bivouacked.
September 22.— Went into camp one and one-half miles from Jacinto.
September 28.— Remained in camp.
September 29.— Marched to and bivouacked at Rienzi, distance nine miles.
September 30.— In bivouac at Rienzi.
October 1.— Marched through Kossuth and bivouacked on the Tuscumbia River.
October 3.— Marched to Corinth and took position in line of battle on the west side of the town in support of Battery Robinett, the enemy in front.
October 4.— Participated in the battle of Corinth.
October 5-7.— Pursued the enemy; marched forty miles.
October 8.— The regiment ordered on reconnaissance in the direction of Ripley.
October 9.— In bivouac near Ripley.
October 10.— Marched in direction of Corinth, twenty miles.

October 11.— Passed through Kossuth and bivouacked on Tuscumbia River.
October 12.— Marched into Corinth. Encamped on east side of town inside of breastworks.
October 13-31.— In camp and mustered for pay.

Stationed at camp near Corinth, Mississippi, November-December 1862.
[For record of events, see Company B.]

Stationed at camp near Corinth, Mississippi, January-February 1863.
January 1.— Marched from battlefield, Parker's Cross-Roads to Lexington, twelve miles.
January 2.— Marched from Lexington to Snake Creek on Clifton, Tennessee road in pursuit of Forrest's Cavalry, twenty-five miles.
January 3.— Marched to Clifton on Tennessee River. Skirmished across the river with the enemy, they all having crossed. Marched back to Snake Creek.
January 5.— Remained at Snake Creek until marched to Jack's Creek on Purdy Road, seventeen miles.
January 6.— Marched to Robinson's Mills, sixteen miles.
January 7.— Marched to Bethel on Mobile and Ohio Railroad, sixteen miles.
January 8.— Marched towards Corinth, fourteen miles.
January 9-February 28.— Marched to Corinth, seventeen miles. Camped on mile south of town, where regiment remained until mustered February 28.

Stationed at camp near Corinth, Mississippi, April 15, 1863.

Stationed at Big Bear Creek, March-April 1863.
[For record of events, see Regiment.]

Stationed at Memphis, Tennessee, May-June 1863.
May 1.— The regiment continued the march toward Corinth, crossing Bear Creek and marching to Burnsville, sixteen miles.
May 2.— Marched to Corinth, eighteen miles, and went into camp formerly occupied.

May 12-June 30.— Remained until regiment moved to Memphis by rail and encamped one mile south of town, where regiment has since remained doing guard duty until mustered for pay June 30 by Colonel E. F. Noyes of the Thirty-ninth Ohio Volunteer Infantry.

Stationed at Memphis, July-August 1863.

Stationed at Iuka, Mississippi, September-October 1863.

Stationed at Columbia, Tennessee, November-December 1863.
November 20-23.— Left Iuka, Mississippi, place of last muster, and arrived at Prospect, Tennessee via Eastport and Pulaski November 23.
December 29.— Remained at Prospect, Tennessee until the regiment started for Ohio, the company having reenlisted as veteran volunteers. Marched through Pulaski, Tennessee.
December 30.— Marched to Columbia.
December 31.— Mustered for pay and moved from camp about 7 o'clock. Marched to Smith Station some ten miles. Got transportation and started at 9 p.m. for Cairo, Illinois.

Stationed at Athens, Alabama, January-February 1864.
January 3.— Arrived [at Cairo] at noon. Got transportation on cars for Cincinnati, arriving there in the morning on June 6. Proceeded to Camp Dennison to be paid and furloughed.
January 10.— Were paid.
January 11.— Furloughed for thirty days.
February 11.— The regiment reorganized. Was ordered to take the field immediately.
February 12.— The regiment embarked on transports *Arizona* and *Reserve* and proceeded to Nashville and arrived there.
February 18.— Took quarters in city hospital.
February 20-21.— Took cars for Pulaski, Tennessee and arrived there February 21. The regiment marched from there to Prospect, Tennessee about fifteen miles.
February 22.— Arrived there in the evening. Marched from camp at 8 o'clock. Took up line of march for Athens, Alabama and arrived at 4 p.m. February 23.
February 29.— Remained in camp until day of muster.

Stationed at Decatur, Alabama, March-April 1864.

Stationed at Kenesaw Mountain, Georgia, May-June 1864.

Stationed near Jonesborough, Georgia, July-August 1864.
July 1-3.— The company, with the regiment, lay at the foot of Kenesaw Mountain until July 3, when we marched about twelve miles.
July 4.— In the morning the regiment was ordered to advance. After a march of two miles met the enemy and after a severe skirmish drove him into his earthworks. At 6 p.m. changed the enemy and drove him from his works with a loss of three wounded out of company.
July 5.— Marched eight miles.
July 9.— Marched to Marietta, Georgia, a distance of fifteen miles.
July 10.— Marched to Roswell Factory, a distance of twelve miles.
July 11.— Crossed Chattahoochee River.
July 17.— Marched ten miles.
July 18.— Eight miles.
July 19.— Marched to Decatur, Georgia, a distance of ten miles.
July 20.— Marched three miles.
July 21.— Moved in rear of Seventeenth Army Corps.
July 22.— At 10 o'clock the enemy made an attack on our left. We were ordered to move at double-quick to the rear to protect our ammunition and supply train. Met the enemy; fought them three hours and repulsed them with a loss of one noncommissioned officer and three privates out of company.
July 17.— Marched to the right of the Army, a distance of twelve miles.
August 26.— We were engaged in the investment of Atlanta, Georgia until we fell back.
August 27.— Marched eighteen miles.
August 28.— Marched twelve miles.
August 29.— Destroyed Atlanta and Montgomery Railroad.
August 30.— Marched twelve miles.

August 31.— In line of battle on the right flank expecting an attack, the center being heavily engaged with enemy, he having made the attack but was repulsed with great loss at Jonesborough, Georgia.

Stationed at Van's Valley, Georgia, September-October 1864.

In September in front of Jonesborough the enemy evacuated the place during the night southward. Marched in pursuit in vicinity of Lovejoy's Station, four miles. Moved back during the night to Jonesborough.

September 6.— Marched in direction of East Point.

September 7.— Marched eight miles.

September 8.— Marched four miles. Camped one mile south of East Point.

September 10.— Moved to East Point.

September 20.— The regiment lay until it was detailed to put up hospital tents for the Department of Tennessee.

October 4.— Remained on duty at Atlanta until the regiment rejoined the brigade and marched all night and camped five miles north of Chattahoochee.

October 6.— Marched all night and camped three miles from Marietta, eighteen miles. Marched to Big Shanty, nine miles, and bivouacked.

October 10.— Marched to Acworth.

October 11.— Marched to Cartersville, fifteen miles.

October 12.— Marched passing through Kingston, Georgia. Marched eighteen miles from Resaca within seven miles from Rome, Georgia.

October 13.— Started and marched all night to Adairsville.

October 14.— Took the cars for Resaca then marched to Snake Creek Gap. Drove the enemy back and returned to Resaca at 5 a.m.

October 15.— Marched to Snake Creek Gap and drove the enemy through and camped eighteen miles from Resaca.

October 16.— Marched eight miles from Blue Mountains.

October 17.— Marched at daylight passing through Ship's Gap nearly four miles.

October 18.— The regiment ordered to remain and guard cross-roads while the Army passed. Marched at 10 o'clock, passing through Summerville, where rejoined the brigade.

October 20.— Marched to Gaylesville, [Alabama], forty-nine miles.
October 29.— Moved from Gaylesville at 7 o'clock; crossed the Chattooga and Coosa Rivers, passing through Cedar Bluff; marched twelve miles and camped.
October 30.— Marched eighteen miles to Cape Spring and camped.
October 31.— The regiment in camp at Cave Spring, where it was mustered for pay.

Stationed at Savannah, Georgia, November-December 1864.
November 1.— Marched from Van's Valley to Cedartown, ten miles.
November 2.— Marched nine miles.
November 3.— Marched to Dallas, seventeen miles, passing through Van Wert.
November 4.— Marched to Lost Mountain, ten miles.
November 5.— Marched twelve miles.
November 6-12.— In camp. At dark destroyed railroad from Big Shanty to Marietta.
November 13.— Marched to Peach Tree Creek.
November 14.— Marched to Atlanta, eight miles.
November 15-16.— Marched with division train, thirty miles.
November 17.— Marched to Jackson.
November 18.— Marched to Ocmulgee, ten miles.
November 19.— Marched to Monticello.
November 20-22.— Marched southward to Gordon Station.
November 24.— Marched to Oconee River.
November 27.— Marched ten miles.
November 28.— Marched fifteen miles.
November 29.— Marched to Williams' Swamp, thirteen miles.
November 30.— Marched to Ogeechee River at Sebastopol Station, ten miles.
December 1.— Marched seven miles along railroad destroying it. Marched to Millen Station, eleven miles.
December 3.— Marched to Station No. 79.
December 4.— Marched to Cameron Station, fifteen miles.
December 5.— Marched to Horton Station.
December 6.— Drove the enemy out of works at Little Ogeechee River.
December 7.— Marched along railroad, thirteen miles.

December 8.— Marched to Station No. 2, eleven miles.
December 9.— Marched to Station No. 1, ten miles.
December 10.— Marched driving the enemy into his main works four miles from Savannah. During the night built a line of works within 800 yards of the enemy.
December 11.— Still in position. Relieved by Fourteenth Army Corps. Moved to right nine miles.
December 14.— Marched on forage expedition to Midway Church, thirty miles.
December 16-17.— Marched with division to Altamaha River fifty miles to destroy railroad.
December 21.— Returned.
December 22.— Marched to Savannah and camped near Wassaw Sound, three miles out of city.
December 31.— Still in camp.

Stationed near Cheraw, South Carolina, January-February 1865.
January 1.— At Savannah, Georgia.
January 3-4.— Took steamer for Beaufort, South Carolina and arrived January 4.
January 5.— Remained until marched seven miles.
January 14.— Marched ten miles.
January 15.— Marched to Pocotaligo, enemy evacuating.
January 20.— Made a reconnaissance to Salkehatchie River and returned to camp, a distance of eight miles.
January 21.— Marched to Tulifinny.
January 22.— Returned to Pocotaligo.
January 26.— Made a reconnaissance to Salkehatchie. Returned to camp.
January 30.— Marched northwesterly. Camped near Salkehatchie River.
January 31.— Remained in camp.
February 1.— Moved and heavy skirmishing. Marched eight miles.
February 3.— Crossed Whippy Swamp and Salkehatchie River by wading river and drove the enemy from their works.
February 7.— Marched twelve miles. Camped on railroad at Midway. Moved camp one mile.
February 9.— Marched and crossed South Edisto River.
February 12.— Crossed in direction of Columbia. Marched twelve miles.

February 13.— Marched nine miles.
February 16.— Four miles, crossed Congaree River.
February 17.— Crossed Saluda River. Moved and crossed Broad River. Marched through Columbia.
February 18.— Destroyed railroad all day.
February 19.— Remained in camp.
February 20.— Moved and destroyed railroad. Marched twelve miles.
February 21.— Marched twelve miles.
February 22.— Marched through Winnsborough.
February 23.— Crossed the Wateree River. Marched ten miles.
February 24.— Marched through Liberty Hill. Country hilly, rocky. Marched eight miles.
February 25.— Marched fifteen miles.
February 26.— Crossed Little Lynch's Creek. Marched eight miles.
February 27.— Crossed Big Lynch's Creek. Marched four miles.
February 28.— Marched sixteen miles and camped.

Stationed at Neuse River near Raleigh, North Carolina, March-April 1865.

Stationed at Louisville, Kentucky, May-June 1865.

Company F

Stationed at Camp Dennison, Ohio, August 13, 1861.
August 13.— Muster-in roll of Captain Jacob Koenig's Company (F), in the Thirty-ninth Regiment of Ohio Foot Volunteers, commanded by Colonel John Groesbeck, called into the service of the United States by the President from August 13, 1861 (date of this muster) for the term of three years, unless sooner discharged. The company was organized by Captain Jacob Koenig at Marietta, Ohio, in the month of July 1861 and marched thence to Camp Dennison via Camp Colerain, where it arrived August 13, a distance of 180 miles. . . .

T. W. WALKER,
First Lieutenant,
Third Infantry, Mustering Officer.

Stationed at Greenfield, Missouri, October 31, 1861.
August 18-20.— This company left Camp Dennison, Ohio for Camp Benton, Missouri and arrived there August 20.
September 6-8.— Remained until it was ordered to Mexico, Missouri and arrived there on September 8.
September 13-18.— Left Mexico under General Sturgis for Lexington via Hudson and Utica. Arrived in sight of Lexington September 18 but turned off towards Kansas City via Richmond, Camden, and Liberty.
September 21.— Arrived at Kansas City.
October 15.— Left Kansas City to take possession on the extreme right of Frémont's Grand Army by Pleasant Hill, Osceola and Bolivar.
October 30.— Arrived at Greenfield.
October 31.— Inspected and mustered for pay. This company left Greenfield, Missouri at 5 p.m., forming part of Brigadier-General Sturgis' Brigade under orders to join the Army of the West at Springfield.

Stationed at Syracuse, Missouri, November-December 1861.
November 1.— Arrived at Springfield about 5 p.m., marching about thirty-three miles.
November 9.— Remained in that place until it formed part of the brigade commanded by Acting Brigadier-General Totten in the Fifth Division of the Army under Acting Major-General Sturgis and took up the line of march for Warsaw by way of Bolivar and Quincy.
November 14-16.— Arrived at Warsaw and then marched to Sedalia, the terminus of the Pacific Railroad, arriving there November 16. At Sedalia received pay and clothing.
December 8-10.— Remained in camp near Georgetown until we received orders from General Pope to march to Syracuse, forming part of the detachment of the Thirty-ninth Regiment, Ohio Volunteers under command of Lieutenant-Colonel A. W. Gilbert and arrived at Syracuse December 10.
December 31.— Inspected and mustered for pay.

Stationed near Commerce, Missouri, January-February 1862.
February 2.— This company left Syracuse, Missouri, the place of last muster, together with Companies C, D, H, and G, and marched to Boonville, Missouri.
February 7-16.— Crossed the river and marched in the brigade under command of Colonel Worthington, Fifth Iowa Volunteers via Columbia and Fulton to Saint Charles, Missouri, where they arrived February 16. Crossed the river and marched to Benton Barracks, Saint Louis, Missouri.
February 17.— They arrived and rejoined the other half of the regiment under Colonel Groesbeck.
February 22.— Embarked on board steamboat *Gladiator*.
February 24.— Landed and encamped near Commerce, Missouri.
February 28.— Inspected and mustered for pay.

Stationed at camp on Corinth Road, Tennessee, March-April 1862.
March 1-3.— Forming part of the First Brigade, First Division, Army of the Mississippi under General Pope, took up line of march from Hunter's Farm for New Madrid, Missouri, arriving there on March 3. Made a demonstration before the town and was fired upon by Fort Thompson and gunboats. Retired at dark and camped one and one-half miles from the town.
March 7.— Formed part of a reconnaissance in force and was fired upon again from the upper fort and gunboats at 3 a.m.
March 13.— Marched on the forts and town. Took supporting distance in rear of a battery of four siege guns. Remained all day amid a shower of shot and shells and all night in a terrible and drenching rain. Was relieved at daylight.
April 7.— Remained in camp until ordered to the river. Crossed the Mississippi in order to get in position in the rear of Island No. 10. Marched six miles and camped.
April 8.— Marched to Tiptonville, where 6,000 of the enemy had surrendered to the command of General Paine. Marched to Island No. 10 and camped.
April 9.— Took passage on steamer *N. W. Graham* for New Madrid.
April 13.— Remained in camp at New Madrid until embarked on steamer *New Uncle Sam* for Fort Pillow.
April 16.— Arrived above the fort.

April 17-23.— Ordered to Pittsburg Landing and arrived there on April 23.
April 27.— Went into camp at Hamburg. Moved camp five miles in advance.
April 29.— Formed part of a reconnaissance in force. Drove in the pickets of the enemy and captured a number of prisoners. Returned to camp.

Stationed at Camp Clear Creek, six miles south of Corinth, Mississippi, May-June 1862.
May 1.— Left camp about five miles from Hamburg Landing, Tennessee. Marched about five miles on the road to Farmington and encamped.
May 2.— General Tyler assumed command of the First Brigade, Second Division, Army of the Mississippi of which the Thirty-ninth formed a part.
May 8.— Marched to a point within two miles of Farmington, forming a part of the division under General Stanley. Were ordered out on an armed reconnaissance towards Corinth and got within one mile of the outworks and engaged in a skirmish with the enemy and were fired upon with shot and shell. Returned to camp at night.
May 17.— Moved camp to Farmington, where we were protected by entrenchments and batteries.
May 24.— Five companies, of which Company F was one, were ordered out to support a battery and drive in the Rebel pickets, which we accomplished.
May 28.— Marched towards Corinth and took a position about two miles from that place and dug rifle pits. Constant skirmishing going on all day. Four men of the Thirty-ninth wounded.
May 29.— Continued all day in the trenches.
May 30.— Ordered early in the morning to advance towards Corinth. Did so in the main road driving their pickets before us and entered the deserted works of Corinth at 6.40 a.m. The flags of the Thirty-ninth and Forty-second Illinois being the first planted. At 5 p.m. started on pursuit of the enemy. Marched six miles on Danville Road.
June 1.— Marched to within two miles of Booneville and bivouacked.
June 5.— Advanced to Booneville and returned.
June 7.— Moved about two miles to the right.

June 11.— Returned to old camp six miles south of Corinth, marching twenty-six miles round to avoid the dust.
June 12.— Moved camp three-fourths of a mile to the east.
June 15.— Paid off for the months of March and April.
June 30.— Inspected and mustered for pay.

Stationed at Camp Clear Creek, Mississippi, August 18, 1862.

Stationed at camp near Iuka, Mississippi, July-August 1862.
[For record of events, see Company C.]
August 31.— Mustered for pay by Lieutenant-Colonel E. F. Noyes of the Thirty-ninth Ohio Volunteer Infantry, United States Army.

Stationed at Corinth, Mississippi, September-October 1862.
[For record of events, see Company A.]
October 4.— Participated in the battle of Corinth.

Stationed at Corinth, Mississippi, November-December 1862.
[For record of events, see Company A.]
November 17.— Remained in camp near Grand Junction until the camp was removed five miles south.

Stationed at Corinth, Mississippi, January-February 1863.
[For record of events, see Company C.]

Stationed at Corinth, Mississippi, April 15, 1863.

Stationed at Bear Creek, Mississippi, March-April 1863.
[For record of events, see Regiment.]

Stationed at Memphis, Tennessee, May-June 1863.
May 1.— The regiment continued to march toward Corinth, crossing Bear Creek and marching to Burnsville, sixteen miles.
May 2.— Marched to Corinth, eighteen miles, and went into camp formerly occupied.
May 12.— Remained there until the regiment by rail, moved to Memphis and encamped one mile south of Memphis, where the regiment has since remained doing guard duty.
June 30.— Mustered for pay by Colonel E. T. Noyes of the Thirty-ninth Ohio Regiment.

Stationed at Memphis, Tennessee, July-August 1863.
August 31.— The regiment remained in camp, since last muster, doing guard duty until mustered for pay by Lieutenant-Colonel McDowell.

Stationed at Iuka, Mississippi, September-October 1863.
October 18.— Left Memphis and marched to Iuka.

Stationed in the field, November-December 1863.

Stationed at Athens, Alabama, January-February 1864.
[For record of events, see Company D.]

Stationed at Decatur, Alabama, March-April 1864.
March 1-16.— Remained in camp at Athens, Alabama until March 16 when detached to guard the Swan Creek Trestle Works.
April 22.— Rejoined the regiment at Decatur, Alabama.
April 30.— Mustered by Colonel E. F. Noyes at Decatur, Alabama.

Stationed at Kenesaw Mountain, May-June 1864.
May 1-4.— The company, with the regiment, took up line of march from Decatur, Alabama and after three days' successive marching, reached Woods Station on the Memphis and Charleston Railroad, a distance of fifty miles from Decatur. There took the cars and reached Chattanooga, Tennessee on May 4, a distance of fifty miles.
May 5.— Took up the line of march from Chattanooga and brought up at Resaca, Georgia via Snake Creek Gap, a distance of about forty-five miles. Served with the Army of the Tennessee under the command of Major-General McPherson.
May 11.— Was engaged in active operations against the enemy at Resaca until he evacuated. Then proceeded to Lay's Ferry, Oostenaula Creek, Georgia, a distance of five miles.
May 14.— Reached Kingston, Georgia, a distance of fifty miles from Lay's Ferry.
May 23.— Left Kingston and reached Dallas, Georgia on May 26, a distance of fifty miles. Was engaged in the operations against the enemy at Dallas serving with the First Brigade, Fourth Division, Sixteenth Army Corps, Army of the Tennessee.

June 1.— Marched to Pumpkin Vine Creek, a distance of five miles.
June 5-6.— Took up line of march and reached Acworth, Georgia on June 6, a distance of ten miles.
June 10.— Moved to Big Shanty Station, Georgia, a distance of five miles.
June 12-30.— Took position in front of the enemy posted on Kenesaw Mountain and since that time have been engaged in his investment.

Stationed at Jonesborough, Georgia, July-August 1864.

Stationed at Cave Spring, Georgia, September-October 1864.
September 1.— In front of Jonesborough, Georgia.
September 2.— The enemy evacuated the place during the night and retreated southward. Marched in pursuit to vicinity of Lovejoy's Station, four miles.
September 5.— Moved back during the night to Jonesborough.
September 6.— Marched four miles in direction of East Point.
September 7.— Marched eight miles.
September 8.— Marched four miles and camped one mile south of East Point.
September 10.— Moved camp to East Point.
September 20.— The regiment lay until it was detailed to go to Atlanta to put up hospital tents for the Department of Tennessee.
October 4-5.— Remained on duty at Atlanta until the regiment joined the brigade on its northward march. Marched all night and camped five miles north of the Chattahoochee River.
October 6.— Marched all night and camped three miles from Marietta.
October 9.— Marched to Big Shanty, nine miles and bivouacked.
October 10.— Marched at 10 p.m. to Acworth, seven miles.
October 11.— Marched to Cartersville, fifteen miles.
October 12.— Marched at daylight passing through Kingston and marched eighteen miles to a point within seven miles of Rome.
October 13.— Started at 5 p.m. and marched all night to Adairsville, sixteen miles.
October 14.— Took cars for Resaca and after arriving there, marched to Snake Creek Gap, eight miles. Drove the enemy back two miles and returned to Resaca at 5 a.m.

October 15.— Marched at 4 a.m. to Snake Creek Gap and drove the enemy through and camped eighteen miles from Resaca.
October 16.— Marched eight miles and camped near Blue Mountains.
October 17.— Marched at dark passing through Ship's Gap and camped west of the mountains, making four miles.
October 18.— The regiment ordered to remain in rear and guard cross-roads while the whole Army passed.
October 19-20.— Marched at 1 a.m., passing through Summerville and Alpine, where we joined the brigade, and marched to Gaylesville, Alabama on October 20, four miles from the mountains.
October 29.— Moved from Gaylesville at 7 a.m. and crossed the Chattooga River, passing through Cedar Bluff. Marched twelve miles and camped.
October 30.— Marched eighteen miles to Cave Spring and camped.
October 31.— The regiment remained in camp, where it is mustered for pay.

Stationed at camp near Savannah, Georgia, November-December 1864.
November 1.— Marched from Van's Valley to Cedartown, distance ten miles.
November 2.— Marched nine miles.
November 3.— Marched to Dallas, passing Van Wert, distance nineteen miles.
November 4.— Marched to Lost Mountain, distance ten miles.
November 5.— Smyrna Campground, twelve miles.
November 6-12.— Remained in camp until November 12, when marched to tear up railroad from Big Shanty to Marietta.
November 13.— Marched to Peach [Tree] Creek.
November 14.— Marched to Atlanta, eight miles.
November 15-16.— With provision train, distance twenty miles.
November 17.— Marched to Jackson, seventeen miles.
November 18.— To Ocmulgee River.
November 19.— To Monticello and to Hillsborough, thirteen miles.
November 20-22.— Marched southwest to Gordon, distance thirty-three miles.
November 23.— In camp.

November 24— Marched to Edwards Station, distance ten miles.
November 25.— To Sandersville, nine miles.
November 27-29.— Northwest to Williams' Swamp, thirty-eight miles.
November 30.— Crossed Ogeechee River at Sebastopol Station, ten miles.
December 1.— Along railroad, seven miles, diminishing it.
December 2.— To Millen, Station No. 8, eleven miles.
December 3.— To Station No. 7, nine miles.
December 4.— To Cameron Station, fifteen miles.
December 5-17.— To Horton Station. Marched and went driving the enemy to December 17, when went foraging back from [Savannah, Albany and] Gulf Railroad, forty miles
December 24-31.— Marched to Savannah in camp three miles of city and remained until December 31.

Stationed at Cheraw, South Carolina, January-February 1865.
The command accompanied General Sherman in his campaign through North and South Carolina.

Station not stated, March-April 1865.

Stationed at Louisville, Kentucky, May-June 1865.

Company G

Stationed at Camp Dennison, Ohio, July 31, 1861.
July 31.— Muster-in roll of Captain Charles W. Pomeroy's Company, in the Thirty-ninth Regiment of Ohio Foot Volunteers, commanded by Colonel John Groesbeck, called into the service of the United States by the President from July 31, 1861 (date of this muster) for the term of three years, unless sooner discharged. The company was organized by Captain Charles W. Pomeroy at Cincinnati, Ohio in the month of July and marched thence to Camp Colerain and thence to Camp Dennison, where it arrived August 2, distance thirty miles. . . .

T. W. WALKER,
First Lieutenant,
Third Infantry, Mustering Officer.

Stationed at Greenfield, Missouri, July 1-October 31, 1861.
August 18-20.— This company left Camp Dennison, Ohio for Camp Benton, Missouri, where it arrived August 20.
September 6-8.— Remained until it was ordered to Mexico, Missouri, arriving there on September 8.
September 13.— Left Mexico under General Sturgis for Lexington via Hudson and Utica.
September 18-21.— Arrived in sight of Lexington but turned off toward Kansas City via Richmond, Camden and Liberty and arrived at Kansas City September 21.
October 15-30.— Left Kansas City to take position on the extreme right of Frémont's Grand Army via Pleasant Hill, Osceola and Bolivar. Arrived at Greenfield October 30.
October 31.— Inspected and mustered for pay. The company left Greenfield, Missouri at 5 p.m. forming part of Brigadier-General Sturgis' Brigade under orders to join the Army of the West at Springfield.

Stationed at Syracuse, Missouri, November-December 1861.
November 1.— Arrived about 5 p.m., marching about thirty-three miles.
November 9.— Remained in camp at that place until it formed part of the brigade commanded by Acting Brigadier-General Totten in the Fifth Division of the Army under Acting Major-General Sturgis and took up the line of march for Warsaw by way of Bolivar and Quincy.
November 14-16.— Arrived at Warsaw; thence marched to Sedalia, the terminus of the Pacific Railroad, November 16.
December 3.— At Sedalia received pay and clothing.
December 8.— Remained in camp near Georgetown until we received orders from Brigadier-General Pope to march to Syracuse, forming part of the detachment of the Thirty-ninth Regiment, Ohio Volunteers under command of Lieutenant-Colonel A. W. Gilbert.
December 9.— Arrived at Syracuse. Went into camp.
December 31.— Was inspected and mustered for pay.

W. H. LATHROP,
Commanding Company.

Stationed at camp in the field, Missouri, January-February 1862.
[For record of events, see Company D.]

W. H. LATHROP,
Commanding Company.

Stationed with Army in the field, March-April 1862.
[For record of events, see Company C.]
April 13.— Remained in camp at New Madrid until embarked on steamer *Admiral* for Fort Pillow.

W. H. LATHROP,
Commanding Company.

Stationed at Camp Clear Creek, May-June 1862.
[For record of events, see Company C.]

W. H. LATHROP,
Commanding Company.

Stationed at Camp Clear Creek, Mississippi, August 18, 1862.

Stationed at Iuka, Mississippi, July-August 1862.
[For record of events, see Company C.]
August 18.— The regiment mustered by Colonel Gilbert in accordance with General Orders No. 71, District of West Tennessee.
August 21.— Arrived at Iuka, Mississippi about 10 a.m. Camped on ridge south of springs.

JOHN W. ORR,
First Lieutenant,
Commanding Company.

Stationed at Corinth, Mississippi, September-October 1862.
[For record of events, see Company A.]
October 4.— Participated in the battle of Corinth.

Stationed at Corinth, Mississippi, November-December 1863.
November 2-7.— The regiment marched from Corinth, Mississippi, the last place of muster, and arrived at Grand Junction, Tennessee November 7 and encamped near Grand Junction.
November 17.— Remained until the camp was removed five miles south.

November 28.— The regiment moved; marched seven miles south of Holly Springs.
November 30.— The regiment joined part of a reconnaissance in force in the direction of the Tallahatchie River.
December 10.— The regiment moved to Oxford and encamped two [miles] south of Oxford.
December 18.— The regiment moved by rail to Jackson, Tennessee, leaving camp and garrison equipage behind.
December 20.— Formed part of force under command of General Sullivan and marched nineteen miles toward Lexington, Tennessee.
December 21.— Returned to Jackson.
December 27.— Remained in Jackson until the regiment moved to Trenton by rail.
December 28-29.— Formed part of a force that marched in the direction of Huntingdon, Tennessee, arriving there December 29.
December 31.— Remained there until resumed the march with First Brigade, Colonel Fuller commanding, toward the Tennessee River. Sixteen miles from Huntingdon came upon the enemy under command of General Forrest, who had been engaged with Colonel Dunham's Union Brigade during the day. Assisted to put the enemy to rout, in recapturing prisoners, guns and train and in capturing a portion of the enemy's artillery and forces.

Stationed at Corinth, Mississippi, January-February 1863.

Stationed at Corinth, Mississippi, April 15, 1863.

Stationed at Bear Creek, Alabama, March-April 1863.
April 20.— The company remained in camp at Corinth from last muster (February 28) until we marched with the brigade to Burnsville, twenty-one miles over a very bad road.
April 21.— Marched by way of Iuka to Bear Creek, seventeen miles, and joined General Dodge's Division.
April 23.— Remained in bivouac until we marched sixteen miles in the direction of Tuscumbia.
April 24.— Marched to Tuscumbia and bivouacked on the west side of town.
April 27.— Marched twelve miles in an easterly direction.

April 28.— Moved five miles to the front and took position on west bank of Town Creek, the enemy having made his appearance at that place. Retired after a slight skirmish.
April 29.— Marched twenty miles westward and bivouacked five miles west of Tuscumbia.
April 30.— Marched to Bear Creek, seventeen miles.

Stationed at Memphis, Tennessee, May-June 1863.
May 1.— The regiment continued the march towards Corinth crossing Bear Creek and marching to Burnsville, sixteen miles.
May 2.— Marched to Corinth, eighteen miles, and went into camp formerly occupied.
May 12.— Remained until the regiment moved by rail to Memphis and encamped one mile south of Memphis, where the regiment has since remained doing guard duty until mustered for pay June 30 by Colonel Edward F. Noyes, Thirty-ninth Ohio Regiment.

Stationed at Memphis, Tennessee, July-August 1863.
[For record of events, see Company B.]

Stationed at Iuka, Mississippi, September-October 1863.

Stationed at Columbia, Tennessee, November-December 1863.

Stationed at Athens, Alabama, January-February 1864.

Stationed at Decatur, Alabama, March-April 1864.

Stationed near Kenesaw Mountain, Georgia, May-June 1864.
[For record of events, see Company B.]
May 23.— Left Kingston and reached Dallas, Georgia, a distance of fifty miles.

Stationed near Jonesborough, Georgia, July-August 1864.
July 1.— The company, with the regiment, lay at the foot of Kenesaw Mountain, Georgia.
July 3.— We marched twelve miles.
July 4.— In the morning the regiment was ordered to advance. After a march or two miles met the enemy and after a severe

skirmish, drove him into his earthworks. At 6 p.m. charged the enemy and drove him from his works with a loss of four men wounded out of the company.
July 5.— Marched eight [miles].
July 9.— Marched to Marietta, Georgia, a distance of fifteen miles.
July 10.— Marched to Roswell Factory, a distance of twelve miles.
July 11.— Crossed Chattahoochee River.
July 17.— Marched ten miles.
July 18.— Eight miles.
July 19.— Marched to Decatur, Georgia, a distance of ten miles.
July 20.— Marched three miles.
July 21.— Moved in rear of the Seventeenth Army Corps.
July 22.— At 1 o'clock the enemy made an attack upon our left. We were ordered to move at a double-quick to the rear to protect our ammunition and supply train and there met the enemy. Fought him three hours and repulsed him with a loss of one non-commissioned officer and thirteen privates out of the company.
July 29.— Marched to the right of the Army.
August 26.— We were engaged in the investment of Atlanta, Georgia until we fell back.
August 27.— Marched fifteen miles.
August 28.— Marched eight miles.
August 29.— Destroyed the Atlanta and Montgomery Railroad.
August 30.— Marched twelve miles.
August 31.— In line of battle on the right flank expecting an attack, the center being heavily engaged with the enemy, he having made the attack but was repulsed with great loss at Jonesborough, Georgia.

Stationed at Beaufort, Georgia, September 30-December 31, 1864.
November 1.— Marched from Van's Valley to Cedartown, twenty miles.
November 2.— Marched nine miles.
November 3.— Marched to Dallas, nineteen miles, passing through Van Wert.
November 4.— Marched to Lost Mountain, ten miles.
November 5.— Marched twelve miles south, camping at Smyrna Campground.

November 12.— In camp. At dark marched and destroyed railroad from Big Shanty to Marietta.
November 13.— Marched to Peach Tree Creek.
November 14.— Marched to Atlanta, eight miles.
November 15-16.— Marched with division train, twenty miles.
November 17.— Marched to Jackson, seventeen miles.
November 18.— Marched to Ocmulgee River, ten miles.
November 19.— Marched to Monticello via Hillsborough.
November 20-22.— Marched southward to Gordon.
November 23.— Remained in camp.
November 24.— Eastward ten miles. Camped near Station No. 16.
November 25.— Marched to Summerville.
November 26.— Marched to Oconee River.
November 27.— Marched ten miles.
November 28.— Marched fifteen miles.
November 29.— Marched to Williams' Swamp.
November 30.— Marched to Ogeechee River.
December 1.— Marched seven miles along railroad, destroying it.
December 2.— Marched to Millen, eleven miles.
December 3.— Marched to Station No. 11, nine miles.
December 4.— Marched to Eumans Station, fifteen [miles].
December 5.— Marched to Horton Station, ten miles, driving enemy out of their works at Little Ogeechee River.
December 7.— Marched thirteen miles along railroad.
December 8.— Marched to Station No. 2, nine miles.
December 9.— Marched to Station No. 1, ten miles.
December 10.— Marched driving enemy out of their new works before Savannah. Dark night built line of works within 800 yards of enemy.
December 11.— Still in position relieved by Fourteenth Army Corp. Marched to rear, nine miles.
December 14.— Marched, foraging to Midway Chapel, thirty miles. Returned.
December 16-17.— Marched to Anderson to Altamaha River to destroy railroad.
December 21.— Marched to Savannah and camped near Wassaw Sound three miles out of city.
December 31.— Still in camp.

Stationed in the field, January-February 1865.
January 1.— At Savannah, Georgia.
January 3-4.— Took steamer for Beaufort and arrived January 4.
January 13.— Remained until moved at 6 p.m. Marched nine miles.
January 14.— Moved at 10 a.m. Marched ten miles.
January 15.— Marched to Pocotaligo. Enemy evacuating. Remained in camp.
January 20.— Made a reconnaissance to Salkehatchie River and returned to camp, distance eight miles.
January 21.— Marched to Tulifinny River, raining.
January 22.— Returned to Pocotaligo.
January 26.— Made a reconnaissance to Salkehatchie River and returned to camp.
January 30.— Marched northwesterly and camped near Salkehatchie River.
January 31.— Remained in camp.
February 1.— Moved at 7 o'clock.
February 2.— Marched 7.30 a.m., skirmishing with enemy. Marched eight miles.
February 3.— Crossed swamp and Salkehatchie River by wading and saw the enemy from their works.
February 7.— Moved at 12 m., camped on the C. and R. Railroad near Midway. Marched twelve miles.
February 8.— Moved camp one mile and threw up works.
February 9.— Crossed the Salkehatchie River and waded the swamp. Enemy evacuating. Marched ten miles.
February 10.— Remained in camp.
February 11.— Moved at 12 m. Camped two miles of North Edisto River.
February 12.— Crossed the river and camped north of Orangeburg.
February 13.— Destroyed railroad.
February 14.— Marched in direction of [Columbia], South Carolina. Marched twelve miles.
February 15.— Marched nineteen miles.
February 16.— Crossed the Congaree Creek.
February 17.— Crossed Saluda River at 11 a.m. Crossed Broad River at 4 p.m. Marched through [Columbia], South Carolina.

February 18.— Destroyed railroad.
February 19.— Remained in camp.
February 23.— Crossed the Wateree River.
February 24.— Marched through Liberty Hill.
February 25.— Marched fifteen miles.
February 26.— Marched through Lynch's Creek. Marched eight miles.
February 27.— Moved at 7 a.m. Crossed Big Lynch's Creek. Marched four miles.
February 28.— Marched sixteen miles and camped.

Stationed in the field, March-April 1865.
March 1.— Remained in camp.
March 2-24.— Marched to Cheraw, from thence to Fayetteville, from there to Goldsborough, North Carolina, where we arrived March 24.
April 10-14.— Remained until we marched for Raleigh, North Carolina and arrived April 14.
April 29.— Remained, then we marched fourteen miles.
April 30.— We remained until we were mustered for pay.

Stationed near Louisville, Kentucky, May-June 1865.

Company H

Stationed at Camp Dennison, Ohio, July 31, 1861.
July 31.— Muster-in roll of Captain Adam Koogle's Company (H), in the Thirty-ninth Regiment of Ohio Foot Volunteers, commanded by Colonel John Groesbeck, called into the service of the United States by the President from July 31, 1861 (date of this muster) for the term of three years, unless sooner discharged. The company was organized by Captain Adam Koogle at Wilmington, Ohio in the month of July and marched thence to Camp Dennison, where it arrived August 5, a distance of thirty-six miles. . . .

T. W. WALKER,
First Lieutenant,
Third Infantry, Mustering Officer.

Station not stated, July 31-October 31, 1861.
August 18-20.— The company left Camp Dennison, Ohio for Camp Benton, Saint Louis, Missouri at which place we arrived August 20.
September 6-8.— Remained until we were ordered to Mexico, Missouri, arriving there on September 8.
September 13-18.— Left Mexico under General Sturgis for Lexington, Missouri via Hudson and Utica. Arrived in sight of Lexington September 18. Went to Kansas City via Camden, Richmond and Liberty.
September 20.— Arrived at Kansas City.
October 15-30.— Left Kansas City to take position on the extreme right of Frémont's Grand Army by way of Pleasant Hill, Osceola and Bolivar. Arrived at Greenfield October 30.
October 31.— Was inspected and mustered for pay. The company left Greenfield, Missouri at 5 p.m. forming part of Brigadier-General Sturgis' Brigade under orders to join the Army of the West at Springfield.

Stationed at Syracuse, Missouri, November-December 1861.
[For record of events, see Company C.]

SAMUEL H. RULON,
Lieutenant,
Commanding Company.

Stationed near Commerce, Missouri, January-February 1862.
February 2.— The company remained at Syracuse, Missouri, the place of last muster, until formed part of the detachment of the Thirty-ninth Ohio Regiment under Lieutenant-Colonel Gilbert. We took up the line of march for Saint Louis via Boonville, Columbia, Fulton, Danville, Warrenton, and Saint Charles.
February 3.— We arrived at Boonville in the afternoon.
February 7.— We remained until we crossed the Missouri River forming part of a column under command of Colonel Worthington of the Fifth Iowa Volunteers and encamped near Franklin.
February 10.— We passed through Columbia.
February 12.— Through Fulton.
February 13.— Through Danville.

February 14.— Warrenton.
February 17.— Arrived at Saint Charles.
February 18.— Crossed the Missouri River.
February 19.— Arrived at Saint Louis. Took up quarters in Benton Barracks, where the regiment was reunited under command of Colonel Groesbeck.
February 22.— Left Benton Barracks for Commerce, Missouri, taking passage on the steamer *Gladiator*.
February 24.— Arrived at Commerce, where we encamped.
February 28.— Remained until we took up the line of march for New Madrid, forming part of the First Brigade, First Division of the Army of the Mississippi under General Pope and were mustered for pay while encamped on Colonel Hunter's Farm.

Stationed at camp near Hamburg, Tennessee, March-April 1862.
March 3.— The regiment, forming part of the First Brigade, First Division of the Army of the Mississippi, arrived at New Madrid, Missouri and immediately made a demonstration at the works of the enemy.
March 14.— Took possession of them and went into camp.
April 7-8.— Remained in camp until formed part of the division under General Stanley. Crossed the Mississippi River for the purpose of attacking Island No. 10. Heard the enemy had evacuated and marched to Tiptonville. We marched to Tiptonville and arrived there about 11 a.m. of April 8 and found the enemy about 3,000 strong had surrendered to General Paine. Marched thence to Island No. 10. Slept that night on the shore opposite to the island.
April 9.— Returned in the morning to camp at New Madrid.
April 12.— Remained in camp until formed part of General Stanley's Division. Left on steamboat *Admiral* for some point down the river.
April 13.— Arrived at a point near Osceola, Arkansas and about seven miles above Fort Pillow, Tennessee.
April 17.— Remained there on the boat until we started up the river.
April 19-20.— We arrived at Cairo and left on April 20.
April 23.— Arrived at Hamburg, Tennessee and went into camp.
April 27.— Remained in camp until we moved to a point five miles distant on the road to Corinth, where we again encamped.

April 29.— The regiment, Lieutenant-Colonel Gilbert commanding, formed part of Colonel Groesbeck's Brigade, General Stanley's Division, made a reconnaissance towards Corinth. Marched to Monterey, five miles from Corinth, and returned to camp about 2 p.m. of the same day.

Stationed at Camp Clear Creek, Mississippi, May-June 1862.
May 1.— Left our camp and marched about five miles on the road to Farmington, Mississippi and encamped.
May 2.— In camp. General Tyler assumed command of the First Brigade, Second Division of the Army of the Mississippi of which the Thirty-ninth forms a part.
May 4.— Marched to a point within two miles of Farmington.
May 8.— Formed part of General Stanley's Division, were ordered out on an armed reconnaissance towards Corinth and got to within one mile of the outworks, when we opened upon a body of Rebel Cavalry and immediately were opened upon in turn by a field battery of two pieces with shot and shell. Returned to camp at night.
May 9.— Battle of Farmington.
May 17.— Moved our camp to Farmington and during the night, threw up entrenchments and planted batteries.
May 24.— Five companies ordered out to support a battery and drive in the Rebel pickets.
May 27.— Advanced on Corinth and took a position about two miles from it where we dug rifle pits, skirmishing all day with the Rebels.
May 28-29.— Four were wounded in the pits.
May 30.— Ordered early in the morning towards Corinth and after some skirmishing with pickets entered Corinth at 6.40 a.m. The flag of the Thirty-ninth being the first one raised. At 5 p.m. started in pursuit, marching on the Danville Road.
June 1.— Marched on toward Booneville and encamped within two miles of it.
June 3.— Marched to Booneville and back to camp.
June 11.— Returned to our old camp within six miles from Corinth.
June 15.— Received pay for March and April.
June 23.— Had regimental inspection.
June 30.— Inspected and mustered for pay.

Stationed at Camp Clear Creek, Mississippi, August 18, 1862.

Stationed at Iuka, Mississippi, July-August 1862.
[For record of events, see Company C.]
August 18.— The regiment mustered by Colonel Gilbert in accordance with Orders No. 71 to ascertain absentees.

Stationed at camp at Corinth, Mississippi, September-October 1862.
September 11.— Remained at Iuka.
September 12.— Marched to Clear Creek, a distance of twenty-four miles, and bivouacked.
September 14-17.— On a reconnaissance in direction of Iuka.
September 18.— Rejoined the division at Jacinto.
September 19.— Marched with the division a distance of sixteen miles; had an engagement with the enemy near Iuka.
September 20.— Entered Iuka (the enemy withdrew during the night); followed the retreating enemy ten miles from Iuka and bivouacked.
September 21.— Marched toward Jacinto, twenty miles, and bivouacked.
September 22.— Went into camp one and one-half miles from Jacinto.
September 28.— Remained in camp until marched to and bivouacked at Rienzi, a distance of nine miles.
September 30.— In bivouac at Rienzi.
October 1.— Marched through Kossuth and bivouacked on the Tuscumbia River.
October 3.— Marched to Corinth and took a position in line of battle on west side of town in support of Battery Robinett.
October 4.— Participated in the battle of Corinth.
October 5-7.— In pursuit of the retreating enemy marching forty miles.
October 8.— On a reconnaissance in direction of Ripley.
October 9.— In bivouac near Ripley.
October 10.— Marched in direction of Corinth (twenty miles).
October 11.— Passed through Kossuth; bivouacked near Tuscumbia River.
October 12.— Marched into Corinth and encamped on east side of town.

October 13-31.— In camp at Corinth when the company was mustered for pay.

Stationed at Corinth, Mississippi, November-December 1862.
November 2-7.— The regiment marched from Corinth, Mississippi, place of last muster, and arrived at Grand Junction, Tennessee November 7 and encamped near Grand Junction.
November 17.— Remained until the company was removed five miles south of Holly Springs.
November 30.— The regiment formed part of a reconnaissance in force in the direction of the Tallahatchie River.
December 10.— The regiment took up line of march and moved to Oxford, Mississippi and encamped two miles south of Oxford.
December 18.— The regiment moved by rail to Jackson, Tennessee leaving camp and garrison equipage behind.
December 20.— Formed part of a force under command of General Sullivan. Marched nineteen miles in direction of Lexington, Tennessee.
December 21.— Returned to Jackson.
December 27.— Remained in bivouac near Jackson until regiment moved by rail to Trenton.
December 28.— Formed part of a force that marched in direction of Huntingdon, Tennessee and arrived there same day.
December 31.— Remained until it again resumed the march with the First Brigade under command of Colonel Fuller, commanding brigade towards the Tennessee River sixteen miles from Huntingdon. Came upon the enemy under the command of General Forrest who had been engaged with Colonel Dunham's Union Brigade. During the day assisted to put the enemy to rout recapturing prisoners, guns and train and in capturing a portion of the enemy's artillery and forces.

Stationed at camp near Corinth, Mississippi, January-February 1863.
[For record of events, see Company C.]

Stationed at camp near Corinth, Mississippi, April 15, 1863.
Remained in camp since last muster.

Stationed at camp at Bear Creek, Alabama, March-April 1863.
[For record of events, see Regiment.]

Stationed at Memphis, Tennessee, May-June 1863.
May 1.— The regiment continued the march towards Corinth, crossing Bear Creek and marching to Burnsville, sixteen miles.
May 2.— Marched to Corinth, eighteen miles, and went into camp, formerly occupied.
May 12.— Remained until the regiment moved by rail to Memphis and encamped one mile south of Memphis, where the regiment has since remained doing guard duty.
June 30.— Mustered for pay by Colonel Edward F. Noyes, Thirty-ninth Ohio Regiment.

Stationed at Memphis, Tennessee, July-August 1863.

Stationed at Iuka, Mississippi, October 31, 1863.
October 18-24.— Remained in camp at Memphis, Tennessee, since last muster, until marched from Memphis to Corinth, Mississippi October 24.
October 26.— Thence to Burnsville.
October 29.— To Iuka, Mississippi and went into camp.
October 31.— Remained until we were mustered for pay.

Stationed at camp in the field near Columbia, Tennessee, November-December 1863.
December 31.— Moved from camp about 7 o'clock and marched to Smith Station some ten miles. Got the regiment on cars and started for Nashville. Experienced very cold weather. Arrived at Nashville about 9 p.m., the regiment quartered in the City Barracks.

Stationed at Athens, Alabama, January-February 1864.
[For record of events, see Company B.]

Stationed at Decatur, Alabama, March-April 1864.

Stationed at Kenesaw Mountain, Georgia, June 30, 1864.

Stationed near Jonesborough, Georgia, July-August 1864.
[For record of events, see Company A.]
July 4.— At 6 p.m. we charged and drove him from his works with the loss of one man killed and six wounded in the company.

July 22.— Fought him three hours and repulsed him with a loss of two men killed and four wounded in the company.
August 29.— Engaged in destroying the Montgomery and West Point Railroad.

Stationed at Van's Valley, Georgia, September-October 1864.
[For record of events, see Company B.]

Stationed near Savannah, Georgia, November-December 1864.
November 1.— Marched from Van's Valley to Cedartown, ten miles.
November 2.— Marched nine miles.
November 3.— Marched to Dallas, ten miles, passing through Van Wert.
November 4.— Marched to Lost Mountain, ten miles.
November 5.— Marched to Smyrna Campgrounds, twelve miles.
November 6-8.— In camp. In evening marched to Atlanta, fourteen miles. Detached from regiment as train guard.
November 15.— Remained until marched with train all night.
November 16.— Marched nine miles and camped near McDonnal.
November 17.— Marched twenty-three miles.
November 18.— Marched to Ocmulgee River, eighteen miles.
November 19.— Marched to Monticello, thirteen miles.
November 20.— Marched nineteen miles.
November 21.— Marched eight miles.
November 22.— Marched to Gordon, eight miles.
November 23.— In camp.
November 24.— Marched ten miles.
November 25.— Marched seven miles.
November 26.— Marched eleven miles. Camped on Oconee River.
November 27.— Marched ten miles.
November 28.— Marched eighteen miles.
November 29.— Moved at 7 a.m. fifteen miles.
November 30.— Marched thirteen miles. Crossed at Sebastopol Station the Ogeechee River.
December 1.— Marched seven miles along the railroad destroying it.
December 2.— Marched to Millen, seven miles.

December 3.— Marched to Station No. 7, nine miles.
December 4.— Marched to Cameron Station, thirteen miles.
December 5.— Marched to Horton Station, fifteen miles.
December 6.— Drove the enemy out of his works at Little Ogeechee River.
December 7.— Marched along the railroad, thirteen miles.
December 8.— Marched to Station No. 3, eleven miles.
December 9.— Marched to Station No. 2, ten miles.
December 10.— Marched six miles. Drove the enemy in his main line of works, four miles from Savannah. During night built line of works within 800 yards of enemy.
December 11.— Still in position. Relieved by Fourteenth Army Corps and moved to the right nine miles.
December 14-16.— Marched on foraging expedition to Midway Church, thirty miles. Returned December 16.
December 17-21.— Marched with division to Altamaha River, fifty miles destroying [Savannah, Albany and] Gulf Railroad and returned December 21.
December 24.— Marched to Savannah near Wassaw Sound. Camped three miles southeast of city.
December 31.— Still in camp.

Stationed in the field, South Carolina, January-February 1865.
January 1.— At Savannah, Georgia.
January 3-4.— Took the steamer *Harvest Moon* for Beaufort, South Carolina and arrived January 4.
January 13.— Moved at 5 p.m. Marched nine miles.
January 14.— Moved at 10 a.m. Marched ten miles.
January 16.— Marched to Pocotaligo, enemy evacuating.
January 20.— Remained until made a reconnaissance to Salkehatchie River and returned to camp, distance eight miles.
January 21.— Marched to Tulifinny River. Raining.
January 22.— Returned to Pocotaligo.
January 26.— Made a reconnaissance to Salkehatchie River and returned to camp.
January 30.— Marched northwesterly to camp near Salkehatchie River.
January 31.— Remained in camp.
February 1.— Moved at 7.30 a.m., heavy skirmishing. Marched thirteen miles.

February 2.— Marched 7.30 a.m., heavy skirmishing. Marched eight miles.
February 3.— Crossed Whippy Swamp and Salkehatchie River by wading and drove the enemy from their works.
February 7.— Moved at 12 m. Camped on the South Carolina Railroad near Midway. Marched twelve miles.
February 8.— Moved camp one mile and threw up works.
February 9.— Marched at 7 a.m. Crossed the South Edisto River and waded the swamp. Enemy evacuated. Marched ten miles.
February 10.— Remained in camp.
February 11.— Moved at 12 m.; camped within two miles of North Edisto River.
February 12.— Crossed the river and camped north of Orangeburg.
February 13.— Moved at 7.30 a.m.; destroyed railroad; marched fourteen miles.
February 14.— Moved in direction of Columbia; marched twelve miles. Raining.
February 15.— Moved at 10 a.m. Marched nine miles.
February 16.— Moved at 9 a.m. Crossed Congaree Creek. Marched ten miles.
February 17.— Crossed Saluda River at 11 a.m. Crossed Broad River at 4 p.m. Marched through Columbia and camped.
February 18.— Destroyed railroad all day.
February 19.— Remained in camp.
February 20.— Moved at 9 a.m. destroying railroad. Marched twelve miles.
February 21.— Moved at 8 a.m. Marched twelve miles.
February 22.— Marched through [Winnsborough] and camped eight miles east; marched thirteen miles.
February 23.— Moved at 8 a.m. Crossed the Wateree River. Raining. Marched ten miles.
February 24.— Marched through Silver Hill. Country hilly and rocky. Marched eight miles.
February 25.— Marched fifteen miles.
February 26.— Crossed Little [Lynch's] Creek. Marched eight miles.
February 27.— Moved at 7 a.m. Crossed Big Lynch's Creek. Marched four miles.
February 28.— Marched sixteen miles and camped.

Stationed in the field, North Carolina, March-April 1865.
[For record of events, see Company G.]

Stationed at Louisville, Kentucky, May-June 1865.

Company I

Stationed at Camp Dennison, Ohio, July 31, 1861.
July 31.— Muster-in roll of Captain David C. Benjamin's Company (I), in the Thirty-ninth Regiment of Ohio Foot Volunteers, commanded by Colonel John Groesbeck, called into the service of the United States by the President from July 31, 1861, for the term of three years, unless sooner discharged. The company was organized by Captain D. C. Benjamin at West Union in the month of July 1861 and marched thence to Camp Colerain; thence to Camp Dennison, where it arrived August 3, a distance of 133 miles. . . .

T. W. WALKER,
First Lieutenant,
Third Infantry, Mustering Officer.

Stationed at Camp Benton, Missouri, July 31-August 31, 1861.

Stationed at Camp Prentiss, Chillicothe, Missouri, October 31, 1861.

Stationed at Palmyra, Missouri, [October] 31-December 31, 1861.
September 7-December 31.— This company in connection with the regiment left Benton Barracks, Saint Louis, Missouri and have since been in active service in the field since that time. Recently under the command of General Prentiss the company marched through the counties of Buchanan, Platte, Clay, Ray, Carroll, and Livingston Counties and aided in driving a band of armed Rebels from said counties. The company is now in winter quarters in Palmyra, Missouri.

Stationed at New Madrid, January-February 1862.
February 10.— This company in connection with part of the regiment left Palmyra, Missouri and went by railroad to Benton

Barracks, Saint Louis, Missouri. Here the regiment was united after a separation of six months.

February 22-28.— The company, with the regiment, left Saint Louis and went by steamer *Gladiator* to Commerce, Missouri. Here the regiment debarked and under the direction of General Pope, marched to New Madrid, a distance of nearly fifty miles. We are now forty-five miles south of Columbus and hope soon to go further south and aid in crushing this wicked rebellion.

Stationed at Hamburg, Tennessee, March-April 1862.

March 13.— This company was in the battle of New Madrid and aided in taking two forts and a large number of siege guns, field pieces, and military stores.

The company also aided in taking 5,500 Rebels at Island No. 10. The company then went down the Mississippi River to near Fort Pillow; thence by order of General [Henry Wager] Halleck to near Corinth, Mississippi to aid in taking that place.

Stationed at Camp Clear Creek, Tishomingo County, Mississippi, May-June 1862.

April 23.— This company arrived at Hamburg, Tennessee.

May 30.— Was before Corinth until participating in the numerous skirmishes which occurred during this time. On this day with the regiment entered Corinth. Finding it evacuated pursued the fleeing enemy as far as Booneville on the Mobile and Ohio Railroad, twenty-five miles south of Corinth, but have returned and encamped five miles south of Corinth.

Stationed at Camp Clear Creek, Mississippi, August 18, 1862.

This company, with the rest of the regiment, has been encamped for the last two months at Camp Clear Creek, Mississippi.

Stationed at Iuka, July-August 1862.

August 26.— This company changed station and marched from Camp Clear Creek to Iuka, Mississippi, a distance of twenty miles.

Stationed at Corinth, Mississippi, September-October 1862.
September 12.— This company left Iuka, Mississippi and marched to Camp Clear Creek near Corinth, a distance of twenty-five miles.
September 14.— It left camp with the regiment and marched in the direction of Iuka.
September 19.— Was on the battlefield near Iuka during the engagement.
September 20.— Was in the pursuit of the enemy.
September 21.— The pursuit was discontinued. Returned to Corinth via Jacinto and Rienzi.
October 4-12.— Was stationed near Battery Robinett during the battle. Was in the pursuit of the enemy from Corinth to Ripley and arrived in Corinth October 12. Total distance traveled during the two months was 160 miles.

Stationed at Corinth, Mississippi, November-December 1862.
November 2.— This company left Corinth, Mississippi; marched to Grand Junction, Tennessee, from thence advanced with main Army of the Tennessee as far south as Oxford, Mississippi.
November 17.— At night with the regiment took the cars for Jackson, Tennessee as trouble was expected there, from thence went to Trenton via railroad.
November 28.— We set out on our expedition in pursuit of Forrest's Cavalry, which had been raiding upon many points on the Columbus Railroad.
December 31.— Were present at the battle of Parker's Cross-Roads, Tennessee. This company has marched a distance of 200 miles during the two months.

Stationed at Corinth, Mississippi, January-February 1863.
This company, with the regiment, has been stationed at Corinth during the last two months.
February 28.— Remained in camp at Corinth until date of muster.

Stationed at Corinth, Mississippi, April 15, 1863.

Stationed at Bear Creek, Alabama, March-April 1863.
April 20.— Remained in camp at Corinth until marched that day to Burnsville, twenty-one miles. A portion of the distance over very bad roads. The line of march was in a northeasterly direction.
April 21.— Marched by way of Iuka to Bear Creek, seventeen miles, and there formed a junction with division of General Dodge. A portion of this day's march was over a very bad and muddy road. It rained most of the afternoon and a part of the following night.
April 22.— Remained in bivouac near Bear Creek.
April 23.— Marched ten miles in direction of Tuscumbia. Passed through a fine section of country.
April 24.— Marched to Tuscumbia, Alabama, eight miles, and bivouacked on the west side of the town. The enemy, who had occupied the place, left there in the morning, making no resistance to our advance.
April 25-26.— Remained bivouacked near Tuscumbia.
April 27.— Resumed the march in an easterly direction. Marched twelve miles. The day was very hot and sultry and the roads were very muddy and heavy, it having rained the night before. Received orders to be ready to move at 5 o'clock in the morning.
April 28.— Remained in bivouac until 11 o'clock. Moved about five miles to the front and took position on the west bank of Town Creek, the enemy having made his appearance on the opposite side during the day but after some shelling and skirmishing, retired.
April 29.— Remained in line until 6 o'clock in the morning, when the regiment took up the line of march in westerly direction. Marched twenty miles and bivouacked five miles west of Tuscumbia, Alabama.
April 30.— Marched to Bear Creek, seventeen miles.

Stationed at Memphis, Tennessee, May-June 1863.
May 1.— The regiment continued towards Corinth, crossing Bear Creek and marched to Burnsville, sixteen miles.
May 2.— Marched to Corinth, eighteen miles, and went into camp formerly occupied.
May 12.— Remained until the regiment moved by rail to Memphis, where the regiment has since remained doing guard duty.

June 30.— Mustered for pay by Colonel Edward F. Noyes, Thirty-ninth Ohio Regiment.

Stationed at Memphis, Tennessee, July-August 1863.

Remained in camp at Memphis during the months of July and August.

Stationed at Iuka, Mississippi, September-October 1863.

Stationed in field near Columbia, Tennessee, November-December 1863.

November 2.— Marched from Iuka, Mississippi to Eastport.
November 4.— Crossed Tennessee River.
November 6.— Marched nine miles.
November 7.— Marched twelve miles.
November 8.— Marched fifteen miles encamping at [Landerdale] Factory, Alabama.
November 9.— Marched sixteen miles passing through Lexington, Tennessee.
November 10.— Marched twenty miles encamping near river, Pulaski, Tennessee.
November 11.— Marched twelve miles, passing through Pulaski.
November 12.— Marched ten miles.
November 13.— Marched to Prospect, Tennessee.
December 29.— Marched to near Pulaski.
December 30.— Marched to near Columbia, where the company was mustered for pay.

Stationed at Athens, Alabama, January-February 1864.

January 1.— The veterans of the company, who exceeded three-fourths of the present, left Nashville, Tennessee en route for Ohio.
January 7.— Reached Camp Dennison, Ohio, having traveled about 800 miles by rail and steamer.
January 10-February 10.— Were furloughed until February 10. Rendezvous at Camp Dennison.
February 13.— The company with the regiment left Camp Dennison again for the field.
February 22.— Reached Athens, Alabama, having traveled about 800 miles since leaving Camp Dennison by rail and steamer, making a total of about 1,600 miles traveled during the months of January and February.

Stationed at Decatur, Alabama, March-April 1864.
March 22-23.— Remained in camp at Athens until marched to Decatur, Alabama during the nights until March 23.
March 24.— Returned to Athens, in all having marched thirty miles.
April 13.— Marched to Decatur, Alabama with camp and garrison equipage, a distance of fifteen miles. During the months of March and April, the company was marched forty-five miles.

Stationed near Kenesaw Mountain, Georgia, May-June 1864.
[For record of events, see Company B.]

Stationed near Jonesborough, Georgia, July-August 1864.
July 3.— Marched from Kenesaw Mountain to Nickajack Creek, a distance of ten miles.
July 4.— Assaulted the enemy in his earthworks near Ruff's Mill with a loss of two men wounded.
July 9-10.— Marched to Roswell on Chattahoochee River via Marietta, Georgia, a distance of twenty-seven miles.
July 17-19.— Remained in camp on south side of Chattahoochee opposite Roswell until marched to Decatur, Georgia, a distance of twenty-one miles.
July 21.— Moved to a position on the left of the Army of the Tennessee near Atlanta, Georgia.
July 22.— Engaged the enemy near Atlanta. Had one man killed and seventeen wounded.
July 27.— Moved with Army of the Tennessee to right wing of Grand Army, a distance of ten miles. Advanced in line of battle and took a position two and one-half miles west of Atlanta.
August 26.— Engaged in the investment there until moved with Army of the Tennessee to the West Point Railroad, a distance of thirty miles.
August 29.— Engaged in destroying railroad track.
August 30-31.— Moved to near Jonesborough, Georgia, a distance of twelve miles, where [we] were engaged in operations against the enemy until the present time.

Stationed at Cave Spring, Georgia, September-October 1864.
September 1.— In front of the enemy at Jonesborough, Georgia.

September 2-3.— Pursued the enemy from Jonesborough to near Lovejoy's Station, distance four miles.
September 5-8.— Returned marching northwest to a point near East Point, Georgia, distance thirty miles.
September 20.— Remained near East Point until detailed to go to Atlanta for the purpose of erecting tents for the Army of the Tennessee.
October 4.— Remained at Atlanta until joined the brigade on its march northward and encamped five miles north of the Chattahoochee River.
October 5.— Marched all night and encamped near Marietta, Georgia.
October 6-11.— Marched to a point within four miles of Rome, Georgia, distance fifty miles.
October 13.— Marched to Adairsville, distance sixteen miles.
October 14.— Took the cars for Resaca. Arrived at Resaca at 12 a.m. Made a reconnaissance to Snake Creek Gap. Skirmished with the enemy and returned to Resaca, twelve [miles].
October 15.— Marched at 7 a.m. Drove the enemy through Snake Creek Gap. Marched eighteen miles.
October 16-17.— Continued the march passing through Ship's Gap, distance twelve miles.
October 19-20.— Marched forty-four miles passing through Summerville.
October 21-31.— Marched to Gaylesville, Alabama, distance twenty-one miles. Lay in camp near Gaylesville until October 31.

Total distance marched during the two months about 280 miles.

Stationed near Savannah, Georgia, November-December 1864.
November 1.— Marched from Van's Valley to Cedartown, twenty miles.
November 2.— Marched nine miles.
November 3.— Marched nineteen miles to Dallas, passing through Van Wert.
November 4.— Marched to Lost Mountain, ten miles.
November 5.— Marched twelve miles south, camping at Smyrna Campgrounds.
November 12.— In camp at dark. Marched and destroyed railroad from Big Shanty to Marietta.
November 13.— Marched to Peach Tree Creek.

November 14.— Marched to Atlanta, eight miles.
November 15-16.— Marched with division train, twenty miles.
November 17.— Marched to Jackson, seventeen miles.
November 18.— Marched to Ocmulgee River, ten miles.
November 19.— Marched to Monticello via Hillsborough.
November 20-22.— Marched southward to Gordon.
November 23.— Remained in camp.
November 24.— Eastward ten miles to Station No. 16.
November 25.— Marched to Summerville.
November 26.— Marched to Oconee River.
November 27.— Marched ten miles.
November 28.— Marched fifteen miles.
November 29.— Marched to Williams' Swamp.
November 30.— Marched to Ogeechee River.
December 1.— Marched seven miles along railroad, destroying it.
December 2.— Marched to Millen, eleven miles.
December 3.— Marched to Station No. 11, nine miles. Marched to Eumans Station, fifteen miles.
December 5.— To Horton Station, ten miles, engaging enemy out of his works at Little Ogeechee River.
December 7.— Marched thirteen miles, destroying railroad.
December 8.— Marched to station, twenty-seven miles.
December 9.— Marched to Station No. 1, ten miles.
December 10.— Drove the enemy out of his new works before Savannah. Dark night built line of works in sight of enemy's works.
December 11.— Still in position. Relieved by Fourteenth Corps. Marched to rear, nine miles.
December 14.— Marched foraging to Midway Church, thirty miles and returned.
December 16-17.— Marched to Anderson, Altamaha River to destroy railroad.
December 21.— Marched to Savannah. Encamped near Wassaw Sound three miles east of city.
December 31.— In camp.

Stationed at Thompson's Creek, South Carolina, January-February 1865.
January 1-3.— Moved by water from camp near Savannah, Georgia to Beaufort, South Carolina.
January 13.— Remained refitting and collecting supplies.

January 14-31.— Moved to Pocotaligo, South Carolina and remained in camp until January 31.
February 1.— Broke up camp and marched.
February 2-3.— Were engaged in brisk skirmishes at Rivers' Bridge, South Carolina.

Were engaged in an active campaign during the entire month in which time we destroyed over fifty miles of railroad track.
February 28.— In the evening were at Thompson's Creek, South Carolina.

Stationed at Neuse River, North Carolina, March-April 1865.
March 21.— The company was engaged in the battle of Bentonville, North Carolina.

Stationed at Louisville, Kentucky, May-June 1865.

Company K

Stationed at Camp Dennison, Ohio, August 13, 1861.
August 13.— Muster-in roll of Captain John Rhoades' Company (K), in the Thirty-ninth Regiment of Ohio Foot Volunteers, commanded by Colonel John Groesbeck, called into the service of the United States by the President from August 13, 1861 (date of this muster) for the term of three years, unless sooner discharged. The company was organized by Captain John Rhoades at Troy Township, Athens County in the month of June and marched thence to Camp Dennison, where it arrived August 9, a distance of 190 miles. . . .

T. W. WALKER,
First Lieutenant,
Third Infantry, Mustering Officer.

Stationed at Benton Barracks, July 31-August 31, 1861.

Stationed at Camp Prentiss, Chillicothe, Missouri, September-October 1861.

Stationed at Palmyra, Missouri, November-December 1861.
December 2.— Left Macon City, Missouri for Saint Joseph.
December 5.— We took the field under General Prentiss. Marched through Buchanan, Platte, Clay, Carroll, Livingston Counties.

December 12.— Bombarded Lexington.
December 15.— Slight affair at Shanghia.
December 18.— Reached the Hannibal and Saint Joseph Railroad at Utica Station.
December 20-21.— Left Utica and arrived at Palmyra, Missouri December 21, having marched 420 miles.

Stationed at Commerce, Missouri, January-February 1862.
February 12-13.— Left winter quarters at Palmyra, Missouri by railroad to Saint Louis, arriving there February 13.
February 22-24.— Left Saint Louis for Dixie Land; arrived at Commerce, Missouri February 24, here to prepare for a campaign south.

Stationed at camp near Hamburg, Tennessee, March-April 1862.
March 1-3.— Formed part of First Brigade, First Division, Army of Mississippi under General Pope. Took up line of march from Hunter's Farm for New Madrid, arriving there on March 3. Made a demonstration before the town and was fired on by Fort Thompson and gunboats. Returned at dusk and encamped one and one-half miles from the town.
March 7.— Formed part of a reconnaissance in force and was fired upon again from upper fort and gunboats.
March 13-14.— At 3 a.m. marched on the forts and town; took supporting distance in rear of a battery of four siege guns. Remained all day amid a shower of shot and shell and all night in a terrible and drenching rain. Was relieved a daylight.
April 7-8.— Remained in camp until ordered to the river. Crossed the Mississippi in order to get position in rear of Island No. 10. Marched six miles and camped. Marched next day to Tiptonville, where 6,000 of the enemy had surrendered to the command of General Paine. Marched to Island No. 10 and camped.
April 9.— Took passage on steamer *N. W. Graham* for New Madrid.
April 13-14.— Remained in camp until embarked on steamer *Admiral* for Fort Pillow and arrived there on April 14.
April 17-23.— Ordered to Pittsburg Landing and arrived there on April 23. Went into camp at Hamburg.
April 27.— Moved camp five miles in advance. Formed part of a reconnaissance.

April 29.— In force drove in the pickets of the enemy and captured a number of prisoners.
April 30.— Returned to camp and was mustered for pay.

Stationed at Camp Big Springs, May-June 1862.
May 1.— Marched five miles on the road to Farmington and encamped.
May 2.— General Tyler assumed command of the First Brigade, Second Division of which the Thirty-ninth formed a part.
May 4.— Marched to a point within two miles of Farmington.
May 8.— Formed part of the division of General Stanley. Were ordered out on an armed reconnaissance toward Corinth and got within one mile of the outworks when we fired on Rebel Cavalry. Immediately a battery opened on us with shot and shell. Returned to camp at night.
May 17.— Moved our camp to Farmington, where we were protected by entrenchments and batteries.
May 28.— Marched out and took a position two miles from Corinth and dug rifle pits, a portion of our forces skirmishing all day. Two men of this company were wounded by a shell.
May 29.— Stayed in the trenches and skirmished.
May 30.— Ordered early in the morning toward Corinth. Marched on main road and after some skirmishing with pickets entered the deserted works at 6.40 a.m. The flags of the Thirty-ninth Ohio and Forty-second Illinois being the first planted. At 5 p.m. same day, started in pursuit of Rebels marching on the Danville Road. Encamped six miles from Corinth.
June 2.— Marched toward Booneville, leaving camp at 7 a.m. Encamped two miles north of Booneville.
June 3.— Marched to Booneville and back to camp.
June 7.— Changed camp about two miles to the right.
June 11.— Returned to our old camp six miles south of Corinth.
June 12.— Changed camp about three-fourths of a mile to the left.
June 15.— Received pay for the months of March and April.
June 22.— Had regimental inspection.

Stationed at Camp Clear Creek, Mississippi, August 18, 1862.

Stationed at Iuka, Mississippi, July-August 1862.
[For record of events, see Company B.]

July 25.— Still at camp Clear Creek. Received Whitney rifles with sword bayonets.

Stationed at Corinth, Mississippi, September-October 1862.
September 1.— Marched from Iuka, Mississippi to Cherokee, Alabama, distance sixteen miles.
September 2.— Encamped at Cherokee.
September 3.— Marched back to Iuka.
September 12.— Remained at Iuka until marched to Clear Creek, distance of twenty-four miles, and bivouacked.
September 14-17.— On a reconnaissance in the direction of Iuka.
September 18.— Rejoined the division at Jacinto.
September 19.— Marched with the division a distance of fourteen miles. Had an engagement with the enemy.
September 20.— Entered Iuka. Enemy withdrew during the night. Followed the retreating enemy ten miles from Iuka and bivouacked.
September 21.— Marched toward Jacinto, twenty miles, and bivouacked.
September 22.— Went into camp one and one-half miles from Jacinto.
September 28.— Remained in camp.
September 29.— Marched to and bivouacked at Rienzi, distance of nine miles.
September 30.— In bivouac at Rienzi.
October 1.— Marched through Kossuth and bivouacked on the Tuscumbia River.
October 2.— Marched to Corinth and took a position in line of battle on the west side of the town in support of Battery Robinett, the enemy being in front.
October 4.— Participated in the battle of Corinth.
October 5-7.— Pursued the retreating enemy marching forty miles.
October 8.— The regiment ordered on a reconnaissance in direction of Ripley.
October 9.— In bivouac near Ripley.
October 10.— Marched in direction of Corinth, twenty miles.
October 11.— Passed through Kossuth. Bivouacked near Tuscumbia River.
October 12.— Marched into Corinth. Encamped east of town inside of outer breastworks.

October 13-31.— In camp at Corinth. Mustered for pay.

Stationed at Corinth, Mississippi, November-December 1862.

November 2-7.— The regiment marched from Corinth, the place of the last muster, and arrived at Grand Junction, Tennessee on November 7.

November 17.— Remained in camp near Grand Junction until the camp was moved five miles south.

November 28.— Remained in camp until the regiment moved seven miles south of Holly Springs.

November 30.— Formed a part of a reconnaissance in force in direction of Tallahatchie River.

December 10.— Remained in camp seven miles south of Holly Springs until took up line of march in direction of Oxford, Mississippi.

December 11.— Marched through the town of Oxford, Mississippi and encamped two miles south of it.

December 18-19.— Remained encamped here until the regiment was ordered to prepare three days' rations and moved by rail to Jackson, leaving camp and garrison equipage behind. Left Oxford at 12 p.m., arriving in Jackson the next day. Bivouacked on the north side of Jackson that night.

December 20.— Formed part of a force under command of General Sullivan and marched nineteen miles in the direction of Lexington, Tennessee.

December 21.— Returned to Jackson.

December 27.— Remained in bivouac near Jackson until the regiment moved to Trenton, Tennessee by rail.

December 28-29.— The regiment formed part of a force under command of General Sullivan and marched in direction of Huntingdon, Tennessee, arriving there December 29.

December 31.— Remained there until the regiment again resumed the march with the First Brigade under command of Colonel Fuller towards the Tennessee River, sixteen miles from Huntingdon. Came upon the enemy under command of General Forrest, who had been engaged with Colonel Dunham's Union Brigade during the day. Assisted to put the enemy to rout in recapturing prisoners, guns, and train and in capturing a portion of the enemy's artillery and force.

Stationed at Corinth, Mississippi, January 10-February 28, 1863.
[For record of events, see Field and Staff.]
February 28.— Remained in camp at Corinth until the date of muster.

Stationed at Corinth, Mississippi, April 15, 1863.

Stationed at Bear Creek, March-April 1863.
[For record of events, see Regiment.]

Stationed at Memphis, Tennessee, May-June 1863.
[For record of events, see Company A.]

Stationed at Memphis, Tennessee, July-August 1863.

Stationed at Iuka, Mississippi, September-October 1863.

Stationed at Columbia, Tennessee, November-December 1863.
December 31.— Moved from camp about 7 o'clock and marched to Smith Station some ten miles. Got regiment on cars and started for Nashville. Experienced very cold weather, arrived at Nashville about 9 p.m., and the regiment quartered in City Barracks.

Stationed at Athens, Alabama, January-February 1864.
[For record of events, see Company B.]

Stationed at Decatur, Alabama, March-April 1864.

Stationed at Kenesaw Mountain, Georgia, May-June 1864.

Stationed near Jonesborough, Georgia, July-August 1864.

Stationed at Cave Spring, Georgia, September-October 1864.
September 1.— In front of Jonesborough, Georgia.
September 2.— The enemy evacuated the place during the night and retreated southward. Marched in pursuit to vicinity of Lovejoy's Station, four miles.

September 5.— Moved back during the night to Jonesborough.
September 6.— Marched four miles in the direction of East Point.
September 7.— Marched eight miles.
September 8.— Marched four miles and camped one mile south of East Point.
September 10.— Moved camp to East Point.
September 20.— Remained until it was detailed to go to Atlanta to put up hospital tents for the Department of the Tennessee.
October 4-5.— Remained there until the regiment joined the brigade on its march northward. Marched all night and camped five miles north of Chattahoochee River.
October 6.— Marched all night and camped nine miles from Marietta, Georgia.
October 9.— Marched to Big Shanty, nine miles, and bivouacked.
October 10.— Marched at 10 p.m. to Acworth, seven miles.
October 11.— Marched at daylight to Cartersville, fifteen miles.
October 12-13.— Marched at daylight passing through Kingston and marched all night to Adairsville, sixteen miles.
October 14.— Took the cars for Resaca and after arriving there marched to Snake Creek Gap, eight miles, and drove the enemy two miles and returned to Resaca at 3 a.m.
October 15.— Marched at 7 a.m. to Snake Creek Gap and drove the enemy through and camped eighteen miles from Resaca.
October 16.— Marched eight miles and camped near Blue Mountain.
October 17.— Marched at dark passing through Ship's Gap and camped west of the mountains, making four miles.
October 18.— The regiment was ordered to remain in rear and guard cross-roads while the whole Army train passed.
October 19.— Marched at 1 a.m. passing through Summerville and Alpine, where we joined the brigade and marched to Gaylesville, Alabama on October 20, forty-nine miles from the mountains.
October 29.— Marched from Gaylesville at 7 a.m. and crossed the Chattooga and Coosa Rivers, passing through Cedar Bluff. Marched twelve miles and camped.
October 30.— Marched eighteen miles to Cave Spring and camped.
October 31.— The regiment in camp at Cave Spring, where it is mustered for pay.

Stationed at Savannah, Georgia, November-December 1864.
November 1.— Marched from Van's Valley to Cedartown, ten miles.
November 2.— Marched nine miles.
November 3.— To Dallas passing Van Wert, nineteen miles.
November 4.— To Lost Mountain, ten miles.
November 5.— To Smyrna Camp Ground, twelve miles.
November 6-12.— In camp. Marched to tear up railroad from Marietta to Big Shanty.
November 13.— Marched to Peach Tree Creek, twenty-five miles.
November 14.— To Atlanta, eight miles.
November 15-16.— Marched with division train, twenty miles.
November 17.— Marched to Jackson, seventeen miles.
November 18.— To Ocmulgee River, ten miles.
November 19.— Through Monticello and Hillsborough, thirteen miles.
November 20-22.— Marched southward to Gordon, thirty-three miles.
November 23.— In camp.
November 24.— Marched eastward ten miles.
November 25.— To Sandersville, nine miles.
November 26.— To Oconee, nine miles.
November 27.— Northwest ten miles.
November 28.— Fifteen miles.
November 29.— To Williams' Swamp, thirteen miles.
November 30.— To Ogeechee River, Sebastopol Station, ten miles.
December 1.— Marched down the railroad eight miles.
December 2.— To Millen, eleven miles.
December 3.— To Station No. 7, nine miles.
December 4.— To Cameron, fifteen miles.
December 5-6.— To Horton Station, ten miles, driving the enemy out of his works at the Little Ogeechee.
December 7.— Marched along the railroad, thirteen miles.
December 8.— To Station No. 2, eleven miles.
December 9.— To [Station] No. 1, ten miles. Marched six miles driving the enemy into his works four miles from Savannah. During the night built a line of works within 800 yards of the enemy.

December 11.— Still in position. Relieved by the Fourteenth Corps.
December 14-16.— Went on a foraging expedition to Midway Church, thirty miles. Returned December 16.
December 17-21.— Marched with division to Altamaha River, destroying railroad. Returned December 21.
December 24.— Marched to Savannah and camped near Wassaw Sound, three miles east of the city.
December 31.— Still in camp.

Stationed at Cheraw, South Carolina, January-February 1865.
This command has marched under Major-General Sherman.

Stationed at Neuse River near Raleigh, North Carolina, March-April 1865.
March 1.— Remained in camp.
March 2-24.— Marched to Cheraw, from there to Fayetteville; thence to Goldsborough, North Carolina, where we arrived March 24.
April 10-14.— Remained until we marched for Raleigh, North Carolina and arrived April 14.
April 29-30.— Remained at Raleigh until marched north fourteen miles, where we remained until April 30, where we mustered for pay.

Stationed at Louisville, Kentucky, May-June 1865.

[M594-Roll #149]

Record of Events for Fortieth Ohio Infantry, September 1861-December 1864.

Field and Staff

Stationed at Licking Station, Kentucky, November-December 1861.

Stationed at Camp Chase, December 11, 1861.
December 11.— Muster-in roll of field and staff and band in the Fortieth Regiment of Ohio Volunteers, commanded by Colonel Jonathan Cranor, called into service of the United States by the President for the term of three years, unless sooner discharged. . . .

ALBERT [BALDWIN] DOD,
Captain,
Fifteenth Infantry, United States Army, Mustering Officer.

Stationed at Prestonburg, Kentucky, May-June 1862.

Stationed at Guyandotte, [West] Virginia, September-October 1862.

Stationed at Louisa, Kentucky, November-December 1862.

Stationed at Nashville, [Tennessee], January-February 1863.

Stationed at Franklin, Tennessee, April 11, 1863.
April 10.— While the regiment was doing guard duty in front of Franklin, Tennessee it was severely attacked by the enemy in command of General [Earl] Van Dorn. The engagement was short and spirited, lasting about two hours, resulting in the repulse of the enemy with severe and heavy loss. The loss of the regiment was four killed, three wounded and ten prisoners.

Stationed at Franklin, Tennessee, March-April 1863.

Stationed at Shelbyville, Tennessee, May-June 1863.

Stationed at Tullahoma, Tennessee, July-August 1863.

Stationed at Chattanooga, Tennessee, September-October 1863.

Stationed at Nickajack Cove, Georgia, November-December 1863.

Stationed at Blue Springs, Tennessee, January-April 1864.

Stationed at Kenesaw [Mountain], Georgia, May-June 1864.

Stationed near Atlanta, Georgia, July-August 1864.

Stationed at Pulaski, Tennessee, September-October 1864.

Regiment

Stationed at Camp Chase, November 1861.

Stationed at Prestonburg, Kentucky, except Company G at Catlettsburg, Kentucky, June 1862.

Stationed at Louisa, Kentucky, except Company G at Catlettsburg, Kentucky, July 1862.

Stationed at Columbus, Ohio, September 30, 1862.
September 30.— Muster-out roll of band in the Fortieth Regiment of Ohio Volunteers, commanded by Colonel Jonathan Cranor, called into the service of the United States by the President of the United States at Camp Chase, Ohio (the place of general rendezvous) to serve for the term of three years from the date of enrollment, unless sooner discharged, from the dates set opposite their names respectively, 1861. The band was organized by Captain Johial G. Dungan. . . .

DAVID M. MEREDITH,
Captain,
Fifteenth Infantry, Mustering Officer.

Stationed at Louisa, Kentucky, November 1862.

Stationed at Louisa, Kentucky, except Companies E and F at Catlettsburg, Kentucky, January 1863.

Stationed at camp near Franklin, Tennessee, March-May 1863.

Stationed at Shelbyville, Tennessee, June 1863.

Stationed at Wartrace, Tennessee, July 1863.

Stationed at Tullahoma, Tennessee except Company E at Manchester, Tennessee; Company F at Crampton's Creek, Tennessee; Company G at Duck River Bridge, Tennessee, August 1863.

Stationed at Chattanooga, September-October 1863.

Stationed near Shellmound, Tennessee, November 1863.

Stationed at Nickajack Cove, Georgia, December 1863.

Stationed near Tyner's Station, Tennessee, January 1864.

Stationed at Blue Springs, Tennessee, February 1864.

Stationed at Blue Springs, Tennessee, except Company E at Versailles, Ohio; Company F at Union City, Indiana; Companies G and K at Greenville, Ohio, March 1864.

Company E
March 1-31.— Company E (Veteran), commanded by Captain James Allen, at home on furlough.

Company F
March 27-31.— Company F (Veteran), commanded by Captain John L. Reeves, at home on furlough.

Company G
March 1-31.— Company G (Veteran), commanded by Captain Charles G. Matchett, at home on furlough.

Company K
March 28-31.— Company K (Veteran), commanded by Lieutenant John W. Smith, at home on furlough.

Stationed at Blue Springs, Tennessee, except Companies F and K at Darke County, Ohio, April 1864.

Station not stated, May 1864.

Stationed near Atlanta, Georgia, July-August 1864.

Stationed near Atlanta, Georgia, except Company F at Division Hospital, September 1864.

Company A

Stationed at Camp Chase, September 19, 1861.
September 19.— Muster-in roll of Captain William Jones' Company, in the Fortieth Regiment of Ohio Volunteers, commanded by Colonel J. Cranor, called into the service of the United States by the President from September 19, 1861 (date of this muster) for the term of three years, unless sooner discharged. The company was organized by Captain William Jones at West Jefferson in the month of September and marched thence to Camp Chase near Columbus where it arrived September 10, a distance of ten miles. . . .

JOHN [RUFUS] EDIE,
Major,
Fifteenth Infantry, United States Army, Mustering Officer.

Stationed at Camp Chase near Columbus, Ohio, September 5-October 31, 1861.

Stationed at Licking Station, December 31, 1861.

Stationed at Prestonburg, Kentucky, May-June 1862.

Stationed Guyandotte, [West] Virginia, September-October 1862.

Stationed at Louisa, Kentucky, November-December 1862.

Stationed at camp near Nashville, Tennessee, January-February 1863.

Stationed at Franklin, Tennessee, March-April 1863.

Stationed at Shelbyville, Tennessee, May-June 1863.

Stationed at Tullahoma, Tennessee, July-August 1863.

Stationed at Camp Clark, Tennessee, September-October 1863.

Stationed at Shellmound, Tennessee, November-December 1863.

Stationed at Blue Springs, January-April 1864.

Stationed in the field, May-August 1864.

Stationed at Atlanta, Georgia, October 7, 1864.
October 7.— Muster-out roll of Lieutenant [Isaac N.] Edwards, late Captain [Clements F.] Snodgrass', Company (A), in the Fortieth Regiment of Ohio Infantry Volunteers, commanded by Colonel [Jacob] E. Taylor, late Cranor, called into the service of the United States by the President at Camp Chase, Ohio (the place of general rendezvous) on September 19, 1861 to serve for the term of three years from the date of enrollment, unless sooner discharged, from September 5, 1861 (when enrolled). The company was organized by Captain William Jones at West Jefferson in the month of September 1861. . . .

JOHN I. MORRIS,
First Lieutenant,
Twentieth Indiana Battery, Mustering Officer.

Company B

Stationed at Camp Chase, September 19, 1861.
September 19.— Muster-in roll of Captain James M. Haworth's Company (B), in the Fortieth Regiment of Ohio Volunteers, commanded by Colonel J. Cranor, called into the service of the United States by the President from September 19, 1861 (date of this muster) for the term of three years, unless sooner discharged. The company was organized by Captain James M. Haworth at Wilmington, Ohio in the month of September and marched thence to Camp Chase, where it arrived September 18, a distance of 108 miles. . . .

JOHN R. EDIE,
Major,
Fifteenth Infantry, United States Army, Mustering Officer.

Stationed at Camp Chase, September 17-October 31, 1861.

Stationed at Licking [Station], Kentucky, November-December 1861.

Stationed at Prestonburg, Kentucky, May-June 1862.

Stationed at Guyandotte, [West] Virginia, September-October 1862.

Stationed at Louisa, Kentucky, November-December 1862.

Stationed at Nashville, Tennessee, January-February 1863.

Stationed at Franklin, Tennessee, March-April 1863.

Station not stated, May-June 1863.

Stationed at Tullahoma, Tennessee, July-August 1863.

Stationed at Chattanooga, Tennessee, September-October 1863.

Stationed at Shellmound, Tennessee, November-December 1863.

Stationed at Blue Springs, Tennessee, January-April 1864.

Stationed in the field, May-August 1864.

Stationed at Atlanta, Georgia, October 7, 1864.
October 7.— Muster-out roll of Captain Charles J. Ent's Company (B), in the Fortieth Regiment of Ohio Infantry Volunteers, commanded by Colonel J. E. Taylor, called into the service of the United States by the President at Camp Chase, Ohio (the place of general rendezvous) on September 19, 1861 to serve for the term of three years from the date of enrollment, unless sooner discharged, from September 17, 1861 (when enrolled). The company was organized by Captain James M. Haworth at Wilmington, Ohio in the month of September 1861. . . .

JOHN I. MORRIS,
First Lieutenant,
Twentieth Indiana Battery, Assistant Commissary of Musters,
First Division, Fourth Corps.

Company C

Stationed at Camp Chase, Ohio, September 21, 1861.
September 21.— Muster-in roll of Captain Thomas Acton's Company (C), in the Fortieth Regiment of Ohio Volunteers, commanded by Colonel Jonathan Cranor, called into the service of the United States by the President from September 21, 1861 (date of this muster) for the term of three years, unless sooner discharged. The company was organized by Captain Thomas Acton at London, Ohio in the month of August and marched thence to Camp Chase, where it arrived September 10, a distance of twenty-five miles. . . .

JOHN R. EDIE,
Major,
Fifteenth Infantry, United States Army, Mustering Officer.

Stationed at Camp Chase, September 11-October 31, 1861.

Stationed at Licking Station, Kentucky, December 31, 1861.

Stationed at Camp Cranor, Prestonburg, Kentucky, May-June 1862.

Stationed at Guyandotte, [West] Virginia, September-October 1862.

Stationed at Camp McClure, Louisa, Kentucky, November-December 1862.

Stationed at camp near Nashville, Tennessee, January-February 1863.

Stationed at camp near Franklin, Tennessee, April 10, 1863.

Stationed at Franklin, Tennessee, March-April 1863.

Stationed at Shelbyville, Tennessee, May-June 1863.

Stationed at Tullahoma, Tennessee, July-August 1863.

Stationed at Chattanooga, Tennessee, September-October 1863.

Stationed at Shellmound, November-December 1863.

Stationed at Camp Blue Springs, Tennessee, January-February 1864.

Stationed at Blue Springs, Tennessee, April 30, 1864.

Stationed in the field, May-June 1864.

Station not stated, July-August 1864.

Stationed at Atlanta, Georgia, October 8, 1864.
October 8.— Muster-out roll of Captain [Delamer] L. De Land's (late Captain Acton) Company (C), in the Fortieth Regiment of Ohio Infantry Volunteers, commanded by Colonel Jacob E. Taylor, called into the service of the United States by the President at Camp Chase, Ohio (the place of general rendezvous). The company was organized by Captain Thomas Acton at Camp Chase, Ohio. . . .

JOHN F. MORRIS,
First Lieutenant,
Twentieth Indiana Battery, Assistant Commissary of Musters,
First Division, Fourth Army Corps.

Company D

Stationed at Camp Chase, Ohio, September 30, 1861.
September 30.— Muster-in roll of Captain James Watson's Company, in the Fortieth Regiment of Ohio Volunteers, commanded by Colonel Jonathan Cranor, called into the service of the United States by the President from September 30 (date of this muster) for the term of three years, unless sooner discharged. The company was organized by Captain James Watson at London, Ohio in the month of September and marched thence to Camp Chase, where it arrived September 10, a distance of twenty-five miles. . . .

JOHN R. EDIE,
Major,
Fifteenth Infantry, United States Army, Mustering Officer.

Stationed at Camp Chase, October 31, 1861.

Stationed at Licking Station, Kentucky, December 31, 1861.

Stationed at Camp Cranor, December 31, 1861-June 30, 1862.

Station not stated, September-October 1862.

Stationed at Camp McClure, Louisa, Kentucky, November-December 1862.

Stationed at camp near Nashville, Tennessee, January-February 1863.

Stationed at camp near Franklin, Tennessee, March-April 1863.

Stationed at Shelbyville, Tennessee, May-June 1863.

Stationed at Tullahoma, July-August 1863.

Stationed at Camp Clark, Tennessee, September-October 1863.

Stationed at Shellmound, [Tennessee], November-December 1863.

Stationed at Camp Blue Springs, Tennessee, January-April 1864.

Stationed in the field, Georgia, May-June 1864.

Stationed at Atlanta, Georgia, July-August 1864.

Stationed at Atlanta, Georgia, October 7, 1864.
October 7.— Muster-out roll of Captain James Watson's Company (D), in the Fortieth Regiment of Ohio Volunteers, commanded by Colonel Jacob E. Taylor, called into the service of the United States by the President at Camp Chase, Ohio (the place of general rendezvous) on September 30, 1861 to serve for the term of three years from the date of enrollment. The company

was organized by Captain James Watson at Camp Chase, Ohio, in the month of September 1861. . . .

JOHN I. MORRIS,
First Lieutenant,
Twentieth Indiana Battery, Assistant Commissary of Musters,
First Division, Fourth Army Corps.

Company E

Stationed at Camp Chase, Ohio, October 5, 1861.
October 5.— Muster-in roll of Captain John D. Gennett's Company, in the Fortieth Regiment of Ohio Volunteers, commanded by Colonel J. Cranor, called into the service of the United States by the President from October 5, 1861 (date of this muster) for the term of three years, unless sooner discharged. The company was organized by captain John D. Gennett's at Versailles, Ohio in the month of September and marched thence to Camp Chase, where it arrived September 19, a distance of 105. . . .

JOHN R. EDIE,
Major,
[Fifteenth] Infantry, United States Army, Mustering Officer.

Stationed at Camp Chase, Ohio, September 18-October 31, 1861.

Stationed at Licking [Station], Kentucky, November-December 1861.

Stationed at Prestonburg, Kentucky, May-June 1862.

Stationed at Guyandotte, [West] Virginia, September-October 1862.

Stationed at Louisa, Kentucky, November-December 1862.

Stationed at camp near Nashville, Tennessee, January-February 1863.

Stationed at Franklin, Tennessee, March-April 1863.

Stationed at Shelbyville, May-June 1863.

Stationed at Manchester, Tennessee, July-August 1863.

Stationed at Nickajack Cove, September-October 1863.

Stationed at Shellmound, Georgia, November-December 1863.

Stationed at Cleveland, Tennessee, January-February 1864.

Stationed at Blue Springs, Tennessee, March-April 1864.

Stationed at Kenesaw Mountain, Georgia, May-June 1864.

Stationed at Atlanta, Georgia, July-August 1864.

Stationed at Chattanooga, Tennessee, September-October 1864.

Stationed at Nashville, Tennessee, December 11, 1864.
December 11.— Muster-out roll of Captain James Allen's Company (E), in the Fortieth Regiment of Ohio Infantry Volunteers, commanded by Lieutenant-Colonel James Watson, called into the service of the United States by the President at Camp Chase, Ohio (the place of general rendezvous) on September 18, 1861 to serve for the term of three years from the date of enrollment, unless sooner discharged. . . .

JOHN I. MORRIS,
First Lieutenant,
Twentieth Indiana Battery, Assistant Commissary of Musters,
First Division, Army Corps.

Company F

Stationed at Camp Chase, October 31, 1861.

Stationed at Camp Chase, December 12, 1861.
December 12.— Muster-in roll of Captain John S. Reeves' Company, in the Fortieth Regiment of Ohio Foot Volunteers, commanded by Colonel Jonathan Cranor, called into service of the

United States by the President from the date opposite their names respectively. . . .

ALEXANDER McBRIDE,
Surgeon,
Fortieth Regiment.

[JOHN] F. MAHON,
Second Lieutenant.

Stationed at Licking Station, Kentucky, November-December 1861.

Stationed at Camp Cranor, Prestonburg, Kentucky, May-June 1862.

Stationed at Guyandotte, [West] Virginia, September-October 1862.

Stationed at Louisa, Kentucky, November-December 1862.

Stationed at camp near Nashville, Tennessee, January-February 1863.

Stationed at Franklin, Tennessee, March-April 1863.

Stationed at camp near Wartrace, Tennessee, May-June 1863.

Stationed at Crampton's Bridge, Tennessee, July-August 1863.

Stationed at Camp Clark, Tennessee, [August 31]-October 31, 1863.
September 19-20.— The company was in the battle of Chickamauga, Georgia.

Stationed at Shellmound, Tennessee, November-December 1863.

Stationed at Blue Springs, Tennessee, January-February 1864.

Stationed in the field, May-June 1864.

Stationed at Kenesaw Mountain, Georgia, July-August 1864.

Stationed at Chattanooga, Tennessee, September-October 1864.

Company G

Stationed at Camp Chase, October 31, 1861.

Stationed at Camp Chase, November 21, 1861.
November 21.— Muster-in roll of Captain Charles G. Matchett's Company, in the Fortieth Regiment of Ohio Foot Volunteers, commanded by Colonel Jonathan Cranor, called into service of the United States by the President from the dates set opposite their names respectively for the term of three years, unless sooner discharged. . . .

CHARLES G. MATCHETT,
Captain,
Company G, Fortieth Regiment, Ohio Volunteers,
Mustering Officer.

Stationed at Licking Station, Kentucky, December 31, 1861.

Stationed at Catlettsburg, Kentucky, December 31, 1861-June 30, 1862.

Continued a march from Camp Brutus, Clay, Kentucky to Paintsville.
January 8, 1862.— Arrived at Paintsville.
January 10.— Was engaged in the battle of Middle Creek.
February 12.— Advanced from Camp Buell to Brownlow.
March 10.— Was in the Round Gap affair.
June 20.— Was engaged in scouts without number until which time this company was ordered as a provisional guard to Catlettsburg, Kentucky. The captain had been appointed [illegible] when the company was first paid by Major McDowell October 31, 1861. They were paid from the date of "mustered into service" and not from that of "joined for service and enrolled."

Stationed at Camp McClure, July-August 1862.

Station not stated, September-October 1862.

Stationed at Camp McClure, Louisa, Kentucky, November-December 1862.

Stationed at camp near Nashville, Tennessee, January-February 1863.

Stationed at Franklin, Tennessee, March-April 1863.

Stationed at Shelbyville, Tennessee, May-June 1863.
June 2.— Left Franklin, Tennessee and arrived at Triune, Tennessee.
June 22-30.— Left Triune and arrived four miles west of Murfreesborough, since which time, except one day, we have been constantly on the move and to-day (June 30) finds us in peaceable possession of the recent Rebel stronghold and Headquarters of the Rebel Army of Tennessee, Shelbyville.

Stationed at Duck River Bridge, Tennessee, July-August 1863.

Station not stated, September-October 1863.

Stationed at Shellmound, Tennessee, November-December 1863.
November 1.— Left camp near Chattanooga, Tennessee for Shellmound, Tennessee, distance twenty-two miles.
November 23.— Left this camp for Chattanooga.
November 24.— Our regiment stormed the heights of Lookout Mountain, being in the advance. Three men, to wit William M. Bailey, Isaac N. Crumrine and Aaron D. Denise, wounded.
November 25.— Was in the battle of Missionary Ridge.
November 26.— Skirmished at Pea Vine Ridge.
November 27.— At Ringgold, Georgia.
December 3.— Returned to this camp.

Total distance marched ninety-eight miles.

Stationed at Blue Springs, Tennessee, January-February 1864.
February 22-28.— The company was engaged in the reconnaissance in force against Dalton, Georgia until February 28. Engaged the enemy on February 25.

Forty enlisted men of the company have reenlisted as veteran volunteers.

Stationed at Blue Springs, Tennessee, March-April 1864.

Forty enlisted men, having on former muster reenlisted as veteran volunteers under the two commissioned officers of the company, went home on veteran furlough of thirty days and returned.

Stationed at front of Kenesaw Mountain, May-June 1864.

Stationed in the field, Georgia, July-August 1864.

Stationed at Chattanooga, Tennessee, September-October 1864.

Company H

Stationed at Camp Chase, September 17-October 31, 1861.

Stationed at Camp Chase, Ohio, November 21, 1861.
November 21.— Muster-in roll of Captain William Cunningham's Company (H), in the Fortieth Regiment of Ohio Volunteers, commanded by Colonel Jonathan Cranor, called into service of the United States by the President for the term of three years, unless sooner discharged. . . .

ALBERT B. DOD,
Captain,
Fifteenth Infantry, United States Army, Mustering Officer.

Stationed at Licking Station, Kentucky, November-December 1861.

Stationed at Prestonburg, May-June 1862.

Stationed at Guyandotte, September-October 1862.

Stationed at Louisa, Kentucky, November-December 1862.
November 14.— Took up line of march from Guyandotte for Catlettsburg, Kentucky, twelve miles, and arrived the same day.
November 19-21.— Took up line of march from Catlettsburg, Kentucky, a distance of about forty miles, and arrived at Louisa, Kentucky November 21.

Stationed at camp near Nashville, Tennessee, January-February 1863.

Stationed at camp near Franklin, March-April 1863.

Stationed at Shelbyville, Tennessee, May-June 1863.

Stationed at Tullahoma, Tennessee, July-August 1863.

Stationed at Chattanooga, Tennessee, September-October 1863.

Stationed at Shellmound, Tennessee, November-December 1863.

Stationed at Blue Springs, Tennessee, January-April 1864.

Station not stated, May-August 1864.

Stationed at Chattanooga, Tennessee, September-October 1864.

Stationed at Nashville, Tennessee, December 6, 1864.
December 6.— Muster-out roll of Lieutenant George D. Stone's Company (H), in the Fortieth Regiment of Ohio Infantry Volunteers, commanded by Lieutenant-Colonel James Watson, called into the service of the United States by the President at camp Chase, Ohio (the place of general rendezvous) to serve for the term of three years from the date of enrollment, unless sooner discharged. . . .

JOHN I. MORRIS,
First Lieutenant,
Twentieth Indiana Battery, Assistant Commissary of Musters,
First Division, Fourth Army Corps.

Company I

Stationed at Camp Chase, December 11, 1861.
December 11.— Muster-in roll of Captain [Andrew] R. Calderwood's Company, in the Fortieth Regiment of Ohio Volunteers, commanded by Colonel Jonathan Cranor, called into service of the United States by the President from the date set opposite their

names respectfully (date of muster) for the term of three years, unless sooner discharged. . . .

ANDREW R. CALDERWOOD,
Second Lieutenant,
Fortieth Regiment, Ohio Volunteers,
United States Army, Mustering Officer.

Stationed at Licking Station, Kentucky, December 31, 1861.

Station not stated, December 31, 1861-June 30, 1862.

Station not stated, September-October 1862.

Stationed at Louisville, Kentucky, November-December 1862.

Stationed at camp near Nashville, Tennessee, January-February 1863.

Stationed at Franklin, Tennessee, March-April 1863.

Stationed at Shelbyville, Tennessee, May-June 1863.

Stationed at Tullahoma, Tennessee, July-August 1863.

Stationed at Camp Clark near Chattanooga, Tennessee, September-October 1863.
September 7.— Left Tullahoma, Tennessee and marched to Rossville, Georgia, a distance of ninety-five miles.
September 18-20.— Encamped there until moved out five miles and opened the battle which terminated in the battle of Chickamauga. We were engaged until September 20, losing two men killed, twelve wounded and two prisoners of war.
September 22.— Fell back to Chattanooga, ten miles.

Stationed at Shellmound, Georgia, November-December 1863.

Stationed at Blue Springs, Tennessee, January-April 1864.

Stationed in the field near Kenesaw Mountain, May-June 1864.

Stationed in the field, July-August 1864.

Stationed at Chattanooga, Tennessee, September-October 1864.

Stationed at Nashville, Tennessee, December 6, 1864.
December 6.— Muster-out roll of Captain Milton Kemper's Company (I), in the Fortieth Regiment of Ohio Infantry Volunteers, commanded by Lieutenant-Colonel James Watson, called into the service of the United States by the President at Camp Chase, Ohio (the place of general rendezvous) to serve for the term of three years from the date of enrollment, unless sooner discharged. . . .

JOHN I. MORRIS,
First Lieutenant,
Twentieth Indiana Battery, Assistant Commissary of Musters,
First Division, Fourth Army Corps.

Company K

Stationed at Camp Chase, November 30, 1861.
November 30.— Muster-in roll of Captain Alexander A. Knapp's Company, in the Fortieth Regiment of Ohio Volunteers, commanded by Colonel Jonathan Cranor, called into service of the United States by the President from the date set opposite their names respectively (date of this muster) for the term of three years, unless sooner discharged. . . .

ALEXANDER A. KNAPP,
Captain,
Company K, Fortieth Regiment, Ohio Volunteers,
Mustering Officer.

Stationed at Licking Station, Kentucky, December 31, 1861.

Stationed at Camp Cranor, May-June 1862.

Stationed at Guyandotte, [West] Virginia, September-October 1862.

Stationed at Camp McClure, Kentucky, November-December 1862.

Stationed at Nashville, Tennessee, January-February 1863.

Stationed near Franklin, Tennessee, April 11, 1863.

Stationed at Franklin, Tennessee, March-April 1863.

Stationed at Shelbyville, Tennessee, May-June 1863.

Stationed at Tullahoma, Tennessee, July-August 1863.

Stationed at Camp Clark, Tennessee, September-October 1863.

Stationed at Camp Nickajack, Georgia, November-December 1863.
November 24.— This company was engaged in the battle of Lookout Mountain.
November 25.— Was engaged in the battle of Missionary Ridge.

Stationed at Blue Springs, Tennessee, January-April 1864.

Stationed in the field, May-August 1864.

Stationed at Chattanooga, Tennessee, September-October 1864.

Stationed at Nashville, Tennessee, December 7, 1864.
December 7.— Muster-out roll of Lieutenant Isaac N. Edwards' Company (K), in the Fortieth Regiment of Ohio Infantry Volunteers, commanded by Lieutenant-Colonel James Watson, called into the service of the United States by the President at Camp Chase, Ohio (the place of general rendezvous). . . .

JOHN I. MORRIS,
First Lieutenant,
Twentieth Indiana Battery, Assistant Commissary of Muster,
First Division, Fourth Army Corps.

[M594-Roll #149]

Record of Events for Forty-first Ohio Infantry,
August 1861-June 1865.

Field and Staff

Stationed at Camp Wood, Ohio, October 29, 1861.
October 29.— Muster-in roll of the Forty-first Regiment of Ohio Volunteers, commanded by Colonel William [Babcock] Hazen, called into service of the United States by the President from October 29, 1861 (date of this muster) for the term of three years, unless sooner discharged. . . .

JAMES P. [WILSON] NEILL,
First Lieutenant,
Eighteenth United States Infantry, Mustering Officer.

Stationed at Camp Wood, Ohio, enrollment to October 31, 1861.

Stationed at Camp Wickliffe, Kentucky, November-December 1861.

Stationed at Andrew Jackson near Nashville, Tennessee, [January]-February 1862.

Stationed at the field of Shiloh, March-April 1862.

Station not stated, May-August 1862.

Stationed at Corinth, Mississippi, June 6, 1862.
June 6.— Muster-out roll of the band of the Forty-first Regiment of Ohio Volunteers, commanded by Colonel William B. Hazen, from October 22, 1861 when mustered in to June 6 when discharged. . . .

[JOHN THOMAS] PRICE,
First Lieutenant,
Fifth Infantry, Aide-de-Camp, Mustering Officer.

Stationed at Columbia, Kentucky, September-October 1862.

Stationed at Murfreesborough, Tennessee, November-December 1862.

December 26-29.— The regiment marched from camp near Nashville, Tennessee and arrived in front of the enemy's lines near Murfreesborough, Tennessee December 29, the distance marched being about twenty-six miles.

December 31.— Was in the battle before Murfreesborough. It became engaged about 8.30 o'clock a.m. and continued so without cessation, except to procure ammunition, until between 2 and 3 p.m.

The regiment is in excellent health and discipline.

Requisitions for clothing, equipments and camp and garrison equipage have generally been promptly supplied and the men have seldom suffered for the want of those articles. The arms are altered flintlock muskets, the same that were issued to the regiment at its first organization, are miserable things, not fit to be in the hands of troops. The ordnance department seems guilty of negligence in the packing of ammunition and we frequently find round and conical balls and of different calibre in the same packing boxes.

In the month of November the regiment marched from Columbia, Kentucky via Glasgow and Gallatin to Nashville, Tennessee.

Stationed at Readyville, Tennessee, January-February 1863.

January 1-3.— The regiment was present at the battle of Stone's River but was held in reserve during January 1, 2 and 3, except in the afternoon of January 2, when the enemy made a vigorous assault on our left and was repulsed. The regiment was then ordered forward and assisted in following up the advantage gained. In this affair it lost four wounded.

January 7.— Marched to Murfreesborough, a distance of three miles.

January 11.— [Marched] to Readyville, a distance of twelve miles, which it, with the regiment and brigade, still occupies.

January 24.— Marched with the division to Woodbury, a distance of seven miles. Attacked a body of the enemy's cavalry, inflicting a loss of four left dead on the field, and returned to Readyville the same day. The loss of the regiment in this affair was one wounded.

Stationed at Readyville, Tennessee, March-April 1863.
April 2.— In the morning the regiment, with the Sixth Kentucky Volunteer Infantry, marched to cooperate in an attack on a Rebel cavalry post at Woodbury, some miles east of this post. The regiment marched a distance of sixteen miles, getting in rear of the Rebels, and the detachment of which it formed part succeeded in capturing their baggage train, killing one and wounding two others. This regiment, however, being on the left and the Rebels leaving the road as soon as they came upon the head of the column, was not engaged.

Stationed at Manchester, Tennessee, May-June 1863.

Stationed at Poe's Tavern, Tennessee, July-August 1863.

Stationed at Brown's Ferry, Tennessee, September-October 1863.
July 1-8.— The regiment marched from Manchester, Tennessee to Elk River and returned to Manchester July 8.
August 16-24.— Marched from Manchester August 16 to Poe's Tavern, Hamilton County, Tennessee, where it arrived August 24.
September 9.— Marched from thence.
September 10.— Forded the Tennessee River at Friar's Island. Marched thence via Tyner's Station, Ringgold and [Lee and] Gordon's Mills to Chattanooga Creek; thence back to Chickamauga River, east of Crawfish Spring.
September 19-20.— Thence to the battlefield of Chickamauga. It was engaged on September 19 and 20, sustaining a loss of six killed, 100 wounded and nine missing. On the evening of September 20 it was withdrawn to Missionary Ridge.
September 21.— At night [withdrew] to Chattanooga.
September 27.— One hundred fifty men embarked in pontoons at Chattanooga for Brown's Ferry, eight miles distant by river, the rest of the regiment marching by land a distance of two miles across Moccasin Point. The boat parties landed at the ferry and gained and held the heights with a loss of one killed, three wounded and two missing. At Chickamauga Lieutenant [Lloyd] Fisher, Acting Adjutant, was severely wounded. Colonel [Aquila] Wiley had one horse killed, Lieutenant-Colonel [Robert

Lewis] Kimberly had two and Major [John H.] Williston one wounded. There was no loss in the field and staff at Brown's Ferry.

Stationed at Blain's Cross-Roads, Tennessee, November-December 1863.

Stationed at Cleveland, Ohio, January-February 1864.
January 1.— The regiment reenlisted as veteran volunteers and from the fact that both officers and men were absent either on duty or on leave, there was no inspection of the regiment.

Stationed at McDonald's Station, Tennessee, March-April 1864.

Station not stated, May-June 1864.

Stationed near Battle Station, Georgia, July-August 1864.
July 3.— The enemy evacuated his position at Kenesaw Mountain and on July 5 in following him the regiment was sharply engaged with his skirmishers, driving them across the Chattahoochee River, causing him to abandon his position, sustaining a loss of one commanding officer wounded and one man killed and three [men] wounded.
July 17.— Having crossed the river at [Pace's] Ferry, the division, with the regiment as skirmishers, moved down the south bank of the river to cover the crossing of other parts of the Army to Pace's Ferry. The skirmishers were hotly engaged with the enemy without loss.
August 25.— The regiment lay before the works of the enemy at Atlanta until the night of August 25, when it, with the Army, moved to the south of Atlanta but was not engaged during the movement.

Stationed at Athens, Alabama, September-October 1864.

Stationed at Lexington, Alabama, November-December 1864.
The regiment has been attached to the Third Division, Fourth Army Corps and has been with it in the retreat from Pulaski, Tennessee to Nashville, Tennessee.
December 15-16.— Took an active part in the battles in front of Nashville. Also in pursuit of the defeated Army, losing five

commanding officers wounded, one enlisted man killed, twenty-eight enlisted men wounded, and three missing.

Stationed at Nashville, Tennessee, March-April 1865.
March 15.— The regiment, with the Third Division, Fourth Army Corps, left Huntsville, Alabama and took the cars for East Tennessee.
March 17.— Encamped at Strawberry Plains, East Tennessee in the morning.
March 18-April 4.— Marched for New Market; thence to Bull's Gap on March 30 and 31; thence to Greeneville on April 4.
April 6-8.— Left there in company with the Second Brigade of the Third Division, Fourth Army Corps for Warm Springs, North Carolina, where it arrived on April 8, distance twenty-five miles.
April 9-10.— Returned to Greeneville.
April 22.— Marched for Bull's Gap and came thence by railroad to Nashville, where it is now encamped.

Stationed near New Orleans, Louisiana, May-June 1865.
April 30.— The regiment was at Nashville, Tennessee.
June 15.— Left with the balance of the Third Division, Fourth Corps for New Orleans, Louisiana, coming down the Ohio River on transport *Echo No. 2*.
June 29.— Off Cairo, Illinois she (the *Echo No. 2*) collided with the Monitor *Oneida* and sank in ten minutes. The regiment lost one man. The rest of the men barely escaped with their lives. All regiment records were lost, also all public and private property belonging to officers and men, including ordnance and stores, camp and garrison equipage, etc. The regiment is now at New Orleans with the Second Brigade, Third Division, of which it forms a part.

Regiment

Stationed at Camp Wood, Cuyahoga County, Ohio, October 1861.

Stationed at Camp Jenkins, November 1861.
November 6-7.— The regiment, having been furnished with fatigue uniforms, knapsacks, haversacks, camp equipage, and the flanking companies with Enfield rifles and accoutrements, moved

from Camp Wood near Cleveland, Ohio November 6 and was reported to Brigadier-General [Melancthon Smith] Wade at Camp Dennison, Ohio November 7. At Camp Dennison rifled muskets (No. 2) and accoutrements were furnished to the companies not previously supplied and transportation wagons for the regiment.

November 14.— The regiment moved from Camp Dennison to Cincinnati by rail; thence by steamboat to Gallipolis, Ohio by orders of General Wade. From Gallipolis two expeditions were sent to Green Bottom, [West] Virginia, the residence of the Rebel Colonel [Albert] Gallatin Jenkins, and a considerable quantity of corn, some horses, hogs, etc., taken.

November 19-20.— Companies A and B, with eighty-four and ninety-eight men, respectively made the first expedition, Companies C, D, E, F, and I, with an aggregate strength of 420 men. The second on November 20. Each expedition occupying one day, somewhat extensive scouts were made during the expedition but without material result.

November 26.— The regiment was supplied with overcoats while at Gallipolis, from whence it moved to Louisville, Kentucky by steamer by orders of Brigadier-General [Don Carlos] Buell November 26.

Stationed at Camp Wickliffe, December 1861.

November 30.— The regiment was attached to the Fifteenth Brigade, temporarily under command of Colonel Milo [Smith] Hascall, O. V.

December 6.— The regiment moved from Camp Jenkins (the place and date of last monthly report) to Camp Quigley (one-half mile from Louisville, Kentucky).

December 10.— The Tenth and Fifteenth Brigades (Fourth Division, Army of the Ohio) left camp at Louisville and under Brigadier-General [William] Nelson, marched to a point about nine miles from New Haven, Kentucky on the Nashville Road, occupying five days in accomplishing the distance, between sixty and seventy miles, and encamping at Camp Wickliffe, the present location. At this place the clothing of the regiment was completed by the issue [of] dress costs and caps.

Stationed at Camp Wickliffe, Kentucky, January 1862.

January 3.— The regiment was made a part of the Nineteenth Brigade, then formed under command of Colonel W. B. Hazen.

January 29.— The Enfield rifles of the following companies were exchanged for Springfield muskets (rifled), making the entire complement of arms of uniform calibre. During the month the sickness existing at the time of last report has increased seriously, impairing the efficiency of the regiment.

Stationed at Camp Andrew Jackson, February 1862.
February 14.— The Forty-first Ohio Volunteers marched from Camp Wickliffe, Kentucky.
February 17-21.— Arrived at West Point, Kentucky. Embarked on steamboats *Silver Moon* and *Lady Jackson*. Was transported to Paducah, Kentucky, arriving there February 21; thence to Nashville, Tennessee, where it disembarked and encamped at Camp Andrew Jackson, one mile from the city.

Stationed at camp near Mount Pleasant, Tennessee, March 1862.

Stationed at field of Shiloh, April 1862.
April 1-6.— The regiment was marched from near Pleasant Hill, Tennessee en route for Savannah, where it arrived April 6. From there it marched to Pittsburg Landing, arriving at night.
April 7.— The regiment was engaged in the battle of the field of Shiloh, losing twenty-four men killed, 110 wounded and one missing in action.

Stationed at camp near Corinth, Mississippi, May 1862.

Stationed at camp near Athens, Alabama, June 1862.

Stationed at Reynolds' Station, Tennessee, July 1862.
Since our last monthly report the regiment has been marched from camp near Iuka, Mississippi to Athens, Alabama, a distance of about 100 miles.
July 17-30.— Were encamped near Athens, Alabama about two weeks, from which place we started July 17 and were on the march nearly three days, when we encamped on the Nashville and Decatur Railroad. We were engaged there in building trestlework and stockades at the tunnel on the road. We remained there from July 20 until July 30, when we moved camp and marched to Reynolds' Station, a distance of sixteen miles. We passed

through Pulaski, Tennessee on the way here. We are awaiting now the arrival of the train to convey us to Murfreesborough, Tennessee via Nashville, Tennessee.

Stationed at Murfreesborough, Tennessee, August 1862.

Since July 31 the regiment has moved from Reynolds' Station, Tennessee to this place, Murfreesborough, by railroad via Nashville, a distance of 112 miles. The wagon train was sent across the country a distance of seventy miles. The health of the regiment is usually good but it is sadly in need of clothing, blankets, etc., and quite a large number of our men are very poorly equipped.

The regiment has been engaged at times in loading and unloading freight at the Nashville and Chattanooga Railroad Depot and for a week past has had very heavy details for the work on the fortifications, which are being erected here.

Stationed at Louisville, Kentucky, September 1862.

September 6-26.— The regiment left Murfreesborough and has marched to Louisville via Nashville, Bowling Green, Munfordville, and Elizabethtown, a distance of 215 miles, arriving there September 26. The march has been a severe one, the whole distance being made on half rations. Our baggage was left at Bowling Green and the men were much in want of clothing on our arrival here. The health of the regiment is extremely good, considering the length of the march and its many disadvantages.

The entire Company D is on guard duty at brigade Headquarters.

Stationed at Columbus, Kentucky, October 1862.

October 1.— The regiment left Louisville in pursuit of the enemy. His rear was constantly harassed and many slight skirmishes ensued, in which at times the regiment bore a part. At the battle of Chaplin Hills, the only engagement of account, we were not engaged, except in slight skirmishing, though in close proximity. Our march through the mountains was constantly impeded by obstructions being thrown across the road and was necessarily slow.

October 20.— What proved to be our journey's end in that direction, Pitman's Cross-Roads near London, was reached.

October 22-31.— A countermarch was commenced and we arrived at Columbia on October 31.

Entire Company D doing guard duty at brigade Headquarters.

Stationed at Nashville, Tennessee, November 1862.
November 2-3.— The regiment in connection with the division left Columbia, Kentucky, arriving at Glasgow, Kentucky, a distance of thirty-six miles, on November 3.
November 12-16.— It again took up its line of march via Scottsville (twenty-five miles) and Gallatin (thirty-two miles) to Silver Springs, Tennessee (fourteen miles), arriving there on November 16.
November 20-26.— From there it moved to a point six miles east of Nashville (twelve miles) and on November 26 to a point on the Nashville and Murfreesborough Pike, three and one-half miles from the former place (seven miles), where it now is.

The condition of the regiment with regard to military appearance and discipline is excellent. The health of the regiment has not been better since its organization. The Sibley tents issued to the regiment in January have become leaky and are not fit for use in the coming winter. The men are entirely destitute of overcoats, they having turned them over for storage in May or June, according to orders of the commander of the department, and they have not been returned nor have they yet received any in place of them. They are also much in want of other clothing, for which requisitions and estimates have been repeatedly made but which the government, on account, I presume, of the limited transportation, have not been able to furnish. The arms and accoutrements are generally in good condition. About twenty of the muskets are without bayonets. The bayonets were lost in the battle of Shiloh and though requisitions have been made repeatedly on the ordnance officer, they have never been furnished.

The entire Company D is on guard duty at Headquarters, Nineteenth Brigade.

Stationed at Murfreesborough, Tennessee, December 1862.
[For record of events, see Field and Staff.]

The entire Company D doing provost guard duty at Headquarters, Nineteenth Brigade.

Stationed at Readyville, January 1863.
December 31, 1862.— The regiment being engaged in the first line of battle and engaged during the greater part of the day at the battle of Stone's River in front of Murfreesborough.
January 1-2, 1863.— The battle still being undecided, it was held in reserve, as it was also on January 2 until about 3 p.m., when the enemy vigorously attacked the left wing, when it was again ordered to the front and assisted in his repulse, sustaining a loss of four wounded.
January 7.— It moved three miles east of Murfreesborough and encamped.
January 10.— From [Murfreesborough] it marched to Readyville, eleven miles east of Murfreesborough, which, with the rest of the brigade, it occupies as an outpost.
January 24.— It marched with the entire division to Woodbury, seven miles east of Readyville, to capture a force of the enemy's cavalry stationed there. On approaching the enemy's pickets the regiment was ordered to the front and drove them in upon the reserve which was posted behind a stone fence. The regiment engaged them, inflicting some loss upon the enemy and dislodging them but the entire force made good its retreat. The only loss the regiment sustained was one man wounded.

Stationed at Readyville, Tennessee, February 1863.
During the month of February no changes of station have been made. The regiment, with the brigade to which it belongs, has occupied the outpost at Readyville, Tennessee.

Stationed at Readyville, Tennessee, March 1863.

Stationed at Readyville, April 1863.
[For record of events, see Field and Staff.]

Stationed at Readyville, Tennessee, May 1863.
The regiment has not changed station during the month. It has received new Springfield rifled muskets in exchange for altered muskets, with which it was formerly armed. Discipline excellent; arms and accoutrements are complete and in good condition; clothing good. Requisitions on the quartermaster and ordnance departments are filled more promptly than at any other time since we have been in the service.

Stationed at camp at Manchester, Tennessee, June 1863.
June 24-28.— The regiment, in company with the division, marched from Readyville, reaching Manchester on June 28, a distance of twenty-five miles.

Stationed at Manchester, Tennessee, July 1863.

Stationed at Poe's Tavern, Tennessee, August 1863.

Stationed at Chattanooga, Tennessee, September-October 1863.

Station not stated, November-December 1863.

Station not stated, January 1864.
January 1.— The regiment reenlisted as veteran volunteers under provisions of General Orders No. 191, War Department, series of 1863 at Blain's Cross-Roads, Tennessee.
January 5-8.— It marched for Chattanooga, Tennessee, where it arrived January 8.
January 26-31.— It left Chattanooga for Ohio, arriving at Columbus, Ohio on January 31.

Station not stated, February-March 1864.

Stationed near McDonald's Station, Tennessee, April 1864.

Station not stated, May 1864.

Stationed near Marietta, Georgia, June 1864.

Since June 1 this regiment has moved from near Dallas, Georgia to Kenesaw Mountain and during that time has been constantly at the front and under fire of the enemy, having one commissioned officer and four men wounded in different skirmishes.

Station not stated, July 1864.

Station not stated, August 1864.
August 1-25.— The regiment remained in front of the enemy's works before Atlanta. On the night of August 25 it, with the rest of the Army, commenced the movement to the south of Atlanta.

August 29.— It assisted in the destruction of the Montgomery Railroad.
August 31.— The Corps struck the Macon Railroad at Battle Station. It was not engaged during the movement, except as skirmishers before the enemy's position, six miles south of Jonesborough.

Stationed near Atlanta, Georgia, September 1864.

Station not stated, October 1864-February 1865.

Stationed at New Market, East Tennessee, March 1865.

Stationed at Camp Harker, Tennessee, April 1865.

Station not stated, May 1865.

Stationed at Green Lake, Texas, June 1865.

Company A

Stationed at Camp Wood, Ohio, August 26, 1861.
August 26.— Muster-in roll of Captain [Seth] A. Bushnell's Company, in the Forty-first Regiment of Ohio Volunteers, commanded by Colonel William B. Hazen, called into service of the United States by President Abraham Lincoln from August 26, 1861 (date of this muster) for the term of three years, unless sooner discharged. . . .

JAMES P. W. NEILL,
First Lieutenant,
Eighteenth United States Infantry, Mustering Officer.

Stationed at Camp Wood, Ohio, August 26-October 31, 1861.

Stationed at Camp Wickliffe, Kentucky, November-December 1861.

Since date of last payroll this company has changed station from Camp Wood, Ohio to Camp Dennison, Ohio by railroad, 250 miles.
November 6.— From last-named camp to Gallipolis, Ohio by railroad, fifteen miles.

November 15-16.— By steamer *Telegraph No. 3*, a distance of 210 miles.
November 17.— Steamed down the Ohio thirty miles at night to surprise the Rebel leader Jenkins in [West] Virginia. Surrounded and thoroughly examined the house but found no trace of the object of our search. The scrupulous obedience to orders on the part of the men under my command, especially as to silence and caution, gave me great confidence in the efficiency of the company for service.
November 27-28.— Left Gallipolis by steamer *Telegraph No. 3* for Louisville, Kentucky, 356 miles, where we arrived November 28. Marched six miles same day and stopped at Camp Jenkins. This camp being, in every respect, bad.
December 5.— We went to Camp Quigley, a few miles distant.
December 10-14.— We left the latter place for Camp Wickliffe, Kentucky, where we arrived on December 14, a distance of about sixty-four miles. The men carried their arms and accoutrements, knapsacks and forty rounds of cartridges. Very few fell out, to be carried by vehicles.
December 30.— The men are now in bad condition. Many are ill, several severely. An increase of one-fourth in the quantity of their food and tent protection would, in my judgment, give a [likewise and] happy proportionate increase of vigor to the men.

Stationed at Camp Andrew Jackson, January-February 1862.

Changed stations, since last roll, from Camp Wickliffe, Kentucky to Camp Andrew Jackson, Tennessee near Nashville by a march of forty miles and by steamer the balance of the distance.

Stationed at field of Shiloh, Tennessee, March-April 1862.

Changed station, since last roll, from Camp Andrew Jackson, Tennessee by a march to the field of Shiloh, Tennessee, where the company was engaged in the battle of April 7.

Stationed at camp near Athens, Alabama, May-June 1862.

Stationed at Murfreesborough, Tennessee, July-August 1862.

Changed station, since last muster, from Athens, Alabama by march to Reynolds' Station, Tennessee; thence by rail to Murfreesborough, Tennessee via Nashville, Tennessee. The discipline and efficiency of the company has materially improved and its strength increased by the arrival of convalescent soldiers.

Stationed at Columbus, Kentucky, September-October 1862.

Changed stations, since last muster, from Murfreesborough, Tennessee to Louisville, Kentucky by march of 215 miles via Nashville and Bowling Green.

October 1.— Left Louisville in pursuit of the enemy. The company was engaged in several skirmishes with the enemy's rear guard during the march to Pitman's Cross-Roads near London, Kentucky. From this place the regiment marched to Columbus, Kentucky via Mount Vernon and Somerset. The company has been strengthened by the arrival of fourteen recruits, enlisted by the recruiting officers detailed from the regiment.

Stationed at camp near Murfreesborough, Tennessee, November-December 1862.

Changed station, since last muster, from Columbia, Kentucky by march to Nashville, Tennessee via Glasgow and Gallatin.

December 26-31.— Left Nashville and marched twenty-eight miles toward Murfreesborough, where the company was engaged in the great battle of December 31. Whole number engaged in action, forty-eight. Whole number killed in action, three. Whole number severely wounded, nine. Whole number slightly wounded, six.

Stationed at Readyville, Tennessee, January-February 1863.

Changed stations, since last muster, from Murfreesborough, Tennessee to Readyville, Tennessee, twelve miles. The brigade, constituting an outpost, formed an entrenched camp.

January 2.— The company was engaged in the battle at Stone's River. Lost one wounded.

January 24.— The company was engaged in a sharp skirmish with the enemy at Woodbury, Tennessee.

Stationed at Readyville, Tennessee, April 11, 1863.

No change of station since last muster. Occupy an entrenched camp at Readyville, Tennessee, an outpost of the Union Army.

The company has been engaged in several skirmishes with the enemy while on scouting expeditions or guard for forage trains.

Stationed at Readyville, Tennessee, March-April 1863.
No change of station since last muster.

Stationed at Manchester, Tennessee, May-June 1863.
Changed stations, since last muster, from Readyville, Tennessee to Manchester, Tennessee by march.
June 24-29.— Left Readyville and arrived at Manchester June 29.

Stationed at Poe's Tavern, Tennessee, July-August 1863.

Stationed at Brown's Ferry, Tennessee, September-October 1863.

Stationed at Blain's Cross-Roads, Tennessee, November-December 1863.

Stationed at Cleveland, Ohio, January-February 1864.
January 5-8.— The company and regiment left Blain's Cross-Roads. Arrived at Chattanooga on January 8.
January 26-February 1.— Left Chattanooga; arrived in Cleveland, Ohio on February 1; went into barracks at Camp Cleveland.
February 3.— The company was furloughed for thirty days.

Stationed at McDonald's Station, Tennessee, March-April 1864.
March 5.— The company rendezvoused at Camp Cleveland, Ohio.
March 8-18.— Left that place for the seat of war. It was transported to Loudon, Tennessee, at which place it arrived on March 18, a distance of 850 miles. From there it marched to Powder Springs Gap via Knoxville, a distance of sixty miles.
April 6.— Leaving there it marched to McDonald's Station near Cleveland, Tennessee by way of Knoxville and Loudon, along the East Tennessee and Georgia Railroad, a distance of 123 miles.

Stationed near Kenesaw Mountain, Georgia, May-June 1864.
May 3-5.— The company, with the regiment, left McDonald's Station. Marched to Catoosa Springs, arriving there on May 5.
May 7-13.— Left Catoosa Springs, skirmishing with the enemy through Tunnel Hill to Rocky Face Ridge. Confronted the enemy at the latter place until May 13, losing two men wounded. Then marched in the direction of Dalton. Passed through Dalton on May 13.

May 14-15.— Engaged the enemy at Dalton, Georgia.
May 16-20.— Left Resaca, skirmishing constantly with the enemy until May 20, when it arrived at Cassville, Georgia.
May 23.— Left the latter place.
May 25-June 5.— Marched in the direction of Dallas. Came upon the enemy at Pumpkin Vine Creek. Engaged the enemy May 27, suffering severely, losing two killed, eleven wounded and two prisoners. Held a position in front of the enemy from May 27 until June 5, when he evacuated. Followed him to Kenesaw Mountain, skirmishing constantly most of the way. The whole distance marched was over 100 miles. The company is now on duty with the regiment at this place.

Stationed near Battle Station, July-August 1864.
July 3.— The company and regiment left Kenesaw Mountain. Followed the enemy to the Chattahoochee River, skirmishing with the enemy and driving them across the river.
July 5-18.— We moved up the river about eight miles and crossed it on July 8. Remained there until July 18, when we moved to Peach Tree Creek, skirmishing with the enemy until they were in their works near Atlanta, Georgia.
August 25.— We remained before Atlanta until the night of August 25, when we moved to the right of Atlanta. Was engaged in destroying the Montgomery Railroad.
August 29.— Marched towards the Macon Railroad, within three miles of it.

Stationed at Athens, Alabama, September-October 1864.
September 1.— The company and regiment marched to Jonesborough, Georgia.
September 2-5.— [Marched] to Lovejoy's [Station] and there fronted the enemy until September 5, when it returned to Jonesborough.
September 6.— [Marched] to Rough and Ready [Station].
September 7.— [Marched] to Atlanta, where it remained.
October 3-31.— Marched to Marietta to intercept the Rebel General [John Bell] Hood's Army from there to Kingston; thence to Rome; thence to Resaca; thence across the country to Summerville and Gaylesville, Alabama; thence to Chattanooga, where it took the cars for Athens, Alabama, where we arrived October 31. Distance marched about 190 miles, by rail about 100 miles.

Stationed at Lexington, Alabama, November-December 1864.
November 2.— Changed stations from Athens, Alabama to Pulaski, Tennessee. Arrived at the latter place November 2. Left Pulaski and marched to Nashville, Tennessee. Arrived at the latter place November —.
December 15-16.— Remained in camp until December 15, when we moved out and attacked the enemy, Hood's Army. Fought them to hell and gone December 15 and 16. Afterwards followed the retreating Army to Lexington, Alabama. Whole distance marched 212 miles.

Stationed at Huntsville, Alabama, January-February 1865.
January 31.— The company, with the regiment, marched from Lexington, Alabama (place of last muster) to Huntsville, Alabama, where it remained in winter quarters until January 31, when it marched for Eastport, Mississippi as guard to the Third Division train. On reaching Blue Water [Creek], thirty miles from Eastport, received orders to return to Huntsville.
February 8.— Arrived [at Huntsville] and have remained up to present date in comfortable winter quarters.

Stationed at Nashville, Tennessee, March-April 1865.
March 15.— The company, with the regiment, left Huntsville, Alabama. Took the cars for Bull's Gap.
March 17.— Arrived at Strawberry Plains.
March 18.— Left the Plains. Marched to New Market. Went into camp.
March 29-31.— Marched to Bull's Gap. Arrived there March 31.
April 4.— We marched for Greeneville, Tennessee. Arrived there the same day.
April 6-7.— We marched for [Warm] Springs, North Carolina. Arrived there April 7.
April 9-10.— We marched for Greeneville again. Arrived there April 10.
April 22.— Marched for Bull's Gap.
April 25-28.— Took cars for Nashville, Tennessee, arriving there April 28, where we lie quietly in camp.

Stationed near New Orleans, Louisiana, May-June 1865.
June 16-17.— The company, with the regiment, broke camp near Nashville, Tennessee and on June 17 took the cars for Johnsonville on the Tennessee River, arriving there on the evening of June 17. We embarked on the steamer *Echo No. 2* for New Orleans, Louisiana.
June 19-24.— In the morning the boat collided with a Monitor near Cairo, Illinois and sank, the men barely having time to escape on the Monitor. During the day we were placed on board the steamer *Atlantic* and again under way for New Orleans, arriving there on June 24, where we have lain in camp until the present time, eight miles below the city. Whole distance traveled 1,298 miles.

Company B

Stationed at Camp Wood, August 27, 1861.
August 27.— Muster-in roll of Captain William R. Tolles' Company B, in the Forty-first Regiment of Ohio Volunteers, commanded by Colonel William B. Hazen, called into service of the United States by orders of the President, approved by Congress July 22, 1861 from August 27, 1861 (date of this muster) for the term of three years, unless sooner discharged. . . .

JAMES P. W. NEILL,
First Lieutenant,
Eighteenth United States Infantry, Mustering Officer.

Stationed at Camp Wood, Ohio, August 27-October 31, 1861.

Stationed at Camp Wickliffe, Kentucky, November-December 1861.
November 6-7.— The company left Camp Wood, Cleveland, Ohio per railroad for Camp Dennison, Ohio. Arrived at Camp Dennison November 7.
November 14-16.— Left Camp Dennison, Ohio for Gallipolis, Ohio per railroad and steamboat, arriving November 16.
November 19.— The company was employed in a scouting expedition to Green Bottom, [West] Virginia.
November 26-27.— Left Gallipolis by steamboat. Arrived at Louisville November 27.

November 28.— Marched to Camp Jenkins, Kentucky.
December 5.— Marched to Camp Quigley, Kentucky.
December 10-14.— Marched from Camp Quigley and arrived on December 14 at Camp Wickliffe, Kentucky.

The company has performed the various marches without leaving any men on the route, save those who were sick and left in the hospital at Louisville, and is in a good state of discipline and efficiency.

Stationed at Camp Andrew Jackson, Tennessee, [January]-February 1862.
February 14.— The company marched from Camp Wickliffe, Kentucky.
February 15-17.— Marched to West Point on the Ohio, embarking there and by steamboat down the Ohio [River] to Paducah; thence up the Cumberland River to Nashville, Tennessee.
February 25.— Landed and encamped at Camp Andrew Jackson near Nashville.

Stationed at field of Shiloh, March-April 1862.
March 17-April 6.— The company left Camp Andrew Jackson, Tennessee. Marched three days; encamped near Spring Hill, Tennessee. Arrived there April 6.
April 7.— Engaged in action. The efficiency of the company is much weakened by sickness and loss of wounded and killed in action.

Stationed near Athens, Alabama, May-June 1862.

Marched from the field of Shiloh, Tennessee to within three miles of Corinth, Mississippi and engaged in throwing up earthworks.

May 30.— Entered Corinth, the enemy having evacuated it.
June 4.— Marched from camp before Corinth. Marched south (below Danville, Mississippi); thence to Jacinto; thence to camp near Iuka, Mississippi.
June 23-30.— Marched from camp near Iuka, arriving at this camp near Athens, Alabama June 30.

Stationed at camp, Murfreesborough, Tennessee, July-August 1862.

The company marched from camp near Athens to camp near Pulaski, Tennessee and engaged there in working on the railroad. Marched from thence to Reynolds' Station and was transported to this place by the way of Nashville on the railroad. The company is gaining in efficiency of drill also in health and numbers.

Stationed at Columbia, Kentucky, September-October 1862.
September 6-26.— The company started from Murfreesborough, Tennessee and marched to Louisville, Kentucky, a distance of about 215 miles, arriving September 26.
October 1.— Lay at Louisville until October 1 and were ordered eastward. Marched east as far as Pitman's Cross-Roads, Laurel County, Kentucky, having been engaged in several skirmishes with the enemy.
October 21-31.— Left Pitman's Cross-Roads, marching through Mount Vernon and Somerset, arriving at Columbia, Kentucky October 31, making about 450 miles marched during the months of September and October. The company received eight recruits at Louisville and twenty-three at Columbia, Kentucky.

Stationed at camp at Readyville, Tennessee, January-February 1863.

The company marched from camp near Murfreesborough, Tennessee to camp near Readyville, Tennessee.
January 1-3.— The company was at the battle of Stone's River.
January 24.— Was in a skirmish with the enemy near Woodbury, Tennessee.

Stationed at camp at Readyville, Tennessee, March-April 1863.

Stationed at camp at Manchester, Tennessee, May-June 1863.
[For record of events, see Company A.]

Stationed at Poe's Tavern, Tennessee, July-August 1863.

During the month of August the company, with the regiment, marched from Manchester, Tennessee to Poe's Tavern, Tennessee near Tennessee River, at which place it was on August 31.

Stationed at Chattanooga, Tennessee, September-October 1863.
September 7.— The company left camp at Poe's Tavern, Tennessee.
September 10-11.— Crossed the Tennessee River above Chattanooga, arriving at Ringgold, Georgia September 11.
September 12.— Skirmished with the enemy near [Lee and] Gordon's Mills.
September 19-20.— Marched and countermarched until September 19. Were engaged in action September 19 and 20 at Chickamauga.
September 21.— Skirmished with the enemy near Rossville.
September 22.— Arrived at Chattanooga, Tennessee.

Stationed at Blain's Cross-Roads, November-December 1863.

Stationed at Cleveland, Ohio, January-February 1864.
January 1.— Seventeen men of the company reenlisted at Blain's Cross-Roads, Tennessee. They proceeded to Chattanooga via Knoxville, where they were mustered out and mustered in and paid to January 31.
January 26-February 1.— They left Chattanooga for Ohio, which state they entered February 1.
February 3.— They were furloughed for thirty days.

Stationed at McDonald's Station, Tennessee, March-April 1864.
[For record of events, see Company A.]

The total distance transported was 850 miles. The total distance marched is 183 miles.

Stationed at Marietta, Georgia, May-June 1864.
May 3.— The company belongs to the Second Brigade, Third Division, Fourth Army Corps, which took up its line of march from Cleveland, Tennessee and has been with [William Tecumseh] Sherman's advance on Atlanta, Georgia. The company was engaged at Buzzard Roost, Resaca, Adairsville, and Cassville, losing eight wounded.

Stationed at Battle Station, Georgia, July-August 1864.
July 1.— The company was in position in front of Marietta, Georgia.

July 3.— Marched towards Atlanta eight miles.
July 5.— Marched three miles to the front to the Chattahoochee River, where they had a sharp skirmish with the enemy.
July 10.— Moved to the left about six miles.
July 12.— Crossed the Chattahoochee River.
July 17.— Moved to the right with the Second Brigade, Third Division, Fourth Army Corps and drove the enemy from the river at [Pace's] Ferry and effected a crossing for the Fourteenth Army Corps.
July 19.— The company was engaged at Peach Tree Creek.
July 22-August 28.— Went into position in front of Atlanta, Georgia, where we remained until August 28. Was with the Third Division, Fourth Army Corps in the movements south of Atlanta. Lost one man killed and one wounded.

Stationed at Athens, Alabama, September-October 1864.

During the last two months the company has marched from Atlanta, Georgia to Gaylesville, Alabama and from thence to Chattanooga, Tennessee, where it took the cars and was transported to Athens, Alabama, where it arrived on October 31.

Stationed near Lexington, Alabama, November-December 1864.

November 23.— The company, with the regiment, left Pulaski, Tennessee and went with the Army on its retreat to Nashville, Tennessee.
December 15-16.— It was engaged in the battle near Nashville, which resulted in the defeat of Hood's Army. It joined in the pursuit of the enemy.
December 25-31.— Passed through Pulaski and then went to Lexington, Alabama, near which place it was on December 31.

Stationed near Huntsville, Alabama, January-February 1865.

January 5.— During the months of January and February the company, with the regiment, marched from Elk River near Athens, Alabama to Huntsville, Alabama, at which place it arrived January 5.
January 31-February 8.— Near this place it remained until January 31, when it left Huntsville and went as train guard with wagon train to within about twelve miles of Florence, Alabama. Both train and guard were then ordered back to Huntsville, where they arrived February 8, at which place it was on day of muster ——.

Stationed near Nashville, Tennessee, March-April 1865.
March 14.— The company, with the regiment, left Huntsville, Alabama for East Tennessee by railroad.
March 17-April 28.— Arrived at Strawberry Plains, East Tennessee in the morning. From there it marched to New Market; thence to Bull's Gap; thence to Greeneville; thence to Warm Springs, North Carolina; thence back to Greeneville, East Tennessee to Bull's Gap, where it took the cars for Nashville, Tennessee, where it arrived on the morning of April 28 and near which place it is now encamped.

Stationed at New Orleans, Louisiana, May-June 1865.
During the month of May the company, with the regiment, was encamped near Nashville, Tennessee.
June 17.— Remained there until June 17, when it took the cars for Johnsonville, Tennessee, where it took boats for New Orleans.
June 19.— When opposite Cairo, Illinois the transport *Echo No. 2*, on which it was embarked, collided with the Monitor *Oneida*, anchored in the river and sank in a few minutes, carrying down all company records and property.
June 24.— Arrived at New Orleans, near which place it is now encamped.

Company C

Stationed at Camp Wood, Ohio, September 19, 1861.
September 19.— Muster-in roll of Captain Aquila Wiley's Company, in the Forty-first Regiment of Ohio Volunteers, commanded by Colonel William B. Hazen, called into the service of the United States by the President from September 19, 1861 (date of this muster) for the term of three years, unless sooner discharged. The company was organized by Captain Aquila Wiley at Wooster, Ohio in the month of September and marched thence to Camp Wood, where it arrived September 19. . . .

JAMES P. W. NEILL,
First Lieutenant,
Eighteenth United States Infantry, Mustering Officer.

Stationed at Camp Wood, Ohio, September 19-October 31, 1861.

Stationed at Camp Wickliffe, Larue County, Kentucky, [November]-December 1861.
November 6-7.— The company left Camp Wood, Ohio. Proceeded by railroad to Camp Dennison, Ohio, where it arrived November 7.
November 15-16.— Left Camp Dennison. Proceeded by railroad to Cincinnati, Ohio; thence by steamboat to Gallipolis, Ohio, where it arrived November 16.
November 26-27.— Left Gallipolis. Proceeded by steamboat to Louisville, Kentucky, where it arrived November 27.
November 28.— Marched from Louisville to Camp Jenkins, Kentucky.
December 5.— Marched from Camp Jenkins to Camp Quigley, Kentucky, a distance of four miles.
December 10-16.— Marched from Camp Quigley to Camp Wickliffe, Larue County, Kentucky, a distance of sixty-six miles, where it arrived December 16.

Stationed at Camp Andrew Jackson, Tennessee, January-February 1862.
February 14-16.— The company left Camp Wickliffe, Kentucky and marched via Elizabethtown to West Point, Kentucky, a distance of forty miles, where it arrived February 16.
February 17-21.— Embarked on steamboat at West Point with nine regiments of General Wilson's Division and proceeded to Paducah, Kentucky, where it arrived February 21. Left Paducah February —— on board steamboat for Nashville, Tennessee.
February 25.— The fleet, consisting of ten steamboats, carrying parts of several brigades, the whole under command of General Nelson reached Nashville February 25. Found the fortifications on the Cumberland, six miles below Nashville, deserted by the Rebel troops, many of the field and siege guns still remaining in the works. Found Nashville had been evacuated by the Rebel troops. The division took possession of Nashville without resistance.

Stationed at the field of Shiloh, Pittsburg Landing, Tennessee, March-April 1862.

The company marched from Nashville, Tennessee to Pittsburg Landing via Columbia and Savannah.

April 6.— It reached Pittsburg Landing Sunday evening, April 6.

April 7.— Was engaged in the action, in which our second lieutenant and three men were killed and fifteen wounded, two of which mortally.

Stationed at camp near Athens, Alabama, May-June 1862.

May 2-30.— The company left the field of Shiloh and moved toward Corinth by regular advance until it was evacuated May 30, when the company marched into the enemy's deserted works.

The company marched about twenty-five miles in a southwesterly direction in pursuit of the retreating Rebels. It then marched eastward to its present camp near Athens, Alabama via Iuka, Tuscumbia and Florence.

Stationed at Murfreesborough, Tennessee, July-August 1862.

July 17-August 3.— The company left Athens, Alabama, where last mustered on July 17. Marched northward twenty-five miles to the tunnel on the Central Southern Railroad and for ten days assisted in repairing trestlework; thence marched to Reynolds' Station and was transported by railroad to Murfreesborough, Tennessee, where it arrived August 3.

August 18.— On the muster of August 18 sixteen were absent without authority as required by General Orders, War Department. Most of them are sick in the various hospitals in Ohio.

Stationed at Columbia, Tennessee, September-October 1862.

Stationed at the battlefield, Murfreesborough, Tennessee, November-December 1862.

The company marched from Columbia, Kentucky, where last mustered, to Nashville, Tennessee via Glasgow, Scottsville, Gallatin, and Silver Springs.

December 26.— It commenced march in the direction of Murfreesborough, Tennessee.

December 31.— It was engaged in the battle of Murfreesborough, in which engagement eleven were wounded, four severely and six slightly. The number taken into the engagement was one commissioned officer and thirty-nine enlisted men.

Stationed at camp at Readyville, Tennessee, January-February 1863.

On December 31, the day of last muster, the company was engaged in the battle of Stone's River. It remained on the field until after Murfreesborough was evacuated.

January 2.— It took part in the action on Friday evening, January 2, when the enemy attacked the left and were so terribly repulsed. One man was slightly wounded.

January 10.— The company remained in the vicinity of Murfreesborough until January 10, when it marched to its present station, Readyville, Tennessee, twelve miles southeast of Murfreesborough.

January 24.— The company was engaged in a skirmish at Woodbury, Tennessee, in which the enemy was routed with a loss of four left dead on the field.

Stationed at camp at Readyville, Tennessee, March-April 1863.

The company occupies the same camp that it did at last muster.

April 2.— It took part in a reconnaissance beyond Woodbury, Tennessee, which resulted in the rout of the enemy [and] the capture of some prisoners and property.

Stationed at Manchester, Tennessee, May-June 1863.
[For record of events, see Company A.]

Stationed at Poe's Tavern, Tennessee, July-August 1863.

Stationed at Chattanooga, Tennessee, September-October 1863.

Stationed at Blain's Cross-Roads, Tennessee, November-December 1863.

Stationed at Cleveland, Ohio, January-April 1864.

Stationed near Kenesaw Mountain, Georgia, May-June 1864.
May 3.— The company belongs to the Second Brigade, Third Division, Fourth Army Corps, which took up its line of march from Cleveland, Tennessee May 3 and has been with Sherman's advance on Atlanta, Georgia.

The company was engaged at Buzzard Roost, Resaca, Adairsville, Cassville, Pickett's Mills, and in front of Kenesaw Mountain, Georgia, losing four killed; four mortally, several severely and three slightly wounded; total fifteen.

Stationed near Battle Station, Georgia, July-August 1864.
The company has been in the trenches in front of Atlanta, Georgia most of the time, since last mustered, and was engaged in various demonstrations on the enemy's lines, losing two men wounded. It was with Sherman in his last grand flank movement, which resulted in the fall of Atlanta, Georgia.

Stationed at Athens, Alabama, September-October 1864.

Stationed at Lexington, Alabama, November-December 1864.
November 2.— Changed station from Athens, Alabama to Pulaski, Tennessee, arriving at the latter place November 2.
November 15-December 1.— Left Pulaski. Marched to Nashville, Tennessee. Arrived there December 1.
December 15-16.— Remained in camp until December 15, when it moved out and attacked the enemy, Hood's Army. Fought them December 15 and 16. Afterwards followed the retreating enemy to Lexington, Alabama, in all a distance of over 200 miles.

Stationed near Huntsville, Alabama, January-February 1865.
The company marched from Lexington, Alabama, where last mustered, to Huntsville, Alabama, a distance of over fifty miles.

Stationed near Nashville, Tennessee, March-April 1865.
March 15-April 4.— The company left Huntsville, Alabama and by railroad to Strawberry Plains, Tennessee and marched from thence to Greeneville, Tennessee, arriving April 4.

April 10-28.— Marched from Greeneville, Tennessee to Warm Springs, North Carolina and returned April 10. Marched from Greeneville, Tennessee to Bull's Gap, Tennessee and took cars for Nashville, Tennessee, arriving April 28.

Stationed at New Orleans, Louisiana, May-June 1865.
June 6.— The company broke camp near Nashville, Tennessee and proceeded by railroad to Johnsonville, Tennessee. There embarked on the steamer *Echo No. 2.*
June 19-24.— At Cairo, Illinois the morning of June 19 she collided with a monitor lying at anchor opposite the city and immediately sank. All the records, camp equipage and ordnance of the company were lost. The company then embarked on the steamer *Atlantic* and proceeded down the river to New Orleans, Louisiana, arriving there June 24. Went into camp near the Chalmette battleground.

Company D

Stationed at Camp Wood, Ohio, October 29, 1861.
October 29.— Muster-in roll of Captain James H. Cole's Company, in the Forty-first Regiment of Ohio Volunteers, commanded by Colonel William B. Hazen, called into service of the United States by the President under the Act of Congress approved September 22 1861 from October 29, 1861 (date of this muster) for the term of three years, unless sooner discharged. . . .

JAMES P. W. NEILL,
First Lieutenant,
Eighteenth United States Infantry, Mustering Officer.

Stationed at Camp Wood, Cuyahoga County, Ohio, enrollment to October 31, 1861.

Stationed at Camp Wickliffe, Larue County, Kentucky, November-December 1861.
November 6-7.— The company left Camp Wood, Ohio. Transported to Camp Dennison, Ohio, arriving there November 7.
November 15-16.— Left Camp Dennison; transported to Gallipolis, Ohio by rail to Cincinnati and boat to destination, arriving there November 16.

November 26-27.— Left Gallipolis, Ohio for Louisville, Kentucky via steamboat. Arrived there November 27. The company was then marched to Camp Jenkins near Louisville, Kentucky.
November 28.— Marched from Camp Jenkins to Camp Quigley, Kentucky, a distance of four miles.
December 10-16.— To camp Wickliffe, Larue County, Kentucky, a distance of sixty-six miles, where it arrived December 16.

Stationed at Camp Andrew Jackson, Tennessee, January-February 1862.
February 14-16.— The company was marched from Camp Wickliffe, Kentucky en route to West Point, Kentucky, where it arrived February 16. It was then embarked on board the steamer *Silver Moon* and was transported to Nashville, Tennessee without an incident of note.
February 25-26.— Was disembarked and marched to Camp Andrew Jackson near Nashville, Tennessee, where it arrived February 26. Distance unknown.

Stationed at the field of Shiloh, Tennessee, March-April 1862.
March 17-April 6.— The company was marched en route from Camp Andrew Jackson, Tennessee and proceeded to Savannah, Tennessee, where we arrived April 6. The company then proceeded on to Pittsburg Landing, Tennessee.
April 7.— Was engaged in the action in which nine of the company were wounded.

Stationed near Athens, Alabama, May-June 1862.
May 30.— The company marched into the evacuated city of Corinth.
June 4.— The regiment left Corinth and after marching about five days camped near Iuka, thirty miles from Corinth, where we remained ten days, then moved in an easterly direction, when we reached Athens, Alabama after marching eight days, [generally] averaging about thirteen miles a day.

Stationed at Murfreesborough, Tennessee, July-August 1862.

The company was marched from Athens, Alabama, where last mustered, to the tunnel on the Tennessee and Alabama Railroad and from thence to Pulaski and Reynolds' Station and from thence it was transported by rail to Murfreesborough, Tennessee, where it now is.

Stationed at Columbia, Kentucky, September-October 1862.

Since the last muster the company has been marched from Murfreesborough, Tennessee to Columbia, Kentucky via Louisville, Kentucky.

October 19.— Was engaged in a skirmish with the enemy. None hurt.

Station not stated, November-December 1862.

Station not stated, January-February 1863.

January 2.— It was engaged with the regiment in the fight at Stone's River. The casualties were one wounded, First Sergeant Floyd Fisher, in the foot, slightly.

January 24.— The company was engaged with a portion of [John Hunt] Morgan's (Rebel) Cavalry at Woodbury, Tennessee and had one man wounded (William Smilie) in the right hip. It is now encamped at Readyville, Tennessee with the regiment.

Stationed at Readyville, Tennessee, March-April 1863.

The company Roll of Honor selected, in accordance with General Orders No. 19, Headquarters, Department of the Cumberland, of February 14, 1863 is hereby announced as required by said order: Sergeant Elon G. Boughton, Private William Marshall, Private Albert Herriman, Private William H. Diesman, Private Spencer A. Sawyer, and Private [illegible] C. Fancher.

Stationed at Manchester, Tennessee, May-June 1863.

The company was marched from Readyville, Tennessee to Manchester, Tennessee, about thirty miles, where it arrived June 29.

Stationed at Poe's Tavern, Tennessee, July-August 1863.

June 20-July 1.— The company, with the regiment, at Manchester, Tennessee, from which place it moved in the direction of Tullahoma. That place being evacuated, it returned to Manchester. Arrived there July 1. Went into camp.

August 16-23.— Broke camp and marched to this place, crossing the Cumberland Mountain at Dunlap. Arrived here August 23, since which time it has been engaged in scouting and reconnoitering the Tennessee River. The company is on duty with the regiment.

Stationed at Chattanooga, Tennessee, September-October 1863.

Stationed at Blain's Cross-Roads, November-December 1863.

Stationed near Cleveland, Ohio, January-April 1863.

Stationed near Kenesaw Mountain, Georgia, May-June 1864.
[For record of events, see Company A.]

Stationed at Battle Station, Georgia, July-August 1864.
June 30-July 3.— The company was on duty with the regiment at Kenesaw Mountain, confronting the enemy, where it remained until July 3, when the enemy evacuated and it, in connection with the rest of the Army, followed him to the Chattahoochee, skirmishing most of the way.
July 10.— About July 10 it crossed the river five miles above Pace's Ferry and took a position on the other side.
July 18-August 26.— The rest of the Army being in position, we advanced on the enemy and found him strongly entrenched at Peach Tree Creek. He was compelled to leave the position and retreat to his works in front of Atlanta. We followed; fortified and remained until the night of August 26, when the whole Army was shoved to the south. On July 18 Second Lieutenant [George] C. Dodge was sent to the hospital and has since gone home on sick [leave].
August 29.— We tore up part of the Montgomery Railroad and are now confronting the enemy near Jonesborough.

Stationed at Athens, Alabama, September-October 1864.
September 1.— The company, with the regiment, was at Jonesborough, Georgia, from which place it marched to Lovejoy's [Station], distant eight miles, and took up a position in front of the enemy.
September 5-8.— At night we left for Atlanta, distant twenty-five miles. Arrived in Atlanta September 8.

October 3-21.— Started north, marching to Rome, Georgia; thence to Resaca and Summerville, Georgia and as far as Gaylesville, Alabama, which place it reached October 21. From Gaylesville it marched to Chattanooga, from Chattanooga it came to Athens, Alabama by rail. It marched from the latter place to Pulaski, Tennessee, where it is now on duty with the regiment. The whole distance marched by this company since August 31, about 300 miles.

Stationed at Lexington, Alabama, November-December 1864.

Stationed at Huntsville, Alabama, January-February 1865.
The company has been on detached duty as provost guards at Headquarters, Third Division, Fourth Army Corps since last muster.

Stationed near Nashville, Tennessee, March-April 1865.
The company has been on detached duty as provost guards at Headquarters, Third Division, Fourth Army Corps since last muster.

Stationed at camp, Chalmette, Louisiana, May-June 1865.
The company has been on detached service as provost guard, Headquarters, Third Division, Fourth Army Corps, per Special Orders No. 32, Headquarters, Third Division, Fourth Army Corps, March 1, 1865 since last muster.

Company E

Stationed at Camp Wood, Ohio, October 29, 1861.
October 29.— Muster-in roll of Captain [Frank] D. Stone's Company, in the Forty-first Regiment of Ohio Volunteers, commanded by Colonel William B. Hazen, called into service of the United States by the President approved by Act of Congress July 22, 1861 from October 29, 1861 (date of this muster) for the term of three years, unless sooner discharged. . . .

JAMES P. W. NEILL,
First Lieutenant,
Eighteenth United States Infantry, Mustering Officer.

Stationed at Camp Wood, Cuyahoga County, Ohio, enrollment to October 31, 1861.

Stationed at Camp Wickliffe, Larue County, Kentucky, November-December 1861.
November 1-6.— From November 1 to 6 the company was at Camp Wood, Cleveland, Ohio. On November 6 it started for Camp Dennison.
November 14-16.— Left Camp Dennison for Gallipolis via Cincinnati on board steamer *Telegraph No. 3*. Arrived at destination November 16.
November 27-28.— Left for Kentucky. Arrived at Louisville November 28. Pitched tents at Camp Jenkins same day.
December 6.— Struck tents and pitched at Camp Quigley near Louisville.
December 10-16.— Again struck tents and took up march for Camp Wickliffe, where we arrived December 16, after five days' march.
December 22.— The company was out on picket duty, two miles from camp.

Station not stated, January-February 1862.

Stationed at Shiloh, Tennessee, March-April 1862.
March 18-April 6.— The company left Camp Andrew Jackson near Nashville and proceeded by way of Columbia to Savannah, Tennessee, where it arrived April 6.
April 7.— Was engaged in the battle of Shiloh. Fifty-four members of the company entered the fight. Of these, three were killed and thirteen wounded. The men behaved with great gallantry and did themselves much honor. Health of the company, which was injured by the exposure of the time and after the battle, is improving.

Stationed at camp near Athens, Alabama, May-June 1862.
May 8.— The company left the vicinity of the field of Shiloh and during the month approached Corinth with the Army. Before Corinth were engaged with the enemy in several skirmishes while picketing.

June 4.— Left Corinth with Nelson's Division to go [to] the support of General [John] Pope.
June 12.— Reached Iuka, Mississippi.
June 23-30.— Left Iuka. Passing through Tuscumbia, crossed the Tennessee River at Florence and arrived at Athens June 30.

Stationed at camp near Murfreesborough, Tennessee, July-August 1862.
July 15.— Left Athens, Alabama about July 15 and marched to Richland Creek, a distance of thirty miles. Repaired the Nashville and Decatur Railroad at this point and built a stockade.
July 31.— Left Richland Creek. Marched to Reynolds' Station and from thence by railroad to Murfreesborough, Tennessee.

Stationed at Columbia, Kentucky, September-October 1862.

Stationed at camp near Murfreesborough, Tennessee, November-December 1862.

Stationed at Readyville, Tennessee, January-February 1863.
January 1.— Company E in the battle of Stone's River, Tennessee. The company was in the engagement from December 31, 1862 until the Confederate Army evacuated Murfreesborough.
January 6.— Moved with the regiment one mile east from Murfreesborough.

The company behaved with gallantry during the battle, under command of First Sergeant Frederick A. McKay.
January 10.— Moved to Readyville, Tennessee.
January 24.— Were engaged in a skirmish at Woodbury, Tennessee. Since that time the company has been in camp at Readyville, Tennessee. The health of the company is good, discipline fair, arms poor, accoutrements good.

Stationed at Readyville, Tennessee, March-April 1863.
April 1.— The company marched with the regiment to the rear of Woodbury. Engaged in a skirmish at that place. One man, Kane, fell behind and was probably captured, as he is still missing. Health of the company has been good.

JOHN W. STEELE,
Captain,
Forty-first Ohio Volunteer Infantry, Commanding Company.

Stationed at Manchester, May-June 1863.
June 24.— Left camp at Readyville. Marched for Elk River, from there to Manchester.

Stationed at Poe's Tavern, Tennessee, July-August 1863.

Station not stated, September-October 1863.
August 16-20.— Marched from Manchester, Tennessee, where the regiment had been in camp since July 8. Arrived at Dunlap, Tennessee August 20.
August 24.— Marched from Dunlap and arrived at Poe's Tavern, Tennessee same day.
September 4-10.— Marched from Poe's Tavern September 4 and crossed the Tennessee River September 10.
September 11-12.— Marched, passing through Ringgold, Tennessee and arriving at [Lee and] Gordon's Mills September 12.
September 14-15.— Moved from thence to Chattanooga Valley and back to Chickamauga Creek September 15.
September 17-20.— We were moved back to [Lee and] Gordon's Mills and on September 19 and 20 were engaged with the enemy, losing two wounded and four taken prisoner.

Stationed at Blain's Cross-Roads, Tennessee, November-December 1863.
November 23-25.— Engaged with the enemy, losing one killed and eight wounded.
November 28-December 8.— Started on the march to Knoxville, Tennessee. Arrived at Knoxville December 8 and encamped two miles south of Knoxville.
December 15.— Broke up camp and marched twenty miles north of Knoxville and went into camp.

Stationed at Cleveland, Ohio, February 29, 1864.

Stationed at McDonald's [Station], March-April 1864.

Stationed near Marietta, Georgia, May-June 1864.
May 3.— Left Cleveland, Tennessee. Was engaged in skirmishing all the way to Resaca, where a general engagement took place, in which one man was mortally wounded, since died.

May 27.— Had another battle at Pickett's Mills near Dallas, Georgia. Lost one man killed and two wounded.

Stationed at Battle Station, Georgia, July-August 1864.
July 5.— Skirmished with the enemy near Chattahoochee River. Lost one man killed. Encamped on the riverbank.
July 15.— Crossed the river. Met the enemy at Peach Tree Creek, where a skirmish took place. Drove the enemy.
July 19.— Crossed the creek. Took up position in front of Atlanta.
July 20.— Broke camp and moved to the right, in connection with the balance of the Army.

Stationed at Athens, Alabama, September-October 1864.

Stationed at Lexington, Alabama, November-December 1864.
Was in the retreat from Pulaski, Tennessee to Nashville.
December 15-16.— Also took an active part in the battles in front of Nashville, the company losing one commissioned officer.

Stationed at Huntsville, Alabama, January-February 1865.
January 31-February 8.— The regiment was detailed to go as train guard to Eastport, Mississippi. Went as far as Elk River and got orders to return to Huntsville, Alabama, at which place it arrived on February 8 and remained since.

Stationed at Nashville, Tennessee, March-April 1865.
March 15-17.— The company, with the regiment, left Huntsville for East Tennessee, where it arrived on March 17, having been transported by railroad to Strawberry Plains.
March 18-April 4.— Marched from the Plains to New Market, at which place it remained until March 29, when it left for Bull's Gap, where it arrived April 1 and left April 4 for Greeneville, Tennessee.
April 22-29.— It left Greeneville for Nashville and arrived there on April 29.

Stationed at New Orleans, June 30, 1865.
June 17.— The company, with the regiment and division to which it belongs, left Nashville, Tennessee and were transported

by railroad to Johnsonville, Tennessee, where it, with the regiment, embarked on board the steamer *Echo No. 2* and with the fleet started for New Orleans.
June 19-24.— When near Cairo, Illinois at 2 a.m. the *Echo* collided with the Monitor *Oneida* and sank in a few minutes. The men escaped but the papers and government property pertaining to Company E were lost. The company and regiment reshipped at Cairo and arrived at New Orleans on June 24, where it yet remains.

Company F

Stationed at Camp Wood, Ohio, October 29, 1861.
October 29.— Muster-in roll of Captain Daniel S. Leslie's Company, in the Forty-first Regiment of Ohio Volunteers, commanded by Colonel William B. Hazen, called into service of the United States by the President approved by act of Congress approved July 22, 1861 from October 29, 1861 (date of this muster) for the term of three years, unless sooner discharged. . . .

JAMES P. W. NEILL,
First Lieutenant,
Eighteenth United States Infantry, Mustering Officer.

Stationed at Camp Wood, Cleveland, Ohio, enrollment to October 31, 1861.

Station not stated, November-December 1861.
Since the last muster this company had made the following changes of station, *viz.*:
November 6-9.— Left Camp Wood, Ohio and went by railroad to Camp Dennison, where it arrived November 9.
November 14-16.— Left the last-named camp. Went by railroad to Cincinnati and up the Ohio River on the steamer *Telegraph No. 3* to Gallipolis, Ohio, where we arrived November 16.
November 20.— A part of the company was sent with parts of Companies C and I into Western Virginia, under command of Captains Wiley and Leslie, on a scouting expedition. We marched until near night and encamped until 9 o'clock p.m.,

when we received orders to return and marched back to the landing. After waiting several hours we went up the river to Gallipolis on a little steamer, *Castle Garden*.
November 26-28.— We embarked on the *Telegraph No. 3* for Louisville, Kentucky, where we arrived November 28 and marched out about six miles and encamped at Camp Jenkins.
December 5.— Left Camp Jenkins and marched back towards the city of Louisville and encamped at Camp Quigley.
December 10-14.— We commenced our march southward and arrived here (Camp Wickliffe) December 14.

Stationed at camp near Nashville, Tennessee, January-February 1862.
February 14-17.— Left Camp Wickliffe. Arrived at West Point February 17. Embarked on the steamboat *Silver Moon*.
February 21.— Arrived at Paducah.
February 23-25.— Left and arrived at Nashville February 25, where we immediately went into camp.

Stationed at the field of Shiloh, March-April 1862.

Stationed in camp near Athens, Alabama, May-June 1862.

Stationed at Murfreesborough, Tennessee, July-August 1862.
No change of station since last muster.
July 17-20.— Left Athens, Alabama for the tunnel on Nashville and Decatur Railroad. Arrived at the tunnel July 20.
July 30-August 2.— Left the tunnel; arrived at Murfreesborough August 2.

Stationed at Columbia, Kentucky, September-October 1862.
The condition of the company is good.

Stationed at the battlefield of Stone's River, November-December 1862.
November 2-3.— Marched from Columbia, Kentucky to Glasgow, thirty-six miles.
November 12-13.— Marched from Glasgow, Kentucky to Silver Springs, Tennessee, seventy-two miles.

November 19.— Marched to Stone's River, ten miles.
November 26.— Moved camp to Murfreesborough Pike, eight miles.
December 26-29.— Marched to the battlefield of Stone's River, twenty-eight miles.
December 31.— Engaged in action.

Stationed at Readyville, Tennessee, January-February 1863.
January 2.— Engaged in action in the battle of Stone's River.
January 10.— Marched twelve miles and encamped near Readyville, Tennessee.
January 24.— Made a reconnaissance; had a sharp skirmish with the enemy near Woodbury, Tennessee.

Stationed at Readyville, Tennessee, March-April 1863.

The regiment has been encamped near Readyville since last muster. No change of station has been made.

Stationed at Manchester, Tennessee, May-June 1863.
[For record of events, see Company A.]

Stationed at Poe's Tavern, Tennessee, July-August 1863.

Stationed at Brown's Ferry, Tennessee, September-October 1863.

Stationed at Blain's Cross-Roads, Tennessee, November-December 1863.

Stationed at Cleveland, Ohio, January-February 1864.
January 1.— The regiment reenlisted at Blain's Cross-Roads, Tennessee.
January 5-8.— Left Blain's Cross-Roads. Arrived at Chattanooga January 8.
January 26-February 1.— Left Chattanooga, Tennessee and arrived at Cleveland, Ohio February 1.
February 3.— Was furloughed at Cleveland, Ohio for a period of thirty days.

Stationed at McDonald's Station, Tennessee, March-April 1864.

Stationed near Marietta, Georgia, May-June 1864.
May 3.— The company left McDonald's Station, Tennessee with the Forty-first Regiment, Ohio Volunteer Infantry en route for Tunnel Hill, Georgia. Were engaged in the skirmishes near Tunnel Hill.
May 13.— Left Tunnel Hill.
May 14-15.— Arrived at Resaca on May 14. Was engaged there on May 14 and 15.
May 16.— Left Resaca.
May 17.— Arrived near Adairsville. Were engaged in a sharp skirmish.
May 18-19.— Left Adairsville. Arrived at Cassville, Georgia on the evening of May 19. Were again engaged with the enemy.
May 22-25.— Left Cassville. Arrived on the battlefield of Pickett's Mills near Dallas, Georgia May 25.
May 27.— Had a severe engagement in which the company lost four men killed and seven wounded. The company participated in every engagement in which the regiment was engaged during the month of June and was with the advance of the Army in Sherman's campaign in Georgia during the months of May and June.

Stationed near Jonesborough, Georgia, July-August 1864.
July 1.— The company was in position in front of Marietta, Georgia.
July 3.— Moved towards Atlanta, distance eight miles.
July 5.— Advanced five miles to the front to the Chattahoochee River, where we had a sharp skirmish with the enemy.
July 10-12.— Moved six miles to the left and crossed the Chattahoochee River on July 12.
July 17.— We moved to the right with the Second Brigade, Third Division, Fourth Army Corps and drove the enemy from the river at Pace's Ferry and effected a crossing for the Fourteenth Army Corps. Had a skirmish with the enemy and returned to camp at 5 o'clock p.m.
July 19.— The company was engaged at Peach Tree Creek.
July 22-August 31.— We took our position in front of Atlanta, where we remained until August 25, with the Third Division, Fourth Army Corps in the movements south of Atlanta and were near Jonesborough, Georgia on August 31.

Stationed at Athens, Alabama, September-October 1864.
September 1.— We left Jonesborough, Georgia and marched south to Lovejoy's Station.
September 5-8.— We commenced the march northward to Atlanta. Arrived there on September 8 and went into camp.
October 3-31.— Left Atlanta. Marched to Pine Mountain and from there to Big Shanty, then to Acworth, Allatoona, Cartersville, Kingston, Rome, Calhoun, and Resaca. From there crossed Horn Mountain through Snake Creek Gap to Summerville and Gaylesville, Alabama, from thence to Alpine, Alabama; La Fayette, Georgia; Gordon's Mills, and Chattanooga and from thence went by railroad to Athens, Alabama, arriving October 31.

Stationed at Lexington, Alabama, November-December 1864.
November 23.— The company, with the regiment and Army, retreated from Pulaski, Tennessee towards Nashville and was engaged in several skirmishes while on the march.
December 15-31.— It was engaged in the battles near Nashville December 15 and 16, in which eight men were wounded. After Hood's defeat it took a part in the pursuit, following him to Pulaski and thence to Lexington, Alabama, where it was on December 31.

Stationed at Huntsville, Alabama, January-February 1865.
December 31, 1864-January 5, 1865.— The company, with the regiment, left Lexington, Alabama for Huntsville, Alabama, where it arrived on January 5 and built winter quarters.
January 31-February 8.— It, with the regiment, went as train guard for the Third Division train, which started for Eastport, Mississippi. After marching four days orders came for the command to return which it did, arriving at Huntsville on February 8, where it has since remained.

Stationed at Nashville, Tennessee, March-April 1865.
March 15-17.— The company left Huntsville, Alabama for Knoxville, Tennessee, where it arrived on March 17. From there we went to New Market, Tennessee and from there to Greeneville, Tennessee, where we remained for some time after the surrender of Lee.

April 22-28.— We were then ordered back and arrived at Bull's Gap. At this point we took the cars for this place, where we arrived on April 28.

Stationed at New Orleans, Louisiana, May-June 1865.

Company G

Stationed at Camp Wood, Ohio, October 29, 1861.
October 29.— Muster-in roll of Captain Martin H. Hamblin's Company, in the Forty-first Regiment of Ohio Volunteers, commanded by Colonel William B. Hazen, called into service of the United States by the President from October 29, 1861 (date of this muster) for the term of three years, unless sooner discharged. The company was organized by Captain Martin H. Hamblin at Chardon in the month of September and marched thence to Camp Wood, Cleveland, Ohio, where it arrived September 12, a distance of thirty miles. . . .

JAMES P. W. NEILL,
First Lieutenant,
Eighteenth United States Infantry, Mustering Officer.

Stationed at Camp Wood, Ohio, October 29-31, 1861.

Stationed at Camp Wickliffe, Kentucky, November-December 1861.
November 1.— The company at Camp Wood, Cleveland, Ohio.
November 6-14.— Started for Camp Dennison. Arrived at Camp Dennison November 7. Remained there until November 14.
November 15-16.— Left Camp Dennison for Gallipolis by way of Cincinnati November 15 on board steamer *Telegraph No. 3.* Arrived at destination November 16.
November 26-27.— Left for Kentucky. Arrived at Louisville November 27.
November 28.— Pitched tents at Camp Jenkins.
December 6.— Struck tents and pitched at Camp Quigley near Louisville.
December 10-15.— Again struck tents and took up march for Camp Wickliffe, where we arrived December 15 after five days' march.

Stationed at Camp Andrew Jackson, January-February 1862.
February 14.— Commenced march from Camp Wickliffe, Kentucky. Marched fourteen or fifteen miles.
February 15.— Marched near seven miles.
February 16-17.— Marched twenty miles, arriving at West Point, Kentucky February 17. Embarked aboard transports and started down the Ohio.
February 25.— Arrived at Nashville, Tennessee. Selected our camping ground, termed Camp Andrew Jackson, where we still remain.

Stationed at the field of Shiloh, Tennessee, March-April 1862.
March 17-April 14.— The company left Nashville, Tennessee. Arrived at Savannah, Tennessee April 6, having stopped in camp nine days during the time. Was detained as train guard at Savannah, Tennessee from April 6 until April 14.
April 15.— Rejoined the regiment on the field of Shiloh, Tennessee.

Station not stated, May-June 1862.

Stationed at camp at Murfreesborough, July-August 1862.
July 17-30.— Marched from Athens, Alabama. Arrived at the tunnel south of Pulaski, Tennessee on the Nashville and Decatur Railroad July 20. From this date until July 30 were employed repairing the tunnel and trestlework. Marched from the tunnel July 30.
August 2.— Arrived at Murfreesborough, Tennessee.

Stationed at Columbia, September-October 1862.

Stationed at Murfreesborough, Tennessee, November-December 1862.

Stationed at Readyville, Tennessee, January-February 1863.
January 2.— The company was engaged at the battle of Stone's River.
January 10.— Marched from Murfreesborough, Tennessee to Readyville, a distance of twelve miles, at which place the company is now encamped.

January 24.— Engaged in a brisk skirmish at Woodbury, while making a reconnaissance to said place.

Stationed at Readyville, Tennessee, March-April 1863.

Stationed at Manchester, Tennessee, May-June 1863.

Stationed at Poe's Tavern, Tennessee, July-August 1863.

During the month of August the company, with the regiment, marched from Manchester, Tennessee to Poe's Tavern, Tennessee near the Tennessee River, at which place it was on August 31.

Stationed at Chattanooga, Tennessee, September-October 1863.

Stationed at Blain's Cross-Roads, November-December 1863.

Stationed at Cleveland, Ohio, January-February 1864.
January 1.— Eighteen members of the company reenlisted as veterans while in camp at Blain's Cross-Roads, Tennessee.
January 5.— The regiment started for home on furlough of thirty days after being mustered, paid, etc.
February 1.— They arrived at Cleveland, Ohio, their place of rendezvous, where organized.
February 3.— They were furloughed.

Stationed at camp near Cleveland, Tennessee, March-April 1864.

Stationed near Marietta, Georgia, May-June 1864.
May 3.— Marched from Cleveland, Tennessee to Ringgold, Georgia.
May 7.— Marched from Ringgold, Georgia.
May 14-15.— Was engaged in battle of Resaca. Two men were wounded.
May 27.— Also [engaged in] the battle of Pickett's Mills near Dallas, Georgia. Three were killed, five wounded and one missing.

Stationed at Battle Station, Georgia, July-August 1864.

The company, since last muster, has marched from Kenesaw Mountain to and around Atlanta.

Stationed at Athens, Alabama, September-October 1864.

During the last two months the company has marched from Atlanta, Georgia to Gaylesville, Alabama and from there to Chattanooga, Tennessee, where it took the cars and was transported to Athens, Alabama, where it arrived on October 31.

Stationed near Lexington, Alabama, November-December 1864.

November 25.— The company, with the regiment, left Pulaski, Tennessee and marched with the Army on its retreat to Nashville, during which it was engaged in several skirmishes.

December 15-31.— It was engaged in the battle near Nashville December 15 and 16, in which it had two men wounded. After the defeat of Hood's Army the company, with the remainder of the Army, marched to Pulaski, Tennessee; thence to Lexington, Alabama, near which place it was on December 31.

Stationed near Huntsville, Alabama, January-February 1865.

January 5.— During the months of January and February the company, with the regiment, marched from Elk River near Athens, Alabama to Huntsville, Alabama, at which place it arrived January 5.

January 31.— It left Huntsville and went as train guard to within about twelve miles of Florence, Alabama, then the train guards were ordered back to Huntsville.

February 8-28.— It arrived at Huntsville, at which place it was on day of muster, February 28.

Stationed near Nashville, Tennessee, March-April 1865.

March 15-April 10.— The company, with the regiment, left Huntsville, Alabama, where it was on March 1 and was transported on cars to Strawberry Plains, Tennessee. It marched thence to Greeneville, East Tennessee; thence to Warm Springs, North Carolina and back to Greeneville, Tennessee, where it arrived April 10.

April 22-30.— It left Greeneville and marched to Bull's Gap, Tennessee and was thence transported on cars to Nashville, Tennessee, near which place it was on the day of muster, April 30.

Stationed near New Orleans, Louisiana, May-June 1865.
June 16-30.— The company, with the regiment, broke up camp near Nashville, Tennessee, at which place it had been encamped since April 28, and started with the Corps en route for New Orleans, Louisiana, at which place it arrived on June 24. It remained there until after the muster of June 30.

Company H

Stationed at Camp Wood, October 29, 1861.
October 29.— Muster-in roll of Captain H. Alonzo Pease's Company, in the Forty-first Regiment of Ohio Volunteers, commanded by Colonel William B. Hazen, called into service of the United States by the President from October 29, 1861 (date of this muster) for the term of three years, unless sooner discharged. The company was organized by Captain H. Alonzo Pease at Oberlin in the month of September and marched thence to Camp Wood, where it arrived September 16. . . .

JAMES P. W. NEILL,
First Lieutenant,
Eighteenth United States Infantry, Mustering Officer.

Stationed at Camp Wood, enrollment to October 31, 1861.

Stationed at Camp Wickliffe, Kentucky, November-December 1861.
[For record of events, see Company E.]

Stationed at Camp Andrew Jackson, Tennessee, January-February 1862.

Stationed at the field of Shiloh, Tennessee, March-April 1862.
Since last muster the company has marched from Nashville (125 miles) and was engaged in the battle here April 7.

Stationed at camp near Athens, Alabama, May-June 1862.

Stationed at Murfreesborough, Tennessee, July-August 1862.
July 17-August 3.— The company left Athens, Alabama, where last mustered. Marched north twenty-five miles to the tunnel on

the Tennessee and Central Alabama Railroad, where for ten days it assisted in repairing trestlework; thence to Reynolds' Station and was transported by railroad to Murfreesborough via Nashville, Tennessee, where it arrived August 3.

Stationed at camp at Columbia, Kentucky, September-October 1862.

Stationed at camp near Murfreesborough, Tennessee, November-December 1862.

Stationed at Readyville, January-February 1863.
January 10.— Marched to Readyville, Tennessee.
January 24.— Marched to Woodbury, Tennessee. Engaged the enemy and routed him. Returned to Readyville the same day, where we still remain. Sustained no loss at Woodbury.

Stationed at camp at Readyville, April 10, 1863.

Station not stated, March-April 1863.

The company, with the remainder of the regiment, is attached to the Second Brigade, Second Division, Twenty-first Army Corps, Department of the Cumberland. It is stationed at Readyville, Tennessee, twelve miles east from Murfreesborough doing post duty.
April 2.— Nothing of importance has transpired with the last two months, with the exception of a reconnaissance on April 2 to Woodbury, distance seven miles, and return.

Stationed at Manchester, Tennessee, May-June 1863.
June 24-29.— The company occupied the same camp that it did last muster until June 24, at which time it commenced movements southward, arriving at Manchester, Tennessee June 29.

Stationed at Poe's Tavern, Tennessee, July-August 1863.

Stationed at Brown's Ferry, September-October 1863.
July 1-3.— Commenced march from Manchester, Tennessee, arriving at Duck River on July 3.
July 6.— Marched back to Manchester.

August 16.— We again commenced march.
August 22.— Arrived at Dunlap, Sequatchie Valley.
August 24.— Marched from Dunlap and arrived at Poe's Tavern, Tennessee Valley, the same day.
September 7.— Again commenced march. Passed through the towns of Graysville and Ringgold, Georgia.
September 12.— Arrived at [Lee and] Gordon's Mills on the Chickamauga. Engaged in the battle on the Chickamauga.
September 22.— Fell back to Chattanooga.
October 26.— At night we paddled pontoons down the Tennessee [River], passing under the batteries on the above lookout. Effected a landing at Brown's Ferry. Had sharp skirmishing. The discipline of the company is good.

Stationed at Blain's Cross-Roads, Tennessee, November-December 1863.

Stationed at Cleveland, Ohio, January-February 1864.

Stationed near McDonald's Station, Tennessee, March-April 1864.

Stationed near Marietta, Georgia, May-June 1864.
May 3.— The company marched from McDonald's Station.
May 14-15.— Was in the engagement at Resaca, Georgia and later at Pickett's Mills. At the latter place out of fourteen men engaged, four were killed and seven wounded. Besides these the company has been engaged in numerous skirmishes.
June 20.— Arrived at Kenesaw Mountain near Marietta, Georgia, where we still remain.

Stationed near Battle Station, Georgia, July-August 1864.
The company has marched from near Marietta, Georgia to and around Atlanta.

Stationed at Athens, Alabama, September-October 1864.

Stationed at Lexington, Alabama, November-December 1864.
The company marched from Athens, Alabama, where last mustered, to Nashville, Tennessee, a distance of over 100 miles.

December 15-16.— Was engaged in the battles in front of Nashville, Tennessee and in the pursuit of Hood's Army, a distance of over 100 miles, having one man slightly wounded.

Stationed near Huntsville, Alabama, January-February 1865.
The company marched from Lexington, Alabama, where last mustered, to Huntsville, Alabama, a distance of over fifty miles.

Stationed at Nashville, Tennessee, March-April 1865.

Stationed at New Orleans, Louisiana, May-June 1865.
June 16.— The company broke camp near Nashville, Tennessee and went on rail to Johnsonville, Tennessee. There it embarked on the steamer *Echo No. 2*.
June 19-24.— At Cairo, Illinois on the morning of June 19 the steamer *Echo No. 2* collided with a monitor lying at anchor opposite that place and immediately sank. All of the company records, camp equipage and ordnance of the company were lost. At Cairo, Illinois the company embarked on the steamer *Atlantic* and arrived at New Orleans, Louisiana June 24 and went into camp south of the city.

Company I

Stationed at Camp Wood, Ohio, October 29, 1861.
October 29.— Muster-in roll of Captain J. H. Williston's Company, in the Forty-first Regiment of Ohio Volunteers, commanded by Colonel William B. Hazen, called into service of the United States by the President from October 29, 1861 (date of this muster) for the term of three years, unless sooner discharged. The company was organized by Captain J. H. Williston at Port Clinton in the month of September and marched thence to Camp Wood, where it arrived September 18, a distance of seventy-five miles. . . .

JAMES P. W. NEILL,
First Lieutenant,
Eighteenth United States Infantry, Mustering Officer.

Stationed at Camp Wood, Ohio, enrollment to October 31, 1861.

Stationed at Camp Wickliffe near New Haven, Kentucky, November-December 1861.
November 6-7.— Left Camp Wood, Cleveland, Ohio. Arrived at Camp Dennison November 7.
November 14-16.— Left Camp Dennison. Arrived at Cincinnati November 15. Left for Gallipolis, Ohio same day, arriving there November 16.
November 27-28.— Left Gallipolis and arrived at Camp Jenkins near Louisville, Kentucky November 28.
December 5.— Left Camp Jenkins and marched to Camp Quigley, within one mile of Louisville.
December 10-15.— Left Camp Quigley and marched thence to Camp Wickliffe near New Haven, Kentucky, occupying five days in the march, arriving December 15.

Stationed at Camp Andrew Jackson near Nashville, Tennessee, February 28, 1862.
February 14-21.— Left Camp Wickliffe and marched thence to West Point on the Ohio River, arriving there Monday at noon, February 17, where we embarked on board steamer *Silver Moon*. Sailed up and down the river until Friday night, February 21, when we arrived at Paducah, Kentucky.
February 23-25.— Left Paducah Sunday morning, February 23, and sailed thence up the Cumberland River, arriving at Nashville, Tennessee Tuesday morning, February 25, near where we are now encamped.

Stationed at the field of Shiloh, Tennessee, March-April 1862.
March 17-April 6.— Since last muster marched from Camp Andrew Jackson near Nashville, Tennessee, leaving there March 17 and arriving at Pittsburg Landing April 6.
April 7.— Took part in the battle of Shiloh, losing four men killed, ten wounded and one missing.

Stationed at camp near Athens, Alabama, May-June 1862.
May 2-June 30.— Marched from the field of Shiloh to camp near Athens, Alabama, at which place the company arrived June 30.

Stationed at camp at Murfreesborough, Tennessee, July-August 1862.
July 19-August 3.— The company left Athens, Alabama, where last mustered on July 19. Marched northward twenty-five miles to the tunnel on the Central Southern Railroad and for ten days assisted in repairing trestlework; thence marched to Reynolds' Station and was transferred by railroad to Murfreesborough, Tennessee, where it arrived August 3. At the muster of August 1862 eighteen were absent without authority, as required by General Orders, War Department. Most of them are sick in the various hospitals in Ohio.

Stationed at camp at Columbia, Kentucky, September-October 1862.

Stationed at Murfreesborough, Tennessee, November-December 1862.
Marched from Columbia, Kentucky, where last mustered, to Murfreesborough, Tennessee.
December 31.— Were engaged in the battle before [Murfreesborough]. Lost enlisted men, one killed and two wounded; also first lieutenant wounded.

Stationed at Readyville, Tennessee, January-February 1863.
January 2.— The company was engaged in the battle of Stone's River on Friday, January 2 but sustained no loss. Marched from battlefield to Readyville, Tennessee, where it is now encamped.
January 26.— Advanced to Woodbury, Tennessee and was there engaged in a skirmish with the enemy. Returned to Readyville same day. The company sustained no loss.

Stationed at Readyville, Tennessee, March-April 1863.
April 2.— The company took part in a reconnaissance to Woodbury April 2, which resulted in the routing of the enemy and the capture of a few of the enemy and a part of its train and returned to camp on the same day.

Stationed at camp near Manchester, Tennessee, May-June 1863.
[For record of events, see Company A.]

Stationed at Poe's Tavern, Tennessee, July-August 1863.

The company marched from camp near Manchester, Tennessee to Poe's Tavern in the Tennessee Valley.

Stationed at Brown's Ferry, September-October 1863.
[For record of events, see Company E.]
September 19-20.— Were engaged with the enemy, having four men wounded and one missing.
September 22.— Arrived at Chattanooga, Tennessee.
October 27.— On expedition with the brigade under the command of General [William Farrar] Smith. Effected a landing at Brown's Ferry and went into camp.

Stationed at camp near Strawberry Plains, November-December 1863.
November 6.— Marched from Brown's Ferry, Tennessee to Chattanooga, Tennessee and went into camp.
November 23, 25.— Was engaged in the battle of Chattanooga, Tennessee, having three men killed and three wounded.
November 28-December 7.— Left Chattanooga, Tennessee and arrived at Knoxville, Tennessee December 7 and went into camp.
December 15-16.— Marched from Knoxville, Tennessee and arrived at camp near Strawberry Plains December 16 and went into camp.

Stationed at Cleveland, Ohio, January-February 1864.
January 1.— Twenty-eight of the company reenlisted as veterans at Blain's Cross-Roads, Tennessee.
January 5.— Marched to Knoxville, Tennessee.
January 6-8.— From thence by rail to Loudon, Tennessee. Took steamer for Chattanooga, Tennessee. Arrived January 8 and went into camp.
January 16.— The company was mustered into the veteran service.
January 26-February 1.— Started for Cleveland, Ohio, at which place it arrived February 1.
February 3.— Were furloughed for thirty days, in accordance with Special Orders No. 28, Headquarters, Ohio Volunteer Recruiting Service.

Stationed at McDonald's Station, Tennessee, March-April 1864.
March 5.— The company reported at Camp Cleveland, Ohio, having been home on furlough as veterans in accordance with Special Orders No. 28, Headquarters, Ohio Volunteer Recruiting Service.
March 8-17.— Started for the front, arriving at Loudon, Tennessee by rail March 17.
March 19-20.— Marched from Loudon, arriving at Knoxville, Tennessee March 20.
March 25.— Joined the brigade at Powder Springs Gap.
April 5-17.— Marched from Powder Springs Gap, arriving at Cleveland, Tennessee April 17 and went into camp.

Stationed near Marietta, Georgia, May-June 1864.
May 3.— The company and regiment left camp at Cleveland, Tennessee.
May 14-15.— Took part in the battles of Resaca, Georgia.
May 27.— [Engaged at] Pickett's Mills, Georgia.

Are now in front of Kenesaw Mountain near Marietta, Georgia. Total loss during the campaign was three killed and nineteen wounded.

Stationed near Atlanta, Georgia, July-August 1864.
July 3-6.— Marched from camp in front of Kenesaw Mountain, Georgia. Pursued the enemy to the Chattahoochee River and went into camp July 6.
July 10-24.— Crossed the Chattahoochee River and pursued the enemy to Atlanta, Georgia, where we went into camp July 24. The company was engaged in several skirmishes without loss.
August 24.— Marched, passing to the right of Atlanta, Georgia and are now on the march.

Stationed at Athens, Alabama, September-October 1864.

The company marched from Jonesborough, Georgia to Lovejoy's Station, Georgia.
September 8.— From thence withdrew to Atlanta, Georgia, where it arrived September 8.
October 3-31.— Left Atlanta and marched to Chattanooga, Tennessee by way of Marietta, Georgia; Resaca, Georgia and Gaylesville, Alabama. Went from Chattanooga by rail to Athens, Alabama, where it arrived the morning of October 31.

Stationed at Lexington, Alabama, November-December 1864.
December 1.— The company marched from near Athens, Alabama to Pulaski, Tennessee and from thence to Nashville, Tennessee, where it arrived December 1.
December 15-16.— Took part in the battle before Nashville and marched to Lexington, Alabama. Whole distance marched about 222 miles. Loss of the company was one captain and five men wounded and one man killed.

Stationed at Huntsville, Alabama, January-February 1865.
The company marched from Lexington, Tennessee to Huntsville, Alabama, where it arrived January 5.

Stationed near Nashville, Tennessee, March-April 1865.
March 15-April 4.— Left Huntsville, Alabama and went by railroad to Strawberry Plains, Tennessee and marched from thence to Greeneville, Tennessee, arriving April 4.
April 10.— Marched from Greeneville to Warm Springs, North Carolina and returned April 10.
April 28.— Marched from Greeneville to Bull's Gap, Tennessee and took cars for Nashville, arriving April 28.

Stationed near New Orleans, Louisiana, May-June 1865.
June 17.— In the morning the company left Nashville, Tennessee and went by rail to Johnsonville, Tennessee, where it was placed on board the steamer *Echo No. 2.*
June 19-26.— The steamer, on arriving off Cairo, Illinois the morning of June 19, collided with a monitor lying at anchor up the river opposite that place and immediately sank. The company records and all the camp and garrison equipage and ordnance stores belonging to the company were lost. The company was then placed on board the steamer *Atlantic* and arrived at New Orleans, Louisiana June 26.

Company K

Stationed at Camp Wood, Ohio, October 29, 1861.
October 29.— Muster-in roll of Captain William Goodsell's Company, in the Forty-first Regiment of Ohio Volunteers, commanded by Colonel William B. Hazen, called into service of the

United States by the President under the act of Congress of July 22, 1861 from October 29, 1861 (date of this muster) for the term of three years, unless sooner discharged. . . .

JAMES P. W. NEILL,
First Lieutenant,
Eighteenth United States Infantry, Mustering Officer.

Stationed at Camp Wood, Ohio, enrollment to October 31, 1861.

Stationed at Camp Wickliffe, Kentucky, December 31, 1861.
[For record of events, see Company E.]
December 26-27.— The company was out about two miles from camp on picket duty.

Stationed at Camp Andrew Jackson, January-February 1862.

Changed station, since last roll, from Camp Wickliffe, Kentucky to Camp Andrew Jackson near Nashville, Tennessee by a march of forty miles to West Point on the Ohio River; thence by steamboat to this place.

Stationed at the field of Shiloh, March-April 1862.
April 6-7.— Since last muster have marched from Nashville to Pittsburg Landing. Arrived April 6. Took part in the battle of April 7. Lost one private killed and ten privates wounded.

Stationed at camp near Athens, Alabama, May-June 1862.

Stationed at Murfreesborough, Tennessee, July-August 1862.
July 17-30.— At the date of last muster the company and regiment was at Athens, Alabama, where it remained until July 17, when it proceeded with the regiment to a point on Richland Creek on the line of the Tennessee and Alabama Railroad and was employed in rebuilding bridges, etc., until July 30, when it started for Murfreesborough, Tennessee (via Nashville by rail), where it has since been stationed. The discipline and efficiency of the company is fully equal to that of other companies of the volunteer troops.

Stationed at Columbia, Kentucky, September-October 1862.
September 6-26.— The company (in connection with the regiment) left Murfreesborough, Tennessee and marched thence via

Nashville, Bowling Green and Munfordville to Louisville, Kentucky, where it arrived on September 26.
October 1-19.— Left Louisville (with the regiment) and marched via Bardstown, Perryville, Danville, Crab Orchard, Mount Vernon, and Wild Cat to Pitman's Cross-Roads, where it arrived on October 19.
October 23.— Returned to Wild Cat and marched thence via Mount Vernon and Somerset to Columbia, Kentucky. During the march from Louisville to Pitman's Cross-Roads the company was brought under fire several times at different points along the route while deployed as skirmishers but without casualty.

Stationed at battlefield of Murfreesborough, November-December 1862.
November 2-3.— The company in connection with the regiment left Columbia, Kentucky and marched to Glasgow, Kentucky, a distance of thirty-six miles, where it arrived on November 3.
November 12-16.— It again took up its line of march via Scottsville (twenty-five miles) and Gallatin (thirty-two miles) to Silver Springs, Tennessee (fourteen miles), arriving there on November 16.
November 20.— From there it moved to a point six miles east of Nashville (twelve miles).
November 26-December 26.— [Moved] to a point on the Nashville and Murfreesborough Pike (three and one-half miles) south of the former place (seven miles). Stopped until December 26, when it took up line of march to Murfreesborough via La Vergne (fifteen miles), where the company was brought under fire. Casualties none.
December 27-30.— Moved again to within two and one-half miles of Murfreesborough (twelve and one-half miles).
December 31.— Was engaged. Lost Second Lieutenant H. P. Walcott, two sergeants and four privates wounded.

Stationed at Readyville, Tennessee, January-February 1863.
January 1-3.— The company was in the battle of Stone's River; no casualties. Since December 31, 162 most of the time under fire.
January 6.— The company, in connection with the regiment, left the battlefield and marched to a point two miles east of Murfreesborough (four miles) on the Woodbury Pike, where it remained

two days and it again took up its line of march for Readyville (twelve miles), where it has since been in camp.

Stationed at Readyville, Tennessee, March-April 1863.

Stationed near Manchester, Tennessee, May-June 1863.
June 24-29.— The company in connection with the regiment left its camp at Readyville, Tennessee on its way south. It arrived at Manchester, Tennessee, a distance of twenty miles, on June 29.

Stationed at Poe's Tavern, Tennessee, July-August 1863.

Station not stated, September-October 1863.
The company marched from Manchester, Tennessee August 16. Arrived at Poe's Tavern August 24.
[For record of events, see Company B.]

Stationed at Blain's Cross-Roads, Tennessee, November-December 1863.

Stationed at Cleveland, Ohio, January-February 1864.

Stationed near McDonald's Station, March-April 1864.

Stationed near Marietta, Georgia, May-June 1864.

Stationed in the rear of Atlanta, Georgia, July-August 1864.
Company K was with its regiment at last muster, which was more or less engaged in skirmishing with the enemy before Kenesaw.
July 3.— In the morning it advanced with its regiment after the retreating Rebels.
July 5.— Skirmished with them, when we reached the Chattahoochee River near Vining's Station. Here we remained a few days and finally crossed the river.
July 22.— We moved up in front of Atlanta. Built a line of works. Skirmished occasionally with the enemy. When our Army made its grand flank movement to the rear of Atlanta, my company went along and was engaged in tearing up the Montgomery Railroad.

August 31.— At the time of muster we lay about four miles from the Macon Railroad.

Stationed at Athens, Alabama, September-October 1864.

When last mustered the company was at Athens, Alabama, where it just arrived with its regiment after marching from Atlanta, Georgia, where it was engaged with the balance of the Army under General Sherman in driving the enemy from that stronghold. After the capture of Atlanta our regiment, with the Fourth and Twenty-third Corps, returned to Chattanooga, from thence we arrived here, where we were mustered.

Stationed at Lexington, Alabama, November-December 1864.

The company was with the regiment on its retreat from Athens, Alabama to Nashville, Tennessee and was engaged in skirmishing with the enemy at various points on the route. Was in the battle of Nashville and participated in storming the enemy's works. The enemy was obliged to retreat and were closely pursued by our Army as far as the Tennessee River. In these various movements my company, with its regiment, took an active part.

Stationed near Huntsville, Alabama, January-February 1865.

December 31, 1864.— The company, when last mustered December 31, 1864, was at Lexington, Alabama.

January 5, 1865.— Since then we marched for this place, where we arrived January 5. Here we went into winter quarters and have since remained drilling every day and preparing ourselves for the better discharge of our duties in soldiering.

Stationed at Nashville, Tennessee, March-April 1865.

[For record of events, see Company C.]

Stationed at New Orleans, Louisiana, May-June 1865.

[M594-Roll #150]

Record of Events for Forty-second Ohio Infantry, September 1861-December 1864.

Field and Staff

Stationed at Camp Chase, to October 31, 1861.

Stationed at Camp Chase, November 27, 1861.
November 27.— Muster-in roll of the field and staff and band in the Forty-second Regiment of United States Volunteers, commanded by Colonel James [Abram] Garfield, called into service of the United States by the President from November 27, 1861 (date of this muster) for the term of three years, unless sooner discharged. . . .

ALBERT [BALDWIN] DOD,
Captain,
Fifteenth Infantry, United States Army, Mustering Officer.

Stationed at Camp Brownlow, January-February 1862.

Stationed at Camp Patton, March-April 1862.

Stationed at Camp Virginia, May-June 1862.

Stationed at Cumberland Gap, July-August 1862.

Stationed at Charleston, [West] Virginia, September-October 1862.

Stationed at Oak Hill, Ohio, October 18, 1862.
Muster-out roll of the band in the Forty-second Regiment of Ohio Volunteers, commanded by Colonel Lionel [Allen] Sheldon, called into the service of the United States by the President at Camp Chase (the place of general rendezvous) on September 10, 1861 to serve for the term of three years from the date of enrollment, unless sooner discharged. The company was organized by Lieutenant J. W. Ford at Elyria in the month of September 1861

and marched thence to Camp Chase, where it arrived September 28, a distance of 120 miles. . . .

ALBERT B. DOD,
Captain,
Fifteenth Infantry, United States Army, Mustering Officer.

Stationed on board steamer Des Moines, November-December 1862.

Stationed at Young's Point, Louisiana, January-February 1863.

Stationed at Port Gibson, Mississippi, March-April 1863.

Stationed at Black River Bridge, May-June 1863.

Stationed at Carrollton, Louisiana, July-August 1863.

Stationed at New Iberia, Louisiana, September-October 1863.

Stationed at Plaquemine, Louisiana, November 1863-February 1864.

Stationed at Baton Rouge, Louisiana, March-April 1864.

Stationed at Morganza, Louisiana, May-August 1864.

Stationed at Devall's Bluff, Arkansas, September-October 1864.

Stationed at Columbus, Ohio, December 2, 1864.
December 2.— Muster-out roll of Colonel Lionel A. Sheldon's, late Colonel James A. Garfield's, field and staff in the Forty-second Regiment of Ohio Infantry Volunteers, commanded by Colonel Lionel A. Sheldon, late Colonel James A. Garfield, called into the service of the United States by the President at Columbus, Ohio (the place of general rendezvous) on November 27, 1861 to serve for the term of three years from the date of enrollment, unless sooner discharged, from April 30, 1864 (when last paid) to December 2, 1864 when discharged. The regiment was organized by Colonel James A. Garfield at Camp Chase,

Ohio in the month of November 1861 and marched thence to Camp Chase, Ohio, where it arrived November 27. . . .

[PATRICK] W. HORRIGAN,
Second Lieutenant,
Second United States Cavalry, Mustering Officer.

Regiment

Stationed at Camp Chase, October-November 1861.

Stationed at camp, George's Creek, December 1861.

Two privates' names in Company H stricken from the roll by order of colonel.

Stationed at Camp Buell near Paintsville, Kentucky, January 1862.

Stationed at Camp Virginia, Kentucky, June 1862.

Stationed at Memphis, November 1862.

Stationed near Vicksburg, December 1862.

Stationed at Young's Point, Louisiana, January-February 1863.

Stationed at Milliken's Bend, Louisiana, March 1863.

Stationed at Port Gibson, Mississippi, April 1863.

Stationed at the rear of Vicksburg, May 1863.

Stationed at Camp Alice, Mississippi, June 1863.

Stationed at Vicksburg, Mississippi, July 1863.

Stationed at Carrollton, Louisiana, August 1863.

Stationed at Berwick, Louisiana, September 1863.

Stationed at New Iberia, Louisiana, October 1863.

Stationed at Plaquemine, Louisiana, November 1863-February 1864.

Stationed at Baton Rouge, Louisiana, March 1864.

Stationed at Morganza, Louisiana, May-June 1864.

Stationed at Saint Charles, Arkansas, July 1864.

Stationed at Morganza, Louisiana, August 1864.

Stationed at the mouth of White River, Arkansas, September 1864.

Stationed at Devall's Bluff, Arkansas, en route for Columbus, Ohio, October 1864.

Company A

Stationed at Camp Chase, Ohio, September 25, 1861.
September 25.— Muster-in roll of Captain Frederick A. Williams' Company A, in the Forty-second Regiment of Ohio Volunteers, commanded by Colonel J. A. Garfield, called into the service of the United States by the President from September 25, 1861 (date of this muster) for the term of three years, unless sooner discharged. The company was organized by Captain F. A. Williams at Ravenna, Ohio in the month of September and marched thence to Camp Chase, where it arrived September 21, 1861, a distance of 180 miles. . . .

JOHN [RUFUS] EDIE,
Major,
Fifteenth Infantry, United States Army, Mustering Officer.

Stationed at Camp Chase, September 20-October 31, 1861.

Station not stated, December 31, 1861.

Stationed at Camp Brownlow, Piketon, Pike County, Ohio, January-February 1862.

Stationed at Camp Patton, Kentucky, March-April 1862.

Stationed at Cumberland Gap, May-June 1862.

Stationed at Cumberland Gap, Tennessee, July-August 1862.

Stationed at Camp Charleston, [West] Virginia, September-October 1862.

Stationed at Chickasaw Bayou, [October] 31-December 31, 1862.

Stationed at Young's Point, Louisiana, January-February 1863.

Stationed at Richmond, Louisiana, April 10, 1863.

Stationed at Port Gibson, Mississippi, March-April 1863.

Stationed at Big Black River, Mississippi, May-June 1863.

Stationed at Carrollton, Louisiana, July-August 1863.

Stationed at New Iberia, Louisiana, September-October 1863.

Stationed at Plaquemine, Louisiana, November 1863-February 1864.

Stationed at Baton Rouge, Louisiana, March-April 1864.

Stationed at Morganza, Louisiana, May-August 1864.

Stationed at Columbus, Ohio, September 30, 1864.

Muster-out roll of Captain Jasper S. Ross' Company A, in the Forty-second Regiment of Ohio Infantry Volunteers, commanded by Colonel Lionel A. Sheldon, called into the service of the United States by the President at Ravenna, Ohio (the place of general rendezvous) on September 20, 1861 to serve for the term of three years from the date of enrollment, unless sooner discharged, from September 25, 1861 (when mustered) to — 2, 1864. The company was organized by Captain Fred A. Williams at Ravenna, Ohio in the month of September 1861 and marched thence to Camp Chase, Ohio, where it arrived September 23, a distance of 100 miles. . . .

[JOHN FOSTER] SMALL,
Second Lieutenant,
First Cavalry, Mustering Officer.

Company B

Stationed at Camp Chase, Ohio, September 25, 1861.
September 25.— Muster-in roll of Captain William H. Williams' Company B, in the Forty-second Regiment of Ohio Volunteers, commanded by Colonel J. A. Garfield, called into the service of the United States by the President from September 25, 1861 (date of this muster) for the term of three years, unless sooner discharged. The company was organized by Captain William H. Williams at Whittlesey, Ohio in the month of September and marched thence to Camp Chase, where it arrived September 25, 1861, a distance of 133 miles. . . .

JOHN R. EDIE,
Major,
Fifteenth Infantry, United States Army, Mustering Officer.

Stationed at Camp Chase, enlistment to October 31, 1861.

Stationed at the mouth of George's Creek, December 31, 1861.

Stationed in the field, January-February 1862.

Stationed at Camp Patton, Kentucky, March-April 1862.

Stationed near Cumberland Gap, May-August 1862.

Stationed at Charleston, [West] Virginia, September-October 1862.
September 8.— This company left the Cumberland Gap and marched to Manchester. Camped there until the evacuation of the Gap, when we were rejoined by the forces under General Morgan. From thence we marched to the Ohio River, distance 240 miles, without rations and but a scanty supply of water. The whole march from the Gap was accomplished in sixteen days. From the Ohio River marched to Charleston, [West] Virginia,

distance eighty-five miles. Thence back to the Ohio River, again to Point Pleasant, from which place we were transported on boats to Memphis, Tennessee. Remarks beginning with thence and ending with Memphis, Tennessee are canceled.

Stationed in the field, November-December 1862.

Were transported by water from Memphis, Tennessee to near Vicksburg. The expedition, under command of General [William Tecumseh] Sherman, met the enemy. There engaged them. Were under fire five days. On the second day made a desperate charge on Rebel works but were repulsed with loss. The expedition retired up the Mississippi on the sixth day, January 2.

Stationed at Young's Point, Louisiana, January-February 1863.

Stationed at Richmond, Louisiana, April 10, 1863.

Stationed in the field, March-April 1863.

Stationed near Black River Bridge, May-June 1863.

The company was with the regiment in the grand rear movement on Vicksburg by General Grant and was in the following actions, *viz.*:
May 1.— Battle of Port Gibson.
May 16.— Battle of Champion's Hill.
May 17.— Battles of Black River Bridge.
May 19.— Advance on Vicksburg.
May 22.— Charge on works.

Stationed at Carrollton, Louisiana, July-August 1863.

Stationed at New Iberia, September-October 1863.

Stationed at Plaquemine, Louisiana, November 1863-February 1864.

Stationed at Baton Rouge, Louisiana, March-April 1864.

Stationed at Morganza Bend, Louisiana, May-August 1864.

Stationed at Camp Chase, Ohio, September 30, 1864.
September 24.— Muster-out roll of Captain Horace Potter's Company B, in the Forty-second Regiment of Ohio Infantry Volunteers, commanded by Colonel Lionel A. Sheldon, called into the service of the United States by the President at Camp Chase, Ohio (the place of general rendezvous) on September 25, 1861 to serve for the term of three years from the date of enrollment, unless sooner discharged, from September 25, 1861 (when mustered) to September 24, 1864. The company was organized by Captain William W. Williams at Whittlesey, Ohio in the month of September 1861 and marched thence to Camp Chase, Ohio, where it arrived September 22, 1861, a distance of 133 miles. . . .

J. F. SMALL,
Second Lieutenant,
First Cavalry, Mustering Officer.

Company C

Stationed at Camp Chase, Ohio, October 2, 1861.
October 2.— Muster-in roll of Captain Tully C. Bushnell's Company C, in the Forty-second Regiment of Ohio Volunteers, commanded by Colonel J. A. Garfield, called into the service of the United States by the President from October 2, 1861 (date of this muster) for the term of three years, unless sooner discharged. The company was organized by Captain Tully C. Bushnell at Ashland in the month of September and marched thence to Camp Chase, where it arrived September 25, a distance of 101 miles. . . .

JOHN R. EDIE,
Major,
Fifteenth Infantry, United States Army, Mustering Officer.

Stationed at Camp Chase, Ohio, enlistment to October 31, 1861.

Stationed at the mouth of George's Creek, December 31, 1861.

Stationed at Camp Brownlow near Piketon, Kentucky, January-February 1862.

This company marched from Catlettsburg to Louisa, Kentucky, a distance of twenty-six miles, in one day without injury. *February 10.*— Were engaged in the action of Middle Creek near Prestonburg. Henry Forney of this company was slightly wounded.

Stationed at Flat Lick, March-April 1862.

Stationed at Camp Virginia near Cumberland Gap, Kentucky, May-June 1862.

Station not stated, July-August 1862.

Stationed at camp near Charleston, [West] Virginia, September-October 1862.

Stationed at Chickasaw Bayou, Mississippi, November-December 1862.

Stationed at Young's Point, Louisiana, January-February 1863.

Stationed at Richmond, Louisiana, April 10, 1863.

Stationed at Port Gibson, Mississippi, March-April 1863.

Stationed at Camp Alice, Mississippi, May-June 1863.

Stationed at Carrollton, Louisiana, July-August 1863.

Stationed at camp near New Iberia, Louisiana, September-October 1863.

Stationed at Plaquemine, Louisiana, November 1863-February 1864.

Stationed at Baton Rouge, Louisiana, March-April 1864.

Stationed at Morganza, Louisiana, May-August 1864.

Stationed at Camp Chase, Ohio, September 30, 1864.

Muster-out roll of Captain [William] N. Starr's Company C, in the Forty-second Regiment of Ohio Infantry Volunteers, commanded by Colonel L. A. Sheldon, called into the service of the United States by the President at Camp Chase, Ohio (the place of general rendezvous) on September 25, 1861 to serve for the term of three years from the date of enrollment, unless sooner discharged, from September 25, 1861 (when mustered). The company was organized by Captain Tully C. Bushnell at Ashland, Ohio in the month of September 1861 and marched thence to Camp Chase, Ohio, where it arrived September 24. . . .

J. F. SMALL,
Second Lieutenant,
First Cavalry, Mustering Officer.

Company D

Stationed at Camp Chase, Ohio, September 25, 1861.
September 25.— Muster-in roll of Captain James H. Riggs' Company, in the Forty-second Regiment of Ohio Volunteers, commanded by Colonel J. A. Garfield, called into the service of the United States by the President from September 25, 1861 (date of this muster) for the term of three years, unless sooner discharged. The company was organized by Captain James H. Riggs at Mount Ephraim, Ohio in the month of September and marched thence to Camp Chase, where it arrived September 24, 1861, a distance of 105 miles. . . .

JOHN R. EDIE,
Major,
Fifteenth Infantry, United States Army, Mustering Officer.

Stationed at Camp Chase, enlistment to October 31, 1861.

We would be happy to furnish the War Department any information that might be useful but as we have not been engaged in any scouts, marches, changes of station or anything of the kind. We are wholly unable to give any such information. But if the War Department will only give us half a chance we hope to tell you a few things next time that will make you feel miserable good.

Stationed at the mouth of George's Creek, December 31, 1861.

Stationed at Camp Brownlow, January-February 1862.

Stationed at Camp Patton, Cumberland Ford, Kentucky, March-April 1862.

Station not stated, May-June 1862.

Stationed at camp, Cumberland Gap, Tennessee, July-August 1862.

Stationed at Charleston, [West] Virginia, September-October 1862.

Stationed at Arkansas Post, November-December 1862.
December 28-29, 1862.— The company was engaged in the battle of Chickasaw Bayou near Vicksburg.
January 11, 1863.— Also present at the surrender of the Rebel fort at Arkansas Post.

Stationed at Young's Point, Louisiana, January-February 1863.

Stationed at Richmond, Louisiana, April 10, 1863.

Stationed in the field, Mississippi, March-April 1863.

Stationed at Camp Alice, Mississippi, May-June 1863.

Stationed at Carrollton, Louisiana, July-August 1863.

Stationed at New Iberia, Louisiana, September-October 1863.

Stationed at Plaquemine, Louisiana, November 1863-February 1864.

Stationed at Baton Rouge, Louisiana, March-April 1864.

Stationed at Morganza, Louisiana, May-August 1864.

Stationed at Camp Chase, September 30, 1864.

Muster-out roll of Captain George K. Pardee's Company D, in the Forty-second Regiment of Ohio Infantry Volunteers, commanded by Colonel L. A. Sheldon, called into the service of the United States by the President at Camp Chase, Ohio (the place of general rendezvous) on September 25, 1861 to serve for the term of three years from the date of enrollment, unless sooner discharged. The company was organized by Captain James H. Riggs at Mount Ephraim, Ohio in the month of September 1861 and marched thence to Columbus, Ohio, where it arrived September 24, a distance of 105 miles. . . .

J. F. SMALL,
Second Lieutenant,
First Cavalry, Mustering Officer.

Company E

Stationed at Camp Chase, October 30, 1861.

Muster-in roll of Captain Charles H. Howe's Company, in the Forty-second Regiment of Ohio Volunteers, commanded by Colonel J. A. Garfield, called into the service of the United States . . . for the term of three years, unless sooner discharged. The company was organized by Captain Charles H. Howe at Elyria, Ohio in the month of September and marched thence to Camp Chase, where it arrived October 3, a distance of 120 miles. . . .

ALBERT B. DOD,
Captain,
Fifteenth Infantry, United States Army, Mustering Officer.

Stationed at Camp Chase, enlistment to October 31, 1861.

Stationed at the mouth of George's Creek, December 1861.

Stationed at Camp Brownlow, January-February 1862.

Stationed at Camp Patton, March-April 1862.

Stationed at Camp Morgan, Kentucky, May-June 1862.

Stationed at Cumberland Gap, Kentucky, July-August 1862.

Stationed at camp, Charleston, [West] Virginia, September-October 1862.

Stationed in the field near Vicksburg, November 1862-February 1863.

Stationed at camp near Richmond, Louisiana, April 10, 1863.

Stationed at Port Gibson, Mississippi, March-April 1863.

Stationed at Camp Alice, Mississippi, May-June 1863.

Stationed at Carrollton, Louisiana, July-August 1863.

Stationed near New Iberia, Louisiana, September-October 1863.

Stationed at Plaquemine, Louisiana, November 1863-February 1864.

Stationed at Baton Rouge, Louisiana, March-April 1864.

Stationed at Morganza, Louisiana, May-August 1864.

Stationed at Devall's Bluff, September-October 1864.

Stationed at Columbus, Ohio, November 15, 1864.
November 15.— Muster-out roll of Captain Melvin L. Benham's, late Captain Howe's, Company E, in the Forty-second Regiment of Ohio Volunteers, commanded by Colonel L. A. Sheldon, late Colonel J. A. Garfield, called into the service of the United States by the President at Camp Chase (the place of general rendezvous) on October 30, 1861 to serve for the term of three years from the date of enrollment, unless sooner discharged, from April 30, 1864 (when last paid) to November 15, 1864 when discharged.

The company was organized by Captain C. H. Howe at Camp Chase in the month of October 1861. . . .

J. F. SMALL,
First Lieutenant,
First Cavalry, Mustering Officer.

Company F

Stationed at Camp Chase near Columbus, Ohio, not dated.

Muster-in roll of Captain Horace H. Willard's Company F, in the Forty-second Regiment of Ohio Foot Volunteers, commanded by Colonel James A. Garfield, called into the service of the United States by the President from the dates set opposite their names, respectively, for the term of three years, unless sooner discharged. . . .

HORACE H. WILLARD,
Mustering Officer.

[SAMUEL] H. COLE.

L. D. BOOTH.

Stationed at Camp Chase, enlistment to October 31, 1861.

Stationed at the mouth of George's Creek, December 31, 1861.

Stationed at Camp Brownlow, January-February 1862.

Stationed at Camp Patton, March-April 1862.

Stationed at Camp Virginia, Kentucky, May-June 1862.

Station not stated, July-August 1862.

Stationed at Camp ——, September-October 1862.

Station not stated, November-December 1862.

Stationed at Young's Point, Louisiana, January-February 1863.

Station not stated, March-April 1863.

Stationed at Camp Alice, Mississippi, May-June 1863.

Stationed at Carrollton, Louisiana, July-August 1863.

Stationed at New Iberia, Louisiana, September-October 1863.

Stationed at Plaquemine, Louisiana, November 1863-February 1864.

Stationed at Baton Rouge, Louisiana, March-April 1864.

Stationed at Morganza, Louisiana, May-August 1864.

Stationed at Devall's Bluff, September-October 1864.

Stationed at Camp Chase, November 19, 1864.
November 19.— Muster-out roll of late Captain Horace H. Willard's Company F, in the Forty-second Regiment of Ohio Volunteers, commanded by Colonel L. A. Sheldon, late Colonel J. A. Garfield, called into the service of the United States by the President at Camp Chase (the place of general rendezvous) on November 18, 1861 to serve for the term of three years from the date of enrollment, unless sooner discharged, from April 30, 1864 (when last paid) to November 19, 1864 when discharged. The company was organized by Captain Horace H. Willard at Camp Chase in the month of November 1861. . . .

J. F. SMALL,
First Lieutenant,
First Cavalry, Mustering Officer.

Company G

Stationed at Camp Chase, November 27, 1861.
September 19.— Muster-in roll of Captain [Charles] P. Jewett's Company, in the Forty-second Regiment of Infantry Ohio Volunteers, commanded by Colonel J. A. Garfield, called into the service of the United States by the President from September 19,

1861 (date of this muster) for the term of three years, unless sooner discharged. . . .

ALBERT B. DOD,
Captain,
Fifteenth Infantry, United States Army, Mustering Officer.

Stationed at the mouth of George's Creek, December 31, 1861.

Stationed at Camp Brownlow, Pikeville, Kentucky, January-February 1862.
January 10.— The company was engaged in the battle of Middle Creek near Prestonburg, Kentucky. Three of its members were wounded in the engagement; two seriously.

Stationed at Camp Patton, March-April 1862.
March 14.— The company was last mustered at Piketon, Kentucky. Accompanied a detachment of the regiment on an expedition to Pound Gap, a distance of forty miles, to rout a body of Rebels encamped there. After successfully accomplishing their object, totally defeating and routing the enemy and burning their camp, the company returned to Piketon, making the round march a distance of over eighty miles through a rough, mountainous country, in five days. Were then ordered with the regiment to Louisville, Kentucky.
April 29.— From there to Lexington, Kentucky, from Lexington marched to Cumberland Ford, a distance of 120 miles, arriving on April 29, at which place the company is stationed at the date of this muster.

Stationed at Cumberland Gap, May-August 1862.

Stationed in camp near Charleston, [West] Virginia, September-October 1862.

Stationed in the field near Vicksburg, Mississippi, November-December 1862.

Stationed at Young's Point, Louisiana, January-February 1863.

Stationed at Richmond, Louisiana, April 10, 1863.

Stationed in the field, March-April 1863.

Stationed at Camp Alice, Mississippi, May-June 1863.

Stationed at Carrollton, Louisiana, July-August 1863.

Stationed at New Iberia, September-October 1863.

Stationed at Plaquemine, Louisiana, November 1863-February 1864.

Stationed at Baton Rouge, Louisiana, March-April 1864.

Stationed at Morganza, Louisiana, May-August 1864.

Stationed at Devall's Bluff, Arkansas, September-October 1864.

Stationed at Columbus, Ohio, December 2, 1864.
December 2.— Muster-out roll of First Lieutenant Calvin Pierce's, late Captain [Edward] B. Campbell's, Company G, in the Forty-second Regiment of Ohio Infantry Volunteers, commanded by Colonel L. A. Sheldon, late James A. Garfield, called into the service of the United States by the President at Columbus, Ohio (the place of general rendezvous) on November 27, 1861 to serve for the term of three years from the date of enrollment, unless sooner discharged, from April 30, 1864 (when last paid) to December 2, 1864 when discharged. The company was organized by Captain C. P. Jewett at Newburgh, Ohio in the month of September 1861 and marched thence to Camp Chase, Ohio, where it arrived October 4, a distance of 140 miles. . . .

P. W. HORRIGAN,
Second Lieutenant,
Second United States Cavalry, Mustering Officer.

Company H

Stationed at Camp Chase, September 19-October 31, 1861.

Stationed at Camp Chase, November 27, 1861.
November 27.— Muster-in roll of Captain Seth M. Barber's Company, in the Forty-second Regiment of Infantry, Ohio Volunteers, commanded by Colonel James A. Garfield, called into the service of the United States by the President from November 27, 1861 (date of this muster) for the term of three years, unless sooner discharged. . . .

ALBERT B. DOD,
Captain,
Fifteenth Infantry, United States Army, Mustering Officer.

Stationed at camp at the mouth of George's Creek, Lawrence County, Kentucky, December 31, 1861.
This is the payroll made out for this company and hence there are no charges to record.

Stationed at Camp Brownlow, January-February 1862.
Since making out last roll the regiment has marched from the mouth of George's Creek to Paintsville and from thence to Piketon.
January 10.— In the meantime the regiment has been in one engagement at Middle Creek. In this engagement the Rebels, under Humphrey Marshall, were defeated. The field was won by our force under Colonel J. A. Garfield.

Stationed at Camp Patton near Cumberland Ford, Kentucky, March-April 1862.
The captain, with twenty-two men, formed part of the column that marched from Pikeville, Kentucky to Pound Gap, routing the Rebels stationed there.
March 14-19.— Left Pikeville. Reached the Gap March 17. Returned March 19.
April 1.— Left Pikeville for Louisville about April 1 by rail to Lexington; thence by marches to this camp.

Stationed at Camp Virginia, May-June 1862.
Marched from Cumberland Ford to Wilson's Gap, twenty miles west of Cumberland Gap, then to Cumberland Gap. At Wilson's Gap part of the company engaged in skirmish with

Rebel cavalry. Distance about thirty-five miles to Wilson's Gap. Then to Cumberland Gap, twenty miles.

Stationed at Cumberland Gap, Tennessee, July-August 1862.

Stationed at Charleston, [West] Virginia, September-October 1862.

Stationed at Chickasaw Bayou near Vicksburg, November-December 1862.

Stationed at Young's Point, Louisiana opposite Vicksburg, January-February 1863.

Stationed at Richmond, Louisiana, April 10, 1863.

Station not stated, March-June 1863.

Stationed at Carrollton, Louisiana, July-August 1863.

Stationed at New Iberia, Louisiana, September-October 1863.

Stationed at Plaquemine, Louisiana, November 1863-February 1864.

Stationed at Baton Rouge, Louisiana, March-April 1864.

Stationed at Morganza, Louisiana, May-August 1864.

Stationed at Devall's Bluff, Arkansas, September-October 1864.

Stationed at Columbus, Ohio, December 2, 1864.
December 2.— Muster-out roll of Captain John R. [Helman's] Company H, in the Forty-second Regiment of Ohio Infantry Volunteers, commanded by Colonel L. A. Sheldon, called into the service of the United States by the President at Columbus, Ohio (the place of general rendezvous) on November 27, 1861 to serve for the term of three years from the date of enrollment, unless sooner discharged, from April 30, 1864 (when last paid) to

December 2, 1864 when discharged. The company was organized by Captain S. M. Barber at Ashland, Ohio in the month of November 1861 and marched thence to Camp Chase, Ohio, where it arrived November 26, a distance of eighty-two miles. . . .

P. W. HORRIGAN,
Second Lieutenant,
Second United States Cavalry, Mustering Officer.

Company I

Station not stated, not dated.
November 27.— Muster-in roll of Captain Rollin B. Lynch's Company, in the Forty-second Regiment of Ohio Volunteers, commanded by Colonel James A. Garfield, called into the service of the United States by the President from November 27, — (date of this muster) for the term of three years. . . .

JOHN R. EDIE,
Major,
Fifteenth Infantry, United States Army, Mustering Officer.

ALBERT B. DOD,
Captain,
Fifteenth Infantry, United States Army, Mustering Officer.

Stationed at the mouth of George's Creek, December 31, 1861.

Stationed at Camp Brownlow near Piketon, Kentucky, January-February 1862.

Stationed at Camp Patton near Cumberland Ford, Kentucky, March-April 1862.

Stationed at Cumberland Gap, May-August 1862.

Stationed at Charleston, [West] Virginia, September-October 1862.

Station not stated, November-December 1862.

Stationed at camp, Young's Point, Louisiana, January-February 1863.

Stationed at Richmond, Louisiana, April 10, 1863.

Stationed in the field, March-April 1863.

Stationed at camp on Black River, May-June 1863.

Stationed at Carrollton, Louisiana, July-August 1863.

Stationed at New Iberia, Louisiana, September-October 1863.

Stationed at Plaquemine, Louisiana, November 1863-February 1864.

Stationed at Baton Rouge, Louisiana, March-April 1864.

Stationed at Morganza Bend, Louisiana, May-August 1864.

Stationed at Devall's Bluff, Arkansas, September-October 1864.

Stationed at Columbus, Ohio, December 2, 1864.
December 2.— Muster-out roll of Captain David N. Prince's, late Rollin B. Lynch's, Company I, in the Forty-second Regiment of Ohio Infantry Volunteers, commanded by Colonel L. A. Sheldon, late Colonel James A. Garfield, called into the service of the United States by the President at Columbus, Ohio (the place of general rendezvous) on November 27, 1861 to serve for the term of three years from the date of enrollment, unless sooner discharged, from April 30, 1864 (when last paid) to December 2, 1864 when discharged. The company was organized by Captain Rollin B. Lynch at Camp Chase, Ohio in the month of November 1861. . . .

P. W. HORRIGAN,
Second Lieutenant,
Second United States Cavalry, Mustering Officer.

Company K

Station not stated, not dated.

Muster-in roll of Captain Andrew Gardner's, Jr., Company K, in the Forty-second Regiment of Ohio Infantry Volunteers, commanded by Colonel James A. Garfield, called into the service of the United States . . . for the term of three years, unless sooner discharged. . . .

ALBERT B. DOD,
Captain,
Fifteenth Infantry, United States Army, Mustering Officer.

Stationed at Camp Chase, enlistment to October 31, 1861.

Stationed at the mouth of George's Creek, December 31, 1861.

Stationed at Camp Brownlow, January-February 1862.

Stationed at Camp Patton, Kentucky, March-April 1862.

Stationed at Camp Virginia, May-June 1862.

Stationed at Cumberland Gap, Kentucky, July-August 1862.

Stationed at camp, Charleston, [West] Virginia, September-October 1862.

Stationed in the field near Vicksburg, Mississippi, November-December 1862.

Stationed at Milliken's Bend, Louisiana, January-February 1863.

Stationed at Richmond, Louisiana, April 10, 1863.

Station not stated, March-April 1863.

Stationed at Big Black River, May-June 1863.

Stationed at Carrollton, Louisiana, July-August 1863.

Stationed near New Iberia, Louisiana, September-October 1863.

Stationed at Plaquemine, Louisiana, November 1863-February 1864.

Stationed at Baton Rouge, Louisiana, March-April 1864.
March 26.— Left Plaquemine; arrived at Baton Rouge, Louisiana same day, distance thirty miles. Marched to the rear of the city and camped.

Station not stated, May-June 1864.

Stationed at Morganza, Louisiana, July-August 1864.

Stationed at Devall's Bluff, Arkansas, September-October 1864.

Stationed at Columbus, Ohio, December 2, 1864.
December 2.— Muster-out roll of Captain Thomas L. Hutchins', late Captain Andrew Gardner's, Jr., Company K in the Forty-second Regiment of Ohio Volunteers, commanded by Colonel L. A. Sheldon, late Colonel James A. Garfield, called into the service of the United States by the President at Columbus, Ohio (the place of general rendezvous) on November 27, 1861 to serve for the term of three years from the date of enrollment, unless sooner discharged, from April 30, 1864 (when last paid) to December 2, 1864 when discharged. The company was organized by Captain Andrew Gardner, Jr. at Bellefontaine, Ohio in the month of September 1861 and marched thence to Camp Chase, Ohio, where it arrived September 27, a distance of sixty-nine miles. . . .

P. W. HORRIGAN,
Second Lieutenant,
Second United States Cavalry, Mustering Officer.

[M594-Roll #150]

Record of Events for Forty-third Ohio Infantry, October 1861-June 1865.

Field and Staff

Station not stated, not dated.

Muster-in roll of the field and staff in the Forty-third Regiment of Ohio Infantry . . . called into service of the United States by the President from. . . .

[UNSIGNED.]

Stationed at Camp Andrews, Mount Vernon, Ohio, to December 31, 1861.

Station not stated, January-February 1862.

Stationed at camp near Clear Creek, Tishomingo County, Mississippi, March-June 1862.

Stationed at camp on Bear Creek, Mississippi, July-August 1862.

Stationed near Corinth, Mississippi, September-October 1862.

Stationed at Bolivar, Tennessee, November 1862-February 1863.

Stationed at Bethel, Tennessee, March-April 1863.

Stationed at Memphis, Tennessee, May-August 1863.

Stationed at Iuka, Mississippi, September-October 1863.

Stationed at Prospect, Tennessee, November-December 1863.

Stationed at Decatur Junction, Alabama, January-February 1864.

Stationed at Decatur, Alabama, March-April 1864.

Stationed near Kenesaw Mountain, Georgia, May-June 1864.

Stationed in the field near Jonesborough, Georgia, July-August 1864.

Stationed at Cave Spring, Georgia, September-October 1864.

Stationed at Dillon's Bridge, Georgia, November-December 1864.

Station not stated, March-April 1865.
February 3.— The regiment was in action engaged in crossing the Salkehatchie River, South Carolina and capturing the Rebel works.

Stationed at Louisville, Kentucky, May-June 1865.

Regiment

Stationed at Camp Chase near Columbus, Ohio, October 1861.

Stationed at camp near New Madrid, Missouri, March 1862.

Stationed at camp on Corinth Road, April 1862.

Stationed near Booneville, Mississippi, May 1862.

Stationed at camp on Clear Creek, Mississippi, June-July 1862.

Stationed at camp on Bear Creek, Mississippi, August 1862.

Stationed at Rienzi, Mississippi, September 1862.

Station not stated, October 1862-January 1863.

Stationed at Bolivar, Tennessee, February 1863.

Stationed at Bethel, Tennessee, March-April 1863.

Stationed at Memphis, Tennessee, May-September 1863.

Stationed at Iuka, Mississippi, October 1863.

Stationed at Prospect, Tennessee, November 1863.

Stationed at Decatur Junction, Alabama, December 1863.

Station not stated, January 1864.

Stationed at Decatur Junction, Alabama, February 1864.

Stationed at Decatur, Alabama, March-April 1864.

Stationed in the field near Dallas, Georgia, May 1864.

Station not stated, June 1864.

Stationed in the field, Georgia, July-August 1864.

Stationed at East Point, Georgia, September 1864.

Stationed near Cave Spring, Georgia, October 1864.

Station not stated, November 1864.

Stationed at Dillon's Bridge, Georgia, December 1864.

Stationed at Goldsborough, March 1865.

Stationed in the field, North Carolina, April 1865

Stationed near Washington, District of Columbia, May 1865.

Stationed at Louisville, Kentucky, June 1865.

Company A

Stationed at Camp Andrews, Mount Vernon, Ohio, December 31, 1861.
November 6.— Muster-in roll of Captain Jacob M. Spangler's Company A, in the Forty-third Regiment of Ohio Foot Volunteers, commanded by Colonel [Joseph Lee Kirby] Smith, called

into the service of the United States by the President from November 6, 1861 (date of this muster) for the term of three years, unless sooner discharged. . . .

JOHN [RUFUS] EDIE,
Major,
Fifteenth Infantry, United States Army, Mustering Officer.

ALBERT [BALDWIN] DOD,
Captain,
Fifteenth Infantry, United States Army, Mustering Officer.

J. L. KIRBY SMITH,
Colonel,
Forty-third Ohio Volunteer Infantry,
Second Lieutenant, Topographical Engineers.

Station not stated, muster-in to December 31, 1861.

Stationed at Commerce, Missouri, February 28, 1862.

Stationed at Camp Clear Creek, near Danville, Mississippi, March-June 1862.

Stationed at camp on Clear Creek, Mississippi, August 18, 1862.

Stationed at Bear Creek Bridge, Alabama, July-August 1862.

Station not stated, September-October 1862.

Stationed at Bolivar, Tennessee, November 1862-February 1863.

Stationed at Bethel, Tennessee, March-April 1863.

Stationed at Memphis, Tennessee, May-August 1863.

Stationed at Iuka, Mississippi, September-October 1863.

Station not stated, November-December 1863.

Stationed at Decatur Junction, Alabama, January-April 1864.

Station not stated, May-June 1864.

Stationed in the field, Georgia, July-August 1864.

Stationed at Cave Spring, Georgia, September-October 1864.

Stationed at Dillon's Bridge, Georgia, November-December 1864.

Stationed at camp in the field, South Carolina, January-February 1865.

Stationed in the field, North Carolina, April 30, 1865.

Stationed at Louisville, Kentucky, June 30, 1865.

Company B

Station not stated, not dated.
December 5, 1861.— Muster-in roll of Captain James Marshman's Company B, in the Forty-third Regiment of Ohio Volunteers, commanded by Colonel J. L. K. Smith, called into the service of the United States by the President from December 5, 1861 (date of this muster) for the term of three years, unless sooner discharged. . . .

JOHN R. EDIE,
Major,
Fifteenth United States Infantry, Mustering Officer.

ALBERT B. DOD,
Captain,
Fifteenth United States Infantry, Mustering Officer.

J. L. KIRBY SMITH,
Colonel,
Forty-third Ohio Volunteer Infantry, Topographical Engineers, Mustering Officer.

Stationed at Camp Anderson, Ohio, muster-in to December 31, 1861.

Stationed at Commerce, Missouri, February 28, 1862.

Stationed at camp near Corinth, Mississippi, March-April 1862.

Station not stated, May-June 1862.

Stationed at camp on Clear Creek, Mississippi, August 18, 1862.

Stationed at camp on Bear Creek, Mississippi, July-August 1862.

Stationed at Corinth, Mississippi, September-October 1862.

Stationed at Bolivar, Tennessee, November 1862-February 1863.

Stationed at Bethel, Tennessee, March-June 1863.

Stationed at Memphis, Tennessee, July-August 1863.

Stationed at Iuka, Mississippi, September-October 1863.

Stationed at Prospect, Tennessee, November-December 1863.

Stationed at Decatur Junction, January-February 1864.

Stationed at Decatur, Alabama, March-April 1864.

Stationed at Kenesaw Mountain, May-June 1864.

Stationed near East Point, Georgia, July-August 1864.

Stationed near Marietta, Georgia, September-October 1864.

Stationed at Dillon's Bridge, Georgia, November-December 1864.

Stationed at camp in the field, North Carolina, January-February 1865.

Stationed at Raleigh, North Carolina, March-April 1865.

Stationed at Louisville, Kentucky, May-June 1865.

Company C

Stationed at Camp Andrews, Mount Vernon, Ohio, December 31, 1861.

Muster-in roll of Captain Moses J. Urquhart's Company C, in the Forty-third Regiment of Ohio Foot Volunteers, commanded by Colonel J. L. Kirby Smith, called into service of the United States by the President, thereof, from the dates set opposite their names respectively . . . for the term of three years, unless sooner discharged. . . .

MOSES J. URQUHART,
Mustering Officer.

SANFORD F. TIMMONS,
Mustering Officer.

WILLIAM B. THORNHILL,
Mustering Officer.

Stationed at Camp Andrews, Mount Vernon, Ohio, December 31, 1861.

Stationed at Commerce, Missouri, February 28, 1862.

Station not stated, March-April 1862.

Stationed at Camp Clear Creek, near Danville, Mississippi, May-June 1862.

Stationed at camp near Iuka Springs, July-August 1862.

Stationed at Corinth, Mississippi, September-October 1862.

Stationed at Bolivar, Tennessee, November 1862-February 1863.

Stationed at Bethel, Tennessee, March-April 1863.

Stationed at Memphis, Tennessee, May-August 1863.

Stationed at Iuka, Mississippi, September-October 1863.

Stationed at Prospect, Tennessee, November-December 1863.

Stationed at Decatur, Junction, January-February 1864.

Stationed at Decatur, Alabama, March-April 1864.

Stationed at camp in the field, Georgia, May-August 1864.

Stationed at Cave Spring, Georgia, September-October 1864.

Stationed at Dillon's Bridge, Georgia, November-December 1864.

Stationed in the field, South Carolina, January-February 1865.

Stationed near Raleigh, North Carolina, March-April 1865.

Stationed at Louisville, Kentucky, May-June 1865.

Company D

Stationed at Camp Andrews, Ohio, December 21, 1861.

Muster-in roll of Captain [Christian] L. Poorman's Company, in the Forty-third Regiment of Ohio Foot Volunteers, commanded by Colonel J. L. K. Smith, called into the service of the United States by the President from date set opposite their names respectively, for the term of three years, unless sooner discharged. . . .

C. L. POORMAN,
Mustering Officer.

Stationed at Camp Andrews, Mount Vernon, Ohio, December 31, 1861.

Stationed at Commerce, Missouri, February 28, 1862.

Stationed at Camp Clear Creek, near Danville, Mississippi, March-April 1862.

Station not stated, May-June 1862.

Stationed at camp near Bear Creek, Mississippi, July-August 1862.

Stationed at Corinth, Mississippi, September-October 1862.

Stationed at camp near Bolivar, Tennessee, November 1862-February 1863.

Stationed at Bethel, Tennessee, March-April 1863.

Stationed at Memphis, Tennessee, May-June 1863.

Stationed at Memphis, Tennessee, July-August 1863.
The company has been doing garrison duty at Memphis since last muster.

Stationed at Iuka, Mississippi, September-October 1863.

Stationed at Prospect, Tennessee, November-December 1863.
Last mustered at Iuka, Mississippi.
November 2.— Marched to Eastport, Mississippi.
November 4.— Crossed the Tennessee River from Eastport.
November 6-13.— Marched toward Stevenson, Alabama in Left Wing, Sixteenth Army Corps, Brigadier-General [Grenville Mellen] Dodge commanding, continuing until November 13, when ordered to camp at Prospect, Tennessee.
December 31.— The regiment engaged in garrisoning and repairing the Alabama and Tennessee Central Railroad until December 31, when the company having entered the veteran service, it was ordered to Ohio with the regiment on furlough.

Stationed at Junction Memphis and Charleston and Tennessee and Alabama Central Railroad, January-February 1864.
January 1-22.— Fifty-eight members of the company having reenlisted as veteran volunteers, they were ordered to Ohio in charge of Lieutenant [Thomas G.] Harper, where they were furloughed for thirty days. The company left Prospect, Tennessee January 1 and returned to that place February 22.

February 24-25.— Marched for the junction of Memphis and Charleston and Tennessee and Alabama Central Railroad and arrived there February 25, where this muster is dated.

Stationed at Decatur, Alabama, March-April 1864.

Stationed at Kenesaw Mountain, May-June 1864.
May 1-5.— Marched from Decatur, arriving at Chattanooga May 5.
May 9-16.— Participated in the operations at Resaca May 9, 13, 14, 15, and 16.
May 26-29.— [Participated] at Dallas and at Kenesaw Mountain to date.

Stationed near Jonesborough, Georgia, July-August 1864.

Stationed at Cave Spring, Georgia, September-October 1864.

Stationed at Dillon's Bridge, Georgia, November-December 1864.

Stationed in the field, South Carolina, January-February 1865.

Stationed at Raleigh, North Carolina, March-April 1865.

Stationed at Louisville, Kentucky, May-June 1865.

Company E

Stationed at Camp Andrews, Ohio, December 31, 1861.
Muster-in roll of Captain Harley H. Sage's Company, in the Forty-third Regiment of Ohio Volunteers, commanded by Colonel J. L. Kirby Smith, called into the service of the United States by the President from the dates set opposite their names respectively . . . for the term of three years, unless sooner discharged. . . .

[DAVID] F. PHILLIPS,
Mustering Officer.

JOHN P. KINNEY,
Mustering Officer.

Stationed at Camp Andrews, Mount Vernon, Ohio, December 31, 1861.

Stationed at Commerce, Missouri, January-February 1862.

Station not stated, March-April 1862.

Stationed at Camp Clear Creek, May-June 1862.

Stationed at camp on Bear Creek, Alabama, July-August 1862.

Stationed at Corinth, Mississippi, September-October 1862.

Stationed at Bolivar, Tennessee, November 1862-February 1863.

Stationed at Bethel, Tennessee, March-April 1863.

Stationed at Memphis, Tennessee, May-August 1863.

Stationed at Prospect, Tennessee, November-December 1863.

Stationed at Decatur Junction, Alabama, January-February 1864.

Stationed at Decatur, Alabama, March-April 1864.

Stationed at Kenesaw Mountain, Georgia, May-June 1864.

Stationed near East Point, Georgia, July-August 1864.

Stationed at Cave Spring, Georgia, September-October 1864.

Stationed at Dillon's Bridge, Georgia, November-December 1864.

Stationed in the field, South Carolina, January-February 1865.

Stationed in the field, North Carolina, March-April 1865.

Stationed at Louisville, Kentucky, May-June 1865.

Company F

Stationed at Camp Andrew, Mount Vernon, Ohio, December 31, 1861.

Muster-in roll of Captain James H. Coulter's Company F, in the Forty-third Regiment of Ohio Foot Volunteers, commanded by Colonel J. L. Kirby Smith, called into the service of the United States by the President from the dates set opposite their names respectively, for the term of three years, unless sooner discharged. . . .

J. H. COULTER,
Mustering Officer.

Stationed at Camp Andrews, Mount Vernon, Ohio, to December 31, 1861.

Station not stated, January-April 1862.

Stationed at camp on Clear Creek, near Danville, Mississippi, May-June 1862.

Stationed at camp near Davis' Mill, July-August 1862.

Stationed at camp near Corinth, September-October 1862.

Stationed at Bolivar, Tennessee, November 1862-February 1863.

Stationed at Henderson's [Station], Tennessee, April 14, 1863.

Company F on detached duty at Henderson's Station, Mobile and Ohio Railroad since March 11, 1863.

Stationed at Henderson's [Station], Tennessee, March-April 1863.

The company has been on detached service at Henderson's since March 11.

Stationed at Memphis, Tennessee, May-August 1863.

Stationed at Iuka, Mississippi, September-October 1863.

Stationed at Prospect, Tennessee, November-December 1863.

Stationed at Decatur Junction, Alabama, January-February 1864.

Stationed at Decatur, Alabama, March-April 1864.

Stationed near Kenesaw Mountain, Georgia, May-June 1864.

Stationed in the field, Georgia, July-August 1864.

Stationed near Cave City, Alabama, September-October 1864.

Stationed at Dillon's Bridge, Georgia, November-December 1864.

Stationed in the field, South Carolina, January-February 1865.

Stationed near Raleigh, North Carolina, March-April 1865.

Stationed at Louisville, Kentucky, May-June 1865.

Company G

Stationed at Camp Andrews, Ohio, December 31, 1861.

Muster-in roll of Captain John Ferguson's Company G, in the Forty-third Regiment of Ohio Foot Volunteers, commanded by Colonel J. L. Kirby Smith, called into service of the United States by the President from the dates set opposite their names respectively, for the term of three years, unless sooner discharged. . . .

ALBERT B. DOD,
Captain,
Fifteenth Infantry, United States Army, Mustering Officer.

Stationed at Camp Andrews, Mount Vernon, Ohio, December 31, 1861.

Station not stated, January-February 1862.

Stationed at Camp Clear Creek, March-June 1862.

Stationed at camp near Bear Creek Bridge, July-August 1862.

Stationed at camp, Corinth, Mississippi, October 31, 1862.
September 12-October 4.— The company was engaged at the battle of Corinth, Mississippi October 4 and were on the march from the first appearance of the enemy near Iuka about September 12 until our forces returned to Corinth, pursuing the enemy after their repulse and retreat on October 4.

Stationed at Bolivar, Tennessee, November 1862-February 1863.

Stationed at Bethel, Tennessee, March-April 1863.

Stationed at Memphis, Tennessee, May-August 1863.

Stationed at Iuka, Mississippi, September-October 1863.

Stationed at Prospect, Tennessee, November-December 1863.

Station not stated, January-February 1864.

Stationed at Decatur, Alabama, March-April 1864.

Stationed at Kenesaw Mountain, Georgia, May-June 1864.

Stationed at Chattahoochee River, Georgia, July-August 1864.

Stationed at Cave Spring, Georgia, September-October 1864.

Stationed at Dillon's Bridge, Georgia, November-December 1864.

Stationed in the field, South Carolina, January-February 1865.

Stationed at Raleigh, North Carolina, March-April 1865.

Stationed at Louisville, Kentucky, May-June 1865.

Company H

Station not stated, not dated.
Muster-in roll of Captain Joel [Allen] Dewey's Company, in the Forty-third Regiment of Ohio Foot Volunteers, commanded

by Colonel J. L. Kirby Smith, called into the service of the United States by the President from the dates set opposite their names respectively, for the term of three years, unless sooner discharged. . . .

J. A. DEWEY,
Mustering Officer.

[SAMUEL] K. WILLIAMS,
Mustering Officer.

Station not stated, to December 31, 1861.

Stationed at Commerce, Missouri, January-February 1862.

Station not stated, March-June 1862.

Stationed at Camp Clear Creek, Mississippi, August 18, 1862.

Stationed at camp on Bear Creek, Mississippi, July-August 1862.

Stationed at camp at Corinth, Mississippi, September-October 1862.

Stationed at camp at Bolivar, Tennessee, November 1862-February 1863.

Stationed at Henderson's Station, March-April 1863.

Company H, Forty-third Regiment Ohio Volunteers, has been on detached service since March 11 at Henderson's Station, Tennessee.

Stationed at Memphis, Tennessee, May-August 1863.

Stationed at Iuka, Mississippi, September-October 1863.

Stationed at Prospect, Tennessee, November-December 1863.

Stationed at Decatur Junction, Alabama, January-February 1864.

Stationed at Decatur, Alabama, March-April 1864.

Stationed near Kenesaw Mountain, Georgia, May-June 1864.

Stationed near Atlanta, Georgia, July-August 1864.

Stationed at Cave Spring, Georgia, September-October 1864.

Stationed at Dillon's Bridge, Georgia, November-December 1864.

Stationed in the field, South Carolina, January-February 1865.

Stationed near Washington, District of Columbia, March-April 1865.

Stationed at Louisville, Kentucky, May-June 1865.

Company I

Stationed at Camp Andrews, Mount Vernon, Ohio, February 12, 1862.

Muster-in roll of Captain Peter Brown's Company, in the Forty-third Regiment of Ohio Foot Volunteers, commanded by Colonel J. L. Kirby Smith, called into the service of the United States by the President from the dates set opposite their names respectively, for the term of three years, unless sooner discharged. . . .

PETER BROWN,
Second Lieutenant,
Forty-third Ohio Volunteer Infantry, Mustering Officer.

WILLOUGHBY W. WEBB,
Mustering Officer.

PETER HEWETSON,
Mustering Officer.

Stationed at Commerce, Missouri, February 28, 1862.

Stationed at Camp Clear Creek, March-June 1862.

Stationed at Corinth, Mississippi, July-October 1862.

Stationed at Bolivar, Tennessee, November 1862-February 1863.

Stationed at Bethel, Tennessee, March-April 1863.

Stationed at Memphis, Tennessee, May-August 1863.

Stationed at Iuka, Mississippi, September-October 1863.

Stationed at Prospect, Tennessee, November-December 1863.

Stationed at Decatur Junction, January-February 1864.

Stationed at Decatur, Alabama, March-April 1864.

Stationed at Kenesaw Mountain, Georgia, May-June 1864.

Stationed at Jonesborough, Georgia, July-August 1864.

Stationed at Cave City, Alabama, September-October 1864.

Stationed at Dillon's Bridge, Georgia, November-December 1864.

Stationed at camp in the field, South Carolina, January-February 1865.

Stationed at camp in the field, North Carolina, March-April 1865.

Stationed at Louisville, Kentucky, May-June 1865.

Company K

Stationed at Camp Andrews, Mount Vernon, Ohio, February 14, 1862.

Muster-in roll of Captain William Walker's Company, in the Forty-third Regiment of Ohio Foot Volunteers, commanded by Colonel J. L. Kirby Smith, called into the service of the United States by the President from the dates set opposite their names respectively, for the term of three years, unless sooner discharged. . . .

WILLIAM WALKER,
Second Lieutenant,
Mustering Officer.

[MOSES] R. SHALTERS,
Second Lieutenant,
Mustering Officer.

ISAAC YOUNG,
Second Lieutenant,
Mustering Officer.

Stationed at Commerce, Missouri, February 28, 1862.

Station not stated, March-April 1862.

Stationed at camp on Clear Creek, Mississippi, May-June 1862.

Stationed at camp on Bear Creek, Mississippi, July-August 1862.

Stationed at camp at Corinth, Mississippi, September-October 1862.

Stationed at Bolivar, Tennessee, November 1862-February 1863.

Stationed at Fort Hooker, Tennessee, March-April 1863.

Stationed at Memphis, Tennessee, May-August 1863.

Stationed at Iuka, Mississippi, September-October 1863.

Stationed at Prospect, Tennessee, November-December 1863.

Stationed at Decatur Junction, January-February 1864.

Stationed at Decatur, Alabama, March-April 1864.

Stationed at Kenesaw Mountain, near Marietta, Georgia, May-June 1864.

Stationed near Jonesborough, Georgia, July-August 1864.

Stationed at Cave Spring, Georgia, September-October 1864.

Stationed at Dillon's Bridge, Georgia, November-December 1864.

Stationed at camp in the field, South Carolina, January-February 1865.

Stationed at camp in the field, North Carolina, March-April 1865.

Stationed at Louisville, Kentucky, May-June 1865.

[M594-Roll #150]

[Note: no record of events were reported for the Forty-fourth Ohio Infantry.]

Record of Events for Forty-fifth Ohio Infantry, August 1862-June 1865.

Field and Staff

Stationed at Camp Chase, Columbus, Ohio, August 19, 1862.

Muster-in roll of the field and staff of the Forty-fifth Regiment of Ohio Volunteers, commanded by Colonel [Benjamin Piatt] Runkle, called into service of the United States by the President . . . for the term of three years or during the war, unless sooner discharged. . . .

ALEXANDER [EDWIN] DRAKE,
Captain,
United States Army, Mustering Officer.

Stationed on the march, October 31, 1862.

Stationed at Camp Ella Bishop, Lexington, Kentucky, November-December 1862.

Stationed at Danville, Kentucky, January-February 1863.

Station not stated, March-April 1863.

Stationed at Jamestown, Kentucky, May-June 1863.

Stationed on the march to Tennessee, July-August 1863.

Stationed at Knoxville, Tennessee, September-October 1863.

During the month the regiment was constantly in active service.

October 20.— At Philadelphia, Tennessee engaged largely superior numbers of the enemy. After a severe contest [were] compelled to fall back to Loudon, Tennessee with the loss of six wagons and all the camp and garrison equipage and officers' baggage and regimental and company records. Left three killed and twenty-two wounded, including Captain [Comfort] E. Stanley and 150 missing (including the two assistant surgeons and chaplain).

October 26.— First Lieutenant Thomas H. B. Jones of Company B, was killed in action near Philadelphia, Tennessee.

October 28.— The regiment moved with the rest of [Frank] Wolford's Brigade to Knoxville, Tennessee to obtain necessary arms, clothing, etc.

Stationed at Massengale's Mill, East Tennessee, November-December 1863.

Stationed at Mount Sterling, Kentucky, January-February 1864.

Stationed at Jacksborough, Tennessee, March-April 1864.

Stationed in the field near Kenesaw Mountain, Georgia, May-June 1864.

Stationed before Atlanta, Georgia, July-August 1864.

Stationed at Chattanooga, Tennessee, September-October 1864.

Stationed at Duck River, Tennessee, November-December 1864.

Stationed at Huntsville, Alabama, January-February 1865.

Stationed at Camp Harker, Tennessee, March-April 1865.

Stationed at Camp Harker, Tennessee, June 12, 1865.

Muster-out roll of the field and staff in the Forty-fifth Regiment of Ohio Infantry Volunteers, commanded by Lieutenant-Colonel John H. Humphrey, called into the service of the United States by the President at Camp Chase, Ohio (the place of general rendezvous) on August 19, 1862 to serve for the term of three years from the date of enrollment, unless sooner discharged. . . .

JOHN I. MORRIS,
Captain and Assistant Commissary of Musters,
Twentieth Indiana Battery, First Division, Fourth Army Corps,
Mustering Officer.

Regiment

Stationed at Camp Ella Bishop, October-December 1862.

Stationed at Camp Gillmore, Danville, Kentucky, January 1863.

Stationed at Danville, Kentucky, February 1863.

Station not stated, March-May 1863.

Stationed at Somerset, Kentucky, June 1863.

Station not stated, July-November 1863.

Stationed at Massengale's Mill, East Tennessee, December 1863.

Stationed at Cumberland Gap, Tennessee, January 1864.

Stationed at Mount Sterling, Kentucky, February-March 1864.

Station not stated, May 1864.

Stationed in the field near Kenesaw Mountain, Georgia, June 1864.

Stationed near Atlanta, Georgia, July-September 1864.

Station not stated, October-December 1864.

Stationed at Huntsville, Alabama, January-February 1865.

Stationed at Bull's Gap, Tennessee, March 1865.

Stationed at Nashville, Tennessee, April 1865.

Stationed at Camp Harker, Tennessee, May 1865.

Company A

Stationed at Camp Chase, August 19, 1862.
August 19.— Muster-in roll of Captain George E. Ross' Company, in the Forty-fifth Regiment (First Brigade) of Ohio Volunteers, commanded by Colonel Ben P. Runkle, called into service of the United States . . . from August 19, 1862 (date of this muster) for the term of three years, unless sooner discharged. . . .

ALEX. E. DRAKE,
Captain,
United States Army, Mustering Officer.

Stationed on the march from Falmouth, Kentucky, October 31, 1862.

Stationed at Camp Ella Bishop, Lexington, Kentucky, November-December 1862.

Stationed at Danville, Kentucky, January-February 1863.

Stationed at Camp Burnside, Kentucky, April 10, 1863.

Stationed at Somerset, Kentucky, March-June 1863.

Stationed on the march to East Tennessee, July-August 1863.

Stationed at Knoxville, [September]-October 1863.

Stationed at Buffalo [Creek], November-December 1863.

Stationed at Mount Sterling, Kentucky, January-February 1864.

Stationed near Jacksborough, Tennessee, March-April 1864.

Stationed at Kenesaw, May-June 1864.

Stationed at Atlanta, Georgia, July-August 1864.

Stationed at Chattanooga, Tennessee, September-October 1864.

Stationed at Lexington, Tennessee, November-December 1864.

Stationed at Huntsville, Alabama, January-February 1865.

Stationed near Nashville, Tennessee, March-April 1865.

Stationed at Camp Harker, Tennessee, June 12, 1865.

Muster-out roll of Captain William H. Allen's Company A, in the Forty-fifth Regiment of Ohio Infantry Volunteers, commanded by Lieutenant-Colonel J. H. Humphrey, called into the service of the United States by the President at Camp Chase, Ohio (the place of general rendezvous) on August 19, 1862 to serve for the term of three years from the date of enrollment, unless sooner discharged. . . .

JOHN I. MORRIS,
Captain and Assistant Commissary of Musters,
Twentieth Indiana Battery, First Division, Fourth Army Corps,
Mustering Officer.

Company B

Stationed at Camp Chase, Columbus, Ohio, August 19, 1862.
August 19.— Muster-in roll of Captain Daniel Amerman's Company B, in the Forty-fifth Regiment of Ohio Volunteers, commanded by Colonel Ben P. Runkle, called into service of the

United States by August 19, 1862 (date of this muster) for the term of three years, unless sooner discharged. . . .

ALEX. E. DRAKE,
Captain,
United States Army, Mustering Officer.

Stationed on the march, October 31, 1862.

Stationed at Camp Ella Bishop, Lexington, Kentucky, November-December 1862.

Stationed at Camp Gillmore, Danville, Kentucky, February 28, 1863.

Stationed at Camp Burnside, Kentucky, March-April 1863.
March 30.— Twenty-five of my company were engaged at the battle of Dutton's Hill near Somerset, Kentucky. They acted like veterans and fought with great coolness. The remainder of my company was engaging the force under Colonel [Roy S.] Cluke at or near Owensville, Kentucky the same day.

JAMES T. JENNINGS,
Captain,
Commanding Company B, Forty-fifth Regiment,
Ohio [illegible], Mustering Officer.

Stationed at camp near Somerset, Kentucky, May-June 1863.

Stationed at camp on the road, East Tennessee, July-August 1863.

Stationed at camp near Knoxville, Tennessee, September-October 1863.
October 20.— Engaged in an action at Philadelphia, Tennessee. Lost all company books and rolls.

Stationed at Buffalo Creek, Tennessee, November-December 1863.

Stationed at Mount Sterling, Kentucky, January-February 1864.

Stationed at Jacksborough, Tennessee, March-April 1864.

Stationed near Kenesaw Mountain, Georgia, May-June 1864.

Stationed near Rough and Ready [Station], Georgia, July-August 1864.

Stationed at Chattanooga, Tennessee, September-October 1864.

Stationed on the march, November-December 1864.

Stationed at Huntsville, Alabama, January-February 1865.

Stationed at Nashville, Tennessee, [March]-June 1865.

Stationed at Camp Harker, Tennessee, June 12, 1865.

Muster-out roll of —'s Company B, in the Forty-fifth Regiment of Ohio Infantry Volunteers, commanded by Lieutenant-Colonel J. H. Humphrey, called into the service of the United States by the President at Camp Chase, Ohio (the place of general rendezvous) on August 19, 1862 to serve for the term of three years from the date of enrollment, unless sooner discharged. The company was organized by Captain Daniel Amerman at Kenton, Ohio in the month of August 1862 and marched thence to Camp Chase, Ohio, where it arrived August 12, a distance of eighty-six miles. . . .

JOHN I. MORRIS,
Captain and Assistant Commissary of Musters,
Twentieth Indiana Battery, First Division, Fourth Army Corps,
Mustering Officer.

Company C

Stationed at Camp Chase, Columbus, Ohio, August 19, 1862.
August 19.— Muster-in roll of Captain James D. Stover's Company C, in the Forty-fifth Regiment of Ohio Volunteers, commanded by Colonel Ben P. Runkle, called into service of the United States by August 19, 1862 (date of this muster) for the term of three years, unless sooner discharged. . . .

ALEX. E. DRAKE,
Captain,
United States Army, Mustering Officer.

Stationed on the march, October 31, 1862.

Stationed at Camp Ella Bishop, Lexington, Kentucky, December 31, 1862.

Stationed at Danville, Kentucky, January-February 1863.

Stationed at Camp Burnside, Kentucky, April 10, 1863.

Stationed at Somerset, Kentucky, March-April 1863.

Stationed at Jamestown, Kentucky, May-June 1863.

Station not stated, July-October 1863.

Stationed at Buffalo Creek, Tennessee, November-December 1863.

Stationed at Mount Sterling, Kentucky, January-February 1864.

Stationed on the march, March-April 1864.

Stationed near Kenesaw Mountain, Georgia, May-June 1864.

Stationed at Atlanta, Georgia, July-August 1864.

Stationed at Chattanooga, Tennessee, September-October 1864.

Stationed at Lexington, Alabama, November-December 1864.

Stationed at Huntsville, Alabama, January-February 1865.

Stationed at Nashville, Tennessee, March-April 1865.

Stationed at Camp Harker, Tennessee, June 12, 1865.

Muster-out roll of Captain Joseph R. Smith's Company C, in the Forty-fifth Regiment of Ohio Infantry Volunteers, commanded by Lieutenant-Colonel John H. Humphrey, called into the service of the United States by the President at Camp Chase, Ohio (the place of general rendezvous) on August 19, 1862 to serve for the term of three years from the date of enrollment, unless sooner discharged. The company was organized by Captain James D. Stover at Bellefontaine, Ohio in the month of August 1862 and marched thence to Camp Chase, Ohio, where it arrived August 12, a distance of sixty-six miles. . . .

JOHN I. MORRIS,
Captain and Assistant Commissary of Musters,
Twentieth Indiana Battery, First Division, Fourth Army Corps,
Mustering Officer.

Company D

Stationed at Camp Chase, Columbus, Ohio, August 19, 1862.
August 19.— Muster-in roll of Captain Robert Dow's Company D, in the Forty-fifth Regiment of Ohio Volunteers, commanded by Colonel Benjamin P. Runkle, called into service of the United States by August 19, 1862 (date of this muster) for the term of three years, unless sooner discharged. . . .

ALEX. E. DRAKE,
Captain,
United States Army, Mustering Officer.

Stationed on the march, October 31, 1862.

Stationed at Camp Ella Bishop, Lexington, Kentucky, November-December 1862.

Stationed at Danville, Kentucky, January-February 1863.

Stationed at Camp Burnside, Kentucky, April 10, 1863.

Stationed on the march, March-April 1863.

Stationed at Jamestown, Kentucky, May-June 1863.

Station not stated, July-August 1863.

Stationed at Knoxville, Tennessee, September-October 1863.

Stationed in the field, November-December 1863.

Stationed at Mount Sterling, Kentucky, January-February 1864.

Stationed near Jacksborough, East Tennessee, March-April 1864.

Stationed at the foot of Kenesaw Mountain, Georgia, May-June 1864.

Stationed near Rough and Ready [Station], Georgia, July-August 1864.

Stationed at Chattanooga, Tennessee, September-October 1864.

Stationed in the field, November-December 1864.

Stationed at Huntsville, Alabama, January-February 1865.

Stationed at Nashville, Tennessee, March-April 1865.

Stationed at Camp Harker, Tennessee, June 12, 1865.

Muster-out roll of Captain Nelson G. Franklin's Company D, in the Forty-fifth Regiment of Ohio Infantry Volunteers, commanded by Lieutenant-Colonel J. H. Humphrey, called into the service of the United States by the President at place of organization . . . to serve for the term of three years from the date of enrollment, unless sooner discharged. . . .

JOHN I. MORRIS,
Captain and Assistant Commissary of Musters,
Twentieth Indiana Battery, First Division, Fourth Army Corps,
Mustering Officer.

Company E

Stationed at Camp Chase, Columbus, Ohio, August 19, 1862.

August 19.— Muster-in roll of Captain Lewis Taylor's Company, in the Forty-fifty Regiment of Ohio Volunteers, commanded by Colonel Ben P. Runkle, called into service of the United States . . . from August 19, 1862 (date of this muster) for the term of three years, unless sooner discharged. . . .

ALEX. E. DRAKE,
Captain,
United States Army, Mustering Officer.

Stationed on the march, October 31, 1862.

Stationed at Camp Ella Bishop, Lexington, Kentucky, November-December 1862.

Stationed at Danville, Kentucky, January-February 1863.

Stationed at Camp Burnside, Kentucky, April 10, 1863.

Stationed at camp on the march, March-April 1863.
March 30.— Captain Taylor's Company was engaged at the battle on Dutton's Hill near Somerset, Kentucky. They acted with coolness and determination; charged and routed the enemy with great gallantry. William Rea and Elijah Peace received flesh wounds during the action. No other casualties.

JOSEPH R. SMITH,
First Lieutenant,
Commanding Company E, Forty-fifth Regiment,
Ohio Volunteer M. Infantry.

Stationed at Jamestown, Kentucky, May-June 1863.

Captain Taylor and company were engaged at the battle near Captain West's under my command on June 9 and fought, with great courage, a vastly superior force of the enemy and finally routed them. Corporal Joseph Sailor and Private Jacob Wise were both seriously wounded.

JOSEPH R. SMITH,
First Lieutenant,
Commanding Company E, Forty-fifth Regiment,
Ohio Volunteer M. Infantry.

Stationed on the march, July-August 1863.

Company E was engaged in the chase after John [Hunt] Morgan through the states of Kentucky, Indiana and Ohio during the month of July.
July 20.— Assisted the regiment in the capture of about 1,200 of Morgan's command near Buffington Island.

Stationed at Knoxville, Tennessee, September-October 1863.
September 26.— Met the enemy at Athens, Tennessee and fell back to Sweet Water, Tennessee.
October 20.— Surrounded by the enemy at Philadelphia, Tennessee, where we lost fourteen men, all supposed to be prisoners. Also lost all the camp and garrison equipage.
October 21.— Marched out and drove the enemy out of Philadelphia, Tennessee and fell back to Loudon, Tennessee.
October 26.— Engaged the enemy at the same place as last stated and fell back to Loudon, Tennessee at night. The three last engagements met with no loss.

Stationed at camp at Buffalo Creek, November-December 1863.
November 15.— Our forces on the south side of the Holston River being compelled to fall back to Knoxville, our regiment was ordered by General [William Price] Sanders to the rear to check the enemy and cover the retreat. Company E lost during the engagement seven men, supposed to be captured: Corporals Lappon and Loffer; Privates Solomon Hartle, Hirman H. Hostetter, John W. Irwin, Philip O. Jacobs, and Jabez Town.
November 17.— The regiment again engaged [James] Longstreet's advance between Knoxville and Lenoir's Station and fought them from 10 o'clock a.m. until 8 o'clock p.m. without serious loss to the company. Hedgman Jeffers and Leonidas T. Stoutmyer were slightly wounded.
November 18.— Engaged the enemy again in front of Fort Saunders at 10 o'clock a.m. and continued fighting until dark, protected by rail barricades. Lost Corporal Clinton D. Henderson, mortally wounded; and William Rea, slightly wounded and captured; and Corporal P. B Wells, slightly wounded.
December 14.— Our regiment was attacked by a superior force of the enemy at Bean's Station at 2 o'clock p.m. We fought them until after dark without casualty to the company.

JOSEPH R. SMITH,
First Lieutenant,
Commanding Company E.

Stationed at Mount Sterling, Kentucky, January-February 1864.

Stationed on the march, April 30, 1864.

Stationed in the field, May-August 1864.

Stationed at Chattanooga, Tennessee, September-October 1864.

Stationed at Lexington, Alabama, November-December 1864.

Stationed at Huntsville, Alabama, January-February 1865.

Stationed at Nashville, Tennessee, March-April 1865.

Stationed at Camp Harker, Tennessee, June 12, 1865.

Muster-out roll of Captain [Alfred] K. Rarey's Company E, in the Forty-fifth Regiment of Ohio Infantry Volunteers, commanded by Lieutenant-Colonel J. H. Humphrey, called into the service of the United States by the President at Camp Chase, Ohio (the place of general rendezvous) on August 19, 1862 to serve for the term of three years from the date of enrollment, unless sooner discharged from August 19, 1862 (when mustered in). The company was organized by Captain Lewis Taylor at De Graff, Ohio in the month of August 1862 and marched thence to Camp Chase, Ohio, where it arrived August 12, a distance of seventy-six miles. . . .

JOHN I. MORRIS,
Captain and Assistant Commissary of Musters,
Twentieth Indiana Battery, First Division, Fourth Army Corps,
Mustering Officer.

Company F

Stationed at Camp Chase, Columbus, Ohio, August 19, 1862.

August 19.— Muster-in roll of Captain Miles V. Payne's Company, in the Forty-fifth Regiment of Ohio Volunteers, commanded by Colonel Ben P. Runkle, called into service of the United States . . . from August 19, 1862 (date of this muster) for the term of three years, unless sooner discharged. . . .

ALEX. E. DRAKE,
Captain,
United States Army, Mustering Officer.

Stationed at camp on the road, October 31, 1862.

Stationed at Camp Ella Bishop, Lexington, Kentucky, November-December 1862.

Stationed at Danville, Kentucky, January-February 1863.

Stationed at Camp Burnside, Kentucky, April 10, 1863.

Stationed at Somerset, Kentucky, April 30, 1863.

Stationed at Jamestown, Kentucky, May-June 1863.

Stationed at Kingston, Tennessee, July-August 1863.

Stationed at Knoxville, Tennessee, September-October 1863.

Stationed at Massengale's Mill, November-December 1863.

Stationed at Mount Sterling, Kentucky, January-February 1864.

Stationed on the march, March-April 1864.

Stationed near Kenesaw Mountain, Georgia, May-June 1864.

Stationed at Smithfield, July-August 1864.

Stationed at Chattanooga, Tennessee, September-October 1864.

Stationed in the field, November-December 1864.

Stationed at Huntsville, Alabama, January-February 1865.

Stationed at Nashville, Tennessee, March-April 1865.

Stationed at Camp Harker, Tennessee, June 12, 1865.

Muster-out roll of First Lieutenant Frederick L. Dunning's Company F, in the Forty-fifth Regiment of Ohio Infantry Volunteers, commanded by Lieutenant-Colonel J. H. Humphrey, called into the service of the United States by the President at Camp Chase, Ohio (the place of general rendezvous) on August 19, 1862 to serve for the term of three years from the date of enrollment, unless sooner discharged. . . .

JOHN I. MORRIS,
Captain and Assistant Commissary of Musters,
Twentieth Indiana Battery, First Division, Fourth Army Corps,
Mustering Officer.

Company G

Stationed at Camp Chase, Columbus, Ohio, August 19, 1862.
August 19.— Muster-in roll of Captain John H. Humphrey's Company, in the Forty-fifth Regiment . . . commanded by Colonel Ben P. Runkle, called into the service of the United States . . . from August 19, 1862 (date of this muster) for the term of three years, unless sooner discharged. . . .

ALEX. E. DRAKE,
Captain,
United States Army, Mustering Officer.

Stationed on the march, October 31, 1862.

Stationed at Camp Ella Bishop, December 31, 1862.

Stationed at Danville, Kentucky, January-February 1863.

Stationed at Camp Burnside, Kentucky, April 10, 1863.

Stationed on the march, March-April 1863.

Stationed at Jamestown, Kentucky, May-June 1863.

Stationed at Kingston, Tennessee, July-August 1863.

Stationed at Knoxville, Tennessee, September-October 1863.

Stationed in the field, Tennessee, November-December 1863.

Stationed at Mount Sterling, Kentucky, January-February 1864.

Stationed at Jacksborough, Tennessee, March-April 1864.

Stationed at Kenesaw [Mountain], May-June 1864.

Stationed near Rough and Ready [Station], Georgia, July-August 1864.

Stationed at Chattanooga, Tennessee, September-October 1864.

Stationed in the field, November-December 1864.

Stationed at Huntsville, Alabama, January-February 1865.

Stationed at Nashville, Tennessee, March-April 1865.

Stationed at Camp Harker, Tennessee, June 12, 1865.

Muster-out roll of Captain [Thomas] W. Hodges' Company G, in the Forty-fifth Regiment of Ohio Infantry Volunteers, commanded by Lieutenant-Colonel J. H. Humphrey, called into the service of the United States by the President at Camp Chase, Ohio (the place of general rendezvous) on August 19, 1862 to serve for the term of three years from the date of enrollment, unless sooner discharged, from August 19, 1862 (when mustered in). The company was organized by Captain John H. Humphrey at Delaware, Ohio in the month of August 1862 and marched thence to Camp Chase, Ohio, where it arrived August 12, a distance of twenty-five miles. . . .

JOHN I. MORRIS,
Captain and Assistant Commissary of Musters,
Twentieth Indiana Battery, First Division, Fourth Army Corps,
Mustering Officer.

Company H

Stationed at Camp Chase, Columbus, Ohio, August 19, 1862.
August 19.— Muster-in roll of Captain William Rhoads' Company H, in the Forty-fifth Regiment of Ohio Volunteers, commanded by Colonel Ben P. Runkle, called into service of the

United States . . . from August 19, 1862 (date of this muster) for the term of three years, unless sooner discharged. . . .

ALEX. E. DRAKE,
Captain,
United States Army, Mustering Officer.

Stationed on the march, October 31, 1862.

Stationed at Camp Ella Bishop, Lexington, Kentucky, November-December 1862.

Stationed at Danville, Kentucky, January-February 1863.

Stationed at Camp Burnside, Kentucky, April 10, 1863.

Stationed at camp near Somerset, Kentucky, March-April 1863.

Stationed at Jamestown, Kentucky, May-June 1863.

Stationed on the march, July-August 1863.

Stationed at Knoxville, Tennessee, September-October 1863.

Stationed at Buffalo Creek, Tennessee, November-December 1863.

Stationed at Mount Sterling, January-February 1864.

Stationed at Jacksborough, Tennessee, March-April 1864.

Stationed at Kenesaw Mountain, Georgia, May-June 1864.

Stationed near Rough and Ready [Station], Georgia, July-August 1864.

Stationed at Chattanooga, Tennessee, September-October 1864.

Stationed at Lexington, Alabama, November-December 1864.

Stationed at Huntsville, Alabama, January-February 1865.

Stationed at Nashville, Tennessee, March-April 1865.

Stationed at Camp Harker, Tennessee, June 12, 1865.
June 12.— Muster-out roll of Captain Adam R. Eglin's Company H, in the Forty-fifth Regiment of Ohio Infantry Volunteers, commanded by Lieutenant-Colonel J. H. Humphrey, called into the service of the United States by the President. . . .

JOHN I. MORRIS,
Captain and Assistant Commissary of Musters,
Twentieth Indiana Battery, First Division, Fourth Army Corps,
Mustering Officer.

Company I

Stationed at Camp Chase, Columbus, Ohio, August 19, 1862.
August 19.— Muster-in roll of Captain Comfort E. Stanley's Company, in the Forty-fifth Regiment of Ohio Volunteers, commanded by Colonel Ben P. Runkle, called into service of the United States . . . from August 19, 1862 (date of this muster) for the term of three years, unless sooner discharged. . . .

ALEX. E. DAVIS,
Captain,
United States Army, Mustering Officer.

Stationed on the march from Paris to Lexington, October 31, 1862.

Station not stated, November-December 1862.

Stationed at Danville, Kentucky, January-February 1863.

Stationed at Camp Burnside, Kentucky, April 10, 1863.

Stationed at camp near Somerset, Kentucky, March-April 1863.

Stationed at Camp Carter, Somerset, Kentucky, May-June 1863.

Stationed at Kingston, Tennessee, July-August 1863.

Stationed at Knoxville, Tennessee, September-October 1863.

Stationed near Massengale's Mill, Tennessee, November-December 1863.

Stationed at Mount Sterling, Kentucky, January-February 1864.

Stationed near Jacksborough, Tennessee, March-April 1864.

Stationed at Kenesaw Mountain, Georgia, May-June 1864.

Stationed at Rough and Ready [Station], Georgia, July-August 1864.

Stationed at Chattanooga, Tennessee, September-October 1864.

Stationed in the field, Alabama, November-December 1864.

Stationed at Huntsville, Alabama, January-February 1865.

Stationed near Nashville, Tennessee, March-April 1865.

Stationed at Camp Harker, Tennessee, June 12, 1865.

Muster-out roll of Captain William [Morrow] Williams' Company I, in the Forty-fifth Regiment of Ohio Infantry Volunteers, commanded by Lieutenant-Colonel J. H. Humphrey, called into the service of the United States by the President at Camp Chase, Ohio (the place of general rendezvous) on August 19, 1862 to serve for the term of three years from the date of enrollment, unless sooner discharged, from August 19, 1862 (when mustered in). The company was organized by Captain Comfort E. Stanley at Patterson, Ohio in the month of August 1862 and marched thence to Camp Chase, Ohio, where it arrived August 12, 1862, a distance of 100 miles. . . .

JOHN I. MORRIS,
Captain and Assistant Commissary of Musters,
Twentieth Indiana Battery, First Division, Fourth Army Corps,
Mustering Officer.

Company K

Stationed at Camp Chase, Columbus, Ohio, August 19, 1862.
August 19.— Muster-in roll of Captain James E. Marsh's Company, in the Forty-fifth Regiment of Ohio Volunteers, commanded by Colonel Ben P. Runkle, called into service of the United States . . . from August 19, 1862 (date of this muster) for the term of three years, unless sooner discharged. . . .

ALEX. E. DRAKE,
Captain,
United States Army, Mustering Officer.

Stationed at Lexington, Kentucky, October 31, 1862.

Stationed at Camp Ella Bishop, November-December 1862.

Stationed at Danville, Kentucky, January-February 1863.

Stationed at Camp Burnside, Kentucky, April 10, 1863.

Stationed on the march, March-April 1863.
March 30.— Forty-three of my company were engaged in the battle of Dutton's Hill near Somerset, Kentucky. They acted with great coolness, fought like veterans and took the hill at the point of the bayonet.
April 28.— We were engaged in a skirmish with the enemy in Wagner County, Kentucky and a few days after in another near Monticello, Kentucky. We have scouted over a large portion of the state.

DAVID SPARKS,
First Lieutenant,
Commanding Company K, Forty-fifth Regiment,
Ohio Volunteer Infantry.

Stationed at Jamestown, May-June 1863.

Stationed on the road in East Tennessee, July-August 1863.

Stationed at Maryville, Tennessee, September-October 1863.

Stationed at Tazewell, Tennessee, November-December 1863.

Stationed at Mount Sterling, Kentucky, January-February 1864.
March 31, 1863.— Engaged in action at Dutton's Hill, Kentucky. During the months of April, May and June of the same year frequently engaged in scouts and skirmishes with the enemy south of the Cumberland River. Also engaged in the chase after Morgan in July through Kentucky, Indiana and Ohio and with others of the regiment succeeded in capturing over 1,100 of his men.
October 20.— Engaged in action near Philadelphia, Tennessee and lost heavily. Also engaged in fighting the advance of General Longstreet in his advance on Knoxville, Tennessee and throughout the siege and afterwards with severe loss to the company. Since its organization this company has probably traveled over 6,000 miles.

Stationed at Jacksborough, Tennessee, March-April 1864.

Stationed at Kenesaw Mountain, Georgia, May-June 1864.

Stationed in the field, July-August 1864.

Stationed at Chattanooga, Tennessee, September-October 1864.

Stationed at Lexington, Alabama, November-December 1864.

Stationed at Huntsville, Alabama, January-February 1865.

Stationed at Nashville, Tennessee, March-April 1865.

Stationed at Camp Harker, Tennessee, June 12, 1865.
Muster-out roll of Captain David Sparks' Company K, in the Forty-fifth Regiment of Ohio Infantry Volunteers, commanded by Lieutenant-Colonel J. H. Humphrey, called into the service of the United States by the President at Camp Chase, Ohio (the place of general rendezvous) on August 19, 1862 to serve for the term of three years from the date of enrollment, unless sooner discharged, from August 19, 1862 (when mustered in). The company was organized by Captain James E. Marsh at Bucyrus, Ohio in the

month of August 1862 and marched thence to Camp Chase, Ohio, where it arrived August 12, 1862, a distance of seventy-five miles. . . .

JOHN I. MORRIS,
Captain and Assistant Commissary of Musters,
Twentieth Indiana Battery, First Division, Fourth Army Corps,
Mustering Officer.

[M594-Roll #150]

Record of Events for Forty-sixth Ohio Infantry, September 1861-June 1865.

Detachment

Stationed at Chattanooga, Tennessee, October 26, 1864.

The company was mustered into the United States service September 10, —.

April 6-7, 1862.— Was in the engagement at Shiloh, Tennessee April 6 and 7, 1862 and lost its captain and two men killed, five wounded and four taken prisoner. Participated in the siege of Corinth, Mississippi. Also the siege of Vicksburg.

July 6-15, 1863.— Was in the battle of Black River July 6, 1863 and Jackson July 13, 14 and 15, losing two men wounded.

November 25.— Was in battle of Missionary Ridge. One lieutenant and three men were wounded.

Was in the following battles in Georgia in the spring campaign: Resaca, Dallas, Noonday Creek, Kenesaw Mountain and before Atlanta July 22. August 3 Jonesborough and Cedar Bluff, losing one lieutenant and eight men killed and nine wounded.

Field and Staff

Stationed at Camp Lyon, near Worthington, Ohio, October 31-December [31], 1861.

Stationed at Columbus, Ohio, February 4, 1862.

Muster-in roll of the field and staff and band in the Forty-sixth Regiment of Ohio Infantry Volunteers, commanded by Colonel Thomas Worthington, called into service of the United States by the President from the dates set opposite their names, respectively, for the term of three years, unless sooner discharged. . . .

[UNSIGNED.]

Stationed at Paducah, Kentucky, January-February 1862.

Stationed at Camp No. 2, Tennessee, March-April 1862.

Station not stated, May-June 1862.

Stationed at Fort Pickering, Memphis, Tennessee, August 27, 1862.

Muster-out roll of the regimental band of the Forty-sixth Regiment of Ohio Volunteer Infantry, commanded by Colonel Thomas Worthington, called into the service of the United States . . . from June 30, 1862 (when last mustered). . . .

[WILLIAM] D. SANGER,
Major and Aide-de-Camp,
Inspector and Mustering Officer.

Stationed at Fort Pickering, Tennessee, July-August 1862.

Stationed at Fort Pickering, Tennessee, September-October 1862.

Stationed at Holly Springs, Mississippi, November-December 1862.

Stationed at Grand Junction, Tennessee, January-February 1863.

Stationed at La Grange, Tennessee, March-April 1863.

Stationed at Oak Ridge, Mississippi, May-June 1863.

Stationed at Camp Sherman, Mississippi, July-August 1863.

Stationed at Florence, Alabama, September-October 1863.

Stationed at Scottsborough, Alabama, November-December 1863.

Stationed at Scottsborough, Alabama, January-February 1864.

Since last muster the regiment has been encamped at Scottsborough, Alabama, performing the usual duties of camp and picket guard and occasionally going out with forage trains.

January 1.— Two hundred seventy-eight members of the regiment were discharged by virtue of reenlistment as veteran volunteers.

The regiment has lately received new arms (the Spencer rifles) procured from the United States government by Charles [Carroll] Walcutt, Colonel commanding.

Stationed at Scottsborough, Alabama, March-April 1864.

March 8-20.— Since last muster the regiment has been home on a veteran furlough, leaving Scottsborough, Alabama on March 8, returning April 20.

Stationed near Kenesaw [Mountain], Georgia, May-June 1864.

May 1.— The regiment left Scottsborough, Alabama.

May 13-15.— Marched to Resaca, Georgia and participated in the battle of Resaca on May 13, 14 and 15. Lost one killed and sixteen wounded. From thence marched to Dallas, Georgia.

May 27-28.— Participated in the battle of Dallas. Lost twenty-three killed and wounded. From thence marched to Big Shanty, Georgia.

June 15.— Participated in a charge upon the enemy and captured 207 prisoners, including two colonels, a number of line officers and 150 stands of small arms. Lost two killed and seven wounded.

June 27.— The regiment participated in a charge upon Kenesaw Mountain. Lost eight killed and thirty wounded. Since June 27 the regiment remained in front of the enemy.

Stationed in the field, Georgia, July-August 1864.

Stationed in the field, Georgia, September-October 1864.
September 1.— The regiment was in the action at Jonesborough.
September 2.— [In action] at Ccdar Bluffs, Georgia.
September 8-October 4.— Returned to East Point, Georgia, arriving September 8 and remained there in camp until October 4, when it started with the command in pursuit of General [John Bell] Hood's Army to northern Georgia and Alabama.
October 31.— Then returned toward Atlanta, Georgia, arriving at Cave Spring, Georgia October 31, having marched during this time a distance of 200 miles.

Stationed at Savannah, Georgia, November-December 1864.
November 1.— The regiment moved from Cave Spring, Georgia on the return from the campaign in pursuit of the Rebel General Hood into northern Georgia and Alabama.
November 5-12.— Arrived at Vining's Station. Remained there in camp preparing for future operations until November 13, when it started with the Army of General [William Tecumseh] Sherman on the campaign through Georgia.
November 19-22.— Crossed the Ocmulgee River and participated in the battle of Duncan's Farm November 22.
December 10-21.— Crossed the Ogeechee River and encountered the enemy at Anderson's Plantation, eight miles from Savannah, and participated in the skirmishes and maneuvers before the city until December 21, when the enemy having evacuated [we] moved up with the command and encamped one and one-half miles from the city, having marched a distance of near 400 miles.

Stationed in the field, South Carolina, January-February 1865.
January 1.— The regiment was encamped near Savannah, Georgia.
January 10.— Broke camp and marched with the brigade to Thunderbolt.
January 12.— Embarked and arrived at Beaufort, South Carolina the same date.
January 27.— Broke camp at Beaufort and started with the command on the South Carolina campaign.
February 15-17.— Participated in the action at Congaree Creek [River] near Columbia, South Carolina and entered the city with the command on February 17.

February 25.— Reached Lynch's Creek, South Carolina, having marched a distance of 300 miles.

Stationed at Raleigh, North Carolina, March-April 1865.
March 1.— The regiment, with the command, moved from Lynch's Creek, South Carolina.
March 4.— Arrived at Cheraw, South Carolina.
March 12-13.— [Arrived at] Fayetteville, North Carolina, from where it moved on March 15.
March 20-21.— Participated in the battle of Bentonville, North Carolina, losing four men killed and eleven wounded.
March 23-24.— Moved from Bentonville, arriving at Goldsborough, North Carolina March 24.
April 10-14.— Remained in camp until April 10, when the command moved against the enemy's forces at Smithfield and Raleigh, quietly entering the latter on April 14.

Stationed at Louisville, Kentucky, May-June 1865.
May 1-7.— The regiment, with the brigade, broke camp near the Neuse River. Marched to Petersburg, Virginia, where it arrived on May 7.
May 9-10.— Renewed the march to Richmond, arriving on May 10.
May 12-22.— Recommenced the march to Washington, District of Columbia via Alexandria, arriving on May 22.
May 24-31.— Participated in the Grand Review and encamped until May 31, when it was transported by rail to Parkersburg, West Virginia.
June 4-30.— From thence by steamer to Louisville, Kentucky, arriving June 4, since when it has remained encamped in the vicinity of the city.

Regiment

Stationed at Camp No. 1, Tennessee, April 1862.

Stationed at camp, La Fayette, Tennessee, May 1862.

Station not stated, June-August 1862.

Station not stated, September 1862.
September 24.— By orders of Major-General W. T. Sherman, eight companies embarked on board the steamer *Ohio Belle* and two companies on board steamer *Eugene* and proceeded to Randolph, Tennessee, being a distance of sixty-five miles from Memphis.
September 25-26.— We landed [at Randolph] at about 7 a.m. to destroy the town, which was done, leaving but one house and a small church to mark the place. We also captured four prisoners, eighteen horses and mules and took possession of twenty-one bales of cotton. The regiment reembarked at 6 p.m., arriving in Memphis the next morning.

Station not stated, October-December 1862.

Stationed at Grand Junction, Tennessee, January 1863.

Station not stated, February-May 1862.

Stationed at Oak Ridge, Mississippi, June 1863.

Stationed at Camp Sherman, Mississippi, July-August 1863.

Station not stated, September-October 1863.

Stationed at Charleston, Tennessee, November 1863.

Stationed at Scottsborough, Alabama, December 1863-January 1864.

Station not stated, February-April 1864.

Stationed at camp in the field, near Dallas, Georgia, May 1864.

Station not stated, June-August 1864.

Stationed at East Point, Georgia, September 1864.

Stationed in the field, Georgia, October-November 1864.

Stationed at Savannah, Georgia, December 1864.

Stationed in the field, South Carolina, January-February 1865.

Stationed at Goldsborough, North Carolina, March 1865.

Stationed in the field, North Carolina, April 1865.

Stationed at Crystal Springs, District of Columbia, May 1865.

Stationed near Louisville, Kentucky, June 1865.

Company A

Stationed at Camp Lyon, near Worthington, Ohio, September 10-December 31, 1861.

Stationed at Camp Lyon, near Worthington, Ohio, October 15, 1861.
October 15.— Muster-in roll of Captain Joshua W. Heath's Company, in the forty-sixth Regiment of Ohio Foot Volunteers, commanded by Colonel Thomas Worthington, called into the service of the United States by the President from October 15, 1861 (date of this muster) for the term of three years, unless sooner discharged. The company was organized by Captain Joshua W. Heath at Van Wert in the month of September and marched thence to Camp Lyon, where it arrived September 16, a distance of 150 miles. . . .

[UNSIGNED],
Major,
Fifteenth Infantry, United States Army, Mustering Officer.

Stationed at Camp Washington, near Paducah, Kentucky, January-February 1862.

Station not stated, March-April 1862.

Stationed at camp, La Fayette, Tennessee, May-June 1862.

Stationed at Fort Pickering, July-August 1862.

Stationed at Fort Pickering, October 31, 1862.

Stationed at Holly Springs, November-December 1862.

Stationed at Grand Junction, Tennessee, January-February 1863.

Stationed at La Grange, Tennessee, March-April 1863.

Stationed at Oak Ridge, Mississippi, May-June 1863.

Stationed at Camp Sherman, Mississippi, July-August 1863.

Stationed at Florence, Alabama, September-October 1863.
September 28-29.— The company marched from camp, Big Black River, Mississippi to Vicksburg, arriving at Vicksburg on September 29. Embarked on steamer *John H. Groesbeck.*
October 9.— Arrived at Memphis, Tennessee on Friday, October 9.
October 11.— Started from Memphis going east on the State Line Road Sunday, October 11. Arriving at Collierville was started in pursuit of General [James Ronald] Chalmers after his attack on General Sherman, taking the road through Mount Pleasant to La Grange, Tennessee, then to Iuka, Mississippi via Corinth and from Iuka to Florence, Alabama via Eastport, Mississippi.

Stationed at Scottsborough, Alabama, November-December 1863.

The regiment marched from Florence, Alabama via Rogersville to Winchester, Tennessee, from there to Stevenson, Alabama, from there to Bridgeport. Crossed the Tennessee River. Passed over Sand Mountain to Trenton, Georgia. The regiment marched from there to Johnson's Gap. Ascended Lookout Mountain and drove off a regiment of Rebels. Marched back to Chattanooga via Trenton. Crossed the river. Was in the engagement of Missionary Ridge for two days. Followed the enemy as far as Graysville, Georgia. Marched from there to the relief of General [Ambrose Everett] Burnside at Knoxville, going within fourteen miles of Knoxville. Marched back to Bridgeport, Alabama and from there to Scottsborough, Alabama.

Stationed at Scottsborough, Alabama, January-February 1864.
[For record of events, see Field and Staff.]
January 1.— Forty members of the company were discharged by virtue of reenlistment as veteran volunteers.

Stationed at Scottsborough, Alabama, March-April 1864.

Stationed at camp in the field, near Kenesaw Mountain, Georgia, May-June 1864.
May 1-15.— The company marched from Scottsborough, Alabama, arriving at Resaca, Georgia and participated in the engagement there May 13, 14 and 15.
May 27-28.— From there the company marched to Dallas, Georgia and participated in the engagement at that place on May 27 and 28. Marched from thence to New Hope Chapel.
June 7.— From there to Acworth.
June 9.— Marched to Big Shanty on a reconnaissance. Returned to Acworth the same day.
June 10-15.— Marched to Big Shanty. Bivouacked until June 15, then moved to the extreme left of our lines and charged the enemy's outpost and took thirty-six prisoners. Had one man slightly wounded.
June 27-30.— The company participated in the charge on the Kenesaw Ridge [Mountain]. Had one corporal and one private killed and one first lieutenant and five privates wounded. From June 27 to 30 the company has been lying bivouacked with the regiment in front of Kenesaw Ridge [Mountain].

Stationed at Jonesborough, Georgia, July-August 1864.
July 2.— The company marched with the regiment in pursuit of the enemy from Kenesaw Mountain to the Chattahoochee River.
July 14.— Crossed the Chattahoochee.
July 22.— Marched to Atlanta via Decatur and participated in the battle at Atlanta Railroad July 22.
July 28.— [Engaged at] Ezra Church.
August 3-26.— [Engaged at] Lick Skillet Hollow. [Also engaged in] the numerous skirmishes near Atlanta August 3 to 26.
August 31.— [Engaged at] Jonesborough, Georgia.

Stationed in the field, Georgia, September-October 1864.
[For record of events, see Field and Staff.]

Stationed at Savannah, Georgia, November-December 1864.
[For record of events, see Field and Staff.]

Stationed in the field, South Carolina, January-February 1865.
[For record of events, see Field and Staff.]

Stationed at camp, near Raleigh, North Carolina, March-April 1865.
[For record of events, see Field and Staff.]
April 10-29.— Remained in camp until April 10, when with the regiment moved against the enemy at Smithfield and Raleigh, quietly entering the latter on April 14, where it lay in camp until April 29.

Stationed near Louisville, Kentucky, May-June 1865.
[For record of events, see Field and Staff.]

Company B

Station not stated, not dated.

Muster-in roll of Captain [Alonzo] G. Sharp's Company, in the Forty-sixth Regiment of Ohio Infantry Volunteers, commanded by Colonel Thomas Worthington, called into the service of the United States by the President from the dates set opposite their names, respectively, for the term of three years, unless sooner discharged. . . .

A. G. SHARP,
Second Lieutenant,
Recruiting Officer, Mustering Officer.

JACOB LOHRER,
Second Lieutenant,
Recruiting Officer, Mustering Officer.

GEORGE F. CRARY,
Recruiting Officer, Mustering Officer.

Stationed at Camp Lyon, near Worthington, Ohio, enrollment to December 31, 1861.

Stationed at Camp Washington, Kentucky, January-February 1862.

Station not stated, March-April 1862.
April 6-7.— The company was engaged in the battle of Pittsburg Landing, in which three men were killed.

Stationed at Fort Fayette, Tennessee, May-June 1862.

Stationed at Fort Pickering, July-October 1862.

Stationed at Holly Springs, November-December 1862.

Stationed at Grand Junction, Tennessee, January-February 1863.

Stationed at La Grange, Tennessee, March-April 1863.

Stationed at Oak Ridge, Mississippi, May-June 1863.

Stationed at Camp Sherman, Mississippi, July-August 1863.

Stationed at Florence, Alabama, September-October 1863.
[For record of events, see Company A.]

Stationed at Scottsborough, Alabama, November-December 1863.
The regiment marched from Florence, Alabama via Rogersville to Winchester, Tennessee, from Winchester to Stevenson, Alabama; thence to Bridgeport. Crossed the Tennessee River and Sand Mountain going to Trenton, Georgia. The regiment then marched to Johnson's Gap. Ascended Lookout Mountain at night, driving the enemy. We then proceeded to Chattanooga via Trenton, Georgia, crossing the river.
November 24.— In the morning we recrossed the river above Chattanooga and were detailed as skirmishers on that day.
November 25.— Were in the fight on Missionary Ridge. Followed the enemy two days, going as far as Graysville, Georgia.

From Graysville we marched to the relief of General Burnside at Knoxville, going within twelve miles of the city of Maryville. From Maryville to Athens; thence to Chattanooga; thence to Bridgeport, Alabama. From Bridgeport we marched to Scottsborough.

Stationed at Scottsborough, Alabama, January-February 1864.

The company has been encamped at Scottsborough, Alabama performing the duties of camp and picket guard, frequently going out with forage trains.

During January eighteen privates and ten noncommissioned officers were honorably discharged by virtue of reenlisting as veteran volunteers. The company has lately received new arms (Spencer rifles) from the United States government by Colonel Charles C. Walcutt, commanding company. The regiment has not yet received its furlough.

Stationed at Scottsborough, Alabama, March-April 1864.

March 8-April 21.— During the last two months the regiment has been at home on a veteran furlough, leaving Scottsborough March 8 and returning April 21.

Stationed in the field, Georgia, May-June 1864.

May 1-15.— The company marched with the regiment from Scottsborough, Alabama to Resaca, Georgia. Participated in the engagements on May 13, 14 and 15.

May 27-28.— From there to Dallas, Georgia, taking part in the battle on May 27 and 28.

June 10.— Thence to [Big Shanty], Georgia, participating in the fighting at Kenesaw [Mountain] from June 10 up to the present time.

Stationed at Jonesborough, Georgia, July-August 1864.

July 3.— In the a.m., the enemy having evacuated Kenesaw Mountain, the [company] marched in pursuit.

July 4.— Made a forced march and came upon the enemy late that night upon the Chattahoochee River and entrenched ourselves.

July 12.— Withdrew from our works and marched back to Marietta; thence to Roswell. Crossed the river and marched on the road to Decatur.

July 19.— Skirmished with the enemy at Cross Keys. Took possession of the Augusta Railroad leading to Atlanta, coming upon their works about sundown.
July 22.— Was attacked by the enemy in force but held our line.
July 27.— Marched from the left flank of the Army to the extreme right.
July 28.— Attacked the enemy, whom we repulsed with heavy loss.
August 3.— The company, with the regiment, charged the enemy's outer works, taking them with many prisoners.
August 26-31.— Withdrew from works before Atlanta and marched for some time for Jonesborough, coming upon the enemy in force, who attacked us on August 31 but were repulsed. Casualties, since last muster, four.

Stationed in the field, Georgia, September-October 1864.

Stationed at Savannah, Georgia, November-December 1864.
November 1.— The company was returning from the campaign after the Rebel General Hood in north Georgia.
November 5-13.— Reached Vining's Station on the Chattahoochee River and remained in camp until November 13, when we started with General Sherman's Army on the campaign through Georgia.
November 19.— Crossed Ocmulgee River.
November 22.— Participated in the battle at Duncan's Farm (Griswoldville).
December 10.— Crossed the Great Ogeechee River and encountered the enemy at Anderson's Plantation, eight miles from Savannah.
December 11-21.— Participated in the skirmishes and maneuvers before the city until December 21, when the enemy having evacuated, moved up with the regiment and encamped near the city.

Stationed at Lynch's Creek, South Carolina, January-February 1865.
[For record of events, see Field and Staff.]

Stationed in the field, North Carolina, March-April 1865.

Continued our march which at last muster was not completed.

March 4.— Entered Cheraw, South Carolina.
March 12.— [Entered] Fayetteville, North Carolina.
March 20.— Was engaged in the battle of Bentonville.
March 24.— Camped at Goldsborough, North Carolina.
April 11-29.— Resumed our march, entering Raleigh, North Carolina and remained in its vicinity until April 29, when we resumed our march northward.

Stationed near Louisville, Kentucky, May-June 1865.
[For record of events, see Field and Staff.]

Company C

Station not stated, not dated.

Muster-in roll of Captain John Wiseman's Company, in the Forty-sixth Regiment of Ohio Infantry Volunteers, commanded by Colonel T. Worthington, called into the service of the United States by the President from the dates set opposite their names, respectively, for the term of three years, unless sooner discharged. . . .

ALBERT [BALDWIN] DOD,
Captain,
Fifteenth Infantry, United States Army, Mustering Officer.

Stationed at Camp Lyon, near Worthington, Ohio, to October 31, 1861.

Stationed at Camp Lyon, near Worthington, Ohio, November-December 1861.

Station not stated, January-February 1862.

Stationed at Camp No. 4, March-April 1862.
April 6-7.— Fifty-nine of the company were engaged in the battle of Shiloh, Tennessee. Six were killed and twenty-three wounded.

Station not stated, May-June 1862.

Stationed at Fort Pickering, Memphis, Tennessee, July-October 1862.

Stationed at Holly Springs, Mississippi, November-December 1862.

Stationed at Grand Junction, Tennessee, January-February 1863.

Stationed at La Grange, Tennessee, March-April 1863.

Stationed at Snyder's Bluff, Mississippi, May-June 1863.

Stationed at Camp Sherman, Mississippi, July-August 1863.

Stationed at Florence, Alabama, September-October 1863.
September 29-30.— The company marched with the regiment from camp at Big Black River, Mississippi to Vicksburg, Mississippi. Started September 29 and arrived the following day, distance fifteen miles. Was put aboard the steamer *J. H. Groesbeck* September 30 and transported to Memphis, Tennessee.
October 9.— Arrived at the latter place, distance 400 miles. Marched from thence to Florence, Alabama via Corinth, Iuka and Eastport.
October 30.— Arrived at Florence, distance 160 miles.

Stationed at Scottsborough, Alabama, November-December 1863.
[For record of events, see Company A.]

Stationed at Scottsborough, Alabama, January-February 1864.
[For record of events, see Field and Staff.]
December 31.— Twenty-five members of the company were discharged by virtue of reenlistment as veteran volunteers. The company has lately received new arms. The Spencer rifles [were] procured from the United States government by C. C. Walcutt. The regiment has not as yet received its furlough.

Stationed at Scottsborough, Alabama, March-April 1864.

Stationed near Kenesaw Mountain, May-June 1864.
[For record of events, see Company B.]

Stationed in the field, Georgia, July-August 1864.
[For record of events, see Company A.]

Stationed in the field, Georgia, September-October 1864.
[For record of events, see Field and Staff.]

Stationed at Savannah, Georgia, November-December 1864.

Stationed in the field, South Carolina, January-February 1865.
[For record of events, see Field and Staff.]

Stationed at camp in the field, North Carolina, March-April 1865.
[For record of events, see Company A.]

Stationed near Louisville, Kentucky, May-June 1865.
[For record of events, see Field and Staff.]

Company D

Stationed at Camp Lyon, not dated.

Muster-in roll of Captain Harding C. Geary's Company, in the Forty-sixth Regiment of Ohio Infantry Volunteers, commanded by Colonel Thomas Worthington, called into the service of the United States by the President from the dates set opposite their names, respectively . . . for the term of three years, unless sooner discharged. . . .

ALBERT B. DOD,
Captain,
Fifteenth Infantry, United States Army, Mustering Officer.

Stationed at Camp Lyon, near Worthington, Ohio, to October 31, 1861.

Stationed at Camp Lyon, near Worthington, Ohio, November-December 1861.

Stationed at Paducah, January-February 1862.

Stationed at Camp No. 2, near Shiloh, Tennessee, March-April 1862.

April 6-7.— This company was in the battle of Shiloh, Tennessee on April 6. On April 7 most of the men served in different regiments, having been scattered the day before while retreating.

EDWARD N. UPTON,
First Lieutenant,
Commanding Company D, Forty-sixth Regiment,
Ohio Volunteer Infantry.

Stationed at La Fayette, Tennessee, May-June 1862.

Stationed at Fort Pickering, Memphis, Tennessee, July-October 1862.

Stationed at Holly Springs, Mississippi, November-December 1862.

Stationed at Grand Junction, Tennessee, January-February 1863.

Stationed at La Grange, Tennessee, March-April 1863.

Stationed at Oak Ridge, Mississippi, May-June 1863.

Stationed at Messinger's Ford, Mississippi, July-August 1863.

Stationed at Florence, Alabama, September-October 1863.
[For record of events, see Company A.]

Stationed at Scottsborough, Alabama, November-December 1863.
[For record of events, see Company A.]

Stationed at Scottsborough, Alabama, January-February 1864.
[For record of events, see Field and Staff.]
January 1.— Thirty-two members of the company and two from the noncommissioned staff were discharged by virtue of reenlistment as veteran volunteers. The company has lately received new arms, the Spencer rifles, procured from the United States government by Charles C. Walcutt, Colonel commanding. The regiment has not yet received its furlough.

Stationed at Scottsborough, Alabama, March-April 1864.
[For record of events, see Field and Staff.]

Stationed at Kenesaw Mountain, Georgia, May-June 1864.
May 1.— The company started with the regiment from Scottsborough, Alabama on the spring campaign and has marched from that place to Kenesaw Mountain, Georgia, where it is now stationed in front of the enemy.
May 14-15.— Participated in the battles of Resaca, Georgia.
May 25-June 4.— [Engaged at] Dallas, Georgia.
June 10-27.— [Engaged in] the battles in front of Big Shanty, Georgia since June 10, including a charge on Kenesaw Mountain June 27.

Stationed at Jonesborough, Georgia, July-August 1864.
[For record of events, see Company A.]

Stationed in the field, Alabama, September-October 1864.
[For record of events, see Field and Staff.]

Stationed at Savannah, Georgia, November-December 1864.
When last mustered the company, with the regiment, was returning from the pursuit of the Rebel General Hood.
November 6.— Arrived at Vining's Station near the Chattahoochee River, Georgia. The company went into camp. The company assisted in destroying the Atlanta Railroad. The company then drew clothing, every man fully equipped.
November 13-21.— The company campaigned against this city. Passing through the city of Atlanta the same [day], encamped opposite the city for two days, then took up our line of march through the state of Georgia on different roads too numerous to mention, meeting a force near Griswoldville, Georgia November 21.
November 22-December 11.— Was attacked by the Georgia Militia, which we repulsed with heavy loss, and arrived within eight miles of this city on December 11.
December 20.— At night the enemy evacuated the city. Marched since leaving Vining's Station 337 miles.

Stationed at Lynch's Creek, South Carolina, January-February 1865.
[For record of events, see Field and Staff.]

Stationed at Rogers' Cross-Roads, North Carolina, March-April 1865.
[For record of events, see Field and Staff.]

Stationed near Louisville, Kentucky, May-June 1865.
May 1-8.— The company, with the regiment, broke camp on the Neuse River and marched to Petersburg, Virginia, where it arrived on May 8 and bivouacked.
May 10-22.— It marched to Richmond, Virginia, arriving there on May 12, when it left for Washington, District of Columbia via Alexandria. Arrived there on May 22.
May 24.— Participated in the Grand Review.
May 31-June 30.— Commenced transportation by rail to Parkersburg, [West] Virginia, where it embarked on steamers for Louisville, Kentucky, where it arrived on June 4. Encamped near the city, where it remained until June 30.

Company E

Station not stated, not dated.

Muster-in roll of Captain William Pinney's Company, in the Forty-sixth Regiment of Ohio Infantry Volunteers, commanded by Colonel Thomas Worthington, called into the service of the United States by the President from the dates set opposite their names, respectively, for the term of three years, unless sooner discharged. The company was organized by Captain William Pinney at Worthington, Ohio in the months of September, October and November and marched thence to Camp Lyon. . . .

WILLIAM PINNEY,
Mustering Officer.

WILLIAM NESSLER,
Lieutenant,
Mustering Officer.

[WILLIAM] W. WATTS,
Lieutenant,
Mustering Officer.

Stationed at Camp Lyon, near Worthington, Ohio, to December 31, 1861.

Stationed at Camp Washington, Paducah, Kentucky, January-February 1862.

Stationed at Camp No. 2, Tennessee, March-April 1862.
April 6-7.— The company was engaged in the battle at Shiloh or Pittsburg Landing, in which engagement those marked wounded received their injuries.

Station not stated, May-June 1862.

Stationed at Fort Pickering, July-October 1862.

Stationed at Holly Springs, Mississippi, November-December 1862.

Stationed at Grand Junction, Tennessee, January-February 1863.

Stationed at La Grange, Tennessee, March-April 1863.

Stationed at Oak Ridge, Mississippi, May-June 1863.

Stationed at Camp Sherman, Mississippi, July-August 1863.

Stationed at Florence, Alabama, September-October 1863.
Marched with the regiment from Camp Sherman, Mississippi to Florence, Alabama via Memphis, Tennessee.

Stationed at Scottsborough, Alabama, November-December 1863.

Stationed at Scottsborough, Alabama, January-February 1864.
[For record of events, see Field and Staff.]
January 1.— Thirty-seven members of the company were discharged by virtue of reenlistment as veteran volunteers. The company has lately received new arms (Spencer repeating rifles) from the United States government by Colonel Charles C. Walcutt, commanding Second Brigade, Fourth Division, Fifteenth Army Corps. The regiment has not yet received its furlough.

Stationed at Scottsborough, Alabama, March-April 1864.

Stationed in the field, near Kenesaw Mountain, Georgia, May-June 1864.
[For record of events, see Company A.]
June 10.— Had one man killed and three wounded.
June 27.— Lost two men missing in action, supposed to be killed.

Stationed at Jonesborough, Georgia, July-August 1864.
July 3.— The company marched in company with the regiment via Kenesaw Mountain to Marietta, Georgia. Bivouacked for the night.
July 4.— Made a forced march, coming up with the enemy at the Chattahoochee River at dark. Threw up entrenchments during the night.
July 12.— Marched via Marietta and Roswell, crossing the Chattahoochee River at Roswell, marching out on the Stone Mountain Road.
July 18.— Skirmished with the enemy at Cross Keys.
July 19.— Participated in the occupation of the Augusta Railroad at Decatur.
July 20.— Skirmished with the enemy in front of Atlanta.
July 22.— Was engaged in repulsing an attack of the enemy and succeeding in holding our line.
July 21.— Marched to Ezra Chapel.
July 28.— Was engaged for six hours in repulsing an attack of the enemy.
July 31.— Advanced the line. Had one man killed.
August 3-25.— Charged the enemy's outer line and driving him from and holding it had one man killed and two wounded. Until August 25 were engaged in entrenching the line, constantly skirmishing with the enemy.
August 26-30.— Marched via . . . to Jonesborough, Georgia, twenty-six miles southeast of Atlanta, arriving at dark on August 30.
August 31.— Participated in repulsing an attack of the enemy, holding our line and capturing five prisoners.

Stationed in the field, Georgia, September-October 1864.
[For record of events, see Field and Staff.]

Stationed at Savannah, Georgia, November-December 1864.
[For record of events, see Company B.]

Stationed in the field, South Carolina, January-February 1865.
[For record of events, see Field and Staff.]

Stationed near Raleigh, North Carolina, March-April 1865.
[For record of events, see Field and Staff.]

Stationed at Louisville, Kentucky, May-June 1865.
[For record of events, see Company D.]

Company F

Stationed at Camp Lyon, December 16, 1861.

Muster-in roll of Captain Henry H. Giesy's Company F, in the Forty-sixth Regiment of Ohio Volunteers, commanded by Colonel Thomas Worthington, called into the service of the United States by the President from the dates set opposite their names, respectively, for the term of three years, unless sooner discharged. . . .

H. H. GIESY,
Second Lieutenant,
Forty-sixth Regiment, Ohio Volunteer Infantry, Mustering Officer.

[CHARLES] H. RICE,
Second Lieutenant,
Forty-sixth Regiment, Ohio Volunteer Infantry, Mustering Officer.

Stationed at Camp Lyon, near Worthington, Ohio, December 31, 1861.

Stationed at Camp Washington, Paducah, Kentucky, January-February 1862.

Stationed at Camp No. 2, March-April 1862.
April 6-7.— This company in the battle of Shiloh, Tennessee.

H. H. GIESY,
Captain.

Stationed at La Fayette Station, Tennessee, May-June 1862.

Stationed at Fort Pickering, August 18, 1862.

Stationed at Memphis, Tennessee, July-August 1862.

Stationed at Fort Pickering, Memphis, Tennessee, September-October 1862.

Stationed at Holly Springs, November-December 1862.

Stationed at Grand Junction, Tennessee, January-February 1863.

Stationed at La Grange, Tennessee, March-April 1863.

Stationed at Oak Ridge, Mississippi, May-June 1863.

Stationed at Camp Sherman, Mississippi, July-August 1863.

Stationed at Florence, Alabama, September-October 1863.
[For record of events, see Company A.]

Stationed at Scottsborough, Alabama, November-December 1863.
November 1.— The company left Florence, Alabama on or about November 1. Marched to Bridgeport, Alabama via Rogersville and Winchester. Crossed the Tennessee River there and marched to Trenton, Georgia, across Sand Mountain; thence to Johnson's Gap. Ascended Lookout Mountain. Skirmished with and routed a portion of the enemy there. Crossed the Tennessee River below Chattanooga and moved up the north bank of the Tennessee River above Chattanooga to the mouth of Chickamauga River.
November 24-25.— Crossed the Tennessee River there again and was engaged two days in the action of Missionary Ridge November 24 and 25. From thence followed the retreating enemy to

Graysville, Georgia; thence proceeded towards Knoxville via Cleveland, Charleston and Morganton.
December 5.— Arrived at Maryville.
December 7-19.— Left Maryville for Bridgeport, Alabama via Chattanooga, Tennessee and arrived there December 19.
December 24-28.— Left Bridgeport and arrived at Scottsborough via Stevenson December 28.

Stationed at Scottsborough, Alabama, January-February 1864.

The company has been stationed at this place doing guard and picket duty the past two months.
January 1.— It reenlisted as veteran volunteers.
January 25.— Was mustered into service by Lieutenant Carn, Assistant Commissary of Musters.

Stationed at Scottsborough, Alabama, March-April 1864.

Stationed in the field, near Kenesaw Mountain, Georgia, May-June 1864.
May 1.— Since May 1 the company marched with the regiment from Scottsborough, Alabama via Chattanooga, Tennessee to Resaca, Georgia.
May 13-15.— Participated in the battle of Resaca.
May 27-28.— Thence to Dallas, Georgia and participated in the battle of Dallas.
June 15, 27.— From thence to Kenesaw Mountain and participated in the charges made on the enemy June 15 and 27 and are now in line of battle in front of the enemy at Kenesaw Mountain.

Stationed at Jonesborough, Georgia, July-August 1864.
[For record of events, see Company A.]

Stationed in the field, Georgia, September-October 1864.
[For record of events, see Field and Staff.]

Stationed at Savannah, Georgia, November-December 1864.
[For record of events, see Company B.]

Stationed in the field, South Carolina, January-February 1865.
[For record of events, see Field and Staff.]

Stationed at camp in the field, North Carolina, March-April 1865.
[For record of events, see Field and Staff.]

Stationed at Louisville, Kentucky, May-June 1865.
[For record of events, see Company D.]

Company G

Station not stated, not dated.

Muster-in roll of Captain Philip A. Crow's Company, in the Forty-sixth Regiment of Ohio Infantry Volunteers, commanded by Colonel Thomas Worthington, called into the service of the United States by the President from the dates set opposite their names, respectively, for the term of three years, unless sooner discharged. The company was organized by Captain Philip A. Crow at Worthington, Ohio . . . and marched thence to Camp Lyon. . . .

PHILIP A. CROW,
Mustering Officer.

ALONZO G. SHARP,
Mustering Officer.

Stationed at Camp Lyon, near Worthington, Ohio, to December 31, 1861.

Stationed at Paducah, Kentucky, January-February 1862.

Station not stated, March-June 1862.

Stationed at Fort Pickering, Tennessee, July-August 1862.

Stationed at Memphis, Tennessee, September-October 1862.

Stationed at Holly Springs, November-December 1862.

Stationed at Grand Junction, Tennessee, January-February 1863.

Stationed at La Grange, Tennessee, March-April 1863.

Stationed at Oak Ridge, Mississippi, May-June 1863.

Stationed at Camp Sherman, Mississippi, July-August 1863.

Stationed at Florence, Alabama, September-October 1863.
September 28-29.— The company marched from camp on Big Black River, Mississippi towards Vicksburg. Arrived at Vicksburg on September 29. There embarked on the steamer *J. H. Groesbeck*. Proceeded up the Mississippi River.
October 9.— Arrived at Memphis, Tennessee. Went into camp east of the city.
October 11-27.— Marched from Memphis east to Collierville, Tennessee. Thence south to Mount Pleasant, Tennessee, following up General Chalmers immediately after his attack on Collierville; thence to La Grange, Tennessee; thence east to Iuka, Mississippi via Corinth, Mississippi; thence east to Florence, Alabama via Eastport, Mississippi. Arrived at Florence on October 27.

Stationed at Scottsborough, Alabama, November-December 1863.
The regiment marched from Florence, Alabama via Rogersville to Winchester, Tennessee. From there to Stevenson, Alabama. From there to Bridgeport. Crossed the Tennessee River. Passed over Sand Mountain to Trenton, Georgia. The regiment marched from there to Johnson's Gap. Ascended Lookout Mountain and drove off a regiment of Rebels. Marched back to Chattanooga via Trenton. Crossed the river. Was in the engagement of Missionary Ridge for two days. Followed the enemy as far as Georgia. Marched from there to the relief of General Burnside at Knoxville, going within sixteen miles of Knoxville. Marched back to Athens, Tennessee. From there to Chattanooga. From there to Bridgeport, Alabama and from there to Scottsborough, Alabama.

Stationed at Scottsborough, Alabama, January-February 1864.
[For record of events, see Company C.]
December 31.— Twenty-four members of the company were discharged by virtue of reenlistment as veteran volunteers. . . .

Stationed at Scottsborough, Alabama, March-April 1864.

Stationed near Kenesaw Mountain, May-June 1864.
[For record of events, see Company D.]

Stationed in the field, Georgia, July-August 1864.
[For record of events, see Company A.]

Stationed at Cave Spring, Georgia, September-October 1864.
[For record of events, see Field and Staff.]

Stationed at Savannah, Georgia, November-December 1864.
[For record of events, see Company B.]

Stationed in the field, North Carolina, January-February 1865.
[For record of events, see Field and Staff.]

Stationed near Raleigh, North Carolina, March-April 1865.
[For record of events, see Field and Staff.]

Stationed at Louisville, Kentucky, May-June 1865.

Company H

Station not stated, not dated.

Muster-in roll of Captain Mitchel C. Lilley's Company H, in the Forty-sixth Regiment of Ohio Foot Volunteers . . . called into the service of the United States by the President . . . for the term of three years, unless sooner discharged, from the dates set opposite their names, respectively. . . .

M. C. LILLEY,
Mustering Officer.

Stationed at Camp Lyon, near Worthington, Ohio, enrollment to December 31, 1861.

Stationed at Camp Washington, Kentucky, January-February 1862.

Stationed at Camp No. 2, Tennessee, March-April 1862.

Stationed at La Fayette, Tennessee, May-June 1862.

Stationed at Fort Pickering, July-August 1862.

Stationed at Fort Pickering, September-October 1862.
September 25-27.— Marched with the regiment to the town of Randolph, Tipton County, Tennessee and returned to Fort Pickering on September 27.

Stationed at camp, near Holly Springs, Mississippi, November-December 1862.

Stationed at Grand Junction, Tennessee, January-February 1863.

Stationed at La Grange, Tennessee, March-April 1863.

Stationed at Oak Ridge, Mississippi, May-June 1863.

Stationed at Camp Sherman, Mississippi, July-August 1863.

Stationed at Florence, Alabama, September-October 1863.

Stationed at Scottsborough, Alabama, November-December 1863.
[For record of events, see Company G.]

Stationed at Scottsborough, Alabama, January-February 1864.
[For record of events, see Field and Staff.]
January 1.— Twenty-three members of the company and one from the noncommissioned staff were discharged by virtue of reenlistment as veteran volunteers with the agreement that they were to have a furlough of thirty days within the limits of their respective states, which they have not yet received. . . .

Stationed at Scottsborough, Alabama, March-April 1864.
March 8-12.— Since last mustered the company remained at Scottsborough, Alabama doing the usual camp duties until March 8, when they started homeward on their veteran furlough, arriving at Columbus, Ohio on the evening of March 12 and reported to the governor of the states.
March 14.— The veterans were furloughed on March 14 for thirty days.

April 14-15.— The veterans reported for duty at the Tod Barracks. Remained at Tod Barracks April 15.
April 16.— Started for the front by the way of Cincinnati and Nashville.
April 20.— Arrived at Scottsborough. Remained in camp since we came back, doing the usual camp duties.

Stationed near Big Shanty, Georgia, May-June 1864.
[For record of events, see Company A.]
June 27.— Had one sergeant killed.

Stationed at Jonesborough, Georgia, July-August 1864.

Stationed in the field, Georgia, September-October 1864.
[For record of events, see Field and Staff.]

Stationed at Savannah, Georgia, November-December 1864.
[For record of events, see Company D.]

Stationed at Lynch's Creek, South Carolina, January-February 1865.
[For record of events, see Field and Staff.]

Stationed at Rogers' Cross-Roads, March-April 1865.
[For record of events, see Field and Staff.]

Stationed at Louisville, Kentucky, May-June 1865.
[For record of events, see Company D.]

Company I

Station not stated, not dated.

Muster-in roll of Captain [Charles] L. Ly Brand's Company, in the Forty-sixth Regiment of Ohio Foot Volunteers . . . called into the service of the United States by the President from the dates set opposite their names, respectively, for the term of three years, unless sooner discharged. . . .

C. L. LY BRAND,
Mustering Officer.

M. C. LILLEY,
Captain,
Company H, Mustering Officer.

P. A. CROW,
Captain,
Company F, Mustering Officer.

W. W. WATTS,
Lieutenant,
Company C, Mustering Officer.

GEORGE P. CRAY,
Mustering Officer.

A. G. SHARP,
Captain,
Company B, Mustering Officer.

JOHN WISEMAN,
Captain,
Company C, Mustering Officer.

[AMOS] G. [or L.] PARKS,
Lieutenant,
Company I, Mustering Officer.

WILLIAM PINNEY,
Captain,
Company E, Mustering Officer.

Stationed at Camp Washington, near Paducah, Kentucky, January-February 1862.

Stationed at camp, Headquarters, First Brigade, Fifth Division, west of Pittsburg, Tennessee, March-April 1862.

Stationed at Memphis, Tennessee, May-June 1862.

Stationed at Fort Pickering, July-October 1862.

Stationed at Holly Springs, Mississippi, November-December 1862.

Stationed at Grand Junction, Tennessee, January-February 1863.

Stationed at La Grange, Tennessee, March-April 1863.

Stationed at Oak Ridge, Mississippi, May-June 1863.

Stationed at Camp Sherman, Mississippi, July-August 1863.

Stationed at Florence, Alabama, September-October 1863.
[For record of events, see Company A.]

Stationed at Scottsborough, Alabama, November-December 1863.
The company marched from Florence, Alabama to Bridgeport, Alabama via Fayetteville, Tennessee. From thence to Trenton, Georgia. Thence to Johnson's Creek.
November 20.— Was in the regiment when engaged in driving a Rebel regiment of mounted infantry from the top of Lookout Mountain. Held that point two days to November 20.
November 22.— Marched via Trenton to near Chattanooga.
November 24.— Crossed the Tennessee River against the enemy. Was in the advance to take the first point of Missionary Ridge.
November 25.— Was with the regiment in action on Missionary Ridge.
November 26.— Marched at 6 a.m. for Knoxville. Marched as far as Maryville, 100 miles from Chattanooga.
December 5.— Marched back on the road to Chattanooga via Madison and from thence to Scottsborough via Bridgeport and Stevenson, Alabama, making a march of about 450 miles.

Stationed at Scottsborough, Alabama, January-February 1864.
[For record of events, see Company E.]

January 1.— Nineteen members of the company and one from noncommissioned staff were discharged by virtue of reenlistment as veteran volunteers. . . .

Stationed at Scottsborough, Alabama, March-April 1864.

Stationed in the field, Georgia, May-June 1864.
[For record of events, see Company B.]

Stationed at Jonesborough, Georgia, July-August 1864.
[For record of events, see Company B.]

Stationed in the field, Georgia, September-October 1864.
October 2.— In the morning we found the enemy had evacuated their line of works at Jonesborough under cover of the night. The company with the regiment went in pursuit. Came upon the enemy's rear guard just south of Jonesborough, Georgia. Drove them some three miles south, where we discovered they have formed in line of battle. The company with the regiment charged and carried the enemy's outer line of works, taking many prisoners.
September 5-8.— We entrenched ourselves, where we remained until September 5, when the Army was withdrawn to East Point, Georgia, where we arrived on September 8.
October 4.— We rested here until October 4, when the company with the regiment was again put on the move in pursuit of the Rebel General Hood, who was attempting a raid upon our communications. The company with the regiment participated in all the marches after Hood, performing a march of over 300 miles. Casualties, since last muster, one man.

Stationed at Chattanooga, Tennessee, October 26, 1864.
October 26.— Muster-out roll of Captain Lucius A. Bowers' Company I, in the Forty-sixth Regiment of Ohio Infantry Volunteers, commanded by Lieutenant-Colonel [Isaac] N. Alexander, called into the service of the United States by the President, thereof, at Worthington, Ohio (the place of general rendezvous) on January 24, 1862 to serve for the term of three years from the date of enrollment, unless sooner discharged, from December 31, 1863 (when last paid) to October ——, 1864 when discharged.

The company was organized by Captain C. S. Ly Brand at Worthington, Ohio in the month of December 1861. . . .

RICHARD ROWAN,
Lieutenant,
Thirteenth Infantry, Assistant Commissary of Musters,
First Division, Fifteenth Army Corps, Mustering Officer.

Stationed at Savannah, Georgia, November-December 1864.
[For record of events, see Company B.]

Stationed in the field, South Carolina, January-February 1865.
[For record of events, see Field and Staff.]

Stationed near Raleigh, North Carolina, March-April 1865.
[For record of events, see Field and Staff.]

Stationed at Louisville, Kentucky, May-June 1865.
[For record of events, see Company D.]

Company K

Station not stated, not dated.

Muster-in roll of Captain William Smith's Company, in the Forty-sixth Regiment of Ohio Infantry Volunteers, commanded by Colonel T. Worthington, called into the service of the United States by the President from the dates set opposite their names, respectively, for the term of three years, unless sooner discharged. . . .

WILLIAM SMITH,
Captain,
Forty-sixth Regiment, Ohio Volunteer Infantry, Mustering Officer.

Stationed at Camp Lyon, near Worthington, Ohio, to December 31, 1861.

Station not stated, January-April 1862.

Stationed at Fort La Fayette, Fayette County, Tennessee, May-June 1862.

Stationed at Fort Pickering, near Memphis, Tennessee, August 18, 1862.

The company engaged in the Tennessee expedition.

April 6-7.— [Engaged in the] battle of Shiloh.

July 21.— Thence marched on Corinth; thence to Chewalla, La Grange, La Fayette, and Memphis, where it arrived July 21.

Stationed at Fort Pickering, Memphis, Tennessee, July-August 1862.

Stationed at Fort Pickering, Tennessee, September-October 1862.

The clothing account of all the members of the company is correctly stated in the column of figures above. No deduction is made for their allowance but the men having stated by affidavit under oath the cash value of clothing unavoidably lost by them in action at Shiloh April 6 and 7. The cash value is deducted therefrom.

I. N. ALEXANDER,
Captain,
Company K.

Station not stated, November-December 1862.

Stationed at Grand Junction, Tennessee, January-February 1863.

Stationed at La Grange, Tennessee, March-April 1863.

Stationed at Oak Ridge, Mississippi, May-June 1863.

June 11.— Since last muster the regiment has moved from La Grange, Tennessee to Snyder's Bluff, Mississippi on the Yazoo River, where it arrived June 11.

June 23.— Again marched and arrived at Oak Ridge Post Office, Mississippi.

Stationed at Camp Sherman, Mississippi, July-August 1863.

Stationed at Florence, Alabama, September-October 1863.

[For record of events, see Company A.]

Stationed at Scottsborough, Alabama, November-December 1863.
[For record of events, see Company G.]

Stationed at Scottsborough, Alabama, January-March 1864.

Stationed at camp in the field, near Kenesaw Mountain, Georgia, May-June 1864.
[For record of events, see Company F.]

Stationed at Jonesborough, Georgia, July-August 1864.

Stationed in the field, Georgia, September-October 1864.
[For record of events, see Field and Staff.]

Stationed at Savannah, Georgia, November-December 1864.
[For record of events, see Company B.]

Stationed in the field, South Carolina, January-February 1865.
[For record of events, see Field and Staff.]

Stationed in the field, North Carolina, March-April 1865.
[For record of events, see Field and Staff.]

Stationed at Louisville, Kentucky, May-June 1865.
[For record of events, see Company D.]

[M594-Roll #150]

Record of Events for Forty-seventh Ohio Infantry, June 1861-June 1865.

Field and Staff

Stationed at Camp Anderson, [West] Virginia, June 15-October 31, 1861.

Stationed at Camp Dennison, Ohio, August 27, 1861.
August 27.— Muster-in roll of the commissioned and noncommissioned staff officers of the Forty-seventh Regiment of Ohio Volunteers, commanded by Colonel [Frederick] Poschner, called into the service of the United States by the President from August 27, —— (date of this muster) for the term of three years, unless sooner discharged. . . .

[THOMAS WOODRUFF] WALKER,
Mustering Officer.

Station not stated, January-February 1862.

Stationed at Gauley Mountain, March-April 1862.

Stationed at Meadow Bluff, [West] Virginia, May-June 1862.

Stationed at Post Ewing, [West] Virginia, August 18, 1862.

Station not stated, July-October 1862.

Stationed at Gauley Mountain, [West] Virginia, November-December 1862.

Stationed at camp in front of Vicksburg, January-February 1863.

Station not stated, March-April 1863.

Stationed at Walnut Hill, Mississippi, May-June 1863.

Stationed at Camp Sherman, Mississippi, July-August 1863.

Stationed at Chickasaw, Alabama, September-October 1863.

Stationed at Bellefonte, Alabama, November-December 1863.

Stationed at Cleveland, Tennessee, January-February 1864.

Stationed near Jonesborough, Georgia, July-August 1864.

Stationed at Cave Spring, Georgia, September-October 1864.

Stationed near Savannah, Georgia, November-December 1864.

Stationed at Lynch's Creek, [South] Carolina, January-February 1865.

Stationed in the field, Wake County, North Carolina, March-April 1865.

Stationed at Memphis, Tennessee, May-June 1865.

Regiment

Stationed at Gauley Mountain, [West] Virginia, April 1862.

Stationed at camp, Cotton Hill, [West] Virginia, October 1862.

Stationed at Gauley Mountain, [West] Virginia, November 1862.

Stationed at camp opposite Vicksburg, Mississippi, January 1863.

Stationed at camp at Young's Point, Louisiana, February 1863.

Stationed at camp at Young's Point, Louisiana, March 1863.
March 17.— In the morning the entire regiment left camp at Young's Point, Louisiana to join an expedition under command of Major-General [William Tecumseh] Sherman. We embarked at the landing and proceeded thirty-three miles up the Mississippi River to Eagle Bend, where we constructed bridges across two crevasses in Muddy Bayou. From thence we proceeded up Steele's and Black Bayous until arriving at the junction of Deer Creek and Black Bayou. We remained there nearly three days, when we received orders to embark.
March 27.— We started down Steele's Bayou and reached our camp at Young's Point on the afternoon of March 27, after being absent ten days.

Stationed at camp at Young's Point, Louisiana, April 1863.

Stationed at camp at Walnut Hill, Mississippi, May 1863.

I have the honor to make the following report of the Forty-seventh Regiment, Ohio Volunteer Infantry in the marches from Young's Point, Louisiana to our present position in the rear of Vicksburg. Also the part taken by said regiment in the late engagements at this place.

May 13-15.— We left Young's Point, Louisiana and reached Bowers' Landing, Louisiana in the afternoon of the same day. We remained there until May 15, when we embarked on transports and were conveyed to Grand Gulf, Mississippi, arriving there at 2 o'clock p.m. We marched seven miles farther and encamped for the night.

May 18.— We reached camp in the rear of Vicksburg in the evening, having marched seventy miles in three days. We caught about 200 Rebels on the march.

May 19.— Made a charge on the enemy's works. Were repulsed with a loss of fifty-one killed, wounded and missing.

May 22.— Made another charge and were repulsed as before with a loss of thirty-three killed and wounded. Lost in skirmishing from May 19 to the present time two killed and wounded. The names of the wounded and missing are stated above.

Stationed at Walnut Hill, Mississippi, June 1863.

Stationed at Camp Sherman, Mississippi, July 1863.

I have the honor to make the following report of the part taken by the Forty-seventh Regiment of Ohio Infantry Volunteers in the late expedition to Jackson, Mississippi.

July 4.— In the evening we received orders to march on the following morning. The column was put in motion.

July 6-18.— Crossed the Black River in the afternoon and were assigned to a position in front of Jackson, Mississippi, where we remained skirmishing with the enemy until the morning of July 18, when we marched into town, the enemy having fled the night previous.

July 23-25.— We remained in Jackson doing provost duty until the morning of July 23, when the column was again put in motion. Arrived at our present encampment in the afternoon of July 25.

Stationed at Camp Sherman, August 1863.

Stationed on board steamer [Benjamin] J. Adams, September 1863.

September 26-28.— The regiment received marching orders on the evening of September 26. Left Camp Sherman, Mississippi on the following morning en route for Vicksburg. Arrived there on the afternoon of the same day and embarked from thence September 28 on steamer *Benjamin J. Adams*.

Stationed at Chickasaw, Alabama, October 1863.

October 3.— We disembarked from steamer *Benjamin J. Adams* at Memphis, Tennessee.

October 6-15.— In the afternoon received orders to march immediately. We left Memphis at 4 o'clock p.m. and marched to Germantown, where we were detailed to guard the Fifteenth Army Corps train to Corinth, Mississippi, a distance of ninety-six miles, arriving there on October 15.

October 17-19.— We left Corinth. Arrived at Iuka on October 18 and on October 19 took up our march to Tuscumbia, Alabama.

October 27-31.— We entered the town after a brisk skirmish by the advance of our brigade and in the afternoon marched to South Florence on the Tennessee River, returning to Tuscumbia the same evening. On the morning of the next day we commenced to retrace our steps as far as Cherokee Station and on the following morning took up our march again, arriving at this place on October 31 at 11 o'clock p.m.

Stationed in the field, November 1863.

November 2.— We crossed the Tennessee River on steamer *Masonic Gem* and went into camp four miles from Waterloo, Alabama.

November 3-4.— In the morning we took up our march to Florence, Alabama, where we arrived on November 4, a distance of twenty-seven miles from Waterloo.

November 5.— In the morning we left for Athens but at Rogersville our march was changed towards Pulaski, thus leaving the Huntsville Road.

November 8.— At 10 a.m. we passed through Pulaski, fifty miles distant from Florence by the route traveled. At Pulaski our line of march was changed to Bellefonte.
November 10-12.— We passed through Gaylesville, camping at New Market on the night of November 12, reaching Bellefonte, distant 106 miles from Pulaski.
November 15-17.— At noon, on reaching Bellefonte, received orders to march to Bridgeport, Alabama and passed Stevenson on November 16 and reached Bridgeport, distance twenty-eight miles from Bellefonte on November 17.
November 19-20.— We took up our march for Chattanooga, Tennessee, camping in Lookout Valley on November 20.
November 21.— Crossed the pontoon bridge and went into camp with the rest of our Corps.
November 23.— During the night we crossed the Tennessee River near the mouth of the Chickamauga Creek in pontoon boats and built works in the valley near to and facing the left of Missionary Ridge.
November 24.— In the morning we took possession of a portion of Missionary Ridge, driving the enemy before us, having one man slightly wounded. At night we threw up temporary works.
November 25.— In the morning six companies were sent out as skirmishers to protect the flank of the Thirtieth and Thirty-seventh Ohio, who had orders to drive the enemy from an important position in our immediate front. Two [of] our men were wounded this day. The remaining four companies were left in support of a battery in the works thrown up the night previous. During the night the Rebels evacuated their works.
November 26.— At 7 a.m. we left our position and started in pursuit, camping for the night two miles beyond Chickamauga Station.
November 28.— Reached Graysville or Johnson's Station, where we burned a mill, railroad depot building and factory used for making gun stocks, etc. by the so-called Confederate States.
November 29-30.— Started for Cleveland through which we passed on November 30, camping for the night eight miles beyond Cleveland on the road to Charleston and three miles from the latter place. Distance marched from Bridgeport, Alabama to our bivouac of the night of November 30, eighty-seven miles. Whole distance marched during the month 308 miles.

Stationed at camp at Bellefonte Station, Alabama, December 1863.
December 1.— In the morning we commenced our march for the relief of General [Ambrose Everett] Burnside at Knoxville with orders to subsist on the country through which we should pass. We crossed the Hiwassee River at Charleston and passed Sweet Water Station on the East Tennessee and Georgia Railroad.
December 3-9.— Reached the Little Tennessee River at Morgantown, having marched fifty miles. Built a bridge over the Little Tennessee River and reached Maryville, seventeen miles beyond, on December 5. General [James] Longstreet having fallen back from Knoxville, we recrossed the Tennessee River and started for Tellico Iron Works, arriving there on December 9, having marched forty-one miles since leaving Maryville. Our cavalry [was] out on the Murphy Pike as a support to within one mile of the North Carolina Line. Upon their return we commenced our return to Chattanooga.
December 17.— We reached the latter place, having marched ninety-eight miles since leaving Tellico Iron Works.
December 18-29.— We left Chattanooga and reached this place (Bellefonte Station, Alabama) on December 29, having marched fifty-five miles since leaving Chattanooga. Whole distance marched during the month 261 miles.

Stationed in the field, January 1864.
January 9.— The regiment remained at Bellefonte Station, Alabama until the morning of January 9, when we left camp pursuant to orders and started for Larkinsville, Alabama, arriving there on the afternoon of the same day.
January 24-25.— At 6 o'clock p.m. we left camp at Larkinsville and started on an expedition to Larkin's Ford, Alabama on the Tennessee River, distant eleven miles, arriving there at midnight. Scouted along the riverbank and returned to camp on the afternoon of January 25.
January 26-27.— On our return received marching orders and left camp in the morning, taking again the road to Larkin's Ford. The same evening we crossed the Tennessee River in pontoons and reached Wakefield, Alabama, distant sixteen miles, at 7

o'clock a.m. of January 27. About noon we started on our return and reached Larkin's Ford at 6 p.m., where we recrossed the river.
January 30-31.— We started with a detachment of the Corps. Crossed the river on a pontoon bridge and camped that night and the following day near Jones' Gap, or the Narrows, distant from the river twelve miles. Whole distance marched during the month 100 miles.

Stationed at Cleveland, Tennessee, February 1864.
February 1-2.— We left Jones' Gap, or the Narrows, in the morning and reached Lebanon, Alabama on February 2.
February 3-6.— At noon we started on our return to Larkinsville, where we arrived on February 6, having marched sixty-two miles since leaving Jones' Gap.
February 11-17.— Received marching orders and started for Bridgeport. Arrived there on February 13 and were put under the command of Brigadier-General [Charles Leopold] Matthies, commanding a detachment of the Fifteenth Army Corps. Proceeded then with the command to Chattanooga and thence to Cleveland, Tennessee, where we arrived on February 17, having marched 100 miles since leaving Larkinsville. Whole distance marched during the month 162 miles. The regiment reenlisted as veterans during the month and await muster.

Station not stated, March-April 1864.
The regiment on veteran furlough to Ohio.

Stationed in the field, near Dallas, Georgia. May 1864.
March 1-5.— We received orders to move. Left Cleveland, Tennessee the same morning and arrived at Larkinsville, Alabama on March 5, a distance of 100 miles.
March 18.— The regiment started as an organization on veteran furlough to Ohio.
April 24.— Said furlough expired.
April 27-May 6.— We assembled at Camp Dennison, Ohio and started from thence to the front. Reaching Stevenson, Alabama, we rejoined our division and Army Corps, which was en route for

Chattanooga. We arrived at the latter place on May 6. Moved thence through Snake Creek Gap to within six miles of Resaca, Georgia, where we fortified.

May 13.— The whole column started and moved on the enemy's works at Resaca. We had five men wounded that day, one of whom since died.

May 14.— Our division (Second Division, Fifteenth Army Corps) gained an advanced and important position, which we fortified during the night. This day we had two wounded.

May 15-16.— We remained in our position. Had one man wounded. The following night the Rebels evacuated their works and we took possession of the town on the morning of May 16. The same afternoon we again left Resaca.

May 19.— After several skirmishes reached Kingston, Georgia in the afternoon.

May 23-26.— Left the latter place en route for Dallas, Georgia, where we arrived May 26.

May 28.— The enemy attacked our lines but was repulsed with a heavy loss. Our regiment had one wounded.

May 31.— We again had two men killed and two wounded by Rebel sharpshooters.

Stationed in the field, near Kenesaw Mountain, June 1864.

June 1-6.— Received orders to march in the morning. Moved to the left towards New Hope Church, where our Corps relieved the Twentieth Corps. Remained there until the morning of June 5, when it was discovered that the enemy had disappeared in our front. During our stay here we had four men wounded. Immediately we were put under marching orders and moved towards Acworth, Georgia, where we arrived the next morning.

June 10.— In the vicinity of the latter place we encamped until the morning of June 10, when we started for Big Shanty, Georgia, distant four miles from Kenesaw Mountain. We arrived there about noon on the same day and afterwards participated in the various movements near Kenesaw Mountain.

June 27.— [Participated] in the attack on the enemy's works on Little Kenesaw, where we sustained a loss of three killed and thirteen wounded. During the remainder of the month our division was in reserve.

Stationed at camp, near Atlanta, Georgia, July 1864.

July 2.— In the morning our division received orders to march. We left bivouac at 5 a.m. and moved to our extreme right, where we relieved a portion of the Twenty-third Army Corps.

July 3.— At dawn it was ascertained that the enemy had left Kenesaw Mountain and was falling back towards the Chattahoochee River. In the afternoon we advanced our lines and drove the enemy in our front, consisting of cavalry and a few pieces of artillery.

July 5-10.— After a severe skirmish from a selected position near Nickajack Creek we moved farther to the right and encamped near Nickajack Creek about —— miles from the Chattahoochee River. Here we remained until the morning of July 10, when it was discovered that the entire Rebel force had fallen back across the river.

July 11-13.— We left our position on the right and moved en route for Marietta, Georgia, where we arrived at 2 a.m. on July 13; thence took the road to Roswell on the Chattahoochee River and encamped the same evening in the vicinity of the latter place.

July 14.— In the afternoon we crossed the Chattahoochee and fortified about 500 yards from the riverbank.

July 16-18.— We again moved forward and struck the Georgia Railroad between Decatur and Stone Mountain on July 18, where we destroyed the track for several miles.

July 19-21.— We took possession of Decatur, six miles east of Atlanta, and on July 20 advanced on Atlanta. After considerable skirmishing we succeeded in driving the [enemy] back to within one and one-half miles of Atlanta. During the following night we fortified our position.

July 22.— In the morning the enemy had again abandoned the works in our front. We immediately followed them up and found that they had fallen back to their works within the corporation of the city. Skirmishers were advanced as far as practicable but the main column formed in line along the works the enemy had abandoned. In the afternoon the enemy concentrated his forces and attacked our whole left wing. Several furious assaults were made but finally the Rebels were driven back with dreadful slaughter. The battle lasted all afternoon. Our regiment sustained a loss of 104 killed, wounded and captured.

July 27-28.— We left our position east of Atlanta and moved to the extreme right, where we again encountered the enemy on the afternoon of July 28, when the Rebels once more received a severe punishment. In this day's fight we lost ten wounded and three missing.
July 29.— We fortified our position.
July 30-31.— We advanced our lines about 500 yards, where we again fortified and in which position we remained up to the evening of July 31.

Stationed at Jonesborough, Georgia, August 1864.
August 2.— We moved our lines about 600 yards forward, where we again erected a line of field works.
August 5.— Our skirmishers were ordered to advance but, as the enemy showed too much resistance, we had to reinforce the skirmishers, which brought on a short but severe engagement wherein six companies of our regiment participated. Finally the enemy was compelled to fall back and our forces occupied the ground.
August 7-9.— During the night of August 7 and 8 we had heavy fatigue details out to build a new line of works, which we occupied early in the morning of August 9.
August 26.— Here we remained, participating in the daily skirmishes, etc., until the evening of August 26, when we left our works before Atlanta.
August 28.— Marched around the enemy's left flank and struck the West Point Railroad in the afternoon.
August 30.— In the morning we again moved forward towards the Macon Railroad. In the afternoon our regiment was deployed as skirmishes. The Rebels showed themselves in considerable force but were steadily driven back to within half a mile of Jonesborough, when darkness closed in. During the night we fortified our position.
August 31.— In the afternoon the enemy massed his forces in our front and at 3 p.m. made a furious assault on our lines but was repulsed and driven back in confusion with a terrible loss after one hour's fighting.

Stationed at East Point, Georgia, September 1864.
September 1.— In the afternoon when the Fourteenth Army Corps was assaulting the Rebels' works we also made a demonstration in our front in compliance with orders.

September 2-5.— Early in the morning it was demonstrated that the Rebels had left our front. Immediately we were put under marching orders. Passed through Jonesborough; pursued and skirmished with the enemy until we reached Lovejoy's Station, four miles beyond, where our advance was checked by a strong line of Rebel works. We remained there until the morning of September 5, when orders for a retrograde movement was received.
September 6-8.— Reached Jonesborough at 5 a.m. in the morning. We remained there until the morning of September 7, when we continued our march en route for East Point, Georgia, our present location, where we arrived and went into camp at noon of September 8.

Stationed at Cave Spring, Georgia, October 1864.
October 3.— In the afternoon received orders to be ready to move early the next morning to start on an expedition to intercept the Rebel General [John Bell] Hood, who was then on his way with a formidable Army to cut our lines of communication in our rear.
October 4-8.— Accordingly, left camp at East Point, Georgia at 7 o'clock a.m. Crossed that evening the Chattahoochee River and encamped near Marietta, Georgia the following night. Remained there until the afternoon of October 8, when we moved to Kenesaw Valley.
October 10.— Marched from there to Allatoona Mountains and the next day encamped near Kingston.
October 14.— In the evening reached the vicinity of Calhoun.
October 15.— Passed Resaca in the morning and encamped that night in Sugar Valley.
October 16-17.— Passed through Gordon's Gap on the road to La Fayette and reached the latter place the following day.
October 18-20.— Were ordered to Summerville. Remained there until the morning of October 20, when we marched to Gaylesville, Alabama.
October 21.— Moved about five miles beyond that place on the road to Little River.
October 24.— Started from there toward Gadsden.

October 25.— Came up with the enemy and had a brisk skirmish with him near Turkeytown, Alabama, in which we suffered a loss of two wounded.
October 26.— Marched again towards Little River.
October 29-31.— Started from there on the road towards Rome, Georgia in the morning and reached Cave Spring, Georgia, our present place of encampment on the morning of October 31.

Stationed in the field, November 1864.
November 1-5.— Started from Cave Spring, Georgia in the morning; passed through Cedartown and Powder Springs and reached a place called Smyrna Campground near Rough and Ready [Station], Georgia on the afternoon of November 5, where we remained for several days.
November 7.— A lot of drafted men and substitutes, who were assigned to the regiment, arrived in camp.
November 12.— In the evening received orders to destroy the railroad near the Chattahoochee River.
November 13.— In the morning the whole command started for Atlanta, but our regiment was ordered to complete the destruction of the railroad, then to rejoin the division in the vicinity of Atlanta, which was done in the evening of the same day.
November 14.— Received another installment of drafted men and substitutes.
November 15-30.— In the morning started on an expedition under command of Major-General William T. Sherman through the state of Georgia. In the following days passed through the counties of Fulton, Henry, Butts, Jasper, Jones, Wilkinson, Washington, Johnson, and encamped on the evening of November 30 at a place called Summertown in Emanuel County, having marched a distance of 248 miles during the month.

Stationed near Savannah, Georgia, December 1864.
December 1.— Started from Summertown, Emanuel County, in the morning. Crossed the headwaters of the Cannouchee River on the afternoon of the same day.
December 4-8.— Passed through Statesborough, Bulloch County, and reached Eden, Bryan County, on the afternoon of December 8.

December 9.— In the morning crossed the Cannouchee River. Marched to the Savannah, Gulf and Albany Railroad. Destroyed a portion of it and returned to the river the same night.
December 10.— In the morning recrossed the Cannouchee and marched for the Ogeechee River. Crossed the latter on Dillon's Bridge and encamped that night, ten miles from Savannah.
December 13.— In the morning the division was ordered to march to and assault Fort McAllister, on the south bank of the Ogeechee. Crossed the river on King's Bridge. Reached the Fort about 1 p.m. and assaulted and carried the same at 4.30 p.m. In this assault we had the honor of planting the first Stars and Stripes on the parapet of the doomed Fort.
December 17-21.— Participated in the destruction of the Savannah, Gulf and Albany Railroad.
December 31.— Encamped at night four miles southwest of Savannah, Georgia, having marched about 168 miles during the month.

Stationed at Pocotaligo Station, South Carolina, January 1865.
January 2.— The regiment entered the city of Savannah, Georgia.
January 7.— Nothing of importance transpired until January 7, when we were reviewed by Generals Sherman, [Oliver Otis] Howard and [John Alexander] Logan.
January 14.— Started for Fort Thunderbolt in Wassaw Sound.
January 15-30.— Started for Beaufort, South Carolina on board of transports. Reached there on January 16 and camped on the outskirts of the town. Nothing else of importance except opening of the campaign on January 30.

Stationed at Lynch's Creek, South Carolina, February 1865.
February 11.— Nothing of importance transpired until our reaching the North Edisto River, where the Rebels were entrenched on the opposite side.
February 12.— Commenced to move up the river about three miles. Crossed over and waded a swamp about a mile in width, then put up works for protection and advanced down the riverbank, driving the Rebels before us and capturing several prisoners. Our progress was not impeded until our arrival at the Saluda River, where there was artillery used to help force a crossing,

after which we had nothing to stop our march into Columbia, South Carolina.
February 18-19.— Destroyed the Savannah and Columbia Railroad. Nothing else of importance occurred during the month of February.

Stationed at Goldsborough, North Carolina, March 1865.
March 5.— Nothing of importance transpired until March 5, when we found the enemy entrenched. Slight skirmishing ensued, when the Rebels evacuated their position and we entered Cheraw, South Carolina.
March 9-11.— Repairing roads. In the evening of March 11 entered Fayetteville, North Carolina.
March 13.— Moved towards Bentonville.
March 14.— Received orders to report for reinforcements, as they were hard pressed, and were placed in reserve waiting for further development from the enemy.
March 21.— Took our position in line. Advanced our skirmishers and put up light breastworks. Slight skirmishing all day.
March 22.— The Rebels evacuated their works and we took up our march towards Goldsborough.
March 26.— Went out foraging to procure feed for the animals and was attacked by a few Rebel skirmishers but did not sustain a very heavy loss. Returned and encamped on the east side of Goldsborough, North Carolina. Nothing else transpired during the remainder of the month.

Stationed in the field, Wake County, North Carolina, April 1865.

Stationed near Washington, North Carolina, May 1865.

Stationed at Memphis, Tennessee, June 1865.

Company A

Stationed at Camp Dennison, Ohio, July 29, 1861.
July 29.— Muster-in roll of Captain Samuel L. Hunter's Company, in the Forty-seventh Regiment of Ohio Volunteers, commanded by Colonel Frederick Poschner, called into the service of

the United States by the President from July 29, 1861 (date of this muster) for the term of three years, unless sooner discharged. . . .

T. W. WALKER,
First Lieutenant,
Third Infantry, Mustering Officer.

Stationed at Camp Anderson, [West] Virginia, October 31, 1861.

Stationed at camp, Gauley Mountain, November 1861-April 1862.

Stationed at camp at Meadow Bluff, [West] Virginia, May-June 1862.

Stationed at Post Ewing, [West] Virginia, August 18, 1862.

Stationed at Camp Lookout, [West] Virginia, July-August 1862.

Stationed at camp, near Brownstown, [West] Virginia, September-October 1862.

Stationed at camp, Gauley Mountain, November-December 1862.

Stationed at camp before Vicksburg, Mississippi, January-February 1863.

Stationed at Young's Point, Louisiana, March-April 1863.

Stationed at Walnut Hill, Mississippi, May-June 1863.

Stationed at Camp Sherman, Mississippi, July-August 1863.

Stationed at Chickasaw, Alabama, September-October 1863.

Stationed at Bellefonte Station, Alabama, November-December 1863.

Stationed at Cleveland, Tennessee, January-February 1864.

Stationed at Kenesaw Mountain, May-June 1864.

Stationed before Atlanta, Georgia, August 20, 1864.
August 20.— Muster-out roll of a detachment of Captain Lewis [or Louis] D. Graves', late Hunter's, Company A, in the Forty-seventh Regiment of Ohio Infantry Veteran Volunteers, commanded by Colonel Augustus [Commodore] Parry, late Poschner, called into the service of the United States by the President at Camp Dennison, Ohio (the place of general rendezvous) on June 15, 1861 to serve for the term of three years from the date of enrollment, unless sooner discharged, from December 31, 1863 (when last paid) to August 20, 1864 when mustered out. The company was organized by Captain S. L. Hunter at Cincinnati, Ohio in the month of June 1861 and marched thence to Camp Dennison, Ohio, where it arrived July 29, 1861, a distance of sixteen miles. . . .

[CHARLES JOHN] DICKEY,
First Lieutenant and Assistant Commissary of Musters, Thirteenth Infantry, Second Division, Fifteenth Army Corps, Mustering Officer.

Stationed at Jonesborough, Georgia, July-August 1864.

Stationed at Cave Spring, Georgia, September-October 1864.

Stationed at Savannah, Georgia, November-December 1864.

Stationed at Lynch's Creek, South Carolina, January-February 1865.

Stationed at Neuse River, Wake County, North Carolina, March-April 1865.

Stationed on board the steamer Delaware, Mississippi River, May-June 1865.

Company B

Stationed at Sutton, [West] Virginia, June 15-October 31, 1861.

Stationed at Camp Dennison, Ohio, July 29, 1861.
July 29.— Muster-in roll of Captain William H. Ward's Company, in the Forty-seventh Regiment of Ohio Volunteers, commanded by Colonel Frederick Poschner, called into the service of the United States by the President from July 29, 1861 (date of this muster) for the term of three years, unless sooner discharged. The company was organized by Captain William H. Ward at Adrian, Michigan in the month of June and marched thence to Camp Dennison, where it arrived July 29, a distance of 250 miles. . . .

T. W. WALKER,
First Lieutenant,
Third Infantry, Mustering Officer.

Stationed at Post Gauley Mountain, [West] Virginia, November 1861-April 1862.

Stationed at camp at Meadow Bluff, [West] Virginia, May-June 1862.

Stationed at Post Ewing, [West] Virginia, August 18, 1862.

Stationed at Camp Lookout, Fayette County, [West] Virginia, July-August 1862.

Stationed at camp at Brownstown, [West] Virginia, September-October 1862.

Stationed at camp, Gauley Mountain, [West] Virginia, November-December 1862.

Stationed at camp before Vicksburg, January-February 1863.

Stationed at camp at Young's Point, Louisiana, March-April 1863.

Stationed at Walnut Hill, Mississippi, May-June 1863.
May 3.— At night Captain Ward, with six noncommissioned officers and seven privates, volunteered to run blockade at Vicksburg, Mississippi in two boats loaded with hay and provisions and

were all captured but one private and paroled at Annapolis, Maryland.
May 18-19.— The company left Young's Point, Louisiana, where last mustered, and marched to this station, arriving here late on the night of May 18 and was in the assault on Vicksburg on May 19. The balance of the company was in the assault on Vicksburg May 19 and had four enlisted men wounded.

Stationed at Camp Sherman, Mississippi, July-August 1863.

Stationed at Chickasaw, Alabama, September-October 1863.

Stationed at Bellefonte, Alabama, November-December 1863.
November 2.— The company was at Chickasaw Landing, Alabama when last mustered. Marched from that place on November 2, passing through on our line of march the following named places, *viz.*: Florence, Alabama; Pulaski and Fayetteville, Tennessee; New Market and Stevenson, Alabama.
November 17.— Arrived at Bridgeport, Alabama.
November 19-21.— Left Bridgeport for Chattanooga. Reached there on November 21.
November 24-25.— Crossed the Tennessee at a point opposite the eastern extremity of Missionary Ridge in pontoon boats at 3 o'clock a.m. Was in the engagement on November 25.
November 26-27.— In the morning found that the enemy had retreated during the night. Marched in pursuit that morning, reaching Graysville about 10 a.m. November 27. Destroyed mills and other property of value to the enemy.
November 28-29.— Changed our line of march towards Cleveland, Tennessee. Reached that place on November 29. Found a strong union sentiment in that town. Passed through the place on the same day towards Charleston, Tennessee. When near that place received orders to march to the relief of Burnside at Knoxville, Tennessee.
December 6.— Continued our march towards that place and reached Maryville, fifteen miles from Knoxville on December 6, learning there that Longstreet had raised the siege. We were ordered to return to Chattanooga. On our return march we went by the way of Tellico Plains and within three miles of the North Carolina state line.

December 17.— We arrived at Chattanooga.
December 19.— Marched to Bridgeport and reached that place on December 19.
December 26-30.— Left there, passing through Stevenson, Alabama same day and reaching Bellefonte on December 30, having marched, since last muster, the distance of 569 miles.

Stationed at Cleveland, Tennessee, January-February 1864.

Stationed near Big Shanty, Georgia, May-June 1864.

Stationed near Jonesborough, Georgia, July-August 1864.

Stationed at Atlanta, Georgia, August 20, 1864.
August 20.— Muster-out roll of Captain William H. Ward's Company B, in the Forty-seventh Regiment of Ohio Infantry Veteran Volunteers, commanded by Colonel Augustus C. Parry, late Poschner, called into the service of the United States by the President at Camp Dennison, Ohio (the place of general rendezvous) on June 15, 1861 to serve for the term of three years from the date of enrollment, unless sooner discharged, from December 31, 1863 (when last paid) to August 20, 1864 when mustered out. . . .

C. J. DICKEY,
First Lieutenant and Assistant Commissary of Musters,
Thirteenth Infantry, Second Division, Fifteenth Army Corps,
Mustering Officer.

Stationed at Cave Spring, Georgia, September-October 1864.

Stationed at Savannah, Georgia, November-December 1864.

Stationed at Lynch's Creek, South Carolina, January-February 1865.
January 2-14.— Left our camp, four miles west of Savannah, and moved into camp at the suburbs of the city. Remained there until January 14, during which period we worked several days on fortifications. On the aforesaid date moved down to the Thunderbolt on Wassaw Sound.

January 15-16.— Embarked from there on board the steamer *Ceres* in the afternoon and reached Beaufort, South Carolina at noon of January 16.
January 24-27.— Orders were received to corduroy a certain portion of the road leading to Port Royal Ferry. Finished this job on January 27.
January 31.— Started on our campaign through South Carolina. Reached Pocotaligo Station the same afternoon.
February 17.— In the following month passed through the counties of Beaufort, Barnwell, Orangeburg, and Lexington and reached Columbia, the capital, on February 17.
February 18-19.— Participated in the destruction of the South Carolina Railroad.
February 20-26.— Resumed our march. Passed through Richland and Kershaw Counties and arrived at Lynch's Creek, which we crossed at Kelly's Bridge and where we are now encamped on the afternoon of February 26, having marched during the whole period a distance of about 295 miles over a country exceedingly rich in rivers, creek and swamps, many of the latter we had to wade.

Stationed near Raleigh, North Carolina, March-April 1865.

Stationed on board transports, Memphis, Tennessee, May-June 1865.

Company C

Station not stated, June 15-October 31, 1861.

Stationed at Camp Dennison, Ohio, August 16, 1861.
August 16.— Muster-in roll of Captain Alexander Froelich's Company of Ohio Volunteers, commanded by Colonel Frederick Poschner, called into the service of the United States by the President from August 16, 1861 (date of this muster) for the term of three years, unless sooner discharged. . . .

T. W. WALKER,
First Lieutenant,
Third Infantry, Mustering Officer.

Stationed at Post Gauley Mountain, [West] Virginia, November 1861-February 1862.

Stationed at Camp Gauley Mountain, [West] Virginia, April 30, 1862.

Stationed at Meadow Bluff, [West] Virginia, May-June 1862.

Stationed at Post Ewing, [West] Virginia, July-August 1862.

Stationed at Montgomery Landing, [West] Virginia, September-October 1862.

Stationed at Camp Gauley Mountain, [West] Virginia, November-December 1862.

Stationed at camp, near Vicksburg, Mississippi, January-April 1863.

Stationed at Walnut Hill, Mississippi, May-June 1863.

Stationed at Camp Sherman, Mississippi, July-August 1863.

Stationed at Chickasaw, Alabama, September-October 1863.

Stationed near Bellefonte, Alabama, November-December 1863.

Stationed at Cleveland, Tennessee, January-February 1864.

Stationed at Nashville, Tennessee, March-April 1864.

Stationed at Jonesborough, Georgia, July-August 1864.

Stationed at Cave Spring, September-October 1864.

Stationed at Savannah, Georgia, November-December 1864.

Stationed near Lynch's Creek, South Carolina, January-February 1865.

Stationed in the field, Wake County, North Carolina, March-April 1865.

Stationed on transport steamer Delaware, Memphis, Tennessee, May-June 1865.

Company D

Stationed at Camp Anderson, June 15-October 31, 1861.

Stationed at Camp Dennison, Ohio, August 7, 1861.
August 7.— Muster-in roll of Captain John Wallace's Company, in the Forty-seventh Regiment of Ohio Volunteers, commanded by Colonel Frederick Poschner, called into the service of the United States by the President from August 7, 1861 (date of this muster) for the term of three years, unless sooner discharged. . . .

T. W. WALKER,
First Lieutenant,
Third Infantry, Mustering Officer.

Stationed at Camp Gauley Mountain, November 1861-April 1862.

Stationed at Meadow Bluff, [West] Virginia, May-June 1862.

Stationed at Camp Ewing, [West] Virginia, July-August 1862.

Station not stated, September-October 1862.

Stationed at Camp Gauley Mountain, November-December 1862.

Station not stated, January-February 1863.

Stationed at Young's Point, Louisiana, March-April 1863.

Stationed at camp at Walnut Hill, Mississippi, May-June 1863.

Stationed at Camp Sherman, Mississippi, July-August 1863.

Stationed at Chickasaw, Alabama, September-October 1863.

Stationed at camp, near Bellefonte, Alabama, November-December 1863.

Stationed at Cleveland, Tennessee, January-February 1864.

Stationed at Nashville, Tennessee, March-April 1864.

Stationed near Kenesaw Mountain, Georgia, May-June 1864.

Stationed at Jonesborough, Georgia, July-August 1864.

Stationed before Atlanta, Georgia, August 20, 1864.
August 20.— Muster-out roll of Captain Joseph L. Pinkerton's Company D, in the Forty-seventh Regiment of Ohio Infantry Veteran Volunteers, commanded by Colonel Augustus C. Parry, late F. Poschner, called into the service of the United States by the President at Camp Dennison, Ohio (the place of general rendezvous) on August 7, 1861 to serve for the term of three years from the date of enrollment, unless sooner discharged, from December 31, 1863 (when last paid) to August 20, 1864 when mustered out. The company was organized by Captain John Wallace at Morning Sun, Ohio in the month of July 1861 and marched thence to Camp Dennison, Ohio, where it arrived July 30, a distance of sixty miles. . . .

C. J. DICKEY,
First Lieutenant and Assistant Commissary of Musters,
Thirteenth Infantry, Second Division, Fifteenth Army Corps,
Mustering Officer.

Stationed at Cave Spring, [Georgia], September-October 1864.

Stationed at Savannah, Georgia, November-December 1864.

Stationed at Lynch's Creek, South Carolina, January-February 1865.

Stationed in the field, Wake County, North Carolina, March-April 1865.

Stationed on board steamer Delaware, Memphis, Tennessee, May-June 1865.

Company E

Station not stated, June 15-October 31, 1861.

Stationed at Post Gauley Mountain, [West] Virginia, November 1861-April 1862.

Stationed at camp at Meadow Bluff, [West] Virginia, May-June 1862.

Stationed at Post Ewing, August 18, 1862.

Stationed at Camp Lookout, [West] Virginia, July-August 1862.

Stationed at Brownstown, September-October 1862.

Stationed at Camp Gauley Mountain, November-December 1862.

Stationed at camp before Vicksburg, January-February 1863.

Stationed at camp before Vicksburg, April 10, 1863.

Stationed at Young's Point, Louisiana, March-April 1863.

Stationed at Walnut Hill, Mississippi, May-June 1863.
May 18.— The company marched from Grand Gulf, Mississippi by way of Rocky Springs, Big Black River Bridge, etc., and arrived in the rear of Vicksburg May 18 and, in connection with the Army, invested the city May 18 and has been closely and unceasingly engaged in the siege to the present date.

Stationed at Camp Sherman, Mississippi, July-August 1863.

Stationed at Chickasaw Landing, Alabama, September-October 1863.

Stationed at camp, near Bellefonte, November-December 1863.
November 2-20.— The company, since last muster, has marched from Eastport, Alabama (crossing the Tennessee River on November 2) through Waterloo, Gravelly Springs and Florence, Alabama; Pulaski and Fayetteville, Tennessee; New Market, Brownstown, Bellefonte, Stevenson, and Bridgeport, Alabama and on to Chattanooga, which place we reached on November 20, making a distance of 264 miles. Crossed the Tennessee River in pontoon boats.
November 24-25.— At 3 o'clock a.m. threw up entrenchments and then moved forward with the division and took possession of the northern extremity of Missionary Ridge. Were in the battle of Chattanooga on November 24 and 25.
November 26-27.— Started in pursuit of [Braxton] Bragg's retreating Army, chasing the enemy for two days. Changed our line of march for Knoxville to relieve General Burnside, who was besieged by General Longstreet.
December 5-30.— Reached Maryville (within one day's march of Knoxville). General Longstreet having raised the siege, the company returned to this point by way of Chattanooga, reaching here on December 30, having marched a distance of 275 miles.

Stationed at Cleveland, Tennessee, January-February 1864.

Stationed at Nashville, Tennessee, March-April 1864.
February 11.— The company reenlisted as veterans during the months of January and February and was mustered as such on February 11.
March 19-April 29.— Started from Larkinsville, Alabama on veteran furlough on March 19. Returned to the field April 29.

Stationed near Kenesaw Mountain, Georgia, May-June 1864.

Stationed at Jonesborough, Georgia, July-August 1864.

The company has been actively engaged in the front lines during the whole of the two months, has marched 200 miles and has fought four regular battles, besides being engaged in various severe skirmishes. It has lost three men killed, ten wounded and ten captured during the two months, making a total loss of twenty-three enlisted men out of thirty-four on duty carrying muskets.

Stationed at Atlanta, Georgia, August 20, 1864.
August 20.— Muster-out roll of a detachment of Captain Webster Thomas', late Allen S. Bundy's, Company E, in the Forty-seventh Regiment of Ohio Infantry Veteran Volunteers, commanded by Colonel Augustus C. Parry, late Poschner, called into the service of the United States by the President at Camp Dennison, Ohio (the place of general rendezvous) on June 15, 1861 to serve for the term of three years from the date of enrollment, unless sooner discharged, from December 31, 1863 (when last paid) to August 20, 1864 when mustered out. The company was organized by Captain Allen S. Bundy at Westborough, Ohio in the month of June 1861 and marched thence to Camp Dennison, Ohio, where it arrived August 7, a distance of twenty miles. . . .

C. J. DICKEY,
First Lieutenant and Assistant Commissary of Musters, Thirteenth Infantry, Second Division, Fifteenth Army Corps, Mustering Officer.

Stationed at Cave Spring, Georgia, September-October 1864.

Stationed near Savannah, Georgia, November-December 1864.

Stationed at Lynch's Creek, South Carolina, January-February 1865.

Stationed in the field, North Carolina, March-April 1865.

Stationed on board transport, Memphis, Tennessee, May-June 1865.

Company F

Station not stated, June 15-October 31, 1861.

Stationed at Camp Dennison, Ohio, August 7, 1861.
August 7.— Muster-in roll of Captain Thomas [Thompson] Taylor's Company, in the Forty-seventh Regiment of Ohio Volunteers, commanded by Colonel Frederick Poschner, called into the service of the United States by the President from August 7, 1861

(date of this muster) for the term of three years, unless sooner discharged. The company was organized by Captain Thomas T. Taylor at Georgetown, Ohio in the month of July and marched thence to Camp Dennison, where it arrived July 29, 1861, a distance of sixty-nine miles. . . .

T. W. WALKER,
First Lieutenant,
Third Infantry, Mustering Officer.

Stationed at Post Gauley Mountain, November 1861-April 1862.

Stationed at camp, Meadow Bluff, [West] Virginia, May-June 1862.
May 1.— The captain started with fifteen men on a scout. Joined Captain Wallace. Explored several mountain ranges. Drove guerrillas therefrom and passed into the county of Greensborough.
May 11.— Scouted through the western part of the country until the night of May 11, when the whole expedition, under command of Lieutenant-Colonel [Lyman] S. Elliott made an attack on Lewisburg.
May 12.— In the morning drove the Rebels from the town and to White Sulphur Springs. Captured some baggage stores. Took several prisoners and horses. Occupied the town.
May 21.— Received orders to march to Meadow Bluff, which we reached during the day.
June 22-26.— On Sunday, June 22, the company received orders to march with the brigade. Marched via Alderson's Ferry to Centerville; thence via Salt Sulphur Springs to Union, Monroe County and thence by Greenfield or Rocky Point to Alderson's Ferry to this place. The expedition resulted in driving the Rebels under General [Henry] Heth and others in the direction of Salt Pond Mountain and clearing the section through which we passed of all hostile bands. We took some stores, wagons, horses, and a large lot of cattle. Also a few prisoners. Were fired on a few times. Roads good, water generally abundant. Returned to camp June 26. Don't know distance marched.

Stationed at Camp Ewing, [West] Virginia, July-August 1862.

Stationed at Clifton, [West] Virginia, September-October 1862.

Stationed at Camp Gauley Mountain, [West] Virginia, November-December 1862.

Stationed at camp opposite Vicksburg, Mississippi, January-February 1863.

Stationed at Young's Point, Louisiana, March-April 1863.

Stationed at camp, Walnut Hill, Mississippi, May-June 1863.

Stationed at Camp Sherman, Mississippi, July-August 1863.

Stationed at Chickasaw, Alabama, September-October 1863.

Stationed at Bellefonte Station, Alabama, November-December 1863.

Stationed at Cleveland, Tennessee, January-February 1864.

Stationed at Kenesaw Mountain, Georgia, May-June 1864.

Stationed at Jonesborough, Georgia, July-August 1864.

Stationed at Atlanta, Georgia, August 20, 1864.
August 20.— Muster-out roll of a detachment of non-veterans of Captain Henry N. King's, late Taylor's, Company F, in the Forty-seventh Regiment of Ohio Infantry Volunteers, commanded by Colonel Augustus C. Parry, called into the service of the United States by the President at Camp Dennison, Ohio (the place of general rendezvous) on June 15, 1861 to serve for the term of three years from the date of enrollment, unless sooner discharged, from December 31, 1863 (when last paid) to August 20, 1864 when mustered out. The company was organized by Captain Thomas T. Taylor at Georgetown, Ohio in the month of June 1861 and marched thence to Camp Dennison, Ohio, where it arrived July 20, a distance of sixty-nine miles. . . .

C. J. DICKEY,
First Lieutenant and Assistant Commissary of Musters,
Thirteenth Infantry, Second Division, Fifteenth Army Corps,
Mustering Officer.

Stationed at Cave Spring, Georgia, September-October 1864.

Stationed near Savannah, Georgia, November-December 1864.

Stationed at Lynch's Creek, South Carolina, January-February 1865.

Stationed at Raleigh, North Carolina, March-April 1865.

Stationed on board transport, Memphis, Tennessee, May-June 1865.

Company G

Stationed at Cross-Lanes, [West] Virginia, June 15-October 31, 1861.

Stationed at Camp Dennison, Ohio, August 17, 1861.
August 17.— Muster-in roll of Captain Valentine Rapp's Company, in the Forty-seventh Regiment of Ohio Volunteers, commanded by Colonel Frederick Poschner, called into the service of the United States by the President from August 17, 1861 (date of this muster) for the term of three years, unless sooner discharged. . . .

T. W. WALKER,
First Lieutenant,
Third Infantry, Mustering Officer.

Stationed at Camp Gauley Mountain, [West] Virginia, November 1861-April 1862.

Stationed at camp, Meadow Bluff, May-June 1862.

Stationed at Post Ewing, [West] Virginia, August 18, 1862.

Stationed at Camp Lookout, July-August 1862.

Stationed at camp opposite Cannelton, [West] Virginia, September-October 1862.

Stationed at Camp Gauley Mountain, [West] Virginia, November-December 1862.

Stationed at camp opposite Vicksburg, January-February 1863.

Stationed at Young's Point, Louisiana, March-April 1863.

Stationed at Walnut Hill, Mississippi, May-June 1863.
May 19-20.— The company was engaged in action at Walnut Hill, Mississippi.

Stationed at Camp Sherman, Mississippi, July-August 1863.

Stationed at camp at Chickasaw, Alabama, September-October 1863.

Stationed at Bellefonte, Alabama, November-December 1863.

Stationed at Cleveland, Tennessee, January-February 1864.

Stationed at Nashville, Tennessee, March-April 1864.

Stationed at Big Shanty, Georgia, May-June 1864.

Stationed in the field, near Jonesborough, Georgia, July-August 1864.

Stationed at Atlanta, Georgia, August 20, 1864.
August 20.— Muster-out roll of Captain Henry H. Sinclair's, late Rapp's, Company G, in the Forty-seventh Regiment of Ohio Infantry Volunteers, commanded by Colonel Augustus C. Parry, late Poschner, called into the service of the United States by the President at Camp Dennison, Ohio (the place of general rendezvous) on June 15, 1861 to serve for the term of three years from the date of enrollment, unless sooner discharged, from December 31, 1863 (when last paid) to August 20, 1864 when mustered out. The company was organized by Captain Valentine

Rapp at Cincinnati, Ohio in the month of June 1861 and marched thence to Camp Dennison, Ohio, where it arrived July 29. . . .

C. J. DICKEY,
First Lieutenant and Assistant Commissary of Musters,
Thirteenth Infantry, Second Division, Fifteenth Army Corps,
Mustering Officer.

Stationed at Cave Spring, Georgia, September-October 1864.

Stationed near Savannah, Georgia, November-December 1864.

Stationed at Lynch's Creek, South Carolina, January-February 1865.

Stationed at Raleigh, North Carolina, March-April 1865.

Stationed on board steamer Delaware, Memphis, Tennessee, May-June 1865.

Company H

Stationed at Camp Dennison, Ohio, August 21, 1861.
August 21.— Muster-in roll of Captain Charles [N.] Helmerich's Company, in the Forty-seventh Regiment of Ohio Volunteers, commanded by Colonel Frederick Poschner, called into the service of the United States by the President from August 21, 1861 (date of this muster) for the term of three years. . . .

T. W. WALKER,
First Lieutenant,
Third Infantry, Mustering Officer.

Station not stated, October 31, 1861.

Station not stated, November-December 1861.

Stationed at Gauley Mountain, [West] Virginia, January-April 1862.

Stationed at Meadow Bluff, [West] Virginia, May-June 1862.

Stationed at Post Ewing, [West] Virginia, July-August 1862.

Stationed at Brownstown, [West] Virginia, September-October 1862.

Stationed at Gauley Mountain, [West] Virginia, November-December 1862.

Stationed at camp opposite Vicksburg, [Mississippi], January-February 1863.

Stationed at Young's Point, Louisiana, March-April 1863.

Stationed at Walnut Hill, Mississippi, May-June 1863.

Stationed at Camp Sherman, Mississippi, July-August 1863.

Stationed at Chickasaw, Alabama, September-October 1863.

Stationed at camp, near Bellefonte, Alabama, November-December 1863.

Stationed at Cleveland, Tennessee, January-February 1864.

Stationed at Nashville, Tennessee, March-April 1864.

Stationed at Kenesaw Mountain, Georgia, May-June 1864.

Station not stated, July-August 1864.

Stationed at Atlanta, Georgia, August 28, 1864.
August 20.— Muster-out roll of a detachment of Captain Charles N. Helmerich's Company H, in the Forty-seventh Regiment of Ohio Infantry Veteran Volunteers, commanded by Colonel A. C. Parry (late Frederick Poschner), called into the service of the United States by the President at Camp Dennison, Ohio (the place of general rendezvous) on June 15, 1861 to serve for the term of three years from the date of enrollment, unless sooner discharged, from December 31, 1863 to August 20, 1864 when mustered out.

The company was organized by Captain Charles N. Helmerich at Cincinnati, Ohio in the month of June 1861 and marched thence to Camp Dennison, Ohio, where it arrived July 29, 1861. . . .

C. J. DICKEY,
First Lieutenant and Assistant Commissary of Musters,
Thirteenth Infantry, Second Division, Fifteenth Army Corps,
Mustering Officer.

Stationed at Cave Spring, Georgia, September-October 1864.

Stationed near Savannah, Georgia, November-December 1864.

Stationed at Lynch's Creek, South Carolina, January-February 1865.

Stationed in the field, Wake County, North Carolina, March-April 1865.

Stationed on board transport, Memphis, Tennessee, May-June 1865.

Company I

Stationed at Cross Lanes, [West] Virginia, June 15-October 31, 1861.

Stationed at Post Gauley Mountain, [West] Virginia, November-December 1861.

Station not stated, January-February 1862.

Stationed at Post Gauley Mountain, [West] Virginia, March-April 1862.

Stationed at Meadow Bluff, May-June 1862.

Stationed at Camp Ewing, [West] Virginia, September-October 1862.

Stationed at Gauley Mountain, [West] Virginia, November-December 1862.

Stationed before Vicksburg, January-February 1863.

Stationed at Young's Point, Louisiana, April 10, 1863.

Station not stated, March-April 1863.

Stationed at Walnut Hill, Mississippi, May-June 1863.

Stationed at Camp Sherman, Mississippi, July-August 1863.

Stationed at Chickasaw Landing, Alabama, September-October 1863.
September 27.— At last muster this company was at Camp Sherman on Black River, Mississippi, from whence it marched with the regiment to Vicksburg.
September 28.— Embarked on board transport in the evening.
October 3-6.— Arrived at Memphis, Tennessee. Landed and remained there until October 6, when we marched for Corinth with the brigade as convoy to Corps train.
October 15-18.— Arrived at Corinth. Remained here until October 17, when we marched towards Iuka, reaching there October 18.
October 19-27.— Marched to Cherokee Station, remaining here until October 26, when with the regiment marched to Tuscumbia, arriving there October 27.
October 28.— Marched out to Florence, returning to Tuscumbia the morning of October 28 and falling back arrived at Cherokee the evening of October 28.
October 30-31.— Marched in the morning, arriving at this station October 31.

Stationed at Bellefonte Station, November-December 1863.
At the date of last muster the company was at Chickasaw Landing, Alabama.
November 2-21.— We crossed the Tennessee [River] at [Chickasaw Landing] and took up the march for Chattanooga, passing through Florence, Alabama and Pulaski and Fayetteville, Tennessee; thence to New Market, Alabama; thence to Stevenson and Bridgeport. Reached Chattanooga November 21. Distance marched 568 miles.

November 24-25.— Before any light, crossed the Tennessee [River] in boats with the regiment, forming a part of the Second Brigade, Second Division, Fifteenth Army Corps and gaining a position to the left of Missionary Ridge the same day. Participated in the engagement of November 25, the enemy being defeated and retreating the night of November 25.

November 26.— We marched in pursuit of the enemy.

November 30-December 6.— When near Charleston, received orders to march toward Knoxville to the relief of General Burnside's Army. Started the same day and continued the march to Maryville, reaching there December 6.

Information being received that the enemy had raised the siege of Knoxville, we started on the return march, passing through Tellico Plains, where we remained three days to forage. Since leaving Charleston we have subsisted off the country.

December 10-12.— The command marched over the North Carolina line, returning on December 12.

December 13-17.— Marched for Chattanooga, reaching there December 17.

December 18-19.— Marched, reaching Bridgeport December 19.

December 26-30.— We marched, reaching this station December 30.

Stationed at Cleveland, Tennessee, January-February 1864.

The company, at date of last muster, was at Bellefonte, Alabama.

January 9.— Marched with the regiment to Larkinsville, Alabama, eleven miles, and went into winter quarters.

February 11-17.— From that place we marched and reached this station; distance marched ninety miles.

Stationed at Nashville, Tennessee, March-April 1864.

At date of last muster the company was at Cleveland, Tennessee with a detachment of the Fifteenth Army Corps.

March 1-5.— Marched from that place, arriving at Larkinsville, Alabama on March 5.

March 18-23.— The company and regiment having reenlisted as veterans, left for Ohio. Arrived at Cincinnati on March 23.

March 24.— The men were furloughed for thirty days.

April 25-30.— Rendezvoused at Camp Dennison on April 25 and left there for the front on April 26, arriving at Nashville, Tennessee April 29 and remaining there April 30 to muster.

Stationed at East Point, Georgia, May-June 1864.

Stationed at Jonesborough, Georgia, July-August 1864.

Stationed at Cave Spring, Georgia, September-October 1864.

Stationed at Savannah, Georgia, November-December 1864.

Stationed at Lynch's Creek, South Carolina, January-February 1865.

Stationed in the field, Wake County, North Carolina, March-April 1865.

Stationed on board transport, Memphis, Tennessee, May-June 1865.

Company K

Stationed at Camp Anderson, [West] Virginia, September-October 1861.

Stationed at Post Gauley Mountain, [West] Virginia, November 1861-April 1862.

Stationed at Meadow Bluff, [West] Virginia, May-June 1862.

Stationed at camp at Huff's Branch, West Virginia, August 18, 1862.

Stationed at Post Ewing, July-August 1862.

Stationed at camp opposite Piatt, [West] Virginia, September-October 1862.

Stationed at Camp Gauley, [West] Virginia, November-December 1862.

Stationed at camp in front of Vicksburg, [Mississippi], January-February 1863.

Stationed at camp, Young's Point, Louisiana, April 10, 1863.

Station not stated, March-April 1863.

Stationed at Walnut Hill, Mississippi, May-June 1863.

Stationed at Camp Sherman, Mississippi, July-August 1863.

Stationed at Chickasaw, Alabama, September-October 1863.

Stationed at camp, near Bellefonte, Alabama, November-December 1863.

Stationed at Cleveland, Tennessee, January-February 1864.

Stationed at Nashville, Tennessee, March-April 1864.
March 18.— The regiment went on veteran furlough and was mustered on his return to the field at Nashville, Tennessee. The non-veterans of the regiment were left at Larkinsville, Alabama.

Stationed at the foot of Kenesaw Mountain, May-June 1864.

Stationed near Jonesborough, Georgia, July-August 1864.

Stationed near Cave Spring, Georgia, September-October 1864.

Stationed near Savannah, Georgia, November-December 1864.

Stationed at Lynch's Creek, South Carolina, January-February 1865.

Stationed at Wake County, North Carolina, March-April 1865.

Stationed aboard the steamer Delaware, Memphis, Tennessee, May-June 1865.

Stationed at Atlanta, Georgia, August 20, 1864.
August 20.— Muster-out roll of a detachment of Captain Charles Haltenhof's Company K, in the Forty-seventh Regiment of Ohio Infantry Veteran Volunteers, commanded by Colonel Augustus C, Parry, called into the service of the United States by the President at Camp Dennison, Ohio (the place of general rendezvous) on July 18, 1861 to serve for the term of three years from the date of enrollment, unless sooner discharged, from December 31, 1863 (when last paid) to August 20, 1864 when mustered out. The company was organized by Captain Frederick Hesser at Hamilton and Cincinnati, Ohio in the month of July 1861 and marched thence to Camp Dennison, where it arrived July 18, 1861. . . .

C. J. DICKEY,
First Lieutenant and Assistant Commissary of Musters, Thirteenth Infantry, Second Division, Fifteenth Army Corps, Mustering Officer.

[M594-Roll #150]

Record of Events for Forty-eight Ohio Infantry, September 1861-December 1864.

Detachment

Stationed at Camp Dennison, Ohio, July-August 1863.

This party was detailed by Special Orders No. 112, from Headquarters, Tenth Division, Thirteenth Army Corps, Department of the Tennessee, Vicksburg, August 9, 1863 to conduct to the Forty-eighth Regiment, Ohio Volunteer Infantry, the men of the draft assigned to it and assigned to Recruiting Service by Special Orders No. 253, from Headquarters, Ohio Volunteer Recruiting Service, Columbus, Ohio September 4, 1863.

Field and Staff

Station not stated, not dated.

Muster-in roll of the field and staff of the Forty-eighth Regiment of Ohio Foot Volunteers, commanded by Colonel Peter [John] Sullivan, called into service of the United States by the President . . . for the term of three years, unless sooner discharged. . . .

ALBERT [BALDWIN] DOD,
Captain,
Fifteenth Infantry, United States Army, Mustering Officer.

Station not stated, enrollment to December 31, 1861.

Stationed at Paducah, Kentucky, January-February 1862.
February 17-20.— By orders of Adjutant-General of Ohio, marched by rail and river from Camp Dennison, Ohio and arrived at Paducah, Kentucky, where the regiment is now stationed.

Stationed at Camp No. 2, March-April 1862.
March 6.— The regiment left Paducah, Kentucky in the expedition up the Tennessee River.
April 6-7.— Was engaged in the battle of Shiloh.

Station not stated, not dated.
April 24, 1862.— Muster-out roll of the regimental band in the Forty-eighth Regiment of Ohio Foot Volunteers, commanded by Colonel Peter J. Sullivan, called into the service of the United States by the President at Camp Dennison, Ohio (the place of general rendezvous) on January 23, 1862 to serve for the term of three years from the date of enrollment, unless sooner discharged, from January 23, 1862 (when mustered) to April 24, 1862 when mustered. . . .

[JOHN THOMAS] PRICE,
First Lieutenant and Aide-de-Camp,
Fifth United States Infantry, Mustering Officer.

Stationed at Moscow, Tennessee, May-June 1862.

Stationed at Fort Pickering, Tennessee, July-August 1862.
June 2.— Marched from Camp No. 8 before Corinth and passing through Corinth, bivouacked for the night two miles beyond.
June 3.— Marched to Chewalla, Tennessee.
June 9.— Marched to Tuscumbia River, six miles.
June 11.— Marched to Muddy Creek, six miles.
June 12.— Marched to Porter's Creek.
June 13.— Marched to Spring Creek No. 2, seven and one-half miles.
June 14.— Marched to La Grange, ten miles.
June 16.— To Moscow, ten miles.
June 22.— To La Fayette, ten miles.
June 26.— To Moscow, ten miles.
June 30-July 1.— To Holly Springs, twenty-five miles.
July 6-7.— To Moscow, twenty-five miles.
July 19.— To Collierville, fifteen miles.
July 20.— To White's Station, twelve miles.
July 22.— To Memphis, Tennessee, eight miles. Distance marched 151 1/2 miles.

Stationed at Fort Pickering, Tennessee, September-October 1862.

Stationed before Vicksburg, Mississippi, November-December 1862.
December 20.— Left Memphis, Tennessee on board steamer *City of Alton* with expedition against Vicksburg, commanded by Major-General William [Tecumseh] Sherman.
December 28.— Disembarked on the right bank of Yazoo River.
December 29.— Was in action in front of Vicksburg from the morning of December 29 without loss.

Stationed at Young's Point, Louisiana, January-February 1863.
December 29, 1862-January 9, 1863.— The regiment was engaged before Vicksburg, Mississippi. Debarked on the night of December 30 and proceeded up the Mississippi [River] to the Arkansas River; thence up the Arkansas [River] to Arkansas Post, where the expedition arrived on January 9.
January 11-12.— Disembarked and was engaged on January 12. Lost two killed and fourteen wounded.

January 15-23.— Left Arkansas Post and arrived at Young's Point, Louisiana January 23, where the regiment is now encamped.

Stationed at Milliken's Bend, Louisiana, April 10, 1863.

Stationed at Hard Times Landing, Louisiana, March-April 1863.

Stationed in the rear of Vicksburg, Mississippi, May-June 1863.

Stationed at Carrollton, Louisiana, July-August 1863.

Stationed at Franklin, Louisiana, September-October 1863.

Stationed at Decros Point, Texas, November-December 1863.

Stationed at Berwick City, Louisiana, January-February 1864.

Stationed at Alexandria, Louisiana, March-April 1864.

Stationed at Natchez, Mississippi, June 30-October 31, 1864.

Regiment

Stationed at Fort Pickering, near Memphis, Tennessee, July-November 1862.

Stationed near Vicksburg, Mississippi, December 1862.

Stationed at Young's Point, Louisiana, January-February 1863.

Stationed at Milliken's Bend, Louisiana, March 1863.

Stationed at Hard Times [Landing], Louisiana, April 1863.

Stationed in the rear of Vicksburg, Mississippi, May-July 1863.

Stationed at Carrollton, Louisiana, August-September 1863.

Stationed at Franklin, Louisiana, October 1863.

Stationed at New Iberia, Louisiana, except Company A at Franklin, Louisiana, November 1863.

Stationed at Decros Point, Texas, December 1863-January 1864.

Stationed at Berwick City, Louisiana, February 1864.

Stationed at Cane River, Louisiana, March 1864.

Stationed at Alexandria, Louisiana, April 1864.

Stationed at Baton Rouge, Louisiana, May-June 1864.

Stationed on board steamer, Mississippi River, July 1864.

Stationed at New Orleans, Louisiana, August-September 1864.

Stationed at Natchez, Mississippi, October-December 1864.

Company A

Stationed at Camp Dennison, Ohio, September 9-December 31, 1861.

Stationed at Paducah, Kentucky, January-February 1862.
[For record of events, see Field and Staff.]

Stationed at Camp Shiloh, near Pittsburg, Tennessee, March-April 1862.
April 6-7.— With the regiment in the expedition up the Tennessee and was engaged in the battle of Shiloh April 6 and 7.

Stationed at Moscow, Tennessee, May-June 1862.

Stationed at Fort Pickering, Tennessee, July-August 1862.

Stationed at Memphis, Tennessee, September-October 1862.

Station not stated, November-December 1862.

Stationed at Young's Point, Louisiana, January-February 1863.
January 11.— Engaged in the capture of Fort Hindman, Post Arkansas.

Stationed at Milliken's Bend, Louisiana, April 10, 1863.

Stationed near Grand Gulf, Mississippi, March-April 1863.
May 9.— Was transported by water from Young's Point to Milliken's Bend, Louisiana.

Marched from Milliken's Bend to near Grand Gulf in April 1863.

Stationed near Vicksburg, Mississippi, May-June 1863.
May 1-22.— Engaged at Magnolia Hills. Marched with Army when maneuvering, fighting in rear of Vicksburg, and was engaged in the desperate charge of May 22.

Stationed at Greenville, Louisiana, July-August 1863.

Engaged in the siege at Vicksburg until July 4. Marched to Jackson, Mississippi. Was engaged at that place and marched to Vicksburg again in July. Was transported from Vicksburg to Carrollton, Louisiana in August.

Stationed at Franklin, Louisiana, September-October 1863.
October 3-4.— Transported by water and rail from Carrollton, Louisiana to Berwick City, eighty-eight miles.
October 7-11.— Marched from Berwick City to New Iberia and from New Iberia to Franklin, eighty miles. Now on provost guard.

Stationed at Decros Point, Texas, November-December 1863.
November 1-December 10.— The company was provost guard at Franklin, Louisiana. Marched from Franklin to Berwick City December 9 and 10, twenty-eight miles.
December 12-18.— Was transported thence to Algiers, Louisiana and from that point by steamer *Continental* to Decros Point, Texas, landing December 18.

Stationed at Berwick City, Louisiana, January-February 1864.
February 21-25.— Was transported on steamer *Albany* from Decros Point, Texas to Algiers, Louisiana; thence by rail to Brashear City, Louisiana and by steamer to Berwick, Louisiana.

Stationed at Alexandria, Louisiana, March-April 1864.

Station not stated, May-June 1864.

Stationed at Natchez, Mississippi, June 30-October 31, 1864.

Company B

Station not stated, not dated.

Muster-in roll of Captain William L. Warner's Company B, in the Forty-eighth Regiment of Ohio Foot Volunteers, commanded by Colonel Peter J. Sullivan, called into the service of the United States by the President from the dates set opposite their names, respectively, for the term of three years, unless sooner discharged. . . .

[FRANCIS] M. POSEGATE,
Lieutenant,
Forty-eighth Regiment, Ohio Volunteers, Mustering Officer.

[JOB] R. PARKER,
Captain,
Forty-eighth Regiment, Ohio Volunteer, Mustering Officer.

[JOSEPH] W. LINDSEY,
Lieutenant,
Forty-eighth Regiment, Ohio Volunteers, Mustering Officer.

[ROBERT] T. WILSON,
Lieutenant,
Forty-eighth Regiment, Ohio Volunteers, Mustering Officer.

Stationed at Camp Dennison, Ohio, to December 31, 1861.

Stationed at Paducah, Kentucky, January-February 1862.
[For record of events, see Field and Staff.]

Stationed at Camp No. 4, near Monterey, Tennessee, March-April 1862.
March 7-19.— This company, with the regiment, left Paducah and was transported on the steamer *Empress* up the Tennessee River to Pittsburg Landing, Tennessee and encamped March 19 about one mile west of the river.
March 24.— Marched about four miles to Shiloh and camped.
April 6-7.— Was in the battle, having the captain and two men killed and the first and second lieutenants and thirteen men wounded. One man who was wounded is missing.
April 29.— Left Camp Shiloh and marched five miles.
April 30.— Marched three and one-half miles farther.

Stationed at Moscow, Tennessee, May-June 1862.

Stationed at Fort Pickering, Tennessee, Memphis, Tennessee, July-October 1862.

Stationed at camp in the field, near Vicksburg, Mississippi, November-December 1862.

Stationed at Young's Point, Louisiana, January-February 1863.
This company participated in the attack on Vicksburg, Mississippi during the last three days of the year 1862.
January 11.— Also in the capture of Post Arkansas.

Stationed at Milliken's Bend, Louisiana, April 10, 1863.

Stationed near Grand Gulf, Mississippi, March-April 1863.

Stationed at camp, near Vicksburg, Mississippi, May-June 1863.

Stationed at Carrollton, Louisiana, July-August 1863.
[For record of events, see Company A.]

Stationed at Franklin, Louisiana, September-October 1863.
October 3.— Remained in camp at Carrollton, Louisiana until October 3. Moved by steamer to Algiers, from thence to Brashear City by rail. Crossed Berwick Bay to Berwick City; thence marched to new New Iberia, Louisiana; thence returned to Franklin, Saint Mary Parish, Louisiana, where the company is now camped.

Stationed at Decros Point, Texas, November-December 1863.
Last mustered at Franklin, Louisiana.
November 11-12.— Marched for New Iberia, Louisiana, which place we reached on November 12.
December 7-11.— Remained there until December 7, on which day the company marched to Brashear City, which place it reached December 11. Thence went by rail to Algiers, Louisiana, reaching that city on December 11.
December 13-18.— The company started on board the steamship *Continental* for Matagorda Peninsula, Texas and reached that peninsula at Decros Point on December 18, where the company is now encamped.

Station not stated, January-February 1864.

Stationed at Alexandria, Louisiana, March-April 1864.

Stationed at Baton Rouge, Louisiana, May-June 1864.

Stationed at Natchez, Mississippi, June 30-October 31, 1864.

Company C

Stationed at Camp Dennison, October 14, 1861.
Muster-in roll of Captain John W. Frazee's Company, in the Forty-eighth Regiment of Ohio Foot Volunteers, commanded by Colonel Peter J. Sullivan, called into the service of the United States from the dates set opposite their names, for the term of three years, unless sooner discharged. . . .

JOHN W. FRAZEE,
Second Lieutenant,
Mustering Officer.

Stationed at Camp Dennison, Ohio, to December 31, 1861.

Stationed at Paducah, Kentucky, January-February 1862.
[For record of events, see Field and Staff.]

Stationed at camp in the field, March-April 1862.
March 6-18.— The company left Paducah, Kentucky with the regiment for Savannah, Tennessee, from thence thirty miles above Pittsburg, returning and landing at Pittsburg Landing, Tennessee on March 18. From the transport *Empress* camped near the Landing.
April 6-7.— Moved from thence to Camp Shiloh. Was engaged in the battle of April 6 and 7, losing one killed and ten wounded.
April 8.— A portion of the company was engaged in a scout.
April 29-May 1.— Moved from Camp Shiloh on the march for Corinth, Mississippi, camping again at Camp No. 4 May 1.

Stationed at camp, near Moscow, Tennessee, May-June 1862.

Stationed at Fort Pickering, near Memphis, Tennessee, July-October 1862.

Stationed on board steamer City of Alton, November-December 1862.

Stationed at Young's Point, Louisiana, January-February 1863.

Stationed at Milliken's Bend, Louisiana, April 10, 1863.

Stationed near Grand Gulf, Mississippi, March-April 1863.

Stationed in the rear of Vicksburg, Mississippi, May-June 1863.

Stationed at Greenville, Louisiana, July-August 1863.
July 4.— The company was engaged at the siege of Vicksburg, Mississippi until the surrender of the place July 4.
July 5.— Started for Jackson, Mississippi, forty-six miles east of Vicksburg.

July 10-16.— Arrived near Jackson. Were engaged at the siege of Jackson until the evacuation July 16.
July 21-23.— Started back for Vicksburg. Arrived there July 23.
August 23-27.— Started for New Orleans on the steamer *Atlantic*, a distance of 400 miles. Arrived at Carrollton, Louisiana, five miles above the city, August 27. Disembarked the same day and encamped two miles south of Carrollton, Louisiana.

Stationed at Franklin, Louisiana, September-October 1863.
October 3-4.— The company, with the regiment, embarked on the steamer *North America* at Carrollton, Louisiana. Ran down the Mississippi River to Algiers, Louisiana, a distance of eight miles. Disembarked the same evening at Algiers and traveled by rail to Brashear City, a distance of eighty miles, where the regiment arrived early on the morning of October 4. Crossed Berwick Bay the same day and encamped at Berwick City, Louisiana.
October 7-11.— Left Berwick City for New Iberia, a distance of fifty-eight miles. Marched to within three miles of the latter place, where the regiment with the Second Brigade, Fourth Division, Thirteenth Army Corps was ordered back to Franklin, Louisiana, a distance of twenty-five miles, arriving at the latter place October 11.

Stationed at Decros Point, Texas, November-December 1863.
November 11-12.— Left Franklin; arrived at New Iberia, Louisiana, distance twenty-eight miles, November 12.
December 7-11.— Left New Iberia; arrived at Berwick December 10, distance fifty-eight miles. Crossed the bay the same evening on a steamer. Were transported by rail from Brashear to Algiers, Louisiana, distance eighty miles, arriving at the latter place December 11.
December 13-18.— Embarked on the steamship *Continental*. Arrived off Matagorda Bay, Texas December 15, distance 490 miles from Algiers, Louisiana. Disembarked December 18 at Decros Point, Texas.

Stationed at Berwick City, Louisiana, January-February 1864.
February 2-24.— The company, with the regiment, was encamped at Decros Point, Texas until February 2, when the

regiment received marching orders for Berwick City, Louisiana. Embarked the same day on the steamer *Albany* and arrived at Algiers, Louisiana February 24, a distance of 490 miles.
February 25.— Traveled from thence by rail to Brashear City, Louisiana, a distance of eighty miles, where the regiment arrived the same evening. Crossed Berwick Bay on a steamer and encamped at Berwick City, Louisiana.

Stationed at Alexandria, Louisiana, March-April 1864.

Stationed at Baton Rouge, Louisiana, May-June 1864.

Stationed at Natchez, June 30-December 31, 1864.

Company D

Station not stated, not dated.

Muster-in roll of Captain Cyrus Elwood's Company D, in the Forty-eighth Regiment of Ohio Foot Volunteers, commanded by Colonel Peter J. Sullivan, called into the service of the United States by the President from the dates set opposite their names, respectively. . . .

F. M. POSEGATE,
Lieutenant,
Forty-eighth Regiment, Mustering Officer.

J. R. PARKER,
Captain,
Forty-eighth Regiment, Mustering Officer.

CYRUS ELWOOD,
Lieutenant,
Forty-eighth Regiment, Mustering Officer.

Stationed at Camp Dennison, Ohio, to December 31, 1861.

Station not stated, January-February 1862.

Stationed at Camp No. 4 in the field, March-April 1862.
April 6-7.— The company, with the regiment, accompanied the expedition up the Tennessee [River] and was engaged in the battle of Shiloh April 6 and 7.

Stationed at Moscow, Tennessee, May-June 1862.

Stationed at Fort Pickering, Tennessee, July-October 1862.

Stationed on board the transport City of Alton, November-December 1862.
Left Memphis, Tennessee on board transport *City of Alton* in company with the fleet under General Sherman, destined for operations against Vicksburg. Our regiment held the extreme right of General [Andrew Jackson] Smith's Division before that city.

Stationed at Young's Point, Louisiana, January-February 1863.

Stationed at Milliken's Bend, Louisiana, April 10, 1863.

Stationed at camp opposite Grand Gulf, Mississippi, March-April 1863.
April 15.— Left Milliken's Bend.
May 1.— Engaged in the battle of Port Gibson.

Stationed at the rear of Vicksburg, May-June 1863.

Stationed at Carrollton, Louisiana, July-August 1863.
This company, with the regiment, took an active part in the siege of Vicksburg, Mississippi until the surrender of that place to the United States forces and from thence to Jackson, Mississippi with the Army under Major-General Sherman. After the evacuation of that place by the enemy it was ordered to Vicksburg and from there to Carrollton, Louisiana.

Stationed at Franklin, Louisiana, September-October 1863.

Stationed at Decros Point, Texas, November-December 1863.

Stationed at Berwick City, Louisiana, January-February 1864.

Stationed at Alexandria, Louisiana, March-April 1864.

Station not stated, May-June 1864.

Stationed at Natchez, Mississippi, June 30-December 31, 1864.

Company E

Station not stated, not dated.

Muster-in roll of Captain John J. Ireland's Company, in the Forty-eighth Regiment of Ohio Foot Volunteers, commanded by Colonel Peter J. Sullivan, called into the service of the United States by the President from the dates set opposite their names, respectively, for the term of three years, unless sooner discharged. . . .

F. M. POSEGATE,
Lieutenant,
Forty-eighth Regiment, Mustering Officer.

JOHN J. IRELAND,
Lieutenant,
Forty-eighth Regiment, Mustering Officer.

Stationed at Camp Dennison, Ohio, to December 31, 1861.

Stationed at camp at Paducah, Kentucky, January-February 1862.
[For record of events, see Field and Staff.]

Stationed at Camp Shiloh, Tennessee, March-April 1862.
March 6-April 7.— The company left Paducah, Kentucky with the regiment for Savannah, Tennessee. From thence to Pittsburg Landing on transport *Empress*. Disembarked and camped near the landing a few days; thence four miles to Camp Shiloh, where the company was engaged in the battle of April 6 and 7. Lost in killed, one; wounded and afterwards died, one; wounded, seven; and four missing.
April 8.— A portion of this company was engaged in a scout.
April 29.— Moved from Camp Shiloh towards Corinth.

Stationed at Moscow, Tennessee, May-June 1862.

Stationed at Fort Pickering, Tennessee, July-October 1862.

Stationed on board the steamer City of Alton, [November]-December 1862.

Stationed at Young's Point, Louisiana, January-February 1863.
January 11.— Engaged in the capture of Arkansas Post.

Stationed at Milliken's Bend, Louisiana, April 10, 1863.

Stationed in the field opposite Grand Gulf, Louisiana, March-April 1863.

Stationed at the rear of Vicksburg, Mississippi, May-June 1863.

Stationed at Carrollton, Louisiana, July-August 1863.
The company was engaged in all the engagements prior to the siege of Vicksburg, Mississippi in which the company took an active part during the siege, which ended July 4. Was then ordered to Jackson, Mississippi.
July 5-9.— Started [for Jackson], where we arrived on July 9.
After a siege of seven days, the Rebel Army under General [Joseph Eggleston] Johnston evacuated the place and the Federal Army took possession; thence returned to Vicksburg and went into camp.
August 25.— We were ordered on the steamer *Atlantic* and steamed down to Carrollton, Louisiana, where we are at present.

Stationed at Franklin, Louisiana, September-October 1863.

Stationed at Decros Point, Texas, November-December 1863.

Stationed at Berwick, Louisiana, [January]-February 1864.

Stationed at Alexandria, Louisiana, March-April 1864.

Stationed at Natchez, Mississippi, June 30-October 31, 1864.

Company F

Station not stated, not dated.

Muster-in roll of Captain Virgil H. Moats' Company, in the Forty-eighth Regiment of Ohio Foot Volunteers, commanded by Colonel Peter J. Sullivan, called into the service of the United States by the President from date set opposite their respective names, unless sooner discharged. . . .

VIRGIL H. MOATS,
Captain,
Commanding Company, Mustering Officer.

Stationed at Camp Dennison, Ohio, to December 31, 1861.

Stationed at Paducah, January-February 1862.
[For record of events, see Field and Staff.]

Stationed at Camp Shiloh, Tennessee, March-April 1862.

Left camp at Paducah with the regiment on transport *Empress* for Savannah, Tennessee. From there to Pittsburg Landing, where we encamped.

April 6-7.— [Were engaged in] the battle of Shiloh, in which we were engaged. The men fought well.

April 29.— From thence we moved toward Corinth.

Stationed at Moscow, Tennessee, May-June 1862.

Stationed at Memphis, Tennessee, August 18, 1862.

Stationed at Fort Pickering, Tennessee, July-October 1862.

Stationed before Vicksburg, Mississippi, November-December 1862.

December 20.— The company left Memphis with the regiment on the expedition against Vicksburg under command of Major-General W. T. Sherman.

Station not stated, January-February 1863.

Stationed at Milliken's Bend, Louisiana, April 10, 1863.

Station not stated, March-April 1863.

Stationed at camp, near Vicksburg, Mississippi, May-June 1863.

Stationed at Carrollton, Louisiana, July-August 1863.
July 4.— Was at Vicksburg during the [siege], which ended July 4.
July 5.— Started to Jackson, Mississippi.
July 9.— Reached [Jackson] and found the place occupied by General Johnston and his Army and after a siege of seven days the Confederate Army evacuated the place.
July 24-27.— We returned to Vicksburg, Mississippi, where we arrived July 24 and encamped until August 25, when we were ordered on board the steamer *Atlantic* and started down the Mississippi River. We landed August 27 at Carrollton, Louisiana.

Stationed at Franklin, Louisiana, September-October 1863.

Stationed at Decros Point, Texas, November-December 1863.

Stationed at Berwick, Louisiana, January-February 1864.

Stationed at Alexandria, Louisiana, March-April 1864.

Stationed at Natchez, Mississippi, June 30-December 31, 1864.

Company G

Stationed at Camp Dennison, Ohio, December 24, 1861.
Muster-in roll of Captain George A. Miller's Company G, in the Forty-eighth Regiment of Ohio Foot Volunteers, commanded by Colonel Peter J. Sullivan, called into service of the United States by the President from the dates set opposite their names, respectively, for the term of three years, unless sooner discharged. . . .

GEORGE A. MILLER,
Mustering Officer.

J. W. FRAZEE,
Mustering Officer.

[CHARLES] A. PARTRIDGE,
Mustering Officer.

Stationed at Camp Dennison, Ohio, to December 31, 1861.

Stationed at Paducah, Kentucky, February 28, 1862.
February 17-20.— Were transported by railroad from Camp Dennison, Ohio to Cincinnati, Ohio and thence by steamboats *Hastings* and *Argonaut* to Paducah, Kentucky.

Stationed at Camp No. 2, March-April 1862.
March 7-9.— This company, with the regiment, left Paducah and was transported by steamer *Empress* up the Tennessee River. Landed at Pittsburg Landing March 9.
March 21.— Camped at Shiloh.
April 6-7.— Was engaged in the battle of Shiloh, having two men severely wounded and one corporal missing.
April 29-30.— Marched from Shiloh and camped on April 30 about eight miles toward Corinth.

Stationed at Moscow, Tennessee, May-June 1862.

Stationed at Fort Pickering, Memphis, Tennessee, July-October 1862.

Stationed at Young's Point, Louisiana, January-February 1863.

Stationed at Milliken's Bend, Louisiana, April 10, 1863.

Stationed opposite Grand Gulf, Louisiana, March-April 1863.

Stationed near Vicksburg, Mississippi, May-June 1863.

Stationed at Carrollton, Louisiana, July-August 1863.
July 4.— This company, with the regiment, was at the siege of Vicksburg, Mississippi until the surrender July 4.
July 5-17.— Started for Jackson, Mississippi and was engaged in the siege of Jackson until it was evacuated July 17.

July 24.— Marched back to Vicksburg again and encamped there July 24.
August 25-27.— Embarked on the steamer *Atlantic* and arrived at Carrollton, Louisiana August 27, where we are still encamped yet.

Stationed at Franklin, Louisiana, September-October 1863.
October 3-4.— Was encamped near Carrollton, Louisiana until October 3, when we crossed the Mississippi River to Algiers and took the cars for Brashear City and arrived there October 4. Crossed Berwick Bay and encamped near Berwick City.
October 7.— Started on the march up Bayou Teche. Passed through Pattersonville, Centerville and Franklin, Louisiana.
October 9-11.— We caught up with the Thirteenth Army Corps near Iberia, Louisiana. Was ordered back to Franklin. Arrived there October 11, where we are at present encamped, making a march of seventy-five miles.

Stationed at Decros Point, Texas, November-December 1863.

Stationed at Berwick City, Louisiana, January-February 1864.

Stationed at Alexandria, Louisiana, March-April 1864.

Stationed at Baton Rouge, Louisiana, May-June 1864.

Stationed at Natchez, Mississippi, [July]-December 1864.

Company H

Station not stated, not dated.

Muster-in roll of Captain J. C. Bond's Company H, in the Forty-eighth Regiment of Ohio Foot Volunteers, commanded by Colonel Peter J. Sullivan, called into the service of the United States by the President from the dates set opposite their names, respectively, for the term of three years, unless sooner discharged. . . .

J. R. PARKER,
Captain,
Forty-eighth Regiment, Mustering Officer.

R. T. WILSON,
Lieutenant,
Forty-eighth Regiment, Mustering Officer.

F. M. POSEGATE,
Lieutenant,
Forty-eighth Regiment, Mustering Officer.

[SAMUEL] G. W. PETERSON,
Captain,
Forty-eighth Regiment, Mustering Officer.

J. W. FRAZEE,
Commanding Company C, Forty-eighth Regiment, Mustering Officer.

Stationed at Paducah, Kentucky, January-February 1862.
February 17-20.— This company, with the regiment, was transported by the government by rail and steamboat from Camp Dennison, Ohio to this place.

Stationed at Camp No. 4, Tennessee, March-April 1862.
This company was transported from Paducah, Kentucky with the regiment to Pittsburg Landing, Tennessee on board the steamer *Empress*.
April 6-7.— Was engaged in the battle at Shiloh, Tennessee.

Stationed at Moscow, Tennessee, May-June 1862.

Stationed at Fort Pickering, Tennessee, July-October 1862.

Stationed near Vicksburg, Mississippi, November-December 1862.

Stationed at Young's Point, Louisiana, January-February 1863.

Stationed at Milliken's Bend, Louisiana, April 10, 1863.

Station not stated, March-April 1863.

Stationed at camp, near Vicksburg, Mississippi, May-June 1863.

Stationed at Carrollton, Louisiana, July-August 1863.

The company participated in the siege of Vicksburg, Mississippi. Marched to Jackson, Mississippi and took an active part in driving the enemy from that place.

July 23.— Returned to Vicksburg.

August 25-27.— Embarked on board transport *Atlantic* and landed at Carrollton, Louisiana August 27.

Stationed at Franklin, Louisiana, September-October 1863.

Stationed at Decros Point, Texas, November-December 1863.

November 11.— The company was last mustered at Franklin, west Louisiana, from whence we received marching orders November 11.

November 12-December 7.— We arrived at New Iberia, Louisiana. We encamped at New Iberia until December 7, when we received orders to march at 2 o'clock p.m.

December 10-11.— We arrived at Brashear City and were transported by rail from there to Algiers on December 11.

December 12-18.— We embarked on board the steamer *Continental* at night and sailed on the morning of December 13, anchoring off Decros Point, Texas on December 15. Owing to a rough sea we were not landed until December 18, since then we have been encamped at this place.

Stationed at Berwick City, Louisiana, January-February 1864.

Since last muster the company has sailed from Decros Point, Texas to Algiers, Louisiana. Was then transported by railroad to Brashear City, Louisiana and from thence ferried across Berwick Bay to our present camp.

Stationed at Alexandria, Louisiana, March-April 1864.

Stationed at Natchez, Mississippi, June 30-October 31, 1864.

Stationed at Natchez, Mississippi, December 31, 1864.

Transferred from Camp Dennison, Ohio to Paducah, Kentucky in February 1862. Thence to Pittsburg Landing in March 1862.

April 2, 7, 1862.— Engaged in the battle of Shiloh April 2 and 7, 1862.

Thence to the siege of Corinth during May 1862. Thence to Holly Springs, Mississippi; thence to Memphis, Tennessee in July 1862. Thence to Vicksburg, Mississippi December 1862.

Engaged in battle of Chickasaw Bayou; thence to Arkansas Post.

January 11, 1863.— Engaged there January 11, 1863; thence to the siege of Vicksburg.

May 1-23.— Engaged the enemy at Magnolia Hills May 1. Also Raymond, Champion's Hill, Black River Bridge and at the charge of Vicksburg May 23; thence to Jackson, Mississippi.

July 16.— Engaged the enemy July 16; thence to Vicksburg.

From there to New Orleans in August 1863.

October 3.— Thence to Brashear City, Louisiana.

Thence to New Iberia, Louisiana in November 1863. Thence to New Orleans, Louisiana in December 1863. Thence to Decros Point, Texas in December 1863.

Thence back to New Orleans February 1864. From there on the Red River campaign in March and April 1864.

April 8, 1864.— At the battle of Sabine Cross-Roads April 8, where nine commissioned officers and 168 enlisted men were taken prisoners out of the regiment.

Thence back to Baton Rouge, Louisiana May 1864; thence to New Orleans June 1864, where the veteran portion was ordered home on furlough in June 1864. Returned to New Orleans September 1864; thence to Natchez, Mississippi September 1864.

November 3.— Prisoners taken at Sabine Cross-Roads returned to the regiment. We are at present date doing provost duty in the city of Natchez, Mississippi.

Company I

Station not stated, not dated.

Muster-in roll of Captain Isaac J. Ross' Company I, in the Forty-eighth Regiment of Ohio Foot Volunteers, commanded by

Colonel Peter J. Sullivan, called into the service of the United States by the President from the dates set opposite their names, respectively, for the term of three years, unless sooner discharged. . . .

CYRUS ELWOOD,
Captain,
Forty-eighth Regiment, Mustering Officer.

R. M. POSEGATE,
Lieutenant,
Forty-eighth Regiment, Mustering Officer.

J. R. PARKER,
Captain,
Forty-eighth Regiment, Mustering Officer.

S. G. W. PETERSON,
Captain,
Forty-eighth Regiment, Mustering Officer.

J. W. LINDSEY,
Lieutenant,
Forty-eighth Regiment, Mustering Officer.

JOHN J. IRELAND,
Captain,
Company E, Mustering Officer.

V. H. MOATS,
Captain,
Forty-eighth Regiment, Mustering Officer.

Stationed at Paducah, Kentucky, February 28, 1862.
[For record of events, see Field and Staff.]

Stationed at Camp Shiloh, Department of West Tennessee, March-April 1862.
[For record of events, see Field and Staff.]

Stationed at Moscow, Tennessee, May-June 1862.

Stationed at Fort Pickering, Tennessee, July-October 1862.

Stationed in the field, near Vicksburg, November-December 1862.

Stationed at Young's Point, Louisiana, January-February 1863.

Stationed at Milliken's Bend, Louisiana, April 10, 1863.

Station not stated, March-April 1863.

Stationed at camp, near Vicksburg, Mississippi, May-June 1863.

Stationed at Greenville, Louisiana, July-August 1863.

The company was last mustered in the rear of Vicksburg, Mississippi, where they were present at the siege and surrender of the place.

July 5-16.— We started to Jackson, Mississippi and took part in all the skirmishes and in the siege of that place until the evacuation on July 16. We then returned to Vicksburg, Mississippi.

August 25-27.— We started for Carrollton, Louisiana, arriving August 27.

Stationed at Franklin, Louisiana, September-October 1863.

October 3-4.— Left Carrollton, Louisiana and reached Brashear City by railroad October 4. Marched from Brashear City to New Iberia, distance fifty-eight miles.

October 12.— Countermarched to Franklin, Louisiana, distance thirty miles, at which place we encamped October 12 and have since remained.

Stationed at Decros Point, Texas, November-December 1863.

Last mustered at Franklin, Louisiana.

November 11-12.— Left Franklin for New Iberia, which place we reached on November 12, distance thirty miles.

December 7-11.— Left New Iberia and arrived at Brashear City December 11, distance fifty-eight miles. Left Brashear City December 11 by railroad. Reached Algiers the evening of the same day.

December 13-18.— Left Algiers by steamship *Continental* and arrived at Decros Point, Texas December 18, where we still remain.

Stationed at Berwick City, Louisiana, January-February 1864.

Stationed at Alexandria, Louisiana, March-April 1864.

Stationed at Baton Rouge, Louisiana, May-June 1864.

Stationed at Natchez, Mississippi, [July]-December 1864.

Company K

Station not stated, not dated.

Muster-in roll of Captain Samuel G. W. Peterson's Company K, in the Forty-eighth Regiment of Ohio Volunteers, commanded by Colonel Peter J. Sullivan, called into the service of the United States by the President from the dates set opposite their names, respectively, for the term of three years, unless sooner discharged. . . .

F. M. POSEGATE,
Lieutenant,
Forty-eighth Regiment, Mustering Officer.

SAMUEL G. W. PETERSON,
Lieutenant,
Forty-eighth Regiment, Mustering Officer.

Stationed at Camp Dennison, Ohio, from muster-in to December 31, 1861.

Stationed at Paducah, Kentucky, January-February 1862.
[For record of events, see Field and Staff.]

Stationed at Camp No. 3, Tennessee, March-April 1862.
March 6.— The company was transported by steamboat from Paducah, Kentucky to Pittsburg Landing, Tennessee.
April 6-7.— Was in the battle of Shiloh.
April 29.— Marched to Camp No. 3 from Shiloh on the way to Corinth, Tennessee.

Stationed at Moscow, Tennessee, May-June 1862.

The company, since last muster, has marched from Camp No. 2 to Corinth, fortifying every few miles. Were in advance in several skirmishes before Corinth, before it at the evacuation and among the foremost to mount the fortifications. Have marched from Corinth towards Memphis as far as La Fayette, Tennessee and countermarched as far back as Moscow.

Stationed at Fort Pickering, Tennessee, July-August 1862.

Marched from Moscow, Tennessee to Holly Springs, Mississippi in the advance. Brisk skirmish with Rebel cavalry. Returned to Moscow. Marched from Moscow to Memphis, Tennessee.

Stationed at Fort Pickering, Tennessee, [September]-October 1862.

Stationed at Fort Pickering, Tennessee since July 23.

Stationed on board steamer City of Alton, November-December 1862.

Stationed at Young's Point, Louisiana, January-February 1863.

Since last muster was transported by steamboat up Arkansas River to Fort Hindman. Was in the fight. Lost one man killed and three slightly wounded. Came down the Mississippi River to Young's Point, Louisiana and have been engaged at the work on the canal.

Stationed at Milliken's Bend, Louisiana, April 10, 1863.

Stationed at Hard Times Landing, Louisiana, March-April 1863.

Stationed near Vicksburg, Mississippi, May-June 1863.

Stationed at Carrollton, Louisiana, July-August 1863.

The company participated in the siege of Vicksburg. Marched to Jackson, Mississippi. Took an active part in driving the enemy from that place.

July 23.— Returned to Vicksburg.

August 2.— Embarked on board the transport *Atlantic* and arrived at Carrollton, Louisiana August 2.

Stationed at Franklin, Louisiana, September-October 1863.

Stationed at Decros Point, Texas, November-December 1863.

Stationed at Berwick City, Louisiana, January-February 1864.

Stationed at Alexandria, Louisiana, March-April 1864.

Stationed at Baton Rouge, Louisiana, May-June 1864.

Stationed at Natchez, Mississippi, [July]-October 1864.

[M594-Roll #150]

Record of Events for Forty-ninth Ohio Infantry, August 1861-June 1865.

Detachment

Stationed at Tiffin, Ohio, January 1, 1864.
January 1.— This party was detailed on special recruiting services by virtue of Special Orders No. 193, Headquarters, Department of the Cumberland, Nashville, July 23, 1863, and assigned to duty in Ohio by Special Orders No. 345, Headquarters, Ohio Volunteer Recruiting Services, Columbus, Ohio, December 30, 1863.

Field and Staff

Station not stated, October 31, 1861.

Stationed at Camp Wood, Kentucky, [November 1]-December 31, 1861.

Stationed at Camp Wood, Kentucky, January 14, 1862.
January 14.— Muster-out roll of regimental band, Forty-ninth Regiment of Ohio Infantry Volunteers, commanded by Colonel William [Harvey] Gibson, called into the service of the United States by the President at Tiffin, Ohio (the place of general rendezvous) on August 15, 1861 to serve for the term of three years from the date of enrollment, unless sooner discharged, from August 15, 1861 (when enrolled) to January 14, 1862. The regiment was organized by Colonel William H. Gibson at Tiffin, Ohio. . . .

The band was organized by Homer W. Gifford in the month of August 1861, and mustered in Company C, Forty-ninth Regiment, Ohio Volunteers on which the members were transferred to the regimental band by order of the colonel, September 4, 1861 . . . with the exception of those noted as "absent sick at Louisville," it is hereby honorably discharged from the service of the United States.

[REUBEN] DELAVAN MUSSEY,
Captain,
Nineteenth [Infantry], United States Army,
Mustering Officer.

Stationed at Louisville, Kentucky, January 16, 1862.
January 16.— I certify that I have this day duly mustered out of service those members of the above band noted as "absent sick at Louisville."

R. DELAVAN MUSSEY,
Captain,
Nineteenth [Infantry], United States Army,
Mustering Officer.

Stationed in the field, January-February 1862.

Station not stated, March 1-August 31, 1862.

Stationed at Bowling Green, [Kentucky], September-October 1862.

Stationed near Murfreesborough, Tennessee, November-December 1862.

Stationed at Camp Sill, Tennessee, January-February 1863.

Stationed at Camp Drake, Tennessee, April 10, 1863.

Station not stated, March-August 1863.

Stationed at Chattanooga, Tennessee, September-October 1863.

Stationed at McDonald's Station, Tennessee, November 1863-April 1864.

Stationed at Kenesaw Mountain, Georgia, May-June 1864.

Stationed near Atlanta, Georgia, July-August 1864.
July 1-3.— Confronted the enemy at Kenesaw Mountain, Georgia. Enemy evacuated the night of July 2. Pursued the following morning at 12 m.
July 6.— Reached the Chattahoochee River.
July 12-August 24.— Crossed [the river]. Participated in the siege of Atlanta.
August 25.— The same was raised. The regiment, with the other forces, performed the circuit of Atlanta, passing around to the right and struck first the West Point and Montgomery Railroad, then the Macon Railroad, the only remaining one by which Atlanta communicated with the Confederacy.
August 31.— Reached the latter road. The regiment marched during July and August sixty miles.

Stationed at Athens, Alabama, September-October 1864.

The regiment participated in no general engagements. Marched as follows: from Rough and Ready [Station] to Jonesborough, twelve miles; thence to Lovejoy's Station, four miles; back to Atlanta, twenty-eight miles; thence to Kingston, ninety-eight miles; thence to Rome, twenty-three miles; thence to Resaca, twenty-five miles; thence to Summerville; thence to Gaylesville, Alabama; thence to Chattanooga, Tennessee; thence by rail to Athens, Alabama.
October 31.— We arrived in the morning [at Athens].

Stationed near Huntsville, Alabama, November 1864-February 1865.

Stationed near Nashville, Tennessee, March-April 1865.

Stationed near New Orleans, Louisiana, May-June 1865.

Regiment

Stationed at Camp Wood, December 1861-February 1862.

Stationed at Camp Andrew Johnson, March 1862.

Stationed before Corinth, April-May 1862.

Stationed near Huntsville, June 1862.

Stationed at Battle Creek, Tennessee, July 1862.
July 5.— Marched to Huntsville, distance eight miles.
July 6.— Marched to Hurricane Creek, distance thirteen miles.
July 7.— Marched to Paint Rock Creek, distance twelve miles.
July 8.— Marched to Larkinsville, distance fourteen miles.
July 9.— Marched to Bellefonte, distance twelve miles.
July 10.— Marched to Crow Creek, distance nine miles.
July 18.— Marched to Battle Creek, distance fifteen miles, total eighty-three miles.

Stationed at Battle Creek, August 1862.

Station not stated, September 1862.
Return dated Camp Drake, Tennessee June 8, 1863.

Station not stated, October 1862.
Return dated Camp Drake, Tennessee June 8, 1863.

Stationed at Nashville, November 1862.

Stationed near Murfreesborough, Tennessee, December 1862-January 1863.

Stationed at Camp Sill, Tennessee, February 1863.

Stationed at Camp Drake, Tennessee, March-April 1863.

Stationed at Murfreesborough, Tennessee, May 1863.

Stationed at Manchester, Tennessee, June 1863.

Stationed at Camp Reed, Tullahoma, Tennessee, July 1863.

Stationed at Bellefonte, Alabama, August 1863.

Stationed at Chattanooga, Tennessee, September-October 1863.

Station not stated, November 1863.
Return dated Chattanooga, Tennessee January 30, 1864.

Stationed at Strawberry Plains, December 1863.

Stationed at Chattanooga, January 1864.

Stationed at Tiffin, Ohio, February 1864.
February 2.— The regiment reenlisted and left Chattanooga for Ohio. They were furloughed for thirty days at Tiffin, Ohio from February 15, 1864.

Stationed at Nashville, Tennessee, March 1864.

Stationed in the field, April-June 1864.

Stationed near Atlanta, Georgia, July-September 1864.

Stationed at Athens, Alabama, October 1864.

Stationed at Franklin, Tennessee, November 1864.

Stationed at Lexington, Alabama, December 1864.

Stationed at Camp Green, near Huntsville, Alabama, January 1865.

Stationed at Camp Green, Alabama, February 1865.

Stationed at Bull's Gap, East Tennessee, March 1865.

Stationed near Nashville, Tennessee, April-May 1865.

Stationed near New Orleans, Louisiana, June 1865.

Company A

Stationed at Camp Noble, Tiffin, Ohio, August 15, 1861.
August 15.— Muster-in roll of Captain Albert Langworthy's Company [A], in the Forty-ninth Regiment (—— Brigade) of Ohio Volunteers, commanded by Colonel William H. Gibson, called into the service of the United States by [the President] from August 15, 1861 (date of muster) for the term of three years, unless sooner discharged. The company was organized by Captain Albert Langworthy at Findlay, Ohio in the month of August and marched thence to Tiffin, Ohio, where it arrived August 10, a distance of thirty-two miles. . . .

ANSON MILLS,
First Lieutenant,
Eighteenth Infantry, Mustering Officer.

Stationed at Camp Nevin, Kentucky, August 6-October 31, 1861.

Stationed at Camp Wood, Kentucky, [November 1]-December 31, 1861.

Station not stated, January-February 1862.

Stationed in field of Shiloh, March-April 1862.

Stationed at Louisville, May 1-August 31, 1862.

Stationed near Bowling Green, Kentucky, September-October 1862.

Stationed at Camp Sill, Tennessee, November 1862-February 1863.

Stationed at Camp Drake, Tennessee, March-April 1863.

Station not stated, May-June 1863.

Stationed near Stevenson, Alabama, July-August 1863.

Stationed at Chattanooga, Tennessee, September-December 1863.

Stationed at Camp Green, Alabama, January-February 1864.
January 1.— Reenlisted as veteran volunteers at Strawberry Plains, East Tennessee.

Stationed at McDonald's [Station], Tennessee, March-April 1864.

Stationed near Atlanta, Georgia, May-August 1864.

Stationed at Camp Green, Alabama, September 1864-February 1865.

Stationed near Nashville, Tennessee, March-April 1865.

Stationed near New Orleans, Louisiana, May-June 1865.

Company B

Stationed at Camp Noble, Tiffin, Ohio, August 17, 1861.
August 17.— Muster-in roll of Captain Benjamin Sabin Porter's Company [B], in the Forty-ninth Regiment (—— Brigade) of Ohio Volunteers, commanded by Colonel William H. Gibson, called into the service of the United States by the President from August 17, 1861 (date of muster) for the term of three years, unless sooner discharged. The company was organized by Captain Benjamin S. Porter at Tiffin, Ohio in the month of August and marched thence to Camp Noble, where it arrived August 13. . . .

ANSON MILLS,
First Lieutenant,
Eighteenth Infantry, Mustering Officer.

Stationed at Camp Nevin, Kentucky, [August 17]-October 31, 1861.

Stationed at Camp Wood, Kentucky, [November 1]-December 31, 1861.

Station not stated, [January-February 1862].
Corresponds to roll on file on which company was paid to February 28, 1862.

Station not stated, March 1-August 31, 1862.

Stationed near Bowling Green, Kentucky, September-October 1862.

Stationed at Camp Sill, Tennessee, November 1862-February 1863.

Stationed at Camp Drake, Tennessee, March-April 1863.

Stationed at Camp Reed, Tullahoma, Tennessee, May-June 1863.

Stationed in the field, July-August 1863.

Stationed at Chattanooga, Tennessee, September-December 1863.

Stationed in the field, Georgia, January-February 1864.
January 1.— Reenlisted as veteran volunteers at Strawberry Plains, East Tennessee.
January 27.— Mustered as veteran organization at Chattanooga, Tennessee.

Stationed in the field, Georgia, March-June 1864.

Stationed at camp, near Atlanta, Georgia, July-August 1864.

Stationed in the field, near Athens, Alabama, September-October 1864.

Stationed at Camp Green, Alabama, November 1864-February 1865.

Stationed at Camp Harker, Tennessee, March-April 1865.

Stationed at camp, near New Orleans, Louisiana, May-June 1865.

Company C

Stationed at Camp Noble, Tiffin, Ohio, September 1, 1861.
September 1.— Muster-in roll of Captain [Amos] Keller's Company [C], in the Forty-ninth Regiment (—— Brigade) of Ohio Volunteers, commanded by Colonel W. H. Gibson, called into the service of the United States by the President from September 1, 1861 (date of muster) for the term of three years, unless sooner discharged. The company was organized by Captain Amos Keller at Sulphur Springs in the month of August and marched thence to Tiffin, Ohio, where it arrived August 15, a distance of twenty-eight miles. . . .

ANSON MILLS,
First Lieutenant,
Eighteenth Infantry, Mustering Officer.

Stationed at Camp Nevin, [September 1]-October 31, 1861.

Stationed at Camp Wood, Kentucky, [November 1]-December 31, 1861.

Station not stated, [January-February 1862].

Corresponds to roll on file on which company was paid to February 28, 1862.

Stationed at camp, near Corinth, Mississippi, March-April 1862.

Stationed at Louisville, Kentucky, May 1-August 31, 1862.

Stationed at camp, near Bowling Green, Kentucky, September-October 1862.

Stationed at Camp Sill, Tennessee, November 1862-February 1863.

Stationed at Murfreesborough, Tennessee, April 10, 1863.

Stationed at Camp Drake, Tennessee, March-April 1863.

Stationed at Tullahoma, Tennessee, May-June 1863.

Stationed at camp, near Stevenson, Alabama, July-August 1863.

Stationed at Chattanooga, Tennessee, September-October 1863.

Stationed at Strawberry Plains, East Tennessee, November-December 1863.

Stationed at Tiffin, Ohio, January-February 1864.
[For record of events, see Company B.]

Stationed at McDonald's Station, Tennessee, March-April 1864.

Stationed near Marietta, Georgia, May-June 1864.

Stationed near Atlanta, Georgia, July-August 1864.

Stationed at Athens, Alabama, September-October 1864.

Stationed in the field, November-December 1864.

Stationed near Huntsville, Alabama, January-February 1865.

Stationed at Nashville, Tennessee, March-April 1865.

Stationed near New Orleans, Louisiana, May-June 1865.

Company D

Stationed at Camp Noble, Tiffin, Ohio, August 20, 1861.
August 20.— Muster-in roll of Captain George Washington Culver's Company [D], in the Forty-ninth Regiment (—— Brigade) of

Ohio Volunteers, commanded by Colonel William H. Gibson, called into the service of the United States by the President from August 20, 1861 (date of muster) for the term of three years, unless sooner discharged. The company was organized by Captain George Washington Culver at [illegible], Ohio in the month of August and marched thence to Tiffin, Ohio, where it arrived August 14, a distance of fourteen miles. . . .

ANSON MILLS,
First Lieutenant,
Eighteenth Infantry, Mustering Officer.

Stationed at Camp Nevin, [August 20]-October 31, 1861.

Stationed at Camp Wood, Kentucky, November-December 1861.

Station not stated, January 1-August 31, 1862.

Stationed at camp, near Bowling Green, September-October 1862.

Stationed at Camp Sill, Tennessee, November 1862-February 1863.

Stationed at Camp Drake, Tennessee, March-April 1863.

Stationed at Tullahoma, Tennessee, May-June 1863.

Stationed near Stevenson, Alabama, July-August 1863.

Stationed at Chattanooga, Tennessee, September-October 1863.

Stationed at Strawberry Plains, Tennessee, November-December 1863.

Stationed at Tiffin, Ohio, January-February 1864.
[For record of events, see Company B.]

Stationed at camp, near McDonald's Station, East Tennessee, March-April 1864.

Stationed near Atlanta, Georgia, May-August 1864.

Stationed at Huntsville, Alabama, September-October 1864.

Stationed at Camp Green, Alabama, November-December 1864.

Stationed at Huntsville, Alabama, January-February 1865.

Stationed near Nashville, Tennessee, March-April 1865.

Stationed near New Orleans, Louisiana, May-June 1865.

Company E

Stationed at Camp Noble, Tiffin, Ohio, August 22, 1861.
August 22.— Muster-in roll of Captain William Callihan's Company [E], in the Forty-ninth Regiment (—— Brigade) of Ohio Volunteers, commanded by Colonel W. H. Gibson, called into the service of the United States by the President from August 22, 1861 (date of muster) for the term of three years, unless sooner discharged. The company was organized by Captain William Callihan at Fostoria in the month of August and marched thence to Camp Noble, where it arrived August 22, a distance of fourteen miles. . . .

ANSON MILLS,
First Lieutenant,
Eighteenth Infantry, Mustering Officer.

Stationed at Camp Nevin, Kentucky, August 12-October 31, 1861.

Stationed at Camp Wood, Kentucky, [November 1]-December 31, 1861.

Stationed at Camp Stanton, Tennessee, [January 1]-March 1, 1862.

Stationed at Camp Shiloh, Tennessee, March-April 1862.

Stationed at Louisville, Kentucky, April 30-August 31, 1862.
June 10.— This company left Corinth, Mississippi at 5 o'clock p.m.

July 19.— Arrived at Battle Creek, Tennessee, having marched a distance of 220 miles, passing through the towns of Iuka, Tuscumbia, Florence, Athens, Huntsville, and Stevenson.
August 20.— Left Battle Creek in the night.

Stationed at camp, near Bowling Green, Kentucky, September-October 1862.
September 26.— Arrived at Louisville, Kentucky, having marched a distance of 361 miles, passing through the following named places, *viz.*: Jasper, Altamont, Manchester, Murfreesborough, Nashville, Bowling Green, Elizabethtown, and West Point.

Stationed at Camp Sill, November-December 1862.
November 4.— The company left Bowling Green, Kentucky.
November 7.— Arrived at Nashville, Tennessee. Marched a distance of sixty-five miles.
November 16.— We left Nashville and marched out on the Murfreesborough Pike six miles and encamped.
December 26.— We marched south on the Nolensville Pike about thirty miles from Nashville. Skirmished with the Rebels daily.
December 29.— We crossed over to the Murfreesborough Pike.
December 31.— Were actively engaged in the battle of Stone's River. Our loss was one killed, fourteen wounded and thirteen missing.

Stationed near Murfreesborough, Tennessee, January-April 1863.

Stationed at Tullahoma, Tennessee, May-June 1863.

Stationed near Stevenson, Alabama, July-August 1863.

Stationed at Chattanooga, Tennessee, September-October 1863.

Stationed at Strawberry Plains, East Tennessee, November-December 1863.

Stationed at Tiffin, Ohio, January-February 1864.
[For record of events, see Company A.]

Stationed in the field, March-April 1864.

Stationed near Atlanta, Georgia, May-August 1864.

Stationed at Camp Green, Alabama, August 31, 1864-February 28, 1865.

Stationed near Nashville, Tennessee, March-April 1865.

Stationed near New Orleans, Louisiana, May-June 1865.

Company F

Stationed at Camp Noble, Tiffin, Ohio, August 26, 1861.
August 26.— Muster-in roll of Captain Joseph R. Bartlett's Company [F], in the Forty-ninth Regiment (— Brigade) of [Ohio] Volunteers, commanded by Colonel William H. Gibson, called into the service of the United States by [the President] from August 26, 1861 (date of muster) for the term of three years, unless sooner discharged. The company was organized by Captain Joseph R. Bartlett at Fremont, Sandusky County, Ohio in the month of August and marched thence to Tiffin, where it arrived August 16, a distance of twenty-four miles. . . .

ANSON MILLS,
First Lieutenant,
Eighteenth Infantry, Mustering Officer.

Stationed at Camp Nevin, Warden County, Kentucky, August 16-October 31, 1861.

Stationed at Camp Wood, Kentucky, November-December 1861.

Stationed at Camp Stanton, Tennessee, January-February 1862.

Stationed at field of Shiloh, Tennessee, March-April 1862.
March 1.— Marched toward Nashville, Tennessee, eleven miles.
March 2.— Marched toward Nashville, Tennessee, fourteen miles.
March 16.— Marched toward Franklin, Tennessee, sixteen miles.
March 17.— Marched toward Columbia, Tennessee, fifteen miles.

March 20.— Marched toward Columbia, Tennessee, six miles.
March 31.— Marched toward Savannah, Tennessee, three miles.
April 1.— Marched toward Savannah, Tennessee, fifteen miles.
April 2.— Marched toward Savannah, Tennessee, fifteen miles.
April 3.— Marched toward Savannah, Tennessee, twenty-three miles.
April 4.— Marched toward Savannah, Tennessee, twelve miles.
April 5.— Marched toward Savannah, Tennessee, five miles.
April 6.— Arrived at Savannah, Tennessee, eighteen miles, total 153 miles.
April 7.— Engaged in battle of Shiloh; had six wounded in action.
April 8.— Removed camp three miles from Tennessee River toward Corinth.
April 19.— Made a reconnaissance three miles toward Corinth.
April 24.— Made a reconnaissance five miles toward Corinth.

Stationed at Louisville, Kentucky, April 30-August 31, 1862.

Stationed at Bowling Green, Kentucky, September-October 1862.

Stationed at Camp Sill, Tennessee, November 1862-February 1863.

Stationed at Murfreesborough, Tennessee, April 10, 1863.

Stationed at Camp Drake, Murfreesborough, Tennessee, March-April 1863.

Stationed at Tullahoma, Tennessee, May-June 1863.

Stationed near Stevenson, Alabama, July-August 1863.

Stationed at Chattanooga, Tennessee, September-October 1863.

Stationed in the field, November-December 1863.

Stationed at Fremont, Ohio, January-February 1864.
[For record of events, see Company B.]

Station not stated, March-April 1864.

Stationed in front of Atlanta, Georgia, May-June 1864.

Stationed near Atlanta, Georgia, July-August 1864.

Station not stated, September-October 1864.

Stationed at Camp Green, Huntsville, Alabama, November-December 1864.

Stationed near Huntsville, Alabama, January-February 1865.

Stationed near Nashville, Tennessee, March-April 1865.

Stationed near New Orleans, Louisiana, May-June 1865.

Company G

Stationed at Camp Noble, Tiffin, Ohio, September 3, 1861.
September 3.— Muster-in roll of Captain Luther Martin Strong's Company [G], in the Forty-ninth Regiment (—— Brigade) of Ohio Volunteers, commanded by Colonel William H. Gibson, called into the service of the United States by the President from September 3, 1861 (date of muster) for the term of three years, unless sooner discharged. The company was organized by Captain L. M. Strong at Lodi, Ohio in the month of August and marched thence to Tiffin, Ohio, where it arrived ——, a distance of fifteen miles. . . .

ANSON MILLS,
First Lieutenant,
Eighteenth Infantry, Mustering Officer.

Station not stated, [September 3]-October 31, 1861.

Stationed at Camp Wood, Kentucky, [November 1]-December 31, 1861.

Stationed at Camp Stanton, January-February 1862.

Stationed at camp, near Corinth, [Mississippi], March-April 1862.
March 1-2.— The company marched with the regiment from Tyree Springs, Tennessee to Camp Andrew Johnson, twenty-four miles.
March 16-17, 20.— [Marched] from Camp Andrew Johnson to Camp Stanton, forty miles.
April 1-7.— [Marched] from Camp Stanton to Shiloh, ninety-five miles; total distance 159 miles. The company was engaged in the battle of Shiloh April 7.

Stationed at Louisville, Kentucky, April 30-August 31, 1862.

Station not stated, September-October 1862.

Stationed at Murfreesborough, Tennessee, November-December 1862.

Stationed at Camp Sill, Tennessee, January-February 1863.

Stationed at Camp Drake, Tennessee, April 11, 1863.
Supposed to be Special Muster for April 10, 1863.

Stationed at Murfreesborough, Tennessee, March-April 1863.

Stationed at Tullahoma, Tennessee, May-June 1863.

Stationed at Crow Creek, Alabama, July-August 1863.

Stationed at Chattanooga, Tennessee, September-December 1863.

Stationed at Tiffin, Ohio, January-February 1864.
[For record of events, see Company B.]

Stationed at camp, near McDonald's Station, Tennessee, March-April 1864.

Stationed in the field, May-June 1864.

Stationed near Atlanta, Georgia, July-August 1864.

Stationed at Huntsville, Alabama, September-October 1864.

Stationed at Huntsville, Alabama, November-December 1864.

Stationed at Camp Green, Alabama, January-February 1865.

Stationed near Nashville, Tennessee, March-April 1865.

Stationed near New Orleans, Louisiana, May-June 1865.

Company H

Stationed at Camp Noble, Tiffin, Ohio, August 30, 1861.
August 30.— Muster-in roll of Captain Orin B. Hays' Company (H), in the Forty-ninth Regiment (—— Brigade) of Ohio Volunteers, commanded by Colonel William H. Gibson, called into the service of the United States by the President from August 30, 1861 (date of muster) for the term of three years, unless sooner discharged. The company was organized by Captain Orin B. Hays at Fostoria in the month of August and marched thence to Camp Noble, Tiffin, Ohio, where it arrived August 30, a distance of fourteen miles. . . .

ANSON MILLS,
First Lieutenant,
Eighteenth United States Infantry, Mustering Officer.

Stationed at Camp Nevin, Kentucky, August 15-October 31, 1861.

Stationed at Camp Wood, Kentucky, November-December 1861.

Station not stated, January-February 1862.

Stationed at Camp Shiloh, March-April 1862.

Stationed at Louisville, Kentucky, May 1-August 31, 1862.
June 10.— This company left camp near Corinth, Mississippi and marched to Battle Creek, Tennessee.
July 20.— Arrived at Battle Creek passing through Iuka, Tuscumbia, Florence, Athens, Huntsville, and Stevenson, Alabama. The whole distance being 225 miles.

August 20.— Left Battle Creek and marched to Louisville, Kentucky passing through Jasper, Altamont, Manchester, Murfreesborough, and Nashville, Tennessee and Franklin, Bowling Green, Munfordville, Elizabethtown, and West Point, Kentucky; in all a distance of 370 miles.

Stationed near Bowling Green, Kentucky, September-October 1862.
September 26.— Arrived at Louisville, Kentucky.

Stationed at camp, near Murfreesborough, Tennessee, November-December 1862.

IN CAMP SILL NEAR MURFREESBOROUGH, TENNESSEE,
January 29, 1863.

November 4.— This company left camp near Bowling Green, Kentucky and marched to Nashville, Tennessee.
November 7.— Arrived at Nashville, a distance of seventy-five miles.
November 16.— Left Nashville and marched seven miles south on the Murfreesborough Pike near the State Lunatic Asylum.
December 26.— Left camp south of Nashville and marched on the Nolensville Pike in the direction of Murfreesborough, Tennessee.
December 31.— Was engaged in the battle of Stone's River near Murfreesborough, Tennessee, where we had fifteen men wounded and eight captured.

HIRAM CHANCE,
First Lieutenant,
Commanding Company,

Stationed at Camp Sill, Tennessee, January-February 1863.

Stationed at Camp Drake, Tennessee, March-April 1863.

Stationed at Manchester, Tennessee, [May 1]-June 30, 1863.

Stationed at Camp Von Trebra, Bellefonte, Alabama, July-August 1863.

Stationed at Chattanooga, Tennessee, September-October 1863.

Stationed at Strawberry Plains, East Tennessee, November-December 1863.

Stationed at McDonald's Station, January-February 1864.
[For record of events, see Company A.]

Stationed at McDonald's Station, Tennessee, March-April 1864.

Stationed near Atlanta, Georgia, May-August 1864.

Stationed at Pulaski, Tennessee, September-October 1864.

Stationed at Camp Green, Alabama, November 1, 1864-February 28, 1865.

Stationed near Nashville, Tennessee, March-April 1865.

Stationed near New Orleans, Louisiana, May-June 1865.

Company I

Stationed at Camp Noble, Tiffin, Ohio, August 26, 1861.
August 24.— Muster-in roll of Captain George E. Lovejoy's Company [I], in the Forty-ninth Regiment (—— Brigade) of Ohio Volunteers, commanded by Colonel W. H. Gibson, called into the service of the United States by the President from August 24, 1861 (date of muster) for the term of three years, unless sooner discharged. The company was organized by Captain [Levi] Drake at Ottawa, Ohio in the month of August and marched thence to Tiffin, Ohio, where it arrived August 23, a distance of ninety miles. . . .

ANSON MILLS,
First Lieutenant,
Eighteenth Infantry, Mustering Officer.

Stationed at Camp Nevin, [August 26]-October 31, 1861.

Stationed at Camp Wood, Kentucky, [November 1]-December 31, 1861.

Station not stated, [January-February 1862].
Corresponds to roll on file on which company was paid to February 28, 1862.

Stationed at camp, near Corinth, March-April 1862.
April 7.— In action at battle of Shiloh.

Stationed at camp, near Louisville, Kentucky, May 1-August 31, 1862.

Stationed at camp, near Bowling Green, Kentucky, September-October 1862.

Stationed at camp south of Murfreesborough, Tennessee, November-December 1862.

Stationed at Camp Sill, Tennessee, January-February 1863.

Stationed at Camp Drake, Tennessee, March-April 1863.

Stationed at camp at Tullahoma, Tennessee, May-June 1863.

Stationed at camp, near Stevenson, Alabama, July-August 1863.

Stationed at camp at Chattanooga, Tennessee, September-October 1863.

Stationed at Strawberry Plains, East Tennessee, November-December 1863.

Stationed at Tiffin, Ohio, January-February 1864.
[For record of events, see Company B.]

Stationed at McDonald's Station, East Tennessee, [March 1]-April 30, 1864.

Stationed near Atlanta, Georgia, May-August 1864.

Stationed near Athens, Alabama, [September 1]-October 31, 1864.

Stationed at Camp Green, Alabama, November 1864-February 1865.

Stationed near Nashville, Tennessee, March-April 1865.

Stationed near New Orleans, Louisiana, May-June 1865.

Company K

Stationed at Camp Noble, Tiffin, Ohio, September 9, 1861.
September 9.— Muster-in roll of Captain [James] M. Patterson's Company [K], in the Forty-ninth Regiment (—— Brigade) of Ohio Volunteers, commanded by Colonel William H. Gibson, called into the service of the United States by the President from September 9, 1861 (date of muster) for the term of three years, unless sooner discharged. The company was organized by Captain J. M. Patterson at Tiffin, Ohio in the month of September and marched thence to Tiffin, Ohio, where it arrived September 9. . . .

ANSON MILLS,
First Lieutenant,
Eighteenth Infantry, Mustering Officer.

Stationed at Camp Nevin, [September 9]-October 31, 1861.

Stationed at Camp Noble, [November 1]-December 31, 1861.

Station not stated, [January-February 1862].
Corresponds to roll on file on which company was paid to February 28, 1862.

Stationed at field of Shiloh, Tennessee, March-April 1862.
March 29.— The company, with the regiment, left Camp Stanton.
April 6.— After a tedious and hard march of ninety-four miles, we reached Savannah, on the Tennessee River, in the night at 10 o'clock. Lay in the streets of the town during the night.

April 7.— In the morning at 8 o'clock marched on board the transport *John J. Roe* and at 11 o'clock a.m. were landed at Pittsburg Landing, a distance of nine miles. Immediately disembarked and proceeded to the fields of Shiloh, where near 1 o'clock p.m. we engaged the enemy, and after a severe conflict of near two hours, the enemy was routed, leaving their dead and wounded upon the field. This company behaved with courage and soldier-like bearing. Loss was one man wounded in thigh with a musket ball.

Stationed at Louisville, Kentucky, April 30-August 31, 1862.

Station not stated, September-October 1862.

Stationed at Camp Sill, Tennessee, November 1862-February 1863.

Stationed at Camp Drake, Tennessee, March-April 1863.

Stationed at Tullahoma, Tennessee, May-June 1863.

Stationed near Stevenson, Alabama, July-August 1863.

Stationed at Chattanooga, Tennessee, September-October 1863.

Stationed at Strawberry Plains, East Tennessee, November-December 1863.

Stationed at Camp Green, Alabama, January-February 1864.
[For record of events, see Company B.]

Stationed near Atlanta, Georgia, March-August 1864.

Stationed at Pulaski, Tennessee, September-October 1864.

Stationed at Camp Green, Alabama, November 1864-February 1865.

Station not stated, March-April 1865.

Stationed near New Orleans, Louisiana, May-June 1865.

[M594-Roll #151]

Record of Events for Fiftieth Ohio Infantry, August 1862-June 1865.

Field and Staff

Stationed at Lebanon, Kentucky, [September 1]-October 31, 1862.
September 4.— The Fiftieth Regiment, Ohio Veteran Infantry left Camp Dennison, Ohio and proceeded to Covington, Kentucky, from thence to Louisville, Kentucky.
October 1.— Left Louisville, Kentucky for the interior of Kentucky.
October 8.— Was engaged in the battle of Chaplin Hills, from thence proceeded to Lebanon, Kentucky, where it now remains.

Stationed at Lebanon, Kentucky, November-December 1862.

Stationed at Big Run Trestle, Louisville and Nashville Railroad, Kentucky, January-June 1863.

Stationed at Fort Boyle, Louisville and Nashville Railroad, Kentucky, July-August 1863.

Guarding Louisville and Nashville Railroad from Rolling Fork Bridge to Elizabethtown, Kentucky.

Stationed at Glasgow, Kentucky, September-October 1863.
September 18.— Marched from Fort Boyle, Kentucky.
September 21.— Arrived at Glasgow, Kentucky, distance fifty-four miles.
September 24.— Marched from Glasgow to Cave City, Kentucky, distance fourteen miles. Took the cars the same evening for Nashville, Tennessee.
September 25.— Arrived at Nashville in the morning. Remained in Nashville.

October 6.— Was ordered back to Munfordville, Kentucky.
October 8.— Arrived at Munfordville, Kentucky and remained.
October 11.— Marched to Glasgow, Kentucky, distance twenty-four miles.

Stationed at Somerset, Kentucky, November-December 1863.
Marched from Glasgow, Kentucky to Somerset, Kentucky, distance ninety-three miles.

Stationed at Knoxville, Tennessee, January-February 1864.

Stationed at Loudon, Tennessee, March-April 1864.

Stationed in the field, Georgia, May-June 1864.

Stationed in the field, near Atlanta, July-August 1864.

Stationed in the field, September-October 1864.

Stationed at Columbia, Tennessee, November-December 1864.

Stationed at Wilmington, North Carolina, January-February 1865.

Stationed at Raleigh, North Carolina, March-April 1865.

Stationed at Salisbury, North Carolina, June 26, 1865.
June 26.— Muster-out roll of field and staff of the Fiftieth Regiment of Ohio Foot Volunteers, commanded by Colonel Silas A. Strickland, called into the service of the United States by President [Abraham] Lincoln at Camp Dennison, Ohio (the place of general rendezvous) on August 27, 1862 to serve for the term of three years from the date of enrollment, unless sooner discharged, from the dates respectively (when last paid) to June 26, 1865 date of this muster out. . . .

BENJAMIN F. BRISCOE,
Captain and Assistant Commissary of Musters,
Second Division, Twenty-third Army Corps,
Mustering Officer.

Regiment

Station not stated, [September]-October 1862.

Return dated Columbia November 20, 1862.

September 4.— The regiment left Camp Dennison, Ohio for Fort Mitchel, Kentucky.

September 21.— Left for Louisville.

October 1.— Started on the grand march after [Braxton] Bragg's forces.

October 8.— In the engagement at Perryville.

Stationed at Columbia, Kentucky, November 1862.

November 3.— [In the engagement] at Lebanon, Kentucky.

November 20.— [In the engagement] at Columbia, Kentucky.

Stationed at Lebanon, Kentucky, December 1862.

Stationed at Big Run Trestle, Kentucky, except Companies A, D, F, and G at Sulphur Fork Trestle, Kentucky; and Company E at Rolling Fork Trestle, Kentucky, March 1863.

Stationed at Big Run Trestle, Louisville and Nashville Railroad, Kentucky, except Companies D, F, G, and K at Sulphur Fork Trestle, Louisville and Nashville Railroad; and Company E at Rolling Fork Trestle, Louisville and Nashville Railroad, April-May 1863.

Stationed at Big Run Trestle, Louisville and Nashville Railroad, Kentucky, except Companies D, G and K at Sulphur Fork Trestle, Louisville and Nashville Railroad; Company E at Rolling Fork Trestle, Louisville and Nashville Railroad; and Companies F and H at Elizabethtown, Louisville and Nashville Railroad, June 1863.

Stationed at Fort Boyle, Kentucky, except Companies D, F, G, and K at Fort Sands, Kentucky; and Company E at Fort McAllister, Kentucky, July 1863.

Stationed at Fort Boyle, Louisville and Nashville Railroad, except Companies B, E, H, and K at Fort Sands, Louisville and Nashville Railroad; Company C at Elizabethtown, Louisville and Nashville Railroad; and Company F at Fort McAllister, Louisville and Nashville Railroad, August 1863.

Stationed at Nashville, Tennessee, except Companies C, D, F, G, H, and I at Gallatin, Tennessee; and Company E at Drake's Creek on Louisville and Nashville Railroad, September 1863.

Stationed at Glasgow, Kentucky, except Company B at Nolin's Station on Louisville and Nashville Railroad, Kentucky; Companies D and F at Gallatin, Tennessee; and Company E at Drake's Creek on Louisville and Nashville Railroad, Tennessee, October 1863.

Stationed at Glasgow, Kentucky, except Company B at Nolin's Station, Kentucky on Louisville and Nashville Railroad, November 1863.

Stationed at Somerset, Kentucky, December 1863.

Stationed at Wheeler's Gap, Cumberland Mountains, Tennessee, January 1864.

Stationed at Knoxville, East Tennessee, February 1864.

Stationed at Knoxville, Tennessee, March 1864.

Stationed at Loudon, Tennessee, April 1864.

Station not stated, May-June 1864.
Return dated Decatur, Georgia September 17, 1864.

Station not stated, July 1864.
Return dated in the field near Atlanta, Georgia August 6, 1864.

Station not stated, August 1864.
Return dated Decatur, Georgia September 20, 1864.

Station not stated, September 1864.
Return dated Gaylesville, Alabama October 20, 1864.

Station not stated, October 1864.
Return dated Spring Hills, Tennessee November 11, 1864.

Stationed in the field, November 1864.

Stationed at Camp Stoneman, Virginia, January 1865.

Stationed at Wilmington, North Carolina, February 1865.

Stationed at Best Station, North Carolina, March 1865.

Stationed at Raleigh, North Carolina, April 1865.

Stationed at Salisbury, North Carolina, May 1865.

Company A

Stationed at Camp Dennison, Ohio, August 27, 1862.
August 27.— Muster-in roll of Captain Thomas P. Cook's Company [A], in the Fiftieth Regiment (—— Brigade) of Ohio Volunteers, commanded by Colonel [Jonah R.] Taylor, called into the service of the United States by the President from August 27, 1862 (date of muster) for the term of three years, unless sooner discharged. . . .

[ADOLPHUS FREEMAN] BOND,
Captain,
Second Infantry, Mustering Officer.

Stationed at Lebanon, Kentucky, [August 27]-October 31, 1862.
August 27.— Mustered into service of United States.
September 3.— Left Camp Dennison, Ohio to camp back of Newport, Kentucky. Proceeded by cars to Cincinnati, Ohio; thence to Camp Taylor, Kentucky.
September 4.— Moved to Camp King.
September 7.— Received $25 United States bounty and moved to Camp Saint John.

September 8.— Moved to Camp Beachwood.
September 17.— Went out on picket on Lexington Pike.
September 20.— Moved to Covington and by pontoon bridge over Ohio River to Cincinnati, where bivouacked in railroad depot.
September 21.— Proceeded by cars to Jeffersonville, Indiana. Went to Louisville, Kentucky, where we camped in various places and remained.
September 30.— Went out on picket.
October 1.— Left Louisville for the interior of Kentucky. Took our place in column and went in pursuit of Bragg. Nothing of interest occurred.
October 8.— Proceeded from bivouac to what proved to be the battle of Chaplin Hills, where we were hotly engaged by the enemy, while supporting the Ninth Indiana Battery. Three men were killed instantly and one seriously wounded. Lost knapsacks and contents and company books and papers. We lost nearly all of our clothing at the battle. The men without an exception behaved nobly.
October 11.— Marched toward Crab Orchard.
October 20.— Left Crab Orchard. Went to Lebanon, Kentucky.
October 24.— Arrived at Lebanon, where we are now.

Stationed at Lebanon, Kentucky, November-December 1862.

Went from Lebanon to Campbellsville, from there to Columbia.
December 24.— Ordered back to Campbellsville.
December 29.— Marched to Lebanon.

Stationed at Big Run Trestle, Louisville and Nashville Railroad, Kentucky, January-June 1863.

Stationed at Fort Boyle, Kentucky, July-August 1863.

Stationed at Fort Boyle, Kentucky to guard trestlework at Big Run, Louisville and Nashville Railroad, Kentucky.

Stationed at Glasgow, Kentucky, September-October 1863.

Stationed at Somerset, Kentucky, November-December 1863.
December 1.— At Glasgow, Kentucky until this date, when were detached and guarded prisoners from Louisville, Kentucky to various points.
December 24.— Rejoined regiment at Columbia, having marched from Lebanon to Columbia, forty miles.
December 29.— Marched from Columbia to Somerset, sixty-eight miles. Arrived at Somerset December 29.

Stationed at Knoxville, Tennessee, January-February 1864.
January 2.— Marched from Somerset, Kentucky to camp three miles beyond Fort Isabel.
January 6.— Continued the march.
January 17.— Arrived at Jacksborough, Tennessee, eighty-eight miles.
January 20.— Commenced making road through Wheeler's Gap.
February 22.— Marched to Clinton.
February 23.— Arrived in Knoxville, forty-four miles.

Stationed at Loudon, Tennessee, March-April 1864.
April 15.— Left Knoxville and marched fifteen miles and went into camp for the night.
April 16.— Started again and marched sixty-five miles. Arrived in Loudon and encamped.

Stationed with the Army in the field, Georgia, May-June 1864.

Stationed at Decatur, Georgia, July-August 1864.

Station not stated, September-October 1864.

Stationed at Columbia, Tennessee, November-December 1864.

Stationed at Wilmington, North Carolina, January-February 1865.

Stationed at Raleigh, North Carolina, March-April 1865.

Stationed at Salisbury, North Carolina, June 26, 1865.
June 26.— Muster-out roll of Captain William T. Exline's Company (A), in the Fiftieth Regiment of Ohio Infantry Volunteers, commanded by Colonel S. A. Strickland, called into the service of the United States by the President at Camp Dennison, Ohio (the place of general rendezvous) on August 27, 1862 to serve for the term of three years from the date of enrollment, unless sooner discharged, from the dates respectively (when last paid) to June 26, 1865 date of this muster out. The company was organized by Captain Thomas P. Cook at Camp Dennison, Ohio in the months of July and August 1862. . . .

BENJAMIN F. BRISCOE,
Captain and Assistant Commissary of Musters,
Second Division, Twenty-third Army Corps,
Mustering Officer.

Company B

Stationed at Camp Dennison, Ohio, August 18, 1862.
August 18.— Muster-in roll of Captain Hamilton S. Gillespie's Company [B], in the Fiftieth Regiment (— Brigade) of Ohio Volunteers, commanded by Colonel J. R. Taylor, called into the service of the United States by the President of the United States from [August 18, 1862] (date of muster) for the term of three years, unless sooner discharged. . . .

[PATRICK HENRY] BRESLIN,
Captain,
Eighteenth Infantry, Mustering Officer.

Stationed at Lebanon, Kentucky, [August 18]-October 31, 1862.
September 4.— Left Camp Dennison, Ohio for Fort Mitchel.
September 21.— Left for Louisville, Kentucky.
October 1.— Started on the grand march after Bragg's forces in Kentucky.
October 8.— Were in the engagement at Chaplin Hills near Perryville, Kentucky. Had one man taken prisoner.

Stationed at Lebanon, Kentucky, November-December 1862.
November 3.— We are now with our regiment near Lebanon, Kentucky.

Stationed at Big Run Trestle, Kentucky, January-June 1863.

Stationed at Fort Boyle, Kentucky, July-August 1863.

Stationed at Nolin's Bridge, Louisville and Nashville Railroad, Kentucky, September-October 1863.

Stationed at Somerset, Kentucky, November-December 1863.

Stationed at Knoxville, Tennessee, January-February 1864.

Stationed at Loudon, Tennessee, March-April 1864.

Stationed in the field, Georgia, May-June 1864.

Stationed at Decatur, Georgia, July-August 1864.

Stationed at Rome, Georgia, September-October 1864.

Stationed at Columbia, Tennessee, November-December 1864.

Stationed at Wilmington, North Carolina, January-February 1865.

Stationed at Raleigh, North Carolina, March-April 1865.

Stationed at Salisbury, North Carolina, June 26, 1865.
June 26.— Muster-out roll of Captain David L. Anderson's (late Captain Gillespie's) Company (B), in the Fiftieth Regiment of Ohio Infantry Volunteers, commanded by Colonel S. A. Strickland, called into the service of the United States by the President at Camp Dennison, Ohio (the place of general rendezvous) on August 18, 1862 to serve for the term of three years from the date of enrollment, unless sooner discharged, from the dates respectively (when last paid) to June 26, 1865 date of this muster out. The company was organized by Captain H. S. Gillespie in Shelby County, Ohio in the months of July and August 1862. . . .

BENJAMIN F. BRISCOE,
Captain and Assistant Commissary of Musters,
Second Division, Twenty-third Army Corps,
Mustering Officer.

Company C

Stationed at Camp Dennison, Ohio, August 25, 1862.
August 25.— Muster-in roll of Captain Patrick McGrew's Company [C], in the Fiftieth Regiment (—— Brigade) of Ohio Infantry Volunteers, commanded by Colonel Jonah R. Taylor, called into the service of the United States by the President of the United States from date of their enrollment respectively (date of muster) for the term of three years, unless sooner discharged. . . .

A. F. BOND,
Captain,
Second Infantry, Mustering Officer.

Stationed at Lebanon, Kentucky, [August 25]-October 31, 1862.
September 3.— The company left Camp Dennison, Ohio.
September 14.— [Left] Camp Taylor.
September 17.— [Left] Camp King.
September 21.— Left Cincinnati for Jeffersonville.
September 23.— Crossed to Louisville.
October 1.— Left Louisville.
October 3.— [Left] Taylorsville, Kentucky.
October 8.— In battle at Perryville, Kentucky.
October 15.— At Crab Orchard.
October 21.— On return march.
October 24.— At Danville, Ohio. In camp four days near Lebanon.

Stationed at Lebanon, Kentucky, November-December 1862.

Stationed at Big Run Trestle, Kentucky, January-June 1863.

Stationed at Fort Boyle, Kentucky, July-August 1863.

Stationed at Gallatin, Tennessee, September-October 1863.

Stationed at Somerset, Kentucky, November-December 1863.

Stationed at Knoxville, Tennessee, January-February 1864.

Stationed at Loudon, Tennessee, March-April 1864.

Stationed in the field, Georgia, May-June 1864.

Stationed near Atlanta, Georgia, July-August 1864.

Stationed in the field, September-October 1864.

Stationed in the field, Tennessee, November-December 1864.

Stationed at Wilmington, North Carolina, January-February 1865.

Stationed at Raleigh, North Carolina, March-April 1865.

Stationed at Salisbury, North Carolina, June 26, 1865.
June 26.— Muster-out roll of Captain Thomas C. Honnell's Company (C), in the Fiftieth Regiment of Ohio Volunteers, commanded by Colonel S. A. Strickland, called into the service of the United States by the President of the United States at Camp Dennison (the place of general rendezvous) on August 27, 1862 to serve for the term of three years from the date of enrollment, unless sooner discharged, from the dates respectively (when last paid) to June 26, 1865 date of this muster out. The company was organized by Captain Patrick McGrew at New Paris, Ohio in the month of August 1862. . . .

BENJAMIN F. BRISCOE,
Captain and Assistant Commissary of Musters,
Second Division, Twenty-third Army Corps,
Mustering Officer.

Company D

Stationed at Camp Dennison, Ohio, August 27, 1862.
August 27.— Muster-in roll of Captain John Carr's Company [D], in the Fiftieth Regiment (—— Brigade) of Ohio Infantry Volunteers, commanded by Colonel Jonah R. Taylor, called into the service of the United States by the President of the United States from August 27, 1862 (date of muster) for the term of three years, unless sooner discharged. . . .

A. F. BOND,
Captain,
Second Infantry, Mustering Officer.

Stationed at Lebanon, Kentucky, [August 27]-October 31, 1862.
September 6-October 7.— Left Camp Dennison, Ohio and marched to Camp Taylor, Kentucky. Left Camp Taylor and marched to Camp King, Kentucky. Left Camp King and marched to Camp Beachwood, Kentucky. Left Camp Beachwood and marched through Cincinnati, Ohio and went to camp near Jeffersonville, Indiana. Left Jeffersonville and went to camp near Jonesville, Kentucky.
October 8.— Went to Chaplin Hills near Perryville, Kentucky. Had a fight and lost Captain John Carr and Private William Sudlow in action on this day.
October 9-31.— Left Perryville, Kentucky and went through Danville, Kentucky to Camp Crab Orchard, Kentucky and [left] Camp Crab Orchard and returned through Danville, Kentucky to Lebanon, Kentucky and are now stationed at camp near Lebanon, Kentucky.

Stationed at Lebanon, Kentucky, November-December 1862.
November 14.— Marched from Lebanon, Kentucky to Campbellsville, Kentucky, distance eighteen miles.
November 16.— Marched from Campbellsville, Kentucky to Columbia, Kentucky, distance twenty miles. Encamped at Columbia, Kentucky.
December 22.— Marched again back to Campbellsville, Kentucky, distance twenty miles, and remained.
December 29.— Marched again to Lebanon, distance eighteen miles.

Stationed at Sulphur Fork Trestle, Louisville and Nashville, Railroad, Kentucky, January-February 1863.

Stationed at Sulphur Tank Trestle, Kentucky, March-April 1863.

Stationed at Sulphur Fork Trestle, Louisville and Nashville Railroad, Kentucky, May-August 1863.

Stationed at Gallatin, Tennessee, September-October 1863.

Stationed in the field, Kentucky, November-December 1863.

Stationed at Jacksborough, Tennessee, January-February 1864.

Stationed at Loudon, Tennessee, March-April 1864.

Stationed in the field, Georgia, May-June 1864.

Stationed at Decatur, Georgia, July-August 1864.

Stationed in the field, Rome, Georgia, September-October 1864.

Stationed at Columbia, Tennessee, November-December 1864.

Stationed at Wilmington, North Carolina, January-February 1865.

Stationed at Raleigh, North Carolina, March-April 1865.

Stationed at Salisbury, North Carolina, June 26, 1865.
June 26.— Muster-out roll of Captain Samuel Bitler's Company (D), in the Fiftieth Regiment of Ohio Infantry Volunteers, commanded by Colonel Silas A. Strickland, called into the service of the United States by the President at Camp Dennison, Ohio (the place of general rendezvous) on August 27, 1862 to serve for the term of three years from the date of enrollment, unless sooner discharged, from the dates respectively (when last paid) to June 26, 1865 date of this muster out. The company was organized by Captain Carr at Cincinnati, Ohio in the month of July 1862. . . .

BENJAMIN F. BRISCOE,
Captain and Assistant Commissary of Musters,
Second Division, Twenty-third Army Corps,
Mustering Officer.

Company E

Stationed at Camp Dennison, Ohio, August 26, 1862.
August 26.— Muster-in roll of Captain Levi C. Guthrie's Company [E], in the Fiftieth Regiment (—— Brigade) of Ohio Volunteers, commanded by Colonel Jonah R. Taylor, called into the

service of the United States by the President of the United States from August 26, 1862 (date of muster) for the term of three years, unless sooner discharged. . . .

A. F. BOND,
Captain,
Second Infantry, Mustering Officer.

Stationed at Lebanon, Kentucky, [August 26]-October 31, 1862.
September 4.— Left Camp Dennison for Fort Mitchel near Covington, Kentucky.
September 20.— Left Fort Mitchel for Louisville, Kentucky.
October 1.— Left Louisville on the grand march after Bragg.
October 8-31.— Participated in the engagement near Perryville, Kentucky October 8. Loss of the company during the engagement, two killed and three wounded. Took part in the pursuit following as far as Crab Orchard, Kentucky. The company is now with the regiment doing provost guard duty at Lebanon, Kentucky.

Stationed at Lebanon, Kentucky, November-December 1862.
December 31.— Took part in the pursuit after [John Hunt] Morgan commencing this date. Left Camp Dennison, Ohio September 3, since which time we have been stationed back of Covington and Newport, at Louisville, Lebanon, Columbia, Campbellsville and this place.

Stationed at Rolling Fork Bridge, Louisville and Nashville Railroad, January-February 1863.

Since last muster have participated in the pursuit of Morgan from Lebanon, Kentucky commencing December 31, 1862, since which time we have been stationed at Campbellsville, Kentucky; New Haven, Kentucky; Louisville, Kentucky; and this place, where we are now engaged in building a fortification.

Stationed at Rolling Fork Bridge, Louisville and Nashville Railroad, March-June 1863.

Stationed at Fort Sands, Kentucky, July-August 1863.

Stationed at Drake's Creek Stockade, Louisville and Nashville Railroad, Tennessee, September-October 1863.

Station not stated, November-December 1863.

Stationed at Knoxville, Tennessee, January-February 1864.

Stationed at Loudon, Tennessee, March-April 1864.

Stationed in the field, near Atlanta, Georgia, May-June 1864.

Stationed in the field, July-August 1864.

Stationed in the field, near Rome, Georgia, September-October 1864.

Stationed at Columbia, Tennessee, November-December 1864.

Stationed at Wilmington, North Carolina, January-February 1865.

Stationed at Raleigh, North Carolina, March-April 1865.

Stationed at Salisbury, North Carolina, June 26, 1865.
June 26.— Muster-out roll of Captain William B. Richards' Company (E), in the Fiftieth Regiment of Ohio Infantry Volunteers, commanded by Colonel Silas A. Strickland, called into the service of the United States by the President at Camp Dennison, Ohio (the place of general rendezvous) on August 26, 1862 to serve for the term of three years from the date of enrollment, unless sooner discharged, from the dates respectively (when last paid) to June 26, 1865 date of this muster out. The company was organized by Captain L. C. Guthrie at Camp Dennison, Ohio in the month of August 1862. . . .

BENJAMIN F. BRISCOE,
Captain and Assistant Commissary of Musters,
Second Division, Twenty-third Army Corps,
Mustering Officer.

Company F

Stationed at Camp Dennison, Ohio, August 30, 1862.
August 30.— Muster-in roll of Captain Thomas Clark's Company [F], in the Fiftieth Regiment (—— Brigade) of Ohio Infantry Vol-

unteers, commanded by Colonel Jonah R. Taylor, called into the service of the United States by the President from date of their enrollment respectively (date of muster) for the term of three years, unless sooner discharged. . . .

A. F. BOND,
Captain,
Second Infantry, Mustering Officer.

Stationed at Lebanon, Kentucky, [August 30]-October 31, 1862.
September 3.— The company left Camp Dennison.
September 14.— [Left] Camp Taylor.
September 17.— [Left] Camp King.
September 21.— [Left] Cincinnati for Jeffersonville.
September 23.— Crossed to Louisville.
October 1.— Left Louisville.
October 3.— [Left] Taylorsville, Kentucky.
October 8.— In battle at Perryville. James Francis killed in battle of Chaplin Hills. Joseph Marple, John Barr and Wilson Cochran, slightly wounded.
October 14.— [Left] Danville.
October 15.— [Left] Crab Orchard. In camp four days on return march.
October 21.— [Left] Danville.
October 28.— [Left] camp near Lebanon.

Stationed at Lebanon, Kentucky, November-December 1862.

Stationed at Big Run Trestle, Louisville and Nashville Railroad, January-February 1863.

Stationed at Sulphur Fork Trestle, Louisville and Nashville Railroad, Kentucky, March-April 1863.

Stationed at Elizabethtown, Kentucky, May-June 1863.

Stationed at Fort McAllister, Louisville and Nashville Railroad, Kentucky, July-August 1863.

Stationed at Gallatin, Tennessee, September-October 1863.

Stationed at Somerset, Kentucky, November-December 1863.

Stationed at Knoxville, Tennessee, January-February 1864.

Stationed at Loudon, Tennessee, March-April 1864.

Stationed in the field in Georgia, May-June 1864.

Stationed in the field in Georgia, July-August 1864.
July 1.— With the regiment marched to the right in front of Kenesaw Mountain, Georgia and assisted in turning the left flank of the enemy.
July 3.— On reconnaissance and skirmish line.
July 4-6.— (The enemy having fallen back from Kenesaw Mountain) marched eighteen miles crossing railroad south of Marietta.
July 11.— Crossed Chattahoochee River at Shank's Ferry. Each day or two advancing and throwing up breastworks.
July 19.— Reached Decatur.
July 20.— Advanced three miles driving enemy into front lines of their works before Atlanta.
July 21.— In the night the enemy fell back. Drove them into their strong works before Atlanta. Threw up strong works occupying left center of lines.
July 31.— Occupied extreme left of lines.
August 2.— In the night commenced flank movement to right. Marched twelve miles.
August 3.— Had heavy skirmishing with enemy. Building breastworks at night.
August 6-7.— Advanced driving the enemy and throwing up works at night.
August 8.— On reconnaissance making three charges and driving the enemy three miles.
August 9.— Advanced throwing up three lines of breastworks.
August 10-28.— Occupied front line facing enemy's works. Commenced moving to right August 28.
August 30.— Crossed Mount [illegible] Railroad.
August 31.— Camped near the Western and Atlantic Railroad.

Stationed in the field in Georgia, September-October 1864.

Stationed in the field, Tennessee, November-December 1864.

Stationed at Wilmington, North Carolina, January-February 1865.

Stationed at Raleigh, North Carolina, March-April 1865.

Stationed at Salisbury, North Carolina, June 26, 1865.
June 26.— Muster-out roll of Captain James G. Theaker's (late Thomas Clark's) Company (F), in the Fiftieth Regiment of Ohio Volunteers, commanded by Colonel Silas A. Strickland, called into the service of the United States by the President at Camp Dennison, Ohio (the place of general rendezvous) on August 30, 1862 to serve for the term of three years from the date of enrollment, unless sooner discharged, from the dates respectively (when last paid) to June 26, 1865 date of this muster out. The company was organized by Captain [Thomas Clark] at Camp Dennison in the month of August 1862. . . .

BENJAMIN F. BRISCOE,
Captain and Assistant Commissary of Musters,
Second Division, Twenty-third Army Corps,
Mustering Officer.

Company G

Stationed at Camp Dennison, Ohio, August 26, 1862.
August 26.— Muster-in roll of Captain James W. Cahill's Company [G], in the Fiftieth Regiment (—— Brigade) of Ohio Infantry Volunteers, commanded by Colonel Jonah R. Taylor, called into the service of the United States by the President from date of their enrollment respectively (date of muster) for the term of three years, unless sooner discharged. . . .

A. F. BOND,
Captain,
Second United States Infantry, Mustering Officer.

Stationed at Lebanon, Kentucky, [August 26]-October 31, 1862.
August 28.— Company G moved from Camp Dennison on or near this date to Covington, Kentucky. Camped four miles back of the city.
September 22.— Was ordered to Louisville via Cincinnati.

September 25.— Arrived at Louisville.
October 1.— Moved from Louisville by the Taylorsville Pike, seventy-five miles, to Chaplin Hills.
October 8.— Went into action at Chaplin Hills at 3.30 o'clock p.m. Withdrawn at sunset (first action).
October 11.— Moved in pursuit of General Bragg's forces. Pursued to Crab Orchard, thirty miles. Halted and returned to Lebanon, Kentucky via Danville and Perryville.

Stationed at Lebanon, Kentucky, November-December 1862.
November 3.— Stationed at Lebanon up to this date.

Stationed at Sulphur Fork Trestle, Kentucky, January-February 1863.

Stationed at Big Run Trestle, Kentucky, March-April 1863.

Stationed at Fort Sands, near Coalsburg, Kentucky, May-June 1863.

Station not stated, July-August 1863.

Stationed at Glasgow, Kentucky, September-October 1863.

Stationed at camp, near Somerset, Kentucky, November-December 1863.

Stationed at camp, near Knoxville, Tennessee, January-February 1864.

Stationed at Loudon, Tennessee, March-April 1864.

Stationed in the field, Georgia, May-August 1864.

Stationed in the field, near Rome, Georgia, September-October 1864.

Stationed near Columbia, Tennessee, November-December 1864.
November 1-29.— The company was at Resaca, Georgia November 1. Marched through Rome to Chattanooga, taking railroad

cars to Nashville, through to Spring Hill, Tennessee; thence to Columbia. Marched back from Columbia to Spring Hill, where we had a skirmish with the enemy.
November 30-December 14.— [Marched] to Franklin, where we had a battle in the evening of November 30. Fell back from Franklin to Nashville and went into camp.
December 15-26.— A forward movement was ordered. Had a skirmish with the enemy on December 15. Followed up the retreat of the enemy to this place.
December 27.— Camped near Columbia.

Stationed at Wilmington, North Carolina, January-February 1865.

Stationed at Raleigh, North Carolina, March-April 1865.

Stationed at Salisbury, North Carolina, June 26, 1865.
June 26.— Muster-out roll of Captain Elmer W. Williams' Company (G), in the Fiftieth Regiment of Ohio Infantry Volunteers, commanded by Colonel Silas A. Strickland, called into the service of the United States by the President at Camp Dennison, Ohio (the place of general rendezvous) on August 27, 1862 to serve for the term of three years from the date of enrollment, unless sooner discharged, from the dates respectively (when last paid) to June 26, 1865 date of this muster out. . . .

BENJAMIN F. BRISCOE,
Captain and Assistant Commissary of Musters,
Second Division, Twenty-third Army Corps,
Mustering Officer.

Company H

Stationed at Camp Dennison, Ohio, August 27, 1862.
August 27.— Muster-in roll of Captain Lewis C. Simmons' Company [H], in the Fiftieth Regiment (—— Brigade) of Ohio Foot Volunteers, commanded by Colonel Jonah R. Taylor, called into the service of the United States by proclamation of the President from August 27, 1862 (date of muster) for the term of three years, unless sooner discharged. . . .

A. F. BOND,
Captain,
Second Infantry, Mustering Officer.

Stationed at Lebanon, Kentucky, [August 27]-December 31, 1862.

Stationed at Sulphur Fort Trestle, Kentucky, January-February 1863.

Stationed at Big Run Trestle, Kentucky, March-June 1863.

Stationed at Fort Sands, July-August 1863.

Stationed at Fort Hobson, Glasgow, Kentucky, September-October 1863.

Stationed at Somerset, Kentucky, November-December 1863.

Stationed at Knoxville, Knox County, Tennessee, January-February 1864.

Stationed at Loudon, Tennessee, March-April 1864.

Stationed in the field, Georgia, May-June 1864.

Stationed near Decatur, Georgia, July-August 1864.

Stationed in the field, near Rome, Georgia, September-October 1864.

Stationed at Columbia, Tennessee, November-December 1864.

Stationed at Wilmington, North Carolina, January-February 1865.

Stationed at Raleigh, North Carolina, March-April 1865.

Stationed at Salisbury, North Carolina, June 26, 1865.
June 26.— Muster-out roll of Captain Harrison M. Shuey's Company (H), in the Fiftieth Regiment of Ohio Infantry Volunteers, commanded by Colonel Silas A. Strickland, called into the service of the United States by President Lincoln at Camp Dennison (the place of general rendezvous) on August 27, 1862 to serve

for the term of three years from the date of enrollment, unless sooner discharged, from the dates respectively (when last paid) to June 26, 1865 date of this muster out. The company was organized by Captain L. C. Simmons at Camp Dennison in the month of August 1862. . . .

BENJAMIN F. BRISCOE,
Captain and Assistant Commissary of Musters,
Second Division, Twenty-third Army Corps,
Mustering Officer.

Company I

Stationed at Camp Dennison, Ohio, August 29, 1862.
August 29.— Muster-in roll of Captain [Isaac] J. Carter's Company [I], in the Fiftieth Regiment (—— Brigade), of [Ohio Infantry] Volunteers. . . .

A. F. BOND,
Captain,
Second United States Infantry, Mustering Officer.

Stationed at Lebanon, Kentucky, [August 29]-October 31, 1862.
September 23.— The company was employed in garrison duty near Cincinnati until this date.
October 1.— [Employed in garrison duty] near Louisville until this date.
October 8.— Was in the battle at Chaplin Hills.
October 15.— Marched to Crab Orchard, Kentucky. Countermarched to Lebanon, Kentucky.
October 22.— Reached Lebanon where it yet remains.

Stationed at Lebanon, Kentucky, November-December 1862.
November 13.— The company was encamped at Lebanon, Kentucky until this date, when it marched to Columbia, Kentucky, forty miles. Remained there.
December 22.— Marched to Campbellsville, twenty-nine miles.
December 29.— In the night marched to Lebanon, twenty miles.
December 31.— In the evening proceeded to New Market, six miles, and bivouacked for the night. Engaged in no battles during the two months.

Stationed at Big Run Trestle, [Kentucky], January-February 1863.
January 1.— Marched from Lebanon in pursuit of John Morgan to Columbia, Kentucky in the night.
January 4.— Marched from Columbia toward Lebanon. Camped near Campbellsville.
January 5.— Started for New Haven.
January 17.— Ordered to prepare for a march.
January 22.— Got on cars for Louisville.
January 24.— Arrived and went into camp at Louisville.
January 26.— Ordered to stockade at Big Run Trestle, where we now are.

Stationed at Big Run Trestle, Kentucky, March-June 1863.

Stationed at Fort Boyle, Kentucky, July-August 1863.

Stationed at Glasgow, Kentucky, September-October 1863.

Stationed at Columbia, Kentucky, November-December 1863.

Stationed at Knoxville, Tennessee, January-February 1864.

Stationed at Loudon, Tennessee, March-April 1864.

Stationed in the field, near Marietta, Georgia, May-June 1864.

Stationed in the field, Georgia, July-August 1864.

Stationed in the field, near Rome, Georgia, September-October 1864.

Stationed at Columbia, Tennessee, November-December 1864.

Stationed at Wilmington, North Carolina, January-February 1865.

Stationed at Raleigh, North Carolina, March-April 1865.

Stationed at Salisbury, North Carolina, June 26, 1865.
June 26.— Muster-out roll of Captain John S. Conahan's Company (I), in the Fiftieth Regiment of Ohio Infantry Volunteers, commanded by Colonel Silas A. Strickland, called into the service of the United States by the President at Camp Dennison, Ohio (the place of general rendezvous) on August 28, 1862 to serve for the term of three years from the date of enrollment, unless sooner discharged, from the dates respectively (when last paid) to June 26, 1865 date of this muster out. The company was organized by Captain Isaac J. Carter at Camp Dennison, Ohio in the month of August 1862. . . .

BENJAMIN F. BRISCOE,
Captain and Assistant Commissary of Musters,
Second Division, Twenty-third Army Corps,
Mustering Officer.

Company K

Stationed at Camp Dennison, August 24, 1862.
August 24.— Muster-in roll of Captain Leonard A. Hendrick's, [Jr.], Company [K], in the Fiftieth Regiment (— Brigade) of Ohio Infantry Volunteers, commanded by Colonel J. R. Taylor, called into the service of the United States by the President from date of their enrollment respectively (date of muster) for the term of three years, unless sooner discharged. . . .

A. F. BOND,
Captain,
Second Infantry, Mustering Officer.

Stationed at Lebanon, Kentucky, [August 24]-December 31, 1862.

Stationed at Big Run Trestle, Louisville and Nashville Railroad, Kentucky, January-February 1863.

Stationed at Sulphur Fork Trestle, Louisville and Nashville Railroad, Kentucky, March-April 1863.

Station not stated, May-June 1863.

Stationed at Fort Sands, Sulphur Fork Trestle, Kentucky, July-August 1863.

Stationed at Glasgow, Kentucky, September-October 1863.

Stationed at Somerset, Kentucky, November-December 1863.

Stationed at Knoxville, Tennessee, January-February 1864.

Stationed at Loudon, Tennessee, March-April 1864.

Stationed near Kenesaw Mountain, Georgia, May-June 1864.

Stationed at Decatur, Georgia, July-August 1864.

I certify that the clothing, books, and records were all destroyed by order of Colonel S. A. Strickland at Cassville Station, Georgia on May 24, 1864, and that I have no means of knowing the amount of clothing drawn by the men since August 31, 1863 up to May 24, 1864.

Stationed in the field, near Rome, Georgia, September-October 1864.

Stationed at Columbia, Tennessee, November-December 1864.

Stationed at Wilmington, North Carolina, January-February 1865.

Stationed at Raleigh, North Carolina, March-April 1865.

Stationed at Salisbury, North Carolina, June 26, 1865.
June 26.— Muster-out roll of Captain Oliver S. McClure's (late Captain Leonard A. Hendrick's, [Jr.], Company (K), in the Fiftieth Regiment of Ohio Infantry Volunteers, commanded by Colonel Silas A. Strickland, called into the service of the United States by the President at Camp Dennison, Ohio (the place of general rendezvous) on August 23, 1862 to serve for the term of three years from the date of enrollment, unless sooner discharged, from the dates respectively (when last paid) to June 26, 1865 date

of this muster out. The company was organized by Captain L. A. Hendrick at Cincinnati, Ohio in the months of July and August 1862. . . .

BENJAMIN F. BRISCOE,
Captain and Assistant Commissary of Musters,
Second Division, Twenty-third Army Corps,
Mustering Officer.

[M594-Roll #151]

Record of Events for Fifty-first Ohio Infantry, September 1861-June 1865.

Field and Staff

Stationed at Canal Dover, Ohio, October 26, 1861.
October 26.— Muster-in roll of the field and staff in the Fifty-first Regiment (— Brigade) of Ohio Volunteers, commanded by Colonel Stanley Matthews, called into the service of the United States by the President from October 26, 1861 (date of muster) for the term of three years, unless sooner discharged. . . .

HENRY BELKNAP,
Captain,
Eighteenth Infantry, Mustering Officer.

Stationed at Camp Meigs, Canal Dover, Ohio, from muster in to October 31, 1861.

Stationed at Camp Wickliffe, Kentucky, November-December 1861.

Stationed at Nashville, Tennessee, January-February 1862.

Station not stated, March-April 1862.

Stationed at Nashville, Tennessee, May-June 1862.

Station not stated, July-August 1862.

Stationed at Nashville, Tennessee, September 10, 1862.
September 10.— Muster-out roll of the regimental band of the Fifty-first Regiment of Ohio Infantry Volunteers, commanded by Lieutenant-Colonel [Richard] W. McClain, called into the service of the United States by the President of the United States at Camp Meigs, Canal Dover, Ohio (the place of general rendezvous) on [September 10, 1862]. . . .

JOHN [HORNE] YOUNG,
Captain,
Fifteenth United States Infantry, Mustering Officer.

Stationed at camp, near Columbia, Kentucky, September-October 1862.

Stationed at camp, near Murfreesborough, Tennessee, [November 1], 1862-June 30, 1863.

Stationed at Chattanooga, Tennessee, [July 1]-October 31, 1863.

Stationed at Shellmound, Tennessee, November-December 1863.

Stationed at Columbus, Ohio, January-February 1864.
January 1.— Was reorganized as a veteran regiment at Shellmound, Tennessee.

Stationed at Blue Springs, Tennessee, March-April 1864.

Stationed near Kenesaw Mountain, Georgia, May-June 1864.

Stationed near Rough and Ready [Station], Georgia, July-August 1864.

Stationed at Chattanooga, Tennessee, September-October 1864.

Stationed at Lexington, Alabama, November-December 1864.

Stationed at Huntsville, Alabama, January-February 1865.

Stationed at Nashville, Tennessee, March-April 1865.

Stationed near New Orleans, Louisiana, May-June 1865.

Regiment

Stationed at Camp Jenkins, near Louisville, Kentucky, November 1861.

Stationed at Camp Wickliffe, Kentucky, December 1861.
December 10.— Broke camp at Camp Jenkins and marched to Camp Oakland and in conjunction with the rest of General [William] Nelson's command, took up the line of march for Camp Wickliffe, Kentucky near New Haven, a distance of sixty-five miles. Marched in five days at which camp the regiment is now stationed.

Stationed at Camp Wickliffe, Kentucky, January 1862.

Stationed at Camp Andrew Jackson, February 1862.

Stationed at Nashville, Tennessee, March 1862.

Stationed at Nashville, Tennessee (Provost Guard), April 1862.

Stationed at camp, near Murfreesborough, Tennessee, July 1862.

Stationed at Camp Rosecrans, Tennessee, November 1862.

Stationed near Murfreesborough, Tennessee, December 1862.

Stationed at camp, near Murfreesborough, Tennessee, January-June 1863.

Stationed at McMinnville, Tennessee, July 1863.

Stationed at camp, near Pikeville, Tennessee, August 1863.

Stationed at Chattanooga, Tennessee, September 1863.

Stationed at Shellmound, Tennessee, October 1863-January 1864.

Stationed at Blue Springs, Tennessee, March-April 1864.

Stationed in the trenches, near Dallas, Georgia, May 1864.

Stationed in the field, near Marietta, Georgia, June 1864.

Stationed near Atlanta, Georgia, July-August 1864.

Stationed at Atlanta, Georgia, September 1864.

Stationed at Franklin, Tennessee, October-November 1864.

Stationed in the field, Alabama, December 1864.

Stationed at Huntsville, Alabama, January-February 1865.

Stationed at Shield's Mills, East Tennessee, March 1865.

Stationed at Nashville, Tennessee, April 1865.

Stationed at Camp Harker, Tennessee, May 1865.

Stationed at camp on Battle Creek, Louisiana, June 1865.

Company A

Stationed at Canal Dover, Ohio, September 17, 1861.
September 17.— Muster-in roll of Captain Mathias H. Bartilson's Company (A), in the Fifty-first Regiment (—— Brigade) of Ohio Volunteers, commanded by Colonel ——, called into the service of the United States by the President from September 17, 1861 (date of muster) for the term of three years, unless sooner discharged. The company was organized by Captain Mathias H. Bartilson at New Philadelphia in the month of September and marched thence to Canal Dover, where it arrived September 9, a distance of [illegible] miles. . . .

HENRY BELKNAP,
Captain,
Eighteenth Infantry, Mustering Officer.

Station not stated, October 31, 1861.

Stationed at Camp Wickliffe, November-December 1861.

Stationed at Camp Andrew Jackson, Tennessee, January-February 1862.

Stationed at Nashville, Tennessee, March-June 1862.

Stationed at McMinnville, Tennessee, July-August 1862.

Stationed at camp, near Columbia, Kentucky, September-October 1862.

Stationed at camp in the field, December 31, 1862.

Stationed near Murfreesborough, January-February 1863.
January 2.— The company was in action (with balance of the regiment) at battle of Stone's River; loss, one killed, nineteen wounded, six missing (taken prisoners), and two have since died of wounds. Went into action with forty-one men.

Stationed at Murfreesborough, Tennessee, February 28-June 30, 1863.

Stationed at Chattanooga, Tennessee, October 31, 1863.

Stationed at Shellmound, Tennessee, November-December 1863.

Stationed at Columbus, Ohio, January-February 1864.
[For record of events, see Field and Staff.]

Stationed at Blue Springs, Tennessee, March-April 1864.

Stationed in the field, May-June 1864.

Stationed near Atlanta, Georgia, July-August 1864.

Stationed in the field, September-October 1864.

Stationed at Huntsville, Alabama, November 1864-February 1865.

Stationed at Nashville, Tennessee, March-April 1865.

Stationed at New Orleans, Louisiana, May-June 1865.

Company B

Stationed at Canal Dover, Ohio, September 17, 1861.
September 17.— Muster-in roll of Captain Charles H. Wood's Company (B), in the Fifty-first Regiment (—— Brigade) of Ohio Volunteers, commanded by Colonel ——, called into the service of the United States by the President from September 17, 1861 (date of muster) for the term of three years, unless sooner discharged. The company was organized by Captain Charles H. Wood at Canal Dover, Ohio in the month of September and marched thence to Canal Dover, Ohio, where it arrived September 9, a distance of no miles. . . .

HENRY BELKNAP,
Captain,
Eighteenth Infantry, Mustering Officer.

Stationed at Camp Meigs, Canal Dover, Ohio, September 17-October 31, 1861.

Stationed at Camp Wickliffe, near New Haven, Kentucky, November-December 1861.

Stationed at Nashville, Tennessee, January-June 1862.

Stationed at McMinnville, Tennessee, July-August 1862.

Station not stated, September-October 1862.

Stationed at camp, near Murfreesborough, Tennessee, [November 1, 1862]-June 30, 1863.

Stationed at camp, near Chattanooga, Tennessee, October 31, 1863.

Stationed at Shellmound, Tennessee, November-December 1863.

Stationed at Columbus, Ohio, January-February 1864.
[For record of events, see Field and Staff.]

Stationed at Blue Springs, Tennessee, March-April 1864.

Stationed at camp in the field in Georgia, May-August 1864.

Stationed at Chattanooga, Tennessee, September-October 1864.

Stationed in the field, Alabama, November-December 1864.

Stationed at Huntsville, Alabama, January-February 1865.

Stationed near Nashville, Tennessee, March-April 1865.

Stationed at New Orleans, Louisiana, May-June 1865.

Company C

Stationed at Canal Dover, Ohio, September 17, 1861.
September 17.— Muster-in roll of Captain Benjamin F. Heskett's Company (C), in the Fifty-first Regiment (— Brigade) of Ohio Volunteers, commanded by Colonel —, called into the service of the United States by the President from September 17, [1861] (date of muster) for the term of three years, unless sooner discharged. The company was organized by Captain Benjamin F. Heskett at Newcomerstown in the month of September and marched thence to Canal Dover, where it arrived September 9, a distance of twenty-five miles. . . .

HENRY BELKNAP,
Captain,
Eighteenth Infantry, Mustering Officer.

Stationed at Camp Meigs, near Canal Dover, Ohio, September 17-October 31, 1861.

Stationed at Camp Wickliffe, Kentucky, November-December 1861.

Stationed at Nashville, Tennessee, January-June 1862.

Stationed at camp, near McMinnville, Tennessee, July-August 1862.

Stationed at camp, near Columbia, Kentucky, September-October 1862.

Stationed at camp, near Murfreesborough, Tennessee, [November 1, 1862]-June 30, 1863.

Stationed at Pikeville, Tennessee, July-August 1863.

Stationed at Chattanooga, Tennessee, October 31, 1863.

Stationed at Shellmound, Tennessee, November-December 1863.

Stationed at Columbus, Ohio, January-February 1864.
[For record of events, see Field and Staff.]

Stationed at Blue Springs, Tennessee, March-April 1864.

Stationed at Kenesaw, Georgia, May-June 1864.

Stationed at camp, near Atlanta, Georgia, July-August 1864.

Stationed at Chattanooga, Tennessee, September-October 1864.

Stationed at Lexington, Tennessee, November-December 1864.

Stationed at Huntsville, Alabama, January-February 1865.

Stationed near Nashville, Tennessee, March-April 1865.

Stationed at New Orleans, Louisiana, May-June 1865.

Company D

Stationed at Canal Dover, Ohio, September 17 and October 26, 1861.

September 17.— Muster-in roll of Captain William Patton's Company [D], in the Fifty-first Regiment (—— Brigade) of Ohio Volunteers, commanded by Colonel Stanley Matthews, called into the service of the United States by the President from September 17, 1861 for the term of three years, unless sooner discharged. The company was organized by Captain William Patton at Coshocton in the month of September and marched thence to Canal Dover, Ohio, where it arrived September 11, a distance of thirty-five miles. . . .

HENRY BELKNAP,
Captain,
Eighteenth Infantry, Mustering Officer.

Stationed at Camp Meigs, Canal Dover, Ohio, September 17-October 31, 1861.

Stationed at Camp Wickliffe, near New Haven, Kentucky, November-December 1861.

Stationed at Camp Andrew Jackson, Tennessee, January-February 1862.

Stationed at Nashville, Tennessee, March-June 1862.

Stationed at McMinnville, Tennessee, July-August 1862.

Stationed at Columbia, Kentucky, September-October 1862.

Stationed at camp, near Murfreesborough, Tennessee, [November 1, 1862]-June 30, 1863.

Stationed at Pikeville, Tennessee, July-August 1863.

Stationed at camp, near Chattanooga, Tennessee, October 31, 1863.

Stationed at Shellmound, Tennessee, November-December 1863.

Stationed at Coshocton, Ohio, January-February 1864.
[For record of events, see Field and Staff.]

Stationed at Blue Springs, Tennessee, March-April 1864.

Stationed near Wasitea, Georgia, June 30, 1864.

Stationed near Atlanta, Georgia, August 31, 1864.

Stationed at Chattanooga, Tennessee, September-October 1864.

Stationed at Huntsville, Alabama, November 1864-February 1865.

Stationed at Nashville, Tennessee, March-April 1865.

Stationed in the field, May-June 1865.

Company E

Stationed at Canal Dover, Ohio, October 3, 1861.
October 3.— Muster-in roll of Captain David Chalfant's Company (E), in the Fifty-first Regiment (—— Brigade) of Ohio Volunteers, commanded by Colonel ——, called into the service of the United States by the President from October 3, 1861 (date of muster) for the term of three years, unless sooner discharged. The company was organized by Captain David Chalfant at Uhrichsville in the month of September and marched thence to Camp Meigs, Canal Dover, Ohio, where it arrived September 20, a distance of thirteen miles. . . .

HENRY BELKNAP,
Captain,
Eighteenth Infantry, Mustering Officer.

Stationed at Camp Meigs, Canal Dover, Ohio, October 3-31, 1861.

Stationed at Camp Wickliffe, November-December 1861.

Stationed at Nashville, Tennessee, January-June 1862.

Stationed at McMinnville, Tennessee, July-August 1862.

Stationed at Columbia, Kentucky, September-October 1862.

Stationed at camp, near Murfreesborough, Tennessee, June 30, 1863.

Stationed at camp, near Pikeville, Tennessee, July-August 1863.

Stationed at Chattanooga, Tennessee, October 31, 1863.

Stationed at Shellmound, Tennessee, November-December 1863.

Stationed at Columbus, Ohio, January-February 1864.

Stationed at Blue Springs, Tennessee, March-April 1864.

Stationed near Marietta, Georgia, May-June 1864.

Stationed near Jonesborough, Georgia, July-August 1864.

Stationed at Chattanooga, Tennessee, September-October 1864.

Stationed in the field, November-December 1864.
A company of the Fortieth Ohio Volunteer Infantry transferred to be known as Company E of the Fifty-first Ohio Veteran Volunteer Infantry by reason of consolidation made by order of General [George Henry] Thomas.

Stationed at Huntsville, Alabama, January-February 1865.

Stationed in Tennessee, March-April 1865.

Station not stated, May-June 1865.

Company F

Stationed at Canal Dover, October 3, 1861.
October 3.— Muster-in roll of Captain David W. Marshall's Company (F), in the Fifty-first Regiment (—— Brigade) of Ohio Volunteers, commanded by Colonel ——, called into the service of

the United States by the President from October 3, 1861 (date of muster) for the term of three years, unless sooner discharged. The company was organized by Captain David W. Marshall at Coshocton in the month of September and marched thence to Camp Meigs near Canal Dover, Tuscarawas County, Ohio, where it arrived September 11, a distance of forty-seven miles. . . .

HENRY BELKNAP,
Captain,
Eighteenth Infantry, Mustering Officer.

Stationed at Camp Meigs, near Canal Dover, Ohio, October 3-31, 1861.

Stationed at Camp Wickliffe, near New Haven, Kentucky, November-December 1861.

Stationed at Camp Andrew Jackson, near Nashville, Tennessee, January-February 1862.

Stationed at Nashville, Tennessee, March-June 1862.

Stationed at McMinnville, Tennessee, July-August 1862.

Stationed at camp at Columbia, Kentucky, September-October 1862.

Stationed at camp, near Murfreesborough, Tennessee, December 31, 1862.
December 9.— The company was in action with the enemy under General [Joseph] Wheeler at Dobson's Ford, Wilson County, Tennessee. Lost two wounded, one of whom (Blaser) has since died of his wounds.

Stationed at camp, near Murfreesborough, Tennessee, January-February 1863.
January 2.— The company was in action (with the regiment) at battle of Stone's River and lost five killed, eleven wounded and two missing, total eighteen. Went into action with forty-five men. Three of the wounded have since died.

Stationed at camp, near Murfreesborough, Tennessee, April 10, 1863.

Stationed at Murfreesborough, Tennessee, March-April 1863.

Stationed at camp, near Murfreesborough, Tennessee, June 30, 1863.

Stationed near Chattanooga, Tennessee, October 31, 1863.

Stationed at Shellmound, Tennessee, November-December 1863.

Stationed at Columbus, Ohio, February 29. 1864.
[For record of events, see Field and Staff.]

Stationed at Blue Springs, Tennessee, March-April 1864.

Stationed at Kenesaw, Georgia, May-June 1864.

Stationed in the field, Georgia, July-August 1864.

Stationed at Chattanooga, Tennessee, September-October 1864.

Stationed near Lexington, Tennessee, November-December 1864.

Stationed at Huntsville, Alabama, January-February 1865.

Stationed at Nashville, Tennessee, March-April 1865.

Stationed near New Orleans, Louisiana, May-June 1865.

Company G

Stationed at Canal Dover, Ohio, October 3, 1861.
October 3.— Muster-in roll of Captain James T. Shanton's Company [G], in the Fifty-first Regiment (—— Brigade) of Ohio Volunteers, commanded by Colonel ——, called into the service of the United States by the President from October 3, 1861 (date of

muster) for the term of three years, unless sooner discharged. The company was organized by Captain James T. Shanton at Shanesville, Ohio in the month of September and marched thence to Canal Dover, Tuscarawas County, Ohio, where it arrived September 19, a distance of ten miles. . . .

HENRY BELKNAP,
Captain,
Eighteenth Infantry, Mustering Officer.

Stationed at Camp Meigs, Canal Dover, Ohio, October 3-31, 1861.

Stationed at Camp Wickliffe, Kentucky, November-December 1861.

Station not stated, January-February 1862.

Stationed at Nashville, Tennessee, March-June 1862.

Stationed at camp, near McMinnville, July-August 1862.

Station not stated, September-October 1862.

Stationed at camp, near Murfreesborough, Tennessee, [November 1, 1862]-April 30, 1863.

Stationed at Murfreesborough, Tennessee, June 30, 1863.

Stationed at Pikeville, Tennessee, July-August 1863.

Stationed at Chattanooga, Tennessee, [September 1]-October 31, 1863.
September 11.— Skirmished with enemy's cavalry at Ringgold, Catoosa County, Georgia.
September 18.— Skirmished with enemy at Crawfish Spring, Walker County, Georgia.
September 19-20.— Engaged in the battle of Chickamauga, Georgia, in which engagement the company lost one corporal killed, two privates wounded and two privates missing.

Stationed at Shellmound, November-December 1863.

Stationed at Columbus, Ohio, January-February 1864.
[For record of events, see Field and Staff.]

Stationed at Blue Springs, Tennessee, March-April 1864.

Stationed at Kenesaw, Georgia, May-June 1864.

Stationed in the field, Georgia, July-August 1864.

Stationed in the field, Tennessee, September-December 1864.

Stationed at Huntsville, Alabama, January-February 1865.

Stationed at Nashville, Tennessee, March-April 1865.

Station not stated, May-June 1865.

Company H

Stationed at Canal Dover, Ohio, October 4, 1861.
October 4.— Muster-in roll of Captain John D. Nicholas' Company (H), in the Fifty-first Regiment (—— Brigade) of Ohio Volunteers, commanded by Colonel Stanley Matthews, called into the service of the United States by the President from October 4, 1861 (date of muster) for the term of three years, unless sooner discharged. The company was organized by Captain John D. Nicholas at Coshocton in the month of September and marched thence to Camp Meigs, Canal Dover, where it arrived September 19, a distance of forty-seven miles. . . .

HENRY BELKNAP,
Captain,
Eighteenth Infantry, Mustering Officer.

Stationed at Camp Meigs, Canal Dover, Ohio, September 10-October 31, 1861.

Stationed at Camp Wickliffe, near New Haven, Kentucky, November-December 1861.

Stationed at Camp Andrew Jackson, near Nashville, Tennessee, January-February 1862.

Station not stated, March-April 1862.

Stationed at Nashville, Tennessee, May-June 1862.

Stationed at McMinnville, Tennessee, July-August 1862.

Stationed at camp, near Columbia, Kentucky, September-October 1862.

Stationed at Murfreesborough, Tennessee, [November 1, 1862]-February 28, 1863.

Stationed at camp, near Murfreesborough, Tennessee, April 10, 1863.

Stationed at Murfreesborough, Tennessee, [March 1]-June 30, 1863.

Stationed at Pikeville, Tennessee, July-August 1863.

Stationed at Chattanooga, Tennessee, October 31, 1863.

Stationed at Shellmound, Tennessee, November-December 1863.

Stationed at Columbus, Ohio, January-February 1864.
[For record of events, see Field and Staff.]

Stationed at Blue Springs, Tennessee, March-April 1864.

Stationed at Kenesaw Mountain, Georgia, May-June 1864.

Station not stated, July-August 1864.

Stationed at Chattanooga, Tennessee, September-October 1864.

Station not stated, November-December 1864.

Stationed at Huntsville, Alabama, January-February 1865.

Stationed at Nashville, Tennessee, March-April 1865.

Stationed at camp, near New Orleans, Louisiana, May-June 1865.

Company I

Stationed at Canal Dover, Ohio, October 3, 1861.
October 3.— Muster-in roll of Captain James M. Crooks' Company [I], in the Fifty-first Regiment (—— Brigade) of Ohio Volunteers, commanded by Colonel Stanley Matthews, called into the service of the United States by the President from October 3, 1861 (date of muster) for the term of three years, unless sooner discharged. The company was organized by Captain James M. Crooks at Spring Mountain in the month of September and marched thence to Camp Meigs near Canal Dover, where it arrived September 25, a distance of fifty miles. . . .

HENRY BELKNAP,
Captain,
Eighteenth Infantry, Mustering Officer.

Stationed at Camp Meigs, Canal Dover, Ohio, October 3-31, 1861.

Stationed at Camp Wickliffe, near New Haven, Kentucky, November-December 1861.

Stationed at Camp Andrew Jackson, near Nashville, Tennessee, January-February 1862.

Stationed at Nashville, Tennessee, March-June 1862.

Stationed at camp, near McMinnville, Tennessee, July-August 1862.

Stationed at camp, near Columbia, Kentucky, September-October 1862.

Stationed near Murfreesborough, Tennessee, [November 1, 1862]-February 28, 1863.

Stationed at camp, near Murfreesborough, Tennessee, April 10, 1863.

Stationed at Murfreesborough, Tennessee, [March 1]-June 30, 1863.

Stationed at Chattanooga, Tennessee, October 31, 1863.
September 12.— Skirmished with the enemy at Ringgold, Georgia.
September 19-20.— Engaged in the fight at Chickamauga, Georgia in which the company lost one sergeant and one private killed; eight privates wounded; one second lieutenant captured; and one corporal, one sergeant and four privates missing.

Stationed at Blue Springs, Tennessee, March-April 1864.

Stationed near Atlanta, Georgia, July-August 1864.
No muster roll for [September]-October 1864.

Stationed in the field, November-December 1864.

Stationed at Huntsville, Alabama, January-February 1865.

Stationed at Nashville, Tennessee, March-April 1865.

Stationed near New Orleans, Louisiana, May-June 1865.

Company K

Stationed at Canal Dover, Ohio, October 26, 1861.
October 26.— Muster-in roll of Captain Charles Mueller's Company (K), in the Fifty-first Regiment (—— Brigade) of Ohio Volunteers, commanded by Colonel Stanley Matthews, called into the service of the United States by the President from October [26], 1861 (date of muster) for the term of three years, unless sooner discharged. The company was organized by Captain Charles

Mueller at New Philadelphia in the month of October and marched thence to Camp Meigs near Canal Dover, Ohio, where it arrived October 12, a distance of no miles. . . .

HENRY BELKNAP,
Captain,
Eighteenth Infantry, Mustering Officer.

Stationed at Camp Meigs, Canal Dover, Ohio, October [26]-31, 1861.

Stationed at Camp Wickliffe, near New Haven, Kentucky, November-December 1861.

Stationed at Camp Andrew Jackson, near Nashville, Tennessee, January-February 1862.

Stationed at Nashville, Tennessee, March-June 1862.

Stationed at camp, near McMinnville, Tennessee, July-August 1862.

Stationed at camp, near Columbia, Kentucky, September-October 1862.

Stationed at camp in the field, near Murfreesborough, Tennessee, December 31, 1862.

Stationed at camp, near Murfreesborough, Tennessee, January 1-June 30, 1863.

Stationed at Chattanooga, Tennessee, [July 1]-October 31, 1863.

Stationed near Atlanta, Georgia, July-August 1864.

No muster roll for [September]-October 1864.

Stationed in the field, Alabama, November-December 1864.

Stationed at Huntsville, Alabama, January-February 1865.

Stationed near Nashville, Tennessee, March-April 1865.

Stationed at New Orleans, Louisiana, May-June 1865.

[M594-Roll #151]

Record of Events for Fifty-second Ohio Infantry, August 1862-June 1865.

Field and Staff

Stationed at Camp Dennison, Ohio, August 23, 1862.
August 23.— Muster-in roll of field and staff in the Fifty-second Regiment (—— Brigade) of Ohio Foot Volunteers, commanded by Colonel Daniel McCook, called into the service of the United States by the President from August 23, 1862 (date of muster) for the term of three years or during the war, unless sooner discharged. . . .

[ADOLPHUS FREEMAN] BOND,
Captain,
Second Infantry, Mustering Officer.

Stationed at Prewitt's Knob, Kentucky, September-October 1862.

Stationed at Nashville, Tennessee, November-December 1862.

Station not stated, January-February 1863.

Stationed at Brentwood, Tennessee, March-April 1863.

Stationed at Nashville, Tennessee, May-June 1863.

Stationed at Columbia, Tennessee, July-August 1863.

Station not stated, September-October 1863.

Stationed at McAfee's Church, Georgia, November 1863-February 1864.

Stationed at [Lee and] Gordon's Mills, Georgia, March-April 1864.

Station not stated, May-June 1864.

Stationed near Rough and Ready, Georgia, July-August 1864.

Stationed at Rome, Georgia, September-October 1864.

Stationed at Savannah, Georgia, November-December 1864.

Stationed in the field, North Carolina, January-April 1865.

Stationed at Washington, District of Columbia, June 3, 1865.
June 3.— Muster-out roll of field and staff in the Fifty-second Regiment of Ohio Volunteers, commanded by Lieutenant-Colonel Charles W. Clancy, late Colonel Daniel McCook, called into the service of the United States by the President at Camp Dennison, Ohio (the place of general rendezvous) on August 21, 1862 to serve for the term of three years from the date of enrollment, unless sooner discharged. . . .

GEORGE SCROGGS,
First Lieutenant,
One Hundred Twenty-fifth [Illinois] Volunteers,
Assistant Commissary of Musters,
Second Division, Fourteenth Army Corps,
Mustering Officer.

Regiment

Stationed at Camp Sheridan, Mill Creek, near Nashville, Tennessee, November 1862.

Stationed at Nashville, Tennessee, December 1862-March 1863.

Stationed at Brentwood, Tennessee, April-May 1863.

Stationed at Nashville, Tennessee, July 1863.

Stationed at Columbia, Tennessee, August 1863.

Stationed at North Chickamauga Creek, near Chattanooga, Tennessee, September 1863.

Stationed at North Chickamauga, Tennessee, October-November 1863.

Stationed at McAfee's Church, Georgia, December 1863-February 1864.

Stationed at Lee and Gordon's Mills, Georgia, March-April 1864.

Stationed near Acworth, Georgia, May 1864.

Stationed near Marietta, Georgia, June 1864.

Stationed at camp in the field, near Atlanta, Georgia, July 1864.

Stationed in the field, near Atlanta, Georgia, August 1864.

Stationed at Atlanta, Georgia, September 1864.

Stationed at Gaylesville, Alabama, October 1864.

Stationed at Louisville, Georgia, November 1864.

Stationed at Savannah, Georgia, December 1864.

Stationed at Sister's Ferry, Georgia, January 1865.

Stationed at Kingsbury's Ferry, South Carolina, February 1865.

Stationed at Goldsborough, North Carolina, March 1865.

Stationed in the field, North Carolina, April 1865.

Stationed near Washington, District of Columbia, May 1865.

Company A

Stationed at Camp Dennison, Ohio, August 20, 1862.
August 20.— Muster-in roll of Captain Israel D. Clark's Company [A], in the Fifty-second Regiment (— Brigade) of Ohio Volunteers, commanded by Colonel Daniel McCook, called into the service of the United States by [the President] from — (date of muster) for the term of three years, unless sooner discharged. . . .

A. F. BOND,
Captain,
Second Infantry, Mustering Officer.

Stationed at Prewitt's Knob, August 20-October 31, 1862.
August 31.— We took part in a skirmish against the Rebels at the Kentucky River, sixteen miles from Lexington, Kentucky.
October 8.— We also had the honor of firing the first shot for the Union at the battle of Perryville, Kentucky this morning at 4 o'clock a.m. skirmishing.
October 31.— We marched about 600 miles since August 30 up to this date.

Stationed at Nashville, Tennessee, November 1862-February 1863.

Stationed at camp, near Brentwood, Tennessee, April 24, 1863.
Supposed to be Special Muster for April 10, 1863.

Stationed at Brentwood, Tennessee, March-April 1863.

Stationed at Nashville, Tennessee, May-June 1863.

Stationed at Columbia, Tennessee, July-August 1863.

Stationed at North Chickamauga, Tennessee, September-October 1863.

Stationed at camp, near McAfee's Church, Georgia, November-December 1863.

Stationed at McAfee's Church, Georgia, January-February 1864.

Stationed at Lee and Gordon's Mills, Georgia, March-April 1864.

Stationed in the field, near Marietta, Georgia, May-June 1864.

Stationed in the field, near Atlanta, Georgia, July-August 1864.

Stationed at Rome, Georgia, September-October 1864.

Stationed at Savannah, Georgia, November-December 1864.

Stationed at Kingsbury's Ferry, South Carolina, [January 1]-February 28, 1865.

Stationed at Mooresville, North Carolina, March-April 1865.

Stationed at Washington, District of Columbia, June 3, 1865.
June 3.— Muster-out roll of Captain William H. Bucke's, late Israel D. Clark's, Company (A), in the Fifty-second Regiment of Ohio Volunteers, commanded by Colonel Charles W. Clancy, late Daniel McCook, called into the service of the United States by the President at Camp Dennison, Ohio (the place of general rendezvous) on August 17, 1862 to serve for the term of three years from the date of enrollment, unless sooner discharged. . . .

GEORGE SCROGGS,
First Lieutenant,
One Hundred Twenty-fifth Illinois Volunteers,
Assistant Commissary of Musters, Second Division,
Fourteenth Army Corps, Mustering Officer.

Company B

Stationed at Camp Dennison, Ohio, August 21, 1862.
August 21.— Muster-in roll of Captain Charles W. Clancy's Company [B], in the Fifty-second Regiment (— Brigade) of Ohio Volunteers, commanded by Colonel Daniel McCook, called into the service of the United States by [the President] from —

(date of muster) for the term of three years, unless sooner discharged. . . .

A. F. BOND,
Captain,
Second Infantry, Mustering Officer.

Stationed at Prewitt's Knob, Kentucky, August 21-October 31, 1862.

Stationed at Nashville, Tennessee, November 1862-February 1863.

Stationed at Brentwood, Tennessee, March-April 1863.

Stationed at Nashville, May-June 1863.

Stationed at Columbia, Tennessee, July-August 1863.

Stationed at North Chickamauga Creek, September-October 1863.

Stationed at McAfee's Church, Georgia, November 1863-February 1864.

Stationed at Lee and Gordon's Mills, Georgia, March-April 1864.

Stationed near Marietta, Georgia, May-June 1864.

Stationed near Atlanta, Georgia, July-August 1864.

Stationed at Rome, Georgia, September-October 1864.

Stationed at Savannah, Georgia, November-December 1864.

Stationed at Catawba River, South Carolina, January-February 1865.

Stationed in the field, North Carolina, March-April 1865.

Stationed at Washington, District of Columbia, June 3, 1865.
June 3.— Muster-out roll of First Lieutenant William A. Judkins', late Captain Charles W. Clancy's, Company (B), in the

Fifty-second Regiment of Ohio Volunteers, commanded by Lieutenant-Colonel Charles W. Clancy, late Colonel Daniel McCook, called into the service of the United States by the President at Camp Dennison, Ohio (the place of general rendezvous) on August 21, 1862 to serve for the term of three years from the date of enrollment, unless sooner discharged. . . .

GEORGE SCROGGS,
First Lieutenant,
One Hundred Twenty-fifth Illinois Volunteers,
Assistant Commissary of Musters, Second Division,
Fourteenth Army Corps, Mustering Officer.

Company C

Stationed at Camp Dennison, Ohio, August 20, 1862.
August 20.— Muster-in roll of Captain Jacob E. Moffitt's Company [C], in the Fifty-second Regiment (—— Brigade) of Ohio Volunteers, commanded by Colonel Daniel McCook, called into the service of the United States by [the President] from —— (date of muster) for the term of three years, unless sooner discharged. . . .

A. F. BOND,
Captain,
Second Infantry, Mustering Officer.

Stationed at Prewitt's Knob, Kentucky, August 21-October 31, 1862.
August 25.— Left Camp Dennison, Ohio for Lexington, Kentucky.
August 26.— Arrived at Lexington, Kentucky.
September 1.— Commenced retreat from Lexington, Kentucky.
October 1.— Commenced march from Louisville, Kentucky.
October 8.— Engaged in the battle of Perryville.

Stationed at Nashville, Tennessee, November-December 1862.
November 8-December 11.— From "Prewitt's Knob" (where we mustered last) we marched to Nashville, Tennessee, where we arrived November 8 and camped at Edgefield (opposite Nashville) two weeks, then crossed the river and marched through Nashville, Tennessee to a point on the Nolensville Pike, seven miles from Nashville, and remained.

December 12.— We changed camp with division and returned to Nashville, where we have since remained stationed.

Stationed at Nashville, Tennessee, January-February 1863.

Stationed at Brentwood, Tennessee, March-April 1863.

Stationed at Nashville, Tennessee, May-June 1863.

Stationed at Columbia, Tennessee, July-August 1863.

Stationed at Chattanooga, Tennessee, September-October 1863.

Stationed at McAfee's Church, Georgia, November-December 1863.
November 24.— Left Camp Chickamauga, Tennessee. Crossed the Tennessee River in the morning.
November 25-December 18.— Engaged in the battle of Missionary Ridge. Pursued [Braxton] Bragg to the northern boundary of Georgia. Skirmished with the enemy's rear guard at Shepherd River; thence via Charleston, Tennessee to Morgan's Farm, Tennessee in pursuit of [James] Longstreet.
December 19.— Returned to Camp North Chickamauga, Tennessee.

Stationed at McAfee's Church, Georgia, January-February 1864.

Stationed at [Lee and] Gordon's Mills, Georgia, March-April 1864.

Station not stated, May-June 1864.

Stationed near Rough and Ready, Georgia, July-August 1864.

Stationed at Rome, Georgia, September-October 1864.

Stationed at Savannah, Georgia, November-December 1864.

Stationed at Kingsbury's Ferry, South Carolina, January-February 1865.

Stationed at Holly Springs, North Carolina, March-April 1865.

Stationed at Washington, District of Columbia, June 3, 1865.
June 3.— Muster-out roll of Captain Abisha C. Thomas', late Captain Jacob E. Moffitt's, Company (C), in the Fifty-second Regiment of Ohio Infantry Volunteers, commanded by Lieutenant-Colonel Charles W. Clancy, late Colonel Daniel McCook, called into the service of the United States by the President at Camp Dennison, Ohio (the place of general rendezvous) on August 20, 1862 to serve for the term of three years from the date of enrollment, unless sooner discharged. . . .

GEORGE SCROGGS,
First Lieutenant,
One Hundred Twenty-fifth Illinois Volunteers,
Assistant Commissary of Musters, Second Division,
Fourteenth Army Corps, Mustering Officer.

Company D

Stationed at Camp Dennison, Ohio, August 20, 1862.
August 20.— Muster-in roll of Captain Matthew L. Morrow's Company [D], in the Fifty-second Regiment (—— Brigade) of Ohio Volunteers, commanded by Colonel Daniel McCook, called into the service of the United States by the President thereof from August 20, 1862 (date of muster) for the term of three years, unless sooner discharged. . . .

A. F. BOND,
Captain,
Second Infantry, Mustering Officer.

Stationed in the field, near Cave City, Kentucky, August 20-October 31, 1862.

Stationed near the city of Nashville, Tennessee, November-December 1862.

Stationed at Nashville, Tennessee, January-February 1863.

Stationed at Brentwood, Tennessee, March-April 1863.

Stationed at Nashville, Tennessee, May-June 1863.

Stationed at Columbia, Tennessee, July-August 1863.

Stationed at North Chickamauga, September-October 1863.

Stationed at McAfee's Church, Georgia, November 1863-February 1864.

Stationed at Lee and Gordon's Mills, Georgia, March-April 1864.

Stationed in the field, May-October 1864.

Stationed at Savannah, Georgia, November-December 1864.

Stationed at Kingsbury's [Ferry] Ferry, South Carolina, January-February 1865.

Stationed at Mooresville, North Carolina, March-April 1865.

Stationed at Washington, District of Columbia, June 3, 1865.
June 3.— Muster-out roll of Lieutenant William H. Ray's, late Captain Matthew L. Morrow's, Company (D), in the Fifty-second Regiment of Ohio Volunteers, commanded by Lieutenant-Colonel Charles W. Clancy, late Colonel Daniel McCook, called into the service of the United States by the President at Camp Dennison, Ohio (the place of general rendezvous) on August 20, 1862 to serve for the term of three years from the date of enrollment, unless sooner discharged. . . .

GEORGE SCROGGS,
First Lieutenant,
One Hundred Twenty-fifth Illinois Volunteers,
Assistant Commissary of Musters, Second Division,
Fourteenth Army Corps, Mustering Officer.

Company E

Stationed at Camp Dennison, Ohio, August 21, 1862.
August 21.— Muster-in roll of Captain Parker A. Elson's Company (E), in the Fifty-second Regiment (Ohio Brigade) of Ohio

Infantry Volunteers, commanded by Colonel Daniel McCook, called into the service of the United States by Governor David Tod from August 21, 1862 (date of muster) for the term of three years, unless sooner discharged. . . .

A. F. BOND,
Mustering Officer.

Stationed at Prewitt's Knob, September-October 1862.

Stationed at Nashville, Tennessee, November 1862-February 1863.

Stationed at Brentwood, Tennessee, March-April 1863.

Stationed at Nashville, Tennessee, May-June 1863.

Stationed at Columbia, Tennessee, July-August 1863.

Stationed at North Chickamauga Creek, Tennessee, September-October 1863.

Stationed at McAfee's Church, Georgia, November 1863-February 1864.

Stationed at [Lee and] Gordon's Mills, Georgia, March-April 1864.

Stationed in the field, near Marietta, Georgia, May-June 1864.

Stationed near Rough and Ready, Georgia, July-August 1864.

Stationed at Rome, Georgia, September-October 1864.

Stationed near Savannah, Georgia, November-December 1864.

Stationed at Kingsbury's Ferry, January-February 1865.

Stationed in the field, North Carolina, March-April 1865.

Stationed at Washington, District of Columbia, June 3, 1865.
June 3.— Muster-out roll of Captain William H. Lane's, late Captain Elson's, Company (E), in the Fifty-second Regiment of Ohio Volunteers, commanded by Lieutenant-Colonel Charles W. Clancy, late Colonel Daniel McCook, called into the service of the United States by the President at Camp Dennison, Ohio (the place of general rendezvous) on August 21, 1862 to serve for the term of three years from the date of enrollment, unless sooner discharged. . . .

GEORGE SCROGGS,
First Lieutenant,
One Hundred Twenty-fifth Illinois Volunteers,
Assistant Commissary of Musters, Second Division,
Fourteenth Army Corps, Mustering Officer.

Company F

Stationed at Camp Dennison, Ohio, August 22, 1862.
August 22.— Muster-in roll of Captain James B. Donaldson's Company [F], in the Fifty-second Regiment (— Brigade) of Ohio Volunteers, commanded by Colonel Daniel McCook, called into the service of the United States by the President from — (date of muster) for the term of three years, unless sooner discharged. . . .

A. F. BOND,
Captain,
Second Infantry, Mustering Officer.

Stationed at Prewitt's Knob, Baron County, Kentucky, October 31, 1862.
August 30.— Left Lexington, Kentucky to reinforce the Federal forces at Richmond, Kentucky under General [William] Nelson, then fighting the enemy. Met our Army retreating at Kentucky River. Returned to Lexington.
August 31.— Evacuated the place and commenced retreating to Louisville, Kentucky.
September 4.— Arrived at Camp Gilbert near Louisville. Remained in and about the city.

October 1-7.— Left Louisville in pursuit of General Bragg and his conscript Army. After seven successive days' marching, came up with the enemy's rear.
October 8.— Gave him battle at "Chaplin Heights" near Perryville, Kentucky. The first firing in this battle on part of the Federal forces was done by the skirmishers of the Fifty-second Ohio Volunteer Infantry (Companies A and H). The whole regiment was under a heavy artillery and infantry fire in the afternoon, but one man in this Company (F) wounded in this battle, none killed. Pursued the enemy to Crab Orchard, Kentucky.
October 20.— Let Crab Orchard and returned to Danville, Kentucky, from thence by the way of Bowling Green proceeded to Nashville, Tennessee.

Stationed at Nashville, Tennessee, November-December 1862.
November 29.— Advanced to Camp Sheridan on Mill Creek, six miles south of Nashville, Tennessee.
December 10.— Was transferred from General [Philip Henry] Sheridan's Division to that commanded by General [Robert Byington] Mitchell.
December 11.— Moved from Mill Creek to Nashville.

Stationed at Nashville, Tennessee, January-February 1863.

Stationed at camp, near Brentwood, Tennessee, April 24, 1863.
Supposed to be Special Muster for April 10, 1863.

Stationed at Brentwood, March-April 1863.

Stationed at Nashville, Tennessee, May-June 1863.

Stationed at Athens, Alabama, July-August 1863.

Stationed at North Chickamauga Creek, September-October 1863.

Stationed at McAfee's Church, Georgia, November-December 1863.

Stationed at McAfee's Church, Georgia, January-February 1864.
Company (F) accompanied the late expedition under General [John McCauley] Palmer to near Dalton, Georgia and assisted in

driving the Rebels from the neighborhood of Ringgold and from Tunnel Hill to a gap in a spur of the Blue Ridge Mountains called Buzzard Roost, where we skirmished with the enemy for two days. Our brigade lost between thirty and forty men in killed, wounded and missing.
February 27.— We returned to our camp at McAfee's Church, Georgia after having accomplished the object of the expedition.

Stationed at [Lee and] Gordon's Mills, Georgia, March-April 1864.

Stationed near Marietta, Georgia, May-June 1864.

Stationed in the field, near Atlanta, Georgia, July-August 1864.

Stationed in the field, September-October 1864.

Stationed at Savannah, Georgia, November-December 1864.
This company, F, belongs to the Army of General Sherman and, since last muster, has marched from Rome, Georgia to Savannah, Georgia, upwards of 350 miles tearing up railroads, skirmishing with the enemy, and enduring the other hardships of such a campaign, and has at last, with the balance of the Army, been rewarded by the capture of the city of Savannah and environs.

Stationed in the field, January-February 1865.

Stationed at Holly Springs, March-April 1865.

Stationed at Washington, District of Columbia, June 3, 1865.
June 3.— Muster-out roll of Captain Samuel C. Hutchison's, late Captain James B. Donalson's, Company (F), in the Fifty-second Regiment of Ohio Infantry Volunteers, commanded by Lieutenant-Colonel Charles W. Clancy, late Colonel Daniel McCook, called into the service of the United States by the President at Camp Dennison (the place of general rendezvous) on August 22,

1862 to serve for the term of three years from the date of enrollment, unless sooner discharged. . . .

GEORGE SCROGGS,
First Lieutenant,
One Hundred Twenty-fifth Illinois Volunteers,
Assistant Commissary of Musters, Second Division,
Fourteenth Army Corps, Mustering Officer.

Company G

Stationed at Camp Dennison, Ohio, August 22, 1862.
August 22.— Muster-in roll of Captain [James] Taylor Holmes' Company [G], in the [Fifty-second] Regiment (— Brigade), of [Ohio Volunteers], commanded by [Colonel Daniel McCook], called into the service of the United States by [the President] from — (date of muster) for the term of three years, unless sooner discharged. . . .

A. F. BOND,
Captain,
Second Infantry, Mustering Officer.

Stationed at Prewitt's Knob, September-October 1862.

Stationed at Nashville, Tennessee, November 1862-February 1863.

Stationed at Brentwood, Tennessee, March-April 1863.

Stationed at Nashville, Tennessee, May-June 1863.

Stationed at Columbia, Tennessee, July-August 1863.

Stationed at North Chickamauga Creek, Tennessee, October 31, 1863.

Stationed at McAfee's Church, Georgia, November 1863-February 1864.

Stationed at Lee and Gordon's Mills, Georgia, [March 1]-April 30, 1864.

Station not stated, May-June 1864.

Stationed at camp, near Macon Railroad, July-August 1864.

Stationed at Savannah, Georgia, December 31, 1864.

Stationed at Charleston River, South Carolina, January-February 1865.

Stationed in the field, North Carolina, March-April 1865.

Stationed at Washington, District of Columbia, June 3, 1865.
June 3.— Muster-out roll of First Lieutenant Lemuel W. Duff's, late Captain James T. Holmes', Company (G), in the Fifty-second Regiment of Ohio Volunteers, commanded by Lieutenant-Colonel Charles W. Clancy, late Colonel Daniel McCook, called into the service of the United States by the President at Camp Dennison, Ohio (the place of general rendezvous) on August 22, 1862 to serve for the term of three years from the date of enrollment, unless sooner discharged. . . .

GEORGE SCROGGS,
First Lieutenant,
One Hundred Twenty-fifth Illinois Volunteers,
Assistant Commissary of Musters, Second Division,
Fourteenth Army Corps, Mustering Officer.

Company H

Stationed at Camp Dennison, Ohio, August 21, 1862.
August 21.— Muster-in roll of Captain [Joseph] A. Culbertson's Company [H], in the Fifty-second Regiment (— Brigade) of Ohio Volunteers, commanded by Colonel Daniel McCook, called into the service of the United States by the President from — (date of muster) for the term of three years, unless sooner discharged. . . .

A. F. BOND,
Captain,
Second Infantry, Mustering Officer.

Stationed on the field at Prewitt's Knob, Kentucky, August 21-October 31, 1862.
October 8.— We had the honor of firing the first shot for the Union at the battle of Perryville, Kentucky this morning at 4 o'clock a.m., skirmishing.
October 31.— We marched about 600 miles since August 30, up to this date.

Stationed at Nashville, Tennessee, November 1862-February 1863.

Stationed at Camp Brentwood, Tennessee, March-April 1863.

Stationed at Nashville, May-June 1863.

Stationed at Columbia, Tennessee, July-August 1863.

Stationed at camp on North Chickamauga Creek, September-October 1863.

Stationed at McAfee's Church, Georgia, November 1863-February 1864.

Stationed at Lee and Gordon's Mills, Georgia, March-April 1864.

Stationed at Marietta, Georgia, May-June 1864.

Stationed near Atlanta, Georgia, July-August 1864.

Stationed at Rome, Georgia, September-October 1864.

Stationed at Savannah, Georgia, November-December 1864.

Stationed at Kingsbury's Ferry, South Carolina, January-February 1865.

Stationed at Holly Springs, North Carolina, March-April 1865.

Stationed at Washington, District of Columbia, June 3, 1865.
June 3.— Muster-out roll of Lieutenant Julius Armstrong's, late Captain Culbertson's, Company (H), in the Fifty-second Regiment of Ohio Volunteers, commanded by Lieutenant-Colonel Charles W. Clancy, late Colonel Daniel McCook, called into the service of the United States by the President at Camp Dennison, Ohio (the place of general rendezvous) on August 21, 1862 to serve for the term of three years from the date of enrollment, unless sooner discharged. . . .

GEORGE SCROGGS,
First Lieutenant,
One Hundred Twenty-fifth Illinois Volunteers,
Assistant Commissary of Musters, Second Division,
Fourteenth Army Corps, Mustering Officer.

Company I

Stationed at Camp Dennison, Ohio, August 22, 1862.
August 22.— Muster-in roll of Captain Peter C. Schneider's Company [I], in the Fifty-second Regiment (—— Brigade) of Ohio Volunteers, commanded by Colonel Daniel McCook, called into the service of the United States by [the President] from August 22, 1862 (date of muster) for the term of three years, unless sooner discharged. . . .

A. F. BOND,
Captain,
Second Infantry, Mustering Officer.

Stationed at Prewitt's Knob, August 22-October 31, 1862.

Stationed at Nashville, Tennessee, November 1862-February 1863.

Stationed at camp, near Brentwood, Tennessee, March-April 1863.

Stationed at Nashville, Tennessee, May-June 1863.

Stationed at Columbia, Tennessee, July-August 1863.

Stationed at Camp North Chickamauga [Creek], Tennessee, September-October 1863.

Stationed at McAfee's Church, Georgia, November 1863-February 1864.

Stationed at Lee and Gordon's Mills, Georgia, March-April 1864.

Stationed in the field, Georgia, May-August 1864.

Stationed at Rome, Georgia, September-October 1864.

Stationed at Savannah, Georgia, November-December 1864.

Stationed at Kingsbury's Ferry, South Carolina, January-February 1865.

Stationed at Raleigh, North Carolina, March-April 1865.

Stationed at Washington, District of Columbia, June 3, 1865.
June 3.— Muster-out roll of First Captain Frank B. James's, late Captain Peter C. Schneider's, Company (I), in the Fifty-second Regiment of Ohio Infantry Volunteers, commanded by Lieutenant-Colonel Charles W. Clancy, late Colonel Daniel McCook, called into the service of the United States by the President at Camp Dennison, Ohio (the place of general rendezvous) on August 22, 1862 to serve for the term of three years from the date of enrollment, unless sooner discharged. . . .

GEORGE SCROGGS,
First Lieutenant,
One Hundred Twenty-fifth Illinois Volunteers,
Assistant Commissary of Musters, Second Division,
Fourteenth Army Corps, Mustering Officer.

Company K

Stationed at Camp Dennison, Ohio, August 21, 1862.
August 21.— Muster-in roll of Captain Andrew S. Bloom's Company [K], in the Fifty-second Regiment (—— Brigade) of Ohio

Volunteers, commanded by Colonel Daniel McCook, called into the service of the United States by [the President] from August 21, 1862 (date of muster) for the term of three years, unless sooner discharged. . . .

A. F. BOND,
Captain,
Second Infantry, Mustering Officer.

Station not stated, September-October 1862.

Stationed at Nashville, Tennessee, November [1], 1862-February 27, 1863.

Stationed near Brentwood, Tennessee, April 24, 1863.
Supposed to be Special Muster for April 10, 1863.

Stationed at Brentwood, Tennessee, March-April 1863.

Stationed at Nashville, Tennessee, May-June 1863.

Stationed at Columbia, Tennessee, July-August 1863.

Stationed at Camp North Chickamauga, September-October 1863.

Stationed at McAfee's Church, Georgia, November 1863-February 1864.

Stationed at [Lee and] Gordon's Mills, Georgia, [March 1]-April 30, 1864.

Stationed near Marietta, Georgia, [May 1]-June 30, 1864.

Stationed twelve miles south of Atlanta, July-August 1864.

Stationed at Rome, Georgia, September-October 1864.

Stationed at Savannah, Georgia, November-December 1864.

Stationed at Kingsbury's Ferry, South Carolina, January-February 1865.

Stationed at Holly Springs, North Carolina, March-April 1865.

Stationed at Washington, District of Columbia, June 3, 1865.
June 3.— Muster-out roll of Captain Edward L. Anderson's, late Captain Bloom's, Company (K), in the Fifty-second Regiment of Ohio Infantry Volunteers, commanded by Lieutenant-Colonel Charles W. Clancy, late Colonel Daniel McCook, called into the service of the United States by the President at Camp Dennison, Ohio (the place of general rendezvous) on August 21, 1862 to serve for the term of three years from the date of enrollment, unless sooner discharged. . . .

GEORGE SCROGGS,
First Lieutenant,
One Hundred Twenty-fifth Illinois Volunteers,
Assistant Commissary of Musters, Second Division,
Fourteenth Army Corps, Mustering Officer.

[M594-Roll #151]

Record of Events for Fifty-third Ohio Infantry, October 1861-June 1865.

Field and Staff

Stationed at Camp Diamond, near Jackson, Ohio, December 31, 1861.

Stationed at Camp Sherman, Paducah, Kentucky, January-February 1862.

Stationed at Camp Shiloh, Tennessee, March-April 1862.

Stationed at Moscow, Tennessee, May-June 1862.

Stationed at Fort Pickering, near Memphis, Tennessee, July-October 1862.

Station not stated, November 1862-February 1863.

Stationed at Moscow, Tennessee, March-April 1863.

Stationed at Oak Ridge, Mississippi, May-June 1863.

Stationed at Camp Sherman, Mississippi, July-August 1863.

Station not stated, September-December 1863.

Stationed at Waverly, Ohio, January-February 1864.

Stationed at Scottsborough, Alabama, March-April 1864.

Stationed at Kenesaw Mountain, May-June 1864.

Stationed at Jonesborough, Georgia, July-August 1864.

Stationed at Cave Spring, Georgia, September-October 1864.

Stationed near Savannah, Georgia, November-December 1864.

Stationed at Lynch's Creek, South Carolina, January-February 1865.

Stationed near Raleigh, North Carolina, March-April 1865.

Stationed on board steamer Ontario, May-June 1865.

Regiment

Stationed at Memphis, July 1862.

Stationed at Fort Pickering, Memphis, Tennessee, September-October 1862.

Stationed at Holly Springs, December 1862.

Station not stated, January 1863.

Stationed at La Grange, Tennessee, February 1863.

Station not stated, March 1863.
Return dated Moscow, Tennessee April 1, 1863.

Stationed at Moscow, Tennessee, April 1863.

Station not stated, May 1863.
Return dated Moscow, Tennessee June 1, 1863.

Stationed at Oak Ridge, Mississippi, June 1863.

Stationed at Big Black River, Mississippi, July 1863.

Station not stated, August 1863.
Return dated Camp Sherman, Mississippi September 2, 1863.

Stationed at Camp Sherman, Mississippi, September 1863.

Stationed at Florence, Alabama, October 1863.

Stationed at Graysville, Georgia, November 1863.

Stationed at Scottsborough, Alabama, December 1863.

Stationed at Scottsborough, Alabama, March 1864.

Stationed at Dallas, Georgia, May 1864.

Stationed at Kenesaw Mountain, June 1864.

Stationed before Atlanta, Georgia, July 1864.

Stationed before Jonesborough, Georgia, August 1864.

Stationed at East Point, Georgia, September 1864.

Stationed at Cave Spring, Georgia, October 1864.

Stationed in the field, Georgia, November 1864.

Stationed at Savannah, Georgia, December 1864.

Stationed in the field, South Carolina, January-February 1865.

Stationed at Goldsborough, North Carolina, March 1865.

Station not stated, April 1865.
Return dated Raleigh, North Carolina May 23, 1865.

Station not stated, May 1865.
Return dated Washington, District of Columbia June 9, 1865.

Stationed on board steamboat Ontario, June 1865.

Company A

Stationed at Camp Diamond, Jackson, Ohio, October 3, 1861.
October 3.— Muster-in roll of Captain Wells S. Jones' Company [A], in the Fifty-third Regiment (—— Brigade) of Ohio Foot Volunteers, commanded by Colonel Jesse J. Appler, called into the service of the United States by the President from October 3, 1861 (date of muster) for the term of three years, unless sooner discharged. . . .

[ROBERT BOWNE] HULL,
First Lieutenant,
Eighteenth Regiment, United States Infantry, Mustering Officer.

Stationed at Camp Diamond, near Jackson, Ohio, December 31, 1861.

Stationed at Camp Sherman, Paducah, Kentucky, January-February 1862.

Stationed at Camp Shiloh, Tennessee, March-April 1862.

Stationed at Camp Moscow, Tennessee, May-June 1862.
June 30.— Fifteen enlisted men dropped from roll by Major-General [William Tecumseh] Sherman's [Orders] No. 47 of June 27, 1862.

Stationed at Fort Pickering, Memphis, Tennessee, August 18, 1862.
August 18.— Fifteen enlisted men restored to roll by Major-General Sherman's [Orders] No. 70 of August 12, 1862.

Stationed at Fort Pickering, Tennessee, July-October 1862.

Stationed at Holly Springs, Mississippi, November-December 1862.

Stationed at La Grange, Tennessee, January-February 1863.

Stationed at Moscow, Tennessee, March-April 1863.

Stationed at Oak Ridge, Mississippi, May-June 1863.

Stationed at Camp Sherman, Mississippi, July-August 1863.

Stationed at Florence, Alabama, September-October 1863.

Stationed at Scottsborough, Alabama, November-December 1863.

Stationed at Camp Dennison, Ohio, January-February 1864.

Stationed at Scottsborough, Alabama, March-April 1864.

Stationed at Kenesaw Mountain, Georgia, May-June 1864.

Stationed near Jonesborough, Georgia, July-August 1864.

Stationed at Cave Spring, Georgia, September-October 1864.

Stationed near Savannah, Georgia, November-December 1864.

Stationed at Lynch's Creek, South Carolina, January-February 1865.

Stationed in the field, North Carolina, March-April 1865.

Stationed [on board] steamer Ontario, May-June 1865.

Company B

Stationed at Jackson, Ohio, October 3, 1861.
October 3.— Muster-in roll of the first detachment, Company [B], in the Fifty-third Regiment (—— Brigade) of Ohio Foot Volunteers, commanded by Colonel [Jesse] J. Appler, called into the service of the United States by the President from October 3, 1861 (date of muster) for the term of three years, unless sooner discharged. . . .

R. B. HULL,
First Lieutenant,
Eighteenth United States Infantry, Mustering Officer.

Stationed at Camp Diamond, [Jackson], Ohio, November 6, 1861.
November 6.— Muster-in roll of the second detachment of Captain John I. Parrill's Company [B], in the Fifty-third Regiment (—— Brigade) of Ohio Foot Volunteers, commanded by Colonel J. J. Appler, called into the service of the United States by the President from October 15 and November 6, 1861 for the term of three years, unless sooner discharged. The company was organized by Captain J. I. Parrill at Athens County in the months of October and November and marched thence to Camp Diamond, Jackson, Ohio. . . .

R. B. HULL,
First Lieutenant,
Eighteenth Regiment, United States Infantry, Mustering Officer.

Stationed at Camp Diamond, near Jackson, Ohio, December 31, 1861.

Station not stated, January-February 1862.

Stationed at Camp Shiloh, March-April 1862.

Stationed at Moscow, Tennessee, May-June 1862.

Stationed at Fort Pickering, August 18, 1862.

Stationed at Fort Pickering, Tennessee, July-August 1862.
August 12.— Thirty officers and men reported deserters [last] muster June 30, by order of General W. T. Sherman, are by his Orders No. 70 this date, restored to roll.

Stationed at Fort Pickering, Tennessee, September-October 1862.

Stationed at Holly Springs, Mississippi, November-December 1862.

Stationed at La Grange, Tennessee, January-February 1863.

Stationed at Moscow, Tennessee, March-April 1863.

Stationed at Oak Ridge, Mississippi, May-June 1863.

Stationed at Camp Sherman, Mississippi, July-August 1863.

Stationed at Florence, Alabama, September-October 1863.

Stationed at Scottsborough, Alabama, November-December 1863.

Stationed at Athens, Ohio, January-February 1864.

Stationed at Scottsborough, Alabama, March-April 1864.

Stationed near Kenesaw Mountain, May-June 1864.

Stationed at Jonesborough, Georgia, July-August 1864.

Stationed at Cave Spring, Georgia, September-October 1864.

Stationed at Savannah, Georgia, November-December 1864.

Stationed at Lynch's Creek, South Carolina, January-February 1865.

Stationed near Raleigh, North Carolina, March-April 1865.

Stationed on board steamer Ontario, May-June 1865.

Company C

Stationed at Jackson, Ohio, October 4, 1861.
October 4.— Muster-in roll of the first detachment, Company [C], in the Fifty-third Regiment (— Brigade) of Ohio Foot Volunteers, commanded by Colonel J. J. Appler, called into the service of the United States by [the President] from October 4, 1861, for the term of three years, unless sooner discharged. . . .

R. B. HULL,
First Lieutenant,
Eighteenth Regiment, United States Infantry, Mustering Officer.

Stationed at Camp Diamond, Ohio, November 12, 1861.
November 12.— Muster-in roll of the second and third detachments of Captain Frederick J. Griffith's Company [C], in the Fifty-third Regiment (— Brigade) of Ohio Foot Volunteers, commanded by Colonel J. J. Appler, called into the service of the United States by the President from November 8 and 12, 1861, for the term of three years, unless sooner discharged. The company was organized by Captain F. J. Griffith at Scioto County, Ohio in the months of October and November and marched thence to Camp Diamond, Jackson, Ohio. . . .

R. B. HULL,
Captain,
Eighteenth Regiment, United States Infantry, Mustering Officer.

Stationed at Camp Diamond, December 31, 1861.

Stationed at Camp Sherman, January-February 1862.

Stationed at Camp Shiloh, Pittsburg Landing, Tennessee, March-April 1862.

Stationed at Moscow, Tennessee, May-June 1862.

Stationed at Memphis, Tennessee, July-August 1862.

Stationed at Fort Pickering, Memphis, Tennessee, September-October 1862.

Stationed at Holly Springs, Mississippi, November-December 1862.

Stationed at La Grange, Tennessee, January-February 1863.

Stationed at Moscow, Tennessee, March-April 1863.

Stationed at Oak Ridge, Mississippi, May-June 1863.

Stationed at Camp Sherman, Mississippi, July-August 1863.

Stationed at Florence, Alabama, September-October 1863.

Stationed at Scottsborough, Alabama, November-December 1863.

Station not stated, January-February 1864.

Stationed at Scottsborough, Alabama, March-April 1864.

Stationed in the field, near Atlanta, Georgia, May-June 1864.

Stationed at Jonesborough, Georgia, July-August 1864.

Stationed at Cave Spring, Georgia, September-October 1864.

Stationed at Savannah, Georgia, November-December 1864.

Stationed at Lynch's Creek, South Carolina, January-February 1865.

Stationed in the field, North Carolina, March-April 1865.

Stationed on board steamer Ontario, May-June 1865.

Company D

Stationed at Camp Diamond, Jackson Court-House, November 25, 1861.
November 25.— Muster-in roll of Captain Henry C. Messenger's Company (D), in the Fifty-third Regiment (—— Brigade) of Ohio Infantry Volunteers, commanded by Colonel Jesse J. Appler, called into the service of the United States by William Dennison from the dates set opposite their respective names, for the term of [three years], unless sooner discharged. The company was organized by Captain [Henry] C. Messenger at Jackson Court-House in the month of November 1861. . . .

H. C. MESSENGER,
Mustering Officer.

Stationed at Camp Diamond, Ohio, December 31, 1861.

Stationed at Camp Sherman, Paducah, Kentucky, January-February 1862.
February 17.— Received orders to march to Paducah, Kentucky.
February 18.— Left Camp Diamond, Jackson County, Ohio and marched forty-four miles by railroad to Portsmouth, Ohio; thence 650 miles by steamer to Paducah, Kentucky, where we encamped.

Stationed at Camp Shiloh, Tennessee, March-April 1862.
This company changed station from Camp Sherman, Paducah, Kentucky to Pittsburg Landing, Tennessee in March 1862.
March 20-April 29.— Encamped at Camp Shiloh. During this time the company was engaged in the battle of Pittsburg Landing or "Shiloh." In this action we lost most of our clothing, knapsacks and company books, papers, etc.

Stationed at Moscow, Tennessee, May-June 1862.

Stationed at Fort Pickering, Tennessee, July-October 1862.

Stationed at Holly Springs, Mississippi, November-December 1862.

Stationed at La Grange, Tennessee, January-February 1863.

Stationed at Moscow, Tennessee, [March 1]-April 30, 1863.

Stationed at Oak Ridge, Mississippi, May-June 1863.

Stationed at Camp Sherman, Mississippi, July-August 1863.

Stationed at Florence, Alabama, September-October 1863.

Stationed at Scottsborough, Alabama, November-December 1863.

Stationed at Scottsborough, Alabama, March-April 1864.

Stationed at Kenesaw Mountain, Georgia, May-June 1864.

Stationed at East Point, Georgia, July-August 1864.

Stationed at Cave Spring, Georgia, September-October 1864.

Stationed at Savannah, Georgia, November-December 1864.

Stationed at Lynch's Creek, South Carolina, January-February 1865.

Stationed near Raleigh, North Carolina, March-April 1865.

Stationed [on board] steamer Ontario, May-June 1865.

Company E

Station not stated, not dated.

Muster-in roll of Captain Samuel W. Baird's Company [E], in the Fifty-third Regiment (—— Brigade) of Ohio Foot Volunteers, commanded by Colonel Jesse J. Appler, called into the service of the United States by the President from the date set opposite the names respectively, 1861 (date of muster) for the term of three years, unless sooner discharged. . . .

ROBERT E. PHILLIPS,
Second Lieutenant.

EUSTACE H. BALL,
Mustering Officer.

Stationed at Camp Diamond, near Jackson, Ohio, December 31, 1861.

Stationed at Camp Sherman, Paducah, Kentucky, January-February 1862.

Stationed at Camp Shiloh, Tennessee, March-April 1862.
April 6-8.— The company was in the battle of Shiloh; lost one man killed and four wounded. Marched on several scouts toward Corinth.

Stationed at Moscow, Tennessee, May-June 1862.

Stationed at Fort Pickering, Memphis, Tennessee, August 18, 1862.

Stationed at Fort Pickering, Memphis, Tennessee, July-August 1862.
August 12.— Six enlisted men reported "deserted" at muster June 30, by order of Major-General W. T. Sherman, are by his Orders No. 70 this date, restored to rolls.

Stationed at Fort Pickering, September-October 1862.

Stationed at Holly Springs, Mississippi, November-December 1862.

Stationed at La Grange, Tennessee, January-February 1863.

Stationed at Moscow, Tennessee, March-April 1863.

Stationed at Oak Ridge, Mississippi, May-June 1863.

Stationed at Camp Sherman, Mississippi, July-August 1863.

Stationed at Florence, Alabama, September-October 1863.

Stationed at Scottsborough, Alabama, November-December 1863.

Stationed at Jackson Court-House, January-February 1864.

Stationed at Scottsborough, Alabama, March-April 1864.

Stationed at Kenesaw Mountain, Georgia, May-June 1864.

Stationed at Jonesborough, Georgia, July-August 1864.

Stationed at Cave Spring, Georgia, September-October 1864.

Stationed at Vining's Station, Georgia, November 9, 1864.
November 9.— Muster-out roll of Captain William W. Gilbert's Company (E), in the Fifty-third Regiment of Ohio Infantry Volunteers, commanded by Colonel Wells S. Jones, late J. J. Appler, called into the service of the United States by the President at Camp Diamond, Jackson, Ohio (the place of general rendezvous) on October 13, 1861 to serve for the term of three years from the date of enrollment, unless sooner discharged, from October 31, 1863 (when last paid) to November 9, 1864 when mustered out. The company was organized by Captain Samuel W. Baird at Camp Diamond, Jackson, Ohio in the month of November 1861. . . .

[CHARLES JOHN] DICKEY,
First Lieutenant,
Thirteenth Infantry, Commissary of Musters,
Fifteenth Army Corps, Mustering Officer.

Stationed at Savannah, Georgia, November-December 1864.

Stationed at Lynch's Creek, South Carolina, January-February 1865.

Stationed near Neuse River, North Carolina, March-April 1865.

Stationed [on board] steamer Ontario, May-June 1865.

Company F

Stationed at Camp Diamond, near Jackson, Ohio, January 15, 1862.

January 15.— Muster-in roll of Captain James R. Percy's Company (F), in the Fifty-third Regiment (—— Brigade) of Ohio Foot Volunteers, commanded by Colonel J. J. Appler, called into the service of the United States by the President from the dates set opposite their respective names, 1861 and 1862 (date of this muster) for the term of three years, unless sooner discharged. . . .

THOMAS McINTYRE,
Lieutenant.

[CHARLES] K. CRUMIT,
Lieutenant,
Mustering Officer.

Stationed at Camp Sherman, Paducah, Kentucky, enlistment to February 28, 1862.

Stationed at Camp Shiloh, Tennessee, March-April 1862.

All the company books of Company F were lost during the battle of Shiloh and hence it has been impossible to give true date of furloughs granted previous to April 6, 1862.

Stationed at camp, near Moscow, Tennessee, May-June 1862.

All company books and muster rolls lost at battle of Shiloh, consequently it is impossible to fix dates with certainty.

Stationed at Fort Pickering, Tennessee, July-October 1862.

Stationed at Holly Springs, Mississippi, December 31, 1862.

Stationed at La Grange, Tennessee, February 28, 1863.

Stationed at Moscow, Tennessee, March-April 1863.

Stationed at Oak Ridge, Mississippi, May-June 1863.

Stationed at Camp Sherman, Mississippi, July-August 1863.

Stationed at Florence, Alabama, September-October 1863.

Stationed at Scottsborough, Alabama, November-December 1863.
Marched from Florence, Alabama to Chattanooga. Participated in battle of Missionary Ridge. Marched to Knoxville, Tennessee. Marched back again.
December 26.— Went into winter quarters at Scottsborough, Alabama.

Stationed at Piketon, Ohio, January-February 1864.

Stationed at Scottsborough, Alabama, March-April 1864.

Stationed near Kenesaw Mountain, Georgia, May-June 1864.

Stationed at East Point, Georgia, July-August 1864.

Station not stated, September-October 1864.

Stationed near Savannah, Georgia, November-December 1864.

Stationed in the field, South Carolina, January-February 1865.

Stationed in the field, North Carolina, March-April 1865.

Stationed on steamer Ontario, May-June 1865.

Company G

Station not stated, not dated.
Muster-in roll of Captain Lorenzo Fulton's Company (G), in the Fifty-third Regiment (—— Brigade) of Ohio Infantry Volunteers, commanded by Colonel J. J. Appler, called into the service of the United States by the President from the date set opposite

their name respectively (date of this muster) for the term of three years, unless sooner discharged. . . .

L. FULTON,
Lieutenant.

GEORGE K. HOSFORD,
Lieutenant,
Mustering Officer.

Stationed at Paducah, Kentucky, from muster to February 28, 1862.

Station not stated, March-April 1862.

Stationed at Moscow, Tennessee, June 30, 1862.

Stationed at Fort Pickering, Tennessee, August 18, 1862.

Station not stated, July-August 1862.

Stationed at Fort Pickering, Tennessee, September-October 1862.

Stationed at Holly Springs, November-December 1862.

Stationed at La Grange, Tennessee, January-February 1863.

Stationed at Moscow, Tennessee, March-April 1863.

Stationed at Oak Ridge, Mississippi, May-June 1863.

Stationed at Camp Sherman, Mississippi, July-August 1863.

Stationed at Florence, Alabama, September-October 1863.

Stationed at Scottsborough, Alabama, November-December 1863.

Stationed at Amesville, Ohio, January-February 1864.

Stationed at Scottsborough, Alabama, March-April 1864.

Stationed in the field, near Big Shanty, Georgia, May-June 1864.

Stationed at Jonesborough, Georgia, July-August 1864.

Stationed at Cave Spring, Georgia, September-October 1864.

Stationed near Savannah, Georgia, November-December 1864.

Stationed at Lynch's Creek, January-February 1865.

Stationed near Raleigh, North Carolina, March-April 1865.

Stationed on board steamer Ontario, May-June 1865.

Company H

Station not stated, not dated.

Muster-in roll of Captain David H. Lasley's Company (H), in the Fifty-third Regiment (—— Brigade) of Ohio Foot Volunteers, commanded by Colonel J. J. Appler, called into the service of the United States by the President from the date set opposite their names respectively, 1861, 1862 (date of this muster) for the term of three years, unless sooner discharged. . . .

D. H. LASLEY,
Mustering Officer.

Stationed at Paducah, Kentucky, from enlistment to February 28, 1862.
February 18.— The company was ordered from Camp Diamond, Jackson, Ohio. Arrived at Portsmouth, Ohio, forty-two miles.
February 19.— Left for Cincinnati and Louisville on the steamboat *Ohio No. 3*.
February 20.— Arrived at Louisville in the evening.
February 21.— Left on the steamer *B. J. Adams* for Paducah.
February 23.— Arrived at Paducah. The company is yet unarmed.

Stationed at Camp Shiloh, near Pittsburg Landing, March-April 1862.
[April 6-7].— The company was engaged in the battle of Shiloh throughout both Sunday and Monday being under heavy fire at

different times each day. Four were wounded; second lieutenant severely in the thigh and Corporal E. P. Meek in the leg.
April 8.— Tuesday morning Corporal S. S. Fultz, slightly [wounded] in the back, since recovered, and Private Jacob Heiman, [wounded] in the side. All but Corporal Fultz have been sent to Ohio. Our company being in the advance, fell into the hands of the enemy with all the company books, papers, clothing, and accoutrements except arms; some of these were taken, and the fatigue suit on the backs of the men. Most of the sick absent are awaiting a discharge but the requisite blanks cannot be obtained.

Stationed at Moscow, Tennessee, May-June 1862.

Stationed at Fort Pickering, Memphis, Tennessee, July-October 1862.

Stationed at Holly Springs, Mississippi, November-December 1862.

Stationed at La Grange, Tennessee, January-February 1863.

Stationed at Moscow, Tennessee, March-April 1863.

Stationed at Oak Ridge, Mississippi, May-June 1863.

Stationed at Camp Sherman, July-August 1863.

Stationed at Florence, Alabama, September-October 1863.

Stationed at Scottsborough, Alabama, November-December 1863.

Stationed at Mansfield, Ohio, January-February 1864.

Stationed at Scottsborough, Alabama, March-April 1864.

Stationed at Big Shanty, Georgia, May-June 1864.

Stationed near Jonesborough, Georgia, July-August 1864.

Stationed at Cave Spring, Georgia, September-October 1864.

Stationed near Savannah, Georgia, November-December 1864.

Stationed at Lynch's Creek, South Carolina, January-February 1865.

Stationed near Raleigh, North Carolina, March-April 1865.

Stationed on board steamer Ontario, May-June 1865.

Company I

Station not stated, not dated.

Muster-in roll of Captain David T. Harkins' Company [I], in the Fifty-third Regiment (—— Brigade) of Ohio Foot Volunteers, commanded by Colonel J. J. Appler, called into the service of the United States by the President from the dates set opposite their names respectively, 1861 and 1862, for the term of three years, unless sooner discharged. . . .

DAVID T. HARKINS,
Mustering Officer.

STILES B. MESSENGER,
Mustering Officer.

GEORGE N. GRAY,
Mustering Officer.

Stationed at Camp Sherman, Paducah, Kentucky, [January 1]-February 28, 1862.

Stationed at Camp Shiloh, Tennessee, March-April 1862.

Stationed at Moscow, Tennessee, May-June 1862.

Stationed at Fort Pickering, Memphis, Tennessee, August 18, 1862.

Stationed at Fort Pickering, Tennessee, July-August 1862.
August 12.— One commissioned officer and nineteen enlisted men reported "deserted" on June 30 muster by order of Major-General Sherman, are by his Orders No. 70 restored to rolls.

Stationed at Fort Pickering, Memphis, Tennessee, September-October 1862.

Stationed at Holly Springs, Mississippi, November-December 1862.

Stationed at La Grange, Tennessee, January-February 1863.

Stationed at Moscow, Tennessee, March-April 1863.

Stationed at Oak Ridge, Mississippi, May-June 1863.

Stationed at Camp Sherman, July-August 1863.

Stationed at Florence, Alabama, September-October 1863.

Stationed at Scottsborough, Alabama, November-December 1863.

Stationed at Salem Center, Ohio, January-February 1864.

Stationed at Scottsborough, Alabama, March-April 1864.

Stationed at Kenesaw Mountain, Georgia, May-June 1864.

Stationed at East Point, Georgia, July-August 1864.

Stationed at Cave Spring, Georgia, September-October 1864.

Stationed near Savannah, Georgia, November-December 1864.

Stationed at Lynch's Creek, South Carolina, January-February 1865.

Stationed at camp in the field, near Raleigh, North Carolina, March-April 1865.

Stationed on board steamboat Ontario, May-June 1865.

Company K

Station not stated, not dated.

Muster-in roll of Captain Preston R. Galloway's Company [K], in the Fifty-third Regiment (—— Brigade) of Ohio Foot Volunteers, commanded by Colonel Appler, called into the service of the United States by the President from the date set opposite their names respectively (date of this muster) for the term of three years, unless sooner discharged. . . .

P. R. GALLOWAY,
Mustering Officers.

WILLIAM SHAY,
Mustering Officers.

L. C. SIMMONS,
Mustering Officers.

Stationed at Paducah, Kentucky, from enlistment to February 28, 1862.

Stationed at Camp No. 1, Tennessee, [March 1]-April 30, 1862.

Stationed at Moscow, Tennessee, May-June 1862.

Stationed at Fort Pickering, Memphis, Tennessee, July-October 1862.

Stationed at Holly Springs, Mississippi, November-December 1862.

Stationed at La Grange, Tennessee, January-February 1863.

Stationed at Moscow, Tennessee, March-April 1863.

Stationed at Oak Ridge, Mississippi, May-June 1863.

Stationed at Camp Sherman, July-August 1863.

Stationed at Florence, Alabama, September-October 1863.

Stationed at Scottsborough, Alabama, November-December 1863.

Stationed at Union City, Ohio, January-February 1864.

Stationed at Scottsborough, Alabama, March-April 1864.

Stationed at Kenesaw Mountain, Georgia, May-June 1864.

Stationed at Jonesborough, Georgia, July-August 1864.

Stationed at Cave Spring, Georgia, September-October 1864.

Stationed near Savannah, Georgia, November-December 1864.

Stationed at Lynch's Creek, South Carolina, January-February 1865.

Stationed near Neuse River, North Carolina, March-April 1865.

Stationed [on board] steamer Ontario, May-June 1865.

[M594-Roll #151]

Record of Events for Fifty-fourth Ohio Infantry, September 1861-June 1865.

Field and Staff

Station not stated, December 31, 1861.

Stationed at Paducah, Kentucky, January-February 1862.

Station not stated, March-April 1862.

Stationed at Moscow, Tennessee, May-June 1862.

Stationed at Memphis, Tennessee, July-October 1862.

Stationed at camp before Vicksburg, Mississippi, November-December 1862.

Stationed at Young's Point, Louisiana, January-April 1863.

Stationed at Walnut Hills, Mississippi, May-June 1863.
May 2.— The regiment moved from Young's Point, Louisiana to Milliken's Bend, Louisiana, a distance of twenty miles.
May 7.— Marched from Milliken's Bend, Louisiana.
May 10.— Arrived at Hard Times Landing, Mississippi, having traveled sixty-three miles.
May 11.— Crossed the Mississippi River to Grand Gulf, Mississippi.
May 12.— Marched from Grand Gulf.
May 15.— Arrived at Raymond, Mississippi, a distance of fifty-three miles.
May 16.— Was held in reserve at the battle of Champion's Hill. Marched on the road to Vicksburg.
May 18.— Arrived near the enemy's works, a distance of thirty miles from Raymond.
May 19, 22.— Was engaged in the assault on the enemy's works.
May 26.— Marched from Walnut Hills to Mechanicsburg, Mississippi.
June 3.— Returned to the rear of Vicksburg via Haynes' Bluff, having traveled a distance of ninety miles. Now engaged in the siege of Vicksburg.

Stationed at Camp Sherman, July-August 1863.
July 4.— Engaged at the siege of Vicksburg until this date, when the enemy surrendered.
July 5.— Took up a line of march for Jackson, Mississippi.
July 10.— Arrived in front of the enemy's works about Jackson, having marched forty-five miles.
July 16.— Held a part of the advanced line during the operation against Jackson until this date when the enemy evacuated.
July 17.— Followed the enemy's rear guard to Pearl River.
July 23.— Marched from Jackson.

July 25.— Arrived at Camp Sherman, Mississippi; whole distance traveled since July 5, eighty miles.

Stationed at Eastport, Mississippi, September-October 1863.
September 21.— The regiment marched from Camp Sherman, Mississippi and encamped near Black River Bridge, a distance of seven miles from Camp Sherman, where it remained.
September 27.— Removed to Vicksburg traveling eighteen miles. Embarked on the steamer *Commercial* in the evening.
October 4.— Run up the river to Memphis, Tennessee, where the regiment arrived in the evening, having traveled 400 miles.
October 8.— Traveled by rail to La Grange, East Tennessee, distance forty miles.
October 15.— Moved from La Grange, East Tennessee. Marched to Tuscumbia, Alabama via Corinth, Iuka, and Cherokee Station to Eastport, [Mississippi].
October 31.— Arrived in the morning; entire distance marched 682 miles since September 27.

Stationed at Bellefonte, Alabama, November-December 1863.
November 1.— The regiment crossed the Tennessee River at Eastport, [Mississippi] and on the morning of the third day took up line of march for Chattanooga via Florence, Rogersville, Pulaski, Fayetteville, Bellefonte, and Bridgeport.
November 25.— Arrived at Chattanooga and was ordered to the front in the evening. During the night the enemy evacuated. After evacuation was ordered in pursuit of [Braxton] Bragg.
November 27.— Followed Bragg's Army to Graysville, when ordered to the relief of [Ambrose Everett] Burnside, who was besieged by [James] Longstreet's command at Knoxville. [Marched] via Cleveland and Charleston; here received intelligence that Longstreet was retiring. Returned to Chattanooga on the same route.
December 17.— Arrived and marched to Bellefonte, thirty [miles]; distance traveled since November 1, 600 miles.

Stationed at Larkinsville, Alabama, [January]-April 1864.
January 5.— The regiment left Bellefonte, Alabama and marched to Larkinsville, Alabama, distance eleven miles.

January 22.— Reenlisted as veteran volunteers. Mustered in this date.
January 29.— Left Larkinsville, Alabama to return to Ohio in accordance with General Orders No. 376, from the War Department.
February 5.— Arrived at Cincinnati, Ohio, where the regiment was disbanded on furlough of thirty days. At the expiration of which time the regiment reported to Colonel Potter, superintendent of recruiting service in Ohio and was ordered to report at Camp Dennison, Ohio to reorganize.
March 9.— Left Camp Dennison, Ohio to return to field.
March 30.— Arrived at Larkinsville, Alabama; distance traveled 988 miles.

Stationed near Kenesaw Mountain, Georgia, May-June 1864.
May 1.— Left Larkinsville, Alabama for the spring campaign.
May 6.— Arrived near Chattanooga, Tennessee. After turning over all surplus baggage, took up line of march [to] the front.
May 13-16.— Arrived in front of the enemy's works near Resaca, Georgia. Engaged the enemy losing two killed and eight wounded. Enemy completely routed. Followed in pursuit.
May 27-31.— Engaged them at Dallas, Georgia, losing fourteen wounded. Rebels retreated in direction of Kenesaw Mountain.
June 27.— Again engaged him in his works. Charged the works, losing two killed, twenty wounded and three missing.
June 30.— In bivouac near Kenesaw Mountain, Georgia.

Stationed near Jonesborough, Georgia, July-August 1864.

Stationed at Cave Spring, [Georgia], September-October 1864.
September 1-October 3.— After the fall of Atlanta the regiment followed the enemy south so far as Lovejoy's Station on the Macon and Western Railroad. This station is about thirty miles from Atlanta. Pursuit was here given up and we moved back to East Point, six miles from Atlanta. We remained at East Point in camp.
October 4.— We broke up camp and marched in pursuit of [John Bell] Hood, who was threatening our line of communication. Marched via Marietta, Acworth, Allatoona, Kingston, Resaca, and Snake Creek Gap. This point is twenty-seven miles from

Chattanooga. Then marched through La Fayette, Summerville, and to within eleven miles of Gadsden, Alabama, when we had a slight skirmish with part of [Joseph] Wheeler's Cavalry.
October 31.— From this point we countermarched and arrived at Cave Spring on our return to Atlanta; whole distance marched 200 miles.

Stationed at Savannah, Georgia, November-December 1864.
[November 1-13].— Marched from Cave Spring to Vining's Station, where we remained five days. From there we marched to Turner's Ferry and remained.
November 14.— Marched to Atlanta, Georgia.
November 15.— From there commenced our march in an easterly direction, marching via Jackson, McDonough, Irwinton, Statesborough, and Summerville. Halted eleven miles northwest of Savannah.
December 13.— Here our division was ordered to charge Fort McAllister, which we did on this date and carried the works. From there we marched within three miles of Savannah; distance marched 300 miles.

Stationed at Lynch's Creek, South Carolina, January-February 1865.
January 17.— Broke camp at Savannah, Georgia and proceeded by steamer to Beaufort, South Carolina and went into camp.
January 29-February 11.— Broke camp again and started on another campaign. Marched via Pocotaligo, Bamberg, and Orangeburg to Columbia, South Carolina. Destroyed the city and railroads. From there marched via Liberty Hill and Camden to Lynch's Creek, where we were mustered.
February 12.— Were engaged with the enemy at the North Edisto River. Marched during the two months 200 miles.

Stationed near Raleigh, North Carolina, March-April 1865.
March 2-April 9.— Marched from Lynch's Creek, South Carolina and proceeded to Cheraw, South Carolina. Crossed the Great Pee Dee River and marched to Fayetteville, North Carolina and remained there three days. Marched again and crossed the Cape

Fear River; thence to near Bentonville, where we had a heavy skirmish with the enemy. From there proceeded to Goldsborough, North Carolina and went into camp.
April 10.— Broke camp and marched to Raleigh, North Carolina.
April 14.— Arrived at Raleigh and went into camp. Marched during the two months 300 miles.

Stationed on board steamer Argonaut No. 2, May-June 1865.
May 1.— Broke camp near Neuse River, North Carolina and marched via Warrenton and Lawrenceville.
May 7.— Arrived at Petersburg, Virginia. Here we lay two days.
May 9.— Broke camp.
May 10.— Arrived at Richmond and remained.
May 13.— We again broke camp. Marched via Bowling Green and Fredericksburg.
May 24.— Arrived at Washington, District of Columbia.
June 1.— Broke camp and proceeded to Parkersburg, West Virginia by railroad.
June 6.— Arrived at Louisville, Kentucky and were paid here.
June 25.— Broke camp for Little Rock, Arkansas and went on board steamer *Argonaut No. 2*, where we were mustered; whole distance marched 295 miles and were transported 1,600 miles.

Station not stated, not dated.

Muster-in/out form of the field, staff and band of the Fifty-fourth Regiment of Ohio Infantry Volunteers (Colonel Thomas Kilby Smith), called into the service of the United States by the President for the term of three years, unless sooner discharged, from date set opposite their names respectively. . . .

ALBERT [BALDWIN] DOD,
Captain,
Fifteenth Infantry, United States Army,
Inspector and Mustering Officer.

Regiment

Stationed at Pittsburg Landing, Tennessee, March 1862.

Stationed at Shiloh, April 1862.

Stationed at Moscow, Tennessee, June 1862.

Stationed at camp, near Memphis, Tennessee, July 1862.

Stationed at Memphis, Tennessee, August 1862.

Stationed at Memphis, Tennessee, October 1862.

Stationed at Chulahoma, Mississippi, November 1862.

Stationed at Vicksburg, December 1862.
Return dated steamer *Sunny South*, Mississippi River January 5, 1863.

Stationed at Young's Point, Louisiana, January 1863.
January 2.— The regiment fell back from Chickasaw Bayou in the morning, covering the retreat of the Army. Embarked on the steamer *Sunny South*. Steamed down the Yazoo River and up the Mississippi and [Arkansas] Rivers to Arkansas Post, Arkansas.
January 11.— Was engaged in the battle.
January 14.— Embarked on the steamer and ran down to Young's Point, Louisiana.
January 24.— Arrived at the latter place.

Stationed at Young's Point, Louisiana, February 1863.

Stationed at Young's Point, Louisiana, March 1863.
March 17.— The regiment accompanied the expedition up Steele's Bayou and Deer Creek, leaving Young's Point, Louisiana in the morning.
March 21.— Was engaged in the skirmish on Deer Creek, Mississippi. Returned to Young's Point, Louisiana.
March 27.— Arrived at the latter place.

Stationed at Young's Point, Louisiana, April 1863.

Stationed at Walnut Hills, Mississippi, May 1863.
May 7.— The regiment left Milliken's Bend, Louisiana.

May 10.— Arrived at Hard Times Landing, Mississippi; distance traveled sixty-three miles. The regiment crossed the Mississippi River to Grand Gulf, Mississippi.
May 12.— Marched from Grand Gulf in the morning.
May 15.— Arrived at Raymond, Mississippi, having traveled fifty-three miles.
May 16.— The regiment was held in the reserve at the battle of Champion's Hill, Mississippi.
May 17.— The regiment marched on the road to Vicksburg.
May 18.— Arrived in front of the enemy's works near Vicksburg, distance from Raymond to Vicksburg, thirty miles.
May 19, 22.— The regiment was engaged in the assaults on the enemy's works.
May 26.— Marched from Walnut Hills, Mississippi to Mechanicsburg, Mississippi, leaving the former place on this date.
May 31.— Returned from Mechanicsburg to Haynes' Bluff, Mississippi. Arrived at the latter place, having traveled a distance of seventy-eight miles.

Stationed at Walnut Hills, Mississippi, June 1863.
June 3.— The regiment marched from Haynes' Bluff, Mississippi to Walnut Hills, Mississippi, a distance of fifteen miles.
June 11.— Moved to the front and relieved Colonel Wood's Brigade of General [James Madison] Tuttle's Division, Fifteenth Army Corps and are now engaged in the siege of Vicksburg, Mississippi.

Stationed at Camp Sherman, Mississippi, July 1863.
July 4.— The regiment was engaged in the siege of Vicksburg until the surrender on this date.
July 5.— Took up the march towards Jackson, Mississippi.
July 10.— Arrived in front of Jackson, having traveled a distance of forty-five miles. Held a part of the advanced lines during the operations against Jackson.
July 17.— Entered Jackson.
July 23.— Marched from Jackson.
July 25.— Arrived at Camp Sherman, Mississippi; whole distance traveled eighty-three miles.

Stationed at Camp Sherman, Mississippi, August 1863.

Stationed on steamer Commercial, Mississippi River, September 1863.

Stationed at Eastport, Mississippi, October 1863.
October 4-26.— Arrived at Memphis direct from Vicksburg by steamer *Commercial*. Left Memphis by rail for La Grange. Moved from La Grange. Marched to Tuscumbia via Corinth, Iuka and Cherokee Station.
October 27.— Arrived.
October 28.— Moved for Eastport, [Mississippi] via Cherokee Station.
October 31.— Arrived in the morning; entire distance traveled 600 miles.

Stationed at Cleveland, Tennessee, November 1863.
November 1.— The regiment crossed the Tennessee River at Eastport and took up line of march for Chattanooga via Florence, Pulaski, Bellefonte, and Bridgeport.
November 25.— Arrived at Chattanooga and was ordered to the front of the enemy. During the night the enemy evacuated.
November 26.— In the morning was ordered in pursuit. Followed the enemy to Graysville, at which place we were ordered to the relief of Burnside at Knoxville, the latter being besieged by Longstreet.
November 30.— Arrived at Cleveland, Tennessee in the evening.

Stationed at Bellefonte, Alabama, December 1863.
December 1.— After giving up pursuit of Bragg and his retreating Army from Missionary Ridge, we came to a halt five miles west of Charleston, Tennessee.
December 2.— In the morning received the intelligence that Burnside was besieged by Longstreet's command at Knoxville and immediately took up the line of march for the latter place. Being without transportation we were obliged to subsist entirely upon the country.
December 6.— We arrived at the town of Maryville, sixteen miles west of Knoxville, and halted to await orders.
December 7.— Received orders in the morning with the gratifying intelligence that Longstreet had fallen back into Virginia. We once more turned our face for Chattanooga.

December 17.— Arrived at Chattanooga.
December 19.— Left for Bridgeport.
December 21.— Arrived at Bridgeport, where we remained ten days for the purpose of drawing clothing and pay, of which we were both in need.
December 29.— Left for Bellefonte, Alabama via Stevenson.
December 31.— Arrived after marching some 310 miles.

Stationed at Nashville, Tennessee, January 1864.

Stationed at Camden, Preble County, Ohio, February 1864.

Stationed at Larkinsville, Alabama, March 1864.
March 30.— Left Camp Dennison, Ohio for the front. Arrived at Larkinsville, Alabama this date.

Stationed at Larkinsville, Alabama, April 1864.

Stationed at Dallas, Georgia, May 1864.
Return dated Big Shanty, Georgia June 13, 1864.

HEADQUARTERS,
Fifty-fourth Ohio Veteran Volunteer Infantry,
In the field near Dallas, Georgia,
May 31, 1864.

May 1.— Left Larkinsville, Alabama en route for Atlanta, Georgia.
May 12.— Arrived at Resaca.
May 13-15.— Engaged the enemy. Our loss in action was two killed and eight wounded. In the night of May 15 the enemy evacuated his position and retreated southward. The Federal Army followed in pursuit. At a point near Dallas, the enemy again made a stand.
May 26-31.— The battle commenced and continued up to May 31. The regiment occupied breastworks in front. Our loss was fourteen wounded.

Stationed at Kenesaw Mountain, Georgia, June 1864.
Return dated in the field August 2, 1864.

Stationed before Atlanta, Georgia, July 1864.

Stationed at Jonesborough, Georgia, August 1864.

Stationed at East Point, September 1864.
Return dated near Fort McAllister, Georgia.

Stationed in the field, October 1864.
Return dated near Fort McAllister, Georgia December 20, 1864.

Stationed in the field, November 1864.
Return dated near Savannah, Georgia December 24, 1864.

Stationed near Savannah, Georgia, December 1864.
Return dated Savannah, Georgia January 4, 1864.

Stationed at Pocotaligo, South Carolina, January 1865.
Return dated Goldsborough, North Carolina March 29, 1865.

Stationed at Lynch's Creek, South Carolina, February 1865.
Return dated Goldsborough, North Carolina April 3, 1865.

Stationed at Goldsborough, North Carolina, March 1865.

Stationed in the field, April 1865.
Return dated near Washington, District of Columbia May 27, 1865.

Stationed near Washington, District of Columbia, May 1865.
Return dated near Louisville, Kentucky June 9, 1865.

Stationed on board steamer Argonaut No. 2, June 1865.
Return dated Little Rock, Arkansas July 6, 1865.

Company A

Station not stated, not dated.
September 15.— Muster-in roll of Captain [Stephen] B. Yeoman's Company (A), in the Fifty-fourth Regiment (—— Brigade) of Ohio

Infantry Volunteers, commanded by Colonel Thomas K. Smith, called into the service of the United States by the President from September 15, 1861 (date of this muster) for the term of three years, unless sooner discharged. . . .

ALBERT B. DOD,
Captain,
Fifteenth United States Infantry, United States Army,
Mustering Officer.

Stationed at Camp Dennison, September 5-December 31, 1861.

Stationed at Paducah, January-February 1862.

Station not stated, March-June 1862.

Stationed at Memphis, Tennessee, August 18, 1862.

Stationed near Memphis, Tennessee, July-August 1862.

Stationed at camp, near Memphis, Tennessee, September-October 1862.

Stationed at camp before Vicksburg, November-December 1862.

Stationed at Young's Point, Louisiana, January-April 1863.

Stationed at Walnut Hills, Mississippi, May-June 1863.
May 2.— Moved from Young's Point, Louisiana to Milliken's Bend on steamer *Edward Walsh*, distance twenty miles.
May 3.— Went into camp one mile back from the river.
May 7.— Left Milliken's Bend and marched through to Richmond, near and to the right of Lake Saint Joseph.
May 11.— Arrived at Hard Times Landing on Mississippi River in the evening and crossed over to Grand Gulf, Mississippi on gunboat *Louisville*.
May 15.— Took our line of march again in the morning. Arrived at Raymond in the afternoon.
May 16.— Was held in reserve at battle of Champion's Hill.
May 17.— Crossed Big Black River in the night near Bridgeport.

May 18.— Arrived in front of the enemy's works in rear of Vicksburg in the evening.
May 19, 22.— Was engaged in the assaults.
May 25-June 2.— Marched from Walnut Hills to Mechanicsburg and returned via Haynes' Bluff.
June 3.— Arrived at Walnut Hills again in the evening. Was held in reserve.
June 11.— Have since been to the front working in the trenches. Whole distance marched since May 2, 251 miles.

Stationed at Camp Sherman, Mississippi, July-August 1863.
July 4.— Vicksburg surrendered. On the same day received marching orders.
July 5.— Started to the rear at 5 o'clock a.m.
July 6.— Reached Big Black River and crossed. Found [Joseph Eggleston] Johnston's Army advancing on us. Started them on the retreat toward Jackson, Mississippi, our Army pursuing him.
July 10.— The regiment arrived to within one mile of Jackson when the Second Brigade formed line of battle; Johnston's forces occupying the city. This company, with two others from each regiment, were deployed as skirmishers. We advanced to within 400 yards of the Rebel breastworks, where we remained as pickets the rest of the day. Found it necessary to besiege the city.
July 16.— In the night the Rebels evacuated the city.
July 17.— Our forces took possession of the city. Remained in Jackson.
July 23.— Received orders to return to the Big Black [River] and there to go into camp and remain during the hot season.
July 26.— Reached our camping ground, where the company has since remained. Whole distance marched seventy-five miles.

Stationed at Eastport, Mississippi, September-October 1863.
September 26.— The company received marching orders.
September 27.— Marched from camp near [Big] Black River, Mississippi. Arrived at Vicksburg at 7 o'clock p.m., distance fifteen miles.
September 28.— Embarked on steamer *Commercial*.
October 4-26.— Arrived at Memphis, Tennessee, distance on boat 400 miles. Left Memphis, Tennessee by rail for La Grange, distance forty-eight miles. From La Grange we marched to

Corinth, Mississippi; Iuka, and Cherokee Station, fifty miles. Went into camp four days. Was attacked by General [Philip Dale] Roddey's force. Marched to meet the enemy. Skirmishing commenced at 8 o'clock. Drove the enemy from his position as far as Tuscumbia, Alabama.
October 27.— Arrived at Tuscumbia and encamped.
October 28.— Countermarched to Cherokee Station, forty miles. Received orders to march to Eastport, Mississippi.
October 30.— Arrived at Eastport in the morning, twelve miles.
October 31.— Was mustered for pay. The company has marched 118 miles, traveled by water 400, by rail forty-eight, whole distance 566 miles.

Stationed at Bellefonte, Alabama, November-December 1863.
November 1.— We crossed the Tennessee River en route for Chattanooga.
November 2.— Camped at Waterloo in the evening.
November 3.— [Camped] at Rock Springs in the evening, distance from Eastport seventeen miles.
November 4.— Arrived at Florence, distance thirteen miles.
November 5.— In the evening camped about five [miles] west of Rogersville.
November 6.— Camped eight miles northeast of Rogersville.
November 7.— Camped six miles southwest of Pulaski.
November 8.— Camped twelve miles east of Pulaski.
November 9.— Marched to Fayetteville.
November 10.— Camped about three miles southeast of Fayetteville on a branch of Flint River.
November 12-15.— Marched to Bellefonte and camped eight miles northeast of the town.
November 16-17.— Marched to Bridgeport where we remained.
November 19.— Crossed the [Tennessee] River and arrived at Chattanooga.
November 25.— Crossed the river twice and moved to the front. The enemy evacuated.
November 26-December 6.— We marched after them. Followed after them as far as Graysville. Tore up the railroad. We then started for Knoxville. Arrived to within sixteen miles of that place, when we heard that General Burnside and his Army was relieved.

December 7.— We countermarched.
December 17.— Arrived at Chattanooga.
December 19.— [Arrived] at Bridgeport.
December 30.— [Arrived] at Bellefonte, having marched 630 miles since leaving Eastport.

Stationed at Larkinsville, Alabama, December 31, 1863-April 30, 1864.
January 29.— The company left Larkinsville, Alabama for Ohio.
February 4.— Arrived at Cincinnati, Ohio.
February 7.— Disbanded.
March 9.— Rendezvoused at Camp Dennison, Ohio.
March 18.— Moved from Camp Dennison, Ohio by rail.
March 31.— Rejoined the division at Larkinsville, Alabama.

Stationed near Kenesaw Mountain, Georgia, May-June 1864.
May 1.— Left camp at Larkinsville, Alabama. Marched to Resaca, distance ninety miles.
May 14-16.— Were engaged with the enemy. On the night of May 16 the Rebels evacuated Resaca. We marched from there to Kingston, Georgia, distance thirty miles.
May 18.— Arrived at Kingston. Rested three days.
May 23.— Left Kingston. Encountered the enemy that evening near Dallas, Georgia; distance marched thirty miles.
May 26.— Had one man (Jacob Mistler) severely wounded while engaged in throwing up breastworks.
May 28.— The enemy attacked and charged our works but were repulsed with heavy loss. Our loss was small.
June 1.— Marched again. Marched to Burnt Hickory, distance seven miles.
June 4.— Marched again.
June 6.— Arrived at Acworth, Georgia, distance eighteen miles.
June 9.— Marched again to Big Shanty, distance seven miles. Encountered the enemy then and drove him and fortified near the foot of Kenesaw Mountain.
June 26.— Left there and marched four miles to the right.
June 27.— Attacked and charged the enemy's works on Kenesaw Mountain and were repulsed. Our loss was heavy. Captain [Luther W.] Saxton was wounded; Nathaniel White, killed;

Sergeant W. F. Hill, wounded and taken prisoner; Sergeant D. B. Hedrick, Corporal J. W. Roads, Privates William Dusey, Benjamin Offill and Peter Ulmer were wounded.
June 28-30.— In bivouac seven miles southeast of Big Shanty, Georgia; whole distance [marched], since May 1 to June 30, 175 miles.

Stationed in the field, near Jonesborough, Georgia, July-August 1864.
July 3.— Marched from Kenesaw Mountain to the right of the Army and engaged the enemy at Ruff's Mill and repulsed him. Marched thence to Stone Mountain.
July 18, 20.— [Marched] thence to Decatur, where we destroyed a portion of the Augusta and Atlanta Railroad.
July 22.— Engaged the enemy near the railroad near Atlanta. We [were] driven back a short distance, but formed again and drove the Rebels back to their works. In the engagement loss of company was one man killed, one severely wounded and five taken prisoners.
July 27.— Marched to the right of the Army.
July 28.— The enemy attacked and charged us several times, but was effectually repulsed every time. Their loss was very heavy; ours small.
August 26.— Left from Jonesborough on the Macon Railroad.
August 30.— Arrived there after driving the enemy before us all day to-day. We had two men wounded. Formed our lines after night and threw up temporary works.
August 31.— The enemy attacked and charged us four times and was as often repulsed with heavy loss; our loss small. Distance marched since July 1 to August 31, 180 miles.

Stationed at East Point, Georgia, September 19, 1864.
September 19.— Muster-out roll of a detachment of Captain Luther W. Saxton's, late Yeoman's, Company (A), in the Fifty-fourth Regiment of Ohio Infantry Volunteers, commanded by Lieutenant-Colonel Robert Williams, late Smith, called into the service of the United States by the President at Camp Dennison, Ohio (the place of general rendezvous) on September 15, 1861 to serve for the term of three years from the date of enrollment,

unless sooner discharged, from October 31, 1863 (when last paid) to September 19, 1864 when mustered out. . . .

C. J. DICKEY,
First Lieutenant,
Thirteenth Infantry, Second Division, Fifteenth Army Corps,
Mustering Officer.

Stationed at Cave Spring, [Georgia], September-October 1864.
October 4-30.— Broke up camp at East Point, Georgia and marched via Marietta, Allatoona, Kingston and Resaca; crossed Taylor's Ridge, from thence down the Chattooga Valley through Summerville and Alpine and encountered the enemy near Gadsden, and after a slight skirmish returned. Countermarched and crossed Little River, from there [marched] to Cave Spring, Georgia.
October 31.— Arrived at Cave Springs; distance marched 200 miles.

Stationed at Savannah, Georgia, November-December 1864.
November 1-14.— Moved from Cave Springs to Vining's Station. Remained there five days then marched to Turner's Ferry and then to Atlanta.
November 15-December 12.— Started on our march from Atlanta, Georgia. Marched via McDonough, Clinton, Irwinton, Statesborough, and Summerville. Stopped [eleven] miles northwest of Savannah.
December 13.— Charged and carried Fort McAllister. From there marched to within three miles of Savannah; distance marched 300 miles.

Stationed at Lynch's Creek, South Carolina, January-February 1865.
January 17.— Left Savannah, Georgia and proceeded by steamer to Beaufort, South Carolina and went into camp.
January 29-February 11.— Broke camp and started on a new campaign. Marched via Pocotaligo, Bamberg, and Orangeburg to Columbia, South Carolina. Destroyed the city and railroad and marched thence via Liberty Hill and Camden to Lynch's Creek, where we were inspected and mustered.

February 12.— Had a skirmish with the enemy at the North Edisto River; distance marched 250 miles.

Stationed in the field, March-April 1865.
March 2-20.— Left Lynch's Creek and marched via Cheraw, South Carolina and Fayetteville, North Carolina.
March 21.— Skirmished with the enemy near Bentonville and marched from thence to Goldsborough, North Carolina, where we went into camp.
[April 10].— Broke camp at Goldsborough and marched via Pikeville and Lowell, North Carolina.
April 14.— Arrived at Raleigh and went into camp.
April 29.— Broke camp and marched to a point thirteen miles from Raleigh and went into camp, where we were inspected and mustered; distance marched 300 miles.

Stationed on board steamboat Argonaut No. 2, May-June 1865.
May 1-June 29.— Broke camp at Neuse River and marched via Louisburg and Warrenton, North Carolina, and Petersburg, Richmond, Fredericksburg, and Alexandria, Virginia to Washington, District of Columbia; thence by railway to Parkersburg, West Virginia; thence by steamboat to Louisville, Kentucky and went into camp.
June 30.— Broke camp at Louisville, Kentucky and went on board steamboat *Argonaut No. 2*, where we were mustered and inspected.

Company B

Stationed at Camp Dennison, Ohio, October 31, 1861.
October 31.— Muster-in roll of Captain Robert Williams' Company [B], in the Fifty-fourth Regiment (—— Brigade) of Ohio (Infantry) Volunteers, commanded by Colonel Thomas Kilby Smith, called into the service of the United States by the President from November 1, 1861 (date of this muster) for the term of three years, unless sooner discharged. . . .

[EPHRAIM] MORGAN WOOD,
Captain,
Fifteenth Infantry, United States Army,
Mustering Officer.

Station not stated, from enrollment to December 31, 1861.

Stationed at camp, near Paducah, Kentucky, January-February 1862.

Station not stated, March-April 1862.
April 6-7.— The company was engaged in the battle of Pittsburg [Landing], Tennessee. Went into action Sunday morning with forty-one men and was engaged until the battle ended Monday. Lost in killed and wounded, five killed and fourteen wounded.

Stationed at Moscow, Tennessee, May-June 1862.

Stationed at Memphis, Tennessee, August 18, 1862.

Stationed at camp, near Memphis, Tennessee, July-October 1862.

Stationed in the field, November-December 1862.

Stationed at Young's Point, Louisiana, January-February 1863.

Stationed at Young's Point, Louisiana, April 10, 1863.

Station not given, March-April 1863.

Stationed at Walnut Hills, Mississippi, May-June 1863.
May 1.— Received marching orders at Young's Point, Louisiana.
May 2.— Embarked on transport *Edward Walsh*.
May 3.— Arrived at Milliken's Bend, Louisiana; disembarked and went into camp.
May 7-9.— Marched towards Grand Gulf. Arrived at Hard Times Landing opposite Grand Gulf, sixty-three miles from Milliken's Bend.
May 10.— Crossed the Mississippi River on gunboat *Louisville*.
May 11.— Marched toward Raymond, Mississippi.
May 12.— Arrived at Raymond, fifty-three miles from Grand Gulf.
May 15.— Marched to Champion's Hill.

May 16.— Had an engagement at this place, driving the enemy from the field.
May 17.— Marched towards Vicksburg. Crossed [Big] Black River on a pontoon bridge in the night.
May 18.— Marched to within one half mile of the enemy's works, thirty miles from Raymond.
May 19.— Made an unsuccessful assault upon the enemy's works.
May 22.— Reassaulted them but without success.
May 25-June 1.— Marched towards Yazoo City on a reconnaissance. Were out seven days and to within eighteen miles of Yazoo City.
June 2.— Arrived in camp at Walnut Hills, Mississippi.
June 13.— Moved to the front.

Stationed at Camp Sherman, Mississippi, July-August 1863.
July 4.— Engaged at the siege of Vicksburg. The enemy surrendered.
July 5.— Took up line of march towards Jackson.
July 10.— Arrived in front of the enemy's works at Jackson, a distance of forty-five miles from Vicksburg. Held part of the advanced line while operating against the enemy at Jackson.
July 16.— The enemy evacuated.
July 23.— Marched from Jackson.
July 25.— Arrived at Camp Sherman, Mississippi; distance marched since July 5, eighty miles.

Stationed at Eastport, Mississippi, September-October 1863.
September 26.— Received marching orders.
September 27.— Marched from camp near [Big] Black River. Arrived at Vicksburg same day and embarked on steamer *Commercial*.
October 4.— Arrived at Memphis, Tennessee, distance 400 miles.
October 8.— Left Memphis for the interior by Memphis and Charleston Railroad.
October 9.— Arrived at La Grange, Tennessee.
October 14.— Left La Grange and marched eastward passing through Corinth, Iuka, and Cherokee Station to Tuscumbia, Alabama.

October 27.— Arrived at Tuscumbia.
October 28.— Left Tuscumbia and marched back to Cherokee Station to Eastport, Mississippi on Tennessee River.
October 31.— Arrived at Eastport. Marched about ninety-three miles. Traveled by rail forty-eight miles and by river 400 miles; total distance traveled 541 miles.

Stationed at Bellefonte, Alabama, November-December 1863.
November 1-24.— The regiment crossed the Tennessee River at Eastport, Mississippi, and on the morning of the third day took up line of march for Chattanooga via Florence, Rogersville, Pulaski, Fayetteville, Bellefonte, and Bridgeport, Alabama.
November 25.— Arrived at Chattanooga and was ordered to the front the evening of the same day. The enemy evacuated.
November 27.— After the evacuation was ordered in pursuit of Bragg; followed his Army to Graysville. Were ordered to the relief of Burnside who was besieged by Longstreet's command at Knoxville.
December 6-16.— Marched to Maryville, sixteen miles from Knoxville via Cleveland and Charleston. Here we received the intelligence that Longstreet was retiring. Returned to Chattanooga the same route.
December 17.— Arrived at Chattanooga.
December 19.— Marched to Bridgeport.
December 30.— Marched to Bellefonte; distance traveled, since November 1, 600 miles.

Stationed at Larkinsville, Alabama, December 31, 1863-April 30, 1864.
January 8.— The regiment went into winter quarters at Larkinsville, Alabama after performing the largest march that has ever been made by any troops in the field, from Vicksburg, Mississippi to Knoxville, Tennessee.
January 29.— Three-fourths of the regiment having reenlisted as veterans, the regiment left Larkinsville, Alabama.
February 4.— Arrived at Cincinnati, Ohio.
February 7.— Having received a furlough of thirty days, the regiment disbanded.
March 7.— Our furlough expired this day.

March 19.— Left Camp Dennison, Ohio.
March 22.— Arrived at Nashville, Tennessee. As we could get no transportation, we were ordered to march to Larkinsville.
March 31.— Arrived at Larkinsville, passing through Murfreesborough, Tullahoma, Stevenson, and Bellefonte.
April 1-30.— In the month of April we stayed in camp at Larkinsville preparing for the next campaign.

Stationed before Kenesaw Mountain, Georgia, May-June 1864.
May 1-13.— The company left Larkinsville, Alabama. Marched via Bridgeport, Alabama and Lookout Mountain to Resaca, Georgia.
May 14-15.— Engaged the enemy. Marched from thence to Dallas, Georgia.
May 27-June 1.— Engaged the enemy. [Marched] from thence to Hope Church, Georgia.
June 2-4.— Engaged the enemy. [Marched] from thence to Kenesaw Mountain, Georgia.
June 27.— Engaged the enemy; whole distance marched about 225 miles.

Stationed at Jonesborough, Georgia, July-August 1864.
July 3.— The company marched from Kenesaw Mountain, Georgia to Ruff's Mill and engaged the enemy. Crossed the Chattahoochee at Roswell, Georgia and marched via Decatur to within two miles of Atlanta on the Augusta [and Atlanta] Railroad.
July 22.— Engaged with the enemy. Marched from thence to Ezra Church.
July 28.— Engaged the enemy. Skirmished with the enemy before Atlanta until August 26.
August 26.— Moved to Jonesborough, Georgia.
August 31.— Engaged the enemy; whole distance marched about 180 miles.

Stationed at Cave Spring, Georgia, September-October 1864.
September 1-October 3.— After the fall of Atlanta, Georgia, we followed the enemy south as far as Lovejoy's Station, which is about thirty miles from Atlanta. Here we gave up the chase and returned to East Point, six miles south of Atlanta. We lay here resting and drilling.

October 4-30.— [John Bell] Hood and his Army having gone toward Chattanooga, we followed, passing through Marietta, Acworth, Allatoona, Kingston, Calhoun, Resaca, and Snake Creek Gap. When we were within about twenty-seven miles of Chattanooga, we then marched through La Fayette and Summerville, to within a few miles of Lebanon, Alabama, when we had a slight skirmish with the enemy's cavalry. From here we retreated towards Atlanta leaving General Thomas to look after Hood. Passed to the west of Rome and through Cave Spring.
October 31.— Arrived at Cave Spring.

Stationed near Savannah, Georgia, November-December 1864.
[November 1-13].— Marched from Cave Spring to Vining's Station, where we remained five days. From here we marched to Turner's Ferry and remained.
November 14.— Marched to Atlanta.
November 15-December 12.— Commenced our march. Marched in an easterly direction near Jackson, McDonough, Irwinton, Statesborough, and Summerville. Halted eleven miles northwest of Savannah. Here our division was ordered to charge Fort McAllister.
December 13.— Charged Fort McAllister and carried it by storm. From there we marched to within three miles of Savannah; distance marched 300 miles.

Stationed at Lynch's Creek, South Carolina, January-February 1865.
[For record of events, see Field and Staff.]

Stationed in the field, near Raleigh, North Carolina, March-April 1865.
[For record of events, see Field and Staff.]

Stationed on board steamer Argonaut [No. 2], May-June 1865.
May 1.— Broke camp at Raleigh, North Carolina for Petersburg, marching via Warrenton and Lawrenceville.
May 7.— Arrived at Petersburg. There we lay two days.
May 9.— Broke camp.
May 10.— Arrived at Richmond and remained.

May 13.— We again broke camp for Washington, District of Columbia, marching via Bowling Green and Fredericksburg.
May 24.— Arrived at Washington, District of Columbia.
June 2.— Broke camp for Louisville, Kentucky, passing through Parkersburg, West Virginia and Cincinnati, Ohio.
June 6.— Arrived at Louisville, Kentucky. We were paid here.
June 25.— Broke camp for Little Rock, Arkansas via Ohio, Mississippi and White rivers; whole distance marched 290 miles, were transported 1,600 miles.

Company C

Stationed at Camp Dennison, Ohio, October 31, 1861.
October 31.— Muster-in roll of Captain Charles A. White's Company [C], in the Fifty-fourth Regiment (—— Brigade) of Ohio Infantry Volunteers, commanded by Colonel Thomas Kilby Smith, called into the service of the United States by the President from October 31, 1861 (date of this muster) for the term of three years, unless sooner discharged. . . .

E. M. WOOD,
Captain,
Fifteenth Infantry, United States Army, Mustering Officer.

ALBERT ROGALL,
Second Lieutenant,
[Fifty]-fourth Regiment, Mustering Officer.

Station not stated, from enrollment to February 28, 1862.

Stationed at Camp No. 1, Tennessee, March-April 1862.

Station not stated, May-June 1862.

Stationed at Memphis, Tennessee, July-October 1862.

Stationed in the field before Vicksburg, November-December 1862.

Stationed at Young's Point, Louisiana, January-February 1863.

Station not stated, April 10, 1863.

Stationed at Young's Point, Louisiana, March-April 1863.

Stationed at Walnut Hills, Mississippi, May-June 1863.
May 2.— Left camp at Young's Point, Louisiana and embarked on board steamer *Edward Walsh*.
May 3.— Disembarked at Milliken's Bend, Louisiana and went into camp.
May 7.— Started on our march to Grand Gulf.
May 10.— Arrived at Hard Times Landing opposite Grand Gulf and forty-seven miles from Milliken's Bend. Crossed the Mississippi on gunboat *Louisville* to Grand Gulf.
May 11.— Marched toward Raymond, Mississippi.
May 12.— Arrived.
May 15.— Marched to Champion's Hill.
May 16.— Had an engagement there driving the enemy from the field.
May 17.— Marched towards Vicksburg. Crossed [Big] Black River on a pontoon in the evening.
May 18.— Marched to within one half mile of the enemy's works at Vicksburg and drove in pickets.
May 19.— Made an unsuccessful assault upon the enemy's works; had four men wounded.
May 22.— Assaulted them a second time, but without success.
May 25-June 1.— Marched toward Yazoo City on a reconnaissance. Were out seven days and to within eighteen miles of Yazoo City.
June 2.— Arrived in camp at Walnut Hills.
June 13.— Moved to the front.

Stationed at Camp Sherman, Mississippi, July-August 1863.
July 5.— Marched from our works at Walnut Hills.
July 10.— Arrived before Jackson.
July 13.— Completed breastworks.
July 16.— The enemy evacuated Jackson in the night.
July 17.— We marched into Jackson at 7 o'clock a.m.
July 23.— Marched from Jackson.
July 25.— Arrived at Camp Sherman, Mississippi; total distance marched eighty miles.

Stationed at Chickasaw, September-October 1863.
September 26.— Received marching orders at [Big] Black River Bridge.
September 27.— Marched to Vicksburg and embarked on steamer *Commercial*.
September 29.— Started for Memphis.
October 4.— Arrived at Memphis.
October 8.— Left Memphis by Memphis and Charleston Railroad. Arrived at La Grange same day.
October 14.— Marched eastward from La Grange passing through Corinth, Iuka and Cherokee Station.
October 27.— Arrived at Tuscumbia, Alabama.
October 28.— Marched back through Cherokee Station.
October 31.— Arrived at Eastport or Chickasaw Station; distance traveled by steamer 400; by rail, forty-eight miles; and marched sixty-nine, total 517 miles.

Stationed near Bellefonte, Alabama, November-December 1863.
November 1.— We crossed the Tennessee River en route for Chattanooga.
November 2.— Camped at Waterloo in the evening.
November 3.— [Camped at] Rock Springs, distance from Eastport seventeen miles.
November 4.— Arrived at Florence, distance thirteen miles.
November 5.— In the evening camped about five miles west of Rogersville.
November 6.— Camped about eight miles east of Rogersville.
November 7.— Camped six miles southwest of Pulaski.
November 8.— We marched through Pulaski and camped twelve miles east of that place.
November 9.— Marched to Fayetteville, distance eighteen miles.
November 10.— Camped about fifteen miles southeast of Fayetteville on a branch of Flint River. From this point our course lay south and through a mountainous country, that we made very slow progress.
November 13.— Crossed another branch of Flint River in the evening at a point where the Memphis and Charleston, Railroad crossed it.

November 14.— Marched eastward seventeen miles.
November 15.— Passed through Bellefonte and camped eight miles northeast.
November 16.— Passed through Stevenson and camped four miles northeast arrived at Bridgeport, where we remained.
November 19.— We started again for Chattanooga.
November 25.— Arrived at Chattanooga, having to cross the Tennessee River twice before getting there. We were ordered to the front the same evening. During the night the enemy evacuated.
November 26-December 16.— After drawing rations we started in pursuit of Bragg and his command. Followed them to Perryville where we destroyed the railroad, grist mill, etc. We then started towards Knoxville to relieve General Burnside, who was being besieged by General Longstreet. Arrived within sixteen miles of that place. We here received the intelligence that the siege had been raised and that Longstreet was on the retreat into Virginia. We then countermarched, taking nearly the same road as in coming.
December 17.— Arrived at Chattanooga.
December 19.— [Arrived] at Bridgeport.
December 20.— [Arrived] at Bellefonte. During the two weeks that we were after Bragg and Longstreet, we subsisted almost entirely on the country; whole distance marched since leaving Eastport, 630 miles.

Station not stated, December 31, 1863-April 30, 1864.
January 8.— The regiment went into winter quarters at Larkinsville, Alabama after performing the largest march that has ever been made by any troops in the field, from Vicksburg, Mississippi to Knoxville, Tennessee.
January 27.— Three-fourths of the regiment having reenlisted, the regiment left Larkinsville, Alabama.
February 4.— Arrived at Cincinnati.
February 6.— Having received a furlough for thirty days, the regiment disbanded.
March 7.— Our furlough expired this day.
March 19.— Left Camp Dennison, Ohio.

March 20.— Arrived at Nashville, Tennessee. As we could get no transportation, we were ordered to march on foot to Larkinsville.
March 31.— We arrived at Larkinsville, having passed through Murfreesborough, Tullahoma, Stevenson, and Bellefonte. Prepared for the next campaign.

Stationed near Kenesaw Mountain, Georgia, May-June 1864.
May 1-13.— Left camp at Larkinsville, Alabama. Marched to Resaca, Georgia, distance ninety miles.
May 14-16.— Were engaged with the enemy. From there we marched to Kingston, Georgia, distance thirty miles.
May 19.— Arrived at Kingston and rested three days.
May 23.— Left Kingston and encountered the enemy near Dallas, Georgia; distance marched thirty miles.
May 26.— Arrived and threw up breastworks.
May 27-29.— Were engaged. The enemy attacked and charged our works, but were repulsed.
June 1.— Marched again. Marched to Burnt Hickory, distance seven miles.
June 4.— Marched again.
June 6.— Arrived at Acworth, Georgia, distance eighteen miles.
June 9.— Marched again. Marched to Big Shanty, Georgia, distance seven miles. Encountered the enemy there. Drove them and fortified near the foot of Kenesaw Mountain.
June 26.— Left Kenesaw and marched seven miles to the right.
June 27.— Attacked and charged the enemy's works on Kenesaw Mountain and were repulsed.
June 28-30.— In bivouac seven miles southeast of Big Shanty Station, Georgia.

Stationed at Jonesborough, Georgia, July-August 1864.
July 1.— We left our position in front of Kenesaw Mountain, Georgia and moved to the right of the Army at Nickajack Creek.
July 3.— We charged and drove the enemy from his works. From Nickajack Creek we marched to the front of the enemy's position at the Chattahoochee River and then back to the extreme left of the Army marching via Marietta and Roswell to the Augusta Railroad near Stone Mountain, fifty miles, and after destroying the railroad, marched via Decatur to the enemy's works at Atlanta.

July 22.— The enemy attacked us and was defeated.
July 26.— We moved to the right of the Army.
July 28.— Again we attacked and drove the enemy from the field.
July 29-August 26.— We remained in our entrenchments before Atlanta, Georgia. On August 26 we again marched to the right and after destroying the West Point Railroad, marched to Jonesborough, Georgia.
August 31.— Again met and defeated the enemy; distance marched during the two months, 120 miles.

Stationed at East Point, Georgia, September 19, 1864.
September 19.— Muster-out roll of a detachment of Captain John S. Wells', late Charles A. White's, Company (C), in the Fifty-fourth Regiment of Ohio Infantry Volunteers, commanded by Lieutenant-Colonel Robert Williams, late Smith, called into the service of the United States by the President at Camp Dennison, Ohio (the place of general rendezvous) on September 20, 1861 to serve for the term of three years from the date of enrollment, unless sooner discharged, from October 31, 1863 (when last paid) to September 19, 1864 when mustered out. . . .

C. J. DICKEY,
First Lieutenant,
Thirteenth Infantry, Commissary of Musters,
Fifteenth Army Corps, Mustering Officer.

Stationed at Cave Spring, Georgia, September-October 1864.
[For record of events, see Company A.]

Stationed near Savannah, Georgia, November-December 1864.
[For record of events, see Field and Staff.]

Stationed at Lynch's Creek, South Carolina, January-February 1865.
[For record of events, see Field and Staff.]

Stationed in the field, March-April 1865.
[For record of events, see Field and Staff.]

Stationed on board steamboat Argonaut No. 2, May-June 1865.
[For record of events, see Company A.]

Company D

Stationed at Camp Dennison, October 31, 1861.
October 31.— Muster-in roll of Captain Israel T. Moore's Company (D), in the Fifty-fourth Regiment (—— Brigade) of Ohio Infantry Volunteers, commanded by Colonel Thomas Kilby Smith, called into the service of the United States by the President from [October 31, 1861] (date of this muster) for the term of three years, unless sooner discharged. . . .

E. M. WOOD,
Captain,
Fifteenth Infantry, Mustering Officer.

Stationed at Camp Dennison, December 31, 1861.

Station not stated, January-February 1862.

Stationed at Camp Shiloh, March-April 1862.

Stationed at Moscow, May-June 1862.

Stationed near Memphis, Tennessee, July-October 1862.

Stationed before Vicksburg, Mississippi, November-December 1862.
November 26.— Left Memphis, Tennessee and marched beyond Tallahatchie River, Mississippi. Went into camp three days and then returned.
December 13.— Arrived at Memphis, Tennessee, distance seventy miles.
December 20.— Embarked at Memphis on steamboat *Sunny South*. Ran down Mississippi River to mouth of Yazoo [River] and up Yazoo River ten miles and debarked.
December 28-29.— Took part in action before Vicksburg. Loss in Company D, one killed and four wounded; distance traveled 400 miles.

Stationed at Young's Point, Louisiana, January-February 1863.
January 1.— Retired from before Vicksburg.

January 2.— Embarked on steamboat *Sunny South*; accompanied the fleet to Arkansas Post.
January 10-11.— Debarked and took part in the action. Captured Fort Hindman, etc.; distance traveled 350 miles.
January 13.— Embarked again on *Sunny South* and accompanied the fleet down the Arkansas and Mississippi Rivers to Young's Point, Louisiana; distance traveled 350 miles.

Stationed at Young's Point, Louisiana, March-April 1863.

Stationed at Walnut Hills, Mississippi, May-June 1863.
May 3.— Moved from Young's Point to Milliken's Bend on steamer *Edward Walsh*. Went into camp about one mile back from the river.
May 7.— Left Milliken's Bend and marched through Richmond, near and to the right of Lake Saint Joseph.
May 11.— Arrived at Hard Times Landing on Mississippi River in the evening and crossed over to Grand Gulf, Mississippi on gunboat *Louisville*.
May 12.— Took up our line of march again in the morning.
May 15.— Arrived at Raymond in the afternoon.
[May 16].— Was held in reserve at battle of Champion's Hill.
May 18.— Arrived in front of the enemy's works in rear of Vicksburg in the evening.
May 19, 22.— Was engaged in the assaults. Marched from Walnut Hills to Mechanicsburg and returned via Haynes' Bluff.
June 3.— Arrived at Walnut Hills again in the evening. Was held in reserve.
June 11.— Have since been to the front working in the trenches. Whole distance marched since May 2, 251 miles.

Stationed at Camp Sherman, Mississippi, July-August 1863.
July 5.— Marched from Walnut Hills, Mississippi.
July 10.— Arrived in front of Rebel works in the evening. Threw up earthworks and besieged the city of Jackson.
July 17.— Joseph Johnston evacuated the place and burned several buildings. Marched two and a half miles in pursuit and did not overtake him. We then turned and marched back to Jackson and camped.
July 22.— We then marched to Camp Sherman, Mississippi on [Big] Black River.

July 25.— Arrived at Camp Sherman in the evening; whole distance marched seventy-five miles.

Stationed at Eastport, Mississippi, September-October 1863.
September 26.— The company received marching orders.
September 27.— Marched from camp near [Big] Black River, Mississippi. Arrived at Vicksburg at 1 o'clock p.m.
September 28.— Embarked on steamer *Commercial.*
October 4-20.— Arrived at Memphis, Tennessee, distance by water 400 miles. Traveled by railroad to La Grange, Tennessee, forty-eight miles, from thence to Corinth, Iuka and Cherokee Station.
October 21.— Arrived at Cherokee Station.
October 26.— Marched for Tuscumbia. Was attacked by the enemy at 8 a.m. and skirmished all day as we advanced.
October 27.— In the morning was again attacked. Drove the enemy back and arrived at Tuscumbia at 4 p.m. and found the place evacuated.
October 28.— Countermarched to Cherokee Station making thirty-four miles.
October 30.— Marched again.
October 31.— Arrived at Eastport on the Tennessee River, twelve miles. The company marched ninety-three miles on foot, forty-eight by rail, and 400 on transport.

Stationed at Bellefonte, Alabama, November-December 1863.
November 1.— The company crossed the Tennessee River at Eastport en route for Chattanooga.
November 2.— In evening marched to Waterloo and camped, distance two miles.
November 3.— Marched to Rock Springs, thirteen miles.
November 4.— Arrived at Florence, thirteen miles from [Rock] Springs.
November 5.— Marched to Elk Creek, twenty miles from Florence.
November 6.— Marched from Elk Creek, sixteen miles.
November 8.— Marched through Pulaski.
November 9.— Marched to Fayetteville.
November 10-12.— En route for Flint River, forty miles from Fayetteville.

November 13.— Arrived at Flint River.
November 14.— Marched to Stevenson, Alabama.
November 17.— Arrived at Bridgeport, thirty miles from Chattanooga.
November 18.— Marched and arrived at Tennessee River near Chattanooga.
November 22.— Crossed river on pontoon.
November 24.— In the night was ordered to the front.
November 25-26.— Marched through Chickamauga.
November 28.— Arrived at Graysville. Destroyed a portion of the Atlanta and Cleveland Railroad.
November 29-December 31.— Marched to Cleveland en route for Knoxville through Charleston, Athens, Sweet Water, Philadelphia, and Morganton to Maryville, eighteen miles from Knoxville and ninety miles from Chattanooga. Countermarched to Tellico Iron Works, then east to the North Carolina line and then to Chattanooga, Bridgeport and Stevenson to Bellefonte, marching in all since November 1 to December 31, 630 miles.

Stationed at Larkinsville, Alabama, December 31, 1863-April 30, 1864.
January 8.— Left Bellefonte in the morning and went in camp at Larkinsville, Alabama the same day, marching a distance of twelve miles. The required number of the regiment reenlisted as veteran volunteers.
January 27.— We left Larkinsville.
February 4.— Arrived at Cincinnati.
February 6.— Disbanded.
March 7.— Our furlough having expired, we reported at Camp Dennison, Ohio where we remained until March 19.
March 22.— We arrived at Nashville. There being no transportation for us we were ordered to march to the front.
March 25.— We left Nashville passing through Murfreesborough, Tullahoma, Stevenson and Bellefonte.
March 31.— Arrived at Larkinsville.
April 1-30.— We lay here during the month drilling and preparing for another campaign. Entire distance traveled by rail 716 miles, by water 180 miles, and marched on foot 182.

Stationed near Kenesaw Mountain, Georgia, May-June 1864.
May 1.— The regiment left Larkinsville and marched via Stevenson to Chattanooga, from thence to Gordon's Gap within three miles of Resaca, Georgia.
May 13.— Attacked the enemy's works at Resaca compelling them to evacuate.
May 16.— Resumed our march via Kingston.
May 25.— Arrived near Dallas.
May 26.— Met the enemy one mile beyond Dallas, strongly fortified.
June 1.— They attacked us in force, but we repulsed them after three hours' hard fighting.
June 4-5.— During the nights the enemy evacuated his position at Dallas.
June 7.— We followed passing Acworth on this date. After a short rest we resumed our march.
June 10.— We found the enemy strongly fortified on and around Kenesaw Mountain.
June 27.— We attacked their works, taking their first line of rifle pits, but failed in taking their principal works. In this action the regiment lost in killed, wounded and missing, twenty-seven men.
June 28-30.— Remained in entrenchments in front of Kenesaw Mountain; distance marched from May 1 until June 30 (175) miles.

Station not stated, July-August 1864.
July 3-19.— Marched from Kenesaw Mountain to the right of the Army and engaged the enemy at Ruff's Mill and drove him from his works. Marched then to Stone Mountain, where we tore up a portion of the railroad and then marched to Decatur and destroyed the Augusta and Atlanta Railroad.
July 20.— We skirmished with the enemy all day.
July 21.— Skirmishing and artillery firing all day.
July 22.— In the morning the enemy fell back. We occupied their works at 8 a.m. At 2 p.m. the enemy charged us and drove us from the works; but after we fell back and reformed, we charged in turn and retook our position. The loss of the regiment this day was ninety-four in killed, wounded and missing. The Rebel loss was much heavier.
July 27.— We marched to the right.

July 28.— Engaged the enemy at 11.30 a.m. and fought him until dark, repulsing him with heavy loss. Our loss was very small.
August 26.— Left before Atlanta and marched for Jonesborough.
August 30.— Arrived near Jonesborough driving the enemy before us all day. Made temporary works.
August 31.— Were attacked. They charged our lines four times, but were repulsed with heavy loss; distance marched since July 1 to August 31, 180 miles.

Stationed at Cave Spring, Georgia, September-October 1864.
[For record of events, see Company A.]

Stationed near Savannah, Georgia, November-December 1864.
November 1.— Left Cave Spring, Georgia and marched via Cedartown.
November 5.— Encamped near Vining's Station, Georgia.
November 8.— The regiment was paid.
November 10.— Broke camp and marched via Turner's Ferry, McDonough and Statesborough.
December 9.— Crossed the Cannouchee River and destroyed seven miles of the Gulf Railroad. Marched via Fort McAllister.
December 13-31.— Carried Fort McAllister by assault. Broke camp at Fort McAllister and marched to near Savannah; distance marched from November 1 to December 31, 400 miles.

Stationed at Lynch's Creek, South Carolina, January-February 1865.
[For record of events, see Field and Staff.]

Stationed near Raleigh, North Carolina, March-April 1865.
[For record of events, see Field and Staff.]

Stationed on board the Argonaut No. 2, May-June 1865.
[For record of events, see Company A.]

Company E

Station not stated, January-February 1862.

Station not stated, March-April 1862.

Stationed at Moscow, Tennessee, May-June 1862.

Stationed at Memphis, Tennessee, July-October 1862.

Stationed on board Sunny South, Mississippi River, November-December 1862.
December 27-30.— The company was engaged at the battle near Vicksburg.

Stationed at Young's Point, Louisiana, January-February 1863.
January 10-11.— The company was engaged in the battle at Arkansas Post.

Stationed at camp before Vicksburg, April 10, 1863.

Stationed at camp in the field in front of Vicksburg, March-April 1863.

Stationed at Walnut Hills, Mississippi, May-June 1863.
May 2.— Left camp at Young's Point, Louisiana and embarked on board steamer *Edward Walsh*.
May 3.— Disembarked at Milliken's Bend, Louisiana and went into camp.
May 7.— Started on our march to Grand Gulf.
May 10.— Arrived at Hard Times Landing opposite Grand Gulf and forty-seven miles from Milliken's Bend. Crossed the Mississippi on gunboat *Louisville* to Grand Gulf.
May 11.— Marched toward Raymond, Mississippi.
May 12.— Arrived.
May 15.— Marched to Champion's Hill.
May 16.— Had an engagement there driving the enemy from the field.
May 17.— Marched towards Vicksburg. Crossed [Big] Black River on a pontoon in the evening.
May 18.— Marched to within one half mile of the enemy's works at Vicksburg and drove in pickets.
May 19.— Made an unsuccessful assault upon the enemy's works.
May 22.— Assaulted them a second time, but without success.

May 25-June 1.— Marched toward Yazoo City on a reconnaissance. Were out seven days and to within eighteen miles of Yazoo City.
June 2.— Arrived in camp at Walnut Hills.
June 13.— Moved to the front.

Stationed at Camp Sherman, Mississippi, July-August 1863.
July 4.— Vicksburg surrendered. Received marching orders this day.
July 5.— At 5 o'clock a.m. started on our march toward [Big] Black River.
July 7.— Reached [Big] Black River at 12 o'clock m. Found Rebel pickets on opposite side of the river. At 3 o'clock p.m. they were driven back and our forces started in pursuit. Marched until 12 o'clock midnight. Bivouacked for the night.
July 8.— Started on our march in the morning at 7 o'clock toward Jackson, Mississippi.
July 10.— Arrived in front of and three miles from Jackson, Mississippi, a distance of forty-five miles from Vicksburg, where we held part of the advance line.
July 16.— The enemy evacuated.
July 23.— Marched from Jackson.
July 25.— Arrived at Camp Sherman, Mississippi; distance [marched], since July 5, eighty miles.

Stationed at Chickasaw, Alabama, September-October 1863.
September 26.— Received marching orders.
September 27.— Marched from camp near [Big] Black River Bridge to Vicksburg, Mississippi and embarked on board steamer *Commercial*.
October 4.— Arrived at Memphis, Tennessee.
October 8-19.— Marched into the interior by way of La Grange, Corinth and Iuka.
October 20.— Arrived at Cherokee Station.
October 26.— Marched toward Tuscumbia, Alabama. Skirmished all the way from Cherokee Station to Tuscumbia.
October 28.— Left Tuscumbia and arrived at Cherokee Station same day.
October 29.— Left Cherokee Station.

October 31.— Arrived at Chickasaw, Alabama; total distance by water 400 miles, by rail forty-eight miles, and marched about ninety-five miles.

Stationed near Bellefonte, Alabama, November-December 1863.
November 1.— Crossed the Tennessee River.
November 2.— Bivouacked for the night at Waterloo in the evening.
November 3.— [Bivouacked at] Rock Springs in the evening, distance from Eastport seventeen miles.
November 4.— Arrived at Florence, distance thirteen miles.
November 5.— In the evening bivouacked near Rogersville.
November 6.— Bivouacked about eight miles from Rogersville.
November 7.— Bivouacked near Pulaski.
November 8.— Camped about eight miles from Pulaski.
November 9.— Arrived at Fayetteville.
November 10.— Marched about thirteen miles and bivouacked for the night on branch of Flint River.
November 13.— Crossed another branch of Flint River in the evening.
November 14.— Marched eastward seventeen miles.
November 15.— Passed through Bellefonte and bivouacked eight miles from that place.
November 16.— Passed through Stevenson and camped four miles from there.
November 17.— Arrived at Bridgeport.
November 19.— Started for Chattanooga.
November 25.— Arrived at Chattanooga. Ordered to the front the same evening. During the night the enemy evacuated.
November 26.— Started in pursuit of Bragg. Destroyed the railroad, grist mill, etc. at Graysville.
December 12.— Arrived within sixteen miles of Knoxville.
December 14.— Started back to Chattanooga.
December 17.— Arrived at Chattanooga.
December 19.— Started for Bridgeport. Arrived there same day.
December 26.— Started for Bellefonte.
December 30.— Arrived at Bellefonte; whole distance marched since November 1, 630 miles.

Stationed at Larkinsville, Alabama, December 31, 1863-April 30, 1864.
January 8.— After performing the longest march I think that has ever been made by any troops in this country, *viz.*: from Memphis to Chattanooga, Tennessee via Tuscumbia, Pulaski and Fayetteville, Tennessee; Larkinsville, Alabama and Bridgeport, Alabama; thence to Chattanooga, then to Knoxville, Tennessee and returned to Clarksville by way of Chattanooga, we went into winter quarters on this date. The required number of the regiment reenlisted as veteran volunteers.
January 27.— Left Larkinsville.
February 4.— Arrived at Cincinnati.
February 6.— Disbanded.
March 19.— Furloughs having expired, we left Camp Dennison.
[March] 22.— Arrived at Nashville, Tennessee. There being no transportation, we were ordered to march to the front.
[March] 25.— Left Nashville, passing through Murfreesborough, Tullahoma, Stevenson, and Bellefonte.
March 31.— Arrived at Larkinsville, Alabama.
April 1-30.— We lay here during April preparing for another campaign.

Stationed in the field, May-June 1864.
May 1.— Left Larkinsville at 7 a.m. Marched to Bellefonte, distance twelve miles.
May 2.— Left Bellefonte at 9 a.m. Marched thirteen miles.
May 3.— Left camp and marched to Bridgeport and encamped for the night, distance sixteen miles.
May 4.— Crossed the river; marched twelve miles and went into camp.
May 5.— Left camp at 6 a.m. Marched eleven miles.
May 7.— Left camp at 6 a.m. Went into camp.
May 8.— Left camp at 10.30 a.m. Marched ten miles.
May 9.— Left camp at 5 a.m. Marched three miles and went into camp.
May 10.— Lay in line of battle all day at cross-roads seventeen miles from Dalton.
May 11.— Marched at 3 a.m. to the rear and fortified. Expected an attack.

May 12.— Returned to our former position. All quiet in front.
May 13.— Army advanced and drove the Rebels to their fortifications. Our regiment in reserve.
May 14.— The Rebels evacuated Dalton just before dark. Our division charged and took the hills and went to work fortifying.
May 15.— Lay all day in trenches.
May 16.— Moved toward Rome.
May 17.— Crossed the river and moved on toward Rome.
May 18.— Left camp at 8 a.m. Took the Kingston Road where it was supposed the Rebels were making a stand. Marched nine miles.
May 19.— Still on the road to Kingston. The Rebels evacuated the place and our Army is in pursuit.
May 20-23.— In camp resting.
May 24.— Left camp at 11 a.m. Marched seven miles.
May 25.— Left camp at 6 a.m. Marched eight miles.
May 26.— Left camp at 7 a.m. Marched five miles.
May 27-28.— Our brigade in reserve.
May 29.— Lay in line of battle all day. Enemy charged us seven times but were repulsed with heavy loss.
May 30-31.— The regiment occupied the trenches all day.
June 1.— Army evacuated its works and formed a new line of defense one and a half miles to the rear. Division in reserve.
June 2.— Lay in works all day.
June 3.— The regiment was relieved and in reserve.
June 4.— The regiment returned to works. Enemy evacuated.
June 5.— Left camp at 7 a.m. Marched eight miles.
June 6-7.— Resting. Rebels retreated toward Atlanta.
June 8-9.— Resting.
June 10.— Left camp at 7 a.m. Marched four miles and threw up works.
June 11-15.— In reserve to Seventeen Army Corps.
June 16.— Moved to right in support of General [Peter Joseph] Osterhaus artillery fighting.
June 17.— In same position. Artillery firing.
June 18.— Still in same position. All quiet. Enemy evacuated their works.
June 19.— Left works at 9 a.m. Moved across an open field.
June 20.— At the foot of Kenesaw Mountain. Were engaged. Threw up works.
June 21-25.— Still in same position.

June 26.— Were relieved during the night and moved to the right.
June 27.— At 8 a.m. our division charged the enemy. Went to within 100 yards of enemy's works under a terrific artillery, but owing to the wasted condition of the men, were unable to go further.
June 28-30.— In reserve.

Stationed at Jonesborough, Georgia, July-August 1864.
July 2.— Left our camp at Kenesaw Mountain and marched to Ruff's Mill.
July 3.— We drove the enemy from a strong position. The regiment lost one killed and eleven wounded.
July 5-8.— Lay in reserve.
July 12.— Marched to Rossville via Marietta and crossed the river.
July 18.— Destroyed the Augusta Railroad near Stone Mountain.
July 20.— The regiment skirmished from Decatur to near Atlanta, Georgia.
July 22.— Enemy charged. Severe engagement. Enemy repulsed.
August 1-26.— In same position. On the night of August 26 marched to the Mount [illegible] Railroad.
August 30.— The regiment skirmished.
August 31.— Enemy charged us near Jonesborough and were repulsed; distance marched 106 miles.

Stationed at Cave Spring, Georgia, September-October 1864.
September 5.— We started for East Point, Georgia.
September 9.— Arrived at East Point, where we remained in camp.
October 3.— We started in pursuit of Hood, who was moving his forces towards Chattanooga, Tennessee. We passed through Marietta, Kingston, Resaca, and Snake [Creek] Gap.
October 25.— Engaged the enemy's cavalry near Little River, Alabama. Repulsed them with little loss. From thence we pursued our march to Atlanta, Georgia.
October 29.— Arrived at Cave Spring, marching in all a distance of 200 miles.

Stationed at Savannah, Georgia, November-December 1864.
[For record of events, see Company D.]

Stationed at Lynch's Creek, South Carolina, January-February 1865.
January 17.— Broke camp at Savannah, Georgia and proceeded by steamer to Beaufort, South Carolina and encamped.
January 27-[February 11].— Broke camp and marched via Pocotaligo, Bamberg and Orangeburg to Columbia, from which place we drove the enemy. Marched via Liberty Hill to Camden to Lynch's Creek, distance 200 miles.

Stationed in the field, North Carolina, March-April 1865.
[For record of events, see Field and Staff.]

Stationed on board steamer Argonaut [No. 2] on Mississippi River, May-June 1865.
[For record of events, see Company B.]

Company F

Stationed at Dayton, Ohio, December 21, 1861.
October 31.— Muster-in roll of Captain Peter Bertram's Company [F], in the Fifty-fourth Regiment (—— Brigade) of Ohio Infantry Volunteers, commanded by Colonel Thomas Kilby Smith, called into the service of the United States by the President from October 31 (date of this muster) for the term of three years, unless sooner discharged. . . .

E. M. WOOD,
Captain,
Fifteenth Infantry, United States Army, Mustering Officer.

Station not stated, December 31, 1861.

Stationed at Paducah, Kentucky, January-February 1862.

Station not stated, March-April 1862.
April 6.— Engaged the enemy about 9 a.m. Fought there, retreating slowly, until 3.30 o'clock p.m. Engaged them again in

the evening and fought until dark; loss three killed and ten wounded.
April 7.— Engaged the enemy again about 11 o'clock a.m. Fight lasted until 5 o'clock p.m.; lost one killed and one wounded. Missing from both days, six men. The one killed today was Peter Bertram, commander of the company.

Stationed at Moscow, Tennessee, May-June 1862.

Stationed at Memphis, Tennessee, July-October 1862.

Stationed at camp, near Vicksburg, November-December 1862.

Stationed at Young's Point, Louisiana, January-April 1863.

Stationed at Walnut Hills, Mississippi, May-June 1863.
May 7.— The company marched from Milliken's Bend, Louisiana for Hard Times Landing, Louisiana.
May 10.— Arrived at Hard Times Landing in the evening, distance of sixty-three miles.
May 11.— Crossed the river to Grand Gulf.
May 12.— In the morning we took up our march for Raymond, Mississippi.
May 15.— Arrived at Raymond at 2 o'clock p.m., a distance of fifty-three miles.
May 16.— In the morning we marched for the enemy's fortification in the rear of Vicksburg.
May 18.— Arrived at Vicksburg at 12 o'clock m., a distance of thirty miles. The company skirmished with the enemy from 3 to 6 o'clock p.m. in the afternoon.
May 19, 22.— The company was engaged in the assaults. The loss of the company was one killed and four wounded.
May 26.— In the night we left Walnut Hills, Mississippi and marched to Mechanicsburg. Returned by way of Haynes' Bluff.
June 3-[30].— Arrived at our present position, a distance of ninety miles. Total number of miles marched since May 7 to the present date, 236 miles.

May 16.— Resumed our march via Kingston, Georgia.
May 25.— Arrived near Dallas, Georgia.
May 26.— Met the enemy one mile beyond Dallas, strongly fortified.
May 28.— The enemy attacked us in force, but we repulsed them after three hours fighting.
June 4-5.— During the nights the enemy evacuated his position at Dallas. We followed the enemy on June 5.
June 7.— Passed Acworth, Georgia. After a short rest we resumed our march.
June 10.— We found the enemy strongly fortified on and around Kenesaw Mountain.
June 27.— We attacked the enemy's works, taking their first line of rifle pits, but failed in taking their principal works. In this action the regiment lost in killed, wounded and missing, twenty-seven men.
June 28-30.— Remained in entrenchments in front of Kenesaw Mountain; distance marched from May 1 until June 30, 175 miles.

Stationed at Jonesborough, Georgia, July-August 1864.
July 3-19.— Marched from Kenesaw Mountain to the right of the Army and engaged the enemy at Ruff's Mill and drove him from his works. Marched thence to Stone Mountain, where we took up a portion of the railroad and then marched to Decatur and destroyed more of the Augusta and Atlanta Railroad.
July 20.— We skirmished with the enemy all day.
July 21.— Skirmishing and artillery firing all day.
July 22.— In the morning the enemy fell back. We occupied their works at 8 a.m. At 2 p.m. the enemy charged us and drove us from the works; but after we fell back and reformed, we charged in turn and retook our position. The loss of the regiment this day was ninety-four in killed, wounded and missing. The Rebel loss was much heavier.
July 27.— Marched to the right.
July 28.— Engaged the enemy at (11.30) a.m. and fought him until dark, repulsing him with heavy loss. Our loss was very small.
August 26.— Left before Atlanta and marched for Jonesborough.

August 30.— Arrived at Jonesborough driving the enemy before us all day. Made temporary works.
August 31.— Attacked by the enemy. They charged our lines four times and was as often repulsed with heavy loss; distance marched since July 1 to August 31, 180 miles.

Stationed at Cave Spring, Georgia, September-October 1864.
September 2.— Followed the enemy out from Jonesborough in the morning about five miles.
September 8.— Returned via Jonesborough to East Point.
October 4.— Broke up camp at East Point, Georgia and marched via Marietta, Allatoona, Kingston, and Resaca and crossed Taylor's Ridge, from thence down the Chattooga Valley through Summerville and Alpine. Encountered the enemy near Gadsden, and after a slight skirmish, returned. Countermarched and crossed Little River, from thence to Cave Spring, Georgia.
October 31.— Arrived at Cave Spring; distance marched 200 miles.

Stationed at Savannah, Georgia, November-December 1864.
November 1.— Left Cave Spring, Georgia and marched via Cedartown and Powder Springs.
November 5.— Encamped near Vining's Station, Georgia.
November 8.— The regiment was paid.
November 10.— Broke camp at Vining's Station, Georgia and marched via Turner's Ferry, East Point, McDonough, and Summerville.
December 9.— Crossed the Cannouchee River and destroyed seven miles of the Gulf Railroad. Marched to Fort McAllister.
December 13-31.— Carried Fort McAllister by assault. Broke camp at Fort McAllister and marched to near Savannah; distance marched from November 1 to December 31, 400 miles.

Stationed at Lynch's Creek, South Carolina, January-February 1865.
[For record of events, see Field and Staff.]

Stationed in the field, North Carolina, March-April 1865.
March 2-April 9.— Marched from Lynch's Creek, [South] Carolina. Proceeded to Cheraw, South Carolina and Great Pee Dee

River and marched to Fayetteville, North Carolina. Crossed the Cape Fear River, then thence to Bentonville, North Carolina, where we had a heavy skirmish with the enemy, from thence proceeded to Goldsborough, North Carolina and went into camp.
April 10.— Marched to Raleigh, North Carolina.
April 14.— Arrived at Raleigh and went into camp; marched 300 miles.

Stationed on board the Argonaut No. 2, May-June 1865.
[For record of events, see Company B.]

Company G

Station not stated, December 31, 1861.

Stationed at Paducah, Kentucky, January-February 1862.

Station not stated, March-April 1862.
April 6.— Went into action at the battle of Shiloh with thirty enlisted men. Captain Rogall severely wounded early in the day. Of the enlisted men, two were killed, seven wounded, and three missing.
April 7.— The company was engaged but without any casualties.

Stationed at Moscow, Tennessee, May-June 1862.

Stationed at Memphis, Tennessee, July-August 1862.

Stationed at camp, near Memphis, Tennessee, September-October 1862.

Stationed before Vicksburg, November-December 1862.

Stationed at Young's Point Louisiana, January-April 1863.

Stationed at Walnut Hills, Mississippi, May-June 1863.
May 2.— Moved from Young's Point to Milliken's Bend on steamer *Edward Walsh*.

May 3.— Went into camp about one mile back from the river.
May 7.— Left Milliken's Bend and marched through Richmond, near, and to the right of Lake Saint Joseph.
May 11.— Arrived at Hard Times Landing on Mississippi River in the afternoon and crossed over to Grand Gulf, Mississippi on the gunboat *Louisville*.
May 12.— Took up our line of march again in the morning.
May 15.— Arrived at Raymond in the afternoon.
[May 16].— Was held in reserve at battle of Champion's Hill.
May 18.— Arrived in front of the enemy's works in rear of Vicksburg in the evening.
May 19, 22.— Was engaged in the assaults. Marched from Walnut Hills to Mechanicsburg and returned by way of Haynes' Bluff.
June 3.— Arrived at Walnut Hills again in the evening. Was held in reserve.
June 11.— Have since been to the front working on the approaches, which are progressing finely. Whole distance marched since leaving Young's Point, 251 miles.

Stationed at Camp Sherman, Mississippi, July-August 1863.
[For record of events, see Company B.]

Stationed at Eastport, Mississippi, September-October 1863.
September 26.— Received marching orders.
September 27.— Marched from camp near [Big] Black River, Mississippi and arrived at Vicksburg same day and embarked on steamer *Commercial*.
October 4.— Arrived at Memphis, Tennessee, distance about 400 miles.
October 8.— Left Memphis for the interior by Memphis and Charleston Railroad. Arrived at La Grange, Tennessee same day.
October 14.— Left La Grange and marched eastward passing through Corinth, Iuka and Cherokee Station to Tuscumbia.
October 27.— Arrived at Tuscumbia.
October 28.— Left Tuscumbia and marched back by Cherokee Station to Eastport on Tennessee River.
October 31.— Arrived at Eastport. Marched in all about ninety-three miles. Traveled by rail forty-eight miles and by river 400 miles.

Stationed at Bellefonte, Alabama, November-December 1863.
November 1.— We crossed the Tennessee River en route for Chattanooga.
November 2.— Camped at Waterloo in the evening.
November 3.— [Camped] at Rock Springs, distance from Eastport seventeen miles.
November 4.— Arrived at Florence, distance thirteen miles.
November 5.— In the evening camped about five miles west of Rogersville.
November 6.— Camped eight miles northeast of Rogersville.
November 7.— Camped six miles southwest of Pulaski.
November 8.— Marched through Pulaski and camped twelve miles east of that place.
November 9.— Marched to Fayetteville, distance eighteen miles.
November 10.— Camped about thirteen miles southeast of Fayetteville on a branch of Flint River. From this point our course lay south, and through such a rough and mountainous county, that we made very slow progress.
November 13.— In the evening crossed another branch of the Flint River at the point, where the Memphis and Charleston Railroad crosses it.
November 14.— Marched eastward seventeen miles.
November 15.— Passed through Bellefonte and camped eight miles northeast.
November 16.— Passed through Stevenson and camped four miles northeast.
November 17.— Arrived at Bridgeport, where we remained.
November 19.— We started again for Chattanooga.
November 25.— Arrived at Chattanooga, having crossed the Tennessee River twice before getting there. We were ordered to the front the same evening. During the night the enemy evacuated.
November 26-December 16.— After drawing rations, we started in pursuit of Bragg and his command, followed them to Graysville, where we destroyed the railroad, grist mill, etc. We then started towards Knoxville to relieve General Burnside, who was being besieged by General Longstreet. Arrived to within sixteen miles of that place. We here received the intelligence that the siege had been raised and that Longstreet was on the retreat into Virginia. We then countermarched, taking nearly the same road as in coming.

December 17.— Arrived at Chattanooga.
December 19.— [Arrived] at Bridgeport.
December 30.— [Arrived] at Bellefonte. During the two weeks that we were after Bragg and Longstreet, we subsisted almost entirely on the country; whole distance marched since leaving Eastport, 630 miles.

Station not stated, not dated.

Muster and descriptive roll of an unassigned company of United States Troops forwarded by Lieutenant [Robert] M. Nelson, Thirteen United States Infantry for the Fifty-fourth Regiment of Ohio Volunteer Infantry. . . .

Stationed at Larkinsville, Alabama, March 7-April 30, 1864.
March 7.— The company was organized at Columbus, Ohio by Lieutenant R. M. Nelson, Thirteen United States Infantry and assigned to Fifty-fourth Regiment, Ohio Veteran Volunteer Infantry and is one of the thirty companies called into service by the governor of Ohio.
March 14.— The company joined the regiment at Cincinnati, Ohio. The regiment then proceeded to Camp Dennison to reorganize.
March 19.— We left Camp Dennison.
March 22.— Arrived in Nashville, Tennessee. There being no transportation here for us, we were ordered to march to the front.
March 25.— We left Nashville in the morning, passing through Murfreesborough, Tullahoma, Stevenson, and Bellefonte.
March 31.— Arrived at Larkinsville, Alabama.
April 1-30.— We lay here during the month of April drilling and preparing for another campaign.

Stationed at Kenesaw Mountain, May-June 1864.

Stationed at Jonesborough, Georgia, July-August 1864.
July 3-18.— Marched from Kenesaw Mountain to the right of the Army and engaged the enemy at Ruff's Mill and repulsed him. Our loss one noncommissioned officer killed, one enlisted man mortally and four severely wounded. Marched from there to Stone Mountain by way of Marietta. Crossed the Chattahoochee River at Roswell; thence to Decatur.

July 19-20.— Here we destroyed a portion of the Charleston and Atlanta Railroad.
July 22.— Engaged the enemy on railroad before Atlanta, Georgia. Were compelled to fall back on account of troops on our left giving way. Entered rallying, we charged their front and retook our works. Our loss two killed, three severely wounded, and thirteen prisoners.
July 27.— Marched to extreme right of Army.
July 28.— Engaged the enemy. Fought him seven hours repulsing his repeated charges with heavy loss to the enemy. Our loss one man missing. Remained here.
August 26.— Started for Jonesborough.
August [30].— Arrived within three-quarters of a mile after driving the enemy for eight miles before us. Here we formed lines. Threw up works.
August 31.— Was attacked by enemy who charged four times, and were repulsed with heavy loss each time; distance marched from June 30 to August 31, 175 miles.

Stationed at Cave Spring, Georgia, September-October 1864.
[For record of events, see Company E.]

Stationed at Savannah, Georgia, November-December 1864.
[November 1-12].— Moved from Cave Spring to Smyrna Station, where we remained five days. We were paid here. From here we moved to Turner's Ferry and to Grand Pontoon Bridge, where we remained.
November 13-December 12.— We pursued our course in a southeastward direction passing through Jackson, McDonough, Irwinton, Statesborough, and Eden, halting eleven miles northwest of Savannah. Here our division was ordered to charge Fort McAllister.
December 13.— We charged taking it by storm. From here we moved to within three miles of Savannah. We suffered no loss during the campaign; distance marched 300 miles.

Stationed in the field, January-February 1865.
[For record of events, see Field and Staff.]

Stationed at Raleigh, North Carolina, March-April 1865.
March 2-April 9.— Marched from Lynch's Creek, South Carolina; thence to Cheraw, South Carolina. Crossed the Great Pee Dee River, then to Fayetteville, North Carolina, where we remained three days. Crossed the Cape Fear River; thence to near Bentonville, where we skirmished with the enemy. We then proceeded to Goldsborough, North Carolina and went into camp.
April 10.— Broke camp and marched to Raleigh, North Carolina where we again went into camp; whole distance marched, since last muster, 300 miles.

Stationed on board the Argonaut [No. 2], May-June 1865.
May 1.— Broke camp at Raleigh, North Carolina for Petersburg, marching via Warrenton and Lawrenceville.
May 7.— Arrived at Petersburg. There we lay two days.
May 9.— Broke camp.
May 10.— Arrived at Richmond and remained.
May 13.— We again broke camp for Washington, District of Columbia, marching via Bowling Green and Fredericksburg.
May 24.— Arrived at Washington.
June 2.— Broke camp for Louisville, Kentucky, passing through Parkersburg, West Virginia and Cincinnati, Ohio.
June 6.— Arrived at Louisville, Kentucky. We were paid here.
June 25.— Broke camp for Little Rock, [Arkansas] via Ohio, Mississippi and White rivers; whole distance marched 293 miles; were transported 1,600 miles.

Company H

Station not stated, from enrollment to December 31, 1861.

Stationed at Paducah, Kentucky, January-February 1862.

Stationed at Camp Shiloh, near Pittsburg, Tennessee, March-April 1862.
March 7-16.— Changed station from Paducah, Kentucky to Pittsburg Landing by steamboat up Tennessee River.

March 24.— Marched to Pea Ridge (eleven miles) and returned on reconnaissance under General W. T. Sherman.
April 3.— Made night march to Greier's Ford (eight miles).
April 4.— Returned in the morning.
April 6-7.— The company was in the engagement at Pittsburg. Loss in wounded and missing, eighteen. Number of men in the engagement, fifty-five.

Stationed at Memphis, May-June 1862.
May 17.— Had a skirmish with the enemy near the Russell's House about three miles from Corinth. Drove them out and occupied their position.
May 20.— Moved our camp up to the point and built our third line of breastworks.
May 28.— Moved up about three-quarters of a mile. Had an engagement with the enemy which appeared to be general along the whole line at one time on the right, then on the center, then on the left. On the right we drove the enemy from their position and maintained ours and built our fourth line of breastworks during the night.
May 30.— In the morning were all in line at 3 o'clock ready for action. At 6 o'clock the order came to move forward. Proceeded very cautiously until within sight of the enemy's breastworks. No one in sight, but a few pickets who gave themselves up. Came into Corinth on quick time. Our regiment was the first to enter the town and our flag was the first to wave over it.
June 2.— About 6 o'clock p.m. started for the town of Chewalla on the Memphis and Charleston Railroad, distance ten miles.
June 3.— Arrived at Chewalla about 10 o'clock a.m.
June 4.— In the morning went up the railroad about three miles, where the enemy had burned six trains of cars and four bridges. Worked all day in repairing the road.
June 5.— Was relieved by another regiment. Returned to Chewalla and encamped three-quarters of a mile southwest of the town.
June 11.— Marched about fourteen miles towards Memphis. Repaired a bridge that had been destroyed by the enemy. Halted about 8 o'clock for the night.

June 12.— Marched about twelve miles and halted about sundown.

June 13.— Rested until about 5 o'clock p.m. Marched until 9 o'clock. Halted about half a mile from Grand Junction.

June 14.— Marched to La Grange, about five miles, before breakfast. Encamped in a grove on the edge of town.

June 16.— Started at 4 o'clock p.m. for Holly Springs, Mississippi, twenty-five miles south of La Grange on the Mississippi Central Railroad. Marched twelve miles and halted for the night.

June 17.— Arrived in Holly Springs about 11 o'clock in the morning, but Secesh had evacuated.

June 18.— Our cavalry destroyed some trusselwork on the Mississippi Central Railroad, about eighteen miles south of Holly Springs. Started for La Grange again about 5 o'clock p.m. Marched about six miles. Halted for the night at Coldwater.

June 19.— Marched to La Grange, arriving there about 7 o'clock p.m.

June 22.— Started towards Memphis again at 6 o'clock a.m. Marched ten miles; halted from 11 until 4 o'clock; marched ten miles farther; halted about dark near the town of La Fayette.

June 26.— Marched back again about ten miles to the town of Moscow.

June 30.— Were mustered for pay and at 2 o'clock p.m. started for Holly Springs again. Marched about twelve miles.

Stationed at Memphis, Tennessee, July-August 1862.

July 7.— Marched from Moscow to Ammon's Bridge, six miles.

July 18.— Returned to Moscow.

July 19.— Marched for Memphis.

July 21.— Arrived at Memphis. Went into camp east side of town.

[August] 6.— Marched from Coldwater near Holly Springs to Moscow (twenty miles).

August 8.— Went on a scout beyond Hernando.

August 12.— Returned to camp. Ten men and one sergeant was detailed for this march.

Stationed at Memphis, Tennessee, September-October 1862.
October 14-15.— Went out the Hernando Road ten miles during the night. Returned to camp same morning. Ten men and two commissioned officers detailed for this scout.

Stationed on steamer Sunny South, near Vicksburg, Mississippi, November-December 1862.
November 26.— Left Memphis for Tallahatchie River.
December 13.— Returned to Memphis, having marched 150 miles.
December 20.— Left Memphis for Vicksburg on board steamer *Sunny South*.
December 26.— Landed on the Yazoo River. Marched out six miles.
December 27.— Went into action Sunday morning before daylight.
December 28-29.— Was in action.

Stationed at Young's Point, Louisiana, January-February 1863.
January 1.— Retreated in order to the boats during the night.
January 2.— Left the Yazoo on board transport *Sunny South*.
January 10-11.— Landed at Arkansas Post. Was in the engagement.
January 15.— Reshipped on board transport *Sunny South*.
January 22.— Landed at Young's Point, Louisiana near Vicksburg.

Stationed at Young's Point, Louisiana, March-April 1863.

Stationed at Walnut Hills, Mississippi, May-June 1863.
May 2.— Moved from Young's Point to Milliken's Bend on steamer *Edward Walsh*.
May 3.— Went into camp about one mile back from the river.
May 7.— Left Milliken's Bend and marched through Richmond near and to the right of Lake Saint Joseph.
May 11.— Arrived at Hard Times Landing on Mississippi River in the afternoon and crossed over to Grand Gulf, Mississippi on the gunboat *Louisville*.

May 12.— Took up our line of march again in the morning.
May 15.— Arrived at Raymond in the afternoon.
[May 16].— Was held in reserve at battle of Champion's Hill.
May 18.— Arrived in front of the enemy's works in rear of Vicksburg in the evening.
May 19, 22.— Was engaged in the assaults. Marched from Walnut Hills to Mechanicsburg and returned by way Haynes' Bluff.
June 3.— Arrived at Walnut Hills again in the evening. Was held in reserve.
June 11.— Have since been to the front working on the approaches, which are progressing finely. Whole distance marched since leaving Young's Point, 246 miles.

Stationed at Camp Sherman, Mississippi, July-August 1863.
July 4.— Vicksburg surrendered to General [Ulysses Simpson] Grant.
July 5-6.— Marched from Walnut Hills, Mississippi at 6 a.m. with two days' rations in haversacks and ten days' in wagons. Arrived at [Big] Black River at 10 a.m.; halted four hours; crossed and marched four miles and went into camp the night of July 6.
July 7.— Arrived at Bolton at 3 p.m. Halted for the night.
July 8.— Started from Bolton 5 [a.m.]. Took up our line of march for Clinton.
July 9.— Arrived at Clinton at 9 a.m. but did not camp there.
July 10.— Arrived in front of the Rebel trenches at Jackson. Formed line of battle and threw out skirmishers.
July 11.— Considerable artillery firing on both sides.
July 14-15.— Firing on both sides.
July 16.— Heavy musketry on the left of [Francis Preston] Blair's, [Jr.], Division.
July 17.— Johnston evacuated at 3 a.m. Marched into Jackson early this morning. Private Godfred Gass, wounded by bursting of a torpedo.
July 18-19.— In camp.
July 20.— On picket east of Pearl River.
July 21.— Private William Wilber returned from desertion. Privates John Roth and Martin Ford, missing from picket line.
July 22.— Left Jackson at 4 a.m. Arrived at Clinton at 12 m.
July 23.— Left Clinton at 3 a.m. Arrived at Bolton at 1 p.m.

July 24.— Left Bolton at 1 a.m. Arrived at camp four miles west of [Big] Black River; distance marched eighty miles.

Stationed at Eastport, Mississippi, September-October 1863.
September 26.— The company received marching orders.
September 27.— Marched from camp near [Big] Black River, Mississippi. Arrived at Vicksburg at 1 o'clock p.m.
September 28.— Embarked on steamer *Commercial.*
October 4-20.— Arrived at Memphis, Tennessee, distance on boat 400 miles. Traveled by rail to La Grange, Tennessee, forty-eight miles, from thence to Corinth, Iuka and Cherokee Station.
October 21.— Arrived at Cherokee Station.
October 26.— Marched for Tuscumbia. Was attacked by the enemy at 8 a.m. Skirmished all day.
October 27.— In the morning was again attacked. Drove the enemy back and arrived at Tuscumbia at 4 p.m. Found the town evacuated.
October 28.— Countermarched to Cherokee [Station], making thirty-four miles.
October 29.— Marched.
October 31.— Arrived at Eastport [on the] Tennessee River. The company marched ninety-three miles on foot, fifty by rail, and 400 by boat.

Stationed at Bellefonte, Alabama, November-December 1863.
November 1.— The company crossed the Tennessee River at Eastport en route for Chattanooga.
November 2.— In evening marched two miles and camped at Waterloo.
November 3.— Marched to Rock Springs, thirteen miles.
November 4.— Marched and arrived at Florence, thirteen miles from [Rock] Springs.
November 5.— Marched to Elk Creek, twenty miles from Florence.
November 6.— Marched from Elk Creek, sixteen miles.
November 8.— Marched through Pulaski.
November 9.— Marched to Fayetteville.
November 10-12.— En route [to] Flint River, forty miles from Fayetteville.
November 13.— Arrived at Flint River.

November 14.— Marched to Stevenson, Alabama.
November 17.— Arrived at Bridgeport, thirty miles from Chattanooga.
November 18.— Marched and arrived at Tennessee River near Chattanooga.
November 22.— Crossed the river on pontoon.
November 24.— In the night was ordered to the front.
November 25-26.— Marched through Chickamauga.
November 28.— Arrived at Graysville. Destroyed a portion of the Atlanta and Cleveland Railroad.
November 29-December 31.— Marched to Cleveland en route for Knoxville through Charleston, [Athens], Sweet Water, Philadelphia, and Morganton to Maryville, fifteen miles from Knoxville and ninety miles from Chattanooga. Countermarched to Tellico Iron Works; thence east to the North Carolina line and thence to Chattanooga, Bridgeport and Stevenson and Bellefonte, marching in all, since November 1 to December 31, 630 miles.

Stationed at Columbus, Ohio, April 11, 1864.

Muster and descriptive roll of a detachment of United States Ohio Infantry Volunteers, commanded by Captain Cornelius Neff of the Fifty-fourth Regiment of Ohio Volunteer Infantry, regularly one of the thirty independent companies authorized by the War Department, 1862. . . .

CORNELIUS NEFF,
Captain,
Company H, Fifty-fourth Ohio Volunteer Infantry, Commanding.

Stationed at Larkinsville, Alabama, [March 1]-April 30, 1864.

The company was organized at Camp Dennison, Ohio by the Adjutant-General of Ohio, and assigned to the Fifty-fourth Regiment, Ohio Veteran Volunteer Infantry, and is one of the thirty new companies called into service by the governor of Ohio.
April 30.— The company joined the regiment at Larkinsville, Alabama.

Stationed near Kenesaw Mountain, May-June 1864.
May 1.— Started on march eastward with Fifty-fourth Regiment.
May 5.— Arrived at Lookout Mountain, Tennessee.
May 6.— Reported under orders at Chattanooga and drew arms and equipment for all unarmed men of the regiment.

May 11.— Came up with regiment at Snake [Creek] Gap, Georgia.
May 13.— Advanced in sight of the enemy's works at Resaca.
May 14.— Participated in a charge on to enemy's lines, gaining an advantageous position.
May 16.— Entered Resaca.
May 26.— Arrived in front of the enemy, one mile east of Dallas.
May 28.— Sustained a charge from the enemy, who were effectually repulsed. Captain Neff, Privates Samuel Bringman, Samuel Burrows and Michael Kerby were wounded.
June 11.— Found the enemy entrenched at Kenesaw Mountain.
June 27.— The company participated in the charge at which time Corporal Robert L. Norris, William H. Bringman and Charles Lanhan were severely wounded and Tunis W. Kettle was missing.
June 30.— Captain C. Neff reported to regiment for duty from the hospital.

Stationed at Jonesborough, Georgia, July-August 1864.
July 1.— In bivouac at Kenesaw Mountain.
July 2.— Marched to the right flank about ten miles.
July 3.— The company went into a charge at Nickajack Creek, at which time Lieutenant [Abner] Haines, [Jr.], was severely wounded.
July 4.— Moved to right near Chattahoochee River.
July 15.— Crossed the river at Roswell, Georgia.
July 18.— Moved to Stone Mountain.
July 19.— Arrived at Decatur.
July 20.— Skirmished with the enemy on railroad driving them about three miles.
July 21.— Threw up breastworks. Advanced and reversed the enemy's works.
July 22.— Participated in the memorable battle losing in action Corporal William Osbourne, right hand amputated; and F. G. Brill, O. W. Coone, Charles C. Coles, W. D. Larne, J. S. Reed, Theodore Simpson, and Charles E. Winaus.
July 28.— Moved to the extreme right and took part in battle.
August 1-26.— Lay in breastworks during the siege of Atlanta. Marched to Jonesborough, Georgia.
August 30.— Engaged skirmishing and driving the enemy three miles, during which time Daniel G. Whip and Robertson were severely wounded.

August 31.— Took part in battle near Jonesborough, at which time John Seaman, Corporal, was severely wounded.

Stationed at Cave Spring, Georgia, September-October 1864.
September 2.— Followed the enemy out from Jonesborough in the morning about five miles.
September 8.— Returned via Jonesborough to East Point and went into camp for a short time.
October 4.— Broke up camp at East Point, Georgia and marched via Marietta, Allatoona, Kingston, and Resaca and crossed Taylor's Ridge, from thence down the Chattooga Valley through Summerville and Alpine to Little River. Crossed the river in pursuit of the enemy and encountered them near [Gadsden], and routed them after a slight resistance. Countermarched and recrossed Little River and from thence to Cave Spring, Georgia.
October 31.— Arrived at Cave Spring; distance marched 200 miles.

Stationed at Savannah, Georgia, November-December 1864.
November 15.— Left Atlanta, Georgia in the morning and marched via McDonough, Indian Springs, Hillsborough, Clinton, Irwinton, Statesborough, Eden, etc.
December 9.— Crossed the Ogeechee River.
December 13-27.— Recrossed the river in the morning and assaulted and carried Fort McAllister after a short fight. Moved from Fort McAllister to Savannah.
December 28.— Arrived at Savannah; distance marched 350 miles.

Stationed at Lynch's Creek, South Carolina, January-February 1865.
[For record of events, see Field and Staff.]

Stationed near Raleigh, North Carolina, March-April 1865.
March 2-20.— Marched from Lynch's Creek, South Carolina and proceeded to Cheraw, South Carolina. Crossed the Great Pee Dee River and marched to Fayetteville, North Carolina and remained three days. Marched thence and crossed the Cape Fear River; thence to near Bentonville.

March 21-April 9.— Had a heavy skirmish with the enemy. John Benton Focht, Private, being killed in said skirmish, from there proceeded to Goldsborough, North Carolina and went into camp.
April 10.— Broke camp and marched to Raleigh, North Carolina.
April 16.— Arrived at Raleigh and went into camp. Marched during the two months 300 miles.

Stationed on board steamer Argonaut [No. 2], White River, Arkansas, May-June 1865.
[For record of events, see Company A.]

Company I

Station not stated, to December 31, 1861.

Stationed at Paducah, Kentucky, January-February 1862.

Station not stated, March-April 1862.

Stationed at Moscow, Tennessee, May-June 1862.

Stationed at Memphis, Tennessee, July-August 1862.

Stationed at camp, near Memphis, Tennessee, September-October 1862.

Stationed before Vicksburg, Mississippi, November-December 1862.

Stationed at Young's Point, Louisiana, January-April 1863.

Stationed at Walnut Hills, Mississippi, May-June 1863.
May 2.— [Marched] from Young's Point to Milliken's Bend, distance twenty miles.
May 7-18.— From Milliken's Bend [marched] to Hard Times Landing, sixty-three miles, from Hard Times Landing to Raymond, fifty-three miles, from Raymond to Walnut Hills, thirty miles.
May 19, 22.— The company was in action in the assault in the rear of Vicksburg.

May 26.— [Marched] from Walnut Hills to Mechanicsburg.
June 3.— Returned by Haynes' Bluff.

Stationed at Camp Sherman, Mississippi, July-August 1863.
July 3.— Flag of truce raised by the enemy.
July 4.— Enemy surrenders. Received orders to march with ten days' rations.
July 5.— Marched to within four miles of [Big] Black River.
July 6.— Crossed [Big] Black River at 4 o'clock p.m. Marched until 11 o'clock p.m.
July 7.— Marched to Baker's Creek, thirty miles from Vicksburg.
July 8.— Passed the village of Bolton, traveled eight miles. Army Corps passed to our left.
July 9.— Marched through to Clinton towards Jackson. Army Corps passed to our left.
July 10.— Army Corps passed to our left.
July 11.— Marched towards Jackson. Arrived in front of enemy's works at 11 o'clock a.m.
July 12.— Works thrown up during the night on some parts of the line.
July 13.— Heavy artillery fight.
July 14.— Completed works.
July 15.— Called into line on account of an engagement on the left. Moved up under the works.
July 16.— Formed line of battle twice during the day on account of fighting on our immediate left. Army Corps passed to our left.
July 17.— Enemy evacuated Jackson. Entered the city at 8 o'clock a.m. Followed the rear guard of the enemy to Pearl River. Discovered torpedoes in the bank.
July 22.— Ordered to march.
July 23.— Marched to Clinton, ten miles.
July 24.— Marched to Bolton, eight miles, from thence to Camp Sherman.
July 25.— Arrived at the latter [place] to-day.

Stationed at Eastport, Mississippi, September-October 1863.
September 24.— Received marching orders. Marched to [Big] Black River Bridge.

September 27.— Marched from [Big] Black River Bridge to Vicksburg, fifteen miles, and embarked on the steamer *Commercial.*
September 29.— Left port.
October 3.— Arrived at Memphis.
October 9.— Took the cars. Arrived at La Grange, Tennessee.
October 12.— Took the cars. Arrived at Moscow.
October 13.— Marched to La Grange.
October 14.— Marched fourteen miles.
October 15.— Marched to Pocahontas, eighteen miles.
October 16.— Arrived at Corinth; marched fifteen miles.
October 17.— Marched to Glendale, eight miles.
October 18.— Marched to Iuka, Mississippi, distance seventeen miles. Marched to [Bear] Creek.
October 19.— Arrived at Cherokee Station, Alabama.
October 27.— Marched eight miles.
October 28.— Arrived at Tuscumbia, Alabama, distance seven miles.
October 29.— Marched to Cherokee Station, fifteen miles.
October 30.— Marched ten miles.
October 31.— Arrived at Eastport on the Tennessee River.

Stationed at Bellefonte, Alabama, November-December 1863.
November 1.— The company crossed the Tennessee River at Eastport for Chattanooga.
November 2.— In the evening marched two miles to Rock Springs.
November 4.— [Marched] thirteen miles and camped at Florence, thirteen miles from [Rock] Springs.
November 5.— Marched to Elk Creek, twenty miles from Florence.
November 6.— Marched from Elk [Creek] sixteen miles.
November 8.— Marched through Puckett.
November 9.— Marched to Fayetteville.
November 10-12.— En route for Flint River, forty miles from Fayetteville. Near Flint River.
November 13-14.— Marched to Stevenson, Alabama.
November 17.— Marched to Bridgeport, Alabama, thirty miles from Chattanooga.

November 18.— Marched to Tennessee River near Chattanooga. Crossed the river on pontoons.
November 24.— In the night was ordered to the front.
November 25-26.— Marched across the river and took possession of Missionary Ridge.
November 27.— Marched to Graysville.
November 28.— Destroyed the railroad, Atlanta and Cleveland Railroad.
November 29-December 31.— Marched to Cleveland en route for Knoxville; passed through Charleston, Athens, Sweet Water, Philadelphia, Morganton, Maryville, fifteen miles from Knoxville, ninety miles from Chattanooga. Countermarched to Tellico Plains, then east to North Carolina line, and then back to Chattanooga via Tennessee Iron Works, then to Bridgeport, Stevenson, Bellefonte, Alabama. Marched in all, since November 1 to December 31, 630 miles.

Stationed at Larkinsville, Alabama, December 31, 1863-April 30, 1864.
January 8.— After performing the largest march I think that has ever been made by any troops in this country, *viz.*: from Memphis to Chattanooga, Tennessee by way of Tuscumbia, Alabama; Pulaski and Fayetteville, Tennessee; Larkinsville and Bridgeport, Alabama; thence from Chattanooga to Knoxville, Tennessee and return by way of Chattanooga to Larkinsville, Alabama, we went into winter quarters. The required number of the regiment reenlisted as veteran volunteers.
January 27.— We left Larkinsville.
February 4.— Arrived in Cincinnati, Ohio.
February 6.— Disbanded.
March 19.— Our furlough having expired, we left Camp Dennison.
March 22.— Arrived at Nashville. There being no transportation here for us, we were ordered to march to the front.
March 25.— We left Nashville in the morning, passing through Murfreesborough, Tullahoma, Stevenson, and Bellefonte.
March 31.— Arrived at Larkinsville, Alabama.

April 1-30.— We lay here during the month of April drilling and preparing for another campaign.

Station not stated, May-June 1864.

May 1-13.— The company left Larkinsville, Alabama. Marched via Bridgeport, Alabama and Lookout Mountain to Resaca, Georgia.

May 14-15.— Engaged the enemy. Marched from thence to Dallas, Georgia.

May 27-June 1.— Engaged the enemy. [Marched] from thence to Hope Church.

June 2-4.— Engaged the enemy. [Marched] from thence to Kenesaw Mountain.

June 27.— Engaged the enemy; whole distance marched 228 miles.

Stationed at Jonesborough, Georgia, July-August 1864.

July 3.— Marched from Kenesaw Mountain to the right of the Army and engaged the enemy at Ruff's Mill and repulsed him. Marched thence to Stone Mountain.

July 19-20.— [Marched] thence to Decatur, where we destroyed a portion of the Augusta and Atlanta Railroad.

July 22.— Engaged the enemy on the railroad near Atlanta. Fought him four hours and repulsed him. Our loss in prisoners was twelve enlisted men and one captain.

July 27.— Marched to the right.

July 28.— Engaged the enemy at (11.30 a.m.) and fought him until (7 p.m.) repulsing him with heavy loss; our loss on this day was small.

August 26.— Left before Atlanta and marched for Jonesborough on the Macon Railroad.

August 30.— Arrived there after driving the enemy before us all day. Formed our lines and threw up temporary works.

August 31.— Was attacked by the Rebels who charged us four times and were as often repulsed with heavy loss; distance marched since July 1 to August 31, 180 miles.

Stationed at Cave Spring, Georgia, September-October 1864.

September 1-October 3.— After the fall of Atlanta we followed the enemy south so far as Lovejoy's Station, which is about thirty

miles from Atlanta. Here we gave up the chase, returned, and camped at East Point, six miles south of Atlanta. We lay here resting and drilling.
October 4-30.— Hood and his Army having gone towards Chattanooga, we followed passing through Marietta, Acworth, Allatoona, Kingston, Calhoun, Resaca, and Snake Creek Gap until we were within twenty-seven miles of Chattanooga. We then marched through La Fayette and Summerville, and to within a few miles of Lebanon, Alabama, where we had a slight skirmish with the enemy's cavalry. From here we returned towards Atlanta (leaving General Thomas to look after Hood), passing to the west of Rome and through Cave Spring.
October 31.— Arrived at Cave Spring.

Stationed at Savannah, Georgia, November-December 1864.
November 15.— Marched from Atlanta, Georgia and marched via McDonough, Indian Springs, Hillsborough, Clinton, Irwinton, Summerville, Statesborough, and Eden.
December 9.— Crossed the Ogeechee River.
December 13.— Recrossed the Ogeechee in the morning and assaulted and carried Fort McAllister; distance marched 340 miles.

Stationed in the field, South Carolina, January-February 1865.
[For record of events, see Field and Staff.]

Stationed near Raleigh, North Carolina, March-April 1865.
[For record of events, see Company A.]

Stationed on board steamer Argonaut No. [2], May-June 1865.
May 1.— Broke camp near Raleigh, North Carolina and marched via Louisburg and Warrenton, North Carolina; and Petersburg, Richmond, Fredericksburg, and Alexandria, Virginia to Washington, District of Columbia; thence by railway to Parkersburg, West Virginia; thence by steamboat to Louisville, Kentucky and went into camp.
June 30.— Broke camp at Louisville, Kentucky and went on board steamboat *Argonaut No. [2]*, where we were mustered and inspected.

Company K

Station not stated, to February 28, 1862.

Station not stated, March-April 1862.
March 15.— Second Brigade was ordered to march on a reconnoitering expedition to Pea Ridge, distance of ten miles from Camp Shiloh. Drove in enemy's pickets and returned same day after making all necessary discoveries.
March 24-25.— The regiment was called in line at six o'clock p.m. and marched to 1.30 a.m., when we were ordered to halt in line of battle until daylight. Discovered enemy's cavalry at a distance retreating.
March 30.— The regiment was again called in line on Sunday morning at 9 o'clock by long roll. Were marched to left of line of battle, on extreme left flank. Was there posted and remained until 11 o'clock a.m. when left flank was attacked. Company K marched forty-four men in battle, lost none killed, nine wounded, none mortally.

Stationed at Moscow, Tennessee, May-June 1862.

Stationed at camp, near Memphis, Tennessee, August 18, 1862.

Stationed at Memphis, Tennessee, July-October 1862.

Stationed at camp before Vicksburg, November-December 1862.

Stationed at Young's Point, Louisiana, January-April 1863.

Stationed at Walnut Hills, Mississippi, May-June 1863.
May 7.— The company marched from Milliken's Bend, Louisiana for Hard Times Landing.
May 10.— Arrived at Hard Times Landing in the morning, a distance of sixty-three miles.
May 11.— Crossed the river to Grand Gulf, Mississippi.
May 12.— In the morning we took up our march for Raymond.
May 15.— Arrived at Raymond at 2 o'clock p.m., a distance of fifty-three miles.

May 16.— In the morning we marched for the enemy's fortification in the rear of Vicksburg.
May 18.— Arrived at Vicksburg at 12 o'clock m., a distance of thirty miles. The company skirmished with the enemy from 3 to 6 o'clock p.m. in the afternoon.
May 19, 22.— The company was engaged in the assaults.
May 26.— In the night we left Walnut Hills, Mississippi and marched to Mechanicsburg. Returned via Haynes' Bluff.
June 3-[30].— Arrived at our present position, marching a distance of ninety miles.

Stationed at Camp Sherman, Mississippi, July-August 1863.
July 4.— Vicksburg surrendered. Received marching orders this day.
July 5.— At 5 o'clock a.m. started on our march toward [Big] Black River.
July 7.— Reached [Big] Black River at 12 o'clock m. Found Rebel pickets on opposite side of the river. At 3 o'clock p.m. they were driven back and our forces started in pursuit. Marched until 12 o'clock midnight. Stopped for the night.
July 8.— Started on our march in the morning at 7 o'clock toward Jackson, Mississippi.
July 16.— Arrived in front of and three miles from Jackson, Mississippi, a distance of forty-five miles from Vicksburg, where we held part of the advance line until the enemy evacuated.
July 23.— Marched from Jackson.
July 25.— Arrived at Camp Sherman, Mississippi; distance marched since July 5, eighty miles.

Stationed at Eastport, Mississippi, September-October 1863.
September 26.— The company received marching orders.
September 27.— Marched from camp near [Big] Black River, Mississippi to Vicksburg, Mississippi, fifteen miles.
September 28.— Embarked on steamer *Commercial* for Memphis, Tennessee.
October 4.— Arrived at Memphis, Tennessee (400 miles).
October 7.— Left Memphis and traveled by rail to La Grange, Tennessee (forty-eight miles).
October 10.— Left La Grange and marched to Moscow, Tennessee (ten miles).

October 13.— Left Moscow and marched to Corinth (forty-two miles).
October 17.— Arrived at Corinth.
October 18.— Left Corinth and marched to Iuka, Mississippi (twenty-four miles) in two days.
October 20.— From Iuka we marched to Cherokee Station (sixteen miles) in two days.
October 22.— Stayed at camp.
October 25.— Received orders to march at 3 o'clock a.m.
October 26.— Marched to Tuscumbia, Alabama in two days (eighteen miles). The enemy attacked us on the road both days, but we drove the enemy back.
October 27.— Arrived at Tuscumbia at 4 o'clock and found the town evacuated.
October 28.— Countermarched to Cherokee Station in one day (eighteen miles).
October 29.— Left Camp Cherokee.
October 31.— Arrived at Eastport, Mississippi (twelve miles). Since September 27 the company has marched on foot (152 miles), by rail (forty-eight miles), and (400) by boat, in all (600 miles).

Stationed at Bellefonte, Alabama, November-December 1863.
November 1.— The regiment crossed the Tennessee River at Eastport, [Mississippi] and on the morning of the third [day] took up line of march for Chattanooga via Florence, Rogersville, Pulaski, Fayetteville, Bellefonte, and Bridgeport, Alabama.
November 25.— Arrived at Chattanooga and was ordered to the front in the evening. During the night the enemy evacuated. After the evacuation was ordered in pursuit of Bragg.
November 27.— Followed Bragg's Army to Graysville, where it was ordered to the relief of Burnside, who was besieged by Longstreet's command at Knoxville.
December 6.— Marched to Maryville, sixteen miles from Knoxville via Cleveland and Charleston, and here received intelligence that Longstreet was retreating. Returned to Chattanooga on the same route.
December 17.— Arrived and marched to Bridgeport.
December 30.— [Marched] to Bellefonte; distance traveled, since November 1, 600 miles.

Stationed at Larkinsville, Alabama, December 31, 1863-April 30, 1864.
January 8.— The regiment went into winter quarters at Larkinsville, Alabama after performing the longest march that has ever been made by any troops now in the field, from Vicksburg, Mississippi to Knoxville, Tennessee.
January 27.— Three-fourths of the regiment, having reenlisted as veteran volunteers, the regiment left Larkinsville, Alabama.
February 4.— Arrived at Cincinnati, Ohio.
February 6.— Having received a furlough of thirty days, the regiment disbanded.
March 7.— Our furlough expired this day.
March 19.— Left Camp Dennison, Ohio.
March 22.— Arrived at Nashville, Tennessee. As we could get no transportation, we were ordered to march on foot to Larkinsville.
March 31.— Arrived at Larkinsville, passing through Murfreesborough, Tullahoma, Stevenson, and Bellefonte.
April 1-30.— In the month of April we stayed in camp at Larkinsville preparing for the next campaign.

Stationed near Kenesaw Mountain, Georgia, May-June 1864.
May 1.— The regiment left camp at Larkinsville, Alabama and marched from Larkinsville via Stevenson to Chattanooga, Tennessee, from thence through Gordon's Gap [within] three miles of Resaca, Georgia.
May 13.— Attacked the enemy's works at Resaca compelling them to evacuate.
May 16.— Resumed our march via Kingston, Georgia.
May 25.— Arrived near Dallas, Georgia.
May 26.— Met the enemy one mile beyond Dallas, Georgia, strongly fortified.
May 28.— The enemy attacked us in force and were repulsed after three hours fighting.
June 5.— In the night the enemy evacuated his position at Dallas, Georgia.
June 6-7.— We followed them passing Acworth on June 7. After a short rest we resumed our march.
June 10.— We found the enemy strongly fortified in and around Kenesaw Mountain.

June 27.— We attacked the enemy's works taking their first line of rifle pits but failed to take their principal works. In this action the regiment lost in killed, wounded and missing, twenty-seven men.
June 28-30.— We lay in our entrenchments in front of Kenesaw Mountain; distance marched (175) miles.

Stationed near Jonesborough, Georgia, July-August 1864.
July 1.— We left our position in front of Kenesaw Mountain and moved to the right of the Army at Nickajack Creek.
July 3.— We charged the enemy works and compelled him to evacuate. From Nickajack Creek we marched to the front of the enemy's position at the Chattahoochee River; thence back to the extreme left of the Army marching via Marietta and Roswell to the Augusta Railroad near Stone Mountain, distance (fifty) miles, and after effectively destroying the railroad, marched via Decatur to the enemy's works at Atlanta.
July 22.— The enemy attacked us in force and was defeated.
July 26.— We then marched to the right of the Army.
July 28.— We again were attacked and drove them from the field.
July 29-August 26.— We remained in our entrenchments before Atlanta. On August 26 we again moved to the right, and after destroying the West Point Railroad, we marched to Jonesborough.
August 31.— Again met the enemy and defeated him; distance marched from July 1 to August 31 (115) miles. The regiment lost in killed, wounded and missing, Company K lost eight men in all.

Stationed at Cave Spring, Georgia, September-October 1864.
[For record of events, see Company E.]

Stationed at Savannah, Georgia, November-December 1864.
[November 1-12].— Moved from Cave Spring to Smyrna Station, where we remained five days. We were paid here. From here we moved to Turner's Ferry to guard pontoon bridge, where we remained.
November 13-December 12.— We pursued our course in a south-easterly direction passing through Jackson, McDonough, Irwinton Station, Eden, Walling, thirty-one miles west of Savannah. Here our division was ordered to charge Fort McAllister.

December 13.— We charged taking it by storm. From here we moved to within three miles of Savannah. We suffered no loss during the campaign; distance marched 300 miles.

Stationed at Lynch's Creek, South Carolina, January-February 1865.
[For record of events, see Field and Staff.]

Stationed near Raleigh, North Carolina, March-April 1865.
[For record of events, see Field and Staff.]

Stationed on board steamer Argonaut [No. 2], May-June 1865.
[For record of events, see Company B.]

[M594-Roll #151]
